LEARNING TO TEACH IN THE SECONDARY SCHOOL

A Companion to School Experience

Eighth Edition

Edited by
Susan Capel, Marilyn Leask and
Sarah Younie

Routledge
Taylor & Francis Group

LONDON AND NEW YORK

Eighth edition published 2019
by Routledge
2 Park Square, Milton Park, Abingdon, Oxon, OX14 4RN

and by Routledge
52 Vanderbilt Avenue, New York, NY 10017

Routledge is an imprint of the Taylor & Francis Group, an informa business

First edition published by RoutledgeFalmer 1995

Seventh edition published by Routledge 2016

British Library Cataloguing-in-Publication Data
A catalogue record for this book is available from the British Library

Library of Congress Cataloging-in-Publication Data
A catalog record has been requested for this book

ISBN: 978-1-138-30755-1 (hbk)
ISBN: 978-1-138-30759-9 (pbk)
ISBN: 978-1-315-14240-1 (ebk)

Typeset in Interstate
by Deanta Global Publishing Services, Chennai, India

Visit the companion website: www.routledge.com/cw/capel

LEARNING TO TEACH IN THE SECONDARY SCHOOL

For all undergraduate, postgraduate and school-based routes to qualified teacher status, *Learning to Teach in the Secondary School* is an essential introduction to the key skills and knowledge needed to become a secondary teacher. Underpinned by evidence-informed practice and focussing on what you need to know to thrive in the classroom, the eighth edition is fully updated in light of changes in the field, covers new topics and provides additional guidance on topics such as developing your resilience, using digital technologies, closing the achievement gap and using data to inform your teaching and pupil learning.

The text includes a wealth of examples and tasks to demonstrate how to successfully apply theory to practice and how to critically reflect on and analyse your practice to maximise pupil learning. The wide range of pedagogical features supports both school- and university-based work up to Masters level. Written by experts in the field, the 37 concise units create unit-by-unit coverage that can be dipped into, offering guidance on all aspects of learning to teach including:

- Managing your workload
- Lesson planning
- Curriculum
- Motivating pupils
- Promoting behaviour for learning
- Assessment, marking and feedback
- Special educational needs and disabilities (SEND)
- Applying for jobs, developing as a professional and networking

Learning to Teach in the Secondary School provides practical help and guidance for many of the situations and potential challenges you are faced with in school. The text is extended by a companion website that includes additional information as well as specific units covering England, Northern Ireland, Scotland and Wales. Supported by the subject-specific titles in the *Learning to Teach Subjects in the Secondary School Series*, it is an essential purchase for every aspiring secondary school teacher.

Susan Capel is an Emeritus Professor (Physical Education) at Brunel University, UK.

Marilyn Leask is Chief Editor of the MESHGuides initiative (www.meshguides.org) and visiting professor at the University of Winchester and De Montfort University, UK.

Sarah Younie is Professor of Education Innovation at De Montfort University, UK, and Chair of the Education Futures Collaboration charity.

LEARNING TO TEACH SUBJECTS IN THE SECONDARY SCHOOL SERIES

Series Editors: Susan Capel and Marilyn Leask

Designed for all student teachers learning to teach in secondary schools, including those on school-based initial teacher education programmes, the books in this series complement *Learning to Teach in the Secondary School* and its companion, *Surviving and Thriving in the Secondary School*. Each book in the series applies underpinning theory and evidence to address practical issues to support student teachers in learning how to teach a particular subject.

Learning to Teach Art and Design in the Secondary School, 3rd Edition
Edited by Nicholas Addison and Lesley Burgess

Learning to Teach Citizenship in the Secondary School, 3rd Edition
Edited by Liam Gearon

Learning to Teach Design and Technology in the Secondary School, 3rd Edition
Edited by Gwyneth Owen-Jackson

Learning to Teach English in the Secondary School, 5th Edition
Edited by Jon Davison and Caroline Daly

Learning to Teach Foreign Languages in the Secondary School, 4th Edition
Norbert Pachler, Michael Evans, Ana Redondo and Linda Fisher

Learning to Teach Geography in the Secondary School, 3rd Edition
Mary Biddulph, David Lambert and David Balderstone

Learning to Teach History in the Secondary School, 4th Edition
Edited by Terry Haydn, Alison Stephen, James Arthur and Martin Hunt

Learning to Teach ICT in the Secondary School, 3rd Edition
Edited by Marilyn Leask and Norbert Pachler

Learning to Teach Mathematics in the Secondary School, 4th Edition
Edited by Sue Johnston-Wilder, David Pimm and Clare Lee

Learning to Teach Music in the Secondary School, 3rd Edition
Edited by Carolyn Cooke, Keith Evans, Chris Philpott and Gary Spruce

Learning to Teach Physical Education in the Secondary School, 4th Edition
Edited by Susan Capel and Margaret Whitehead

Learning to Teach Religious Education in the Secondary School, 3rd Edition
Edited by L. Philip Barnes

Learning to Teach Science in the Secondary School, 4th Edition
Edited by Rob Toplis

Surviving and Thriving in the Secondary School, 1st Edition
Edited by Susan Capel, Julia Lawrence, Marilyn Leask and Sarah Younie

CONTENTS

Appendix 4 is on the companion website and can be found at
www.routledge.com/cw/capel

Appendix 4: Guidance for writing
SUSAN CAPEL AND JOHN MOSS

ILLUSTRATIONS

Figures

Tables

TASKS

COMPANION @ WEBSITE

CONTRIBUTORS

Sophy Bassett is a Senior Lecturer in Physical Education at the University of Bedfordshire. For details, please visit www.beds.ac.uk/howtoapply/departments/physical/staff/sophy-bassett

Anna Beck is a Lecturer in Teacher Professional Learning at the University of Strathclyde, Glasgow, with a particular interest in education policy.

Nikki Booth is the Advisor for Assessment Research and Development at Wolgarston High School, Staffordshire, and PhD researcher at Birmingham City University with a particular interest in assessment in music education.

Helen Bowhay is an Assistant Professor at the University of Nottingham. She is the Secondary Phase Leader for the School of Education's PGCE and School Direct PGCE Initial Teacher Education programme.

Mark Bowler is a Senior Lecturer in Physical Education and Leader of the BA (Hons) Secondary Physical Education (with QTS) Degree at the University of Bedfordshire.

Clare Brooks is the Head of Initial Teacher Education, and Head of the Curriculum Pedagogy and Assessment department and Vice Dean International at UCL Institute of Education.

Hazel Bryan is a Professor of Education and the Head of the School of Education at the University of Gloucestershire.

Diana Burton is a higher education consultant and Visiting Professor of Education at the University of Wolverhampton.

Susan Capel is an Emeritus Professor (Physical Education) at Brunel University. For details, please visit http://www.brunel.ac.uk/people/susan-capel

Chris Carpenter is a Tutor in the School of Education at Canterbury Christ Church University. He teaches on undergraduate courses in Physical Education and on the MA Education.

Leora Cruddas is the Chief Executive of Freedom and Autonomy for Schools National Association (FASNA). She was previously Director of Policy for the Association of School and College Leaders.

Andrew Csizmadia is a Senior Lecturer in Computer Science Education at Newman University, Birmingham and Academic Lead for the BCS Certificate in Computer Science Teaching.

Caroline Daly is a Reader in Education at UCL Institute of Education. For details, please visit https://iris.ucl.ac.uk/iris/browse/profile?upi=CDALY47

Paul Davies is the Head of Science at Queen's College and an Associate Senior Lecturer at University College London Institute of Education, with a particular interest in initial teacher education.

Madeleine Findon is a Senior Teaching Fellow in the Centre for Education Studies at the University of Warwick. For further details, please visit
https://warwick.ac.uk/fac/soc/ces/staff/maddyfindon

Philip Garner is a Professor of Education at the University of Northampton and has a research interest in student behaviour and teacher development.

Misia Gervis is a Postgraduate Director of Sport, Health and Exercise Sciences at Brunel University, specializing in sport psychology.

David Grace is a PGCE Physics Tutor at Aberystwyth University and also Physics Network Co-ordinator in West Wales for the Institute of Physics. He had been an A-level Physics examiner for OCR for over 40 years and is a member of the British Astronomical Association.

Graham Haydon has published widely in philosophy of education, particularly on ethics and values, and was formerly a Reader in Philosophy of Education at UCL Institute of Education.

Ruth Heilbronn is a specialist in Philosophy of Education, Linguistics and Teacher Education at the UCL Institute of Education.

Paul Howard-Jones is a Professor of Neuroscience and Education at the School of Education, University of Bristol, with a particular interest in classroom teaching and learning.

Judy Ireson is an Emerita Professor of Psychology in Education at the Institute of Education, UCL, with particular interests in learning, motivation and individual tutoring.

Divya Jindal-Snape is a Professor of Education and the Chair of Education, Inclusion and Life Transitions; and Director of the Transformative Change: Educational and Life Transitions (TCELT) Research Centre at the University of Dundee.

Sue Johnston-Wilder is an Associate Professor of Mathematics Education at the University of Warwick. Sue considers maths anxiety a stress injury; working with Clare Lee, Sue has developed the construct, "mathematical resilience" and developed courses for teachers, parents, learners and coaches to help address maths anxiety.

Jeanne Keay is a Professor of Education and the Pro Vice Chancellor (Global Engagement) at Leeds Beckett University.

Shirley Lawes is an Education Researcher, Consultant and former Teacher Educator at the University College London Institute of Education.

Julia Lawrence is the Head of Teacher Education at the University of Hull. For further details please visit https://www.hull.ac.uk/faculties/staff-profiles/julia-lawrence.aspx

Linda la Velle is the Executive Research Professor at the Institute of Education, University of Plymouth and Visiting Professor at the Institute for Education, Bath Spa University.

Marilyn Leask is a visiting Professor of Education at De Montfort and Winchester universities and Co-chair of the Education Futures Collaboration charity, which is developing MESHGuide research summaries to support evidence informed practice (www.meshguides.org).

Tony Liversidge is the Course Leader for the BSc Secondary Science with QTS course at Edge Hill University. He teaches across a range of undergraduate and postgraduate courses in initial teacher education and has a particular interest in creative science teaching and effective assessment practice in HE.

Susan Lewis is a PGCE Secondary Tutor for Chemistry and Biology at Aberystwyth University, a teacher specialising in A-Level provision at Cardigan Secondary School and an A-level examiner with the WJEC

Ceri Magill is a Senior Lecturer at Liverpool John Moores University in the school of Sport Studies, Leisure and Nutrition with a particular interest in physical education, initial teacher education and nutrition.

Paul McFlynn is a Lecturer in Education and Course Director for PGCE Physical Education at Ulster University, Coleraine.

Cara McLaughlin is a Senior Lecturer for the Institute for Education at Bath Spa University. She is a Subject Tutor for Secondary Chemistry PGCE and a Fellow of the Higher Education Academy.

Paul McQueen is a Lecturer in Education, Course Director for PGCE Music and PGCE Courses Co-ordinator at Ulster University with a particular interest in the use of technology in music education.

John Moss is a Professor of Education and the Dean of the Faculty of Education at Canterbury Christ Church University.

Debra Myhill is a Professor of Education at the University of Exeter and she has a particular interest in the teaching of writing.

Angela Newton is a Principal Lecturer in Physical Education and Postgraduate Portfolio Leader in Teacher Education at the University of Bedfordshire.

Janet Orchard is the Director of the EdD Programme and a Senior Lecturer in the School of Education, University of Bristol. She has a longstanding interest in the role of philosophy in teacher education.

Nick Peacey is an Honorary Research Associate and Fellow of the Centre for Inclusive Education at the University College London Institute of Education.

Clyde Redfern is an Associate Lecturer at the University of Wolverhampton and former Academic Group Leader at Staffordshire University.

Ana Redondo is a Subject Leader of a Secondary PGCE in Modern Foreign Languages. Her scholarly interests include the global dimension in education, international citizenship and developing appropriate pedagogies in technology-enhanced contexts.

Michelle Shaw is a Professor of Education and the Director of Education at the University of Wolverhampton and CEO of the University's Multi Academy Trust.

Stefanie Sullivan is the Associate Professor of Mathematics Education at the University of Nottingham. Stef is Director of Initial Teacher Education and Programme Leader for the Postgraduate Certificate in Mentoring and Coaching Beginning Teachers.

Alexandra Titchmarsh teaches Geography and is the Leader of Learning (pastoral), with additional responsibility for whole school attendance and safeguarding at a secondary school in West London.

Barbara Walsh is the Director of the School of Sport Studies, Leisure and Nutrition at Liverpool John Moores University with a particular interest in Initial Teacher Education.

Annabel Watson is Senior Lecturer in Language Education at the University of Exeter, School Direct Programme Director and Secondary English PGCE Lead.

Carrie Winstanley is a Professor of Pedagogy at Roehampton University, London with interests in all aspects of learning and teaching in schools, in higher education and in non-formal settings beyond the conventional classroom.

Sarah Younie is a Professor of Education Innovation and Co-director of the Institute for Education Futures at De Montfort University. For details please visit http://www.dmu.ac.uk/about-dmu/academic-staff/health-and-life-sciences/sarah-younie/sarah-younie.aspx

Paula Nadine Zwozdiak-Myers is a Senior Lecturer and Director of the Doctor of Education programme within the Department of Education at Brunel University, London. Particular interests include social justice, equity and inclusion; reflective practice; and, the professional development of teachers.

ACKNOWLEDGEMENTS

As we write this eighth edition of the *Learning to Teach in the Secondary School* textbook, we would like to start by thanking those who have contributed to the previous editions.

First, we would like to thank Tony Turner for his vital contribution as editor for editions one to six. We would also like to thank all those people not cited as authors of units in this edition but nevertheless whose work on units in earlier editions has contributed to the underpinning of units in this edition.

Francoise Allen
Michael Allen
Steve Bartlett
Rob Batho
Richard Bennett
Graham Butt
Sue Collins
David Crook
Jon Davison
Jane Dowson
Andrew Green
Terry Haydn
Graham Haydon
Susan Heightman
Margaret Jepson
David Lambert
Dawn Leslie
Ralph Levinson
David Lines
Hilary Lowe
John McCormick
John Moss

Catherine Moorhouse
Colette Murphy
Gill Nicholls
Norbert Pachler
David Pollak
Janet Pritchard
Andrea Raiker
Matti Rautiainen
Jonathan Sharples
Antony Stockford
Roger Strangwick
Alexis Taylor
Allan Thurston
Rob Toplis
Keith Topping
Tony Turner
Gill Watson
Mike Watts
Margaret Whitehead
Barbara Wynn
Bernadette Youens

Introduction

Susan Capel, Marilyn Leask and Sarah Younie

The book introduces the professional knowledge and skills required by teachers, including general principles of effective teaching. The book is backed up by subject-specific and practical texts (*Learning to Teach X Subject in the Secondary School* and *A Practical Guide to Teaching X Subject in the Secondary School*) in the *Learning to Teach in the Secondary School* series by the same editors and by *Surviving and Thriving in the Secondary School: The NQT's Essential Companion*, and *Readings for Learning to Teach in the Secondary School: A Companion to M Level Study*. This reader provides extension reading around key areas of professional knowledge underpinning teaching.

Teaching is a complex activity and is both an art and a science. In this book we show that there are certain essential elements of teaching that you can master through practice and that help you become an effective teacher. An effective teacher is one who can integrate theory with practice, use evidence to underpin their professional judgement and use structured reflection to improve practice. An effective teacher is also comfortable in the presence of young people and is interested in them as individuals as well as learners. An effective teacher motivates and encourages pupils by planning interesting lessons, and links their teaching to the life experiences of pupils. Part of being effective is to respect your pupils and, in turn, earn their respect, not only through the skills mentioned but by maintaining firm but fair discipline.

However, there is no one correct way of teaching, no one specific set of skills, techniques and procedures that you must master and apply mechanically. This is, in part, because your pupils are all different and each day brings a new context in which they operate. Every teacher is an individual and brings something of their own unique personality to the job and their interactions with pupils. We hope that this book helps you to develop skills, techniques and procedures and provides you with ways of understanding what you do and see that you can bring together into an effective whole that is appropriate for your individual personality and style, and helps you to develop your personal philosophy of teaching and learning. We also hope that the text provides the stimulus for you to want to continue to learn and develop throughout your career as a teacher. The book covers enduring principles that underpin effective teaching; however, we acknowledge that teachers work in a political environment where governments may make reforms regularly to change requirements for the curriculum content, assessment and the structure of the education system.

Developing your philosophy of teaching and learning

On your initial teacher education (ITE), much of your time is spent in school. You can expect your ITE not merely to provide *training* but also to introduce you to wider educational issues. What we mean by this is that ITE is not an apprenticeship but a step on the journey of personal development in which your teaching skills develop alongside an emerging understanding of the teaching and learning process and the education system in which it operates. This is a journey of discovery that begins on the first day of your ITE and may stop only when you retire. Teachers are expected to undertake further professional development throughout their career (many join their subject association to keep up to date (http://www.subjectassociation.org.uk/members_links.aspx)). Thus, we use the term 'initial teacher *education*' rather than 'initial teacher training' throughout this book.

The school-based element of your ITE provides the opportunity to appreciate at first hand the complex, exciting and contradictory events of classroom interactions without the immediacy of having to teach all the time. It should allow you time, both in the classroom and the wider school to make sense of experiences that demand explanations. Providing such explanations requires you to have a theory of teaching and learning.

By means of an organised ITE that provides for structured observation, practical experience and reflective activity suitably interwoven with theoretical inputs and evidence, you begin to develop your own theory of teaching and learning that is embedded in your practice. Theoretical inputs and evidence to underpin practice can come from a range of sources including tutors and teachers, lectures and print- and web-based resources. Theory also arises from practice, the better to inform and develop practice.

Everyone who teaches has a theory of how to teach effectively and of how pupils learn. The theory may be implicit in what the teacher does and teachers may not be able to tell you what their theory is. For example, a teacher who is a disciplinarian is likely to have a different theory about the conditions for learning than a teacher who is liberal in their teaching style. Likewise, some teachers may feel that they do not have a philosophy of education. What these teachers are really saying is that they have not examined their views, or cannot articulate them. What is your philosophy? For example, do you consider that your job is to transfer the knowledge of your subject to pupils? Or are you there to lead them through its main features? Are you 'filling empty vessels' or are you the guide on a 'voyage of discovery'? On the other hand, perhaps you are the potter, shaping and moulding pupils.

There are a number of different theories about teaching and learning. You need to be aware of what these are, reflect on them and consider how they help you to explain more fully what you are trying to do and why. Through the process of theorising about what you are doing, reflecting on a range of other theories as well as your own and drawing on the evidence base, you understand your practice better and develop into a reflective practitioner, that is, a teacher who makes conscious decisions about teaching strategies to employ and who modifies their practice in the light of experiences. It is recognised that ITE only enables you to start developing your own personal understanding of the teaching and learning process. Hence, this process must continue throughout your career.

An articulated, conscious philosophy of teaching emerges only if a particular set of habits is developed, in particular, the habit of reviewing your own teaching systematically. It is these habits that need to be developed from the start of your ITE. This is why we (as well as your ITE tutors) ask you to evaluate your own teaching, to keep a diary of your evaluations (reflective practice), a folder of your lesson plans and other material to develop a professional development portfolio (PDP) to record your development and carry that forward from your ITE to your first post. (This is a file where you record evidence of your practice and reflections on practice. Your ITE programme provider will advise you about how to keep these records.)

Many higher education institutions now expect student teachers to develop their PDP or equivalent as an e-portfolio. If you are learning to teach in England, you may be required to compile a self-evaluation tool that includes reflection and evidence.

How to use this book

Structure of the book

The book is laid out so that elements of appropriate background information and theory along with evidence from research and practice introduce each topic. These are interwoven with tasks designed to help you identify key features of the topic.

A number of different enquiry methods are suggested for you to use to generate data, e.g. reflecting on reading and observation or on an activity you are asked to carry out, asking questions, gathering data or discussing with a tutor or another student teacher. Some of the tasks involve you in activities that impinge on other people; for example, observing a teacher in the classroom, or asking for information. If a task requires you to do this, *you must first of all seek permission of the person concerned*. Remember that you are a guest in school(s); you cannot walk into any teacher's classroom to observe. In addition, some information may be personal or sensitive and you need to consider issues of confidentiality and professional behaviour in your enquiries and reporting.

This text is written primarily for student teachers but should also be valuable to teachers in their early years of teaching. Look also for the book in this series, called *Surviving and Thriving: Continuing to learn to teach*, alongside the MESHGuides (Mapping Education Specialist knowHow at www.meshguides.org), which are designed to provide evidence-informed guidance to support you in the early years of your career.

 An appendix on writing and reflection is included on the companion website to help you with the written assignments on your ITE. It also provides advice for you in undertaking the kind of action research project which could lead to M level accreditation. A glossary of terms is also included in the back of the book to help you interpret the jargon of education.

We call school children *pupils* to avoid confusion with *students*, by which we mean people in further and higher education. We refer to those learning to teach as *student teachers*. The important staff in your life are those in your school and higher education institution; we have called all these people *tutors*. Your institution will have its own way of referring to staff.

Meeting the requirements of your ITE

The range and type of requirements (standards) you are expected to meet during your ITE are derived from those for all student teachers in the country in which you are learning to teach. The units in this book are designed to help you work towards meeting these requirements. Your tutors in school and in your institution help you meet the requirements for your ITE. At appropriate points in the text you should relate the work directly to the specific requirements for your ITE.

M Many student teachers are on programmes that provide accreditation towards a Masters degree which can be completed through further research and study focused on the workplace in your early years of teaching. The content of this book, some of the tasks, further readings and the reader, together with the extra materials on the website, are intended to support M level work within your ITE. In this book, we use the symbol shown on the left to denote tasks which can be designed to meet the requirements of M level work, but it is up to your tutors to design assignment titles that meet the requirements of the higher education institution with which you are registered. Once you have qualified as a teacher, M level and Doctorate in Education programmes are designed to support your further professional development through research, reflection and wider reading.

Reflective practice, evidence-informed practice and your professional development portfolio (PDP)

As you read through the book, undertake other readings, complete the tasks and undertake other activities as part of your ITE, we suggest you keep a PDP. You may want to keep a diary of reflective practice to record your reactions to, and reflections on, events, both good and bad, as a way of letting off steam! It enables you to analyse strengths and areas for development, hopes for the future, and elements of your emerging personal philosophy of teaching and learning. Developing the ability to critically appraise research about teaching is integral to many ITE programmes as teaching moves towards being a profession with a publically accessible knowledge base (see www.meshguides.org for background information).

Your PDP holds a selective record of your development as a teacher, your strengths as well as areas for further development, and is something that you continue to develop throughout your teaching career. It is likely that your institution has a set format for a PDP. If not, you should develop your own. You can use any format and include any evidence you think appropriate. However, to be truly beneficial, it should contain evidence beyond the minimum required for your ITE. This further evidence could include, for example, work of value to you, a response to significant events, extracts from your diary of reflective practice, good lesson plans, evaluations of lessons, teaching reports, observations on you made by teachers, outcomes of tasks undertaken and assessed and non-assessed coursework.

At the end of your ITE you can use your PDP to evaluate your learning and achievements. It is also used as the basis for completing applications for your first post, and to take to interview. It can form the basis of a personal statement describing aspects of your development as a teacher during your ITE. Your PDP could include teaching reports written by teachers, tutors and yourself. It can also help provide the basis of your continuing professional development (CPD) as it enables you to identify aspects of your work in need of development and thus targets for induction and CPD in your first post, first through your self-evaluation tool if you are learning to teach in England, and then as part of the appraisal process you will be involved with as a teacher.

Ways you might like to use this book

With much (or all) of your ITE being delivered in school, you may have limited access to a library, to other student teachers with whom to discuss problems and issues at the end of the school day and, in some instances, limited access to a tutor to whom you can refer. There are likely to be times when you are faced with a problem in school that has not been addressed up to that point within your ITE and you need some help immediately, for example before facing a class the next day or next week.

This book is designed to help you address some of the issues or difficulties you are faced with during your ITE, by providing supporting knowledge interspersed with a range of tasks to enable you to link theory with practice.

The book may be useful in a number of ways. You may wish to use it alongside your ITE handbook, which outlines specific ITE requirements, agreed ways of working, roles and responsibilities. It is designed more for you to dip in and out of, to look up a specific problem or issue that you want to consider, rather than for you to read from cover to cover (although you may want to use it in both ways, of course). You can use it on your own as it provides background information and supporting theory along with evidence from research and practice about a range of issues you are likely to face during your ITE.

Using the tasks

Reflecting on an issue faced in school with greater understanding of evidence of what others have written and said about it, alongside undertaking some of the associated tasks, may help you to identify some potential solutions. The tasks can also be used for collaborative work with other student teachers or your tutors. Although you can complete many of the tasks individually, most tasks benefit from wider discussion, which we encourage you to do whenever possible. However, some tasks can be carried out only with other student teachers and/or with the support of a tutor. You should select those tasks that are appropriate to your circumstances.

Further reading

This book will not suffice alone; we have attempted to provide you with guidance to further reading by two methods: first, by references to print and web-based material in the text, the details of which appear in the references; second, by further readings and relevant websites at the end of each unit.

There is much educational material on the Internet. Government, teaching council and subject association websites are useful. And while there are many others, do look at the evidence underpinning the advice on offer, custom and practice in all professions is challenged as expectations for professional practice to be evidence-based rise. Useful websites are listed in each unit in the book. The website which accompanies this text www.routledge.com/cw/capel includes further information and links to useful websites. It also contains several units, including 'Managing yourself and your workload' and 'Using research and evidence to inform your teaching', from the text *Starting to Teach in the Secondary School* (Capel, Heilbronn, Leask and Turner, 2004), which support material in this text and were written specifically to support newly qualified teachers. We suggest you keep a record of useful websites in your PDP.

If you see each unit as, potentially, an open door leading to whole new worlds of thought about how societies can best educate their children, then you have achieved one of our goals: that is, to provide you with a guidebook on your journey of discovery about teaching and learning. Remember, teaching is about the contribution you make to your pupils, to their development and their learning and to the well-being of society through the education of our young people.

Finally, we hope that you find the book useful, and of support in school. If you like it, tell others; if not, tell us.

Susan Capel, Marilyn Leask, Sarah Younie
January 2019

1 Becoming a teacher

The four units in this chapter explore the complexity and breadth of the teacher's role and the nature of teaching. Some of the expectations of you in becoming a teacher include (but are not limited to):

- Dress appropriately (different schools have different dress codes).
- Act in a professional manner; for example, be punctual and reliable; act with courtesy and tact; and respect confidentiality of information.
- Take active steps to ensure that your pupils learn.
- Discuss pupil progress with parents.
- Become familiar with and work within school procedures and policies. These include record-keeping, rewards and sanctions, uniform and relationships between teachers and pupils.
- Be open to new learning: seek and act on advice.
- Be flexible; for example, if there is a change in the timetable on a particular day.
- Accept a leadership role. You may find imposing your will on pupils uncomfortable, but unless you establish your right to direct the work of the class, you are not able to teach effectively.
- Recognise and understand the roles and relationships of staff responsible for your development.
- Keep up to date with your subject.
- Have health and safety of your pupils (and yourself) (including safety) as a priority.

To become an effective teacher, you need to supplement your *subject content knowledge* with *pedagogical knowledge* (about teaching and learning) and to develop your professional knowledge, skills and judgement. Ways of developing these provide themes running throughout the book. Evidence about effective practice is becoming increasingly easy to access to support your development. In the UK, you can find a wealth of material on websites, including government-supported and subject association websites, to support you as a teacher.

Each unit in this chapter examines different facets of the work of student (and experienced) teachers. You are posed questions about your values and attitudes because these influence the type of teacher you become, the ethos of your school and the values and attitudes of pupils in your care.

Unit 1.1 is designed to give you an introduction to what teachers do. We look at teachers as individuals, then your role as a teacher, teacher language, and your work in the classroom. We then consider professional knowledge for teaching generally, followed by specific consideration of one aspect of general pedagogic knowledge – aspects of managing the learning environment. We then introduce classroom rights and responsibilities. Finally, we consider your digital profile.

In Unit 1.2 we discuss your roles and responsibilities as student teachers. This is designed to support you in preparing for school experience and on school experience itself. Your professional relationships with those with whom you work are very important; hence, we look at working with staff and pupils on school experience (including your professional and subject tutors, the class teacher and the pupils themselves). We then consider the expectations, roles and responsibilities of you on school experiences. Finally, phases which mark your development as a teacher are identified. We suggest that, as your own confidence and competence in managing the classroom grow, you can expect the focus of your work to move from your self-image and the mechanics of managing a lesson, to whole class learning and, as you become more experienced, to the learning for the individual pupil.

Unit 1.3 focuses on developing your resilience as a teacher, which is what sustains and enables teachers to thrive rather than just survive in the profession. It helps you to identify when you are stressed and looks at potential causes of stress. It then provides advice on coping with and managing stress proactively. Major causes of stress are workload and time constraints. The unit considers these, focusing on developing ways to manage your time and workload effectively, both inside and outside the classroom. Although approaches to managing your stress, workload and time are individual, being successful in managing these gives you time to enjoy your work and have time for leisure.

Unit 1.4 focuses on helping you to understand the relevance of digital technologies for you and your pupils. It then introduces a framework for auditing your knowledge and understanding of digital technologies, which is important self-knowledge for enhancing your competence in using digital technologies in your lessons to enhance pupils learning. The unit also considers your role and responsibility in promoting online safety for both yourself and the pupils you teach.

1.1 What do teachers do?

Linda la Velle and Marilyn Leask

Now, what I want is, Facts. Teach these boys and girls nothing but Facts. Facts alone are wanted in life. Plant nothing else, and root out everything else. You can only form the minds of reasoning animals upon Facts: nothing else will ever be of any service to them. This is the principle on which I bring up my own children, and this is the principle on which I bring up these children. Stick to Facts, sir!

(Thomas Gradgrind - Dickens, *Hard Times*)

Tell me, I will forget. Show me, I may remember. Involve me, and I will understand.

(Chinese proverb)

Introduction

Education is probably the most powerful influence on the development of our society. The education that young people receive through schooling goes beyond knowledge about a body of academic subjects: it is built upon and shapes the values, rights and responsibilities that make our society distinctive. That is why the form and content of education are so often the focus of scrutiny and are so keenly contested, and why you need to be able to articulate and develop your personal philosophy of education. Your personal views of the purposes of education and of the role of the teacher are major influences on your development in the profession. To enhance your understanding, you may wish to join debates about the form and content of education, which are often held through subject association networks, conferences and, to some extent, social media.

Nobody entering the teaching profession does so as a blank canvas; everyone has experienced education and this shapes their sense of what teachers are and do. Everyone has an opinion of what teachers do. Often these views are formed by personal experiences of school, and they are often idealised by the passage of time. The media, television, cinemas and literature also provide people with many and varied representations of teachers. What examples spring to your mind? However, not all of these views are either valid or useful and it is important to understand these in the context of the current school system, national education policies and the demands they place on teachers. In Units 5.3 and 7.1 you are invited to consider your personal stance on the aims, purposes and practices in education.

The two epigraphs at the beginning of the unit illustrate how different views of education and its functions can be; how differently societies and cultures construct the relationship between teachers and pupils.

Teachers, pupils, parents, carers, politicians, local authorities (LAs)/councils, teachers' unions, professional subject associations and educational researchers may have very divergent views of what teachers should do and how they should do it. Each of these perspectives needs to be considered. What a parent/carer may expect from you as a teacher, what their child may expect and what you as a teacher believe you should provide may differ significantly.

What teachers do, therefore, is complex. How to manage this without compromising the needs either of the individual pupil, the requirements of parents and carers or your own professional integrity is the focus of this unit.

OBJECTIVES

At the end of this unit you should be able to:

- describe your developing vision of yourself as a teacher and the values and ethical code/code of conduct that guide your work;
- describe various aspects of a teacher's academic, pastoral and administrative roles;
- consider effective use of language as a teacher;
- understand the multifaceted nature of the knowledge required for effective teaching;
- explain how teachers can manage proactively the learning environment;
- explain the rights and responsibilities of teachers and pupils within classrooms;
- demonstrate that your digital profile reflects the values and behaviours you aspire to as a teacher.

Check the requirements of your initial teacher education (ITE) programme to see which relate to this unit.

Teachers as individuals: your values and ethics

Teaching is a deeply personal activity. Pupils respond strongly to individual teachers. Think back to your own schooldays and the teachers you had. What do you remember about them? What did they do? Who are the teachers you most liked, and why? Which teachers did you least like, and why? Almost certainly the issues you identify are to do with personality (enthusiasm; intelligence; humour; eccentricity; conformity; efficiency; incompetence, etc.), because in a very real sense, the act of teaching is an extension of the teacher's personality. Similarly, some of the first things *your* pupils notice are your personality and your qualities. Parents and carers look at you as a person, but are also interested in a different set of issues: are you likely to form supportive relationships with their child? Do you communicate with them regularly and clearly? Do they believe you're competent?

Your head of department and senior staff may apply another set of criteria: what skills and interests do you have that could be of benefit to the department or wider school curriculum?

What you do as a teacher, therefore, has to meet a complex set of demands, and your ITE programme should provide you with opportunities both to explore individually the kind of teacher you wish to be, and also to understand the context in which you are working and the demands this places upon you as a teacher to be both professional and collegial (see, for example, the Organisation for Economic Cooperation and Development (OECD) Teaching and Learning International Survey (TALIS), 2015; Wragg, 2004; and the Masterclass series of texts (edited by Brindley)). Unit 8.4 looks at developing a teacher identity in more detail.

Your values and your ethical code

What ethical code guides your practice as a teacher? Adhering to an ethical code of practice is a condition of registration. In the United Kingdom (UK), Teachers' Councils provide ethical codes to which teachers are required to adhere and ethics/professionalism are included in the Teachers' Standards. For example, the General Teaching Council for Scotland (GTCS) has a code of conduct for student teachers that touches on: professionalism, responsibilities, competence, collegiality and working with stakeholders, equality and diversity. Task 1.1.1 asks you to consider this and other codes of conduct to draw up your own ethical code/code of conduct to guide you during your ITE programme and beyond into your teaching career.

 Task 1.1.1   Your code of professional conduct and ethics

Consider some of the professional codes of conduct and ethics on subject association, Teaching Council and Teacher Standards websites (see websites listed in Appendix 3). Review some of the ethical codes to which teachers are required to adhere in different countries. The GTCS (2012a) code of conduct for student teachers provides a starting point (http://www.gtcs.org.uk/web/FILES/teacher-regulation/student-teacher-code-0412.pdf).

Discuss the codes with other student teachers and record your code of conduct in your professional development portfolio (PDP) or equivalent.

Your role as a teacher

Teaching is an intellectual activity. Therefore, a teacher's job is primarily to ensure that pupils learn. Largely, *what* pupils should learn is determined through a published curriculum. The term 'the Hidden Curriculum' refers to what is learned outside the formal curriculum (see Unit 7.2). In England, there is a 'National Curriculum', although many schools, e.g. free schools, independent schools and academies, are not subject to this. Unit 7.2 looks at the curriculum and the companion website for this book (www.routledge.com/cw/capel) has units about the curricula for the different countries making up the UK. *How* you teach, however (i.e. the methods and materials used), is left to your professional judgement (see also Unit 8.4).

Task 1.1.2 focuses on what you personally need to do to become a qualified teacher.

Task 1.1.2   Focusing on the teachers' standards

You need to be familiar with the Teachers' Standards for the country relevant to your ITE programme. These should be in your ITE programme handbook and other documentation provided by your ITE provider. Look at them now. What do they tell you about your role as a teacher? What do they mean to you at the beginning of your ITE programme? Do you feel they capture what you want to be as a teacher? Talk to your tutor about what achieving the standards might look like at the end of your programme.

Which aspects of these Teachers' Standards do you feel most prepared to meet? Which do you believe you need more help to meet? How do you see yourself developing your capability over your ITE and career as a teacher? You may find it useful to discuss these areas with an experienced teacher, thinking about how you can record evidence of your achievements and any areas where you may require additional support.

Store the information in your PDP.

You need to spend time observing experienced teachers. You will not see two teachers the same (see Unit 2.1). Even in the highly unlikely event of you observing the same lesson taught to different classes by a pair of identical twins who are both teachers, they would have their unique take on the preparation for, delivery and evaluation of that lesson. Some of the teaching styles and strategies that you see you will like and relate to; others may not seem as appropriate and comfortable. These preferences and responses are important as you think about your own developing practice. Do not dismiss anything too quickly, however. Just because you do not like a particular approach or because a particular class does not respond well does not necessarily make the approach inappropriate. There is no single correct way to teach. Provided effective teaching and, thus, learning take place, a range of approaches from didactic (formal, instructional, heavy on content) to experiential (learning by discovery and doing) is appropriate – often in the same lesson (see Unit 5.3 on teaching styles and Unit 4.1 on ways to group pupils for learning). You can use video to record your practice so that you can analyse and improve your style as you develop as a teacher, but make sure you gain the necessary permission for video recording lessons in school. An alternative approach is 'micro-teaching'. This is a common practice in many ITE programmes and involves the filming of a short episode of teaching by a student teacher to the rest of the group. The film is then analysed by the student teacher, often with the support and input of the tutor and/or other student teachers.

Teaching is a responsible activity. As well as their academic development, you are also accountable for pupils' pastoral and personal development. In approaching this, you have an important role to play in supporting the school ethos by reinforcing school values, rules and routines, e.g. behaviour, dress, mutual respect, the right to learn and in encouraging pupils to develop self-discipline so that the school can function effectively and pupils can make the most of opportunities that the school and their schooling offers.

Finally, teaching is an administrative activity. You need to develop efficient ways of dealing with educational organisation and management (see Unit 1.3). Developing your information and communications (ICT)/digital technology skills is essential in helping you prepare teaching materials, in supporting pupils learning, in recording and monitoring progress and in keeping up to date with daily administrative tasks. Many teachers keep their pupil records electronically using spreadsheets, and schools normally have Management Information Systems holding data used to monitor pupil performance and assessment. This is essential, not only for accountability, but also for data analysis to support performance improvement (see Unit 6.1). For advice in your subject area, see the subject-specific and practical texts in this *Learning to Teach in the Secondary School* series (see p.ii of this text) and subject association websites (see Appendix 2).

So, your role as a teacher falls into distinct categories. You have responsibility for both the academic and the pastoral development of your pupils. Table 1.1.1 lists the main activities in each of these areas that you are expected to undertake.

Your role in raising attainment and improving life chances

Raising attainment is a collective endeavour involving all in the school working together. The connection between educational attainment and life chances is significant. Pupils obtaining the best grades have more choices, are able to access the top-ranking universities and employment, and so on. It is thus clearly desirable that pupils attain to the very best of their ability through their schooling. It is incumbent on you as a teacher to ensure that every pupil is given the very best opportunity to fulfil his or her potential, and great pressure is often applied to teachers to demonstrate this. Pupil attainment

Table 1.1.1 Some of the activities that teachers undertake in their academic and pastoral roles

The academic role	The pastoral role and spiritual and moral welfare
This encompasses a variety of activities including: ■ subject teaching ■ lesson preparation ■ setting and marking of homework ■ monitoring pupil progress over time ■ assessing pupil progress in a variety of ways, including marking tests and exams ■ writing reports ■ recording achievement ■ working as part of a subject team ■ curriculum development and planning ■ undertaking visits, field courses ■ reporting to parents/carers ■ planning and implementing school policies ■ extra-curricular activities ■ keeping up to date (often through work with your subject association See www.subjectasso ciation.org.uk/members_links) ■ being an examiner for public examination boards, e.g. General Certificate of Secondary Education (GCSE)/General Certificate of Education (GCE) Advanced (A) Level boards	These roles vary from school to school. They often include: ■ getting to know the pupils as individuals ■ helping pupils with problems ■ being responsible for a form/tutor group ■ registering the class, following up absences ■ monitoring sanctions and rewards given to form members ■ reinforcing school rules and routines, e.g. on behaviour ■ writing reports, ensuring records of achievement and/or profiles are up to date ■ working collegially as part of a pastoral team ■ teaching personal, social and health education (PSHE) and citizenship ■ house/year group activities (plays/sports) ■ liaising with parents and carers ■ ensuring school information is conveyed to parents via pupils ■ extra-curricular activities, e.g. educational trips ■ giving careers and subject guidance ■ taking part in a daily act of worship required by legislation ■ liaising with primary schools

Table 1.1.2 'The Average Child'

I don't cause teachers trouble, my grades have been okay.

I listen in my classes and I'm in school every day.

My parents think I'm average, my teachers think so too.

I wish I didn't know that cause there's lots I'd like to do.

I'd like to build a space rocket, I've a book that shows you how.

Or start a stamp collection, well no use trying now.

Cause since I've found I'm average, I'm just not smart enough you see

I know there's nothing special that I should expect of me.

I'm part of that majority that hump part of the bell*,

Who'll just spend all his life in an average kind of hell.

*This refers to the bell shape of a 'normal distribution' curve.

Source: Buscemi (date unknown) in P. Reeve (1992).

is compared internationally, and the results are of great interest and concern for governments (see Unit 7.4). However, where too much attention is paid to raising attainment without corresponding consideration being given to developing pupils' inquisitiveness and autonomy, instrumental practice can easily emerge. 'Spoon-feeding' and 'teaching to the test' may lead to improved attainment in headline examinations, but they do little genuinely to enhance pupils' transferrable abilities as lifelong learners (see, for example, Volante, 2004). For the teacher, the drive to ensure that pupils achieve the best possible results in their assessments must be tempered by the need to provide pupils with the resources they need to be independently functional members of society. This is where educational politics come face to face with educational ethics. The pupils who emerge with the most robust independent abilities are those best placed to meet the increasingly challenging and uncertain demands of employability in the world of the 21st century. Therefore, you need to think very carefully about how you respond to the needs of your pupils and the demands of your employers as you consider issues of raising attainment. Pupils' self-belief and motivation to learn is essential in providing foundations for successful learning, and there is no foundation for the commonly held belief that intelligence is fixed (see Unit 5.6). Your responsibility is to ensure that the pupils themselves realise that they do have considerable capacity and can set high expectations of themselves. The poem 'The Average Child' highlights the damaging effect on pupils of views that intelligence is fixed (see Table 1.1.2). Then complete Task 1.1.3.

 Task 1.1.3   Motivating pupils

Reflect on the poem 'The Average Child' (Table 1.1.2). Think about its implications for your own teaching. In your classroom observations and evaluations, focus on an 'average child' for a number of sessions. Plan your interactions with a small group of these pupils so that you leave them feeling positive about learning and their capacities. Discuss your perceptions with other student teachers and record these in your PDP.

Teacher language

Recognising the social and linguistic disadvantage of a large section of UK society, the Newsom Report recommended to the then Ministry of Education that all secondary subject teachers should also be teachers of English (Newsom, 1963). This still holds true, because language is clearly central to the process of teaching and learning. Whether you are communicating with pupils in the spoken or the written medium, it is essential that you think very carefully about your use of language. It is important to remember that language is used in the classroom for a variety of purposes:

■ to provide direction through the lesson;
■ to question;
■ to impart information;
■ to develop relationships;
■ to give instructions, etc.

An important issue to consider in relation to teacher language is the use of technical subject terminology. Every subject has its own vocabulary, and it is the subject teacher's responsibility to think about this. If science teachers wish their pupils to know how to spell and use the word 'photosynthesis' accurately, it is their job to teach this. Similarly, if you are a business studies teacher and wish your pupils to write reports, you need to equip them with the language tools to do so. Think very carefully about the language and the written forms of your subject. Are these in themselves useful and meaningful, or is it the concepts behind the words and forms that are more important? Think in detail about how and when to introduce subject-specific terminology and develop concise and accurate definitions with which pupils are able to work. Remember that when you introduce a new word, pupils need to be able not only to pronounce, but also to spell it. They need to hear it and see it. Importantly, be aware that terms have different meanings in different subject contexts. Take, for instance, the word 'depression':

■ in geography, a depression is an area of low air pressure;
■ in history, the Depression was a specific era of United States history in the late 1920s and the 1930s;
■ in medicine, depression is a mental state;
■ in English, it may be all of the above, or a hollow in the ground.

As a teacher, it is very important to think about how and when these different language modes are required, and how pupils differentiate between them, whether encountered in the written or the spoken form. It is well worthwhile spending time exploring the range of your voice so that you can develop appropriate varieties of tone and register for these different types of talk. Which tone of voice will you adopt so that pupils know when you are giving instructions? How about when you are disciplining an individual or a class? Your tone of voice reinforces the purposes of language. An important general principle of voice projection is that as you get louder, you should aim to lower the pitch of your voice if possible. This helps to prevent shrillness and strain. (Using your voice is covered in Unit 3.1.)

Additionally, time is well spent in thinking carefully about language formulas that might be useful, recording those used by experienced teachers whom you are observing and practicing using them so as to build your professional toolkit. Such formulas include:

■ I am not happy with…;
■ I want you to think carefully about…;

- Either... or...;
- I want you to make sure that....

These examples illustrate another important general principle in using language to give instructions and manage behaviour; i.e. owning the issue, as in, 'I am not happy about the noise level...' rather than, 'You are getting too noisy...'.

Thinking through both what you want to say and how you want to say it increases your confidence in the use of teacher language. Questions should be planned (see Units 3.1; 5.2), to avoid what might be thought of as 'what's in my head' questions, where the pupils have to guess what you are thinking about. Transactional language (e.g. instructions about how to move into groups) can be prepared ahead. Explanations are usually much clearer if you have thought them through in advance rather than trying to develop them on the spot in the classroom. Much of the language you need to use is firmly within your control and needs to be thought through in detail.

There are, of course, occasions when language needs to be spontaneous, such as when answering unexpected questions, or when dealing with behaviour that doesn't meet the standard you require. This is an aspect of the teacher's job about which student teachers tend to worry most. When managing such behaviours, it is very important to ensure that your language is clear, controlled and respectful - regardless of the language pupils may be using themselves and regardless of your own emotions. Behaviour management situations tend to arise unexpectedly but many of these issues can be prevented by planning ahead and preparing possible responses (see Unit 3.3). The following questions will help you consider use of language in these situations. We also suggest recording the techniques used by experienced teachers whom you are observing and practicing using them. Such formulas include:

- Is a verbal response necessary at all? Would silence or some non-verbal form of communication be more effective? Note stance, facial gestures and arm and hand movements of experienced teachers.
- Which tone of voice is best? A raised voice? A quiet voice? A sympathetic voice?
- Should you speak in front of the whole class so that all can hear, but which may inflame a situation? Would it be more effective to speak to the individual or group of perpetrators quietly, saying perhaps, 'We can discuss this after the lesson'?
- Should a response be immediate or would taking a moment to consider before speaking be more appropriate?

Think through and plan some language formulas that could be used in different situations. This will help you to behave in a calm, controlled and measured way. How and when, for example, might you use the following:

- Either... or...;
- If you cannot calm down, then...;
- You know I do not like it when...;
- Are you refusing to...;
- Would it help if...;
- I think it would be better if....

Teacher language in all its forms needs to be very carefully considered, and is further explored in Unit 3.1 'Communicating with pupils' and Unit 5.8 'Creating a language rich classroom'.

Finally, be clear; your voice is very important to you as a teacher, so you need to look after it. See if your ITE provider puts on sessions on voice projection and voice protection. Voice projection equipment designed for use in classrooms is also available should you need it.

Your work in the classroom – the tip of the iceberg

On the surface, teaching may appear to be a relatively simple process – the view that teachers stand and talk to their classes and that the pupils automatically learn appears to be all too prevalent. (Ask friends and family what they think a teacher does.) The reality is somewhat different.

Classroom teaching is only the most visible part of teachers' work. It may help to consider the cycle of pedagogic reasoning and action set out in Figure 1.1.1 (Shulman, 1987), its elements and the underlying knowledge and skills that drive it.

The cycle begins and ends with an act of **comprehension**. The teacher knows about something to be taught. S/he then has to 'transform' that knowledge into a form that is learnable by the pupils. This **transformation** requires the deployment of several stages and skill sets. In Figure 1.1.1 the sub-cycle to the right shows the process of transformation with the teacher serially *preparing* (critical scrutiny and choice of materials of instruction); *representing* (consideration of the key ideas and how they might best be represented in the form of analogies, examples, etc); *selecting* (choice of teaching strategies) and *adapting*, sometimes called differentiating: tailoring input to pupils' capabilities and characteristics. The teacher sequences a series of teaching/learning episodes to create a logical yet varied lesson. The teacher then provides that lesson (**instruction**), during which there are checks for pupil understanding as well as more formal assessments and feedback (which themselves require all the processes above): **evaluation**. Following the lesson, an effective teacher sets aside time for reconstruction, re-enactment or recapturing of events and accomplishments: **reflection**, which is the critically important process of analysis through which the individual teacher learns from experience. This brings the teacher to a new, more informed and nuanced level of comprehension about the topic of the lesson. The pedagogic cycle should therefore not be thought of as a flat cyclic diagram, but rather as an upward, three-dimensional spiral in which professional knowledge and expertise are continually built.

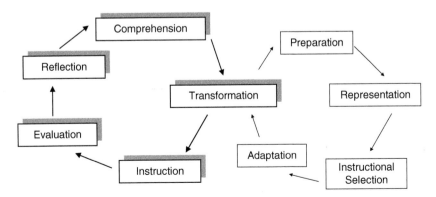

Figure 1.1.1 Shulman's Pedagogic Cycle (after Baggott la Velle, 2001)

The following analogy may help you understand what underpins your work in the classroom. Think of a lesson as being like an iceberg. The work in the classroom represents the tip of an iceberg (20-30 per cent). Supporting this tip, but hidden in the base (70-80 per cent), are the elements of teachers' professional expertise (see Figure 1.1.2). These elements include:

- *planning* a sequence of lessons to ensure learning progresses;
- *evaluation* of previous lessons;
- *planning and preparation* for individual lessons;
- *established routines and procedures* that ensure that the work of the class proceeds as planned;
- *personality*, including the teacher's ability to capture and hold the interest of the class, to establish their authority;
- *professional knowledge*, such as subject content knowledge (SCK); pedagogic knowledge about effective teaching and learning; knowledge of learners; knowledge about the educational context in which you work - local and national;
- *professional judgement* built up over time through reflection on experience.

The contents of this book introduce you to what we see as the invisible foundation of the teacher's work: *professional knowledge* (see Table 1.1.3) about teaching and learning and *professional judgement* about the routines, skills and strategies that support strong teaching (see Unit 8.4). Effective teachers draw on these elements in their planning and preparation to ensure that there is *continuity* and *progression* in pupils' learning. Each lesson is planned as part of a sequence of learning experiences designed to build pupils' engagement with and understanding of the topics they are studying (see Unit 2.2).

Throughout your ITE programme, you should expect to develop confidence and new levels of competence in all the areas in Figure 1.1.2.

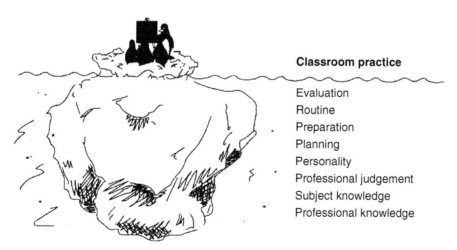

Classroom practice

Evaluation
Routine
Preparation
Planning
Personality
Professional judgement
Subject knowledge
Professional knowledge

Figure 1.1.2 The work in the classroom - the tip of the iceberg
Source: With kind permission of Simon Beer

Professional knowledge for teaching

This section gives an overview of the forms of knowledge you need for teaching.

Teaching requires you to transform the knowledge you possess into suitable tasks that lead to learning (sometimes called pedagogic knowledge). Knowing a lot about your subject does not automatically make you an effective teacher. Your professional knowledge comprises a number of different components.

The forms of knowledge teachers need has been described in different ways. Shulman (1986; 1987) identifies seven knowledge bases that form what he regards as the minimum knowledge for teaching. These are summarised in Table 1.1.3. This is a starting point for thinking about the forms of professional knowledge you may need to acquire.

Subject content knowledge (SCK)

This is a declared body of knowledge about your subject. Within the curriculum for that subject it comprises the concepts and skills pupils are expected to acquire. You amass this knowledge from a variety of sources: your education at home, at school and at university, as well as through personal study and reading. Together, these shape the quantity and quality of your SCK. Your explicit awareness of and engagement with these different sources of SCK vary, but as you begin your career as a teacher, this is likely to be the area in which you are most confident. You should actively seek to extend the

Table 1.1.3 Forms of professional knowledge for teaching (adapted from Shulman, 1986; 1987)

1	*(Subject) Content knowledge*: the content that is to be taught. Schwab (1964) identifies two components of content knowledge:
	■ substantive: core concepts and skills in the subject ■ syntactic: the way these concepts and skills are structured and organised within the subject
2	*General pedagogic knowledge*: broad principles and strategies of classroom management and organisation that apply irrespective of the subject
3	*Pedagogical content knowledge (PCK)*: knowledge of what makes for effective teaching and deep learning, providing the basis for teachers' selection, organisation and presentation of lesson content; i.e. the integration of subject content and its related pedagogy. Grossman et al. (1989) break PCK into four components:
	■ knowledge and beliefs about the *purposes* of teaching a subject at different levels ■ knowledge of pupils' understanding, *conceptions and misconceptions* of subject matter ■ knowledge of *curriculum* materials available for teaching a subject and knowledge of horizontal and vertical curricula for the subject ■ knowledge of *instructional strategies* and representations for teaching particular topics
4	*Curriculum knowledge*: materials and programmes that serve as 'tools of the trade' for teachers
5	*Knowledge of learners and their characteristics*: this comprises a variety of issues – child development; how children develop with age (empirical or social knowledge); cognitive development; knowledge of the needs of particular individuals or groups of pupils
6	*Knowledge of educational contexts*: political, curricular, sociological, cultural, geographical, historical and psychological factors may all be important here
7	*Knowledge of educational ends (aims), purposes, values and philosophical and historical influences*: both short- and long-term goals of education in general and of particular subjects

range of your SCK. This process supports your confidence for teaching and engages you with your subject on a personal level. A word of caution, however: you may see this body of knowledge as the key measure of your likely effectiveness as a teacher, but it is the way you transform that knowledge into effective teaching that is most important. Task 1.1.4 asks you to audit your SCK.

 Task 1.1.4   Auditing your subject content knowledge

Analyse a copy of the curriculum for your subject, identifying areas where your SCK is good now, areas in which you require some additional knowledge and areas in which totally new learning is required. Set yourself targets for developing your knowledge in the areas for development you identify. Discuss these areas for development with your tutor. Plan a course of action for this development. Keep a record of your progress in your PDP.

General pedagogic knowledge (GPK)

This body of knowledge and understanding relates to the effective transformation of your SCK into meaningful learning for pupils, as described above. This knowledge includes the broad principles and strategies that are designed to guide class instruction, organisation and management (e.g. settling a class, managing the learning environment for effective learning, managing resources and other equipment, gaining and sustaining the attention and interest of the whole class, encouraging the disaffected, supporting the less able, extending the most able and motivating each member of the class). By developing your general pedagogic knowledge, your classroom becomes a more varied, stimulating and rewarding place both for yourself and your pupils.

Pedagogical content knowledge (PCK)

This is a combination of SCK and pedagogy that provides the specific knowledge you need for effective teaching and learning in your subject area(s). For example, the ways in which Music teachers shape teaching and learning differs in some ways to the way Design and Technology teachers shape teaching and learning.

Teaching requires you to adapt your PCK to the classroom demands of teaching. It also requires you to consider the processes of your subject and how you can teach these to your pupils. What, for example, are the language and writing demands of your subject, and how are you going to teach them? What research skills and processes should pupils adopt? What forms does assessment (both formative and summative) take in your subject area(s), and how does this relate to content and process? PCK is effectively what pedagogy looks like in your subject area(s). Shulman (1986, p.9) sums it up as follows. PCK is:

> the most useful form of representation of...[the most regularly taught topics in one's subject area]...the most powerful analogies, illustrations, examples, explanations, and demonstrations – in a word, the ways of representing and formulating the subject that makes it comprehensible to others.

You should also think about the historical development of your subject, and think about how it came to be as it is. This dimension enhances your sense of what your subject is about and why it is studied. For further information see the subject-specific textbooks in the Routledge *Learning to Teach* series.

Curriculum knowledge

This is your knowledge of the requirements and range of programmes for teaching your subject(s) across the age ranges that you are preparing to teach. Crucially, this knowledge base includes an understanding of the sequence in which the facts and concepts of a discipline should be taught and learned for greatest understanding. It also encompasses knowledge of the variety of instructional materials available to support the programmes of work. It includes knowledge of the curriculum required in your country and in your school(s), the public examinations they serve and the requirements of those examinations.

Knowledge of learners' and their characteristics

Pupils come with different kinds of knowledge. Shulman (1986; 1987) and Grossman et al. (1989) define this as including empirical and social knowledge, i.e. what children of a particular age range are like, how they behave in classrooms and school, their interests and preoccupations, their social nature, how contextual factors such as weather or exciting events can affect their work and behaviour and the nature of the pupil-teacher relationship, as well as cognitive knowledge.

You need to think about how children develop and what they know, which consists of two elements: knowledge of child development that informs practice; and knowledge of a particular group of pupils, the kind of knowledge that grows from regular contact with these pupils, of what they can and cannot know, do or understand.

Knowledge of educational contexts

Shulman (1986; 1987) and Grossman et al. (1989) define an educational context as any setting where learning takes place. This includes formal settings (schools, nurseries, universities and colleges), informal settings (home, museums, concert halls, art galleries, etc.) and broader educational contexts (social, cultural and communal). The context often has a significant effect on teaching and learning and the work of teachers. In the multicultural classrooms of today, you can expect to be teaching pupils from a wide range of different educational and cultural systems where the expectations of teachers and pupils may be quite different than those you have personally experienced. It is important to think about issues such as:

- the type and size of schools;
- their catchment areas;
- class size;
- the extent and quality of support for teachers;
- the amount of feedback that teachers receive on their performance;
- quality of relationships in schools;
- expectations, philosophies and attitudes of the head teacher;
- schools' policies, curriculum, assessment processes, monitoring and reporting, safety, school rules and expectations;

■ 'hidden' and 'informal' curriculum, which includes the values demonstrated to pupils through the way the school is run (see also Unit 7.2, 'The school curriculum').

The units in Chapter 7 in this book and on the web provide an overview of educational contexts in the four countries of the United Kingdom (England, Northern Ireland, Scotland, Wales).

Knowledge of educational ends (aims), purposes, values and philosophical and historical influences

This includes the values and priorities that shape the education that pupils receive. Teaching is a purposeful activity, both in the short-term (goals for individual lessons or series of lessons) and the long-term (broader purposes, philosophies and functions of education). Views as to the purposes of education vary widely. Some would argue that its long-term goal is to produce efficient workers to serve the needs of society. Others see education as being of intrinsic worth in itself. Aims and purposes tend to be implicit rather than obvious and openly enacted.

Your personal subject construct

All of the above aspects of professional knowledge for teaching are brought together in your *personal subject construct* (Banks et al., 1999), which is the version of the subject that encapsulates your values and assumptions about your subject. This construct provides the basis of your work as a teacher, your understanding of the nature of your subject and how to teach it. Think, for example, about how your political, philosophical, theoretical and religious views shape the version of your subject you wish to teach? Within subject areas specific questions may arise. What, for instance, is the role of sport in physical education? Should creationism be taught alongside evolution and the Big Bang in science lessons? And what about your wider role as a teacher, beyond your subject boundaries? What is your view of supporting language development or teaching mathematical skills as the need arises in your lessons? Such questions have a significant impact on the choices that you make as a teacher. You should ensure that the personal beliefs and subject constructs you use in the classroom do not exclude colleagues and pupils with different views.

Some of the units in this book aim to develop your *general pedagogic knowledge*: your understanding of classroom management and organisation and what makes for effective teaching and deep learning, your *knowledge of learners and their characteristics* and your *knowledge of educational contexts*. Subject-specific pedagogic issues are covered in the subject texts in the *Learning to Teach in the Secondary School* series. Task 1.1.5 asks you to consider PCK.

 Task 1.1.5   Pedagogical Content Knowledge

Look closely at the forms of PCK in Table 1.1.3. Consider carefully how you could apply your knowledge in each of the categories identified by Grossman et al. (1989) to your work with pupils to make them more reflective learners and to personalise their learning experience. Record your notes in your PDP.

Managing the learning environment: a key part of your general pedagogic knowledge

An important aspect of your job is managing the learning environment of your classrooms. *Learning to manage the classroom* is similar in many ways to learning to drive. At the outset there seems so much to remember (using the clutch, brake, changing gear, watching other traffic, looking in the mirror, indicating, obeying the speed limit and so on), but after a short time such skills become part of subconscious, internalised patterns of behaviour.

Much of what experienced teachers do to manage their classes has become part of their unconscious classroom behaviour. So much so that often teachers find it hard to articulate exactly what it is they are doing or why it is successful. This situation, of course, does not help you as a student teacher. It also gives weight to the spurious notion that teachers are born rather than made and that nobody can tell you how to teach.

Some teachers may well begin teaching with certain advantages such as a 'good' voice or organisational skills. Nevertheless, there are common skills and techniques to be learned that, when combined with an awareness of and sensitivity towards the contexts within which you are teaching, enable you to manage your classes effectively. Part of the joy of teaching is that *it is a continuously creative and problem-solving activity*. Pupils and groups of pupils each have their own characteristics and group dynamics, which experienced teachers take into account when planning for teaching and learning. For example, if there has been recent controversy over environmental issues in the local area teachers could adapt their teaching to incorporate this issue, thus allowing pupils to draw on their own contextualised experiences. Although lessons with different groups may have similar content, the same lesson is virtually never delivered in the same way twice because of the variety in relationships between individuals, the whole class and the teacher.

Rogers (2002, p.5) comments:

> Day-to-day school teaching normally takes place in a rather unusual setting: a small room (for what is asked of it), often inadequate furniture and space to move, a 50-minute time slot (or less) to cover set curriculum objectives, and 25 to 30 distinct and unique personalities, some of whom may not even want to be there. Why should there not be some natural stresses and strains associated with a teacher's day-to-day role?

One of your most important roles is to bring together the various personalities of your classroom (including your own) to create from these the best possible context for learning. This requires careful thought, planning and preparation. The key to success is to minimise the element of surprise. Of course, at some point, matters always arise to which you have to react. The majority of events and issues occurring in the classroom are, however, foreseeable and can, therefore, be planned for. It is always better to be proactive than reactive.

When you plan, you should think not only of what you are going to teach and how you are going to teach it, but also of the implications of these choices. If, for example, you want your class to watch (part of) a DVD, have you checked that the equipment works and that you have located the relevant section of the DVD? If you want the class to move into groups halfway through the lesson, have you thought about the rationale for your groups, who is going to work with whom and how you are going to manage their movement? How are you going to manage the distribution of books or worksheets? Are all pupils working from books with the same page numbering? Such questions may seem small, but failure to think about such issues can cause significant interruption and disruption to learning. Effective teachers run efficient classrooms, and efficiency maximises the potential for learning and cooperation.

Some of the important things for you to consider are:

- timing;
- seating plans;
- organisation of desks/materials/texts/etc.;
- how you plan to use Teaching Assistants (TAs) – meeting with them prior to the lesson is always advisable;
- pitch/differentiation/extension of work;
- range of activity;
- likely trouble spots (e.g. using technology, writing on the board, distributing papers, setting homework, moving pupils into groups, etc.).

Units 4.3, 5.1 and 5.3 introduce you to theories underpinning educational practice and ideas that can provide a foundation for your development as an effective teacher, whatever your subject. But what do we mean by effective teaching?

Effective teaching

Effective teaching occurs when the learning experience structured by the teacher matches the needs of each pupil and when tasks effectively build on pupils' knowledge, skills and attitudes. A key feature of effective teaching is balancing pupils' chances of success against the level of difficulty required to challenge them. The units in Chapter 5 provide further information about pupil learning. Understanding the varied ways in which learning takes place and the ways in which pupils' learning styles and preferences can be used is essential.

Classroom rights and responsibilities

It is also important to think about rights and responsibilities in the classroom, including your own. Everyone should understand clearly that rights are counterbalanced by responsibility in terms of behaviour and participation and that in the best interests of everybody, clear and appropriate sanctions will be applied to those who do not comply.

The following are useful areas to consider in relation to the rights and responsibilities of your classroom:

- *Respect*: all pupils and teachers deserve personal respect; everyone should employ respectful language; it is important to respect the views and beliefs of others.
- *Attention*: every pupil has the right to receive a fair share of teachers' attention; when invited to address the class, pupils have the right to be heard; everyone must pay full attention to the requirements of the lesson; when the teacher speaks, all must pay attention.
- *Learning/teaching*: all pupils have the right to learn; teachers have the right to teach; everyone has the responsibility of cooperating so that effective teaching and learning can take place.

- *Safety*: everyone should expect to be safe; everyone must ensure that safety is not compromised. Remember that teachers are responsible for the wellbeing and safeguarding of their pupils. Think carefully about the activities with which pupils engage; consider their risks and take appropriate steps to ensure safe practice. Some subject areas, such as science, technology or physical education carry more inherent risks, but all teachers need to take personal responsibility for ensuring safety and well-being in their lessons. Pupils should be made aware of the risks and take responsibility for acting safely.
- *Safeguarding* of children is an increasingly high-profile issue. Some of the major areas that all teachers must consider are the following:
  - child protection issues;
  - physical abuse and neglect (including female genital mutilation);
  - mental abuse (including forced marriage);
  - sexual abuse and exploitation;
  - emotional well-being;
  - e-safety;
  - accident protection and prevention;
  - drug and alcohol misuse;
  - mental health.

National Institute for Health and Care Excellence (NICE) Pathways provide useful evidence-informed information (http://pathways.nice.org.uk) on many of these topics.

Teachers must be familiar with such issues, the common signs of problems and procedures and channels for dealing with them. Each school is obliged to develop policies to support practice in these areas, and charities exist in some specialist areas.

There may well be other rights and responsibilities that you wish to establish for your classroom. Task 1.1.6 asks you to think now about what these might be and how you are going to establish and maintain them. See Unit 8.3 on your legal responsibilities.

 Task 1.1.6   Classroom rights and responsibilities

Working with fellow student teachers, if possible, consider the rights and responsibilities operating in classrooms that you have observed. Draw up a list for your classes and store it in your PDP to refer to and develop as you progress through your ITE programme.

Your digital profile: what image do you want to project?

Lastly, in developing your professional code of conduct and ethical stance, we suggest you consider what your digital footprint says about you. It is important that you review how you are presented on social media to check that you are portraying the values and behaviours that will earn you the respect of your pupils, parents and carers and your peers and employers.

SUMMARY AND KEY POINTS

So, let us return to the question that is the title of this unit. Becoming a teacher: what do teachers do?

■ In some countries, teachers are free to choose what they teach and how they teach.
■ In others the curriculum is set centrally and teachers' choices about how to teach may be more constrained.
■ Your own philosophy of teaching affects the way you approach your work and develops over time as you acquire further professional knowledge and judgement.
■ As a student teacher, you test out and develop a repertoire of teaching styles and strategies. It may take you considerable time before you can apply the principles of effective teaching to your classroom practice, but you can monitor your development through regular evaluation of lessons. In this book, we aim to provide a basic introduction to what are complex areas, and it is up to you to develop systematically your professional knowledge and judgement by analysing and reflecting on your experience and wider reading.
■ As a teacher you have responsibilities to your pupils, their parents and carers, your head of department, your school, your head teacher and others.
■ Whatever your own subject discipline, all teachers are teachers of literacy, numeracy and ICT/digital skills.
■ Being an effective teacher does not mean simply knowing your subject. It also means:

  ■ knowing how to teach lessons that are intellectually robust, challenging and stimulating;
  ■ managing the classroom effectively and fairly; assessing and monitoring pupils' progress promptly and accurately;
  ■ modelling in your own behaviour and practice what you expect pupils to do; planning for inclusion and the needs of individual pupils;
  ■ managing the rights and responsibilities of the classroom;
  ■ upholding school policies and procedures;
  ■ responding to the pastoral and personal needs of your pupils;
  ■ completing administrative duties;
  ■ contributing to the wider life of the school;
  ■ knowing your legal responsibilities.

As you progress through your ITE programme you develop knowledge, understanding and skills that enable you to fulfil your roles and responsibilities in all of these areas. Through your experiences in school, you should move from knowing about skills to a position where you can use them flexibly and appropriately in a range of situations. In other words, you learn to do what teachers do - the school equivalent of plate-spinning - as you balance the many demands of the wonderful job that is teaching.

Check which requirements for your ITE programme you have addressed through this unit.

 **Further resources**

Association of American Educators (2015) *Code of Ethics for Educators*, **viewed 1 July 2018, from http://www.aaeteachers.org/index.php/about-us/aae-code-of-ethics**
This is an example of a code of ethics for educators. However, this site for professional educators also has a range of other resources.

GTCS (General Teaching Council for Scotland) (2015) *Code of Professionalism and Conduct*, **viewed 8 June 2018, from http://www.gtcs.org.uk/standards/copac.aspx**
This site has a range of resources relevant to educators as well as an ethical code for teachers and student teachers.

Mercer, N. (2015) *Thinking Together Project Materials.* **University of Cambridge Faculty of Education, viewed 8 June 2018, from https://thinkingtogether.educ.cam.ac.uk/**
These materials support a dialogue-based approach to the development of pupil's thinking and learning and include spoken language.

MESHGuide Research Summaries for Teachers, viewed 8 June 2018, from www.meshguides.org

Subject associations, viewed 8 June 2018, from http://www.subjectassociations.org.uk

Teachers Support Network, viewed 8 June 2018, from www.teachersupport.info
Teacher Support Network is a 24-hour confidential counselling, support and advice service. It also offers support lines in England (tel: 08000 562 561), Wales (tel: 08000 855 088) and Scotland (tel: 0800 564 2270).

Appendix 2 lists subject associations and teacher councils and Appendix 3 provides a list of websites.

Capel, S., Leask, M. and Turner, T. (eds.) (2010) *Readings for Learning to Teach in the Secondary School: A Companion to M Level Study*, **Abingdon: Routledge.**
This book brings together essential readings to support you in your critical engagement with key issues raised in this textbook.

Capel, S., Lawrence, J. Leask, M. and Younie, S. (eds.) (2019) *Surviving and Thriving in the Secondary School: The NQT's Essential Companion,* **Abingdon: Routledge.**
This book is designed to support newly qualified teachers in the next phase of development as a teacher. However, you may find it useful as it covers aspects of teaching not included in this book which, nonetheless, you experience on your ITE programme.

The subject specific books in the *Learning to Teach (Subject)* series, the *Practical (Subject) Guides, Debates in (Subject)* and *Mentoring (Subject) Teachers* are also very useful.

Any additional resources and an editable version of any relevant tasks/tables in this unit are available on the companion website: www.routledge.com/cw/capel

1.2 Student teachers' roles and responsibilities

Susan Capel

Introduction

Schools are busy places and teachers are often required to juggle many tasks at once. Unit 1.1 provides some insight into what it is to be a teacher. This unit looks at what it is to be a student teacher in a secondary school and considers the school experience itself. We look at your relationships with both staff and pupils that form part of the busy life of schools, discuss some specific expectations of student teachers in school and offer some guidance about your roles and responsibilities. The unit then considers how your development as a professional is likely to pass through significant changes over your initial teacher education (ITE) programme.

OBJECTIVES

At the end of this unit, you should be able to:

■ prepare for school experience;
■ work with other staff and pupils on school experience;
■ identify expectations, roles and responsibilities of student teachers in school;
■ chart aspects of your development as a teacher over your ITE programme and into your future learning and development.

Check the requirements of your ITE programme to see which relate to this unit.

Preparing for school experience

Before you start any school experience, it is important to know the key players in the school and your ITE programme. Although nomenclature may differ from school to school, the terms given in the first column of Table 1.2.1 are those most used in this unit.

Table 1.2.1 The key players in your ITE programme

Key player	Alternative names	Role
Head teacher	Headmaster; headmistress; head	Carries overall responsibility for the care of pupils, the quality of teaching and learning, and many other aspects of school life.
Professional tutor	Professional coordinating tutor; professional coordinating mentor	Responsible for all student teachers in the school. Organises regular school-wide training sessions. Usually a senior member of staff.
Subject tutor	School-based mentor; class mentor; school tutor; mentor	Your first point of contact within the school. Organises your day-to-day learning in the department, timetabling, weekly meetings and so on.
Class teachers	Teachers; teaching staff	Members of staff whose classes you are given responsibility for during your time in school. Your school mentor may also be one of your class teachers.
Head of department	Head of subject; head of faculty; subject coordinator; subject lead	Responsible for running the subject department where you are placed.
University tutor	Link tutor; tutor	Responsible for your ITE programme both in school and the university. Delegates to school staff during the school experience.
Student teacher	Student; trainee teacher; trainee; beginning teacher	Yourself

It is also important to find out as much as you can about the school and its organisation, as well as the specific department you will be working with.

You can gather information about schools from inspection reports (information about how to access inspection reports and other online information about schools for England, Northern Ireland, Scotland and Wales is in the further resources; alternatively, the school may be able to lend you a copy of the school's last inspection report). Inspection reports provide you with a wealth of information about all aspects of the school as it was assessed at the time of the inspection.

Ideally, you will visit a school at least once before you start any school experience. On any visit, it is helpful to have a list of things you want to find out about the school, department and the activities in which you are going to be engaged. If you are on a university-based ITE programme, you will be given a list of information to gather and questions to ask to help you with this. Further, the inspection report should help you identify questions to discuss with staff and areas to follow up as you learn more about the school. Task 1.2.1 is an orientation activity to help you learn more about your placement school.

 Task 1.2.1   Preparing for school experience

As you work through this unit, and as you read other relevant units in the book, make notes about what you need to do to prepare for, and make the most of, your school experience. Compare your notes with those of other student teachers. Store your notes in your professional development portfolio (PDP) or equivalent.

During your first visit(s), you may be introduced to the head teacher. However, you can expect to talk to the professional tutor and staff with specific areas of responsibility in the school. Every school has many policy and procedure documents, covering a wide range of subjects, for example: school uniform, equal opportunities, behaviour management, marking policy, risk management, safeguarding and e-safety and health and safety information such as the fire assembly points and how to record accidents. Commonly these are included in a staff handbook. You may be issued with a copy of this, or there may be a copy in the staffroom or school office. Your subject tutor may discuss the most relevant sections in the handbook, which you can then read in your own time after the visit. This discussion and reading of the handbook provide you with useful practical information about how the school operates and what you need to do to comply with its policies and procedures and routines. The staff handbook may also include a diagram showing the school's management structure and lines of accountability.

You can also expect to talk to the head of department or faculty, your subject tutor and others in your subject department about the curriculum, schemes of work and your teaching timetable. These discussions are likely to include specific aspects of teaching in the department, for example: safety issues, organisation of equipment and pupils, lesson plans, homework routines, and access to texts and resources, including information and communications technology (ICT)/digital technology. Some of this information may be in a departmental handbook.

On your visits (and later when you start in school), it is important to be aware of staffroom protocols. Some staffrooms are like lounges where teachers can relax and chat safely away from work and pupils during break and lunchtimes. Others have an additional function as a workroom (with or without allocated workspaces) where teachers can do marking and lesson preparation during their free periods. There are still some schools where the same staff have sat in the same chairs for 10, 20 or even 30 years! Colleagues may have brought in their own mugs for tea/coffee. There may or may not be a 'tea/coffee club'. Likewise, if you are planning to drive to school, check out the parking facilities and conventions; there may be reserved spots for some staff. If you check these things, you avoid upsetting the permanent members of staff.

Such visits also enable you to familiarise yourself with the geography of the building. This is particularly important if you are going to teach in a large school, perhaps with several different blocks or operating on more than one site. Secondary schools vary immensely not just in size, but also in physical features, ranging from the small rural or special school with under 100 pupils to the very large school with 1,000–2,000 pupils. Some schools are modern, or comparatively modern, while others are old, dating back to the 1880s, or even earlier. Each type of building has advantages and disadvantages. Whichever type of school you are in, it is important that you locate important facilities, such as the office, lavatories and the staffroom, before you start. The last thing you need to do on your first day is to get lost! Now complete Task 1.2.2.

 Task 1.2.2   Visiting a school prior to school experience

Make a list of information you want to gather about a school and school experience and any observations you would like to undertake on a visit to the school prior to starting a school experience. Compare your list with that of another student teacher and, if you are given a list by your ITE provider, check it against that. Keep the list in your PDP and refer to it when you undertake a visit prior to school experience or as a starting guide for a visit prior to starting a job.

During school experience: work with other staff and pupils in school

Despite the fact that teaching involves spending large amounts of time away from colleagues and working autonomously or just with a teaching assistant, you need to be a team player as you still work closely with other staff. Taking on the role of a teacher as a student teacher means forging and managing professional relationships with adults, as well as pupils. During your initial days in school, you introduce yourself to staff you did not meet on visits prior to school experience, including teaching and support staff in your subject department and key personnel outside the department such as the head teacher, deputies/assistant heads, heads of Key Stage, heads of year and the special educational needs coordinator (SENCO). In addition, you start to build a working relationship with school staff who are supporting you and observing your teaching. Try to make a good first impression on all these people. Figure 1.2.1 suggests some perceived attributes that help convey a positive image of a professional and well-prepared student teacher.

In the next section, advice is presented with regard to developing and managing relationships with specific members of staff who play significant roles in your school experience. Relationships with pupils are also considered.

Relationship with your professional tutor

It is worth remembering that the professional tutor is a key element in your ITE programme, with oversight and management of all student teachers within the school and liaison with your university tutor, if appropriate. You may see the professional tutor in a formal context only once or twice a week, but they are normally a senior member of school staff. They may organise sessions on general school issues. Likewise, you should be able to seek their advice on general school issues, if needed. They expect you to learn school routines, practices and procedures, including rewards/sanctions, and to follow these. They also expect you to engage actively with the school-based programme they have put in place for student teachers.

Figure 1.2.1 Setting out to create a positive image

Relationship with your subject tutor

In the early stages of learning to teach, your subject tutor is an important person (they are often called a mentor). See Unit 8.4 for more about working with your mentor (both as a student teacher and a newly qualified teacher). Your tutor supports your developing practice. As part of this, they observe you teaching and write reports on these observations. Your tutor is responsible for giving you a pass/fail or quantitative grade for your school experience, using these observations and the observations of other staff who have observed you teaching. There are a number of aspects of the relationship that you should consider.

There are likely to be agreed structures for your tutor to give you support, advice and guidance, for example written feedback on one or more lessons each week and a weekly tutorial meeting. For other activities (for example, jointly preparing lessons or approval of lesson plans by your tutor, seeking advice on planning and preparation for lessons or on aspects of teaching with which you are less familiar, completing the required paperwork for your ITE programme, and keeping records of pupil attendance, classwork and homework), you should be clear about what your tutor expects of you and then do what is expected.

You should arrange regular meetings and clarify the purpose of those meetings, so that you are fully prepared for them. Your tutor is an experienced teacher from whom you can learn a lot. Do not think you know it all already and either do not seek advice or ignore your tutor's advice. Do not be afraid to ask for advice if you are not sure about anything, but check when is a convenient time – so that you know when to ask and when is inconvenient.

Also check with your tutor about your status with support staff, such as technical staff and office staff. In some schools, you approach them yourself; in others, you do so via your tutor. Likewise, discuss with your tutor your attendance at school and departmental staff meetings.

Your attendance and punctuality at school (and at lessons when in school) is important. Schools have specific procedures if you find that you are too ill to attend school on any day. Follow that procedure and try to contact your tutor directly by phone/text message; otherwise, speak with the school office staff. Likewise, there are procedures if you are not going to be in school for an important reason (for example, an interview). Let your tutor know of any foreseen absences well in advance. If your ITE programme is in conjunction with a university, you are also required to contact them on the day of absence.

The tutor-student teacher relationship is vital to your success and it is worthwhile taking steps to ensure this remains cordial. However, from time to time, problems do occur. This is often associated with friction generated when a student teacher fails to seek or to act on a tutor's advice. If your relationship with your subject tutor breaks down, you need to contact your university tutor, professional tutor or senior staff member immediately and seek further advice. It is important to be aware that any breakdown in the relationship that ends in a student teacher leaving a placement may subsequently result in failure of the ITE programme.

Relationships with class teachers

You spend the bulk of your time in school in the company of the teachers whose classes you are teaching, so it is important to establish good working relations with them. Remember that they are going to have to teach the class again after you leave, so discuss with them what they want you to do. Some teachers want you to follow their routines, practices and procedures; others allow you to experiment with what is best for you. Plan your lessons well in advance of when they are going to be taught to allow time for any planning meetings with, or checking by, the class teacher and any further planning or adjustment to take place. Collate resources well in advance, especially photocopying, be flexible and prepared to change lesson plans at short notice in the light of unexpected events. Avoid a situation where you are chasing a class teacher 10 minutes before the start of a lesson for an important resource or piece of information. Arrive early before a lesson. Keep teachers fully informed of any new approaches you are taking in your teaching and events that take place with their classes, particularly behavioural issues that need following up.

Relationships with pupils and avoiding difficult association

Your main task as a student teacher is to ensure the pupils in your classes learn. This is most effective when you are able to treat each pupil as an individual. Learning pupils' names is a good first step, as is getting to know something about their interests (learning pupils' names is covered in Unit 2.3). It is important to greet pupils at the beginning of the lesson; this is most easily achieved by standing by the door as the pupils enter.

You also need to gain the respect of the pupils you are teaching. This is not usually automatic; it requires a proactive approach. A general guideline is that if you treat pupils with respect, the feeling is reciprocated (although some pupils may not necessarily respond in this way). For instance, you should be polite when dealing with pupils, and ensure they are polite back to you. At the same time, you should clearly define the boundaries of behaviour. Pupils are sensitive to actions they perceive as being unfair; for example, if one person has been talking, it is unfair to keep the whole class in for a detention.

Make sure you understand the material you are teaching and have planned and prepared your lesson and your resources. Do not be afraid to admit it if you are asked a question to which you do not know the answer, provided you follow it up in a later lesson.

Planning and preparation are essential for learning and to motivate pupils to learn (see planning in Unit 2.2 and motivation in Unit 3.2). During a lesson, you need to keep pupils on task. Encouragement is one effective means of keeping pupils on task in your lesson. To be effective, your approach needs to be tailored to each individual. However, this is difficult early in your school experience when you have little knowledge of individual pupils.

Well-planned lessons support your approach to behaviour for learning (see Unit 3.3). Despite this, you may encounter some behavioural issues in the class; therefore, you should also be clear about how you are going to deal with any poor behaviour, in line with school behaviour policies. In order to deal with poor behaviour, never be drawn into a public confrontation with a pupil because you may lose your authority, which is difficult to recoup later. In any case, you do need to think of the effect on the rest of the class, and also on what the rest of the class is doing when a confrontation is going on. Simply saying 'I will see you later' allows you to choose the time and place to follow up. This enables you to maintain a working relationship with the particular pupil after the event.

Physical contact with pupils should be avoided unless there is an immediate health and safety concern, or is a requirement in a practical lesson, for example supporting a pupil in physical education (see also Unit 8.3). It is unlikely that you will be called on to make decisions in contexts where physical restraint is necessary because the supervising class teacher should be available on the very rare occasion when restraint is the pertinent action. Likewise, any contact with parents/carers in reaction to classroom events, both positive as well as negative, should be undertaken in conjunction with the class teacher. Further, more specific advice on encouraging behaviour to maximise learning is found in Unit 3.3.

A particularly important point to remember is to keep a professional distance in your relationships with pupils. It is easy with some classes to become over-friendly; this is especially the case during the first phase of development (see student teacher development below). To be the target of an adolescent 'crush' is not unusual for young student teachers, and, if this is the case, maintaining an appropriate professional distance is imperative while nurturing mutual respect and good working relationships. In a similar vein, if you are alone in a room with any pupil (or parent), it is good practice to seek the presence of another member of staff or to leave the door wide open. Similarly, you should avoid texting or emailing pupils, or communicating with them via social networking websites (Unit 8.1 looks at your online professional identity). False allegations are uncommon but remain a threat. Task 1.2.3 presents some scenarios you might have to deal with.

 Task 1.2.3   Relationships with pupils

Consider your responses to the following events:

■ there is a struggle between two pupils in the corridor;
■ you observe a pupil going through another pupil's bag/locker.

Discuss your responses with your tutor or another student teacher and record your reflections in your PDP. Identify other scenarios to discuss (these may be real events that have taken place in school).

Expectations, roles and responsibilities on school experience

The main expectation of you as a student teacher is that you promote pupils' learning. To achieve this, there is a range of *structured teaching activities* you are likely to engage in. These include:

■ microteaching: a short teaching episode where you teach peers or small groups of pupils. It might be video recorded to enable analysis of different aspects of teaching;
■ observation of experienced teachers: where you look at specific aspects of teaching in a lesson; for example, how teachers use questions to promote learning (see Unit 3.1);
■ team-teaching: where you share the lesson with others; planning, teaching the lesson and evaluating together;
■ whole-class teaching with the class teacher present;
■ whole-class teaching on your own (as a student teacher, you should always have an experienced teacher nearby).

You should be given feedback on your planning and teaching in each of these situations to enhance your own learning. In practice, there are likely to be agreed conventions governing this aspect of your work. These take into account how you are to achieve the requirements to complete your ITE programme successfully. Further, the amount of feedback you get from teachers observing your lessons varies. However, student teachers also have preferences. If you wish to have feedback on every lesson, ask if this can be done. Some student teachers prefer a small amount of very focused feedback; others can cope with more – a page or more of written comments. Written feedback is essential because it provides a record of your progress and ideas for your development.

Comments on your teaching divide into those relating to tangible technical issues that you can work on relatively easily and those relating to less tangible issues relating to pupils' learning. Technical problems, such as the quality and clarity of your voice, how you position yourself in the classroom, managing transitions from one activity to another, your use of digital technologies and/or audio-visual aids, are easy to spot, so you may receive considerable advice on these issues. Problems with these aspects of your work are usually resolved early in your ITE programme. On the other hand, less tangible issues that are directly related to the quality of pupil learning require ongoing reflection, attention and discussion; these might include your approach to the explanation of lesson content, your style of questioning and your evaluation of pupil learning. You may have access to videos of yourself teaching, in which case you are advised to spend some time in the detailed analysis of your performance in these different aspects of teaching. More detailed advice related to the teaching of your specific subject is given in the subject-specific texts in the *Learning to Teach [Subjects] in the Secondary School* series that accompany this generic text (see list on page ii).

Expectations relating to your social skills in developing relationships with staff and pupils and of your teaching are summarised in Table 1.2.2. Next, complete Task 1.2.4.

 Task 1.2.4   Meeting expectations, roles and responsibilities on school experience

Using Table 1.2.2 as a checklist (to which you can also add any other information on expectations, roles and responsibilities on school experience), identify areas for development. Then identify activities you are going to undertake to develop in the identified areas. Discuss with your tutor the support they can provide. Store the list in your PDP and update as you work on different areas for development.

Thus, your main roles and responsibilities relate to teaching particular classes. Teachers have other roles and responsibilities such as planning the curriculum and liaising with outside agencies, but these are not usually undertaken by student teachers. You become involved in the wider roles and responsibilities of teachers after completing your ITE programme. This is part of your development as a professional (see also Units 8.2; 8.4).

Becoming a member of the teaching profession

The roles and responsibilities of teachers, including student teachers, are underpinned by the concept of *professionalism* (see Unit 8.4). Becoming *a member of the teaching profession* means that you:

■ *reach an acceptable level of competence and skill* in your teaching by the end of your ITE programme. This includes acquiring knowledge and skills that enable you to become an effective teacher and that enable you to understand the body of knowledge about how young people learn and how teachers can teach most effectively;

Table 1.2.2 Schools expectations of student teachers

(i) Social skills

You are expected to:

- develop a good relationship with staff and pupils;
- be able to communicate with adults as well as pupils;
- work well in teams;
- learn to defuse difficult situations;
- keep a sense of humour.

(ii) Planning, teaching and evaluating lessons

You are expected to:

- be well organised;
- know your subject;
- plan and prepare thoroughly. Be conscientious in finding out what lesson content is appropriate to the class you are teaching. For some classes you may be teaching material that is new to you or that you last thought about many years ago. You must know the subject matter you are teaching and you are expected to improve your own subject content knowledge. However, you are also expected to ask if you are unsure about the content for a particular lesson;
- share your plans with the class teacher, explaining why you want to do things the way you plan. Discuss any new/different teaching strategies or innovations in your teaching. Evaluate these carefully afterwards;
- before the day on which you are teaching the lesson check: the availability of books and equipment; test out equipment new to you; talk to staff about the work and pupils' progress; and clarify any safety issues;
- arrive in plenty of time for a lesson in order to arrange the classroom and lay out any equipment or books needed;
- during the lesson learn names of pupils, focus on and assess any learning that is taking place and ensure that good behaviour is maintained during your teaching;
- evaluate the lesson;
- keep good records: have your file of schemes/units of work and lesson plans, pupil attendance and homework up to date. Your evaluations of your lessons are best completed on the same day as the lesson, although sometimes you might want to add to this after you have marked pupils' work.

- *continuously develop your professional knowledge and professional judgement* through experience, further learning and reflection on your work;
- *are publicly accountable for your work.* Various members of the community have the right to inspect and/or question your work: the head teacher, governors, parents and inspectors. You have a professional duty to plan and keep records of your work and that of the pupils. This accountability includes implementation of school policies such as on behaviour and equal opportunities;
- *set personal standards and conform to external standards* for monitoring and improving your work.

Professionalism and developing your professional judgement are considered in Unit 8.4.

It is important to consider the process you go through to become a qualified member of the teaching profession. We do this next.

A model of student teacher development

The aim of your ITE programme is to facilitate your transformation from a student teacher to a competent professional. Plainly, this change is not instantaneous; instead, it proceeds in increments, with each little piece of experience contributing to your development. Your perception of yourself as a teacher alters as different aspects become the focus of concern at different points during your ITE programme (teacher identity is considered in Unit 8.4). A major change for you might be assuming the role of the teacher after being a learner such as in a university course. You become one of them (teachers) instead of being one of us (learners). This role reversal requires significant behaviour modifications by you. Observing other teachers to see how they act in and out of the classroom helps you through these phases of development.

Various models of student teacher development have been identified. For example, Fuller and Brown (1975) described three phases of development: self-concerns, tasks concerns and impact concerns. The three phases identified by Leask and Moorehouse (2005), based on the body of previous work, are in Table 1.2.3.

Thus, your self-perceived role shifts from focusing on yourself to focusing on the whole class, then finally to teaching individual pupils. The model (see Table 1.2.4) does *not* assume that everyone passes through a predetermined, invariable linear process during their ITE programme because individual and contextual aspects (such as the school environment) differ in many respects.

That said, research (for example, Fuller and Brown, 1975; Calderhead and Shorrock, 1997) has suggested that student teachers have common foci for their concerns at different times during their development. Remember, your primary role as expected by a prospective employer is to *teach the curriculum*, with the aspiration being that every pupil in the class achieves the learning outcomes for each of your lessons, over and above any informal pastoral role you may envisage for yourself. Attainment of the final mature stage in Table 1.2.4, with its emphasis on individual pupil learning and the successful achievement of learning outcomes by all pupils, is the aim. You need to start focusing on this third phase right at the start of your school experience; however, you may not reach this completely until after you complete your ITE programme.

Other units in this book cover specific issues described in the model in Table 1.2.4. Timing of the phases is difficult to predict because some student teachers progress more quickly than others during their ITE programme, and because of individual and contextual differences (see above). The three phases may span a single school experience or the whole ITE programme; in some cases,

Table 1.2.3 Phases of student teacher development

Self	Class	Pupil
Self-image and class management	Whole-class learning	Individual pupils' learning
How do I come across?	Are the pupils learning?	What are the different needs of my pupils?
Will they do what I want?	What are the learning outcomes?	How effective are my strategies for ensuring all pupils learn?
Can I plan enough material to last a lesson?	Am I achieving my objectives?	How can I find out?
	How do I know?	

Table 1.2.4 A model of student teacher progression

Phase 1: idealism and insecurity	*Phase 2: getting on top*	*Phase 3: stability and further progression*
■ Desire to portray a caring image ■ Disorientation ■ Feelings of being unable to cope	■ Anxiety about failing ■ Realisation of personal areas for development ■ Drive to impress others brings steady improvements in performance	■ Limited success brings a period of stability and satisfaction ■ Desire to improve wanes ■ External intervention often required to develop further ■ Mature stage involves ensuring learning outcomes have been achieved by *all* pupils

phase 1 occurs at the start of the first school experience, with phase 2 being experienced after a couple of weeks, and with some aspects of phase 3 appearing right at the end. At the start of the second school experience, there may then be a repeat of this process, only the first two phases are shorter. It is important to note that some student teachers who have had difficult and problematic school experiences emerge, after a number of years of qualified experience, as among the best teachers in their schools. Each of these phases is described below.

Phase 1: idealism and insecurity – focusing on yourself/self-development

You may begin your first school experience holding certain idealistic views about your role as teacher, partly based on your own memories of school when you were a pupil. Some student teachers first adopt an empathetic self-image, wanting to create a caring persona, being 'there' for the pupils and hence identifying with the pupils more than the class teacher did, and being popular. You may want to avoid becoming too strict or scary, not wanting pin-drop silence in your classroom, but instead a good-humoured, industrious buzz, so avoiding an atmosphere that negatively affects pupils' emotions. The most important factor determining success is your relationships with pupils. If this can be arranged satisfactorily, you may feel accomplishment in other areas will follow naturally, without a great deal of further effort.

Once you begin your first school experience, these idealistic views may begin to evaporate in the face of immediate issues presented to you. You switch to a more pragmatic stance based on survival, triggered particularly by an urgent need to establish classroom control. You have not yet constructed adequate concepts regarding the boundaries of important features of the modern classroom environment. For instance, when first left alone with a class, you are unclear about whether a particular pupil behaviour such as chatting during written work needs challenging. On top of this, because of the directly challenging nature of some pupils' behaviour, your self-image suffers a blow and there may be insecurity about whether, if you were to challenge behaviours, the pupils would merely ignore you and carry on. Both of these feelings conspire to make you feel reluctant to assert your authority, and student teachers sometimes attempt to justify a failure to challenge poor behaviour by saying they would rather not interrupt the flow of the lesson, or insisting they must keep rigorously to the lesson plan. Pupils actively test your knowledge of these boundaries, as well as your willingness to act on them, and you begin to realise that to be seen as a caring friend and equal by the pupils is not appropriate to a working relationship, and unworkable in practice. Planning issues can also be a cause of anxiety, such as do you have enough work to last the whole lesson, or what if they ask difficult questions?

Thus, the first couple of weeks of school are likely to be a time of insecurity with respect to self-image and readjustment of some prior idealistic notions, and you will at times feel out of your depth and run off your feet. You may have previously felt comfortable handling small groups or one-to-one situations, but whole-class teaching brings fresh and sometimes seemingly insurmountable problems; fortunately, for most student teachers, these feelings are transient.

Phase 2: getting on top – focusing on whole-class learning

An inability to appreciate the limits of certain classroom elements during the first couple of weeks starts to give way in light of your experiences to clearly delineated boundaries of what is judged 'acceptable'. You begin to realise exactly what constitutes, for example, a tolerable level of noise, pupil movement around the classroom and what level to pitch your lessons at. Having said that, realising the boundaries does not mean you can yet find strategies that successfully address every one of these issues. You feel pressure to put on a 'good show' for the significant players in your own assessment as a student teacher, your class teacher, school subject tutor and professional and university tutors, and work hard on your creative planning, delivery and especially your behaviour management, in order to foster these relationships. You are concerned about 'passing your ITE programme', and so do not wish to upset others by, for instance, having a teacher come into your class and complain about the noise. In order to appear to be a competent teacher, you may begin to mimic the behaviours of competent teachers around you or those who taught you in school (for example, their class management routines, personal mannerisms and stock phrases), sometimes unconsciously; although, you may not necessarily fully understand the reasons behind those behaviours.

As a consequence of your hard work in addressing these issues, you begin to experience some successes. The pupils behave better (although perhaps not consistently so), which increases your confidence. Getting to grips with managing behaviour allows you to think more about whether the pupils are achieving learning outcomes, and you begin to adjust your lesson content in the light of this knowledge, although you may avoid differentiating work for individuals. For most student teachers, these successes are inconsistent and largely unpredictable, and some blame may be displaced onto factors beyond your control, such as room arrangement, a lack of resources or a need to fit in with the school's established procedures.

This phase is typified by steady improvements in classroom performance as a result of realising the nature of issues at hand, as well as determining successful strategies to address them. You start to think more about your autonomy as a teacher, about things you would like to do differently, although these desires are tempered by the need to fit in with the clear expectations of your school and tutors.

During the last weeks of your final school experience, there is usually a period of stability. Tried and-tested methods have brought with them hard-won success for you, albeit not consistently, and so your feeling is why fix what isn't broken? Because of this, you may relax or 'cruise' and spend less time on planning and evaluations; you may feel you have 'got there', and will comfortably pass your ITE programme. You are less anxious about managing behaviour, and let slide pupil misbehaviours that you previously might have challenged. However, teaching remains largely at a shallow level. In fact, many student teachers share a common idea that if pupils have enjoyed a lesson, this shows it was successful. Likewise, they might think that because they taught something, pupils have learned it. There is no real effort to ensure *all* pupils are achieving the learning outcomes and there is little differentiation of work for individual pupils. These learning outcomes reflect an epistemology of the transmission of concrete knowledge, with an avoidance of the more abstract ideas, because you judge simple facts to be the material that pupils understand most easily and so can be taught without difficulty. You begin to feel more like a teacher, and believe you outwardly display attributes of a competent professional, although some of these behaviours are merely mimicry, with no real understanding of the professional knowledge that lies behind them.

In order to move on from this phase and progress towards becoming a more effective professional, concerted efforts are necessary, often requiring the intervention of others, such as class teachers or tutors. First, as a student teacher at this phase of your development you may not be aware that further improvements are indeed necessary or even possible, so the first step involves attention being brought to the specific areas where competence could be further advanced. For some, the realisation that there is more to learn about teaching comes as a disappointment after gaining a modicum of proficiency. Critical self-analysis of your own teaching informs these areas for development, and it is vital that *you* recognise the need to make the effort to move on.

You may also realise already that certain aspects of your teaching could be further developed, but your ability to progress is hampered by classroom management issues; for instance, you avoid practical activities, or you do not feel confident enough to experiment with innovative pedagogies. If this is the case, advice from other members of staff will prove invaluable in moving you on to higher levels of achievement.

Phase 3: stability and further progression – focusing on individual pupils' learning

The greatest challenge in order to move on lies in ensuring that each and every member of the class has accessed the learning outcomes. Currently, in English state-maintained schools, the view is one of inclusion of all pupils in the learning process. The purpose of lessons needs to swing towards the needs of individual pupils (away from your early focus on you as a student teacher or even the whole class), with content focused on learning. The first step is determining the extent to which pupils have learned during your lessons. This may be indicated by an effective plenary, end-of-topic test, or more formative types of assessment, all of which need to be referenced in your lesson evaluations. Further steps are covered in the units in Chapter 6.

Task 1.2.5 is designed for you to reflect on the phases of development as a teacher.

 Task 1.2.5   Phases of student teacher development

Consider the three phases of student teacher development above: self, class and individual pupil. Reflect on your strengths and areas for development on each of these. Describe possible strategies for making progress in each of these three phases in the context of the following three areas:

- classroom management and focusing on individuals;
- assessment;
- subject content knowledge.

Discuss your views with another student teacher. As you progress through your ITE programme, record in your PDP what strategies you have used and how they have worked, as well as your progress on the three phases of development.

SUMMARY AND KEY POINTS

This unit has touched on your multiple, changing roles and responsibilities as a student teacher. We hope that it has given you a better understanding of:

- the preparation you need to do prior to school experience;
- what you need to do during school experience, focusing particularly on developing positive working relationships with other staff, including your tutors and class teachers, and with pupils;
- the expectations of you, your roles and responsibilities in school.

The unit has also looked at a model of student teacher development over your ITE programme and beyond. As a result, we hope this has given you a better understanding of your development as a teacher.

Check which requirements for your ITE programme you have addressed through this unit.

Further resources

Brindley, S. (series editor) *Masterclass Series*, **published by Bloomsbury, viewed 1 July 2018, from https:// www.bloomsbury.com/uk/series/masterclass/**

This series takes a practical approach to teaching and learning in different subjects to extend your understanding to enable you to develop effective classroom practice.

Cohen, L., Manion, L., Morrison, K. and Wyse, D. (2010) *A Guide to Teaching Practice*, **5th Edition, Abingdon: Routledge.**

This text covers the important basic skills and issues you need to consider during your school experience, such as planning, classroom organisation, behaviour management and assessment.

Further information about education in the four countries of the UK can be obtained from the websites below. Also see Units 7.3 to 7.6 on the companion website www.routledge.com/cw/capel

England: Department for Education: www.education.gov.uk/

Northern Ireland: the Department of Education Northern Ireland: www.deni.gov.uk/

Scotland: the Scottish Government: http://www.gov.scot/Topics/Statistics/Browse/School-Education

Wales: the Welsh Government: http://wales.gov.uk/topics/educationandskills/?lang=en

School inspection reports in the four countries in the UK can be obtained from:

England: The Office for Standards in Education, Children's Services and Skills (Ofsted): https://www.gov.uk/government/organisations/ofsted

Northern Ireland: The Education and Training Inspectorate Northern Ireland: https://www.etini.gov.uk

Scotland: Education Scotland: https://education.gov.scot

Wales: Estyn (the Office of Her Majesty's Inspectorate for Education and Training in Wales): https://www.estyn.gov.wales/language

To keep up to date, we recommend you join your subject association. A list can be found on the website of the Council for Subject Associations: http://www.subjectassociation.org.uk/members_links.aspx.

Appendix 2 lists subject associations and teacher councils and Appendix 3 provides a list of websites.

Capel, S., Leask, M. and Turner, T. (eds.) (2010) *Readings for Learning to Teach in the Secondary School: A Companion to M Level Study*, **Abingdon: Routledge.**

This book brings together essential readings to support you in your critical engagement with key issues raised in this textbook.

Capel, S., Lawrence, J. Leask, M. and Younie, S. (eds.) (2019) *Surviving and Thriving in the Secondary School: The NQT's Essential Companion*, **Abingdon: Routledge.**
This book is designed to support newly qualified teachers in the next phase of development as a teacher. However, you may find it useful as it covers aspects of teaching not included in this book which, nonetheless, you experience on your ITE programme.

The subject specific books in the *Learning to Teach (Subject)* series, the *Practical (Subject) Guides, Debates in (Subject)* and *Mentoring (Subject) Teachers* are also very useful.

Any additional resources and an editable version of any relevant tasks/tables in this unit are available on the companion website: www.routledge.com/cw/capel

1.3 Developing your resilience

Managing stress, workload and time

Madeleine Findon and Sue Johnston-Wilder

Introduction

Teaching is rewarding, exciting, challenging, demanding and pressured. The latest results from the Teaching and Learning International Survey (The Organisation for Economic Co-operation and Development (OECD), 2013a) showed that over 90% of teachers around the world were satisfied with their job and their performance. Studies over time have also consistently reported that between one-quarter and one-third of teachers report being very or extremely stressed as a result of factors intrinsic to their work (e.g. Mills, 1995; Chaplain, 2008). Proponents of positive psychology suggest when you meet pressure with resilience, you thrive (e.g. Seligman, 2003). However, when the pressure increases beyond your current level of resilience, life becomes stressful, and stress not managed well can cause mental and physical harm. More recently, the Big Question survey carried out by NASUWT (2016) gathered data from over 12,000 teachers in England and found that 85% of respondents experienced their work having negative impacts upon their well-being. In becoming a teacher, you face one of the biggest challenges of your life, perhaps exceeding your existing levels of resilience. The good news is that resilience can be developed; in this unit, we start by considering how to develop personal resilience and how to help you ensure your school promotes resilience.

Throughout the unit, we use analogies of physical endurance activities. While such activities may not be something you would ordinarily choose to do, the motivation, preparation and pacing required to achieve the ultimate goal have many parallels with the teaching challenge. What is needed are: stages of preparation; self-knowledge; taking on fuel before/during the activity; connecting with the community for expertise, assistance and motivation; taking rests, and diligently watching for any warning signs that trouble is building so you can take action: longer breaks or seeking support. You may not be ready to complete an endurance activity yet. However, with the right coaching, training, preparation, support and safeguarding from injury, most people are capable of improving performance and are able to convey themselves further than they might currently imagine.

Like running marathons, teaching can use up inordinate amounts of time and energy, inside and outside the classroom and outside the school day. School days are usually very busy with no time to breathe deeply or eat and drink properly. In order to manage personal well-being, and to preserve time for yourself and your supportive friends or family, you need to use your time and energy effectively. We advise you plan to have at least one day and one evening a week free from school work even during term time, for proper rest.

We encourage you to reflect regularly upon your practice and become aware of available resources, for example, existing lesson plans, homework instructions and resources on the school's intranet or virtual learning environment. Your subject association also provides access to quality assured resources and opportunities for networking. Likewise, you are advised to see yourself as part of a team. The concept of teacher leadership is growing in popularity, a role which can seem quite daunting to a newly qualified teacher: being a teacher leader includes practices such as sharing resources and expertise, being a catalyst for change and committing to life-long learning (Harrison and Killion, 2007). Such actions are well within your capability; being proactive in these areas can help you to develop your skills and promote a healthy work environment.

The unit looks at how you can build your resilience as a teacher, how you can manage stress, workload and time proactively to preserve your well-being, optimise your effectiveness, avoid harm associated with stress or overdoing things, and contribute to an environment that benefits all participants in the school community. In this unit, we distinguish between 'pressure' as a source of motivation, as in 'I work well under pressure', and 'stress' as in 'I feel stressed and not coping so well', indicating pressure is potentially building and becoming harmful over time. Our bodies and minds generally function well under pressure and short bursts of stress, but they are not able to sustain long periods of stress without harm (Siegel, 2010) – much as physical exertion can build our strength and fitness, but too much physical exertion can cause us illness and injury.

OBJECTIVES

At the end of this unit you should know how to develop your resilience as a teacher by:

▪   identifying when you are stressed;
▪   identifying factors that may cause you stress;
▪   developing methods of managing stress proactively;
▪   developing ways to manage your time and workload effectively.

Check the requirements of your initial teacher education (ITE) programme to see which relate to this unit.

What is resilience?

Resilience can be thought of as positive adaptation in the face of adversity, not a personality trait, but a phenomenon that can be encouraged or restricted by a range of internal and external factors (Luthar, 2006). Resilience is often associated with children – in fact, you are probably already familiar with schemes that aim to promote 'growth mindset' or 'grit' in the pupils you teach. However, more recent research has begun to look at resilience in adults, crossing over with newer fields such as positive psychology that are concerned with adult well-being (Luthar, 2006).

Seligman (2003) described resilience as a combination of: confidence (to start a task), persistence (to keep going when things get tough) and perseverance (to recognise when to recruit support and seek alternative approaches). It is important that you build up your resilience, as more resilient teachers are better able to manage the pressures of teaching. Such teachers see periods of when pressure builds up too high as times to proactively manage stress rather than simply having to passively cope with it. The next section looks at building your resilience.

Building your resilience

Resilience is what sustains and enables teachers to thrive rather than just survive under challenge and pressure (see, for example, Kitching et al., 2009). It might be thought of as mental 'fitness'. Resilience can be developed in times of challenge or adversity, where there is appropriate autonomy and support (Masten, 2014). In considering how resilience is built, it is helpful to consider the connection between existing experiences and the ways we deal with new ones, just as prior involvement in sporting activity can equip us with the strength and co-ordination for new challenges. It is helpful to use a framework known as the growth zone model (Johnston-Wilder and Lee, 2008) (see Figure 1.3.1), initially developed by exploring the research around growth mindset, agency, support and inclusion in the context of maths anxiety and avoidance, but found useful in managing other stressful situations.

This model depicts three 'zones' or ways in which an individual experiences and deals with situations, using a psychosocial model of perceived risk. The comfort zone is characterised by feeling safe and confident, being able to use existing knowledge to good effect and not experiencing stress – like an easy run that is well within an individual's capabilities. Conversely, the danger zone is experienced as a place of danger, stress and lack of security. In this zone a 'fight, flight or freeze' reaction may be experienced: perhaps battling against (rather than engaging with) the scenario, fleeing or experiencing an inability to react cogently. Danger zone reactions occur because the primitive part of the brain reacts to physical and social threat (such as being embarrassed or excluded); the amygdala ('the alarm system') triggers the release of chemicals such as adrenaline and cortisol; this is useful for reacting to physical danger but not amenable to pre-frontal cortex activity (Siegel, 2010) such as thinking clearly.

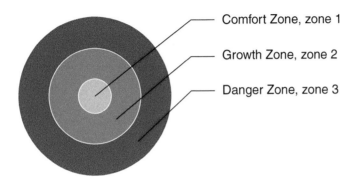

Figure 1.3.1 Growth Zone Model: Johnston-Wilder and Lee (2008)

The zone that lies between these two areas is where optimal growth can be experienced (see also Zaretskii, 2009). There is enough challenge to learn and develop one's skills, including managed risks, meaning mistakes can be learned from. For the would-be athlete, this is where physical limits are stretched under the watchful eye of the coach and team-mates. In becoming a resilient teacher, being in the growth zone is optimised by the support of being part of a learning community, encouraging questioning and exploring strategies, thus helping to mitigate feelings of threat that can prevent healthy engagement. Being in a new school and unsure of the people around you can mean accessing such support is difficult; however, taking the initiative to develop co-operative networks, such as with Harrison and Killion's (2007) teacher leaders, will help you and others to thrive and be resilient under pressure, rather than be harmed by stress.

The most helpful attributes and skills to promote resilience include: altruistic motives, strong intrinsic motivation for teaching, high self-efficacy, feeling confident and competent, having coping strategies, taking credit for and drawing sustenance from accomplishments, collegial support, and learning from mistakes (Ryan and Deci, 2000a; Bandura, 2006; Hinds et al., 2015; Johnson et al., 2016). It is important to note that none of these are present in finite quantities; all can be acquired and developed to an extent, whether through specific strategies or positive environmental conditions. On the other hand, there are certain personal risk factors that include: inability to ask for help (Fantilli and McDougall, 2009; Jenkins et al., 2009), a perceived conflict between personal beliefs and practices being used in school (McCormack and Gore, 2008) and personal challenges or difficulties such as negative self-beliefs or confidence (Kitching et al., 2009), emotional avoidance (Hinds et al., 2015), difficult interpersonal interactions (Burke et al., 1996) and not noticing you have moved into your danger zone.

Day et al. (2011), among others, identified ways to build resilience both in ITE and early in a teaching career, and to stay in your growth zone, which include:

- a formal mentoring programme and collegial support provided in the workplace;
- establishing a mutually respectful, supportive relationship with your tutor, with open, honest, yet sensitive communication that challenges you;
- understanding your role and responsibilities and establishing realistic expectations of your tutor;
- working together with your tutor to improve teaching and learning;
- devising challenging targets for development that also recognise success;
- recognising the challenges in learning to teach and the reasons for these, and establishing a collaborative rather than individualistic approach to seeking solutions;
- developing a reciprocal, mutually supportive, trusting network of peers and colleagues;
- improving self-evaluation of your teaching, e.g. through use of video analysis of teaching or feedback from pupils;
- critiquing your own beliefs, values and practice;
- developing social skills, assertiveness, self-regulation and empathy (Tait, 2008);
- having autonomy and control over key aspects of your work;
- valuing your own well-being.

Naturally, not all of these are necessarily within the control of a student teacher; in terms of building resilience, it is important to attend to aspects of your situation that are within your control, those you can work on at an individual level. In order to achieve this, it is helpful to consider the principles and techniques of reflective practice. The points raised above have much in common with

Schön's (1983) view that good professional practice requires rather more than the application of technical knowledge: it requires you to make sense of complicated matters and engage in careful inquiry about what has happened and what needs to happen next. Such reflection may take place in the moment, or some time afterwards: reflection-in-action and reflection-on-action (Schön, 1983) (see also Unit 5.4).

Now complete Task 1.3.1.

 Task 1.3.1   Building your resilience

Watch neurologist Dr. Daniel Siegel presenting the hand model of the brain on YouTube: https://www.youtube.com/watch?v=gm9CIJ74Oxw

Reflect on how the hand model may explain why you or a pupil may feel stupid or unable to think when confronted with something that relates to a prior bad experience.

Identify times you have been in your comfort, growth and danger zones. Create your own growth zone diagram. Add in key words that help you notice what you are experiencing when you are in each zone. See example below.

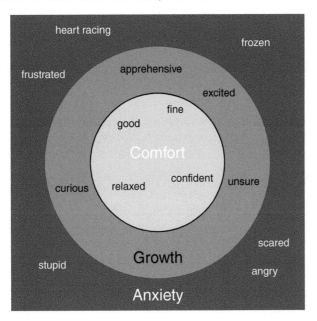

Select some ways to build your resilience from the list from Day et al. (2011) (above). For each, reflect on your own current situation and how you might improve the current situation. For example, you might select devising challenging targets. What are your current targets for development? Are they challenging or are there aspects of your teaching that would be more challenging for you to develop?

Store your reflections in your professional development portfolio (PDP) or equivalent, work on them and review your progress in a month.

Signs that current levels of resilience are not up to current demands

Our bodies and minds cope well with short periods in the danger zone; in fact, being occasionally in the danger zone is a good sign that you are undertaking challenge. However, you need to be able to identify when you are in the danger zone and address the situation by taking a break, breathing (5/7 – the breath out/exhale being slightly longer than the breath in/inhale, e.g. breathe in for 5 counts and out for 7) (a more complete description is available to download free from the international stress management association (ISMA, nd), https://isma.org.uk/nsad-free-downloads, under 'The 60 Second Tranquiliser') or doing some strenuous exercise (Pittman and Karl, 2015).

Prolonged exposure to the danger zone may result in: not thinking clearly, not sleeping well, irritability, tearfulness and stomach pain. These are indicators of problem stress; you are unwell and you need to visit a doctor, just as you would if you had recurring headaches. It is important to note that stress may not be obvious to your employer and maintaining your well-being is, in part, your own responsibility. Historically, teachers we have spoken to have felt shame at this stage, but there should be parity between mental and physical well-being (see Royal College of Psychiatrists, 2013).

Preventing, managing and coping with stress

Whilst teaching can be challenging and rewarding, teaching in the United Kingdom and in many other countries is also ranked as a high stress occupation (see, for example, McCarthy et al., 2012). According to the Health and Safety Executive (HSE, 2016), work-related psychological/emotional ill-health, particularly anxiety and depression, which was caused or made worse by their job, was reported by more people working in the education sector than people working in many other sectors, with only social workers and health professionals reporting higher stress levels.

The percentage of teachers still in post five and ten years after qualifying and entering service was 69 and 60 per cent, respectively (Department for Education (DfE), 2017g). This is not necessarily stress-related; there is no benchmark for 'normal' attrition rates and certainly career change or hiatus may occur for all kinds of reasons. However, in the UK, the mental well-being of teaching staff has historically not been treated as equivalent to physical well-being, and indeed teacher stress is a global phenomenon (McCarthy et al., 2012). The high levels of stress could be related to the teacher concerns that were picked up by the NASUWT (2016) survey, e.g. workload, pupil behaviour, pay, school inspection and curriculum and qualifications changes. Furthermore, stress is 'contagious' 'because [if] the other person seems anxious about something we may conclude that this something may threaten us too (or that the other person's reaction itself is a threat to our well-being)' (Parkinson and Simons, 2012, p.464); thus, student teachers working with teachers who are already stressed may find the stress impacts on their experiences in school.

Things are changing. You and your employer now have joint responsibility to safeguard you; consequently, there has been an increasing focus by employers to take more care, especially in regard to the mental well-being of staff and pupils. However, in law, it is not self-evident that you are overloaded unless you have raised concerns in writing or returned to work after an absence documented as caused by work-based stress (one of the significant cases in this regard is *Walker v. Northumberland County Council*, 1994). Thus, it is important that you identify unnecessary causes of stress for you and develop strategies to be proactive. You might go on a Mental Health First Aid course and certainly should inform yourself about when to seek help and/or medical advice.

Causes of stress

Causes of stress may vary from teacher to teacher or even for the same teacher at different times, depending upon their current level of resilience and the calls upon it. Personal experiences external to school, including physical health, life events or personal finances can all affect your level of resilience. The most frequently reported school-based factors contributing to teacher stress include dealing with pupils' disruptive behaviour, coping with a heavy workload, school ethos and lack of support from colleagues or managers (see, for example, Hinds et al., 2015). A large-scale survey of teacher workload published in February 2017 (DfE, 2017g) reported that teachers in England worked an average of 54.4 hours a week, suggesting that this significantly contributed to increased stress levels. However, over time, there have been many other causes of pressure on teachers identified (see, for example, Akhlaq et al., 2010; Klaasen, 2010; Klaasen and Chui, 2010), including:

- delivering unfamiliar material under pressure of time;
- motivating pupils and maintaining their interest;
- coping with the attainment range of pupils within a class;
- managing the class;
- dealing with conflict and confrontation;
- relationships with parents/guardians;
- maintaining a work-life balance.

In addition to factors that cause stress in all teachers, there may be additional causes of stress for student teachers, for example:

- practical skills of teaching, techniques of lesson preparation and getting the teaching and/or planning right;
- having unrealistic expectations of the profession;
- having high expectations of one's own teaching performance;
- not being regarded as a real teacher;
- disagreement with the tutor;
- observation, evaluation and assessment of teaching by the tutor, particularly receiving the tutor's or class teacher's opinion of classroom competence;
- role ambiguity, role conflict and role overload;
- lack of support in the growth zone.

Some student teachers feel they should know everything, be strong, not make mistakes and, in other words, be constantly in their comfort zone. However, some of the time you should expect to be in your growth zone; you can model being an adult learner to your pupils, sometimes vulnerable, sometimes making mistakes, being resilient. The role of student teacher may thus feel ambiguous, but as a developing teacher you are required to function as both learner and educator. When you are in your growth zone, some of the support that you need will be unambiguous, non-judgemental (unconditional), positive regard (Rogers, 2007), which everyone needs at times, and that may not come from a teacher-tutor with an assessment brief, but is more likely to come from a member of the pastoral team, for example.

In Task 1.3.2, you are asked to look at causes of stress for you.

Task 1.3.2   Identifying causes of stress for student teachers

What causes you to go into your own danger zone at present?

Write a list of factors that cause you stress – both stressors as a student teacher and stressors outside your ITE programme. Compare these with causes of stress identified by another student teacher. Discuss similarities and differences. Store the list in your PDP and use this list for Task 1.3.3.

Reflect on what works for getting you from the danger (stress) to growth (learning) zone.

Reflect on the possibility that sometimes it may be better to take one day off with stress symptoms than be ill for more days later in the year, and consider why teachers might not do this in practice.

How can you cope with the pressures on you?

Long-term stress may result in you being less effective, having more issues with pupils' behaviour, taking time off work or becoming burned out (experiencing emotional exhaustion, or depersonalisation (see, for example, Fernet et al., 2012)). Different ways of coping with stress are appropriate for different people and for the same person at different times.

Ways of coping have been classified differently by different people. For example, Clunies-Ross et al. (2008) referred to proactive and reactive strategies. Lee and Johnston-Wilder (2015) used the term agency and Benson (2001) used the term autonomy. Personal strategies for coping with pressure may be classified as follows: cognitive; physical; behavioural/organisational; emotional. Some examples of specific coping strategies are identified in Table 1.3.1, drawn from a number of sources, e.g. Crothers et al. (2010); Leung et al. (2011); Titchmarsh (2012). Some of these strategies will help you to become more resilient but also help you to promote learning and resilience in your pupils. This list is by no means exhaustive.

It is important to pay attention to your aspirations and hopes as a teacher rather than focusing only on your concerns and fears. Conway and Clark (2003, p.470) suggested that focusing on resolving immediate concerns can result in 'an unduly pessimistic understanding of teachers and teaching'. This is a pertinent observation for many areas of life, including our analogy of endurance activities: it is good to make regular checks on yourself, but to try to keep your focus mostly outwards and enjoy yourself (Latta, 2003). You might find it difficult as a student teacher to focus on your development as a teacher, on the positive aspects of learning to teach and on your long-term goals and aspirations as a teacher. However, if you can do this you are likely to have a more balanced view and be able to put things into perspective and therefore reduce your stress (Unit 8.2 is designed to help you think about your continuing professional development). Task 1.3.3 is designed to help you to cope with your stress.

 Task 1.3.3   Coping with your stress

In Task 1.3.2 you listed causes of stress for you. Now identify ways that you can cope with this stress. Try out different coping methods, and reflect on and evaluate whether these are effective for you. Store your methods and evaluations in your PDP and adapt or try new methods until you find those that work for you to cope with different stressful situations.

Table 1.3.1 Stress coping strategies

Cognitive	■ *Have a good knowledge of what you are teaching.* Read around a topic for which you do not have good knowledge prior to the lesson. ■ *Also have a good knowledge of the structures, organisation and culture of the school.* Understanding how your environment operates can help you to navigate sources of pressure with a little more ease. ■ *Identify where you can get help when needed.* You should get regular feedback on your teaching, but also identify other people who may be able to help. ■ *Take account of the amount and variety of work you are doing to reduce both role overload and conflict.* You might try to take work home less often or take on fewer extra-curricular activities, over a period of time. ■ *Develop attention to now (mindfulness).* ■ *Recognise and try to develop your strengths as well as your weaknesses* so that you can rely on your strengths as you work on improving any weaknesses.
Physical	■ *Take regular exercise.* Exercise releases endorphins in the body, natural pain-relievers and a natural high that making us feel better about ourselves. ■ *Eat regularly and well.* Stress is a drain on the immune system. Look after your immune system by eating well. ■ *Do some proactive relaxation.*
Behavioural/ organisational	■ *Proactively prepare for stressful situations when you are not under pressure*, e.g. prepare lessons days ahead. ■ *Actively prepare for a situation*, e.g. if you are anxious about a particular lesson prepare it more thoroughly than normal. Plan thoroughly how you can reduce the likelihood of a problem occurring or deal with a particular problem. ■ *Role play a situation that is causing you anxiety and/or visualise what you can do to overcome the problem.* This helps you to rehearse how you are going to cope. ■ If you are asked a question which you cannot answer, you can praise the question, encourage pupils to look it up and find the answer before the next lesson. You should then do the same: modelling being a growing learner. ■ *Plan how to work with a teaching assistant (TA) effectively.* Just like anyone else, TAs appreciate knowing what they are doing before they walk into the classroom; otherwise you are putting them on the spot. Depending on the TA, and your relationship with them, they might be happy to team teach, etc. It is important to communicate with them so that you work as a team in the classroom. ■ *Teach pupils to take responsibility for their own learning so that you are facilitating their learning.* Provide them with the resources they need to learn so you do not have to orchestrate everything. This takes the pressure off you and is also effective pedagogically. ■ *Address any behavioural issues as early as possible* because this creates stress and puts pressure on time (see also Unit 3.3). Be ready to investigate why a particular pupil appears not 'ready to learn', e.g. someone at home may be unwell. Remember that aggression often signifies fear. ■ *It is good to consider pupils outside the classroom.* It can help to support their learning if you know something about what pupils do outside the classroom. ■ *Develop effective self-management techniques.* Establish routines so that you can do things automatically, particularly when tired.

Table 1.3.1 continued

Emotional	■ *Develop social support systems that provide a network of people with whom you could talk through problems*, e.g. other student teachers, your tutor, other teachers, a partner or friend. You may talk to different people for help with different problems. You may form a group with other student teachers to provide mutual support, talk about your anxieties/concerns, develop a shared understanding of a problem and provide possible alternative solutions and practical help to address a problem, e.g. a lesson being observed then discussed with another student teacher. ■ *If you worry about incidents that have happened in school, try to keep problems in proportion.* Try not to take problems home. ■ *Try to differentiate between feelings and facts.* You may feel that something has gone dreadfully wrong. If there is no evidence, no need to worry; if there is evidence, then you find out how to improve things. ■ *Try not to worry about things that you cannot change.* Don't worry about things that are not your responsibility. If it is within your gift to act, you should do so, but don't worry about things over the weekend that cannot be dealt with until Monday and dwell only on what can be done, not what has already happened.

Managing your time and workload

As Amos (1998) emphasised, everyone has the same amount of time. However, experience of time is relative, as described in this well-known story of unknown provenance.

> Imagine a teacher of time management standing in front of her class. She picks up a large empty glass jar and fills it with rocks roughly 5cm cubed. She asks the pupils if the jar is full. The pupils say yes.
> Then the teacher picks up a box of small pebbles and pours them into the jar, shaking the jar slightly so the pebbles roll into the spaces between the rocks. Again, she asks the pupils if the jar is full. The pupils say yes, more cautiously this time.
> The teacher picks up box of sand and pours it into the jar. The sand fills the spaces between the pebbles.

The teacher's message is that the jar represents available time. The rocks represent the most important things, whatever they are to you, perhaps family, health and relationships or sense of purpose, the things that make your life meaningful or are critical to your well-being. The pebbles are other things that matter in your life, such as work. The sand signifies the less important things, including possessions that can be replaced. If you put sand into the jar first, there is no room for the rocks or the pebbles. Similarly, if you put the small stuff into your life first, you will have insufficient time for the things that are important to you. Set your priorities. It is important to take control of your workload where you can. Some people always seem to work long hours but achieve little, whereas others achieve a great deal but still appear to have plenty of time to do things other than work. One of the key strategies for reducing stress and increasing productivity is to develop good time management, so in the following sections we discuss strategies for managing time in the classroom, across a half-term, and then across a whole year.

Managing your time in the classroom

Mo Farah: 'As a distance runner, you learn that it is important to rest more and do less. That may sound counterproductive, but it's all about quality over quantity' (Farah with Andrews, 2013, p.173). By cutting out unnecessary tasks and relinquishing some responsibility to others, including the pupils, you can improve the quality of what you do whilst contributing to the holistic development of the pupils in the classroom. As well as managing time more effectively, good time management should enable pupils to:

- spend a high proportion of time engaged on learning tasks;
- experience being part of a challenging, supportive learning community;
- develop self-efficacy and resilience through becoming more autonomous;
- experience a high degree of success during this engaged time;
- demonstrate less adverse behaviour, which is a major stressor for teachers.

You can think of strategies to use classroom time effectively and economically under five headings: pre-emptive, culture setting strategies; supervisory strategies that increase pupil autonomy and responsibility; in-the-moment strategies; balance of time strategies; and reflective strategies. Table 1.3.2 gives examples of ways of using classroom time effectively and economically in these five categories.

There are many other ways of managing time effectively in classrooms, which you develop as you gain experience. Task 1.3.4 is designed to help you look at how you spend your time in lessons.

 Task 1.3.4   How you spend your time in lessons

Observe how several experienced, effective teachers use their time in lessons, how they divide their time between teaching, supervisory, organisational and management activities; how much time is spent listening, observing, providing feedback, explaining and questioning, on routine events such as managing pupils' behaviour, collecting homework or giving back books; what procedures there are for doing this, and what is delegated to TAs or pupils.

Ask another student teacher or tutor to observe how you use your time in the classroom in one lesson or over a series of lessons. Discuss with the observer the findings and possible ways of increasing the pupils' resilience more or using your or the pupils' lesson time more effectively and economically.

Invite feedback from pupils, such as undertaking a brief survey.

Store your findings in your PDP and try these ideas out systematically in your teaching.

Table 1.3.2 Examples of ways of using classroom time effectively and economically

Pre-emptive, culture-setting strategies   ▪ Spend time, especially at the start of the first lesson with the pupils, collecting their ideas and establishing shared ground rules, routines and a safe, inclusive learning environment, which promotes physical and mental well-being in your subject. This saves time on organisation and management, and on addressing affective barriers as you proceed through the year, scheme or unit of work. See Units 1.2 and 2.2 for further information about organisation, rules and routines in the classroom and Unit 3.3 for further information about behaviour for learning.   ▪ Create an expectation that pupils seek answers themselves and amongst peers rather than putting their hand up as soon as they get stuck.   ▪ Keep a section of your mark book for coded comments about progress. As you see pupils' work in class or when you are marking, make brief notes that are then immediately at hand for discussions with parents, head of year, report writing, etc.   ▪ Create an expectation and an environment such that pupils settle down and pack up promptly and manage their behaviour and attention in the lesson.   ▪ Offer transition tasks and productive tasks for pupils to work on outside lessons.   ▪ Devise simple, fast procedures for routine events and dealing with recurring problems.
Supervisory strategies, including delegation and increasing pupil autonomy and responsibility   ▪ Use TAs or pupils to help give out and collect textbooks, pupils' books or equipment, to mark straightforward homework tests in class, to tidy the classroom ready for the next class, all of which also develops pupils' autonomy and ownership of their learning environment.   ▪ Get pupils to do anything they can do to help you, e.g. stick their own worksheets into their books, make wall-posters and videos, make helpful look-up tables or revision guides, copy their notes for absent friends.   ▪ Use peer-, self- or group-marking, e.g. for class tests or homework; it is effective as pupils can be very perceptive when marking work and it saves time; once pupils have learned to do this, with appropriate support, they will get on and do it and learn from the process.   ▪ Ask pupils to ensure that work is dated, each lesson's work is ruled off, and that homework is clearly identified so that it is easy to check what work has been done and what is missing.
In-the-moment strategies   ▪ Carry a marking pen with you as you move around the class checking work. This enables you to make brief notes on the work at that time, after negotiating with the pupil. This provides formative feedback to pupils to promote learning, and it saves you wasting time going back to the work at a later stage.   ▪ Collect in books that are open at the page where you should start marking or where the pupil would particularly like comments.
Balance of time strategies   ▪ Maintain a good balance of time on teaching, supervisory and organisational activities, allocating a high proportion of available time for academic work (sometimes called academic learning time).   ▪ Spend a high proportion of time in 'substantive interaction' with pupils (i.e. listening, observing, providing feedback, explaining, questioning, describing, illustrating).
Reflective strategies   ▪ Regularly review the conduct of lessons in terms of effective use of your own and pupils' time.   ▪ Work to eliminate unnecessary routines and activities from your own teaching.

Managing time outside the classroom effectively across a term

There are so many things for you to do as a teacher in term time that your workload is high. Indeed, 90% of teachers felt that workload was their greatest challenge in their professional role (NASUWT, 2016). A high workload can result in not doing a good job, working very long hours to get the task done and not having enough time mentally and physically to relax for work the following day. All elite athletes recognise the importance of rest time to recuperate and so should you. Thus, it is important to focus on doing 'a good enough' job with excellent elements: not heroic, but providing the necessary conditions for learning (Britzman, 1998).

In order to use your time outside the classroom effectively, you need to plan your use of time and prioritise your work. Preparing as far in advance as you sensibly can and keeping everything up to date means that you do not have to chase around at the last minute, e.g. before a tutor visits. Keeping records of activities can help, for example, keeping a file of activities for the week (e.g. lessons to plan, marking to do, assignments for your ITE programme, specific records of your work, including how you have met certain standards). Also plan time for reflection on your teaching overall and your development as a teacher (what have you learned and how are you going to develop further?).

One person might waste time through, for example, being unsystematic in managing time, handling paperwork or responding to emails, putting off work rather than getting on and doing it, trying to do it all rather than delegating appropriately or not being able to say no to tasks, whereas another person might use time well by, for example, having clear objectives for work to be done, prioritising work, completing urgent and important tasks first and writing lists of tasks to achieve during the day. Which of these descriptions fits you? To check this, you need to analyse the way you work and, if necessary, try to make changes. Task 1.3.5 is designed to help with this.

🖉 Task 1.3.5 Reviewing your use of time in term time

Record for one week in term time the time you spend on school work outside the classroom, both at school and at home, e.g. planning, preparation, marking, record keeping, extracurricular activities, meetings. You might want to use a grid such as the one below, which has been set up with three sessions per day (morning, afternoon, evening).

Day	Work undertaken (along with time for each activity)	Total time
Monday		
Tuesday		
Wednesday		

Day	Work undertaken (along with time for each activity)	Total time
Thursday		
Friday		
Saturday		
Sunday		
Total time for one week		

Then answer the following questions:

■ Did you take one day off?

■ Did you take one evening off?

■ Is the time spent outside the classroom and total hours worked during the week sustainable for you?

■ Are you using this time effectively, i.e. is the balance of time spent on the activities appropriate, e.g. are you spending more time on record keeping or planning and preparation?

■ Do you need to spend more time on some activities?

■ Could you reduce time on some activities, e.g. can some more of the work be delegated to pupils (e.g. mounting and displaying work)?

Compare with other student teachers the time you spent and how you spent it. If time spent is unsustainable, plan what action you will take to reduce the time spent on school-related work each week. Store this in your PDP and recheck the use of time outside the classroom by repeating the log for one week to see whether this has worked and, in light of the results, what further action you will take, for example, might you put up an out-of-office message on your email to say that you will only respond on Saturdays? If all else fails, might you request fewer classes, possibly with the support of a union representative. This would be better than becoming unwell with stress.

Using your time effectively helps you to be more efficient and more productive, better able to plan long term, more satisfied with your work and your job as well as less stressed. In addition, you will have more time for yourself and more opportunity to switch off out of work.

Some specific examples of ways of using your time effectively include:

■ Make a list of activities you are going to complete each day. If there are activities left on the list at the end of the day or the week, ask why this is, e.g. are you spending too much time on each activity? Are you unrealistic in how much you can achieve in a day? Spend five minutes at the end of a day identifying how you will save time the next day.

■ Utilise your non-contact periods effectively (plan what you are going to do in these in advance).

■ Plan to complete your work at time(s) best for you. Some people stay late at school, then do not work during the weekend; other people set aside one day of the weekend and do all their work on that day. Whichever best suits you, remember the glass jar of time, and be strict with yourself; otherwise you will be working all the time. Set yourself things to look forward to, e.g. attending a sports event during the weekend. This helps with time management as it prevents you from working through the weekend.

■ Get to know yourself, your strengths and your weaknesses. Seek advice and suggestions from a range of different people and adopt what works for you.

■ Seek to organise your files and other work so that you can easily locate them (it is as important to organise electronic files and delete those you do not need again as it is to organise paper files and throw away paper you do not need again). This may need dedicated vacation days.

■ You may find that doing more than one job at a time or moving from one thing to another can be disruptive, partly because you may not be concentrating fully on one task, which may result in inefficient use of time. We suggest you switch off your phone or messenger for a time so that you can focus on the task in hand and set aside a time each day to respond to emails, rather than trying to respond as soon as they come into your mail box.

■ Some teachers are now using iPads, Facebook and Twitter to keep up with colleagues, share resources and save time. You need to be careful not to waste time using too many different technologies.

Managing time effectively across a whole year

Teaching is a profession with an uneven profile across the year. This allows for life-style choices in that you can choose to work longer hours in term-time, or you can set aside 'holiday' time for some of the tasks, such as updating subject knowledge and long-term planning for a term. European Union advice suggests that you work no more than 48 hours a week on average– normally averaged over 17 weeks term-time and school vacation. Holidays can be used for an effective balance of recuperation, reflection and preparation, as well as for some larger tasks such as home decorating or learning a new skill that may get put on one side during term time. You might notice a task that could wait and would be helpful to complete longer term, and you might diarise that task to do in a 'holiday'. Task 1.3.6 asks you to look at your work-life balance.

 Task 1.3.6   Coping with your stress through work-life balance

Think about your year as a whole.
What are your own rocks, pebbles and sand? How would you classify:

■ personal administration;
■ family commitments;
■ domestic duties – regular/major;
■ social life/hobbies;
■ holiday;
■ reviewing lifestyle – moving, employment, etc.;
■ upskilling.

How might you decide to spend your year in such a way as to promote your longer-term well-being and achieve an overall balance of your choice between work and leisure time (a work-life balance)?

It may be when you have done all you can, with all the advice you can muster, that your workload or stress level is still unsustainable. Your well-being is important not just to you but to your colleagues, your pupils and the profession you seek to join. Your well-being is a joint responsibility between you and your employer. If you do not do your part in keeping yourself out of harm's way, you cannot be the asset you wish to be to the teaching profession. 'Do not put yourself at risk' (Barraclough, 1996, p.20) is the motto of the first-aider and should equally apply to any individual whose work consists of helping and supporting others. The more teachers who assert their need for well-being, the better it is for all concerned. The employer is not expected to notice if you develop stress symptoms such as not sleeping. Talk to your union representative or a more experienced colleague, read union or HSE guidance on stress management, go and see your GP, and get signed off before you become seriously unwell.

SUMMARY AND KEY POINTS

- As a student teacher on school experience, at times you will be tired, feel as though you do not have enough time to do everything, feel anxious when someone comes in to watch your lessons, particularly if that person has a say in whether you become a qualified teacher, and feel worried about other aspects of your teaching and/or school experience.
- You are not alone in this and many of the causes are the same for other student teachers.
- You can develop effective techniques that work for you to manage your time and cope with stress. Other people can help and support you with this, but nobody else can do it for you because what works for someone else may not work for you. Work at managing your time and stress.
- Build your resilience to enable you to thrive as a teacher. Collegial support in the workplace; a mutually respectful, supportive relationship with your tutor, with open, honest yet sensitive communication which challenges you; and a reciprocal, mutually supportive, trusting network of peers and colleagues are important in doing this. Also, focus on the positive aspects of teaching, your motivation to become a teacher, developing your self-efficacy, confidence and competence, which we hope this book will help you with.
- Stress is contagious, and your pupils and colleagues are vulnerable to stress. Consider how the 'stressed you' responds in everyday classroom occurrences and the impact such responses are likely to have upon the people around you.

Teaching is challenging, rewarding and exhausting. It is a long game, but the skills you gain along the way will help you and your pupils towards fulfilling futures. If insufficient support is in place, there is the potential for aspects of the role to become harmful or injurious, meaning that experienced teachers are lost or the high standards of the profession suffer. Fortunately, it is possible to mitigate these effects by developing your resilience and safeguarding your physical and mental well-being. This will enable you to perform at your best, cultivating, safeguarding and inspiring generations of young people to do the same.

Check which requirements for your ITE programme you have addressed through this unit.

 Further resources

Beltman, S., Mansfield, C. and Price, A. (2011) 'Thriving not just surviving: A review of research on teacher resilience', *Educational Research Review,* **6(3), 185-207.**
This paper reviews recent empirical studies related to the resilience of early career teachers. These show resilience to be the outcome of a dynamic relationship between individual risk and protective factors and contextual challenges or risk factors and contextual supports or protective factors – an understanding of which can help to reduce risk factors and enhance protective factors, and so enable new teachers to thrive, not just survive.

Capel, S. and Al-Mohannadi, A. (2004) 'Managing yourself and your workload', in S. Capel, R. Heilbronn, M. Leask and T. Turner (eds.) *Starting to Teach in the Secondary School: A Companion for the Newly Qualified Teacher,* **2nd Edition, London: RoutledgeFalmer, pp.16-29.**
Although this book is written for newly qualified teachers, this chapter provides guidance on managing stress and time, which is also appropriate for student teachers.

Day, C., Edwards, A., Griffiths, A. and Gu, Q. (2011) *Beyond Survival: Teachers and Resilience,* **Nottingham: University of Nottingham.**
This booklet reports on findings from a series of research seminars focused on addressing the question, 'How does resilience in teaching arise and how is it sustained?' The findings reported should help you to better understand how to build your resilience as a teacher.

Hayes, C. (2006) *Stress Relief for Teachers: The 'Coping Triangle',* **London: Routledge.**
This book looks at the nature of stress in the classroom in a clear, practical way. It focuses on how teachers can help themselves to cope. It focuses on a 'coping triangle'.

Holmes, E. (2009) *The Newly Qualified Teacher's Handbook,* **2nd Edition, Abingdon: Routledge.**
This book covers all aspects of the first few months of teaching. The book is written in light of induction regulations introduced in 2008 for newly qualified teachers in England. Chapter 7 looks at work-life balance. Other chapters are likely to be of use in helping you with aspects of your work that may be stressful.

Johnson, B., Down, B., Le Cornu, R., Peters, J., Sullivan, A., Pearce, J., Hunter, J., Day, C. and Lieberman A. (2016) *Promoting Early Career Teacher Resilience: A Socio-Cultural and Critical Guide to Action,* **Abingdon: Routledge.**
The writers have spent five years exploring conditions that support early career teacher resilience and considering what goes well, intending to help the reader learn from positive experiences and to foster positive environments for early career teachers. They tell the stories of 60 graduate teachers – the struggles and the exhilaration of being an early career teacher. These stories and the associated critical approach will help the reader develop more powerful forms of critical resilience.

McCarthy, C., Lambert, R. and Ulrich, A. (eds.) (2012) *International Perspectives on Teacher Stress (Research on Stress and Coping in Education),* **Kindle Edition.**
This book puts teacher stress into a global context. It includes original research about the ways in which teachers cope and thrive in different cultural contexts.

The Education Support Partnership (https://www.educationsupportpartnership.org.uk/)
Provides information, research evidence and a range of services, including counselling, to help all teachers.

Appendix 2 lists subject associations and teacher councils and Appendix 3 provides a list of websites.

Capel, S., Leask, M. and Turner, T. (eds.) (2010) *Readings for Learning to Teach in the Secondary School: A Companion to M Level Study,* **Abingdon: Routledge.**
This book brings together essential readings to support you in your critical engagement with key issues raised in this textbook.

Capel, S., Lawrence, J. Leask, M. and Younie, S. (eds.) (2019) *Surviving and Thriving in the Secondary School: The NQT's Essential Companion,* **Abingdon: Routledge.**
This book is designed to support newly qualified teachers in the next phase of development as a teacher. However, you may find it useful as it covers aspects of teaching not included in this book which, nonetheless, you experience on your ITE programme.

The subject specific books in the *Learning to Teach (Subject)* series, the *Practical (Subject) Guides, Debates in (Subject)* and *Mentoring (Subject) Teachers* are also very useful.

 Any additional resources and an editable version of any relevant tasks/tables in this unit are available on the companion website: www.routledge.com/cw/capel

1.4 Using digital technologies for professional purposes

Andrew Csizmadia and Sarah Younie

Introduction

Teachers are expected to integrate various forms of information and communications technology (ICT)/ digital technologies into their work in the classroom and promote online safety. The statutory framework of the 2014 National Curriculum Computing Programmes of Study in England states that: 'Pupils should be taught to develop their capability, creativity and knowledge in computer science, digital media and information technology' (Department for Education (DfE), 2013c, p.64). In Wales, a Digital Competence Framework (Welsh Government, 2018) has been developed to enable pupils to thrive in an increasingly digital world. The Welsh Government regard digital competence as one of the three cross-curricular responsibilities for schools, alongside literacy and numeracy. Internationally, European Schoolnet, on behalf of the European Union, advocates digital citizenship as a right for all, and that digital skills enable people to exercise this right. Further, the United Nations Education, Scientific and Cultural Organisation (UNESCO) has developed an ICT Competency Framework for Teachers (ICT-CFT).

The focus for this unit is the use of ICT to facilitate and enhance learning and the learning experience rather than the subject of computing. This aspect of ICT, hereafter referred to as digital technologies, is re-enforced across the curriculum. Digital technologies used innovatively within your subject teaching enhance learning for your pupils. Good subject teachers are already making good use of digital technology and are always looking out for new ways of using digital technologies to stimulate pupils and extend their learning. These teachers understand that digital technologies are a tool to be applied selectively but are not the complete solution to meeting their pupils' needs. They are also able to learn from pupils. Talking with your computing colleagues also helps you identify valuable learning experiences that help your pupils.

One concern for you may be that the pupils know more about digital technologies than you do. If this is a concern, or if you are uncertain about the use of digital technology in your subject area or have not fully embedded it into your teaching, you are not alone, as was noted by the inspectorate in England in their ICT subject report 2008–11 (the Office for Standards in Education, Children's Services and Skills (Ofsted), 2011a, p.42). (There is guidance on using ICT/digital technologies in your subject in the subject books that accompany this generic text, i.e. *Learning to Teach (Subject) in the Secondary School* and *A Practical Guide to Teaching (Subject) in the Secondary School* (both published by Routledge). Subject associations (see Appendix 2) are also a good source of guidance.)

The purpose of this unit is not to turn you into a computing teacher, but to show how you can become a teacher who uses digital technologies creatively in your teaching to enhance pupils' learning. One key objective is to erase some of your fears and present some clear signposts for you to use digital technologies to support your subject teaching. After all, in reality, 'the only thing we have to fear is fear itself' (Roosevelt, 1933, p.1).

OBJECTIVES

At the end of this unit you should be able to:

- understand the relevance of digital technologies for you and your pupils;
- use an appropriate framework for auditing your knowledge and understanding of digital technologies;
- plan to teach using digital technology resources to enhance the pupil learning experience;
- understand your role and responsibility in promoting online safety for both yourself and the pupils you teach.

Check the requirements of your initial teacher education (ITE) programme to see which relate to this unit.

The relevance of digital technologies for you and your pupils

You need to be clear about why you might use digital technologies in teaching your subject lessons. Is it to entertain pupils, is it to engage their curiosity in your subject, is it to enthuse them about your subject, is it to enlighten them about a difficult topic or concept or is it to empower their learning? Hopefully, it is the last four.

Subject associations, Ofsted and technology companies (such as Apple, Google and Microsoft), provide excellent examples of how existing and emerging technologies can be used to support teaching and learning within and outside the classroom. For example, Ofsted (2011a, pp.34-35) reported that for a Key Stage 4 geography coastal study, a pupil used digital technologies to help them both organise a sequence of investigations and also to organise their work. Their use of digital technologies helped deepen their analysis and understanding. This also helped to demonstrate initiative and originality in their work.

Google has developed Google Expeditions (https://edu.google.com/expeditions), which enables a class to be taken on an immersive virtual reality field trip without the need to leave the classroom! For example, in geography, your pupils can explore coral reefs; in RE, pupils can experience festivals from around the world; and, in science, pupils can explore human anatomy.

The key points of the above examples of good practice are that:

- the best use of digital technologies as a resource is context-driven;
- if a pupil sees the benefit, then they are more likely to use the same technologies again elsewhere and more importantly within a different subject.

What is common about the "good practice" cited is that digital technologies were applied in both a contextual and in a practical manner. If you are going to develop your digital confidence, digital capability and digital competence to mirror the good practice presented, understanding the theoretical work that underpins these approaches should help you use them effectively in your teaching. In these cases, the approaches are underpinned by the work of Vygotsky (1978) and, in particular, his theory of the Zone of Proximal Development (ZPD) (see Unit 5.1), and Bruner's (1961) theory of discovery learning. Now complete tasks 1.4.1, 1.4.2 and 1.4.3.

 Task 1.4.1   Using digital technologies to support teaching and learning in your subject

Identify how digital technologies can be used to support teaching and learning in your subject.

Ask other teachers of your subject area and also check out what your subject association identifies as digital resources to support teaching and learning.

Discuss with another student teacher how digital technologies can be used to engage, enthuse and empower pupils in the subject you teach.

Record your findings in your professional development portfolio (PDP) or equivalent for later reference.

 Task 1.4.2   How are digital technologies used in your subject?

Look at one of the examination specifications for your subject and identify where digital technologies can be used to enhance both the teaching and learning experiences within your subject. Remember, not all topics lend themselves equally to the use of digital technologies.

Record your findings in your PDP.

 Task 1.4.3   Planning to teach using digital technology resources

Plan an activity using digital technologies for your subject. Discuss and critique your planned activity with another student teacher. What amendments did you agree should be made? Why?

Record your discussions in your PDP.

In order to use digital technologies effectively to enhance pupils' learning, it is important that you are clear about your own level of knowledge, skills and understanding; the next section of this unit is designed to help you achieve this.

Frameworks for auditing your digital competence

There have been a number of initiatives to support teachers to develop their digital literacy competences, including the DigiLit Leicester project (see Fraser et al., 2013). This was a collaboration between schools, the local authority and De Montfort University to create a framework for assessing teachers' digital literacy skills. This is a helpful evaluation tool that enables you to self-assess your own knowledge and understanding, and also identify which competences you may need to develop further. The framework consists of six strands (Fraser et al., 2013, pp.10-12).

Finding, Evaluating and Organising: Teachers know that the internet has a significant range of information, resources and research that can be used to support and develop learning and teaching. The ***Finding, Evaluating and Organising*** strand of the framework includes the skills required to successfully search for information and resources online, the know-how needed to identify reliable sources of information and the ability to apply a range of approaches for organising online content.

Creating and Sharing: As a teacher you need to be able to manage a wide range of digital information and resources, including those you create yourself. The ***Creating and Sharing*** strand covers using online tools to create original materials, and building on or repurposing existing resources, for the classroom. You should know how to identify resources you have permission to use and remix, and also how to openly share your own materials. You should be able to support pupils in creating their own resources and portfolios of work. You also need to be aware of the legal requirements relating to the use of online and digital resources, for example, copyright law, and the range of open licenses available, for example, Creative Commons licensing.

Assessment and Feedback: Web-based and mobile technologies provide a range of opportunities for teachers and pupils to assess attainment and track progress, to identify where learners are having difficulties and to provide feedback, including peer assessment. The ***Assessment and Feedback*** strand includes how teachers make use of technologies to support learners in monitoring and managing their own learning and to ensure teaching approaches are effective, and adjusting these to suit learners' pace and needs.

Communication, Collaboration and Participation: Digital tools and environments offer teachers and pupils a range of collaborative opportunities, supporting the co-design and co-production of resources, providing new approaches to participation and supporting learner voice. Teachers and learners can use technologies to connect and learn both with and from other learners and experts from around the world. The ***Communication, Collaboration and Participation*** strand involves the use of communication technologies, for example types of social media including wikis, blogs and social networking sites, to support learning activities and enhance school communications, planning and management.

E-Safety and Online Identity: The use of technology is increasingly integrated into everyday life, and the value of using both private and public digital environments to support learning, teaching and communication is well recognised. Schools and teachers support learners in understanding the negative effects of inappropriate online behaviour, and in ensuring learners understand what responsibilities they have as members and representatives of a school community. The ***E-Safety and Online Identity*** strand underpins teachers' and learners' use of digital environments for formal and informal learning, including understanding how to keep both yourself and your learners safe online, and how appropriate and positive online behaviours can be modelled in classroom practice.

Technology-supported Professional Development. For teachers, the challenge with continuous professional development is keeping up to date with subject knowledge and with emerging pedagogic approaches. Web- and mobile-based technologies have changed the landscape in terms of how we can connect to other teachers both locally and globally. Personal Learning Networks (PLN), developed and managed by educators, allow teachers to discover, discuss and share relevant ideas, resources and pedagogic approaches. The ***Technology-supported Professional Development*** strand focuses on how educators can and are making use of technology to take their practice forward.

Please see the companion website for the full Digital Literacy Framework, which you can use as part of a self-assessment audit. Part of this framework is reproduced below in the 'Online safety' section in Task 1.4.6.

There are other frameworks that are worth considering also, for example, see the 'European Framework – Digital Competence for Educators' at:

- https://ec.europa.eu/jrc/en/publication/eur-scientific-and-technical-research-reports/european-framework-digital-competence-educators-digcompedu
- https://ec.europa.eu/jrc/en/digcompedu<https://ec.europa.eu/jrc/en/digcompedu>

There is also 'Learning Wales Digital Competence Framework' at:

- http://learning.gov.wales/resources/browse-all/digital-competence-framework/?lang=en
- Task 1.4.4 is designed to help you develop your digital competence.

 Task 1.4.4   Identify and develop your digital competence

As part of your own professional development and strengthening your subject knowledge, you will be undertaking subject knowledge audits at regular intervals. Periodically, you might wish to review your digital competence and reflect on how your digital competence can impact the teaching and learning that occurs in your classroom.

1   Using one of the digital literacy frameworks above, identify your current digital competences.
2   Create an action plan to develop your digital competences.

Store your table in in your PDP, revisit it, review it and update your knowledge at regular intervals during your ITE programme.

As a teacher, what do I need to know regarding digital technologies?

We live in a world that is influenced by our engagement with digital technologies for the way in which we live, play and work. How would you react to the challenge of 'not using digital technology, including your mobile phone, for a day?' The following section outlines what secondary school teachers will need to know regarding the implications of and guidance for using digital technologies for teaching and learning in the classroom, monitoring pupils' progress and their own professional development:

Data Protection: Be aware of the General Data Protection Regulation (GDPR), which was implemented in May 2018, and its implications for secure storage of and usage of both electronic and manual data related to pupils, as it has superseded the Data Protection Act. You also need to understand how your placement schools meet the requirements of GDPR and the impact of GDPR upon the teaching that you will deliver and usage of any online digital tools that you might use.

Digital Champions: Know who the digital champions are in your subject area; also, subscribe to their blogs and follow them on Twitter. This can keep you up-to-date with developments regarding how digital technologies are being used in your subject.

Digital Resources: Check out what your subject association identifies as digital resources to support teaching and learning.

Digital Tools: Be aware of and able to use digital tools to support teaching and learning inside and outside the classroom. Examples include digital tools for formative assessment, such as Kahoot or Yacapaca, and digital resources such as TED-ED (https://ed.ted.com/) to enhance and enrich both teaching and learning.

Digital Literacy: Ensure you are able to use and promote digital literacy in your subject, just as you would with literacy and numeracy. You are expected to model good practice. This includes the use of office applications for teaching, learning and administrative tasks, i.e. creating resources, planning or tracking pupils' progress.

Digital Footprint: Ensure that you are aware of your digital footprints, especially their imprints across the social media that you use.

Some of these topics are explored in the following sections.

Online safety

In 2015, online safety, previously 'e-safety', was included in Ofsted's common inspection framework (Ofsted, 2015a). Prior to this, in most secondary schools, it was taught predominantly by the computing teacher and occasionally by form tutors as part of an organised personal, social and health education (PSHE) programme. However, it is now recognised as a safeguarding issue due to pupils being at risk of bullying, online grooming, sexual exploitation, changes to sexual behaviour due to sexting, being misled by fake news and radicalisation. As a teacher, it is important to make your pupils aware of not only the benefits of digital technologies but also their potential risks. You should speak openly and honestly about the negative impact of digital technology and peer pressure amongst secondary-school-aged pupils.

You may feel uncomfortable dealing with these issues. Your school may also have its own resources, and we can highly recommend classroom resources produced by Child Exploitation and Online Protection Centre (CEOP), BBC and Safer Internet Day to help you with this. These range from animations to short films. Usually, pupils take these seriously. Pupils can be asked to reflect on what their thoughts are about a video they have seen. Informing pupils that there no right or wrong answers provides an environment in which a mature debate and discussion can take place. You can then ask pupils to devise some general rules or advice based on the videos that other pupils should follow regarding online safety.

Online safety cannot simply be addressed by either one lesson or one form period each year; it should be revisited at regular intervals or when an online safety incident has occurred. If an online safety incident does occur and you are aware of it, then it should be dealt with seriously and you should follow your school's safeguarding procedures as online safety is a whole school issue. As soon as it is practically possible, inform the teacher whose class you are taking what has been disclosed to you. Also, ensure that your subject tutor, the designated school safeguarding lead(s) and, if you are on an ITE programme in partnership with a university, your university tutor are made aware of your discovery so that they can advise and support you. The pupils involved should be asked to reflect on what has occurred and think about the real-life consequences should they be employed as an adult and this incident happened. Now complete Task 1.4.5.

 Task 1.4.5   Safeguarding procedures in your placement school

Ensure you are familiar with the safeguarding procedures specific to each placement school. Summarise this procedure as a flowchart and record who are the designated school safeguarding lead(s). Store this in your PDP.

As schools take preventative measures to ensure pupils' online safety, for example asking pupils to read, sign and abide by an Acceptable User Policy (AUP), adhering to guidance for behaving responsibly online and asking them to select a secure password for their login to the school's network, so should you. You will be required to sign the staff version of your school's AUP at the start of a school placement, prior to being allowed to access the school's network. In addition, you might want to consider what your own digital footprint is by typing your name into a search engine and seeing what information, images and videos are available to be read or viewed. The reason for this is that pupils may well search the web to discover what they can about you. Review your privacy settings on any social media platform (e.g. Facebook) you belong to and any social media apps (e.g. Instagram) you either use or have subscribed to. You should amend your settings on these so that only trusted friends can see what has been posted. Now complete Task 1.4.6.

 Task 1.4.6   Reviewing your digital footprint

We live in an age where we exist simultaneously in two worlds, the physical world and the virtual world. Within the virtual world we exist as a collection of data (i.e. audio, numerical, text, images, videos) and within interdependent, interwoven and interlinked networks which connect us to others within this virtual world. It is not uncommon for employers, pupils and parents to look at what there is about you on social media. It is important, therefore, before you start your ITE programme (and school placement), to ensure photographs and references to you on the internet represent you as the professional you want to be. In order to discover and review your online presence, take the following steps:

1   Google your name and see how many search results relate to you.
2   Which search results would you want the pupils you teach to see? (If there are any you would not want them to see, take them down.)
3   Review your privacy settings on any social media platform that you belong to and any social media apps.

In 2018, the UK Council for Child Safety (UKCCIS) Education Working Group produced *Education in a Connected World*, a framework for online safety. This framework details the knowledge and skills pupils need in order to navigate the internet safely.

As part of your safeguarding training during your ITE, you may undertake online safeguarding training, e.g. CEOP. This training can be submitted as evidence for your Standards. You may also wish to undertake your own self-assessment regarding your digital literacy skills in relation to e-safety and online identity. The self-assessment of E-Safety and Online Identity in Task 1.4.7 is taken from the Digital Literacy Competency Framework (Fraser et al., 2013), which is reproduced in full on the companion website.

 Task 1.4.7   E-Safety and online identity: a self-assessment tool

Assess your own level of competency by completing the self-assessment of E-Safety and Online Identity below. This evaluation tool enables you to self-assess your own knowledge and understanding, and identify which competences you may need to develop further.

E-Safety and Online Identity

Entry

- I have a basic understanding of the definitions of e-safety and cyberbullying.
- I understand basic prevention strategies and safety tips.
- I understand my school's e-safety policies and how these relate to and support safeguarding, and the implications this has for my practice.

Core

- I understand the difference between personal and professional use of online sites and communications technologies.
- I am aware of the importance of looking after my online professional reputation; using privacy settings and 'friending' or connecting to others appropriately.
- I understand my responsibilities under the Data Protection Act with regard to the electronic management and protection of students' information.
- I am able to provide my learners with basic tips about how to stay safe online, including how to deal with online bullying, and how to save evidence.
- I can address cyberbullying disclosures and key e-safety issues (for example, bringing the school's name into disrepute online, accessing inappropriate content in school and sexting) and understand how to report these appropriately.

Developer

- I am aware of what current research tells us about young people's use of technology and the opportunities and risks relating to this.
- I can manage security and privacy settings in a range of platforms and services.

■ I understand issues relating to the management of learner data and information and take responsibility for ensuring it is used appropriately, responsibly and with proper permission.

■ I support my learners in understanding their rights and responsibilities in online environments, and in developing a positive online presence.

Pioneer

■ I understand the importance of modelling the positive use of technologies for young people and I do this in a range of ways.

■ I understand how to identify, manage and address the risks associated with learning and teaching in a range of online environments.

■ I keep up to date with the wide range of online, mobile and gaming technologies young people use and the key ways in which they use them.

■ I ensure the whole school community (learners, staff, parents and carers, governors) are actively involved in understanding and addressing e-safety issues.

Store this in your PDP. Work on any aspects in which you self-assess you need further development and update the self-assessment as appropriate.

SUMMARY AND KEY POINTS

This unit has focused on:

■ reflecting on how to use digital technologies to enhance teaching and learning in your subject area;

■ how digital technology refers to many of the things you may see and use every day, without thinking about it and reflecting on ideas about how you may use them in your teaching;

■ a digital literacy competency audit. This should be encouraging, as it probably showed you knew more than you thought;

■ encouraging you to use digital technologies, including ways in which you are able to control the direction, pace and learning that will keep pupils engaged;

■ the importance of online safety.

Check which requirements for your ITE programme you have addressed through this unit.

Task 1.4.8 is designed to help you reflect on your learning in this unit.

  Task 1.4.8   Reflecting on the use of digital technologies in your subject

Reading this unit and completing the tasks help prepare you for using different IT applications and digital technologies and associated pedagogies to enhance your teaching and your pupils' learning. The following questions are designed to help you reflect on the use of digital technologies in your subject and to critically analyse the potential benefits of doing so.

- Discuss the proposition that using digital technologies to encourage pupils to develop transferable skills is only effective if an application of digital technology is used in different contexts and differing learning environments.
- Critically analyse the statement, 'Understanding what you can do with digital technologies to enhance teaching and learning is more important than knowing how the technologies work'. Support and justify your conclusions.
- Using relevant sources to support your answer, evaluate how the use of different types of digital technologies can be used to enrich the learning experience for pupils with English as an additional language (EAL).
- Pupils who have been diagnosed with autistic disorders typically have limited social interaction, communication or interests and can exhibit repetitive behaviour. Examine, supported by relevant sources, a strategy using forms of digital technologies that you believe will benefit such a pupil's learning experience. Evaluate how you would determine the effectiveness of your strategy.

Record your findings in your PDP.

 ## Further resources

The suggested further resources have been selected to encourage you to think about opportunities for using all types of digital technologies in both an innovative and effective manner to enhance teaching and learning in your subject. They also seek to demonstrate that inspiration can come from an unexpected range of sources, and so pose the question: 'That looks interesting: could I adopt that to enhance my subject teaching?'

Bradshaw, P. and Younie, S. (2018) 'Understanding online ethics and digital identity', in S. Younie and P. Bradshaw (eds.) *Debates in Computing and ICT Education*, Abingdon: Routledge.
This provides an understanding for both pupils and teachers of ethical issues concerning digital technologies and an awareness of our online identities.

Burden, K. and Younie, S. (2014) *Using iPads Effectively to Enhance Learning in Schools MESHGuide*, available at http://www.meshguides.org
This MESHGuide gives a research-informed introduction to the use of iPads for learning.

Cych, L., Williams, L. and Younie, S. (2018) 'Using web 2.0 technologies to enhance learning and teaching', in S. Younie and P. Bradshaw (eds.) *Debates in Computing and ICT Education*, Abingdon: Routledge.
This chapter outlines the use of digital technologies for enhancing teaching and learning across subjects, specifically how Web 2.0 tools can be used to create a social constructivist learning environment. The authors discuss how digital technologies can be used to stimulate pupil engagement and how to deploy Web 2.0 technologies effectively in the classroom.

Fraser, J., Atkins, L. and Hall, R. (2013) DigiLit Leicester: *Initial Project Report*, Leicester: Leicester City Council (CC BY-NC 3.0) (see http://lucyjca.co.uk/publications)
This report contains a digital literacy competency framework with all of its descriptors and statements, which allow you to assess your own digital literacy skills. This also enables you to identify which competences you may need to develop further.

Shea, J. and Stockford, A. (2014) *Inspiring the Secondary Curriculum with Technology: Let the Students Do the Work!* Abingdon: Routledge.
This book explores ways of using everyday technology to enhance pupil learning. The authors illustrate, with examples, a range of activities that pupils become involved in and environments that might be used. The flipped classroom, Interactive White Boards, using mobile devices and social networking are explained in the context of their use to further enhance pupil learning experiences.

Younie, S. and Leask, M. (2013) *Teaching with Technologies: The Essential Guide,* **Maidenhead: Open University Press.**

This book brings together research findings to provide an evidence-based approach to using digital technologies in the classroom and highlights effective practice.

You may find the following resources and websites sources of inspiration as you seek to develop your own digital competence, discover how to embed ICT into your planning and teaching activities and your role and responsibility in promoting e-safety in your classroom and with the pupils you teach.

Child Exploitation and Online Protection (CEOP): https://www.ceop.police.uk/safety-centre

CEOP is a command of the United Kingdom's National Crime Agency (NCA) tasked to bring online sex offenders to the UK courts. One of CEOP's roles is that of public awareness campaigns and educational programmes, including the ThinkUKnow education programme (https://www.thinkuknow.co.uk/), which is currently used in UK schools.

Edutopia: www.eduopia.org

Edutopia is a website published by the George Lucas Educational Foundation, which celebrates and encourages innovation in schools by sharing evidence and practitioner-based learning strategies.

Educational Origami: http://edorigami.wikispaces.com

Educational Origami is a wiki and blog about 21st Century Teaching and Learning, which includes Bloom's Digital Taxonomy.

European Schoolnet (EUN): www.eun.org

EUN is a network of 31 Ministries of Education in Europe, which runs subject-specific projects and online CPD courses for teachers, conducts and publishes research into innovative teaching and supports teachers and pupils working on collaborative projects across Europe (i.e. e-twinning).

Safer Internet Day https://www.saferinternetday.org

This website curates teaching and classroom resources that can be used on Safer Internet Day, which is used to promote more responsible use of online technology and mobile phones.

TED-Ed Lessons Worth Sharing: http://ed.ted.com/

This website provides digital resources to enhance and enrich teaching and learning.

There are also resources to help you with online safety.

UK Council for Child Safety (UKCCIS): https://www.gov.uk/government/groups/uk-council-for-child-internet-safety-ukccis

UKCCIS (2018) wrote *Education in a Connected World,* a framework for online safety, which details the knowledge and skills that a pupil will need in order to navigate the internet safely.

Appendix 2 lists subject associations and teacher councils, and Appendix 3 provides a list of websites.

Capel, S., Leask, M. and Turner, T. (eds.) (2010) *Readings for Learning to Teach in the Secondary School: A Companion to M Level Study*, **Abingdon: Routledge.**

This book brings together essential readings to support you in your critical engagement with key issues raised in this textbook.

Capel, S., Lawrence, J. Leask, M. and Younie, S. (eds.) (2019) *Surviving and Thriving in the Secondary School: The NQT's Essential Companion*, **Abingdon: Routledge.**

This book is designed to support newly qualified teachers in the next phase of development as a teacher. However, you may find it useful as it covers aspects of teaching not included in this book which, nonetheless, you experience on your ITE programme.

The subject specific books in the *Learning to Teach (Subject)* series, the *Practical (Subject) Guides, Debates in (Subject)* and *Mentoring (Subject) Teachers* are also very useful.

Any additional resources and an editable version of any relevant tasks/tables in this unit are available on the companion website: www.routledge.com/cw/capel

2 Beginning to teach

The previous chapter was concerned with the role and responsibilities of the teacher and how you might manage those requirements. In this chapter, we look at how you might learn from observing experienced teachers and then move on to consider aspects of planning and preparing lessons.

For most student teachers, there is a period during which you observe other teachers working, take part in team teaching and take part of a lesson before taking on a whole lesson. During this period, you use observation and critical reflection to build up your professional knowledge about teaching and learning and your professional judgement about managing learning. Unit 2.1 is therefore designed to focus your attention on how to observe the detail of what is happening in classrooms.

It is difficult for a student teacher to become fully aware of the planning that underpins each lesson as planning schemes of work (long-term programmes of work) is usually done by a team of staff over a period of time. The scheme of work then usually stays in place for some time. The extent of the actual planning for each lesson may also be hidden – experienced teachers often internalise their planning so their notes for a lesson are brief in comparison with those that a student teacher needs. Unit 2.2 explains the planning processes. Unit 2.3 combines this advice in an analysis of the issues you need to consider before taking responsibility for whole lessons.

The quality of lesson planning is crucial to the success of a student teacher in enabling the pupils to learn. Defining clear and specific learning objectives and learning outcomes for pupils' learning in a particular lesson is one aspect of planning that many student teachers initially find difficult. The following story (from Mager, 2005: p.v) reinforces this need to have clear objectives and outcomes for lessons:

> Once upon a time a Sea Horse gathered up his seven pieces of eight and cantered out to find his fortune. Before he had travelled very far he met an Eel, who said, 'Psst. Hey, bud. Where 'ya goin'?'
>
> 'I'm going out to find my fortune', replied the Sea Horse, proudly.
>
> 'You're in luck', said the Eel. 'For four pieces of eight you can have this speedy flipper and then you'll be able to get there a lot faster'.
>
> 'Gee, that's swell', said the Sea Horse and paid the money and put on the flipper and slithered off at twice the speed. Soon he came upon a Sponge, who said, 'Psst. Hey, bud. Where 'ya goin'?'

'I'm going out to find my fortune', replied the Sea Horse.

'You're in luck', said the Sponge. 'For a small fee, I will let you have this jet-propelled scooter so that you will be able to travel a lot faster'.

So the Sea Horse bought the scooter with his remaining money and went zooming thru the sea five times as fast. Soon he came upon a Shark, who said, 'Psst. Hey, bud. Where 'ya goin'?'

'I'm going to find my fortune', replied the Sea Horse.

'You're in luck. If you take this short cut', said the Shark, pointing to his open mouth, 'you'll save yourself a lot of time'.

'Gee, thanks', said the Sea Horse and zoomed off into the interior of the Shark and was never heard from again.

The moral of this fable is that if you're not sure where you're going, you're liable to end up somewhere else. We hope that by the end of this chapter, you are able to plan lessons in which both you and the pupils know exactly what they are meant to be learning. Explicitly sharing your learning objectives with pupils provides them with clear goals and, potentially, a sense of satisfaction from your lesson as they achieve the goals set.

2.1 Reading classrooms

How to maximise learning from classroom observation

Ana Redondo

Introduction

How do you actively read a classroom rather than simply watch a teacher at work?

During your school experiences you can expect to observe experienced teachers as well as fellow student teachers. You should have the opportunity to observe lessons within and outside of your subject specialism.

What is important when observing in classrooms is to bear in mind that pupils are not passive recipients nor are they unaware of who is in the classroom. They acknowledge the presence of all adults involved in a lesson, whatever their role, which means that they are in a certain way making a contribution to your learning through observation.

The more observations you carry out, the more comparative information you can gather between pupils, classes, groups, teachers and pedagogical approaches. Asking questions about factors in the local context that have an impact on learning is an important part of the exercise. At the same time, you need to avoid being judgemental about what you observe whilst remaining a critical observer. As a professional you are expected to behave ethically. As examples, see Teachers' Standards Guidance for school leaders, school staff and governing bodies, Part Two, the General Teaching Council for Scotland (2012b) and The Teaching Council (in Ireland) (2012) ethical codes for teachers provide a framework for you to consider. (Weblinks are provided in the 'Further resources' section at the end of this unit.)

It is important to develop a notion of learning as a transformative process and to identify key points in the lesson where learning happens in order to get the most out of the experience of lesson observation. Identifying what learning takes place, when and how by individuals and by the class as a whole is crucial to your understanding of what constitutes evidence of learning.

Teachers and pupils set up a working relationship in which both parties know the rules, the codes of behaviour and boundaries. In most classes, boundaries are kept and teachers work smoothly with the class, apparently without great effort. Beneath that order there is a history of carefully nurtured practice by the teacher in establishing an appropriate atmosphere, usually in the first weeks of the new school year.

Sometimes pupils challenge these boundaries for a whole host of good reasons, and you may have observed ways in which the teacher restores a working atmosphere. Each teacher has his or her own way of dealing with this challenge. Watching the way other teachers deal with such issues helps you widen your own repertoire of skills.

OBJECTIVES

At the end of this unit you should be able to:

- define the focus of your observations to achieve specific learning goals;
- use different strategies for recording your observations in forms that lend themselves to subsequent analysis;
- use observation to analyse teaching strategies and pupil learning behaviours to enhance your ability to plan and teach your own lessons;
- begin to understand the teaching and learning process and gain insights into how you wish to teach.

Check the requirements of your initial teacher education (ITE) programme to see which relate to this unit.

Preparing to observe: some general points

Qualified teachers expect to be observed in the context of continuing professional development (CPD), appraisal, inspections and preparation for inspections. Good practice includes peer observation between colleagues in order to support pupils more effectively. See Dudley's (2014) website on Lesson Study. You should look for opportunities to observe fellow student teachers and experienced teachers.

Teachers may be less used to being observed by people who are concerned about analysing what is happening in the lesson rather than measuring it against predetermined criteria such as teachers' standards. As an observer, it is advisable to engage in a dialogue with the teachers you observe at work, both prior to the lesson and afterwards. Before the lesson you could agree on areas for observation and what you plan to do with the data. After the lesson you may wish to clarify aspects of the lesson you have observed, discussing the rationale for some of the actions taken that lead to a deeper understanding of the nature of learning. Equally, ascertaining their perception of the lesson, which you can then compare to yours, enables you to contextualise events and actions you observed, which at times are not necessarily obvious. *Remember that observation is fundamentally about enquiry: seeking to know what is happening, why it is happening and what its impact is likely to be.* It is not passive. It should focus on perception, i.e. making sense of what you see, rather than judgement. Take an open, positive approach to observation but also be well prepared by reading and discussing key elements of a lesson with other student teachers and your tutor. Developing a kind of literacy by which to 'read' and recognise what takes place in a lesson is a skill you develop gradually, becoming more perceptive as you go along.

The form in which you record your observations varies according to the selected focus. Many schools use their own observation proformas or you may be given a different one by your tutors.

When using either, you should adapt it to your own needs or alternatively create a new one, particularly for collecting and recording specific data in a targeted manner, which, in the flow of the lesson, you might otherwise forget. Lesson observation in pairs has great advantages as sharing an observation activity with another student teacher allows the both of you to compare notes and engage in a discussion about the significance of what was observed. Having a specific structure to collect information in turn can allow for a more focused dialogue and exchange, as well as suggestions to feed into your own teaching. Among other sources, unions such as the National Education Union (NEU) and National Association of School Masters and Union of Women Teachers (NASUWT) provide guidance on lesson observation.

Who should you be observing and why?

Initially in observing lessons, you are naturally concerned with familiarising yourself with the dynamics of the classes with regard to how the pupils interact with each other and with the teacher, and how they respond to learning. These observations will be of particular value in preparing you for teaching these specific classes. However, you should not be observing the teacher with a view to imitating their teaching style but with the idea of analysing what she or he is doing that is effective and from that to make your own decisions as to what you wish to adopt in your own practice (See Unit 2.3 on taking responsibility for whole lessons). Building a rapport with pupils is something you will develop as time goes by and you gain more experience; also, it will occur as you spend more and more time with the same classes.

Through observation you will find ways of developing your own professional practices with which you feel comfortable and which will enable you to be effective in what you teach, what methods and approaches you employ and which teaching strategies you prefer in order to positively impact pupils' experiences. It will also assist you in determining the best way of fostering attitudes in pupils and in creating a learning environment for pupils that is conducive to academic progress. (See Unit 4.2 on adolescent wellbeing and Unit 5.1 on how pupils learn.)

Observing experienced teachers throughout your school experiences exposes you to a range of styles and a variety of strategies for teaching, learning and assessment from which to choose so that you can further develop your practice. (See Unit 5.5 on personalising learning.)

There are many aspects of a lesson that can form the focus for observation. Teachers modelling a respectful attitude towards pupils to enable them to achieve will be an important part of your observation of professional practice as this is an important prerequisite for enjoying the respect of pupils. The learning environment and the ethos that the teacher wishes to create are central. Teachers establish rules and routines which then are often reinforced by just a single gesture or signal, e.g. a raised eyebrow if a pupil speaks out of turn. As a student teacher, you should be observing the routines and teaching strategies of the teacher. This analysis enables you to select those aspects that you wish to adapt and adopt in developing your own approach to teaching. When you start teaching, existing classroom routines should be adhered to at the beginning until pupils are able to adapt to your own routines.

Additionally, you should also observe what and how pupils learn. Use the guidance in Units 4.1 on differentiation, 5.2 on active learning and 5.5 on personalising learning to construct observation schedules. You will have the opportunity to observe either small groups of pupils, outside the mainstream classroom, working with support teachers who are specialist in working with pupils who experience learning difficulties and you will need to understand why that happens; also, you will see

Table 2.1.1 Examples of questions that can assist you in focusing your lesson observations

Briefing and preparing for observation
- ■ Note the date, time and place of the lesson.
- ■ Are you briefed on the topic being taught in the lesson and the composition of the class?
- ■ With respect to professional ethics, have you agreed upon your role: a participant or non-participant?
- ■ Have you agreed upon how and what you will observe?
- ■ Have you agreed upon how you are going to provide feedback to the teacher as well as any future use you may make of your notes?

Teaching and learning questions
- ■ What was the plan/structure/shape of the lesson?
- ■ How was the lesson introduced? How did the pupils know the intended learning outcomes planned for the lesson?
- ■ What were the different learning activities that the pupils undertook?
- ■ Was there group or pair work?
- ■ Did pupils receive a range of tasks, degrees of help and variety of resources?
- ■ What were the different ways that pupils recorded or presented their learning?
- ■ How did the teacher direct the pace of the lesson? Pace refers to the appropriate allocation of time to complete tasks set.
- ■ What form of question and answer sessions did the teacher initiate?
- ■ How were pupils encouraged to ask and answer questions?
- ■ What resources were used to assist in learning and how were they used?
- ■ How did the teacher provide a range of teaching strategies to ensure all pupils can access what has been taught?
- ■ Were digital technologies used during the lesson? How?
- ■ Was the teacher handling the technology used?
- ■ Did the pupils have a hands-on experience to complete tasks?
- ■ What learning was supported through the use of technologies (see Unit 5.3 on teaching strategies)

Management of learning and pupils' dimensions
- ■ What were the teacher's expectations about pupils' responses to what has been taught?
- ■ How did the teacher promote behaviours for learning?
- ■ Were there established routines and codes of conduct? What were they?
- ■ Were issues of health and safety considered during the lesson? What were they? How? When?
- ■ Did the teacher use strategies that promote behaviours conducive to learning? What form did that take and what were the outcomes?
- ■ Is there a rationale for the teacher to use seating plans? Why? Do these favour particular pupils?
- ■ How did the teacher use voice and gesture in the lesson to encourage pupil participation?
- ■ How did the teacher make use of assessment during the lesson and how was this fed back to the pupils?
- ■ Were pupils involved in the assessment process? How? What were the outcomes?

Other professional issues
- ■ Was a teaching assistant or special educational needs teacher also in the room? What was their role and how did they work with the pupils? How did they work with the teacher before and after the lesson?
- ■ Have you identified any gaps in your subject knowledge through observing this lesson? How are you going to address them?
- ■ How has this observation made you consider your future professional practice as a teacher? What professional issues has it raised for you? Discuss these with other student teachers and tutors in relation to the importance of becoming a reflective teacher?

teaching assistants supporting individuals within the classroom (see Unit 4.6 on creating an inclusive classroom and Blamires (2014).) Here you have the opportunity to understand the learning needs of individual pupils in greater depth. Also, it is valuable to follow a class or pupil across the curriculum and observe teachers working in subject disciplines other than your own. That can provide you with a pupils' experience in their school day. All opportunities to observe teachers working with pupils are learning opportunities and you may be able to note similar strategies across disciplines and teaching approaches. Teachers in assembly, on duty at break or working with pupils in an extra-curricular activity are all professionally engaged in their work, and how they work in these contexts directly relates to their work in the classroom. It is therefore a good idea to carry a small notepad with you at all times to record significant observations and any questions that occur to you at the time. These can be followed up later with the teacher or your tutor. Effective observation is an intellectual exercise and, to that end, it requires critical engagement in being able to ask relevant questions and being supported by appropriate reading and discussion with tutors. Table 2.1.1 gives examples of questions to address through observation, perhaps prior to teaching a class. Add questions of your own.

What do classrooms look like?

As part of lesson observation, it is useful to 'read' the impact of the appearance and layout of the room on pupil and teacher learning and their experiences. The classroom or teaching space is more than a room with chairs, desks, boards and screens. It is a learning environment. It should both promote and support effective teaching and effective learning. (See Unit 5.7 on critically appraising learning environments and 5.8 on the language rich classroom.)

Classrooms often express the values and ethos of the school and can reflect and promote specific subjects. You may find the planned approach in Task 2.1.1 useful.

 Task 2.1.1   The learning environment

Consider a classroom or teaching space you are going to be teaching in at your placement school and how you can manage this effectively. Is this space a specialist room or a general classroom? Is the space used mainly by one teacher and for one discipline?

■   Sketch the layout of the space and the seating arrangements. Identify the light source and how this affects visibility of the board, screen and other display boards that you will make use of to support your teaching; also, note other features, resources and the teacher's desk. Check how much space there is for you to move among pupils in order to evaluate what they are doing and support them when needed. Space will be also required by pupils when moving about. Obstacles that can cause concerns from a health and safety point of view, e.g. tripping over chairs, bags, etc, need to be avoided.

■   Note your perceptions of the advantages and limitations of the room layout to pupil and teacher learning and teaching. Does the layout support collaborative group working or not?

■   Describe any displays. Note the different proportions of pupil work and teacher/published material displayed. Are the displays colourful and well looked after? Do the displays prompt pupils to value their own work and the work of other pupils more highly?

▪ What values do display material portray? What potential use can pupils make of them? Do displays portray positive images and information that pupils can use to help with their work? Are they, in that sense, interactive and kept up to date? Are they relevant to the learning experiences of pupils? How can displays prompt pupils to think?

▪ Are any technological tools available in the room? If so, what are they? What can be said about their intended use?

▪ Comment on whether you would like to be taught in this room and whether the environment promotes the subject and pupil learning. Give reasons for your response.

Unit 5.7 provides further guidance about critically appraising learning environments. Record your observations in your professional development portfolio (PDP) or equivalent.

How lessons begin and end

Lessons are structured into different parts after careful consideration of the time dedicated to each to maximise learning opportunities. As with all relationships and activities, how a lesson begins is significant to its success or otherwise. It is usual to begin with a starter task to engage pupils from the very moment that they enter into the classroom, taking them through activities that end with a plenary in which to summarise key points of the lesson and providing pupils with a chance to rationalise for themselves what it is they have learned and how they have learned (see Unit 2.2 for further detail). This can be an opportunity for a teacher's skilful use of questioning in what is a very short period of time, between five and ten minutes of a plenary, highlighting key points and enabling pupils to understand the links between prior and future learning. Questioning (see also Unit 5.2) also provides the teacher with useful information about how pupils have understood what they were asked to do and if they have made sense of the work that they were engaged in. Skilful teachers demonstrate good skills in managing pupils and learning, have good subject knowledge and, at times, give the impression that it is all easy. When you first observe lessons, focusing on each of these parts of a lesson is a useful approach to analyse how timings for tasks, teaching materials and organisation of learning are managed. In addition, you can focus on the type of tasks set and how these can encourage participation, higher order thinking and the acquisition of new concepts with clear understanding an application. You might be asked to make an active contribution to one episode within a lesson as a way of beginning to teach the group that has been allocated to your teaching timetable.

Routines

Routines are important in ensuring a smooth transition between tasks in lessons and to provide a backdrop of familiarity to pupils (see Unit 5.2). They are particularly important when taking up new classes. Have a close look at how it is done. While you should follow routines in the same way at the early stages of taking on a class, you can, from then on, develop your own ways of organising the lesson, following structures and policies set down by the school and subject departments and introduce some of your own ideas as you become more confident and your tutors encourage you to become more assertive and independent, and begin to take some risks - albeit agreed beforehand with your tutor. Experienced teachers are very familiar with their pupils and vice versa and that creates a specific dynamic that you cannot immediately reproduce. Be observant, discuss and ascertain the views of your tutors so as to develop confidence to adopt, to adapt and to align with your own style after a period of practice.

At the end of lessons, after summing up (sometimes called a plenary), it is important to allow enough time for pupils to be dismissed in an orderly manner, ensuring a well-organised exit. Therefore, observe techniques for dismissing pupils.

Timing

When planning lessons, careful attention needs to be paid to how long individual episodes should last. When observing lessons, you are advised to pay attention to the amount of time allocated to individual activities.

Task 2.1.2 is designed to help you to analyse the beginning, middle and end of a lesson.

 Task 2.1.2   Analysing the beginning, middle and end of a lesson

You may hear a lesson being described as being in three parts: starter, main body of the lesson and plenary. However, with experienced teachers the lesson may appear to be a smooth flow of activities and the different features are noticeable in terms of content but not so much in format. For example, at times, some 'mini-plenaries' take place after a task to ensure understanding before moving on so that the end of lesson evaluative time becomes less formal.

1   There are three stages to the beginning of a lesson: first, possibly lining up outside the classroom, particularly with younger pupils, to ensure an orderly entrance and settling them to a prompt start to learning. 'Starter tasks' (or 'hooks', see Unit 5.2) are quick exercises that provide a good opportunity to link to previous learning, e.g. revising work; also, they serve to get pupils to focus on work immediately rather than getting distracted with each other into chatter. Starters need only be between five and seven minutes.

2   The body of the lesson: presenting lesson outcomes, followed by presenting the work through chosen materials (either digital or print and providing instructions to the work).

3   The plenary: invite pupils to provide a summary, highlight key aspects of the lesson and link them to future learning including homework tasks where appropriate.

Useful prompt questions for observations are:

Outside the classroom

■   What procedures were used for pupils gathering outside the classroom? And their rationale?

a) Were pupils free to enter as they arrived or did they have to line up?

b) Did the teacher wait for the class at the classroom door - were they welcomed on arrival outside the classroom or did the teacher stay inside the classroom until the class was directed to enter?

Settling into place

■ Did the pupils sit where they pleased or did they have assigned places? Did they wait to greet the teacher standing before they were asked to sit down?

■ Was a register taken and in what manner?

■ What signals did the teacher use to indicate that the lesson had begun?

The beginning of the lesson

■ How did the teacher explain the intended learning outcomes (see Units 2.2 and 7.4) of the lesson?

■ How long was it before the lesson proper began?

■ What problems or issues did the teacher have to deal with before the lesson began? How did they do this?

■ In settling the class, what praise or conduct reminders did the teacher use and how did pupils respond?

The body of the lesson

■ How effective was the teacher in providing explanations and instructions to pupils to tell them what to do and how?

■ Were pupils encouraged to ask questions?

■ Were pupils expected to work independently from the teacher? Possibly sharing ideas with each other? Or to work quietly? In any other way?

   ■ Were pupils sufficiently challenged and engaged given their prior skills, knowledge and understanding?

   ■ Did pupils understand what they are being asked to do in every stage of the lesson?

   ■ Did pupils have opportunities and means to indicate their understanding (or lack) of the concepts being introduced?

   ■ Did pupils improve their understanding as a result of detailed and accurate feedback on their learning?

   ■ Were pupils who are having difficulty supported to help them understand?

   ■ How well was pupils' subject knowledge developed in terms of concepts, knowledge, skills and understanding?

   ■ Was the management of the pupils' behaviour effective to ensure that they make progress in a safe and secure environment?

The end of a lesson

■ Were pupils able to respond to questions satisfactorily during the plenary, demonstrating they (a) could recall what they have learned and (b) understood what they have learned?

- How did the teacher find out what *most* pupils could recall and understand?
- Were the intended learning outcomes achieved and how did the teacher know that?
- Were pupils dismissed quietly and as a class or in small groups?

If possible, discuss this list of questions with another student teacher and add to them. Then undertake the observation. In carrying out this task you should arrive at least five minutes before the beginning of the lesson.

Using a similar checklist to that drafted below, record your observations.

Observer's name						
Date and Time						
Class name and subject:					Number and Composition of class: ......Males......Female	
Real time	Place	Pupil actions	Teacher	Pupil talk	Teacher talk	Other notes

After the lesson discuss with the teacher what you have noted to check for any misunderstandings and to discuss further the strategies you have observed. Record your observations in your PDP.

The structure of a lesson and transitions

The structure of a lesson is very important to its effectiveness (see Units 2.2 and 2.3). When an experienced teacher teaches a lesson, they work to a plan but, equally, they deviate from the plan when a new learning need becomes apparent. Good teaching is flexible and responsive. Experienced teachers use *transitions* in a lesson to summarise the learning at key points and ascertain understanding before moving on to the next learning activity. Figure 2.1.1 is a flow diagram of a lesson about communication where the transitions are highlighted in bold.

Key parts are:

1   learning objectives and intended learning outcomes for today shared with pupils linking these to longer term objectives. Objectives included: to listen for detail, understand and respond in writing to a recorded conversation, ensuring accuracy;
2   presentation of key concepts and tasks, explaining how to complete these and providing examples, adding visual support as necessary to ensure all pupils can make sense of what is expected of them;
3   pupils complete tasks either individually or collaboratively;
4   pupils can be invited to extend outcomes of tasks if time and expectations for this have been considered and included in your original planning.

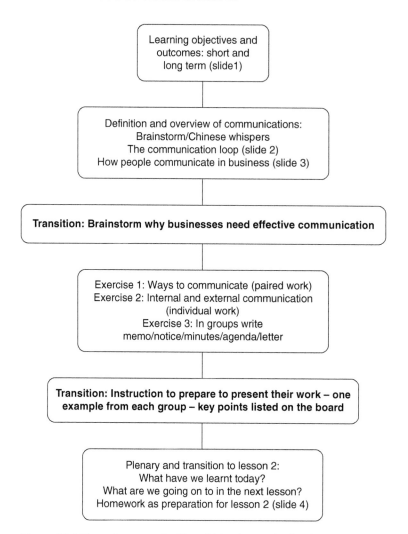

Figure 2.1.1 Flow diagram of a Year 10 business studies lesson, which is the first lesson of a double lesson on communication for business

Teacher talk and oral feedback

It is useful to focus on teacher talk and feedback to pupils during a lesson to enable you to estimate its impact on learning and their responses (see Units 3.1 and 5.8; and also Alexander, 2015; Education Endowment Foundation, 2015; and University of Cambridge, 2015). There are various ways of doing this, including audio or video recordings of a lesson. However, on most occasions, written notes are sufficient. Task 2.1.3 is designed to help you analyse the way teachers talk to pupils. Unit 5.8 provides detail on the use of language in classrooms.

M **Task 2.1.3   Analysis of teacher talk**

Complete the following checklist for a section of the lesson.

Oral feedback	Examples observed in the lesson	Learning impact on pupils
Giving information		
Correcting errors or misapprehensions		
Praising		
Questioning to check understanding		
Questioning to deepen understanding		
Asking pupils to focus on specific aspects		
Summarising learning		
Encouraging pupil reflection		
Coaching in skills		
Answering pupil questions		
Correcting inappropriate behaviour		
Guiding pupils back on task		
Outlining next learning tasks		

Discuss your observations with the teacher after the lesson and record both the checklist and discussion in your PDP.

Task 2.1.4 asks you to focus specifically on questioning. Units 5.1, 5.2 and 5.8 provide more detailed background to the role of questioning in learning.

 Task 2.1.4   Teachers' questions and the development of questioning skills

Questions are often classified into 'closed' and 'open'. Closed questions are those about facts, with a single correct answer. Open questions may not a have a right answer or there may be several ways of responding. They require the pupil to speculate about events or anticipate new ideas or explanations (see Unit 3.1 for further information about questioning).

What types of question do teachers ask? Are they simple questions with one-word answers or are they more complex, involving explanation? Investigate the frequency of different types of questions. The following questions may help to focus your observation. Does the teacher:

■ Ask mainly closed questions?
■ Ask both open and closed questions according to purpose and circumstance? Are only right answers accepted?

- ■ Dismiss wrong answers?
- ■ Give enough time for pupils to give an answer?
- ■ Encourage pupils to frame a reply?
- ■ Provide scaffolding to encourage responses?

How does the teacher respond to right and wrong answers given by pupils?
Discuss your responses and your interpretation of them with the class teacher or your tutor. Record your observations in your PDP.

Pupil talk and interaction

It is equally interesting and highly relevant to analyse pupil talk and interaction, which, if you follow a class or group to lessons in different subjects or with different teachers, can change in significant ways.

You could simply use a class list and place a tick in red next to each pupil's name as they ask for information and a tick in black against each pupil's name as they answer a question or offer information to gauge pupil involvement in lessons.

A more detailed observation with a small group of pupils, one pupil or the entire class can be undertaken using the checklist in Task 2.1.5 over a 20-minute period, recording minute by minute. A three-minute record is shown in the example.

 Task 2.1.5   Analysis of pupil talk

Complete the following checklist to analyse individual, group or whole-class pupil talk over a 20-minute period.

Real time – minute intervals	Pupil(s) initiated questions of teacher	Pupil(s) answering teacher questions	Off task(s) discussion with peers	On task(s) discussion with peers	Other notes about the class activity or other events
9.10	Said B Safia Y				SB not paying attention Safia Y confused
9.11					
9.12		Seth S	Safia B		Good recall by Seth
9.13				Seth S Safia Y	

Discuss your observations with the teacher after the lesson and store both the checklist and the record of your discussion in your PDP.

Observing management of pupils and encouraging learning behaviours that maximise learning

Before beginning lesson observations, you should familiarise yourself with the school's and department's policies about managing learning and pupils to maximise learning. These are used to achieve a common approach to fostering appropriate behaviours for learning. It is essential that you work within these policies (see also Unit 3.3. Task 3.3.2 asks you to record observations of unacceptable behaviours). Discuss with teachers and tutors your own ideas about managing pupils to maximise learning possibly drawn from literature or discussions at seminars so that you can implement and develop your own ways of interacting with pupils and manage learning effectively.

Focus upon pupil learning

Often the instinct of student teachers in the classroom is to focus on the teacher teaching rather than how and what the pupils are learning. This is not surprising. (See Unit 5.7 for a framework for critically analysing the school environment.) How individual pupils respond to the work set is something that needs to be closely observed and then related to their different attainment level, interests and experiences in that subject. This information provides clues about their learning journey and how the teacher makes decisions about how to cater for the diverse needs of all pupils. Hence, you need to shift your focus and observe what and how the pupils are learning. Task 2.1.6 provides some examples of how to do this.

  Task 2.1.6   Analysis of pupil learning

Before beginning your analysis, write down the intended learning outcomes for the lesson (see Unit 2.3) and identify the task/activities on which you are going to focus.

If you are a participant observer, you are able to take notes of key information as the lesson unfolds, look over the work of pupils and be actively engaged with coaching and guiding their learning activities. This enables you to begin to appreciate what strategies and resources are working effectively for their learning and why.

As a non-participant observer, your task becomes subtler. If you are free to move around once pupils are involved in an activity, you can oversee their task completion. If it is appropriate, you can ask them brief questions, but you must not disengage them from their task. Equally, do not be tempted to do the work for them. Always lead them to think through the task with your help.

In highly active lessons there may be considerable chatter and activity, but there may equally be considerable learning taking place. Quiet lessons in which the pupils seem attentive to the teacher are not necessarily lessons where most learning occurs. Different teachers, depending on the subject and specific tasks pupils are engaged in, have different expectations of the degree of talk they allow pupils to have. Observe closely to what extent pupil talk is about the tasks at hand or not and how the teacher responds to that.

> The most flexible way to record pupil learning is to make bullet points as you notice things; a proforma may not be appropriate because pupil learning is so complex. Once the lesson is over, ask the teacher if you may review the work the pupils have completed.
>
> Discuss your observations with the teacher after the lesson and record both your analysis and discussion in your PDP.

The teacher position is also critical in supporting learning. The position of the teacher in the room influences interactions and you should make deliberate decisions about where you will stand and how you move around during lessons. Task 2.1.7 asks you to consider this aspect of classroom management.

 Task 2.1.7   Where is the teacher during a lesson?

The movement of teachers in the classroom may say a lot about their relationship with pupils, about how they keep an eye on activity and behaviour and about their interest in the pupils.

Draw an A4 map of the classroom in which you are observing. Mark on key points: teacher's desk, pupil desks, whiteboard, projector, etc. Have several copies of the map available. At regular intervals throughout the lesson, e.g. every minute or so, mark on your map where the teacher stands and where they have moved from, to build up a picture of position and movement. At the same time, record the time and what is going on in the lesson. This enables you to relate teacher movement to lesson activity. Analyse your map and discuss the following:

- Where is the teacher most often positioned during the lesson? What possible reasons are there for this: writing on the board; explaining with a projector; helping pupils with written work?
- Does the teacher keep an eye on all events in the room and, if so, how? Is it done by eye contact from the front or does the teacher move around the room?
- What does the teacher do to find out whether pupils were on task?
- Were some pupils given more attention than others? What evidence do you have for this? What explanations are there for this?
- Was teacher movement related to pupil behaviour in any way? Examine this idea and look for the evidence.
- Did the nature of the subject matter dictate teacher movement? How do movements change in different subject lessons? Give an example.
- Some teachers use their desk and board and equipment as a barrier between them and pupils; others move in among pupils and desks. Are there 'no-go areas' that the teacher does not visit? Are there similar spaces for teachers that the pupils do not visit?

Summarise your findings for your own records and reflect on what information your 'map' gives you about 'teacher territory' and 'pupil territory'. Share your information with other student teachers. Record your observations in your PDP.

Observing assessment for learning

A common weakness identified in school inspections in England (Office for Standards in Education, Children's Services and Skills; Ofsted, 2014a) is a lack of focus on assessment for learning (see also Unit 6.1). Ensure that you know your school's assessment policies in relation to both teaching and learning as well as national assessments and those of the subject department. Task 2.1.8 asks you to focus on assessment for learning (see Procter, 2013 for an introduction).

 Task 2.1.8   Assessment for learning

Undertake some research about Assessment for Learning choosing reputable sources. Observe a class and, during the lesson, write detailed notes about any activities the teacher uses to assess pupils' understanding of the work. This may include:

1   How does the teacher find out:

   (a) whether the pupils know what they are supposed to be doing?
   (b) whether the pupils understand what they are doing?
   (c) whether the pupils know the possible learning outcomes?

2   Does the teacher:

   (a) talk to individual pupils as they work?
   (b) talk to small groups?
   (c) intervene with questions or suggestions when progress is slow or confused?
   (d) ask challenging questions to individuals or groups to move learning on?
   (e) address the whole class when a common problem emerges?
   (f) accept responses in variety of forms to suit all pupils' preferences in presenting outcomes

   and

3   How does the teacher survey the whole class when working with small groups or individuals?

The teacher may use many strategies but the most common include:

■   direct questions;
■   discussion;
■   asking pupils to present their work to their partner, the whole class or a group;
■   reviewing work on an iPad/tablet, computer, whiteboard or in exercise books;
■   role play or display activities;
■   setting another task to test understanding;
■   posing a problem for pupils to solve in order to evaluate and deepen understanding.

Also note down what the teacher does to correct misconceptions and misunderstandings or to deal with a lack of understanding and to advance learning. How does the teacher reassure and motivate? (See Unit 3.2 on motivation.) How does the teacher consolidate learning? Discuss your observations with the teacher.

Record your observations in your PDP.

How does the teacher use learning resources and aids during the lesson?

Teachers use resources and aids during lessons to help pupils learn most effectively, both by employing a wide range of teaching strategies and differentiating by matching lesson activities to differing levels of attainment, interests and experiences of pupils. All pupils learn best when exposed to a variety of activities at different levels and through many formats and approaches, be they practical, open-ended tasks that require exploring possible solutions or accessing and using audio-visual tools (see Keuchel, Beaudry and Ritz-Swain on Visual Learning in the web references at the end). The important point here is that all pupils are learning and making measurable progress. Providing a range of tasks and formats allows the teacher to be creative and embed variety and differentiation (see Units 4.1 and 5.5) in her/his approach to setting work for all pupils.

Task 2.1.9 provides an example of a proforma to use in analysing how learning resources help pupils learn.

 Task 2.1.9   Learning resources and pupil learning

Identify the teaching/learning resources and aids used in activities in a lesson you observe and describe the benefits for pupil learning. Read Units 5.2, 5.3 and 5.5 for ways of observing learning.

The resource	Learning activity	Learning benefit
Printed texts		
Prepared study guide or worksheet		
Pictures, mind maps, graphics		
Internet and audio-visual material		
Computer programmes including games		
Experiments		
Games, puzzles, models and activity cards		
Digital tools, e.g. interactive whiteboard, iPads/tablets		
Whiteboard		
Other types of equipment		

Discuss the lesson with the teacher and selected pupils. File the data in your PDP.

Subject content-focused observation

All teachers during the early stages of their career have to work hard to fill gaps in subject content knowledge and, as schemes of work and the curriculum change, experienced teachers also need to learn new content. You may want to focus an observation on lesson content concerning a topic in which there is a gap in your own subject content knowledge (see also Unit 1.1).

Using video to support lesson observation

Lesson observation and the subsequent analysis is a very challenging activity. In five minutes of a lesson so much can happen that is of significance and worthy of discussion. Recording part of a lesson for detailed analysis with the teacher is an ideal way of learning. By the same token, taking still images can be a very useful stimulus for post-lesson discussions about aspects of teaching and learning. However, this needs to be discussed and approved by the teacher you are observing, and ethical issues need to be addressed.

Video recording your own lessons enables you to analyse your teaching and to identify ways to improve your practice. You may notice aspects of the lesson that otherwise you may have missed. This process is an effective way to reflect on your practice and set goals for improvement.

Established ethical procedures and guidelines about taking photographs or videos of children need to be adhered to, and you need to gain formal consent from the school to video. Videos of pupils at school need to be kept confidential and within school premises. The use of photographs or video recordings of pupils normally requires parental consent. You need to familiarise yourself, therefore, with school policy and ensure that parental consent has been sought by the school and allows for recordings to be made for the intended purpose. Many schools use video recording of lessons as part of their programme of CPD for all teachers and, in these circumstances, pupils learn to ignore the cameras. Software can be used to annotate videos in real time so that key aspects of the lesson, e.g. questions asked or explanations given, can be easily grouped for playback and analysis. IRIS Connect and D are two commonly used platforms.

Collaborative teaching as a form of observation

Team teaching or collaborative teaching is an interesting approach that can provide you with many interesting ideas about how the teacher and other adults in the classroom, be they another teacher or a classroom assistant, can approach lessons that they have planned together. In that way pupils can gain greater access to adults thereby decreasing the pupil-to-teacher ratio. Individual pupils can be more effectively supported, too. Collaborative or team teaching is an ideal approach by which to organise pupils into small groups to attempt practical work that otherwise is difficult to organise. For example, carousel tasks, discussions in small groups and engaging with work that involves finding solutions are activities that can be far more effectively conducted by more than one teacher.

You should seek every opportunity at your placement school to be involved in collaborative teaching because it is an active and powerful training experience where two-way observation and evaluative feedback can be very constructive, e.g. by co-teaching with another student teacher. Mutual observation can facilitate joint planning, joint lesson evaluation and provide a reassurance that can be helpful when making decisions to inform new planning and teaching. You do need to agree on success criteria for your lesson beforehand so as to help the observer focus on those aspects of your practice.

SUMMARY AND KEY POINTS

■ Lesson observation is something you can expect to take part in throughout your career. You may observe others in order to learn yourself, you may be observed as part of performance management in your school or the inspection process or when you are a supporting student and newly qualified teachers.

■ Observation is an important CPD activity for all teachers. It is also a key tool for reflective practice and practitioner research (see Unit 5.4).

■ Your observation skills will develop with practice and focused effort using some of the methods suggested here over your whole career.

■ The tasks in this unit were designed to help you develop your understanding and get the most out of observation; more importantly, they should enable you to enquire as you seek solutions to challenges arising in your own teaching.

Check which requirements for your ITE programme you have addressed through this unit.

 Further resources

Dudley, P. (2014) *Lesson Study: Professional Learning for Our Time*, **Abingdon: Routledge; see also http://lessonstudy.co.uk/about-us-pete-dudley/ Accessed 8 June 2018.**
Lesson study is widely practiced in schools as an improvement strategy.

Marsden, E. (2009) 'Observing in the classroom', in S. Younie, S. Capel and M. Leask (eds.) *Supporting Teaching and Learning in Schools: A Handbook for Higher Level Teaching Assistants*, **Abingdon: Routledge.**
This chapter should help you to develop your ability to observe in a classroom.

Ofsted (Office for Standards in Education, Children's Services and Skills) (2014b) *Note for Inspectors: Use of Assessment Information during Inspections in 2014/15*, **viewed 8 June 2018, from https://www.gov.uk/government/publications/note-for-inspectors-use-of-assessment-information-during-inspections-in-201415**

O'Leary, M. (2014) *Classroom Observation: A Guide to the Effective Observation of Teaching and Learning*, **Abingdon: Routledge.**
This book should help you to develop your ability to observe in a classroom.

Procter, R. (2013) *Assessment for Learning MESHGuide*, **viewed 8 June 2018, from http://www.meshguides.org/**
This looks at assessment for learning.

The Teaching College of New Jersey (2015) *Anti-Violence Measures*, **viewed 8 June 2018, from http://oavi.tcnj.edu/tools-for-everyone/assertiveness/assertive-nonassertive-and-aggressive-behaviors/**
This site provides examples of classroom issues from an American perspective.

Appendix 2 lists subject associations and teacher councils and Appendix 3 provides a list of websites.

Capel, S., Leask, M. and Turner, T. (eds.) (2010) *Readings for Learning to Teach in the Secondary School: A Companion to M Level Study*, **Abingdon: Routledge.**
This book brings together essential readings to support you in your critical engagement with key issues raised in this textbook.

Capel, S., Lawrence, J. Leask, M. and Younie, S. (eds.) (2019) *Surviving and Thriving in the Secondary School: The NQT's Essential Companion,* **Abingdon: Routledge.**
This book is designed to support newly qualified teachers in the next phase of development as a teacher. However, you may find it useful as it covers aspects of teaching not included in this book which, nonetheless, you experience on your ITE programme.

The subject specific books in the *Learning to Teach (Subject)* series, the *Practical (Subject) Guides, Debates in (Subject)* and *Mentoring (Subject) Teachers* are also very useful.

Any additional resources and an editable version of any relevant tasks/tables in this unit are available on the companion website: www.routledge.com/cw/capel

2.2 Schemes of work, units of work and lesson planning

Sophy Bassett, Mark Bowler and Angela Newton

Introduction

Planning is critical and underpins effective teaching, playing an important role in shaping students' understanding and progression. It is the area of work where teachers can bring their passion for a subject and their desire to make a difference together.

(Department for Education (DfE), 2016c, p.5)

In order to achieve an effectively planned lesson, a number of factors must be considered. These include pupils' prior learning, the ways that pupils learn (see Unit 5.1), the requirements of the curriculum (see units in Chapter 7) and appropriate methods of teaching to suit the needs of all pupils and resources available (see Unit 4.1 on differentiation). In addition to these points, lesson evaluation informs the planning process (see Figure 2.2.1). This unit considers each of these factors in developing medium and short-term plans.

Three levels of planning are particularly relevant to your work in the classroom – the *scheme of work*, which outlines lessons for a term or a year or so, the *unit of work*, which outlines a group of lessons around a particular topic and the *lesson plan* for each individual lesson. You quickly gain experience in planning as you prepare lessons and units of work at your placement school. Evaluation is integrally linked to planning and teaching, and lesson evaluations form the basis of any changes or developments to your plans, both within and between lessons. For this reason, a flexible approach must be adopted.

OBJECTIVES

At the end of this unit you should be able to:

- explain what is meant by the terms: 'aims', 'learning objectives', 'learning outcomes', 'progression' and 'differentiation';
- understand what is meant by a scheme of work, unit of work and lesson plan;
- construct units of work;
- construct effective lesson plans.

Check the requirements for your initial teacher education (ITE) programme to see which relate to this unit.

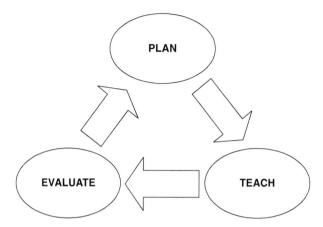

Figure 2.2.1 Plan-teach-evaluate cycle

Planning what to teach and how to teach it

The factors influencing *what* should be taught (content of lessons) are discussed in Unit 1.1 and units in Chapter 7, but how much you teach in each lesson and *how* you teach it (see Unit 5.3) are the teacher's own decisions. At the start of your practical teaching, it is extremely beneficial to plan collaboratively with a more experienced teacher allowing you to access their expert knowledge (the Carter Review (DfE, 2015b)). This collaboration can be used at all stages of your teaching career in order to exchange ideas and increase understanding of pupil learning through mutual support (Dudley, 2011; John, 2006).

Content of lessons

The knowledge, skills, understanding and attitudes appropriate for a young person entering the world of work in the 21st century are vastly different to those that were considered appropriate even 15 years ago. Ideas about what teachers should teach change regularly and the curriculum is under constant scrutiny by those responsible for education.

Before you plan individual lessons, you will require an overall picture of what learning is planned for the pupils over a period of time. As a student teacher, you are usually given clear guidelines about what to teach and the goals for pupils' learning within your subject. These goals are often set out in nationally produced documents; for example, the English National Curriculum, the Northern Ireland Curriculum, the Scottish Curriculum for Excellence, the Welsh School Curriculum, school documents and specifications for accredited courses as issued by examination boards. You should become familiar with the curriculum requirements and the terminology relevant to your subject.

Teaching strategies

To repeat the earlier point, although the learning content may be prescribed, the decision about which teaching strategies to use is usually yours (see Unit 5.3). As you become more experienced as a teacher, you acquire your own personal teaching style. People learn in different ways and different teaching strategies are suitable for different learning objectives and different types of material. You should become familiar with a range of ways of structuring learning experiences in the classroom. For example, you might choose to use discussion, discovery learning or role play to achieve particular learning objectives. Unit 5.3 gives detailed advice on teaching styles and strategies that help you achieve different learning objectives. Task 2.2.1 asks you to reflect on your preferred approaches to learning.

 Task 2.2.1   How do you learn?

Spend a few minutes identifying the methods that help you learn and the teaching strategies used by teachers in situations where you felt you learned effectively (see Unit 5.1). Add notes identifying situations in which you did not learn. Compare these notes with those of other student teachers. People learn in different ways and different learning intentions require different strategies. You should take account of such differences in planning your lessons and demonstrate that you can use a range of teaching methods. This helps you to personalise learning (see Unit 2.1 on observations and 4.1 on differentiation). Record your observations in your professional development portfolio (PDP) or equivalent.

Schemes of work, units of work and lesson plans

There are three main stages to planning for pupil learning:

1   a long-term plan - *the scheme of work;*
2   a medium-term plan - *the unit of work;*
3   a short-term plan - *the lesson plan.*

A number of formats for schemes of work, units of work and lesson plans are in use. We suggest that you read the advice given for the teaching of your subject in the subject-specific texts in this *Learning to Teach* series and gather examples from the teachers and student teachers you are in contact with. However, while the level of detail may vary between different approaches, the purpose is the same - to identify learning objectives and learning outcomes in the long term (scheme of work), in the medium term (unit of work) or in the lesson (lesson plan) and the learning content to achieve these. Your initial teacher education provider may require you to use a specific proforma. However, it would be beneficial to try different approaches to planning in order to find those most appropriate to your situation. The best plans are ones that support you in your teaching so that your pupils learn what you intend them to learn, rather than simply completing a series of tasks. The illustrations in this unit are intended to provide examples with which you can work and later modify.

Scheme of work

This might also be called the 'programme of study' and is usually designed at the department level. Different terms may be used in your school or in your subject, but the purpose is the same - to devise a long-term plan for the pupils' learning, usually across a term, a year or period of years.

The purpose of a scheme of work is to ensure the continuity of pupil learning and build on the learning that has gone before. In some departments, schemes of work are very detailed and include a framework for teaching, learning and assessment as well as safety issues.

Unit of work

As with the scheme of work, different terms may be used for medium-term planning. A unit will normally provide a plan for pupils' learning from a few weeks to an entire term. Units of work are often informed by a department's scheme but will generally be written by an individual teacher.

Both schemes and units of work will plan for the development of pupils' knowledge, skills, capabilities, understanding and attitudes in order to ensure effective progression in learning. The term 'progression' means the planned development of knowledge, skills, understanding or attitudes over time.

Using a scheme of work to plan units of work

Often at your placement school you are given the school's scheme of work to inform your unit planning (see, for example, Table 2.2.1).

The unit itself may be quite brief, but whatever the format, the following questions should be considered when designing units of work:

1   What has been taught before?
2   What do you want the pupils to know, understand and be able to do?
3   How much time is available to do this work?
4   What resources are available?
5   How is the work to be assessed?
6   How does this work fit in with the work pupils are doing in other subjects?
7   What is to be taught later?

Table 2.2.1 Unit of work proforma

Unit of work		
Topic:		
Related prior learning:		
Class:	No in class:	Age:
No of lessons:	Duration:	Dates:
Unit aims: (from the NC or accredited course specification)		
Unit objectives: (in relation to what pupils will know/understand/be able to do)		
Cross curricular links:		
Framework of lessons:		Ref.(NC/Spec)
Resources:		
Assessment strategies:		
Other notes:		

Each question is now discussed in turn.

1   *What has been taught before?* This information should be available from school documentation (for example, the schemes of work) and from staff. In the case of pupils in their first year of secondary education, there is usually a member of staff responsible for liaising with primary schools who may have this information.

2   *What do you want pupils to know, understand and be able to do?* The aims of a unit of work are general statements about the learning that should take place over a period. *Learning objectives* are specific statements that set out what pupils are expected to learn across a unit. Learning outcomes are assessable learning objectives. They describe the action or behaviour of pupils that will provide evidence that they have met the learning objectives. (Learning objectives are also prepared for each lesson and further detail is provided later under lesson planning.) In devising each unit of work, a small aspect of the whole curriculum is selected and a route planned through it to provide the best opportunities for pupils to learn. Progression in pupil learning should be considered and built into units of work.

3   *How much time is available to do this work?* The department or school in which you are working decides the number and length of lessons devoted to a topic. Don't forget that homework has a valuable role to play in enhancing learning, and some time may be taken up by such things as assessments, revision, special events, bank holidays and school training days.

4   *What resources are available?* Resources include material resources as well as human resources, and what is available depends on the school where you are working. You need to find out the procedures for using resources in the school and what is available. You may find there are resources outside the school to draw upon, e.g. parents, governors, charities and subject associations. Many organisations provide schools with speakers on current topics. There may be field study centres or sports facilities nearby. Before planning to use any resources, you should check whether there are any safety issues to consider.

5   *How is the work to be assessed?* Teaching, learning and assessment are interlinked. Most of the work you are doing with pupils is teacher assessed; however, some is externally assessed. A good deal of teacher assessment is formative, often referred to as assessment for learning - to check and guide pupils' progress, e.g. in relation to learning objectives. The key purpose of teacher assessment during a lesson is to check knowledge and understanding of the material and to guide the next steps of teaching.

Teacher assessment may also be summative - undertaken at the end of a piece of work to assess the progress achieved. In any case, you should keep good records of the pupils' progress (homework, class work, assessment results) in your own record book as well as providing these in the form required by the school or department. Unit 6.1 focuses on assessment issues.

Task 2.2.2. asks you to consider how you might record the outcomes of your assessment of pupils.

 Task 2.2.2   Record keeping and assessment

Ask staff in your department how they expect pupil assessment records to be kept and what forms of assessment you should use for the work you are doing. Make notes and compare practice in your school with other schools where your fellow student teachers are working.

Record your observations in your PDP.

6   *How does this work fit in with the work pupils are doing in other subjects?* There are many areas of overlap where it is useful to discuss pupils' work with other departments. For instance, if pupils are having difficulty with measurement in technology, it is worth checking whether and when the mathematics department teaches these skills and how they teach them. Cross-curricular dimensions to the curriculum (see Unit 7.2) are usually considered by the school and responsibilities for different aspects shared among departments. Ask staff in your department what responsibilities the department has in this area.

7   *What is to be taught later?* Progression in pupil learning has to be planned and schemes and units of work are drawn up for this purpose. From these documents, you know what work is to come and the contribution to pupil learning that each lesson is to make.

Task 2.2.3 asks you to draw up a unit of work.

 Task 2.2.3   Drawing up a unit of work

In collaboration with your tutor, draw up a unit of work to last about six to eight lessons. Focus on one particular class that you are teaching. Use the format provided for your ITE programme (or the one in Table 2.2.1). Ensure you consider questions one through to seven above in designing the unit of work. Record your planning in your PDP.

Lesson plan

The lesson plan provides an outline of one lesson within a unit of work. In planning a lesson, you are working out the detail required to teach one aspect of the unit of work. To plan the lesson, it is useful to use a model or framework, an example of which is provided in Table 2.2.2. It is important to note that a range of planning models are available and can be reviewed to find a structure that suits your needs (Capel, et al., 2018).

The following questions should be considered when planning lessons:

1   What is the range of ability of the pupils?
2   What do the pupils know about the topic?
3   What are the aims, learning objectives and outcomes for this lesson?
4   What time is available for the lesson?
5   What resources are available?
6   What approaches to classroom management should I use?
7   What teaching strategies should I adopt?
8   How do I assess pupil learning?
9   What risks are associated with the work?

Table 2.2.2 Planning a lesson: one possible approach

Date:		Class:		Topic:		
Lesson: (e.g. 2/8)		No. pupils:		Focus:		
Duration:		Resources:				
Overall aim						
Learning objectives: (all/most/some)						
Learning outcomes: (all/most/some)						
Learning support requirements:						
Differentiation strategies:						
Assessment for learning strategies:						
Time		Teacher activity/ strategy	Pupil activity (all/ most/some)	Episode evaluation (all/most/some)		
	Starter					
	Main section					
	Plenary					
Lesson evaluation:						
Were objectives/outcomes achieved by all/most/some? What evidence do you have to answer this question with certainty? What went well? What didn't go well? What needs to be addressed next time? What are your priorities for pupil learning in the next lesson? What are your priorities for improving planning, organisation and transitions? What are your teacher performance targets?						

Each question is now discussed in turn.

1   *What is the range of ability of the pupils?* As you develop as a teacher, you are expected to incorporate *differentiation* into your planning. This refers to the need to consider pupils' individual abilities when work is planned so that all pupils, regardless of ability, are challenged and extended by the work. Differentiation can be achieved in different ways depending on the material to be taught. Differentiation may, for example, be achieved by *outcome* (that is, different types or qualities of work may be produced) or by *task* (that is, different tasks may be set for pupils of differing abilities) or by *teacher input* (Unit 4.1 provides further information). You provide continuity of learning for the pupils by taking account of and building on their existing knowledge, skills and understanding.

2   *What do the pupils know about the topic?* As your experience of the curriculum and of pupils' learning develops, it becomes easier to answer this question. You need to consider what has been taught before as well as the experience outside school that pupils might have had. It may be appropriate to do some form of testing or analysis of knowledge, skills, attitudes and understanding or to have a discussion with pupils to discover their prior experience and attitudes regarding the work in question. As a student teacher, you should seek advice from the staff who normally teach your classes, as well as consulting national guidance materials.

3   *What are the aims, learning objectives and outcomes for this lesson?* Learning objectives and outcomes are informed by the aims of the unit. Learning objectives describe the learning intention for the lesson and are recorded in terms of what the pupils are expected to know, understand and be able to do. Objectives describe how pupils' behaviour is expected to change. Learning outcomes are assessable objectives. Drawing up effective objectives and specifying and planning for learning outcomes require considerable thought. Learning objectives are not the same for all pupils and, more often than not, your objectives can be differentiated. One way of achieving this is to write objectives detailing what 'all', 'most' or 'some' pupils should be able to do.

An effective method of presenting learning objectives and outcomes is to begin each statement with, 'By the end of this lesson (all/most/some) pupils should...'. When writing learning outcomes, you should include a verb (and in some subjects a quality) that ensures your outcome is measurable.

Verbs that help you be precise are those such as state, describe, list, identify, prioritise, solve, explain, create and demonstrate. These verbs force you to write outcomes that can be observed or measured. If you think that your learning outcomes are vague, ask yourself whether they make it clear what the pupils have to do to demonstrate their learning. Task 2.2.4 supports your writing of measurable objectives.

 Task 2.2.4   Writing measurable objectives

Using Table 2.2.3, based on research into learning domains, collate a list of useful subject-specific verbs that will help to ensure your outcomes are measurable and progressive. Some generic verbs are provided to help you. Store these in your PDP for use in your lesson plans.

To help pupils understand what is expected of them, you might use the acronym WALT (what am I learning today) and WILF (what am I looking for)? These link with the use of objectives (WALT) and outcomes (WILF).

Task 2.2.5 challenges you to set learning objectives, specify learning outcomes and then analyse the learning that may result.

 Task 2.2.5   Writing learning objectives and learning outcomes

Learning objectives link to the observable outcomes of the lesson, i.e. to what pupils are expected to be able to do. Specifying the expected learning outcomes for the lesson will help you clarify your learning objectives. Discuss the writing of learning objectives with other student teachers in your subject area and your tutor. Choose a particular lesson and, as a group, devise appropriate learning objectives for all/most/some pupils that relate to changes in pupils' learning or behaviour. Pay particular attention to the quality and type of objectives you are setting - are they focused on the pupils' learning? Then identify the learning outcomes related to the learning objectives. How might the pupil demonstrate learning? Record your observations in your PDP.

---

4   *What time is available for the lesson?* On the example lesson plan provided, a timeline is drawn down the left-hand side. You should plan for short learning episodes in order to maintain the engagement of the pupils. At the planning stage, think practically about how long it is likely to

Table 2.2.3 Setting objectives based on learning domains to ensure measurable outcomes

Cognitive Domain *(based on Anderson et al., 2001)*		
Progressive levels	*Example verbs*	*Subject-specific verbs*
Creating	Design, plan, invent	
Evaluating	Judge, assess, identify strengths/weaknesses	
Analysing	Analyse, compare, contrast	
Applying	Apply, use, select	
Understanding	Explain, discuss, identify	
Remembering	Define, list, label	
Affective Domain (based on Krathwohl, Bloom and Masia, 1973)		
Progressive levels	Example verbs	Subject-specific verbs
Characterising by value	Influence, defend, support	
Organising	Modify, relate, integrate	
Valuing	Accept, initiate, endorse	
Responding	Agree to, reply, react	
Receiving	Listen, acknowledge, watch	
Psychomotor Domain (based on Dave, 1975)		
Progressive levels	Example verbs	Subject-specific verbs
Naturalisation	Manage, create, design	
Articulation	Adapt, reorganise, combine	
Precision	Master, refine, control	
Manipulation	Complete, improve, make	
Imitation	Copy, repeat, follow	

take to set up, complete and review each task. During the lesson, the timeline enables you to see easily if it is necessary to adapt the original plan to fit the time available.

5   *What resources are available for the lesson?* It is important to select and make available the most appropriate resources to achieve the learning objectives. Check how resources are reserved in your department and book them early because other staff may need them at the same time. You should also be prepared to adapt resources to suit different classes and to evaluate their suitability (The Carter Review, 2015, DfE, 2015b).

6   *What approaches to classroom management should I use?* You should plan for how you group pupils, integrate resources and manage transitions between activities and stages of the lesson (see Units 2.3 and 4.1).

7   *What teaching strategies should I adopt?* Teaching strategies should be selected as the best method to achieve your learning objectives (see Unit 5.3). Where possible, active learning strategies should be planned to engage all pupils (see Unit 5.2). Relevant questions should be planned for every lesson to assess pupils' knowledge, understanding during the lesson and to develop their higher order thinking skills. Phrasing appropriate questions is a key skill for a teacher (see Unit 3.1).

8   *How do I assess pupil learning?* The assessment methods selected should enable the learning outcomes and thus some learning objectives to be accurately assessed. It is therefore important to choose reliable assessment methods and you should seek advice from the teacher of the class. Ensure that you allocate sufficient time to carry out your chosen assessment methods effectively (see Unit 6.1).

9   *What risks are associated with the work?* Safety is an important issue in schools. In some subjects, the assessment of risk to the pupils and incorporation of strategies to minimise this risk are a necessary part of the teacher's planning. Departmental and national guidelines are provided and should be followed to ensure the safety of pupils. As a student teacher, you should consult your head of department, class teacher or tutor for guidance on safety issues. Never undertake an activity until risk assessment has been considered. For examples of risk assessments see HSE (2015), Eaton Vale Schools Activity Centre (2015) and CLEAPSS (2005). Your subject association will also be able to give you advice.

Lessons have a structure and a rhythm to them. As you read this next section, think about the overall pattern to a lesson and the skills you use at each stage.

Planning parts of a lesson

Planning is an important part of the teaching process. Figure 2.2.1 illustrates the planning, teaching and evaluation cycle that should occur for every lesson that you deliver.

Lessons can be divided into three parts. Each of these must be planned carefully in order that your lesson meets its learning objectives. These parts are called the starter, the main section and the plenary. Although there are three parts to a lesson, the main section usually includes several different activities often referred to as episodes that lead towards the achievement of the planned objectives. Starters and plenaries can also be referred to as episodes.

Starter

In order to actively engage pupils from the outset of the lesson, an interesting and relevant starter activity must be planned. Think of this as the 'hook' to draw pupils in to the lesson. This activity may draw upon and/or assess previous understanding or might present a challenge to pupils. Having such an activity displayed at the start of the lesson will give you time to organise your main activities as the class arrive.

Main section

Before you begin the main activities/episodes of the lesson, you need to clarify your learning objectives for the pupils. Sometimes you may elect to do this before the starter activity, whereas at other times you may complete the starter before explaining the learning objectives. It is considered good practice to display these objectives visually to your pupils. Pupils need to be aware of the purposes of the learning activities/episodes and how they will contribute to their learning journey within the lesson. Activities/episodes need to be 'chunked' as you must bear in mind that pupil concentration span is 10 to 15 minutes. You must also plan for the transitions between each activity/episode and it may be necessary to conduct mini-plenaries at the end of each episode to consolidate learning to ensure a smooth and well-paced lesson. Each episode should build upon the previous one.

Plenary

This is a very important part of the lesson during which learning should be summarised. This involves referring back to the main learning objectives for the lesson. It is an important time for the teacher to check pupil learning and this requires skilful questioning (see Unit 3.1). At this point it may be appropriate to give a brief outline of the next lesson. Enough time should be set aside to record homework tasks and clear away any equipment.

General points to consider

Previous sections of this unit outline the key issues in effective planning. The following section highlights some general points that enhance the likelihood of overall success.

- *Resources*: Make sure your plan identifies the exact number of any resources that are required for the lesson. Ensure that you familiarise yourself with the equipment and know how to use it. If possible, set it up prior to the lesson.
- *Activities*: It is better to plan too many activities than too few. If one of your planned activities does not work or pupils complete the tasks more quickly than you anticipated, additional activities can be used.
- *Homework and forward planning*: Ensure that you plan enough time to set homework and/or remind pupils of any materials that they might require for the next lesson. This can then be recorded in their planner.
- *Group management*: Learn pupils' names as quickly as possible (see Buzan, 2008; TeacherVision, 2015). Consider whether there is a need to design a seating or work space plan for your class. This can have both logistical and learning benefits.
- *Routines*: Classroom routines are important to ensure effective organisation of pupils and resources. These might include distribution and collection of resources; arrival and exit of pupils and movement around the classroom. Ensure that you are at your teaching area before the lesson to greet the pupils on arrival. At the end of the lesson, pupils' departure should be supervised to ensure that they leave your teaching area in a safe and orderly manner. In subjects where there is a level of risk (for example, science or physical education), planning a safe routine is of paramount importance. Where effective routines are already in place, adhere to these: pupils will expect you to use the routines that their teacher will have worked hard to establish. When required, you may need to implement new routines after consultation with your tutor.

Note: the lesson plan should not be regarded as a rigid blueprint for action (John, 2000). Making adaptations during the lesson when necessary should be seen as a positive action rather than a failure (Capel et al., 2018).

Evaluation and planning future lessons

As soon as you can after the lesson, evaluate its success. In the early stages of your practical teaching, this could be in collaboration with your tutor. Were the learning outcomes and, therefore, learning objectives achieved by all/most/some? What went well? What didn't go well? What evidence do you have that allows you to answer these questions with some degree of certainty? Sometimes it is useful to wait until you have reviewed their work before evaluating the lesson (see Unit 5.4). What are your priorities for pupil learning in the next lesson and how do they fit in with the unit of work? What are your priorities for improving planning for organisation and transitions? What are your priorities for your performance as a teacher? If you develop the practice of reflecting on your work as a matter of course, then modifying future practice on the basis of this reflection becomes second nature.

Task 2.2.6 challenges you to plan, teach and evaluate a series of lessons to support pupil progression.

M

✎ Task 2.2.6   Planning for pupil progression

Plan a unit of work to last between three and eight lessons. Plan, teach and evaluate lesson one in conjunction with your tutor. Identify the key points that should be considered when planning lesson two. Repeat this plan-teach-evaluate cycle for the unit of work. Consider any adaptations you will need to make to your planned unit.

Review the quality of your planning and teaching using Brookfield's (1995) four critical reflection lenses of self review, pupil review, peer review and theoretical literature. Identify your areas of strength and development in relation to promoting pupil progression through effective planning. Record this task in your PDP as an example of master's level work.

SUMMARY AND KEY POINTS

You should now be able to:

■ explain the following terms – aims, learning objectives, learning outcomes, progression and differentiation, and;

■ have considered how to construct units of work and lesson plans that are comprehensive and useful.

Check which requirements for your ITE programme you have addressed through this unit.

 Further resources

Butt, G. (2006) *Lesson Planning*, **3rd Edition, London: Continuum.**
This is a comprehensive book supporting both student and qualified teachers to improve their planning in the short, medium and long term. Sections include planning for pupil differences and making plans work within the classroom.

Buzan, T. (2008) *How to Remember Names and Faces*, **viewed 17 June 2015, from http://www.open.edu/ openlearn/body-mind/psychology/buzan-on-how-remember-names-and-faces.**

Capel, S., Bassett, S., Lawrence, J., Newton, A. and Zwozdiak-Myers, P. (2018) 'How trainee physical education teachers in England write, use and evaluate lesson plans', *European Physical Education Review.*
This article looks at how student physical education teachers write, use and evaluate lesson plans.

DfE (Department for Education) (2016c) *Eliminating Unnecessary Workload around Planning and Teaching Resources.* **Report of the Independent Teacher Workload Review Group, London, DfE, viewed 1 July**

2018, from https://assets.publishing.service.gov.uk/government/uploads/system/uploads/attac hment_data/file/511257/Eliminating-unnecessary-workload-around-planning-and-teaching-resou rces.pdf

Jerome, L. and Bhargava, M. (2015) *Effective Medium-Term Planning for Teachers,* London: Sage.
This text provides advice and suggestions for effective medium-term planning. It includes examples of planning, justifications for the importance of medium term plans and explores links between pupil attainment and effective medium-term planning.

Johns, P.D. (2006) 'Lesson planning and the student teacher: re-thinking the predominant model', *Curriculum Studies,* 38(4), 483-489.
This article challenges contemporary ideas on lesson planning.

Kyriacou, C. (2014) *Essential Teaching Skills,* 4th Edition, Cheltenham: Nelson Thornes.
This provides an excellent and readable overview of the key skills that underpin effective teaching.

Lesson plans are widely available on the web but the quality varies. See examples on the Times Educational Supplement (www.tes.co.uk) or the *Guardian Teacher Network* (www.theguarduan.com/teacher-network). Always check the strength of evidence of any advice you find.

Mager, R. (2005) *Preparing Instructional Objectives,* 3rd Edition, Atlanta, GA: Center for Effective Performance.
Making the desired learning objectives and learning outcomes clear to *pupil*s helps ensure effective learning. This text provides useful information about objective setting.

Mutton, T. Hagger, H. and Burn, K. (2011) 'Learning to plan, planning to learn: the developing expertise of beginning teachers', *Teachers and Teaching,* 17(4), 339-416.
This article discusses planning at a variety of levels and recognises the importance of subject knowledge. It suggests that collaborative planning and teaching can allow beginning teachers to access the knowledge and understanding of more experienced professionals.

TeacherVision (2015) *Learning Students' Names Quickly,* viewed 1 July 2018, from https://www.teacherv ision.com/teaching-methods/classroom-management/6708.html

Appendix 2 lists subject associations and teacher councils and Appendix 3 provides a list of websites.

Capel, S., Leask, M. and Turner, T. (eds.) (2010) *Readings for Learning to Teach in the Secondary School: A Companion to M Level Study,* Abingdon: Routledge.
This book brings together essential readings to support you in your critical engagement with key issues raised in this textbook.

Capel, S., Lawrence, J. Leask, M. and Younie, S. (eds.) (2019) *Surviving and Thriving in the Secondary School: The NQT's Essential Companion,* Abingdon: Routledge.
This book is designed to support newly qualified teachers in the next phase of development as a teacher. However, you may find it useful as it covers aspects of teaching not included in this book which, nonetheless, you experience on your ITE programme.

The subject specific books in the *Learning to Teach (Subject)* series, the *Practical (Subject) Guides*, *Debates in (Subject)* and *Mentoring (Subject) Teachers* are also very useful.

> Any additional resources and an editable version of any relevant tasks/tables in this unit are available on the companion website: www.routledge.com/cw/capel

Acknowledgements

The authors would like to thank teachers and student teachers for their contributions to research on lesson planning referenced in this unit.

2.3 Taking responsibility for the whole class

Michelle Shaw and Clyde Redfern

Introduction

This unit draws your attention to issues that have particular relevance to you when you are just starting to take responsibility for whole lessons. It focuses on particular aspects of planning and teaching to which you should pay particular attention. Recall the iceberg image of a teacher's work from Unit 1.1. The delivery of the lesson in the classroom represents the tip of the iceberg, while the bulk of the teacher's work for a lesson - routines, preparation, subject knowledge, professional knowledge and judgement, previous lesson evaluations - is hidden. Sometimes it can be helpful to remember the key elements of complex ideas using an acronym. We want to introduce you to the acronym of PROPS in the first part of this unit. The PROPS we ask you to think about are the following;

P - Personal attributes - being the teacher
R - Routines in the classroom
O - Outcomes
P - Planning
S - Subject

In the first section of the unit we explore the importance of personal attributes and how you personify the role of 'the teacher'. We also look at how you can use verbal and non-verbal communication strategies to develop your confidence to deliver lessons. In the next section we explore further the importance of understanding routines. We then move on to look at the importance of routines for pupils, other adults and on you as a teacher. A key element is to understand what you are trying to achieve in a lesson and the learning outcomes that you intend for pupils. In this unit, we explore effective planning to ensure that learning takes place and introduce you to the concept of the 'LOOP' for planning purposes. We also ask you to think about the importance of subject knowledge in relation to your planning. Finally, we explore the impact your first lesson might have on you personally.

OBJECTIVES

At the end of this unit you should:

- have a greater awareness of your own persona as 'a teacher' and understand the impact that this can have on others;
- have an understanding of the power of routines to support the delivery of effective lessons;
- recognise and apply the core principles in your future planning that ensure pupils can make progress;
- understand some of the barriers and enablers to your own confidence and identify strategies to use these to enhance your professional practice.

Check the requirements of your initial teacher education (ITE) programme to see which relate to this unit.

Personal - being *the* teacher

As a student teacher you may find it hard to imagine yourself as a teacher. You may be asking yourself:

- How do I dress?
- How loudly do I have to talk?
- Will the pupils listen to me?
- Where should I stand?
- How much should I talk?
- What do I do with my hands?
- Will they understand my accent?

This is very common and nothing to worry about. In the section below we provide advice and ask that you explore your perceptions of what it is to be a 'teacher' and how this relates to your assessment of your own communication skills. You are asked to identify your strengths and areas for development. You will also understand how you can get the best out of your relationships with pupils and colleagues.

Personal attributes

First, complete Task 2.3.1.

 Task 2.3.1   What makes a great teacher?

You will already have observed teachers in the classroom. Imagine that you have to describe the key attributes of a great 'teacher' to someone from outer space. Reflect on what you have observed about the attributes that impact upon pupils' learning. Discuss with other student teachers or your tutor. Record the outcomes of your reflections in your professional development portfolio (PDP) or equivalent.

When we talk about personal attributes, we are referring to the mannerisms, values and behaviours that all human beings have. Some people are generous, humorous, animated, smiley, kind, etc. In your description of the 'teacher', you probably had lots of positive words such as these. It may be that some people who enter teaching have a set of personal attributes that pre-dispose them to behaving in certain ways. For most people the attributes needed for teaching, e.g. the ability to explain, to give clear instructions, to appear even-handed in settling disputes, your physical stance and your use of gesture, need to be developed or enhanced. This may take time and you shouldn't expect to have all of the desirable attributes perfected for your first lesson. You do, however, need a plan to enhance your existing personal attributes and to develop others. To do this, you first need to analyse your own personal starting point in a realistic and honest way. A tool used in management to assess personal attributes is the 360° self-evaluation. To complete your own self-evaluation, ask four trusted people to provide you with a list of your top five personal attributes as a teacher. Also ask them to identify three areas for development. Preferably, this would be colleagues in school, but you might also ask your friends or tutors. This will give you a balanced view of how others perceive you. Now complete Task 2.3.2.

 Task 2.3.2   Personal strengths/areas for development

Think back to the description of a great 'teacher' you developed for Task 2.3.1. Use the feedback from the 360° to assess how close you are to this. What do you need to do to close the gap and how will you do this? Store this information in your PDP and update it as you develop as a teacher.

Confidence

When you take responsibility for a class for the first time, this can feel daunting, as all eyes and expectations are upon you. You are no longer assisting someone else in the learning process but are the person responsible for leading it. The most important of the personal attributes you need for this is confidence. To help you feel confident before you stand in front of the class, you need to feel that you understand the following:

- the routines and expectations of the classroom and the wider school – particularly the format and requirements of the lesson plan used in the school;
- knowledge of the pupils – their ability levels and any additional needs they may have;
- knowledge of previous lessons and focus for future lessons;
- what you will be teaching in terms of subject content;
- how both you and the pupils will know that they have made progress;
- the resources needed and available to you;
- which other adults are available to support your lesson and how you will utilise them.

You will already have begun to collect information about your school and the pupils, which should help you with this (see Forms of Professional Knowledge for Teaching in Table 1.1.2). When you plan your first solo lesson it will take a long time and you should be prepared for your tutor to offer advice and guidance. Although this may seem like criticism; remember they have a lot of experience which may be beneficial. This is an investment for the rest of your teaching career. This planning process will probably take longer than you anticipate so allow plenty of quality time for discussion and modifications. Following this advice also means that you develop and display other personal attributes that are valuable as a teacher. You will develop your patience, perseverance, resilience, ability to listen and take advice, and understand the value of reciprocity in professional life. Confidence is a state of mind that is fed by experience. It is not a fixed position and will be affected by how each individual lesson goes. A thorough plan is the key to confident delivery (see Unit 2.2 for the detail of lesson planning) and effective planning, and evaluation of lessons have an impact on your confidence. This is an area that you can develop and control.

Communication

Despite having a good lesson plan, you may still feel a little uncertain about your abilities as a teacher, and it should be remembered that confidence can be affected by factors beyond the classroom. You need to be able to recognise if this happens and seek help and advice as appropriate. There are a number of other strategies that you can employ to develop your confidence. Many of these are linked to verbal and non-verbal communication. In this section, we identify some simple ways in which you can project an image of confidence to your class. Recall the questions at the start of this unit.

How do I dress?

In most schools you will need to conform to a dress code. Make sure you know what this is. Clothing should always be comfortable and practical. This is particularly important in relation to footwear. Similarly, you should also think about jewellery. Functional and in line with school norms is the most appropriate.

You may be a fashionista and tempted to wow pupils with your dress sense. You might argue that your clothing gives you confidence. However, this may not meet the school's dress code or be the best way to start a relationship with a group of pupils. You want them to remember you for the quality of your teaching, not the size of your heels or the pattern on your tie! If you really want to wear distinctive clothing, which is in line with the school's dress code, leave this until you are able to deliver high-quality lessons on a regular basis.

Where should I stand?

Choosing where and how to stand in the classroom is important. Many student teachers position themselves almost exclusively at the front of the class, as if attached to the teacher's desk. This is not helped in some modern classrooms where technology is controlled from a central location. Remember, you can control the computer from anywhere in the classroom using a relatively cheap remote pointer, which is a good investment. You may also be limited by the layout of the classroom. Although it may not be easy to change classroom layout immediately, this might be something that you consider as you reflect on how the classroom layout impacts learning. The most important thing is to position yourself where the pupils can see you and you can see them. You should also consider whether you need to move pupils to facilitate this, e.g. bringing pupils closer to you at the start of a lesson and requiring their full attention on you. If you can plan to keep whole-class activities short and sharp, this will help pupils to maintain their focus on you.

Think of your classroom as a stage. You have the right to work in any part of it that you choose. Do not have the mindset that the teacher and pupil operate in separate zones. There are no teacher zones or pupil zones. Continuing with the analogy of a stage, if you were producing a play you would carefully control as many elements as possible to ensure the audience get a rich experience. The same applies in a classroom. There are some basics. If the room is hot or stuffy you should open a window. Think carefully about lighting – do not stand in front of a bright light or have bright lights shining at your pupils. Acoustics matter in the classroom (see Underwood et al., 2015; Acoustic Accessibility MESHGuide). Make sure your pupils can hear you and you can hear them. It is worth observing how good teachers use the space. Notice how they move and look for the key locations so that they can scan pupil activity on-task (Unit 2.1 gives guidance on observing classrooms).

How loudly do I have to talk? Will the pupils listen to me? Will they understand my accent?

Verbal communication is important (see also Unit 3.1). Many student teachers focus on what they say and can spend a long time perfecting their teacher input, often learning a script like the lines of a play. Over time you will move away from scripted towards a more natural performance. Through your communication style, you are aiming to be authoritative not authoritarian. Teachers need to have clear speech. You need to develop an awareness and control of pace (how fast you talk), volume (how loudly) and tone (the ways in which your voice goes up and down). Some regional accents have particular tonal sounds. For example, some accents can be characterised with a rising inflection towards the end of sentences. This can leave the listener wondering if you have asked a question! You should be particularly aware of your own voice – try recording and listening to yourself and see how this is affected when you feel nervous or under pressure. Pay particular attention to vocalisations. Some people end every sentence with 'ok', 'erm', 'umm', etc. We are not suggesting that you can change the way you speak overnight, but you need to be aware that you are moving from conversational language to presentational language. Just like an actor, you need to change into the character/persona of the teacher.

How much should I talk?

Remember that the aim of every lesson is to enable pupils to make progress in their learning. You have to make an assessment of whether they have done this, and if you dominate the talk in the classroom, it can be difficult to work out what a single pupil or groups of pupils have learned. A good lesson will have a balance of teacher talk and pupil talk and plenty of time for pupil activity. It is often the case in early lessons that the teacher will talk in the belief that this is a safe course of action. You may be scared to allow your pupils some freedoms and worry that they will not do what you ask them to do. A good lesson with engaging activities will keep pupils on-task. Unit 5.2 covers active learning. Over time your role will change from the deliverer of content to the facilitator of learning.

What do I do with my hands?

Our voice is not the only way in which we communicate. Think about when you observe a play. The actions you see are as powerful as the words you hear. It is not just what you say but how you say it.

Our hands are powerful communication tools. For example, if you cross your hands or arms in front of your body, this can be perceived as a sign that you are feeling vulnerable with the cross as a protection. Similarly pointing gestures can be perceived as aggressive and confrontational. You should also think about the eye contact you make with pupils. When you are nervous you might not even look at the pupils, which may be perceived by them as you not being interested in them. Keep eye contact with pupils and link this to facial expression. It is very easy to appear pleased, disappointed, surprised or sad just by changing the position of your mouth or eyebrows. Your aim is not to make pupils your enemies or your best friends. Using a small nod of the head and a smile can be powerful tools in managing a classroom which helps you to maintain your teacher persona. There are many books written about non-verbal communication and we signpost you to one of these in the Further Readings. See also Unit 3.1 on communicating with pupils.

Interpersonal relationships

Student teachers often focus on their relationships with pupils and this is very important to enable you to plan and deliver an effective lesson. You need to know what their abilities are, what personalities they have and what additional needs they may have, etc. Additionally, you will be developing your communication strategies with pupils continually. However, during your first lessons, you may feel nervous about how to use other adults. You are now the leader of learning, which means you need to lead everyone. This can appear daunting. Now complete Task 2.3.3.

 Task 2.3.3   The role of the teaching assistant (TA)

Observe an experienced TA working with a teacher. What do they do? Why is this effective in supporting learning? How does the teacher include them in the lesson?
   Record the outcomes of your reflections on your observations in your PDP.

First of all, establish which adults are available to help you and what their role is. You may have a general TA or a TA to support pupils with additional needs. You may have a technician if you teach a science or an information technology (IT)-related subject. These are highly skilled people who, like your tutor, will be willing to help you plan and deliver your lesson. When you plan your lesson you must plan for what they are going to be doing before, during or after the lesson. Other adults in your classroom will be working with the same school routines and policies that you are, so you can expect them to support decisions that you make in relation to managing behaviour and learning in the classroom. Remember if you plan for and carefully manage the pupils' learning you will have a better chance of managing behaviour. A useful strategy in your early lessons is for you to ask your tutor to act as a TA. They can give you valuable feedback on how effectively you utilised them and included them in your lesson if they act in this role. It will also be helpful as they will be able to provide you with small interventions to keep your lesson on track; for example, they might spot the pupil who finishes the last page in their book and can intervene – you might not even know yet where to get new books! This strategy can also give your tutor a valuable and defined role in what is *their class*.

In this section you have reflected upon your personal attributes and ways in which these can be developed or enhanced. You have also begun to think about how you can ensure that you have the confidence to deliver lessons as the lead teacher. In the next section we explore further the importance of understanding routines.

Routines

Routines for class and lesson management provide a structure where the rules are understood by all so that learning can take place. In time, these routines become instinctive for you. Routines are not established in a vacuum. The pupils you teach have been in schools for at least seven years and they expect the teacher to establish 'norms' for classroom work, talk and movement. You are taking the lead for a class, in a department and school that already has norms, so it would not be appropriate for you to introduce completely new ways of working. School and department routines are normally non-negotiable and can be a support for you. The area in which you can focus and make your own impact over time is the teacher-controlled routines See Unit 2.1 on observation of routines. There are routines for:

- classroom management – the operational management of the physical space;
- relationships in the classroom – the ways in which all people in the classroom interact and relate to each other;
- expectations of and for learning.

Classroom management

You need to think about how the classroom is managed. Completing Task 2.3.4 will help you to identify what current practice is in your school, and it can provide a helpful checklist for you to refer to when you take the lead as the teacher.

 Task 2.3.4   Classroom routines

Make a list of the routines in the classroom for the following:

- entering the room/leaving the lesson;
- getting the teacher's attention/the teacher getting attention;
- pupils moving around the classroom;
- getting equipment out and tidying away;
- leaving the classroom (toilet/illness);
- routine administration – taking registers/keeping records;
- the use of time in the lesson.

Store the list in your PDP to draw on during your school experiences.

For your early lessons, one of your main goals is to get the pupils down to work promptly. To do this, you need to be confident in the operational routines of the classroom. Your concern is to establish yourself as an organised teacher, and earlier in the unit we discussed the idea of the classroom as a stage which you control. Your early lessons will go more easily if you fit in with established routines. You are 'borrowing' this classroom, so always remember to leave it as you would expect to find it.

Relationships in the classroom

Other adults – There may be other adults in the room and your job is to ensure that they are well-utilised in supporting pupil learning. You will need to use or establish a routine for communicating the lesson plan in a timely and appropriate fashion and for gaining feedback from the other adults. Do not expect a TA to be able to do their own preparation if you only give them the lesson plan as the lesson starts!

Pupils – Pupils need to know what the routines are in your classroom. Adopting a *firm, fair, friendly* approach helps you develop good relationships with pupils. Pupils have certain expectations of you. You need to be explicit about your expectations of them and the routines you will use. Above all, they will expect continuity in their experiences at school. It is not helpful for pupils to be given conflicting routines as they move from class to class, subject to subject, teacher to teacher. You do need to know your class and there will be influences on classroom relationships that come from the community. Information about the range of group 'norms' of behaviour for teenagers in the local area and background information about other social relationships (e.g. which pupils are cousins, stepsisters or brothers) may help you understand more easily your pupils and their expectations.

Pupils may ask you inappropriate personal questions. Do not allow yourself to be distracted from the work in the lesson. You can choose whether or not to answer personal questions but do set boundaries beyond which you will not go. Do not be personal, and do not take things personally. If you decide to share personal information with the pupils then choose the time and place.

Routines for behaviour management – In terms of behaviour, pupils expect a teacher to be fair and consistent in applying the school rules. They expect those who comply to be rewarded and those who do not to be sanctioned (reprimanded). You need to think about how you will do this. Schools already have established routines to reward and sanction pupils. You should use these and ensure that you match the reward or sanction to the pupil's action. One of your routines should be to reward rather than sanction to try to create a positive environment for learning in your classroom. Ask your tutor to observe your ratio of rewards to sanctions in your lessons. Behaviour management is cited as an area of concern by student teachers more often than any other area and Units 3.2 and 3.3 provide more detailed guidance.

One of the more challenging areas is how to manage low-level disruptive behaviour. This is where a thorough understanding of the school policy on behaviour is vital. A key strategy is for you to be able to identify and defuse emerging situations. Confrontation in front of the whole class is generally to be avoided. You could use the following ladder of interventions:

- first, try to use non-verbal gestures to remind a pupil to keep working;
- next, a quiet, individual conversation with the pupil. Use your voice sparingly to manage behaviour;
- if this doesn't work, try proximity praise where you reward a pupil nearby who is on-task;
- at the next stage try positioning yourself or another adult near a pupil who needs more encouragement to stay on-task;

■ before you use the school policy on sanctions, try a more detailed conversation where you highlight the issue and give a pupil clear options about how to correct the behaviour and what the consequences of continuing their behaviour will be.

Now complete Task 2.3.5.

 Task 2.3.5   Dealing with swearing

Discuss the following two scenarios with your tutor and identify an appropriate response:

You overhear a pupil use swear words in conversation with another pupil.
A pupil swears at you.
Record the outcomes of your reflections and discussions in your PDP.

You should always try to remain positive and try to hide any frustrations or anger that you might feel. This can be difficult; after all, you have planned a lesson in great detail and you want it to go right. You might be very worried about how a tutor perceives off-task behaviour. Remember, they will want to see that you have a routine for managing behaviour and that you are consistent. Now complete Task 2.3.6.

 Task 2.3.6   School policies: rewards and sanctions

Find out about the policies on rewards and sanctions at your placement school. Make notes of the key issues that affect your work. Check your understanding of the application of these policies with your tutor. Write down the approach you are going to take with respect to rewards and sanctions and discuss this with fellow student teachers and/or your tutor.
    Record your approach, the outcomes, reflections and discussions in your PDP.

Routines for gaining attention – Earlier in the unit we discussed the non-verbal communication skills you can use to keep pupils' attention. Getting pupils' attention at the start of a lesson and at points during the lesson is a skill that experienced teachers do effortlessly. You must decide how you are going to get attention in both situations and then act confidently. You could try a verbal call for attention ('Stop what you're doing and just look here for a minute'). You might have a non-verbal signal (such as raising your hand in the air). You could use an auditory signal (a computer sound). A teacher may then follow this with a focus on an individual ('Guy, that means you too'), which acts as a reminder to all pupils that if they do not want to be the focus of the teacher's attention, then they need to stop what they are doing. Think about what you want to call the class to attention for. You do not want to stop pupils when they are working well but it can be helpful when, for example, pupils come to a difficult point or if you wish to draw their attention to a point on safety.

One of the fundamental rules of the classroom is that pupils should not speak when the teacher is speaking. Spending a few minutes in a lesson waiting for silence until you speak saves a lot of time later, as pupils know what you expect. Pupils may need reminding of your expectations, and you probably need to reinforce the idea that this is one of your basic rules. You must be able to get the class's attention when you require it. When observing classes, the following questions may help you see some of the strategies used by teachers to establish this aspect of their authority.

▪ What verbal cues does the teacher use to establish quiet? Key phrases such as 'Right, then' and 'Put your pens down now', establish that the teacher requires the class to listen. Some student teachers make the mistake of thinking the words 'quiet' or 'shush' repeated over and over will gain the required effect. Units 3.2 and 3.3 provide further advice.
▪ What non-verbal cues does the teacher use to gain attention? Look at the way teachers use gestures - eyes, face, arms, hands - to establish that they require the class to listen. They may stand still and just wait. Unit 3.1 contains more ideas.

There are also routines related to the way pupils gain the teacher's attention. The usual routine is that pupils put up their hands and do not call out. Again, we suggest you find out what the current practice is for the classes you are teaching and make sure you implement this consistently.

Expectations of and for learning

A good teacher has high expectations of and for learning. They plan for learning to take place. You need to establish a routine in your classroom whereby pupils are challenged by you clearly setting out the intended learning objectives for the lesson (see Table 2.2.1), sharing them with the pupils, planning activities that allow the pupils to engage with the learning objectives and assessing the extent to which the objectives have been met by individuals. Individual outcomes and tasks should all be directly related to the objectives and intended learning outcomes for the lesson. This should be reflected in your lesson planning (see Table 2.3.1 'Planning lessons', below). Part of the classroom routine is to help the pupils understand these steps for themselves. Checking and marking pupils' work during the lesson helps improve their work. It also helps if pupils are regularly involved in helping to assess their own work. It is a useful exercise, sometimes, to have pupils swap books so that they can check each other's work. Marking their work routinely helps you to set specific, well-matched and challenging targets for all. Your comments and discussions with pupils help them become aware of where and how to improve their work.

In this section we have explored the importance of routines for pupils, other adults and you as a teacher. Do not underestimate the power of strong and clear routines and strive to achieve these as soon as you can in your practice. You should expect some resistance from tutors and pupils to any change you wish to make as this can create unnecessary disruption.

Outcomes

Now that you have begun to establish your identity as a teacher and have an understanding of the key routines that underpin your performance in the classroom, you can focus on the driver that underpins all lessons - pupil progress. It might seem an obvious statement that in your lessons pupils should make progress; however, achieving this requires a high level of skilful planning and delivery. Pupil progress is evidenced through the outcomes of a lesson. Put simply, outcomes are what pupils achieve in the lesson. There are obvious outcomes, for example the amount of correct completed problems in a mathematics lesson. Outcomes can be planned for and this is known as differentiation (see Unit 4.1). Sometimes there are unanticipated outcomes. When this happens, you need to understand why and adapt future lessons to accommodate this. We can keep the outcomes of a lesson in pupil record files. However, outcomes are often seen as the end product. This is not the case. We would want you to focus more on intended learning outcomes. If a pupil has learned in your lesson, if they have met the intended learning outcomes, they will be able to recall this at a later stage and use it in a variety of other contexts. In the next section we explore the difference between actual outcomes and intended learning outcomes in more detail. You also need to think about outcomes for you. As a student teacher you have to show how you have met the learning outcomes for your ITE programme. The outcomes of your ITE programme may become part of your evidence file against the professional standards. You are likely to feel that your outcomes are under constant scrutiny from many quarters and this is right and proper to ensure that the best teachers enter the profession. Never lose sight of the fact that if you can establish an environment where pupil outcomes and the extent to which pupils achieve the learning objectives set for them are the main focus, then you will be on the right lines to becoming a great teacher, and most other things will fall into place.

Planning

Planning to ensure learning takes place means understanding this LOOP:

L - Learning starting point - what pupils already know
O - Objectives - the new learning for the lesson
O - Outcomes - how you will see the learning happen
P - Progress - how you will know what learning has taken place

The lesson plan is the obvious way in which your tutor can see what you intend to do and may be designed by you for two audiences - your tutor to check your planning and for you to deliver the lesson so that pupils learn (see also Unit 2.2 on lesson planning). It should contain enough information to satisfy both requirements and no more. It should not be a script but the level of detail will vary with time and experience. The lesson plan is the culmination of the research and thinking that you undertake for the lesson and your evaluation of previous lessons. If a lesson is to be effective, you really need to be clear about what you are trying to do with your class and what you will be expecting of them. It is easy to fall into the trap of planning lessons that are relatively superficial but look busy with a series of activities that are not really having an impact on pupils' learning. You can use the checklist in Table 2.3.1 to support you in the planning process.

Table 2.3.1 Planning lessons

- Plan the lesson and ask for advice about your plan. Be clear about what you want to achieve. Have your plan on hand at all times. You need to work with the classroom teacher to understand what next steps pupils need in order to achieve.
- Think about your resource needs – are you using worksheets, pictures, cue cards, video, textbooks, PowerPoint, the interactive whiteboard? Some resources are easier and safer to use than others. You may find that equipment you had planned to use stops working or the specialist in your subject is not available to supervise you.
- Check that you have adequate extension and alternative work. Anticipate that additional work may be needed.
- Link tasks to earlier work (this is known as scaffolding) and set authentic tasks – ones that are relevant to the pupils' lives and locality.
- Make the content challenging. Ensure the challenge is realistic and pupils are productive; do not make the work so difficult that the pupils give up.
- Know the class, if possible, through your observations and have a strategy for using and learning names. Try to learn names quickly – making notes beside the names in the register may help you remember. Draw up a seating plan can help; pupils may always, or at least usually, sit in the same places. In any case, you can ask them to sit in the same seats until you know their names.
- Think about how you are going to assess pupils' work during the lesson. You will need to give them comment and feedback on what they are doing.
- Check which other adults will be in the room, and the need for any materials to help them with particular pupils. It might help, for example, to give them a copy of your lesson plan so that they are aware of what you are trying to do.
- Keep track (in your head, at least) of which activities 'worked' with the class and why.

Now complete Task 2.3.7.

 Task 2.3.7   Comparing lesson plans

Exchange a lesson plan with another student teacher. Discuss some of the questions below together. You can also use Table 2.3.1 to help structure the questions you ask for this task.

Are the learning objectives and intended learning outcomes clearly specified and differentiated? Can you identify the types of outcomes expected?
Are the pupils likely to be actively and appropriately engaged at every opportunity?
Are the tasks 'authentic' tasks?
Have you planned appropriate time sequences into your lesson?
Is there scope for pupils to demonstrate to you what pupils have learned this lesson?

Record the outcomes of your reflections and discussions in your PDP.

Never start your planning just from an activity. You should always ask yourself if the activity that the pupils are doing or your actions as a teacher are directly related to the learning objectives and intended learning outcomes. If they are not, then you are diluting the impact your lesson will have. This is very common and you may do this in the early stages of your planning. You may plan well-meaning activities that deflect pupils from focusing on the learning that you want to take place in your classroom. If you can focus on planning for pupils' learning in your early lessons, you will have a focused impact on your pupils right from the beginning. This inevitably means that you must spend a good deal of time thinking about the learning you want to take place and carefully crafting your learning objectives and intended learning outcomes. Unavoidable incidents occur to interrupt the flow of your carefully prepared lesson. We discuss below some of the more common incidents and possible solutions so that you are not taken by surprise.

Judging the timing during a lesson is one of the most difficult problems initially, and following a timeline on your lesson plan can help you see at a glance how the lesson is progressing in relation to the time allowed. Always keep an eye on the clock and keep your lesson plan on hand. If you spot that you are running ahead or lagging behind you can intervene sooner to get your lesson back on track, but you need to also consider how the pupils are progressing. Monitoring the timing is useful for you and the pupils and it may be that you use a displayed class timer for activities. It may be that you have too much or too little material. Pupils have to get to their next lesson on time and have their break on time. So, you must let them go on time! Five minutes or so before the end of a lesson (more if they have to change or put equipment away), draw the lesson together, reminding them of what's been achieved against the learning objectives and intended learning outcomes, what is expected in the way of homework and perhaps what they will be learning in the next lesson. Table 2.3.2 provides some examples of what you can do if pupils finish work early.

With experience, you acquire the skill of fitting work to the time available so that the problem ceases to cause you anxiety.

Managing behaviour generally has been covered in an earlier section of this unit (it is also covered in Unit 3.3 in more detail). Inevitably, some pupils try to deflect you from your lesson goals. This needs to be addressed. Ignoring deliberately provocative remarks such as, 'This is boring' can help you avoid confrontation. Try to motivate uninterested pupils by linking the work with their interests if possible and ensure the learning is relevant – if you cannot explain to pupils the relevance of the lesson to their current and future lives, then you cannot expect them to be motivated to learn. Ask experienced colleagues for advice if particular pupils constantly cause you trouble. It is likely that they are also causing some other staff difficulties.

You may be worried that you will be asked a question and you do not know the answer. This is bound to happen. You can admit you do not know – 'What an interesting point, I've not thought of it that way Kate'; 'I just cannot remember at the moment'. It is possible to celebrate the moment: 'Paul that is a really good question. Where might we go for an answer to that?'. Make arrangements for the answer to be found. The pupil can follow it up for homework, use the library to look for the answer or write to those who might know. You may also be able to find out from other teachers, student teachers or your subject association.

Table 2.3.2 Backup plans in case pupils finish work quickly

■ Have questions prepared relating to the learning objectives/have a class test ready. ■ Let the pupils peer assess each other's work and feedback against the learning objectives. ■ Go around and look at pupils' work, give constructive comments and share this with the class, if appropriate. ■ Use your lesson objectives and intended learning outcomes to devise questions about the work or get pupils to devise them. For example, devise a quiz related to the lesson; develop a spider diagram for summarising the key points in a topic, producing a mnemonic to aid the recall of key issues. ■ Homework (either past or just set) can be discussed in more detail. You may allow the pupils to discuss this together. ■ Pupils' existing knowledge on the next topics could be discussed through question and answer. (Learning is more certain when you, as the teacher, build on pupils' existing knowledge and experience.)

You may have pupils who are not able to engage with the lesson because they do not have the appropriate equipment. You should aim to get most of the class working so that you can then direct your attention to those who require individual attention. Many schools have systems in place for dealing with pupils' lack of kit and equipment. You need to know what this is so that you follow the school system. It can be less disruptive to your lesson for you simply to supply the missing item for the lesson. But make sure you retrieve what you have loaned and indicate firmly that you expect pupils to provide their own.

You must check equipment in your teaching room beforehand and, in any case, have a backup planned if your lesson is dependent on equipment working, such as information and communications technology software. The more sophisticated your use of technology, the more likely you will encounter technical difficulties. Remember your backup plan should still allow you to deliver the lesson-intended learning outcomes.

Schools have different approaches to dealing with loss and breakage of equipment by pupils. The simple strategy of managing your lesson so that there is sufficient time at the end to check that equipment and books are returned saves you time in the long run. See also Unit 8.3 on health and safety.

Subject knowledge and pedagogy

To use LOOP, you need to be aware of the importance of subject knowledge and specific pedagogic practices linked to your subject. This means that you must ensure your own personal knowledge of the subject is at a suitable level to teach the learning objectives and intended learning outcomes. You should audit your own subject knowledge and fill in any gaps you may have. It is also important for you to think about how you will remain at the forefront of current thinking in your discipline. Joining your subject association provides access to the latest knowledge and networking with colleagues (www.subjectassociations.org.uk). You also need to be aware of the current pedagogic practices in your subject and endeavour to model best practice in your classroom.

Overview

In becoming a teacher, you are more vulnerable than when being educated for many other professions as you are exposed to a discerning audience (the class) early on. So much of your performance in the classroom depends on your own personal qualities and your ability to form good relationships with pupils from a wide range of backgrounds (see Unit 1.2). Your performance is analysed and commented on by those who observe your teaching. You are forced to face your own strengths and weaknesses as a result of this scrutiny. This can be stressful, particularly when you may be given apparently conflicting advice from different observers. As you become more experienced and you develop more analytical skills for use in appraising your performance, you should build your self-belief and confidence.

Despite following all of the advice given, it may be that you may have a poor lesson with a class. This does not mean that all lessons with that class will be like that. What it does mean, however, is that you must analyse the situation and put into place strategies for ensuring that the next lesson is better. Incidents will occur that leave you feeling deflated, unsure or angry. Try to adopt a problem-solving, reflective approach to your work so that you maintain some objectivity and can learn from any difficult experiences you have. You will have seen from this unit that taking responsibility for the class is challenging and delivering your first lesson can call for all of your resilience. Time and stress management and developing resilience are important issues and Unit 1.3 is devoted to them.

SUMMARY AND KEY POINTS

- Your first encounters with the pupils are important in setting the tone for your relationships with them.
- It is worth carefully considering the image you wish to project in these early lessons.
- Aim to give an impression that you have created an organised learning environment.
- Your professional persona as 'the teacher' is something you should create deliberately and not just allow to happen.
- You should not underestimate the importance of planning your lessons to help reinforce this image.
- Time invested in understanding and developing the LOOPS will help you to develop as a skilled practitioner.
- Most student teachers have to work on controlling their nerves and developing their self-confidence.
- Covering the points in Table 2.3.3 in your preparation should prevent some of the difficulties you would otherwise encounter.

Table 2.3.3 Lesson preparations checklist

- Set clear, simple and measurable learning objectives and intended learning outcomes for the lesson that are likely to be achieved.
- Plan the lesson carefully and have extension work ready.
- Obtain pupil lists and know pupils' names.
- Check the room layout: are things where you want them? What about safety issues?
- Know the school, class and lesson routines.
- Be on time.
- Prepare resources beforehand.
- Act as though you are in charge although you probably won't feel that you are.
- Know the subject you are teaching.
- Plan the lesson to give a balance between teacher talk and pupil activity.
- Include a timeline in your lesson plan so that you can check during the lesson how the plan is working. Try not to talk too quickly.
- Be prepared to manage behaviour and remember that learning should drive behaviour not behaviour drive learning.
- Visualise yourself being successful.
- Have a backup plan for the lesson (see Table 2.3.1).

One of the problems you may have will be believing that you are indeed a teacher. This is a mental and emotional transition that you need to make. The pupils, parents and staff see you as a teacher, albeit a new one, and expect you to behave as such.

Check which requirements for your ITE programme you have addressed through this unit.

Further resources

DfE (Department for Education) (2011c) *Getting the Simple things Right - Charlie Taylor's Behaviour Checklists*, viewed 1 July 2018, from https://www.gov.uk/government/uploads/system/uploads/attachment_data/file/283997/charlie_taylor_checklist.pdf

Queensland Government (2015) *Attributes of a Good Teacher*, viewed 4 December 2017, from http://education.qld.gov.au/hr/recruitment/teaching/qualities-good-teacher.html

Pease, A. and Pease, B. (2011) *Body Language in the Workplace,* London: Orion.
This book will give you insights into verbal and non-verbal communication strategies. Further information is on their website and their YouTube videos, viewed 2 July 2018, from http://www.peaseinternational.com/index.php?route=news/headlines

Westwood, P. (2007) *Commonsense Methods for Children with Special Educational Needs*, 5th Edition, Abingdon: RoutledgeFalmer.
Many of the approaches used with pupils with SEN work well with all pupils. This text outlines approaches to effective teaching and provides research to back up different strategies.

YouTube Teachers (https://www.youtube.com/user/teachers) and the **Khan Academy** (https://www.khanacademy.org/) both have short videos explaining core concepts for many subjects. Accessed 4 December 2017.

Appendix 2 lists subject associations and teacher councils and Appendix 3 provides a list of websites.

Capel, S., Leask, M. and Turner, T. (eds.) (2010) *Readings for Learning to Teach in the Secondary School: A Companion to M Level Study*, Abingdon: Routledge.
This book brings together essential readings to support you in your critical engagement with key issues raised in this textbook.

Capel, S., Lawrence, J. Leask, M. and Younie, S. (eds.) (2019) *Surviving and Thriving in the Secondary School: The NQT's Essential Companion*, Abingdon: Routledge.
This book is designed to support newly qualified teachers in the next phase of development as a teacher. However, you may find it useful as it covers aspects of teaching not included in this book which, nonetheless, you experience on your ITE programme.

The subject specific books in the *Learning to Teach (Subject)* series, the *Practical (Subject) Guides*, *Debates in (Subject)* and *Mentoring (Subject) Teachers* are also very useful.

Any additional resources and an editable version of any relevant tasks/tables in this unit are available on the companion website: www.routledge.com/cw/capel

3 Classroom interactions and managing pupils

Introduction

Effective classroom interactions and management are essential to effective learning. Classroom interactions are those with (and between) pupils (and others) in the classroom to support learning. Classroom management refers to arrangements made by the teacher to establish and maintain an environment in which learning can occur, e.g. effective organisation and presentation of lessons so that pupils are actively engaged in learning. Classroom management skills and techniques are addressed throughout this book in a number of different chapters and units. This chapter includes units about different aspects of classroom management related to interacting with pupils. Together they give an insight into the complex relationships which are developed between teachers and pupils, and emphasise the need for well-developed skills and techniques that you can adapt appropriately to the demands of the situation. They reinforce the fact that, although you must plan your lessons thoroughly, not everything you do in the classroom can be planned in advance, as you cannot predict how pupils will react in any situation on any given day.

One commonality of teachers from whom we have learned a lot is their ability to communicate effectively with pupils to enhance their knowledge, skills and understanding. Most of us tend to think we communicate well. However, communication is a complex process. Unit 3.1 is designed to help you communicate effectively in the classroom. The unit looks first at verbal communication, including gaining pupils' attention, using your voice and the language you use. It then considers types of communication, including explaining, questioning, discussion and active listening. Aspects of non-verbal communication are then considered, including showing enthusiasm, confidence and caring and your appearance, gesture, posture, facial expression and mannerisms, particularly in relation to how you present yourself as a teacher.

Some pupils are motivated to learn and maintain that motivation; others are inherently motivated to learn but various factors result in them losing motivation, and still others may not be inherently motivated to learn but their motivation can be increased. A study of motivation, therefore, is crucial to give you some knowledge and insight into how you can create a motivational climate that helps to stimulate pupils to learn. Unit 3.2 looks at what motivation is, presents a number of theories of motivation and considers how these can inform your teaching and pupils' learning. It looks at the motivational learning environment in your classes and how this influences pupil motivation.

It also looks at using performance profiling to enhance motivation. Finally, some specific factors that influence pupils' motivation to learn (e.g. personal achievement (success), rewards, including the use of praise, punishment and feedback) are discussed.

We recognise student teachers' concerns about managing behaviour and misbehaviour. Unit 3.3 looks at adopting a positive approach to behaviour, which focuses on positive relationships with pupils and a positive classroom climate in which all pupils can learn effectively. This approach is more consistent with an inclusive schooling approach. Thus, the focus of the unit is on preventing misbehaviour as far as possible rather than on a reactive approach that focuses on 'discipline' for misbehaviour. The unit starts by giving a brief overview of the policy context for promoting learning in the classroom. It then interrogates the term 'unacceptable behaviour' in order to help you understand the significance of its underlying causes. The unit then looks at factors that may cause unacceptable behaviour and then at the key principles of a behaviour for learning approach which highlights the importance of getting the simple things right, building positive relationships in the classroom, structuring your lessons to promote positive behaviour, and rights, responsibilities, routines and rules in the classroom. It also highlights the importance of pupils' knowing the consequences of sensible or inadvisable choices.

The final unit in this chapter, Unit 3.4, focuses on the transition between primary and secondary schools, recognising that this is only one of the many transitions pupils experience as they go through compulsory schooling. It considers conceptualisations of educational transitions and its impact on planning and preparation, focusing on a maturational and interactionist approach, whether this transition is a one-off event or ongoing event, and academic and life transitions. It highlights issues related to the primary–secondary transition, before considering theoretical perspectives that inform our understanding of transition, considering resilience, self-esteem and emotional intelligence theories. It then provides examples of planning and preparation for primary–secondary transition – focusing on administrative, social/user friendly, curriculum, teaching and learning and managing learning aspects of transition. Finally, it looks at what seems to work for pupils.

3.1 Communicating with pupils

Paula Zwozdiak-Myers and Susan Capel

Introduction

We can all think of people who really understand their subject but cannot communicate it to others. However, effective teachers all have in common the ability to communicate clearly.

Communication is a complex two-way process involving the mutual exchange of information and ideas, written, verbal and non-verbal. Clear and effective communication includes not only delivering, but also receiving information, which involves listening, observation and sensitivity. Although the quality of communication between pupil and pupil in lessons is important in enhancing or hindering learning, the focus of this unit is the quality of communication between a teacher and pupils, which is critical to effective learning.

Although most of us tend to think we communicate well, when we study our communication skills systematically, most of us can find room for improvement. You need well-developed communication skills combined with awareness and sensitivity to the diverse needs, experience and level of understanding of your pupils.

We first consider aspects of verbal communication, including using your voice (volume, projection, pitch, speed, tone, clarity and expressiveness), the language you use and the importance of active listening. We then consider aspects of non-verbal communication (appearance, gesture, posture, facial expression and mannerisms), particularly in relation to how you present yourself as a teacher. Further aspects of communication are addressed in Unit 5.2.

OBJECTIVES

At the end of this unit, you should be able to:

- appreciate the importance of effective verbal and non-verbal communication skills;
- vary your voice consciously to enhance your teaching and pupils' learning;
- appraise your use of language and use questioning more effectively as a teaching and learning tool;
- understand the relationship between verbal and non-verbal communication;
- gain awareness and control over your own self-presentation in order to present yourself effectively.

Check the requirements for your initial teacher education (ITE) programme to see which relate to this unit.

Verbal communication

Gaining attention

You need to establish procedures for gaining pupils' attention at the beginning of a lesson and also when you want the class to listen again after they have started an activity. This latter skill is especially important if there is a safety risk in the activity. Before you start talking to a class, make sure that all pupils can see and hear you, that you have silence and they are paying attention. To initiate and sustain group attention, it may help to stand at the front of the room: 'a centre-front position, facing the class group, standing relaxed and scanning the faces of the students while cueing for attention will normally (and positively) signal the teacher's readiness and expectation' (Rogers, 2015, p.58). Establish a means of getting silence (for example, say, 'quiet please', raise your hand, blow a whistle in physical education or bang on a drum in music), and use this technique with the class each time to ensure consistency of approach. Wait for quiet and do not speak until there is silence. Once you are talking, do not move around. This distracts pupils, who may pay more attention to the movement than to what you are saying.

Using your voice

A teacher's voice is a crucial element in classroom communication. It is like a musical instrument, and if you play it well, then your pupils will be an appreciative and responsive audience. Some people have voices that naturally are easier to listen to than others. Certain qualities are fixed and give your voice its unique character. However, you can alter the volume, projection, pitch, speed, tone, clarity and expressiveness of your voice to use it more effectively and lend impact to what you say. These verbal dynamics are important elements of paralanguage, and your voice, if sensitively tuned, can become a powerful agent of expression and communication.

The most obvious way you can vary your voice is by altering the *volume*. It is useful to have the whole volume range available, from quiet to very loud, but it is rarely a good thing to be loud when it is not needed. Loud teachers have loud classes. If you shout too much, you may get into the habit of shouting all the time – sometimes people know somebody is a teacher because of their loud voice.

Also, if you shout too much, you may lose your voice every September! Of course, you have to be heard, but this is done by projection more than by volume. (If you do have voice problems, see the advice at the end of the unit. Low-cost voice projection equipment is available.)

You *project* your voice by making sure it leaves your mouth confidently and precisely. This needs careful enunciation and breath control. If your voice is projected well, you are able to make a whisper audible at some distance. Equally, good projection brings considerable volume to your ordinary voice without resort to shouting or roaring.

Each group of words spoken has its own 'tune' that contributes to the meaning. A person may have a naturally high or low voice, but everybody can vary the 'natural' *pitch* with no pain. Generally speaking, deep voices sound more serious and significant; high voices sound more exciting and lively. To add weight to what is being said, the pitch should be dropped; to lighten the tone, the pitch should be raised. A voice with a lower pitch can create a sense of importance as it comes across as more authoritative and confident than a high-pitched voice. It can also be raised more easily to command attention, whereas raising a naturally high-pitched voice may result in something similar to a squeak, which does not carry the same weight.

Speed variations give contrast to delivery. You can use pause to good effect. It shows confidence if you can hold a silence before making a point or answering a question. Having achieved silence, do not shout into it. Equally, have the patience to wait for a pupil to respond. Research (for example, Muijs and Reynolds, 2011, p.59) suggests that 'three seconds or slightly longer is the optimal wait-time' for a closed, lower-level factual recall question, whereas a longer wait-time (up to 15 seconds) is required for 'open-ended, higher-level questions'. Speaking quickly can be a valuable skill on occasion; however, this needs concentration and careful enunciation.

To use your voice effectively, these factors need to work together. For instance, you do not communicate effectively if the pitch of your voice is right, but you are not enunciating clearly or the volume is wrong; for example, you are shouting at a group, or pupils at the back cannot hear what you are saying. It is also important to put feeling into what you say to engage pupils so that your voice does not sound dull and monotonous. Often, pupils respond to *how* you say something rather than *what* you say. If you are praising a pupil, sound pleased, and if you are disciplining a pupil, sound firm. If you deliver all talk in the same way without varying the verbal dynamics, do not be surprised if pupil response is undifferentiated since the intended meaning behind the message may not be readily understood. Now complete Task 3.1.1.

 Task 3.1.1   The quality of your voice

Record your voice either reading from a book or a newspaper, or in a natural monologue or conversation. Listen to the recording with a friend or another student teacher. If you have not heard yourself before, the experience may be a little shocking! Your voice may sound different from the way you hear it, and a common response is to blame the recording equipment. This is probably not at fault. Remember that, normally, you hear your voice coming back from the soft tissue and bone in your head. Most of your audience hear it coming forward. As you become used to listening to yourself, try to pick out the good points of your voice. Is it clear? Is it expressive? Is the basic pitch pleasant? When you have built up your confidence, consider areas for improvement. Do you normally speak too fast? Is the tone monotonous?

Repeat the task, but this time trying to vary your voice. For example, try reading at your normal speed, then faster, then as quickly as you can. Remember to start each word precisely and to concentrate on what you are saying. Then try varying the pitch of your voice. You will be surprised at how easy it is. Ask another student teacher to listen to the tape with you, comment on any differences and provide helpful advice for improving. Try these out in your teaching and store in your professional development portfolio (PDP) or equivalent for future reference/ experimentation.

Language of the teacher

Teaching involves communicating with pupils from a variety of backgrounds and with different needs. To effectively support pupils with English as an additional language (EAL), for example, requires specialist knowledge and skill for teaching within the mainstream context in a way that promotes language learning alongside content learning. The learning of English for pupils with EAL takes place as much in the arts, humanities, mathematics and science as it does in the 'subject' of English, as well as the 'hidden curriculum', which implies that all teachers are teachers of language (see Flynn, Pim and Coles, 2015).

In order to develop pupils' language skills, a teacher's language must be accessible (see Unit 5.8 for detailed advice). There is no point in talking to pupils in language they do not understand. That does not mean subject-specific vocabulary cannot be introduced, but rather that you gradually introduce your class to the language of the subject. To do this, you must not assume that everybody knows the words or constructions that you do, including simple connecting phrases, for example, 'in order to', 'so that', 'tends to', 'keep in proportion', and so on. Start with a simple, direct language that makes no assumptions.

It is easier for pupils to understand a new concept if you make comparisons or use examples, metaphors or references to which they can relate. Where appropriate, use a variety of words or explanations that ensure the meaning of what you intend to convey is understood by all pupils. As a teacher, your language must be concise. When you are speaking, you stress or repeat important words or phrases. Placing an accent on certain syllables of the words you use gives rise to rhythmic patterns that affect the meaning of your message. These are important techniques in teaching. If they help learning, then repetition, accentuation and elaboration are valuable, but filling silence with teacher talk is generally unproductive. You take longer to deliver the same information and pupils' time may not be used most effectively. However, it is generally accepted that pupils understand something and learn it better if they hear it a number of times and if it is explained in different ways. A commonly used phrase to explain this is:

- tell them what you are going to tell them;
- tell them;
- then tell them again what you have told them.

Task 3.1.2 focuses on the language of your subject.

Task 3.1.2   The language of your subject

Compile a list of specialist words and phrases used in your subject or in a particular topic that you may be teaching. How many of these might be in the normal vocabulary of an average pupil at your school? In your lesson planning, how might you introduce and explain these words and phrases? How might you allow pupils opportunities to practise their use of the words in the lesson? Tape a lesson that you are teaching, then replay the tape and consider your use of language, including words and phrases identified above. It can be particularly helpful to listen to this with a student teacher learning to teach another subject who does not have the same subject knowledge and language, and who therefore may be nearer to pupils' experience of the subject. How might you improve your use of language in future lessons? Record your responses in your PDP.

As well as conveying content, a teacher's language is also used to create and develop interpersonal relationships with individual pupils that make them more interested and motivated in learning. Using pupils' names, 'saying something positive to every pupil individually over a period of time and thanking pupils at the end of a good lesson' (DfES, 2004e, p.18), showing interest in their lives outside the classroom and valuing their experience are all important in building mutual respect and creating a positive atmosphere for classroom learning (see also Unit 3.2).

Teachers also use language to impose discipline. Often, negative terms are used for this. This is not inevitable, and a positive approach may have more success (see also Unit 3.3). For example, can you suggest a constructive activity rather than condemning a destructive one? Could earlier praise or suggestion have made later criticism unnecessary? Hughes and Vass (2001) provide guidance on types of language that teachers can use to positively enhance pupils' motivation and learning, and Rogers (2015) unpacks the complex, dynamic relationship between language and behaviour management, particularly in relation to effective communication with challenging pupils and pupils with emotional and behavioural difficulties (see also Units 3.2, 3.3 and 5.8).

Types of verbal communication

There are many different ways in which verbal communication is used in teaching. Explaining, modelling, demonstrating, questioning and discussion are core pedagogical tools for teachers and are briefly considered below.

Explaining, modelling and demonstrating

Teachers spend a lot of time explaining to pupils. In some teaching situations, it can be the main form of activity in the lesson, thus being able to explain something effectively is an important skill to acquire. Pupils learn better if they are actively engaged in the learning process and a good explanation actively engages pupils, and, therefore, is able to gain and maintain their attention. You must plan to involve pupils; for example, mix an explanation with tasks, activities or questions rather than relying on long lectures, dictating notes or working something out on the board (see also Unit 5.2).

Explaining provides information about what, why and how. It describes new terms or concepts or clarifies their meaning. Pupils expect teachers to explain things clearly and become frustrated when they cannot understand an explanation. A good explanation is clear and well structured. It takes account of pupils' previous knowledge and understanding, uses language that pupils can understand and relates new work to concepts, interests or work already familiar to the pupils. Use of analogy or metaphor can also help an explanation.

Table 3.1.1 identifies some key characteristic features of effective explanations. You might find this checklist and the sample questions useful when analysing and reviewing both your own and another student teacher's explanations.

Teachers often reinforce verbal explanations by providing pupils with a visual prompt, demonstration or model. Modelling is an effective learning strategy that allows pupils to ask

Table 3.1.1 Characteristic features of effective explanations

Characteristic feature	Sample question to ask yourself
Clear structure	Is the explanation structured in a logical way showing how each part links together?
Key features identified	What are the key points or essential elements that pupils should understand?
Dynamic opening	What is the 'tease' or 'hook' that is used at the start?
Clarity – using voice and body	Can the voice or body be used in any way to emphasise or embellish certain points?
Signposts	Are there clear linguistic signposts to help pupils follow the sequence and understand which are the key points?
Examples and non-examples	Are there sufficient examples and non-examples to aid pupils' understanding of a concept?
Models and analogies	What models might help pupils understand an abstract idea? Are there any analogies you could use? Will pupils understand the analogy? How might you help pupils identify the strengths and weaknesses of the analogy?
Props	What concrete and visual aids can be used to help pupils understand more?
Questions	Are there opportunities to check for pupils' understanding at various points, and to note and act on any misconceptions or misunderstandings? Are there opportunities for pupils to rehearse their understanding?
Connections to pupils' experience	Are there opportunities, particularly at the start, to check pupils' prior knowledge of the subject and to link to their everyday experiences?
Repetition	Are there a number of distinct moments in the explanation when the key points that should be learned are repeated and emphasised?
Humour	When and how might it be appropriate to use humour?

Source: DfES (2004c, p.11)

questions about and hear explanations related to each stage of the process as it happens, since the teacher can:

■ 'think aloud', making apparent and explicit those skills, decisions, processes and procedures that would otherwise be hidden or unclear;
■ expose pupils to the possible pitfalls of the task in hand, showing how to avoid them;
■ demonstrate to pupils that they can make alterations and corrections as part of the process;
■ warn pupils about possible hazards involved in practical activities, how to avoid them or minimise the effects if they occur.

(DfES, 2004a, p.3)

Showing learners what to do while talking them through the activity and linking new learning to old through questions, resources, activities and language is sometimes referred to as scaffolding (see Unit 5.1). The idea is that:

[L]earners are supported in carrying out a task by the use of language to guide their action. The next stage in scaffolding is for the learner to talk themselves through the task. Then that talk can, in turn, become an internalised guide to the action and thought of the learner.

(Dillon and Maguire, 2001, pp.145-146)

Combining verbal and visual explanations can be more effective than using verbal explanations exclusively (see Units 5.1 and 5.3).

Questioning

One technique in the scaffolding process for actively engaging pupils in their learning is questioning. Teachers use a lot of questions; indeed, 'every day teachers ask dozens, even hundreds of questions, thousands in a single year, over a million during a professional lifetime' (Wragg and Brown, 2001, p.1).

Asking questions effectively

Effective use of questioning is a valuable part of interactive teaching. However, if not handled effectively, pupils misunderstand and/or become confused. To use questioning effectively in your lessons requires planning (see Unit 2.2 on lesson planning), as you will need to consider:

■ what type of question(s) you are going to ask;
■ how you are going to ask the question(s);
■ when you are going to ask the question(s);
■ why you are asking the question(s);
■ of whom you are going to ask a question, how you expect the question answered, how you are going to respond if the pupil does not understand the question or gives an inappropriate answer, and how long you are going to wait for an answer.

However, you cannot plan your questioning too rigidly and follow a pre-set agenda, as this may result in pupils asking fewer questions themselves, producing undeveloped responses, rarely discussing ideas with their peers, presenting few thoughts of their own or demonstrating confusion. You must exercise flexibility and adapt your plan during the lesson to take account of the development of the lesson.

Asking questions is not a simple process. Questions are asked for many reasons; for example, to gain pupils' attention or check that they are paying attention, to check understanding of an instruction or explanation, to reinforce or revise a topic, to deepen understanding, to encourage thinking and problem-solving or to develop a discussion. Wragg and Brown (2001, pp.16–17) classified the content of questions related to learning a particular subject, rather than procedural issues, as one of three types: *empirical questions* requiring answers based on facts or on experimental findings; *conceptual questions* concerned with eliciting ideas, definitions and reasoning in the subject being studied; and *value questions* investigating relative worth and merit, moral and environmental issues. These broad categories often overlap, and some questions may involve elements of all three types of question. Consider also the time that a teacher gives, after a question, for pupils to reply. Allowing thinking time is an important aspect of questioning.

Another classification that can be used to help you plan questions with specific purposes in mind is Bloom's (1956) taxonomy of cognitive objectives, through which questions can be arranged into six levels of complexity and abstraction. Lower-level questions usually demand factual, descriptive answers, whereas higher-level questions are more complex and require more sophisticated critical thinking from pupils. Research indicates that pupils' cognitive abilities and levels of achievement can be increased when they are challenged and have regular access to higher-order thinking (Black and Wiliam, 2002; Fisher, 2013; Muijs and Reynolds, 2011). Table 3.1.2 links the hierarchical levels in Bloom's taxonomy with what pupils might be expected to do and the types of question that would help them to realise those tasks. Examples of possible question stems you could draw upon when planning questions to ask pupils in your lessons are provided for each cognitive objective.

There are a number of other ways in which questions can be categorised. Below we consider closed and open questions.

Closed and open questions

The most common reason for asking questions is to check that pupils have learned what they are supposed to have learned or memorised certain facts or pieces of information. These are questions such as: what is the capital of Borneo? What is Archimedes' Principle? How many furlongs are there in a mile? What does the Latin expression, 'Veni, vidi, vici' mean, who first used it and when? How do you spell 'loquacious'? These are called *closed* questions. There is only one correct answer, which limits the scope of the response. The pupil either knows the answer or not; no real thought is required. Closed questions might be given to the whole class, with answers coming instantaneously. A short, closed question-answer session might be used to reinforce learning, refresh pupils' memories or provide a link to new work.

Conversely, *open* questions broaden the scope for response since they have several possible answers and it may be impossible to know whether an answer is 'correct'. These questions are often used to stimulate thinking and learning and challenge pupils' capacity to frame ideas in words. Examples of open questions are: How could we reduce our carbon footprint? Should Western governments intervene in Middle Eastern politics? What words might you use to describe the Olympics? What do we know about the 'Big Bang' theory?

Table 3.1.2 Linking Bloom's (1956) taxonomy to what pupils need to do, thinking processes and possible question stems

Cognitive objective	What pupils need to do	Use of questioning to develop higher-order thinking skills	Links to thinking	Possible question stems
Knowledge	Define Recall Describe Label Identify Match	To help pupils link aspects of existing knowledge or relevant information to the task ahead.	Pupils are more likely to retain information if it is needed for a specific task and linked to other relevant information. Do your questions in this area allow pupils to link aspects of knowledge necessary for the task?	Describe what you see... What is the name for...? What is the best one...? Where in the book would you find...? What are the types of graph...? What are we looking for? Where is this set?
Compre-hension	Explain Translate Illustrate Summarise Extend	To help pupils to process their existing knowledge.	Comprehension questions require pupils to process the knowledge they already have in order to answer the question. They demand a higher level of thinking and information processing than do knowledge questions.	How do you think...? Why do you think...? What might this mean...? Explain what a spreadsheet does... What are the key features...? Explain your model... What is shown about...? What happens when...? What word represents...?
Application	Apply to a New context Demonstrate Predict Employ Solve Use	To help pupils use their knowledge to solve a new problem or apply it to a new situation.	Questions in this area require pupils to use their existing knowledge and understanding to solve a new problem or to make sense of a new context. They demand more complex thinking. Pupils are more likely to be able to apply knowledge to a new context if it is not too far removed from the context with which they are familiar.	What shape of graph are you expecting? What do you think will happen?... Why? Where else might this be useful? How can you use a spreadsheet to...? Can you apply what you now know to solve...? What does this suggest to you? How does the writer do this? What would the next line of my modelled answer be?

Table 3.1.2 continued

Analysis	Analyse Infer Relate Support Break down Differentiate Explore	To help pupils use the process of enquiry to break down what they know and reassemble it.	Analysis questions require pupils to break down what they know and reassemble it to help them solve a problem. These questions are linked to more abstract, conceptual thought that is central to the process of enquiry.	Separate... (for example, fact from opinion) What is the function of...? What assumptions are being made...? What is the evidence...? State the point of view... Make a distinction... What is this really saying? What does this symbolise? So, what is the poet saying to us?
Synthesis	Design Create Compose Reorganise Combine	To help pupils combine and select from available knowledge in order to respond to unfamiliar situations.	Synthesis questions demand that pupils combine and select from available knowledge to respond to unfamiliar situations or solve new problems. There is likely to be a great diversity of responses.	Propose an alternative... What conclusion can you draw...? How else would you...? State a rule... How do the writers differ in their response to...? What happens at the beginning of the poem and how does it change?
Evaluation	Assess Evaluate Appraise Defend Justify	To help pupils compare and contrast knowledge gained from different perspectives as they construct and reflect upon their own viewpoints.	Evaluation questions expect pupils to use their knowledge to form judgements and defend the positions they take up. They demand complex thinking and reasoning.	Which is more important/ moral/logical...? What inconsistencies are there in...? What errors are there...? Why is... valid? How can you defend...? Why is the order important? Why does it change?

Source: Adapted from DfES (2004b, pp.13-14)

Open questions are much more complex than closed questions. They are designed to extend pupils' understanding of a topic. To answer them, the respondent has to think and manipulate information by reasoning or applying information and using knowledge, logic, creativity and imagination. Open questions cannot usually be answered quickly as pupils need time to gather information, sift evidence, advance hypotheses, discuss ideas and plan their answers.

An example from a science lesson shows the difference in purpose between closed and open questions. 'What is the chemical formula of carbon dioxide?' is a closed question requiring factual knowledge, whereas 'How does carbon combine with oxygen during the respiration process?' requires understanding. Further, a question such as 'Do you think that reducing our carbon footprint can slow down global warming?' requires a deeper level of reflection and research by pupils.

You can ask closed or open questions or a combination of the two as *a series of questions*. The questions in the series can start with a few relatively easy closed questions and then move on to more complex open questions. A series of questions takes time to build up if they are to be an integral part of the learning process. They must therefore be planned as an integral part of the lesson, not as a time-filler at the end of a lesson where their effect is lost. Questions at the end of the lesson are much more likely to be closed-recall questions to help pupils remember what they have been taught in the lesson. There are implications for assessment of closed and open questions (see also Unit 6.1).

Other aspects of questioning to consider

There are other aspects of questioning that are important to consider. Questions can be asked to the whole class, to groups, or to specific named individuals. Questions can be spoken, written on (an electronic) whiteboard, or given out on printed sheets. Answers can be given at once or produced after deliberation, either spoken or written. For example, you may set a series of questions for homework and either collect the answers in to mark or go through them verbally with the class at the start of the next lesson.

Effective questioning requires you to be able to ask clear, appropriate questions, use pauses to allow pupils to think about an answer before responding and use prompting to help pupils who are having problems in answering a question. Some key tactics identified by Wragg and Brown (2001, p.28) for asking questions include: structuring; pitching and putting clearly; directing and distributing; pausing and pacing; prompting and pacing; listening and responding to replies; and sequencing. Muijs and Reynolds (2011, p.58) identify three types of prompts to help pupils answer questions: *verbal prompts* (cues, reminders, instructions, tips, references to previous lessons or giving part of a sentence for pupils to complete); *gestural prompts* (pointing to an object or modelling a particular behaviour); and *physical prompts* (guiding pupils explicitly through motor skills).

Follow-up questions can be used to: probe further; encourage pupils to develop their answers; extend their thinking; change the direction of the questioning; and distribute questions to involve the whole class. Non-verbal aspects of communication such as eye contact, gesture, body language, tone of voice, humour, smiles and frowns are important in effective questioning because they go with the words that are used.

Common pitfalls or 'errors' in student teachers' use of questioning, as identified by Wragg and Brown (2001, p.28), include:

- asking too many questions at once;
- asking a question and answering it yourself;
- asking questions only of the brightest or most likeable pupils;
- asking a difficult question too early in the sequence of events;
- asking irrelevant questions;
- always asking the same types of questions (for example, closed ones);
- asking questions in a threatening way;
- not indicating a change in the type of question;
- not using probing questions;
- not giving pupils the time to think;
- not correcting wrong answers;

- ▪ ignoring pupils' answers;
- ▪ failing to see the implications of pupils' answers;
- ▪ failing to build on answers.

Errors of presentation (for example, not looking at pupils when asking a question, talking too fast, talking at the wrong volume or not being clear) are common errors and commonly detected (Wragg, 1984). The second most common type of error is the way student teachers handle responses to questions; for example, they only accept the answer(s) to open-ended questions that they want or expect. Open questions are likely to prompt a range of responses that may be valid but not correspond to the answer expected: avoid the guessing game type of question-and-answer session where you have a fixed answer in mind as pupils then spend their time guessing what the teacher wants.

Other errors identified include pupils not knowing why particular questions were being asked, pupils not being given enough background information to enable them to answer questions, teachers asking questions in a disjointed fashion rather than a logical sequence, jumping from one question to another without linking them together and focusing on a small group of pupils and ignoring the rest of the class. Student teachers tended to focus on those pupils sitting in a V-shaped wedge in the middle of the room.

Some aspects of questioning were not identified as common errors, for example, whether the vocabulary is appropriate for the pupils' level of understanding. Check that your questions are not too long, complex or ambiguous.

You can encourage pupils to actively participate in questioning by listening and responding appropriately to answers, praising good answers, being supportive and respecting answers and not making pupils feel they will be ridiculed if they answer a question incorrectly (see also Units 3.2, 5.2 and 5.5).

Discussion

Questioning may lead naturally into discussion to explore a topic further. Although pupils generally have more control over the material included in, and direction of, a discussion than in many teaching situations, the teacher is still in charge. Discussion should be planned. Seating arrangements and pupil grouping help develop a less structured atmosphere, which can encourage as many pupils as possible to contribute. Plan how you are going to stimulate the discussion and how you are going to respond if a discussion drifts off its main theme. By interjecting suggestions or key questions, you can keep a discussion on the topic.

> For a fruitful discussion that allows pupils some significant say over what is discussed, while at the same time covering the ground that teachers judge to be important, it is best to think of questions that may be perplexing, intriguing or even puzzling to pupils. Skilfully chosen encouraging, broad questions are often effective in sparking off animated conversations. The process may begin with recall questions to extend and activate knowledge and then thought questions to lift the discussion.
>
> (Wragg and Brown, 2001, p.44)

To maximise pupils' learning through discussion you need to be able to chair a discussion effectively. Before you use discussion in your classes, it is wise to observe another teacher use this technique in their teaching. See also Unit 4.5 and the appendix to Unit 4.5, 'Handling discussion with classes'.

Active listening

Listening is not the same as hearing. For effective communication, *being able to actively listen and take account of the response* (for example, what pupils are communicating to you) is as important as being able to send the message effectively. Learn to recognise and be sensitive to whether or not a message has been received correctly by a pupil; for example, you get a bewildered look or an inappropriate answer to a question. Be able to react appropriately; for example, repeat the same question or rephrase it. However, also reflect on why the communication was not effective; for example, was the pupil not listening to you? If so, why? For example, had the pupil 'switched off' in a boring lesson or was the question worded inappropriately? Do not assume that pupils have your grasp of meaning and vocabulary (see 'Language of the teacher', above). It is all too easy to blame a pupil for not listening attentively, but it may be that you had a large part to play in the breakdown of the communication.

Wragg and Brown (2001, p.34) identify four types of listening:

> *Skim listening* – little more than awareness that a pupil is talking (often when the answer seems irrelevant); *survey listening* – trying to build a wider mental map of what the pupil is talking about; *search listening* – actively searching for specific information in an answer; *study listening* – a blend of survey and search listening to identify the underlying meaning and uncertainties of the words the pupil is using.

It is too easy to ask a question and then 'switch off' while an answer is being given, to think about the next question or next part of the lesson. This lack of interest conveys itself to the pupil. It is distracting to the pupil to know that the teacher is neither listening nor responding to what is being said. Also, you may convey boredom or indifference, which has a negative impact on the tone of the lesson. Effective listening is an active process, with a range of non-verbal and verbal responses that convey the message to the pupil speaking that you are listening to what is being said. Effective listening is associated with conveying enthusiasm and generating interest, by providing reinforcement and constructive feedback to pupils. These include looking alert, looking at the pupil who is talking to you, smiling, nodding and making verbal signals to show you have received and understood the message or to encourage the pupil to continue, saying, for example, 'yes', 'I see what you mean', 'go on', 'oh dear', 'mmmm', 'uh-huh'.

Non-verbal communication

When we communicate, non-verbal cues can have as great an impact on the listener as the spoken word. Much teacher-pupil communication is non-verbal (for example, your appearance, gestures, posture, facial expression and mannerisms). Non-verbal communication supports or detracts from verbal communication, depending on whether or not verbal and non-verbal signals match each other; for example, if you are praising someone and smiling and looking pleased or reprimanding them and looking stern and sounding firm, you are sending a consistent message and are perceived as sincere. On the other hand, if you are smiling when reprimanding someone or looking bored when praising someone, you are sending conflicting messages that cause confusion and misunderstanding. As Robertson (1996, p.94) cautions, 'When non-verbal behaviour is not reinforcing meaning...it communicates instead the speaker's lack of involvement. Rather than being the message about the message, it becomes the message about the messenger'.

However, non-verbal communication can also have a considerable impact without any verbal communication; for example, looking at a pupil slightly longer than you would normally communicates your awareness that they are talking or misbehaving. This may be sufficient to gain the pupil's attention. You can probably think of a teacher who stands at the front of the class leaning against the board with arms crossed waiting for silence, the teacher marching down between the desks to tell someone off or the teacher who sits and listens attentively to the problems of a particular pupil. You can indicate your enthusiasm for a topic by the way you use gestures. The meaning of the communication is clear and there is no need to say anything, thus demonstrating that our actions can speak as loudly, if not more loudly, than our words. This illustrates that non-verbal signals are important for good communication, classroom management and control.

Effective communication therefore relies not only on appropriate content, but also on the way it is presented. Mehrabian (1972) found that 93 per cent of the meaning behind verbal messages was received through non-verbal channels: notably, 55 per cent through gesture; 38 per cent through tone of voice; and 7 per cent from the words actually used.

Presenting yourself effectively

There is no single correct way to present yourself as a teacher. Herein lies one of the keys to effective teacher self-presentation: while there are some common constituents and expectations, every teacher is an individual and brings something of their own unique set of characteristics and personality to the job.

Initial impressions are important, and the way you present yourself to a class on first meeting can influence their learning over a period of time. Having prepared the lesson appropriately, the pupils' impressions of the lesson, and also of you, are important. Part of the impression created relates to your appearance and pupils do 'value adults' in school who take pride in their appearance and who are well dressed (Sage, 2000). Pupils expect all teachers to wear clothes that are clean, neat and tidy, and certain teachers to wear certain types of clothes; for example, it is acceptable for a physical education teacher to wear a tracksuit but not a history teacher. Thus, first impressions have as much to do with non-verbal as with verbal communication, but both are important considerations.

How teachers follow up the first impression is equally important, for example, whether you treat pupils as individuals, how you communicate with pupils, whether you have any mannerisms such as constantly flicking a piece of hair out of your eyes or saying 'er' or 'OK' – which reduce or prevent effective communication (pupils tend to focus on any mannerism rather than on what is being said and they may even count the number of times you do it!). It is generally agreed that effective teaching depends on and is enhanced by self-presentation that is *enthusiastic*, *confident* and *caring*. Why are these attributes important? How can you work towards making these attributes part of your self-presentation as a teacher?

Enthusiasm

Before many pupils will make an effort to get to grips with something new, the teacher needs to 'sell' it to them as something interesting and worthwhile. However, your enthusiasm should be sustained throughout a lesson, and in relation to each activity – not only when you are presenting material, but also when you are commenting on a pupil's work, particularly perhaps when a pupil has persevered or achieved a goal.

Your enthusiasm for your subject is infectious. However, there could be a danger of 'going over the top' when showing enthusiasm. If you are overexcited, it can give a sense of triviality, so the enthusiasm has to be measured.

There are perhaps three principal ways in which you can communicate enthusiasm both verbally and non-verbally. The first is via *facial expression*:

> An enthusiastic speaker will be producing a stream of facial expressions which convey his excitement, disbelief, surprise or amusement about his message. Some expressions are extremely brief, lasting about one fifth of a second and may highlight a particular word, whereas others last much longer, perhaps accompanying the verbal expression of an idea. The overall effect is to provide a running commentary for the listener on how the speaker feels about the ideas expressed. In contrast, a speaker who is not involved in his subject shows little variation in facial expression. The impression conveyed is that the ideas are brought out automatically and are failing even to capture the attention of the speaker.
>
> (Robertson, 1996, p.86)

The second way is via the *use of your voice*. The manner in which you speak as a teacher gives a clear indication of how you feel about the topic being taught and is readily picked up by pupils. Your voice needs to be varied and to indicate your feelings about what you are teaching. As you are engaged in something akin to a 'selling job', your voice has to show this in its production and delivery – it has to be persuasive and occasionally show a measure of excitement. A monotone voice is hardly likely to convey enthusiasm as, 'Enthusiastic teachers are alive in the room; they show surprise, suspense, joy, and other feelings in their voices and they make material interesting by relating it to their experiences and showing that they themselves are interested in it' (Good and Brophy, 2007, p.385).

A third way to convey enthusiasm is via your *poise and movement*. An enthusiastic speaker has an alert, open posture and accompanies speech with appropriately expressive hand and arm gestures – sometimes to emphasise a point, at other times to reinforce something that is being described through indicating relevant shape or direction, for example, an arrangement of apparatus or a tactical move in hockey. If you are enthusiastic, you are committed and involved, and all aspects of your posture and movement should display this.

Think back to teachers you have worked with and identify some whose enthusiasm for their subject really influenced your learning. How did these teachers convey their enthusiasm? How do you convey your enthusiasm? To what extent does poise and movement reflect people's attitudes, emotions and intentions?

Confidence

It is very important that, as a teacher, you present yourself with confidence. This is easier said than done because confidence relates both to a sense of knowledgeable mastery of the subject matter and to a sense of assurance of being in control, which takes time to develop and establish within the context of interpersonal relationships built by the teacher.

There is an irony in pupils' response to teacher confidence. Expression of authority is part of the role pupils expect of a teacher, and where exercised with confidence, pupils feel at ease and reassured. In fact, pupils prefer the security of a confident teacher. However, if they sense at any time that a teacher is unsure or apprehensive, it is in young people's nature to attempt to undermine authority (for further information, see Rogers, 2015).

Of course, in many cases, it is experience that brings confidence but, regrettably, pupils seldom allow that to influence their behaviour. Although the key to confident self-presentation is to be well planned, both in respect of material and in organisation, without the benefit of experience, all your excellent plans may not work, and you may have no alternative 'up your sleeve'. Whatever happens, you need to cultivate a confident exterior, even if it is something of an act and you are feeling far from assured inside.

Confidence can be conveyed verbally in clear, purposeful instructions and explanations that are not disrupted by hesitation. Instructions given in a direct and business-like manner, such as, 'Jane, please collect the scissors and put them in the red box', convey a sense of confidence. On the other hand, the same instruction put in the form of a question, such as 'Jane, will you collect the scissors and put them in the red box?' can convey a sense of your being less assured, not being confident that, in fact, Jane *will* cooperate. There is also the possibility of the pupil saying, 'No'! Your voice needs to be used in a firm, measured manner. A slower, lower, well-articulated delivery is more authoritative and displays more confidence than a fast, high-pitched method of speaking. Use of voice is particularly important in giving key instructions, especially where safety factors are involved and in taking action to curtail inappropriate pupil behaviour. This is perhaps the time to be less enthusiastic and animated, and more serious and resolute in your manner.

Non-verbally, confidence is expressed via, for example, posture, movement and eye contact, both in their own right and as an appropriate accompaniment to verbal language. There is nothing agitated about the movement of confident people. They tend to stand still and use their arm gestures to a limited extent to reinforce the message being conveyed.

Eye contact is a crucial aspect of conveying confidence to pupils. A nervous person avoids eye contact, somehow being afraid to know what others are thinking, not wanting to develop a relationship that might ultimately reveal their inability or weakness. Clearly, it is your role as a teacher to be alert at all times to pupil reaction and be striving to develop a relationship with all pupils that encourages them to seek your help and advice. Steady, committed eye contact is usually helpful for both of these objectives. You must, however, also recognise that eye contact is perceived differently by people of different cultures: in certain parts of Africa, Asia and Latin America, avoiding eye contact is the way to show respect, whereas extended eye contact may be perceived as disrespectful or a challenge to authority. You should therefore take into account cultural sensitivities. This also applies to other aspects of non-verbal communication, such as dress, gesture, physical contact and spatial proximity to another person. For further information about cultural differences, take advice from your tutor, a staff member of that culture, staff at the local multicultural centre or the Equality and Human Rights commission (for additional guidance on cultural difference and diversity, see Knapp, Hall and Horgan (2014), as well as the website www.naldic.org.uk).

Caring

It is perhaps not surprising that pupils feel emotional support and a caring approach are important in developing an effective relationship with teachers. Wentzel (1997) described caring teachers as those who demonstrate a commitment to their teaching, recognise each pupil's academic strengths and needs and have a democratic style of interaction. Wilson, Pianta and Stuhlman (2007) found that an emotionally supportive environment in which the teacher also supplies plenty of evaluative feedback has a positive influence on pupils' social competencies. Wragg (1984, p.82) reported that many more pupils preferred teachers who are 'understanding, friendly and firm' than teachers who are 'efficient, orderly and firm' or 'friendly, sympathetic and understanding'. It is interesting to note that firmness is also a preferred characteristic.

Notwithstanding pupils' preferences, interest in pupils as individuals and in their progress is surely the reason most teachers are in teaching. Your commitment to pupils' well-being and learning should be evident in all aspects of your manner and self-presentation. While this attitude goes without saying, it is not as straightforward as it sounds since it demands sensitivity and flexibility. In a sense, it is you, as the teacher, who has to modify your behaviour in response to the pupils, rather than it always being the pupil who has to fall into line with everything asked for by the teacher. There is a potential conflict, and balance to be struck, between firm confidence and flexible empathy. It is one of the challenges of teaching to find this balance and to be able to respond suitably at the appropriate time.

A caring approach is evident in a range of features of teaching, from efficient preparation through to sensitive interpersonal skills such as active listening. Those teachers who put pupils' interests above everything have taken the time and trouble to prepare work thoroughly in a form appropriate to the class. Similarly, the classroom environment shows thoughtful design and organisation. In the teaching situation, caring teachers are fully engaged in the task at hand, observing, supporting, praising, alert to the class climate and able to respond with an appropriate modification in the programme, if necessary. Above all, however, caring teachers know pupils by name, remember their work, problems and progress from previous lessons and are prepared to take time to listen to them and talk about personal things as well as work. In other words, caring teachers show a real sensitivity to pupils' individual needs. They communicate clearly that each pupil's learning and success are valued.

Now complete Tasks 3.1.3 and 3.1.4.

 Task 3.1.3   Communicating effectively

Select in turn each aspect of verbal and non-verbal communication identified above; your use of voice, language, explaining/questioning/discussion, listening, presenting yourself effectively, enthusiasm, confidence and caring. Prepare an observation sheet for your tutors or another student teacher to use when observing you teach a class. Use this as a basis for evaluation and discussion about how you can further develop this aspect of your teaching. Store these in your PDP for future reference.

  Task 3.1.4   Studying one aspect of communication in depth

Select one specific aspect of communication to study in greater depth. Review the literature on that aspect of communication. Design and conduct a piece of action research on that specific aspect of communication with one of your classes. Report critically on your research, identifying issues related to the assumptions underlying the methods of data collection and analysis. Critically analyse the outcomes of the study and reflect on your learning about improving your communication. Store in your PDP.

SUMMARY AND KEY POINTS

■ Good communication is essential for developing sound interpersonal relationships with pupils, a positive classroom climate and effective teaching and learning.

■ This unit has aimed to help you identify both the strengths and weaknesses in your verbal and non-verbal communication, and in your self-presentation, to provide the basis for improving your ability to communicate.

■ Developing your professional knowledge and judgement in this area should enable you to communicate sensitively and to best advantage.

Check which requirements for your ITE programme you have addressed through this unit.

 Further resources

Fisher, R. (2013) *Creative Dialogue: Talk for Thinking in the Classroom*, 2nd Edition, Abingdon: Routledge.
The principles of dialogic learning that underpin this book are drawn from worldwide research, and, in particular, from three successful approaches to teaching through dialogue: Piagetian approaches; Philosophy for Children (P4C) programmes; and Assessment for Learning strategies. Key principles common to these approaches and characteristic of successful lessons and learning conversations incorporate: dialogic challenge; dialogic construction of meaning; and dialogic review.

Knapp, M., Hall, J. and Horgan, T. (2014) *Non-Verbal Communication in Human Interaction*, 8th Edition, Boston, MA: Wadsworth/Cengage Learning.
Chapters embedded within Parts II, III and IV explore the non-verbal elements involved in any interaction, including the environment within which the interaction occurs; the physical features of the participants themselves; and their behaviour (for example, gestures, touching, territory and personal space, facial expressions, eye gazing and vocal sounds).

Muijs, D. and Reynolds, D. (2011) *Effective Teaching: Evidence and Practice*, 3rd Edition, London: Sage.
Chapter 3 considers the important relationship between interactive teaching and pupils' learning. Elements of effective questioning techniques are identified and then reviewed in relation to class discussion. Chapter 11 introduces heuristic problem-solving strategies and guidance on how to promote higher-order thinking skills.

National Association for Language Development in the Curriculum (naldic): www.naldic.org.uk.
This website provides a professional forum for the teaching and learning of EAL, supporting bilingualism and raising the achievement of ethnic minority learners. The 'resources' link enables you to access important key documents and the CPD link navigates you to the ITE section.

Rogers, B. (2015) *Classroom Behaviour: A Practical Guide to Effective Teaching, Behaviour Management and Colleague Support*, 4th Edition, London: Sage.
The author looks at everyday behaviour issues facing teachers in today's classrooms. Describing real dilemmas and situations, he provides theoretically sound strategies and best practices to support you in meeting the challenges of the job, as well as building up a rapport with pupils and colleagues to enable positive and productive learning environments. Examples of verbal and non-verbal communication skills are detailed within case studies that permeate throughout this highly accessible and informative book.

Walsh, J. and Sattes, B. (2005) *Quality Questioning: Research-Based Practice to Engage Every Learner*, London: Sage.
The authors provide an in-depth look at how quality questions can transform classrooms. Drawing from research into teacher effectiveness, they offer strategies that engage all pupils in the teacher's questions and prompt pupils to generate their own questions. For example, quality questioning includes

a comprehensive framework for preparing and presenting questions, prompting and processing pupil responses, teaching pupils to generate questions and reflecting on questioning practice.

Teacher's non-verbal communication in the classroom.wmv (2012) www.youtube.com/watch?v=vnbtxh ZRcEs.

This 11-minute film shows five teachers from secondary schools at Ras Al Khaimah addressing their classes at the beginning of a lesson – the soundtrack has been replaced with music so that the behaviour and body language are the main focus of the film.

Voice Care Network: www.voicecare.org.uk.

Their booklet 'More Care for your Voice' is intended to help people whose voice is needed for their work. This organisation is a registered charity with subscribing members. They provide advice and training. Relatively low-cost equipment is available to help with voice projection and to ensure that all pupils can hear the teacher.

Dylan Wiliam Center Webinar (2015) *The Right Questions, the Right Way*: **Learning Sciences International: www.youtube.com/watch?v=6WFR-ZegH4o**

In this webinar, Wiliam discusses the use of a wide range of classroom techniques to improve questioning, along with ways to create and capitalise upon 'teaching moments', and the defining characteristics of effective diagnostic questions.

Appendix 2 lists subject associations and teacher councils and Appendix 3 provides a list of websites.

Capel, S., Leask, M. and Turner, T. (eds.) (2010) *Readings for Learning to Teach in the Secondary School: A Companion to M Level Study*, **Abingdon: Routledge.**

This book brings together essential readings to support you in your critical engagement with key issues raised in this textbook.

Capel, S., Lawrence, J. Leask, M. and Younie, S. (eds.) (2019) *Surviving and Thriving in the Secondary School: The NQT's Essential Companion*, **Abingdon: Routledge.**

This book is designed to support newly qualified teachers in the next phase of development as a teacher. However, you may find it useful as it covers aspects of teaching not included in this book which, nonetheless you experience on your ITE programme.

The subject specific books in the *Learning to Teach (Subject)* series, the *Practical (Subject) Guides*, *Debates in (Subject)* and *Mentoring (Subject) Teachers* are also very useful.

Any additional resources and an editable version of any relevant tasks/tables in this unit are available on the companion website: www.routledge.com/cw/capel

3.2 Motivating pupils

Misia Gervis and Susan Capel

Introduction

Pupils' attitudes to school and motivation to learn are a result of a number of factors, including school ethos, class climate, past experiences, future expectations, peer group, teachers, gender, family background, culture, economic status and class. As a result, the link between motivation and educational performance and achievement is complex.

Some pupils have a more positive attitude to school and to learning; for example, it is valued at home or they see a link between education and a job. If pupils see a relationship between success at school and economic success, then they are more likely to work hard, behave in the classroom and be more successful. Many pupils want to learn but depend on teachers to get them interested in a subject. Even though some pupils may not be inherently motivated to learn, the school ethos, teachers' attitudes, behaviour, personal enthusiasm, teaching style and strategies in the classroom can increase their motivation to learn (see also, for example, Unit 5.3). On the other hand, pupils who do not feel valued at school are, in turn, unlikely to value school. Therefore, although some pupils may be inherently motivated to learn, they may become demotivated or have low motivation because of a learning environment that does not stimulate them, because a task is too difficult or because there is a negative impact of factors such as those identified above. Pupils for whom the motivational climate is not right are more likely to become disinterested and misbehave. If the teacher does not manage the class and their behaviour effectively, the learning of all pupils in the class can be negatively affected.

Thus, a central aim for you as a teacher is to create a motivational climate that helps stimulate pupils to learn. There is a range of techniques you can use to increase pupils' motivation to learn, for example:

■ showing your enthusiasm for a topic, subject or teaching;
■ treating each pupil as an individual;
■ noticing and valuing effort in the classroom;
■ providing quick feedback by marking work promptly;
■ rewarding appropriate behaviour.

In order to use such techniques effectively, you need some knowledge and insight into ways of motivating pupils to learn. There is a wealth of research and evidence available on motivation. This unit tries to draw out some of the ideas we feel are of most benefit to you as a student teacher. However, the 'Further resources' at the end of this unit, plus other reading in your library, will help you to develop your ability to motivate pupils further.

OBJECTIVES

At the end of this unit, you should be able to:

- understand the role and importance of motivation for effective teaching and learning and classroom management;
- appreciate some of the key elements of motivation for effective teaching;
- understand how to motivate pupils effectively;
- understand how to create a challenging classroom environment.

Check the requirements of your initial teacher education (ITE) programme to see which relate to this unit.

What is motivation?

Motivation 'consists of internal processes and external incentives which spur us on to satisfy some need' (Child, 2007, p.226). Understanding key elements of motivational behaviour can help you to interpret the behaviour of your pupils, i.e.:

- direction (what activities people start);
- intensity (what effort people put in);
- persistence (what activities people continue).

These three key elements determine the activities that people start (direction) and continue (persistence) and the amount of effort they put into those activities at any particular time (intensity). Specifically, persistence has been found to be critical in the achievement of pupils. Duckworth (2016) describes this as 'grit'. She provides a wealth of evidence that shows a willingness to persevere despite encountering initial failure or difficulties is what predicts success. Indeed, this has been found to predict success more reliably than measures of IQ (Duckworth et al., 2007). More importantly, she says that it is something that can be learnt. Creating a learning culture whereby pupils are encouraged to see mistakes as an opportunity for development is an integral part of this process. Fundamentally, it is about developing what Dweck (2006) calls a 'Growth Mindset'. If pupils are able to learn with a growth mindset, then they embrace challenges, recognise that effort is essential to succeed, understand that feedback gives opportunities to learn and improve and that setbacks simply test perseverance.

Motivation can be intrinsic (motivation from within the person; that is, engaging in an activity for its own sake for pleasure and/or satisfaction inherent in the activity; for example, a sense of achievement at having completed a difficult piece of work) or extrinsic (motivation from outside; that is, engaging in an activity for external reasons; for example, to receive a reward, such as praise, or to avoid punishment). Research has found that a person intrinsically motivated is more likely to persist and continue with an activity than a person extrinsically motivated. This can be illustrated by some (intrinsically motivated) pupils succeeding at school/in a subject despite the quality of the teaching, whereas other (extrinsically motivated) pupils succeed because of good teaching. Therefore, intrinsic motivation is to be encouraged in learning. However, pupils are asked to do many activities at school that are new to them, that are difficult, at which they may not be immediately successful or that they may perceive to be of little or no relevance to them. Further, they may have low self-confidence and may feel they have limited capacity to learn. In order to become intrinsically motivated, pupils need encouragement along the way, such as written or verbal praise for effort, making progress or success, feedback on how they are doing or an explanation of the relevance of the work. The quality of feedback pupils receive can directly impact on their self-confidence. Teachers can deliberately plan extrinsic motivators (see below) into their lessons with a view to enhancing both self-confidence and intrinsic motivation (there is a symbiotic relationship between self-confidence and intrinsic motivation, such that high self-confidence increases intrinsic motivation whereas low self-confidence decreases intrinsic motivation). Task 3.2.1 asks you to reflect on what motivates you as a learner.

 Task 3.2.1   What motivates you as a learner?

Reflect on your own experiences at school. What was it that motivated you in the subject you are now learning to teach? Identify another subject in which you were less motivated and reflect on why this was the case. Use the terms identified above and discuss your reflections with another student teacher. Identify anything you can learn from these experiences to build into your own teaching. Keep your notes in your professional development portfolio (PDP) or equivalent for future reference.

Theories of motivation

There are a number of theories of motivation. In addition, we adopt our own, often unconscious, theories. Examples of theories of motivation, along with some of their implications for you as a teacher in determining learning activities, are given in Table 3.2.1 and in the text below.

Table 3.2.1 Important theoretical perspectives and their implications for you as a teacher

Theory	Source	Main points	Implications for teachers
Theory x and theory y	McGregor (1960)	Theory x managers assume that the average worker is lazy, lacks ambition, is resistant to change and self-centred. Theory y managers assume that the average worker is motivated, wants to take responsibility, has potential for development and works for the organisation. Any lack of ambition or resistance to change comes from experience.	A theory x teacher motivates pupils externally through a controlling environment; for example, by directing and controlling pupils' actions, persuading, rewarding and punishing them to modify their behaviour. A theory y teacher encourages intrinsic motivation through, for example, an autonomy-support environment (see below).
Achievement motivation	Atkinson (1964) and McClelland (1961)	Motivation to perform an achievement-oriented task is related to the: (i) need to achieve on a particular task; (ii) expectation of success on the task; and (iii) strength of the incentive after the task has been completed successfully. This results in individuals setting themselves standards of achievement.	Create a learning environment that raises the need for achievement by raising levels of aspiration. Plan tasks that are challenging but attainable with effort. Work should be differentiated according to individual needs.
Achievement goal theory	Ames (1992a, 1992b), Dweck (1986), Dweck and Leggett (1988) and Nicholls (1984, 1989)	A social-cognitive perspective that identifies determinants of achievement behaviour, variations of which result from different achievement goals pursued by individuals. In a task- (or mastery-) oriented setting, the focus is on skill learning and exerting effort to succeed, and success is judged by self-improvement and mastery of a task. In an outcome- (ego- or performance-) oriented setting, individuals compare their performance and ability with others and judge success by beating others with little effort to enhance social status.	Pupils' goal orientation may be influenced by the motivational climate created by what teachers do and say. Therefore, plan a task-oriented learning environment that encourages pupils to improve their performance by trying hard, selecting demanding tasks and persisting when faced with difficulty, rather than an outcome-orientated learning environment that encourages pupils to select easy tasks that they can achieve with minimum effort and on which they are likely to give up when facing difficulties.

Table 3.2.1 continued

Theory	Source	Main points	Implications for teachers
Attribution theory	Weiner (1972)	Success or failure is attributed to ability, effort, difficulty of task or luck, depending on: (i) previous experience of success or failure on the task; (ii) the amount of work put in; or (iii) a perceived relationship between what is done and success or failure on the task.	Reward effort as well as success, as pupils are more likely to try if they perceive success is owing to effort; for example, you can give two marks for work, one for the standard of the work, the other for effort. Use teaching and assessment that is individualised rather than competitive.
Expectancy theory	Rosenthal and Jacobson (1968)	A person uses a range of cues to form expectations (high or low) of another. That person then behaves in a way that is consistent with their expectations. This influences the other person's motivation, performance and how they attribute success or failure. The other person performs according to the expectations, thus creating a self-fulfilling prophecy.	In order to avoid the self-fulfilling prophesy of pupils performing according to the way teachers expect them to perform (high or low), do not prejudge pupils on their past performance. Rather, encourage pupils to work to the best of their ability all the time.
Hierarchy of needs theory	Maslow (1970)	Hierarchy (highest to lowest): (1) self-actualisation (need to fulfil own potential); (2) self-esteem (need to feel competent and gain recognition from others); (3) affiliation and affection (need for love and belonging); (4) need for physical and psychological safety; and (5) physiological needs (for example, food, warmth). Energy is spent meeting the lowest level of unmet need.	If a basic need (for example, sleep, food, warmth) is not met, a pupil concentrates on meeting that need first and is unlikely to benefit from attempts by teachers to meet higher-level needs. Try to create a classroom environment to fulfil basic needs first; for example, rules for using dangerous equipment provide a sense of physical safety, routines give a sense of psychological security, group work can give a sense of belonging/affiliation (Postlethwaite, 1993). Schools also try to meet pupils' basic needs through, for example, providing breakfast.

Table 3.2.1 continued

Theory	Source	Main points	Implications for teachers
Behavioural learning theories	Skinner (1953)	Activity or behaviour is learned and maintained because of interaction with the environment. An activity or behaviour reinforced by a pleasurable outcome is more likely to be repeated.	Positive reinforcement (reward, such as praise) generally increases motivation to learn and behave. This has a greater impact if the reward is relevant to the pupils, they know how to get the reward and it is given fairly and consistently (there are, however, exceptions: see 'praise' below).
Self-determination theory	Deci and Ryan (1985) and Ryan and Deci (2000a)	A broad framework that considers both social and environmental factors that contribute to either enhancing or diminishing intrinsic and extrinsic motivation. Key themes relating to intrinsic motivation are autonomy, competence and relatedness. Extrinsic motivation operates by engaging pupils in tasks so that they can willingly accept the value of the task even if the task itself may not hold any specific interest to them. This can lead to greater persistence and better engagement in the task. Key themes relating to extrinsic motivation are internalisation and integration.	In a teaching context, it is acknowledged that interpersonal interactions (for example, communication and feedback) between teachers and pupils are critical in facilitating or impeding feelings of competency in pupils. As a consequence, intrinsic motivation can be elevated or diminished. Elevated intrinsic motivation does not occur unless also accompanied by a sense of autonomy. Research shows that autonomy-supportive teachers catalyse pupils' intrinsic motivation (Deci et al., 1981).
Positive Psychology	Seligman (2011)	The key to flourishing is that an individual finds meaning and purpose in the activities they are doing. Further, the key to individual enhancement is that they are fully engaged in what they are doing.	For teachers, the challenge is to help pupils find meaning and purpose in each lesson, for example, by using relevant and up-to-date examples to support a particular topic. If this does not happen there is likely to be less engagement and less focus during the lesson.

Applying theories of motivation to your teaching

It is often difficult for a teacher to identify the exact reason for a particular pupil's behaviour at a particular time, and, therefore, what is motivating them. Likewise, it is often difficult for a pupil to identify exactly what is motivating them. As a teacher, you can often only infer whether or not a pupil is motivated by observing their behaviour. Although there may be other reasons for a pupil not listening to what you are saying, talking, looking bored or staring out of the window, one reason may be that the motivational climate is not right and, therefore, the pupil is not motivated to learn.

Some of the factors that have been found to be motivating include: positive teacher–pupil relationships; supportive peer relationships; a sense of belonging; pupils' beliefs about their abilities; pupils' beliefs about the control they have over their own learning; pupils' interest in the subject; and the degree to which the subject or specific tasks are valued. Such factors have been categorised as:

- achievement (for example, completing a piece of work that was difficult or has taken a lot of effort);
- pleasure (for example, getting a good mark or praise from a teacher for a piece of work);
- preventing or stopping less pleasant activities/punishment (for example, avoiding getting a detention);
- satisfaction (for example, feeling that progress is being made);
- success (for example, doing well in a test).

The need to achieve can be encouraged by creating a learning environment in which 'the need for achievement in academic studies is raised' (Child, 2007, p.254). Each individual sets for themselves a standard of achievement, according to their level of aspiration. It is therefore important to raise pupils' levels of aspiration. Research has shown that when people experience an activity as 'challenging', they have higher levels of self-confidence, feel more in control, experience more positive emotions and have reduced levels of the stress hormone cortisol. Conversely, when people experience an activity as 'threatening', their self-confidence is reduced, they perceive themselves to have limited control, experience more negative emotions and cortisol levels increase, which ultimately reduces their performance (Jones et al., 2009). Thus, setting tasks that are challenging but achievable for each individual pupil (that is, individualised tasks) can be used to raise aspirations. Tasks on which pupils expect to achieve/succeed approximately 50 per cent of the time are the most motivating. However, this means that pupils are likely to fail on the task approximately 50 per cent of the time, so it is important to plan to reduce loss of motivation when pupils fail (for example, by praising effort, giving feedback on performance, and so on).

Intrinsic motivation in pupils is related to interest in the activity and to effort (hard work), which leads to deep learning (Entwistle, 1990; see also deep and surface learning in Units 5.2 and 5.3). Deep learning means that learners try to understand what they are doing, resulting in greater understanding of the subject matter. This is a prerequisite for high-quality learning outcomes (that is, achievement). Drawing on achievement goal theory, Covington (2000) reported deep learning as being associated with task (or mastery) goals, whereas surface (superficial or rote) learning is associated with outcome (or performance) goals. In line with other studies, Lam et al. (2004) found that pupils with an outcome orientation were more likely to focus on better performance than on mastering a task.

Consideration of the types of goal that pupils use is important not only for their achievement, but also in determining the climate you create in the classroom. Research has shown that people's achievement is directly related to the types of goal they adopt (Elliot and McGregor, 2001). Essentially, there are two key considerations when understanding the type of goal being used. First, is it a mastery or performance referenced goal? And second, is it an approach or avoid type of goal? These different components combine to create four possible types of goal: mastery-approach; mastery-avoid; performance-approach; and performance-avoid (see Figure 3.2.1). There seems to be a relationship between the types of goal adopted and whether pupils find an activity challenging or threatening. For example, work by Elliot and McGregor (2001) identified that pupils who set mastery-approach goals perceived an examination situation to be challenging (positive), whereas those who adopted performance-avoid goals perceived it as threatening (negative). Individuals who set mastery-approach goals have the most control over their achievement, and consequently understand that their efforts determine their success. Thus, it is important to work with your pupils to help them adopt mastery-approach goals but also to be mindful of pupils who are only focusing on performance-avoid goals, as these are also associated with contributing to pupils experiencing higher levels of threat.

Once a pupil has identified their mastery goal, how this is used to develop their skills is also important. The work of Ericsson and Poole (2016) on the science of expertise highlighted that the most critical factor in whether someone becomes an expert or not is how they actually practice. The notion of practicing with purpose is essential in this process. Purposeful practice encourages a person to leave their comfort zone, to risk making mistakes but to challenge themselves. In essence, there are three key principles to becoming purposeful, referred to as the 3Fs.

1   Focus: set mastery-approach goal.
2   Feedback: use all available feedback to see how you did.
3   Fix-it: solve the problems and find a solution.

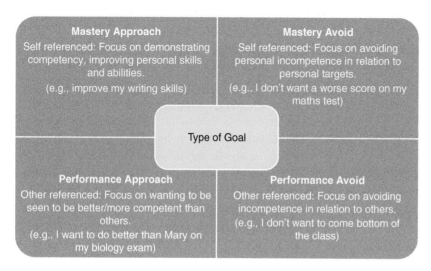

Figure 3.2.1 A representation of the different types of goals; adapted from Elliot and McGregor, 2002

If this approach is continuously employed, it helps to change the way pupils use goal setting to develop their skills and competencies. The recent work of Gervis and Williams (2017) has shown how these principles develop expertise in coaching. However, they can be applied to a different context, including developing your expertise as a teacher. Pupils' perceptions of the motivational climate (that is, the goal orientation of the classroom and school) has been found to be important for their motivation and adjustment to school. There is a relationship between pupils' perceptions of a lesson as being task-oriented and adaptive motivational responses, including increased intrinsic motivation. Pupils are motivated by teachers who know, support, challenge and encourage them to act independently from each other and from the teacher. An autonomy-supportive environment is one in which the teacher gives increasing responsibility to pupils (for example, for choices/options about what they want to do); encourages pupils' decision-making by spending less time talking, more time listening, making less directive comments, asking more questions and not giving pupils solutions; allows pupils to work in their own way; and offers more praise and verbal approval in class. Such an environment supports pupils' academic and social growth by increasing intrinsic and self-motivation to succeed at school, self-confidence, perceived competence and self-esteem. On the other hand, there is a relationship between pupils' perceptions of a lesson as being outcome-oriented and maladaptive motivational responses. Such a lesson focuses on individual achievement and competition between individuals. This may foster extrinsic motivation and discourage hard work and effort to achieve success by pupils who fail to achieve the outcome. Further, controlling environments (teachers attempt to guide pupils' thinking by providing specific guidelines for their academic and personal behaviours in class) have been found to have a negative effect on perceived competence and participation, which results in decreased intrinsic and self-motivation. Research by Manouchehri (2004) has found a relationship between the motivational style adopted by teachers of mathematics and their commitment to implementing new teaching methods. Those adopting an autonomy-supportive style of motivation increase pupils' participation and engagement by, for example, creating more opportunities for pupils to examine and develop their understanding of mathematical ideas, to listen to the arguments and to ask questions of other pupils.

Figure 3.2.2 illustrates the link between teachers' actions in creating the motivational climate and pupils' responses, which influences their intrinsic motivation.

Although their motivations change with age, it is generally accepted that pupils are more likely to try harder if they can see a link between the amount of effort they make and success in the activity. Indeed, there is a link between achievement goal theory and attribution theory in that pupils with a high need to achieve attribute their success to internal causes (for example, aptitude and effort), while they attribute failure to lack of effort. On the other hand, pupils with a low need to achieve attribute their failure to external factors (for example, bad luck). Therefore, as a teacher, you should design activities that encourage pupils to attribute success or failure to effort. However, this is not always easy. Postlethwaite (1993) identified the difficulty of determining how much effort a pupil has made on a piece of work (especially that done at home) and hence the problems of marking the work. No doubt you can think of occasions where one person has made a lot of effort on a piece of homework, but missed the point and received a low mark, whereas another person has rushed through the homework and managed to achieve a good mark. In 'norm-referenced' marking, a certain percentage of the class are given a designated category of mark, no matter how good each individual piece of work. Thus, each pupil's mark for a piece of work is given solely for their performance compared to that of the rest of the group. This encourages success or failure to be attributed to ability or luck. In 'criterion-referenced' marking, all pupils who meet stated criteria for

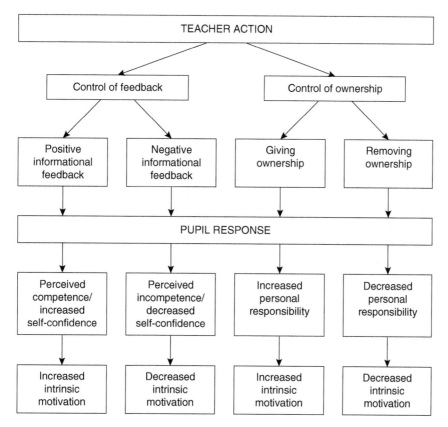

Figure 3.2.2 Creating a motivational climate

a particular category of mark are marked in that category. Thus, pupils are given a mark that reflects how closely the criteria for the assessment have been met, irrespective of the performance of other pupils. Although this overcomes some of the disadvantages of norm-referenced marking, it does not reflect how much effort the pupil has put into the work. Postlethwaite (1993) went on to say that effort can best be judged by comparing different pieces of the same pupil's work, as the standard of work is likely to reflect the amount of effort put in (that is, ipsative assessment). Giving two marks for the work, one for content and standard of the work and one for effort and presentation, can encourage effort. Thus, even if the content and standard are poor, it may be possible to praise the effort. This praise can motivate the pupil to try harder, especially if the pupil values the mark for effort. He suggested that another way of encouraging pupils to attribute success to effort is to ask them to write about the way they tackled the task (see also Units 6.1 and 6.2 on assessment).

According to expectancy theory, a teacher forms an impression of a pupil on which they base their expectations of that pupil; the teacher's verbal and non-verbal behaviour is based, consciously or unconsciously, on those expectations; the pupil recognises, consciously or unconsciously, the teacher's expectations of them from their behaviour and responds in a way that matches these expectations. Thus, there is a self-fulfilling prophecy. It is generally accepted that if a teacher expects high achievement and good behaviour, pupils perform to the best of their ability and behave well. Murdock (1999) found that when teachers held high expectations of pupils, they were more engaged academically. If, on the other hand, teachers have low expectations of pupils' achievement and behaviour, pupils achieve little and behave badly. In the same way, teachers can develop stereotypes of how different groups of pupils perform or behave; stereotypes can direct expectations (see also Unit 4.4).

One aspect of the organisation of a school that may particularly influence teachers' expectations of pupils is the way pupils are grouped. Pupils streamed by ability remain in the same group throughout the year, whatever their ability in different subjects. Whatever the labels attached to each stream, pupils are perceptive and judge their abilities by the stream they are in. This may be partly because teachers' verbal and non-verbal behaviour communicates clearly their expectations. Teachers expect pupils in the 'top' stream to do well; therefore, they behave accordingly; for example, actively encouraging pupils, setting challenging work. Teachers do not expect pupils in the 'bottom' stream to do as well; therefore, they behave accordingly; for example, constantly nagging pupils, setting easy work (or none at all). Both groups of pupils tend to fulfil the expectations of teachers. No doubt, many of you have heard of the notorious 'bottom' stream in a school. Setting (or banding) pupils for different subjects can overcome problems of streaming; that is, recognising pupils' ability in different subjects and changing the grouping of pupils according to their ability in a specific subject. The problem can also be overcome by grouping pupils in mixed-ability classes and providing differentiated work to enable pupils of different abilities to work alongside each other on tasks that are challenging but achievable for each pupil (see achievement motivation above). For further information about grouping and differentiation, see Unit 4.1.

Self-determination theory has contributed significantly to the current understanding of motivation to learn in a classroom setting. As mentioned earlier, two distinct, yet interrelated, aspects of motivation need to be considered: intrinsic and extrinsic motivation. Unlike other one-dimensional theories, both are considered to be important in establishing an effective motivational climate in the classroom. There is an accepted view that intrinsic motivation refers to activities that an individual engages in because they find them inherently interesting and satisfying. We know that teachers can be instrumental in creating the 'right' conditions for intrinsic motivation to flourish. Furthermore, research has found that teachers have a significant contribution to make in either undermining or facilitating intrinsic motivation in their pupils (Ryan and Stiller, 1991). When intrinsic motivation is increased, pupils demonstrate high-quality learning and high levels of creativity, both of which are desirable and should be cultivated by teachers in the classroom. In order to understand why this happens, we need to look further into self-determination theory.

Ryan and Deci (2000b) highlight three important innate needs that underpin motivation; these are: competence, autonomy and relatedness. While each of these may appear to be separate and distinct, they interact with each other and mediate behavioural outcomes. Therefore, the motivation of an individual is a function of these factors. In order to enhance motivation in a pupil, the teacher needs to consider how they are working in relation to each of these. So, for example, effective positive feedback can enhance an individual's feeling of competence and, consequently, intrinsic motivation is increased. However, this does not occur unless accompanied by an increased sense of autonomy. The role of a teacher can be instrumental in enhancing feelings of competence through their interpersonal interactions with pupils and frameworks, such as reward systems, that they put in place. There is substantive evidence to support the notion that teachers who adopt an autonomy-supportive approach are catalysts for their pupils' intrinsic motivation (Deci et al., 1981).

In self-determination theory, extrinsic motivation is also considered to be an important factor in regulating behaviour. The key factor is the degree to which an individual has 'internalised' the extrinsic factor as this directly impacts autonomy. The greater the internalisation, the more autonomous the individual feels, which, in turn, enhances intrinsic motivation. Specifically, it is the relationship between 'internalisation' and 'integration' that is seen to be essential in contributing to how individuals perceive their own competence and self-determination. Figure 3.2.3 relates self-determination theory to flying a kite; it is important for a teacher to focus on developing both competence and autonomy at the same time (as it is important to pull both strings on a kite to keep it in the air).

In order for positive psychology to make a contribution in the classroom, you need to consider five critical elements that are the foundations for well-being and flourishing: positive emotion, engagement, relationships, meaning and achievement (PERMA). If you create a classroom environment where pupils are engaged and find purpose and meaning in the activities you ask them to do, this will offer opportunities for them to achieve and flourish. Furthermore, the quality of the relationship between teacher and pupil also impacts on their learning and well-being. A relationship that is open, trusting and supportive helps your pupils flourish.

Task 3.2.2 asks you to think about the hierarchy of needs theory. Task 3.2.3 asks you to think about the application of these theories to your teaching.

 Task 3.2.2   Hierarchy of needs

Consider some of the home conditions likely to leave pupils with unmet needs that prevent effective learning at school. Discuss with your tutor or another student teacher what can be done in the school and what you can do in your lessons that may help pupils to meet these basic needs to provide a foundation for effective learning. Discuss when and to whom you should report if you suspect pupils' most basic needs are not being met, as this may require the skills of other professionals. Store the information in your PDP.

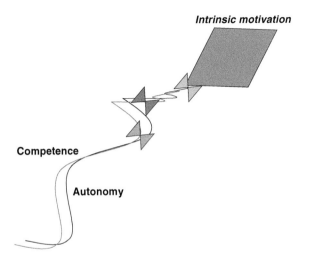

Figure 3.2.3 Developing competence and autonomy to enhance intrinsic motivation

> ✎ **Task 3.2.3   Using theories of motivation in your teaching**
>
> Review a range of literature on theories of motivation. Write a reflective commentary on these.
>
> Work in a group with other student teachers. Each select one theory of motivation. Use the information and the implications for teachers in Table 3.2.1 and in the text above as a basis for identifying practical implications of the theory for your lessons. Use this as the basis for planning for motivating pupils in one of your lessons based on this theory of motivation. Ask your tutor to observe the lesson and give you feedback on the effectiveness of your motivation. Record your own reflections. Meet with your group and discuss the theory, your lesson and reflection, then identify ways that you can improve. Repeat the cycle of planning, teaching the lesson, reflecting and evaluating your effectiveness. Record the outcomes of your own and other student teachers' work in your PDP.
>
> You might then like to try this using other theories of motivation.

Some specific factors that influence pupils' motivation to learn

One newly qualified teacher highlighted the following as factors that she has found important in motivating pupils to learn (Titchmarsh, 2012):

- if you are enthusiastic, pupils are enthusiastic;
- if you are in a bad mood, pupils pick up on it. You therefore need to cultivate a 'game face' for your teaching that does not show how you feel behind it;
- if pupils are bored, they are not going to be motivated. On the other hand, if they are doing an activity they enjoy, they are going to be motivated to learn;
- give pupils ownership of tasks to enhance feelings of autonomy;
- pupils should not copy from a textbook as it is boring and does not encourage enquiry-based learning, which is generally more motivating;
- many pupils find difficulty with independent learning as they have not learned how/not been encouraged, to do it. It takes time and effort to teach pupils how to be independent learners, but it is worth it in the long run. If you do this from the start, they know what to expect. This then needs to be reinforced and they need to be encouraged to be independent;
- in subjects where it is applicable (for example, geography), taking pupils out of the classroom motivates them. However, once you get them out of the classroom, you need to have a good lesson plan for them;
- pupils have to see the point in the activity, what they are going to have achieved and how they are going to have achieved it. There is no point in having an all-singing-and-dancing lesson if the pupils do not see the point. This has to be clear;
- pupils will not be motivated or engaged if the work is too hard and they cannot access it, or it is too easy. Therefore, you need to differentiate the work;
- some pupils are difficult. Sit and have a frank discussion with them about what interests them, what helps them learn, and so on so you can tailor your lessons for them;

- give pupils (part of) a topic each to research and teach to others. This can be tailored to their ability. Tell them that what they teach will form the foundation for all pupils in the class. Normally, pupils do not want to let their peers down, so they work hard at this task;
- using examples of good work gives a lift to those whose work is highlighted but also shows other pupils what is needed;
- give verbal praise in the classroom;
- give merits or credits, following the school's rewards and sanctions policy;
- give stickers to younger pupils (for example, stars or smiley faces) for good work/answers.

Extrinsic motivation is sometimes used to encourage intrinsic motivation. However, it is important to recognise that motivating pupils extrinsically can have a detrimental effect when a pupil is already motivated intrinsically (see also Unit 5.6 on neuroscience).

Personal achievement (success)

Personal achievement (generally called 'success' in an outcome-oriented learning environment) is generally motivating in itself. Some pupils struggle to succeed, whereas others succeed much more quickly. There are many ways to help pupils succeed, such as using whole-part-whole teaching. In this, pupils are shown the whole activity first so that they know what they are trying to achieve. The activity is then broken down into small, self-contained, achievable parts, which allows pupils to receive reinforcement for each small, successful step. The separate parts of the activity are gradually put together until the whole activity has been built up. Pupils are given appropriate feedback at each stage (see giving feedback below); therefore, when they attempt the whole, they are more likely to succeed. You may relate to this by thinking about when you learned (or tried to learn) front crawl in swimming. You probably practiced your arms, legs and breathing separately before you tried to put it all together (see Task 3.2.4). What other techniques can you use to help pupils succeed? (See also Unit 2.2 on lesson planning.)

 Task 3.2.4   Whole-part-whole teaching

As part of your normal lesson planning with a class, select one activity you can break down into small, self-contained, achievable parts, which can be put together to build up gradually to the whole. Ask your tutor or another student teacher to observe you teaching this activity using whole-part-whole teaching. At the end of the lesson, discuss with some of the pupils how this went. Discuss with the observer how the pupils responded and how well they learned the task. Evaluate the lesson yourself, store in your PDP and build on this experience in future lessons.

The use of performance profiling techniques to enhance pupils' motivation by engaging them in self-assessment, but also in the process of goal setting, can be a valuable tool. This helps pupils identify their own personal successes but also areas for development. Performance profiling is based on Kelly's (1955) personal construct theory, which maintains that each individual holds unique cognitive constructs about the world and the self. It is through these that we all construct our own reality, and, consequently, we are the best experts on ourselves. As we develop, these constructs are changed and modified through our experiences and knowledge and understanding of the world. This theory suggests that, in order to understand another, first we have to be able to see the world from their perspective. Thus, for the teacher to enhance motivation, it is helpful if they have an understanding of their pupils' perspectives. (Bourdieu's theory may give you a framework to identify factors influencing pupils' motivation.)

The process entails first asking pupils to identify key factors that they think are essential to be successful learners; these could be subject-specific or more generic. This discussion should focus on identifying key factors perceived to be critical from the pupils' perspective. Through class discussion, you can agree on the final list. This can be as long or short as you want.

Once identified, these key factors can be added to the profile chart (see Figure 3.2.4). Each pupil can then complete their own profile by identifying their perceived strengths and weaknesses in relation to each of the key factors. The teacher can also complete their own chart for each pupil.

This creates a means to compare the pupil perspective with that of the teacher and can be a starting point for discussion. Through discussion, pupil and teacher can gain better insight and understanding into how the pupil sees themself. So, for example, if a pupil has rated themself as a '4' on one factor and the teacher rated them as a '7', this provides a useful framework for mutual understanding. It also provides a clear visual representation of the pupil's strengths and weaknesses, which makes it tangible. Strengths and weaknesses can be recorded in a table such as Table 3.2.2.

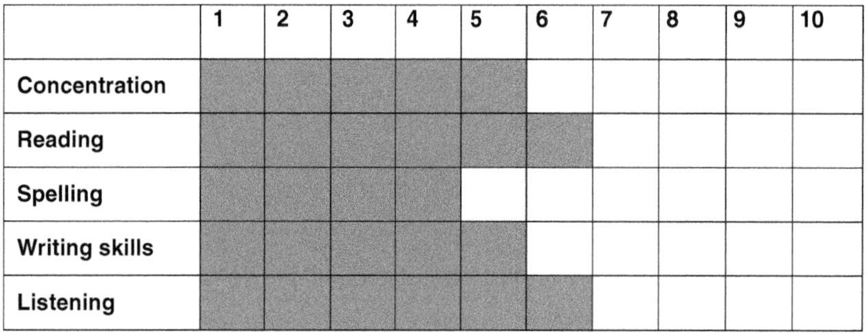

	1	2	3	4	5	6	7	8	9	10
Concentration	■	■	■	■	■					
Reading	■	■	■	■	■	■				
Spelling	■	■	■	■		■				
Writing skills	■	■	■	■	■					
Listening	■	■	■	■	■	■				

Figure 3.2.4 Example performance profile (1 = very poor, 10 = excellent)

Table 3.2.2 Identifying key areas of excellence and key areas of improvement

Key areas of excellence	Key areas for improvement
For example, listening	For example, spelling

Once the profile has been created, it can become an effective monitoring system and a focal point for goal setting. By agreeing the actions that need to be taken to address the profile and set goals, the pupil is able to take ownership of the process. In accordance with self-determination theory, we know that, by increasing autonomy, intrinsic motivation is increased. This process creates a platform from which this can develop. Furthermore, we know that changes in behaviour can only be initiated with the complete agreement of the individual, and this process ensures that the pupil is able to 'buy into' their own action plan to achieve success. Progress can be monitored through repeated profiles, which can provide a direct comparison to previous profiles, and serve to visibly map change and achievement towards the agreed goals.

Rewards

Although personal achievement or success is motivating in itself, pupils may not be immediately successful on activities that they undertake at school; therefore, they may need external rewards (positive reinforcements) to motivate them. Bull and Solity (1987) identified four types of rewards, listed below in the order in which they are used most often:

- social rewards (social contact and pleasant interactions with other people, including praise, a smile to recognise an action or achievement or to say thank you, encouraging remarks or a gesture of approval);
- token rewards (house points, grades, certificates);
- activity rewards (opportunities for enjoyable activities);
- material rewards (tangible, usable or edible items).

Task 3.2.5 focuses on these four types of reward.

 Task 3.2.5   Using rewards

Develop an observation schedule with sections for the four types of reward listed above. Observe a class and mark in the appropriate category any reward used by the teacher in the class. Discuss with the teacher the variety and frequency of use of the different possible methods of reward, as well as why a particular type of reward was used to achieve a particular purpose. Ask your tutor or another student teacher to undertake the same observation on one of your lessons. Discuss the differences in variety and frequency of reward used. As you plan your lessons, consider how you might use rewards. Ask the same person to observe a lesson a couple of months after the first one and see if you have changed your use of reward in your lessons. Relate this to what you know about behavioural learning theories. Record your notes in your PDP.

Praise

Generally, pupils respond more positively to praise and positive comments about their work or behaviour than to criticism and negative comments. This, in turn, may produce a motivational learning environment in which pupils work harder and behave better. If pupils misbehave in a classroom in which there is a positive motivational learning environment, Olweus (1993, p.85) suggested that the use of praise makes pupils feel appreciated, which may make it easier for them to accept criticism of inappropriate behaviour and to attempt to change.

However, the Office for Standards in Education, Children's Services and Skills (Ofsted, 1993) reported that teachers give relatively little praise and that their vocabulary is generally more negative than positive. Praise is given more often for academic than social behaviour, and social behaviour is more likely to be criticised than praised. One reason for this may be that teachers expect pupils to behave appropriately in the classroom.

Some teachers use very few different words to praise pupils; for example, 'good', 'well done', 'OK'. What other words can you use to praise someone or give feedback? Try to develop a list of such words because if you use the same word to praise pupils all the time, the word loses its effect. The range of words must be accompanied by appropriate non-verbal communication signals (see non-verbal communication in Unit 3.1 and Task 3.2.6).

 Task 3.2.6   The language of praise

Use the observation schedule below (or develop a similar one of your own with categories for praise and negative comments given to an individual, a group or the whole class, for both academic work and behaviour).

Tick each time praise or negative comment is given in each category					
Praise to individual for academic work					
Praise to group for academic work					
Praise to whole class for academic work					
Praise to individual for effort					
Praise to group for effort					
Praise to whole class for effort					
Praise to individual for perseverance					
Praise to group for perseverance					
Praise to whole class for perseverance					
Praise to individual for behaviour					
Praise to group for behaviour					
Praise to whole class for behaviour					
Negative comment to individual for academic work					
Negative comment to group for academic work					
Negative comment to whole class for academic work					
Negative comment to individual for effort					
Negative comment to group for effort					
Negative comment to whole class for effort					
Negative comment to individual for perseverance					
Negative comment to group for perseverance					

Negative comment to whole class for perseverance					
Negative comment to individual for behaviour					
Negative comment to group for behaviour					
Negative comment to whole class for behaviour					

Observe a class taught by an experienced teacher. Sit in a place where you can hear everything that is said. Record the number of times the teacher gives praise and makes negative comments to individuals, groups and the whole class in relation to academic work, effort, perseverance and behaviour. Observe the same experienced teacher in another lesson. This time, write down the different words, phrases and actions the teacher uses to give praise and negative comments in each of these categories and the number of times each is used.

Ask someone to conduct the same observations on your lessons. Discuss the differences with your tutor and, if appropriate, develop strategies to help you improve the amount of praise you give and the range of words, phrases and actions you use to give praise (you might be surprised to find that you use a phrase such as 'good' or 'OK' very frequently in your teaching). Record these strategies in your PDP and gradually try to incorporate them into your teaching.

Although it is generally accepted that praise aids learning, there are dangers in using praise. There are times when it may not be appropriate. For example, pupils who become lazy about their work as a result of complacency may respond by working harder if their work is gently criticised on occasion. If praise is given automatically, regardless of the work, effort or behaviour, pupils quickly see through it and it loses its effect. Praise should only be used to reward appropriate achievement, effort or behaviour.

Some pupils do not respond positively to praise; for example, they are embarrassed, especially if they are praised in front of their peers. Others perceive praise to be a form of punishment; for example, if they are teased or rejected by their peers for being 'teacher's pet' or for behaving themselves in class. Thus, conforming to the behaviours and values promoted in school results in negative social consequences. Therefore, although pupils know that they will be rewarded for achievement, effort or behaviour, they may also be aware of the norms of the peer group, which discourage them from achieving academically, making an effort or behaving well.

Other pupils do not know how to respond to praise because they have not received much praise in the past; for example, because they have continually received low marks for their work or because they have been in the bottom stream. They have therefore learned to fail. Some of these pupils may want to attribute failure to not caring or not trying to succeed. One way they may do this is by not making an effort with work; another way is misbehaving in the classroom.

Thus, pupils respond differently to praise. In the same class, you may have some pupils working hard to receive praise from the teacher or a good mark on their homework, while others do not respond well to praise or are working hard at avoiding praise. You have to use your judgement when giving praise; for example, if you praise a pupil who is misbehaving to try to encourage better behaviour, you may be seen to be rewarding bad behaviour, thereby motivating the pupil to continue to misbehave in order to get attention. If you are not immediately successful in your use of praise, do not give up using it, but consider whether you are giving it in the right way; for example, would it be better to have a quiet word, rather than praise pupils out loud in front of their peers? As your professional knowledge and judgement develop, you become able to determine how best to use praise appropriately to motivate pupils in your classes.

Punishment

As well as using praise, teachers also use punishment to try to change behaviour. However, reward, most frequently in the form of praise, is generally considered to be more effective because it increases appropriate behaviour, whereas punishment decreases inappropriate behaviour. If pupils are punished, they know what behaviour results in punishment and, therefore, what not to do, but may not know what behaviour avoids punishment.

However, there are times when punishment is needed. At such times, make sure that you use punishment to best effect; for example, avoid punishing a whole class for the behaviour of one or a few pupil(s), always make it clear which pupil(s) are being punished for what behaviour and always give punishment fairly and consistently and in proportion to the offence. Also, make sure that the punishment does not include the behaviour you want exhibited (for example, do not punish a pupil by requiring them to run around the football pitch if that is what you had wanted them to do). This sends mixed messages and is likely to put the pupil off that activity. Do not make idle threats to pupils by threatening them with punishment you cannot carry out. In order to increase appropriate behaviour, identify to the offender any positive aspects of the behaviour being punished and explain the appropriate behaviour (see also Units 3.3 and 4.5).

Feedback

It may be that pupils who do not respond positively to praise are underperforming and have been doing so for a long time. You may be able to check whether they are underperforming by comparing assessment data over a period of time to measure current achievement with past achievement. The achievement of all pupils, including underperforming pupils, can be enhanced by receiving feedback on their work. Feedback is a formative process that gives pupils information about how they are doing and whether they are on the right track when learning something. This motivates them to make an effort and to continue.

A pupil is more likely to learn effectively or behave appropriately if feedback is used in conjunction with praise. A sequence in which feedback is sandwiched between praise (that is, praise-constructive feedback-praise) is designed to provide encouragement and motivation, along with information to help the pupil improve the activity or behaviour. Giving praise first is designed to make pupils more receptive to the information and, afterwards, to have a positive approach to try again. Try combining feedback with praise in your teaching. Be careful how you use the word 'but' when giving feedback, especially when using the sandwich approach. The power of this small word has the effect of devaluing everything that comes before it. So, for example, if you said, 'Well done for your concentration in class today *but* your writing needs attention', the pupil will not acknowledge the praise; it is as if you have not said it. If, however, you replace 'but' with 'and', it changes the message and the emotional response to it. If you said, 'Well done for your concentration in class today *and* your writing needs attention', the praise element will still be acknowledged.

By observing pupils very carefully, you are able to spot small changes or improvements, which allows you to provide appropriate feedback (Unit 2.1 looks at observation techniques and Unit 6.1 focuses on assessment for learning). Feedback can be used effectively with the whole-part-whole teaching method (see above). If you give feedback about how a pupil has done on each part, this part can be improved before going on to the next part. If you give feedback immediately (that is, as an attempt is being finished or immediately after it has finished, but before another attempt is started), pupils can relate the feedback directly to the outcome of the activity. Thus, pupils are more likely to succeed if they take small steps and receive immediate feedback on each step. This success can, in turn, lead to increased motivation to continue the activity.

One problem with giving immediate feedback is how you can provide feedback to individual pupils in a class who are all doing the same activity at the same time. There are several methods you can use to provide feedback to many pupils at the same time; for example, getting pupils to work through examples in a book that has the answers in the back, or setting criteria and letting pupils evaluate themselves against the criteria or having pupils assess one another against set criteria (Unit 5.3 covers teaching strategies and styles, including the reciprocal teaching style of Mosston and Ashworth, 2002). If they have been properly prepared for it, pupils are generally sensible and constructive when given responsibility for giving feedback. In Task 3.2.7, the focus is on pupils giving feedback to each other.

 Task 3.2.7   Pupils giving feedback

As an integral part of your lesson planning, select one activity in which pupils can observe each other and provide feedback. Devise a handout with the main points/criteria to be observed. Plan how you are going to introduce this activity into the lesson. Discuss the lesson plan with your tutor. Ask your tutor to observe the lesson. Discuss the effectiveness of the strategy afterwards, determining how you can improve its use. Also, try to observe teachers who plan for pupils to observe and give feedback to each other. Try the strategy at a later date in your school experience. Identify other ways in which you can get more feedback to more pupils when they are doing an activity and record in your PDP. Include these in your lesson plans, as appropriate (see also teaching styles in Unit 5.3).

However, it is not always appropriate to give immediate feedback.

Not all feedback comes from another person (for example, the teacher or another pupil); feedback also comes from the activity itself. The feedback from an activity may be easier to identify for some activities than others; for example, a pupil gets feedback about their success if an answer to a mathematics problem matches that given in the book or the wicket is knocked down when bowling in cricket. In other activities, right or wrong, success or failure, is not as clear-cut; for example, there is often no right or wrong answer to an English essay. In the early stages of learning an activity, pupils find it hard to use the feedback from the activity; for example, they may notice that they were successful at the activity, but not be able to identify why. Normally, therefore, they need feedback from another person. This immediate, external feedback can be used to help pupils become more aware of what they are doing, how they are improving, why they were successful or not at the activity, and therefore to make use of feedback from the activity. Later in the learning (for example, when refining an activity), pupils should be able to benefit from feedback from the activity itself, and, therefore, it is better to encourage this internal feedback by, for example, asking appropriate questions, such as, 'How did that feel?' In this situation, the teacher should not give immediate feedback.

Finally, to be effective, feedback should be given about pupils' work or behaviour, not about the pupils themselves. It must convey to pupils that their work or behaviour is satisfactory or not, not that they are good (or bad), per se.

Motivating individuals and the class as a whole

As the discussion above has highlighted, there is no one correct way to motivate pupils to learn. Different motivation techniques are appropriate and effective in different situations; for example, pupils of different ages respond differently to different types of motivation, reward, punishment or feedback. Likewise, individual pupils respond differently. Further, any one pupil may respond to the same motivator differently at different times and in different situations.

Pupils need to feel that they are individuals, with their needs and interests taken into account, rather than just being a member of a group. Pupils need to be given opportunities to take ownership of the tasks in which they are engaged. If pupils are not motivated or bored, do not let them avoid doing an activity, but try to find ways of motivating them, such as by relating it to something in which they are interested. You can motivate pupils most effectively by using motivation techniques appropriate for a particular pupil in a particular situation.

Therefore, you need to get to know pupils as individuals. Learning pupils' names quickly gives you a start in being able to motivate pupils effectively (Unit 2.2 provides advice on learning pupils' names). Observation of pupils, talking to them and discussing a pupil with the form tutor or other teachers all help. As you get to know your pupils well, you can identify what motivates them by finding out what activities they enjoy, what they choose to do and what they try to avoid, and what types of reward they work for and to what they do not respond, as well as their needs and interests.

The sooner you can relate to pupils individually, the sooner you can manage a class of individuals effectively. However, this does not occur at an early phase of your development as a teacher. As a student teacher, you are at a disadvantage here because you do not usually spend enough time in one school to get to know the pupils well, and, therefore, you can only try to motivate individual pupils by using your knowledge and understanding of pupils of that age.

However, there is one further element to motivation to consider briefly here. The same principles can also be applied to enhance the collective motivation of a class. By engaging pupils in discussions about 'what kind of a class' they want to be, you can encourage pupils to elicit qualities that they think are necessary to enable all members of the class to succeed; for example, everyone to be on time and with the right materials, to respect others (and hence to listen quietly when someone else is talking), to work hard, to do their homework, and so on. Thus, in essence, they create a class profile (similar to that in Figure 3.2.4 created for an individual pupil) that enables the collective perspective to be represented. Giving pupils ownership of the profile they create contributes significantly towards collective motivation and behaviour modification in line with the desired outcome. Consequently, if there is collective buy-in, pupils monitor each other's behaviour and work to reinforce the key aspects identified on the profile. The benefit for you is that the pupils can help you with class management.

SUMMARY AND KEY POINTS

- This unit has identified some theoretical underpinnings, general principles and techniques for achieving an appropriate motivational climate in your lessons to increase pupils' motivation to learn. However, you need to be able to use these appropriately. For example, if you praise a group for working quietly while they are working, you may negatively affect their work. It is better in this situation to let the group finish their work and then praise them.
- In addition, pupils are individuals and therefore respond differently to different forms of motivation, reward, punishment and feedback. Further, the same pupil responds differently at different times and in different situations.
- To motivate each pupil effectively, therefore, requires that you know your pupils so that you can anticipate how they will respond.
- Motivation is supported by good formative assessment techniques (see Unit 6.1). Your developing professional knowledge and judgement enables you to combine theory with practice to motivate pupils effectively in your classes, which raises the standard of their work.

Check which requirements for your ITE programme you have addressed through this unit.

 Further resources

Child, D. (2007) *Psychology and the Teacher*, **8th Edition, London: Continuum.**
   Chapter 8 provides in-depth consideration of motivation in education. It starts by considering three broad types of theories of motivation, then looks specifically at how some of the theories of motivation impact on you as a teacher and on your pupils.

Gilbert, I. (2002) *Essential Motivation in the Classroom*, **London: RoutledgeFalmer.**
   This book covers strategies, ideas and advice to help teachers understand how to motivate pupils and how pupils can motivate themselves.

Kyriacou, C. (2014) *Essential Teaching Skills*, **4th Edition, Cheltenham: Stanley Thornes.**
   This book contains chapters on lesson management and classroom climate, both of which consider aspects of motivation, such as whether lesson management helps to maintain pupils' motivation and whether the opportunities for learning are challenging and offer realistic opportunities for success.

Appendix 2 lists subject associations and teacher councils and Appendix 3 provides a list of websites.

Capel, S., Leask, M. and Turner, T. (eds.) (2010) *Readings for Learning to Teach in the Secondary School: A Companion to M Level Study*, **Abingdon: Routledge.**
   This book brings together essential readings to support you in your critical engagement with key issues raised in this textbook.

Capel, S., Lawrence, J. Leask, M. and Younie, S. (eds.) (2019) *Surviving and Thriving in the Secondary School: The NQT's Essential Companion*, **Abingdon: Routledge.**
   This book is designed to support newly qualified teachers in the next phase of development as a teacher. However, you may find it useful as it covers aspects of teaching not included in this book which, nonetheless you experience on your ITE programme.

The subject specific books in the *Learning to Teach (Subject)* series, the *Practical (Subject) Guides*, *Debates in (Subject)* and *Mentoring (Subject) Teachers* are also very useful.

 Any additional resources and an editable version of any relevant tasks/tables in this unit are available on the companion website: www.routledge.com/cw/capel

3.3 Managing classroom behaviour

Adopting a positive approach

Philip Garner

Introduction

This unit is designed to enable you to enhance your knowledge and skills in classroom management, and especially to support the development of positive approaches for dealing with pupil behaviour. It takes account of some of the most recent shifts in thinking and policy in this important dimension of your initial teacher education (ITE) programme. This includes the most recent advice from the Department for Education (DfE) in England, providing practical, hands-on information to teachers (DfE, 2014f). This essential guidance reinforces earlier information (DfE, 2014a,b, p.6), which emphasised that '[t]eachers have statutory authority to discipline pupils whose behaviour is unacceptable, who break the school rules or who fail to follow a reasonable instruction'.

There has been a noticeable move away from reactive approaches to dealing with unwanted behaviour over the last 20 or more years. Such approaches were characterised by a preoccupation with 'discipline' being something that the teacher imposes on pupils (Robertson, 1996). Instead, a greater awareness of 'behaviour for learning' has become apparent, which is consistent with an accompanying quest to develop inclusive schooling for all pupils (Cheminais, 2010). Even so, it should be clearly understood that such an approach to pupil behaviour does not diminish the importance of clear and explicit classroom rules to govern pupil behaviour – and their consistent application. You need to ensure that pupils are under no illusions that, as class teacher, you are in control; it is, after all, what they expect of you!

A 'behaviour for learning' approach emphasises the teacher's role in creating an appropriate climate in which all pupils can learn effectively. It encourages you to link pupil behaviour with their learning via three interlinked relationships: how pupils think about themselves (their relationship with themselves); how they view their relationship with others (both teachers and fellow pupils); and how they perceive themselves as a learner, relative to the curriculum (their relationship with the learning they are undertaking). Recognition of the interplay between these three relationships is seen as the basis of a preventative approach. It also places importance on the role of the pupils themselves in learning to manage their own behaviour (Morgan and Ellis, 2011).

Understanding this way of working remains an important aspect of a teacher's role in managing pupil behaviour. The most recent advice continues to balance this with a requirement that all teachers – and especially new teachers – understand some basic guidelines regarding the way in which the occurrence of unacceptable behaviour by pupils in a classroom can be minimised. Such behaviour has been a consistent cause of concern on the part of teachers themselves, educational professionals, parents and politicians for many decades; some aspects of these concerns are dealt with in the section dealing with 'policy context'.

Current approaches to 'behaviour' in ITE programmes reflect the shift in emphasis in the way that the issue is being tackled. The focus is on a middle ground between the earlier focus on 'control' and 'discipline' and a more recent holistic approach that focuses more upon linking behaviour with achievement. This is captured, for example, in Tom Bennett's (2018) behaviour blog (http://behaviourguru.blogspot.co.uk/).

This unit does not provide detailed accounts of individual behavioural needs or characteristics. There is now an extensive literature relating to the practical aspects of behaviour management, which is widely accessible elsewhere (see, for example, Dix, 2010; Haydn, 2012). Rather, the unit concentrates on both the principles underpinning the links between pupil behaviour and the taught curriculum, as well as some of the important practical dimensions involved in effectively managing 'pupil discipline' in the classroom.

OBJECTIVES

At the end of this unit, you should be able to:

■ recognise the policy context in England for promoting pupil learning in classrooms;
■ interrogate a definition of the term 'unacceptable behaviour' and understand the significance of its underlying causes;
■ recognise the importance of the links between pupil behaviour and their curriculum learning;
■ understand the classroom implications of the current guidance to teachers regarding pupil behaviour;
■ develop positive approaches to unacceptable behaviour that are based on relationships with pupils.

Check the requirements for your ITE programme to see which relate to this unit.

The current context: official advice and guidance in England

This section outlines the policy context in England. If you are learning to teach outside England, ask your tutors about policy in your context. There has been an increasing emphasis upon the inclusion of a greater diversity of pupils in mainstream schools in the last 20 years (Department for Education and Employment (DfEE), 1999; Department for Education and Skills (DfES), 2001c, 2003a, DfE, 2014k). The underpinning ideology of educational inclusion is that the educational needs of all pupils in schools should be met, irrespective of their level of achievement or the nature of their behaviour (Winter, 2006). Thus, you will encounter a wide range of pupil needs in your first encounters in the classroom. Some pupils who exhibit what were termed social, emotional and behavioural difficulties (SEBD) and are now referred to as experiencing 'social, emotional and mental health' (SEMH) issues, will almost certainly be present in your classroom, even though recent changes in the Special Educational Needs and Disability (SEND) code of practice (DfE, 2014k) have resulted in this category of pupils being removed from the remit of Special Education Needs (SEN) provision. Such pupils have traditionally represented as many as 20 per cent of all pupils who have SEN (DfE, 2014k). The challenging behaviour of these pupils is usually accompanied by underachievement or a specific educational need. In consequence, they will most likely be supported by the special educational needs coordinator (SENCO), teaching assistants and by other key workers in the school (Webster, 2018).

SEMH, and formerly SEBD, are terms that refer to a continuum of behaviours, from relatively minor behaviour problems to serious mental illness (DfE, 1994b). In this unit, the focus is principally on pupil behaviours that are viewed as low-level unacceptable behaviours – in other words, not those towards the more serious end of the continuum. However, you may sometimes encounter pupils who present more challenging behaviours in your classroom, including some who may abuse drugs and other substances; pupils with mental health needs and pupils who experience behaviour-related syndromes, such as attention deficit hyperactivity disorder (ADHD) or autistic spectrum disorders (ASD). Many of these behaviours, including those that are sometimes intense and very challenging to teachers, can be more effectively managed if you build proactive, positive strategies into your teaching. There are also existing school strategies and support (including a key teacher or tutor) who are directly involved in dealing with these more extreme behaviours: these form part of a range of interventions, as noted by DfE (2017f). In addition, in instances when such pupils are present, support will frequently be available from a teaching assistant who will work with the pupil in your classroom.

One related aspect of pupil behaviour that requires special mention is bullying. Like other unacceptable behaviours, bullying varies in its type and intensity. The current guidance on bullying in schools, which you should become familiar with, is provided in *Preventing and Tackling Bullying: Advice for Headteachers Staff and Governing Bodies* (DfE, 2017d).

Finally, you are reminded that the Office for Standards in Education, Children's Services and Skills (Ofsted) handbook includes 'personal development, behaviour and welfare' as one of its key areas for each evaluation of schools (Ofsted, 2018b). As well as being intrinsic to becoming a successful classroom teacher, there is a statutory emphasis that behaviour is a feature of teaching that will be under continuing close scrutiny in England, and no doubt in other countries, in the years ahead.

Whole school behaviour policy

An important feature of a school's promotion of a 'positive climate', as well as its response to unacceptable behaviour, is the 'whole school behaviour policy' (DfE, 2014a,b; Bennett, 2017a). Moreover, everyone has a role to play in creating an appropriate behaviour culture in the school: 'It is vital that the behaviour policy is clear, that it is well understood by staff, parents and pupils, and that it is consistently applied' (DfE, 2014a,b, pp.5-6). As a matter of course, you should therefore make sure that you familiarise yourself with the content of the whole school behaviour policy in your placement school. Clear guidelines regarding its content are now widely understood (see Table 3.3.1); however, you should also recognise that individual schools vary according to the behaviour routines and rules they put in place.

Now complete Task 3.3.1.

Table 3.3.1 Content of a whole-school behaviour policy

1   a consistent approach to behaviour management;
2   strong school leadership;
3   classroom management;
4   rewards and sanctions;
5   behaviour strategies and the teaching of good behaviour;
6   staff development and support;
7   pupil support systems;
8   liaison with parents and other agencies;
9   managing pupil transition;
10   organisation and facilities.

 Task 3.3.1   School policy on pupil behaviour

Familiarise yourself with your placement school's whole-school policy on behaviour and attendance. Discuss it with another student teacher who is placed in a different school. Consider both the similarities and differences in the two policies. What are the implications of the document for you as a student teacher, particularly in respect of classroom management?

Record your reflections in your professional development portfolio (PDP) or equivalent.

A whole-school behaviour policy provides some of the basic building blocks that you use to help establish a positive classroom 'climate'; this term refers to the character or 'feel' of your classroom, as experienced by all those who come in contact with it – teachers, pupils and any classroom visitors. A major influence on this is the class teacher's own repertoire of knowledge, skills and understanding about pupil behaviour and classroom management. To assist you in acquiring these attributes, you may be assisted by lead behaviour teachers, tutors and other suitably experienced professionals who provide practical support in positively managing behaviour (Department for Children, Schools and Families (DCSF), 2008c; DfE, 2017a). In addition, further support can be provided by teachers from other educational settings, such as pupil referral units (PRUs), special schools for pupils experiencing SEMH, teaching assistants and local authority (LA) personnel who have a specific brief for work in SEMH (Walker, 2004).

Behaviour policies aim, among other things, to help teachers to promote positive behaviour and to support them in tackling issues of low-level unacceptable behaviour. They point to the importance of providing creative and positive learning environments for all pupils. They also provide a framework that you can use in order to develop a set of rules and routines based on the development of a positive relationship between yourself and the pupils. This is the first step in helping to insulate pupils from those factors (discussed later in this unit), which might cause them to behave inappropriately and, in consequence, fail to thrive as learners.

What is unacceptable behaviour?

Recent national advice and guidance on behaviour management in England emphasises the development of appropriate, positive behaviour that brings significant benefits for all pupils (Garner, 2011).

The guidance invites teachers to be clear about what behaviour they want pupils to engage in, and to model this as part of their teaching.

However, the term 'behaviour' has traditionally been taken to mean unacceptable behaviour. The Elton Report (Department of Education and Science (DES), 1989a) refers to misbehaviour as 'behaviour which causes concern to teachers'. The term is one that can variously be replaced by a range of other expressions that teachers use to describe unwanted, unacceptable behaviour by pupils. Thus, disruptive, challenging, antisocial, off-task, unwanted 'acting out' and withdrawn behaviours are all terms that are widely used, according to the personal orientation of the teacher concerned and to the type of problem behaviour being described.

The term 'unacceptable behaviour', as with its companion descriptors (see above), is often used as a catch-all expression for pupil behaviours that span a continuum (DfE, 1994b). The continuum ranges from low-level unacceptable behaviour at one end (such as talking out of turn, distracting others, occasionally arriving late in class) to more serious, sometimes acting out behaviour, at the other (such as non-attendance, verbal or physical aggression, wilful disobedience and bullying). This confusion was recognised by DfE (1994b), which described emotional and behavioural difficulties (EBD) as all those behaviours that comprise a continuum from 'normal though unacceptable' to mental illness. Confusion rather than clarity over definitions seemed to increase when the term EBD subsequently incorporated social and mental health difficulties into the spectrum, so that it is now referred to as SEMH – an even broader spectrum of behaviours.

A previous version of the current *SEN Code of Practice* (DfES, 2001a, p.93) defined 'children and young people who demonstrate features of emotional and behavioural difficulties' as those who are 'withdrawn and isolated, disruptive and disturbing, hyperactive and lacking concentration'. The definition also included those who display 'immature social skills and those who present challenging behaviours arising from other complex special needs'.

One of the major difficulties in defining what inappropriate behaviour constitutes is that it varies according to the perception, tolerance threshold, experience and management approach of individual teachers. What might be an unacceptable behaviour in your own classroom may be viewed in another context, or by another (student) teacher, as quite normal. Alternatively, what you accept as normal may be seen as unacceptable in another context or by another (student) teacher. This leads to confusion in the mind of pupils, and to potential tension between individual teachers in a school or between a student teacher and tutor or other experienced teacher. So, it is important to recognise that: (a) pupil behaviour is described explicitly in terms of observable actions; and (b) responses to it take full regard of a school's policy concerning behaviour and apply it with consistency. When you describe a pupil behaviour, you should always ensure that your definition is of the behaviour itself and not a description of the pupil as a whole. This avoids any likelihood of the pupil being labelled as a disruptive pupil or a problem pupil.

The Qualifications and Curriculum Authority (QCA, 2001b) usefully identified 15 behaviours by which a pupil's emotional and behavioural development might be defined and assessed. These were divided into learning behaviours, conduct behaviours and emotional behaviours. Each group is subdivided into sets of criteria, depicting desirable and undesirable behaviours (see Figure 3.3.1).

Task 3.3.2 helps you to develop a definition of unacceptable behaviour.

DESIRABLE BEHAVIOUR	**UNDESIRABLE BEHAVIOUR**
L1. Attentive/interested in schoolwork • attentive to teacher, not easily distracted • interest in most schoolwork/starts promptly on set tasks/motivated • seems to enjoy school	• verbal off-task behaviours • does not finish work/gives up easily • constantly needs reminders/low attention span • negative approach to school
L2. Good learning organisation • competent in individual learning • tidy work at reasonable pace • can organise learning tasks	• forgetful, copies or rushes work • inaccurate, messy and slow work • fails to meet deadlines, not prepared
L3. Effective communicator • good communication skills (peers/adults) • knows when it's appropriate to speak • uses non-verbal signals and voice range • communicates in 1:1 or group settings	• poor communication skills • inappropriate timing of communication • constantly talks • lack of use of non-verbal skills
L4. Works efficiently in a group • works collaboratively • turn-takes in communication/listens • takes responsibility within a group	• refuses to share • does not take turns
L5. Seeks help where necessary • seeks attention from teacher when required • works independently or in groups when not requiring help	• constantly seeking assistance • makes excessive and inappropriate demands • does not ask 'finding out' questions
C6. Behaves respectfully towards staff • cooperative and compliant • responds positively to instruction • does not aim verbal aggression at teacher • interacts politely with teacher • does not deliberately try to annoy or answer the teacher rudely	• responds negatively to instruction • talks back impertinently to teacher • aims verbal aggression, swears at teacher • deliberately interrupts to annoy
C7. Shows respect to other pupils • uses appropriate language; does not swear • treats others as equals • does not dominate, bully or intimidate	• verbal violence at other pupils • scornful, use of social aggression (e.g. 'pushing in') • teases and bullies • inappropriate sexual behaviour
C8. Seeks attention appropriately • does not attract inappropriate attention • does not play the fool or show off • no attention-seeking behaviour • does not verbally disrupt • does not physically disrupt	• hums, fidgets, disturbs others • throws things, climbs on things • calls out. eats, runs around the class • shouts and otherwise attention seeks • does dangerous things without thought

Figure 3.3.1 Desirable and undesirable behaviour

Source: Adapted from QCA (2001b)

Key: L = learning behaviour; C = conduct/behaviour; E = emotional behaviour

DESIRABLE BEHAVIOUR	UNDESIRABLE BEHAVIOUR

C9. Physically peaceable
- does not show physical aggression
- does not pick on others
- is not cruel or spiteful
- avoids getting into fights with others
- does not have temper tantrums

- fights, aims physical violence at others
- loses temper, throws things
- bullies and intimidates physically
- cruel/spiteful

C10. Respects property
- takes care of own and others' property
- does not engage in vandalism
- does not steal

- poor respect for property
- destroys own or others' things
- steals things

E11. Has empathy
- is tolerant and considerate
- tries to identify with feelings of others
- tries to offer comfort
- is not emotionally detached
- does not laugh when others are upset

- intolerant
- emotionally detached
- selfish
- no awareness of feelings of others

E12. Is socially aware
- understands social interactions of self and peers
- appropriate verbal/non-verbal contacts
- not socially isolated
- has peer-group friends; not a loner
- doesn't frequently daydream
- actively involved in classroom activity
- not aloof, passive or withdrawn

- inactive, daydreams, stares into space
- withdrawn or unresponsive
- does not participate in class activity
- few friends
- not accepted or well-liked
- shows bizarre behaviour
- stares blankly, listless

E13. Is happy
- smiles and laughs appropriately
- should be able to have fun
- generally cheerful; seldom upset
- not discontented, sulky, morose

- depressed, unhappy or discontented
- prone to emotional upset, tearful
- infers suicide
- serious, sad, self-harming

E14. Is confident
- not anxious
- unafraid to try new things
- not self-conscious, doesn't feel inferior
- willing to read aloud, answer questions in class
- participates in group discussion

- anxious, tense, tearful
- reticent, fears failure, feels inferior
- lacks self-esteem, cautious, shy
- does not take initiative

E15. Emotionally stable/self-controlled
- no mood swings
- good emotional resilience, recovers quickly from upset
- manages own feelings
- not easily flustered or frustrated
- delays gratification

- inappropriate emotional reactions
- does not recover quickly from upsets
- does not express feelings
- frequent mood changes; irritable
- over-reacts; does not accept punishment or praise
- does not delay gratification

Figure 3.3.1 continued

Task 3.3.2   What is unacceptable behaviour?

It is important that you arrive at a personal definition of what comprises unacceptable behaviour. Divide a blank sheet of paper into three. Head the left-hand section 'Totally unacceptable' and the right-hand section 'Acceptable'. The middle section is reserved for 'Acceptable in certain circumstances'. Now examine your own classroom teaching, and complete each section. Remember, behaviour is as much about positive learning behaviour as it is those pupil actions that you regard as unacceptable or challenging. Reflect on your responses, discuss with your tutor and record in your PDP. Should the opportunity arise, you might wish to undertake this exercise with your pupils, in order to gather their thoughts. Comparing your list to theirs is likely to prove very revealing! You may also wish to discuss your responses with another student teacher.

Scoping the causal factors

As Ayers and Prytys (2002, p.38) noted, 'The way in which behaviour is conceptualised will determine the treatment of emotional and behavioural problems'. There are a number of causal factors that assist in explaining unwanted behaviour, disaffection and disengagement among some pupils; these are often multivariate and overlapping. The attribution of a cause can frequently result in the acquisition of a negative label by the pupil. But, on the other hand, understanding and recognising the causes can give you clues as to what might be successful interventions. A brief outline of causal factors is given below. There is more exhaustive coverage in a variety of other sources (for example, Garner et al., 2014).

Factors that may cause unacceptable behaviour

Unacceptable behaviour may be caused by several of the factors identified in Table 3.3.2.

One aspect of causality that needs further consideration is that the influences on pupil behaviour have been interpreted as forming three interlinked relationships, first identified in what Bronfenbrenner (1979) called the *ecosystemic theory of relationships*. In the case of a pupil who is consistently behaving inappropriately, it is suggested that there has been a breakdown in one (or more) of these three relationships:

- pupils' relationship with themselves (how pupils feel about themselves, their self-confidence as learners and their self-esteem);
- pupils' relationship with others (how they interact socially and academically with all others in their class and school);
- pupils' relationship with the learning they are undertaking (the curriculum) (how accessible they feel a lesson is and how best they think they learn).

Table 3.3.2 Some causes of unacceptable behaviour

Individual factors

- ◼ A pupil believes that the work is not within their grasp and, as a result, feels embarrassed and alienated and lacks self-esteem as a learner.
- ◼ A pupil may well experience learning difficulties.
- ◼ A pupil may have mental health, stress and possible drug misuse issues, all of which are important factors explaining underachievement and inappropriate behaviour in adolescence.

Cultural factors

- ◼ Adolescence can be a period of rebellion or resistance for many young people.
- ◼ Possible tension between societal expectation and the beliefs and opinions of the pupil.
- ◼ Group/peer pressure can result in various forms of alienation to school.
- ◼ Negative experience of schooling by parents, siblings or other family members.

Curriculum relevance factors (linked to both individual and cultural)

- ◼ The curriculum may be seen by a pupil to be inaccessible and irrelevant.
- ◼ The school may give academic excellence more value than vocational qualifications or curriculum options.

School ethos and relationships factors

- ◼ Some schools can be 'deviance provocative'; their organisational structures and procedures are viewed by pupils as oppressive and negative.
- ◼ Some schools are less inclusive, both academically and socially, to pupils who behave 'differently'.

External barriers to participation and learning factors

- ◼ Family breakdown or illness usually impacts negatively on a pupil's mental health, and often on their sense of priority.
- ◼ Poverty and hardship can mean that a pupil's physiological needs are not met – such pupils may be tired, hungry and consequently easily distracted (see also Maslow, 1970 in Unit 3.2).
- ◼ Sibling and caring responsibilities may mean that some pupils arrive late in your lesson – or not at all.

The interrelationship between these is shown in Figure 3.3.2.

Subsequently, this theory was adapted in strategies to address pupil behaviour, for example in what was termed 'behaviour for learning' (Ellis and Tod, 2009). This approach argues that all three 'relationships' need to be taken into account when planning your strategy to tackle unacceptable behaviour. The emphasis upon positive relationships is an integral component of the approach, with individual pupils as well as whole classes. This effort needs to begin from your first encounter with a group of pupils; over time, it will enable you to establish a classroom climate in which pupil learning can flourish.

Task 3.3.3 links causes to possible teaching strategies.

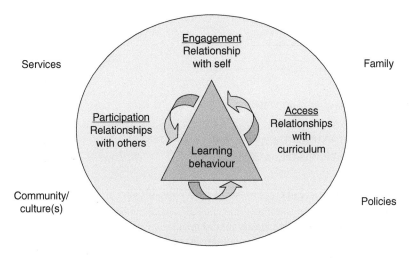

Figure 3.3.2 The behaviour for learning model

Source: After Tod and Powell (2004)

 Task 3.3.3   Linking causes to possible teaching strategies

Consider one pupil that you are teaching who sometimes exhibits behaviour(s) unacceptable to you. Write a brief description of each of the behaviours, making sure that your language is clear and describes clearly observable pupil actions. Taking each behaviour in turn and referring to the causal factors identified above, assess which factors you feel might underlie that particular behaviour. Consider how amenable to change each of the causal factors you have identified is. Also, identify any other teachers (for example, the SENCO) who might be able to provide you with advice and support. Finally, reflect on how your interpretation of cause might inform the way in which you choose to address the behaviour(s) shown.

Make notes in your PDP and discuss your responses with your tutor.

Key principles of a behaviour for learning approach

There has been an increasing interest amongst educators in the 'social and emotional aspect of learning' (SEAL) over the last 10 years. This approach incorporates a long-standing awareness of aspects of 'emotional intelligence' (Goleman, 1995), which can assist teachers in helping to create a positive climate or culture for learning in which good relationships between them and their pupils are paramount (see also Unit 3.2 on motivation). It is based, in part, on the premise that 'generally a punitive approach tends to worsen or sometimes even create the very problems it is intended to eradicate...punishment alienates children from their teachers and does nothing to build up trust that is the bedrock of relationships' (Weare, 2004, p.63). Crucially, and linking SEAL to the notion of 'behaviour for learning', an understanding of 'self' is a cornerstone of pupil motivation. As a result, pupils can:

■ be effective and successful learners;
■ make and sustain friendships;
■ deal with and resolve conflict effectively and fairly;
■ solve problems with others or by themselves;
■ manage strong feelings such as frustration, anger and anxiety;
■ recover from setbacks and persist in the face of difficulties;
■ work and play cooperatively;
■ compete fairly and win and lose with dignity and respect for competitors.

Although each of these represents a complex undertaking, your use of them as guidelines in developing your thinking about pupil behaviour will pay rich dividends as you progress in your teaching career. Discuss with your tutor how you might be able to do this.

A behaviour for learning approach accepts that most SEAL are learned and, therefore, can be taught or modelled by the teacher. Evidence strongly suggests that the most successful strategies for developing a positive learning environment are those that incorporate the promotion of positive relationships (Burnett, 2002). As has been suggested, each of the three (interlinked) relationships is important in developing a positive learning environment in the classroom, and, as a teacher, you are at the very heart of orchestrating them. Although some pupils have relatively advanced 'social and emotional' skills when they arrive at school, others (often pupils who can sometimes behave unacceptably) might need support and the direct teaching of the specific skills they have not yet learned. So, your task is to focus on helping to develop appropriate skills that enable each pupil to learn within a variety of learning contexts. This can be in whole-class or small-group situations in the classroom and elsewhere in the school. Some of the basic principles which inform the way in which this can be done are:

■ behaviour for learning is a positive description. It tells pupils what you want them to do and why this helps them to learn, rather than focusing on behaviours that you do not want in your classroom;
■ it requires that you place value on (and praise appropriately) pupil behaviour that enables and maximises learning;
■ effective behaviour for learning strategies can range from high-level listening and collaborative learning skills to remaining seated for two minutes. The emphasis is upon setting targets that are reachable by pupils.

Getting the simple things right!

So far in this unit, the focus has been placed upon the underlying principles of creating a positive learning environment. But your understanding of these must coincide with a parallel focus on the strategies that you can implement practically in order to establish yourself as a teacher who can manage pupil behaviour effectively.

Classroom

- ☐ Know the names and roles of any adults in class.
- ☐ Meet and greet pupils when they come into the classroom.
- ☐ Display rules in the class – and ensure that the pupils and staff know what they are.
- ☐ Display the tariff of sanctions in class.
- ☐ Have a system in place to follow through with all sanctions.
- ☐ Display the tariff of rewards in class.
- ☐ Have a system in place to follow through with all rewards.
- ☐ Have a visual timetable on the wall.
- ☐ Follow the school behaviour policy.

Pupils

- ☐ Know the names of pupils.
- ☐ Have a plan for pupils who are likely to misbehave.
- ☐ Ensure other adults in the class know the plan.
- ☐ Understand pupils' special needs.

Teaching

- ☐ Ensure that all resources are prepared in advance.
- ☐ Praise the behaviour you want to see more of.
- ☐ Praise pupils doing the right thing more than criticising those who are doing the wrong thing (parallel praise).
- ☐ Differentiate.
- ☐ Stay calm.
- ☐ Have clear routines for transitions and for stopping the class.
- ☐ Teach pupils the class routines.

Parents

- ☐ Give feedback to parents about their child's behaviour – let them know about the good days as well as the bad ones.

Figure 3.3.3 Behaviour checklist for teachers

Source: DfE (2011c)

It is important that, whilst you recognise that managing a class is complex, you should concentrate on getting the simple, but essential, things right (DfE, 2011c). Bennett (2017b) emphasises the importance of planning for each individual pupil especially when setting behaviour goals, rather than just reacting to misbehaviour when it occurs.

As a student teacher, you need to fit in with the practice in the classrooms you work in. However, to assist you in avoiding some of the more obvious pitfalls and to aid planning, Figure 3.3.3 provides a helpful checklist.

Each of the items in the checklist will most likely become 'second nature' to you; they are commonly understood by successful teachers as being crucial to organising effective learning in their classrooms. What you will notice is that each of the recommendations in the behaviour checklist (DfE, 2011c) connects well with both Bronfenbrenner's ecosystem theory and the relationships that underpin a 'behaviour for learning' approach. Now complete Task 3.3.4.

Task 3.3.4   Relationships and pupil behaviour

We have noted that promoting positive behaviour requires the teacher to understand three sets of relationships, with *self*, *others* and with the *curriculum*. But we have also noted that you need to take some practical steps in order to make these relationships happen. Examine the behaviour checklist (see Figure 3.3.3) and allocate each of the items in it to one or more of these relationship areas. Reflect on their distribution, compare and discuss your findings with another student teacher and store your findings in your PDP.

Incorporating both a set of clear principles and some straightforward actions enables you to prevent the occurrence of unacceptable behaviour by pupils. It also assists you in giving a firm and consistent response to any instances of problem behaviour that might arise. As a student teacher, keep things simple and avoid overuse of sanctions by giving pupils ways of getting out of a situation leading to sanctions. This also enables you to present yourself in a classroom leadership role. Most pupils will come to your classroom wanting to learn, although there will be times when some will either be unable or unwilling to learn on account of some of the factors described earlier in this unit. In dealing with this situation, it is important to develop certain classroom leadership skills that contribute to your being able to establish a well-organised environment for learning, forge positive relationships with all pupils, and establish a classroom ethos that allows pupils to demonstrate positive behaviour and optimum attainment.

A classroom leader needs to address three broad elements that help to define the ethos of the classroom. While these issues are important for all pupils, they are essential elements for promoting the engagement and positive behaviour of pupils who are at risk of misbehaviour. They are:

- motivation: you need to provide time at the start of each lesson to tell pupils what they are learning and why. Pupils need to be involved at every stage in assessing whether these learning intentions have been met (Unit 3.2 looks at motivation in more depth);
- emotional well-being: to help reduce pupil anxiety, you should share the lesson structure with pupils at the start, so they know what is going to happen during the lesson;
- expectations: you need to give time at the start of the lesson and before each new activity to make clear what behaviours are needed for this piece of learning to be successful.

These three underpinning elements are embedded in more specific teacher actions that allow you to demonstrate your role as the classroom leader to your pupils. These include:

- good communication between yourself and your pupils (see Unit 3.1);
- secure subject knowledge;
- providing lively, well-paced lessons;
- understanding and meeting the learning needs of all pupils in your class;
- acting on your reflections and evaluations of previous lessons (feedback loop) (see also Unit 2.1);
- demonstrating confidence and direction in managing pupils;
- modelling desired behaviours yourself.

It is unlikely that, as a student teacher, everything clicks into place straight away; some actions develop with experience. Research has shown that student teachers who display confidence in managing their classes are less likely to encounter problem behaviour by pupils (Giallo and Little, 2003).

Building positive relationships in classrooms

As has been discussed earlier in this unit, promoting positive behaviour places emphasis on the relationships you form with your pupils. Ineffective interventions are usually the product of unsatisfactory relationships with individual pupils. These interventions, even though they are ultimately unsuccessful, take up valuable teaching time and impact negatively on the learning of an individual pupil, the rest of the class and also on your own confidence. Most interventions should take the form of positive actions that fit somewhere on a continuum from *positive reinforcement* through to *positive correction*. The actions you select should be those that enable learning to continue. They usually include eye contact, use of pupil name, description of the appropriate behaviour you would like the pupil to demonstrate, praise and affirmation (see also Units 3.1 and 3.2). For example:

■ modelling appropriate behaviour;
■ positive reinforcement and the appropriate use of targeted praise;
■ consistent and firm application of rules;
■ use of verbal and non-verbal communication;
■ listening to pupils and respecting their opinions;
■ remaining vigilant (pre-empting unacceptable behaviour);
■ dealing decisively with lateness and non-attendance.

By consistently using these approaches in your teaching, you are more likely to forge meaningful and positive relationships with your pupils. In sum, effective relationships mean that there is common ground between pupil and teacher. This is as vital in securing appropriate conditions for learning as it is for managing those behavioural issues that may be potentially problematic.

Structuring your lessons to promote positive behaviour

The design of effective lessons is fundamental to high-quality teaching and learning. Effective lesson design takes into account behavioural differences between pupils as much as it does their levels of achievement or the subject or skill they are learning. Your teaching should be characterised by:

■ focus and structure so that pupils are clear about what is to be learned and how it fits with what they know already;
■ actively engaging pupils in their learning so that they make their own meaning from it;
■ developing pupils' learning skills systematically so that their learning becomes increasingly independent (see also Unit 5.2);
■ using assessment for learning to help pupils reflect on what they already know, reinforce the learning being developed and set targets for the future (Units 6.1 and 6.2 discuss assessment);
■ having high expectations of the effort that pupils should make and what they can achieve (see also Unit 3.2);
■ motivating pupils by well-paced lessons, using stimulating activities that encourage attendance;
■ creating an environment that promotes learning in a settled and purposeful atmosphere.

You can further promote a positive approach to behaviour by building individual teaching sequences within an overall lesson. The lesson (or a sequence of lessons) needs first of all to be firmly located, in the mind of the pupil, in the context of: (a) a scheme of work; (b) pupils' prior knowledge; and (c) their preferred ways of learning. It is also important to identify clear learning outcomes. Structuring your lesson as a series of 'episodes' by separating pupil learning into distinct stages or steps, and then planning how each step should be taught, enables those pupils who are at risk of distraction or lack of concentration to regard the lesson as a series of 'bite-sized chunks'. Finally, you can secure overall coherence by providing: (a) a stimulating start to the lesson; (b) transition 'signposts' between each lesson episode, which reviews pupil learning until now and launches the next episode; and (c) a final plenary session that reviews learning (lesson planning is covered in Unit 2.2).

Rights, responsibilities, routines and rules

A framework for promoting positive classroom behaviour has been commonly constructed around the so-called 4Rs: rights, responsibilities, rules and routines (Hook and Vass, 2000). You should recognise that such a focus operates best within the context of a fifth 'R', already encountered in this unit – 'relationships'. In applying aspects of the 4Rs, you need to be very sensitive, as a student teacher, to the existing arrangements in any class that you work in. These will have been established over a long period of time by the permanent class teacher. But you can begin by being conscious of how each of these 'Rs' can have a positive impact on your teaching.

Rights (R1) and responsibilities (R2)

Both rights and responsibilities are inextricably linked. They refer equally to teacher and pupils, and are the basis on which classroom relationships, teaching and learning are built.

■ Teacher's responsibilities – you must seek to enable all pupils to learn, to seek out and celebrate improvements in learning, to treat pupils with respect and to create a positive classroom environment in which pupils feel safe and able to learn.
■ Teacher's rights – you must be allowed to teach with a minimum of hindrance, to feel safe, to be supported by colleagues and to be listened to.
■ Pupils' responsibilities – pupils must be willing to learn, to allow others to learn, to cooperate with teaching and other staff and peers, and to do their best at all times.
■ Pupils' rights – pupils should be treated with respect, be safe, be able to learn and be listened to.

Rules (R3)

These are the mechanisms by which rights and responsibilities are translated into adult and pupil behaviours. They are best constructed collaboratively, so that the views of all pupils are taken into account.

Routines (R4)

These are the structures that underpin the rules and reinforce the smooth running of the classroom. The more habitual the routines become, the more likely they are to be used. Pupils who behave inappropriately often do so because they are unsure of what is happening in the classroom at a given time. Consistent application of your classroom rules will constitute a major step in establishing a routine in your class.

In using the 4Rs as a basis for promoting positive pupil behaviour, you should be encouraged to provide opportunities for your pupils to make choices about their behaviour, thus allowing them to take responsibility for their own actions. Choice is guided by their responsibilities and leads to positive or negative consequences according to the choice made by the pupil.

Consequences

Pupils need to know the consequences of sensible or inadvisable choices. Responsible choices lead to positive consequences; conversely, a choice to behave inappropriately leads to a known negative consequence.

Now complete Task 3.3.5, which is designed to help you to focus on the ways you use encouragement, positive feedback and praise in the classroom, and Task 3.3.6, which focuses on the impact of praise on your pupils.

 Task 3.3.5   Monitoring your use of praise and encouragement in the classroom

A very useful starting point to promote the notion of positive approaches to behaviour is to examine the ways in which you provide encouragement, positive feedback and praise to your pupils. You can assess this by developing a log of praise and encouragement to use as a tool for measuring these positive interactions.

Add to the list of positive pupil behaviours identified below, which you can use to give praise. Underneath each one, note the words or actions you might use to convey to the pupil that your recognition carries value and meaning in that they are clearly directed towards a particular pupil and are linked to the positive behaviour that the pupil has demonstrated.

1   Queuing sensibly and quietly to enter the classroom.
2   Allowing another pupil to go first.
3   Lending an item of equipment to another pupil.
4   Putting waste paper in the bin.
5   Supporting another pupil's learning.
6   _____
7   _____
8   _____
9   _____
10 _____

During your observation of a lesson taught by a more experienced teacher in your placement school, record other ways in which that teacher acknowledges positive behaviour by pupils. Compare your notes on this topic with another student teacher working in a different setting. Store in your PDP for later reference.

Task 3.3.6   The impact of praise

Undertake a small-scale project designed to establish the impact of 'praise' on pupils in your class. In doing this, you should: (a) develop one or more research questions, so that your data collection has a focus; (b) identify a small, but recent and relevant, set of literature that contributes to a theoretical understanding of the issue; (c) define and provide a rationale for your methodology (including coverage of any ethical issues that might emerge in such a study); (d) gather and analyse data; and (e) consider the relevance of your findings to your practice. Store this in your PDP.

Among the possible research questions you might wish to consider are:

■   Do boys prefer different kinds of praise and encouragement than girls?
■   Does the nature and type of praise change according to age?
■   What types of praise do pupils prefer?
■   Is praise evenly distributed among your teaching group?
■   Is praise carefully targeted and in response to specific pupil actions?
■   Does personal praise link closely with a whole-school approach?

In Task 3.3.7, you are asked to explore the links between behaviour and learning. Task 3.3.8 asks you to consider different definitions of unacceptable behaviour.

 Task 3.3.7   Exploring further the links between behaviour and learning

To explore further the links between behaviour and learning, select one or more pupils who you currently teach in your placement school and who present you with a particular challenge on account of their unacceptable behaviour. You should explore the learning and behaviour interface by responding to the following key questions:

■   Does the educational achievement of this pupil vary from one curriculum subject to another?
■   What are the characteristics of those curriculum subjects in which the pupil appears to perform more effectively?
■   Has the pattern of educational achievement been inconsistent over time? Are there any logical explanations for this?
■   Do you know anything about the pupil's preferred ways of learning?
■   What are your own views about the capabilities of this pupil?
■   What do other subject teachers say about the educational achievements of this pupil?

Each of the above questions can form the basis of a small-scale classroom enquiry. For each, you could: (a) gather evidence from the school's pupil data; (b) obtain information from key personnel (for instance, the pupil's form tutor, or the SENCO); and (c) secure inputs from the pupil directly (subject to the appropriate permissions).

On the basis of what you discover, try to formulate a theoretical model for both the unacceptable behaviours displayed and their relationship with more positive aspects of this pupil's school performance. Store this in your PDP.

M   🖉 Task 3.3.8   Interpretations of unacceptable behaviour

Interpretations of 'unacceptable behaviour', and the ways in which it has been defined, have changed over time. In spite of this, the educational literature is replete with material (research papers, books, official reports and guidance documents) looking at ways in which schools and teachers can manage behaviour more effectively. Two examples of this, separated by nearly 20 years, are the Elton Report (1989) and the Steer Report (DCSF, 2009). Using the links provided below, consider the similarities and differences in the recommendations of each report. What does the content of these documents tell you about official policy on pupil behaviour? Are there many commonalities regarding the practical advice that these reports offer to classroom teachers? Are you able to draw any inferences from the generic commentaries given concerning the nature and extent of pupil behaviour in schools?

Write up your analysis, discuss with your tutor or other student teachers and store in your PDP.

The Elton Report is available at: http://www.educationengland.org.uk/documents/elton/elton1989.html

The Steer Report is available at: www.educationengland.org.uk/documents/pdfs/2005 steer-report-learning-behaviour.pdf

---

SUMMARY AND KEY POINTS

- Adopting a positive approach to managing pupil behaviour is crucially important.
- Become familiar with your school's policies regarding behaviour management.
- Take steps to understand what are the underlying causes of the problem behaviour in your class. This is the first step in taking positive action.
- Try to establish a clear set of classroom rules and rewards and sanctions and ensure that they are applied consistently and fairly.
- Focus on your relationships with pupils. Establishing an effective working relationship is crucial to a positive classroom 'ethos'.
- Always try to lead by example. Try to model the kinds of positive behaviours you want to see from your pupils.
- Seek guidance and support from more experienced teachers in your placement school, and make use of all opportunities for professional development.

Check which requirements for your ITE programme you have addressed through this unit.

 Further resources

Dix, P. (2010) *Taking Care of Behaviour*, **Harlow: Pearson Education Limited.**
This practical, skills-based book gives you a wide range of useful behaviour management strategies that you can establish in your classroom. It can be used alongside, and can enhance, the inputs you receive from tutors, mentors and other staff. The content can be individualised to your current situation to enable you to develop your own 'behaviour plan'. This is a crucial dimension of your confidence-building.

Above all, it will inspire you to recognise that you can begin to play an active part in responding to some of the most challenging behaviour.

Ellis, S. and Tod, J. (2014) *Promoting Behaviour for Learning in the Classroom*, **Abingdon: Routledge.**
This book provides a concise analysis of established behaviour management strategies that you can use in your own classroom. It recognises that no single approach will work for *all* pupils and that it is important to understand the individual needs, attributes and personalities of your pupils when deciding how best to intervene. The book covers a range of issues, including developing positive relationships in the classroom, understanding personal style and self-management, making use of effective feedback and rewards, individual differences and special educational needs, and dealing with challenging behaviour.

Haydn, T. (2012) *Managing Pupil Behaviour: Improving the Classroom Atmosphere*, **2nd Edition, Abingdon: Routledge.**
This book provides some practical insights into how best you can manage behaviour effectively in your classroom. It encourages you to think about the degree to which you are relaxed and in assured control of your class so that you can really enjoy your teaching.

Managing Pupil Behaviour uses the views of over 140 teachers and 700 pupils to provide insights into factors that enable teachers to manage learning effectively in their classrooms to enable pupils to learn and achieve. Key issues explored include factors that influence the working atmosphere in the classroom, the impact of that atmosphere on teaching and learning, as well as tensions around inclusive practice and situations where some pupils may be spoiling the learning of others.

Rogers, W. (2015) *Classroom Behaviour: A Practical Guide to Effective Teaching, Behaviour Management and Colleague Support*, **London: Sage.**
This book explores some of the issues that you will face when working in today's classrooms. It describes real situations and dilemmas and offers advice on dealing with the challenges of the job. Emphasis is placed on how to establish and enhance your relationships with pupils. The book also considers some more specialist aspects of teaching pupils who have additional needs, including sections looking at dealing with bullying, teaching pupils on the autistic spectrum in a mainstream classroom and working with very challenging pupils.

Key policy documents relating to pupil behaviour

Bennett, T. (2017) *Creating a Culture: How School Leaders Can Optimise Behaviour*, **London: DfE, viewed 3 July 2018, from https://www.gov.uk/government/uploads/system/uploads/attachment_data/file/ 602487/Tom_Bennett_Independent_Review_of_Behaviour_in_Schools.pdf**
Status: Independent report, March 2017.

DfE (Department for Education) (2011c) *Getting the Simple Things Tight: Charlie Taylor's Behaviour Checklists*, **London: DfE, viewed 3 July 2018, from www.education.gov.uk/schools/pupilsupport/ behaviour/a00199342/getting-the-simple-thingsright-charlie-taylors-behaviour-checklists**
Status: Departmental advice, April 2012

DfE (Department for Education) (2012b) *Behaviour and Discipline in Schools: Guidance for Governing Bodies*, **London: DfE, viewed 7 July 2018, from www.gov.uk/government/publications/behaviour- and-discipline-in-schools-guidance-for-governing-bodies**
Status: Statutory guidance, September 2015.

DfE (Department for Education) (2013g) *Use of Reasonable Force: Advice for Headteachers, Staff and Governing Bodies*, **London: DfE, viewed 3 July 2018, from www.gov.uk/government/publications/ use-of-reasonable-force-in-schools**
Status: Departmental advice, July 2013

DfE (Department for Education (2016a) *Behaviour and Discipline in Schools: Advice to Headteachers and School Staff*, **London: DfE, viewed 3 July 2018, from www.gov.uk/government/publications/ behaviour-and-discipline-in-schools**
Status: Departmental advice, January 2016.

DfE (Department for Education (2017d) *Preventing and Tackling Bullying: Advice for Headteachers, Staff and Governing Bodies*, **London: DfE, viewed 2 July 2018, from https://www.gov.uk/government/uploads/ system/uploads/attachment_data/file/623895/Preventing_and_tackling_bullying_advice.pdf**
Status: Departmental advice, July 2017

DfE (Department for Education (2018a) *Screening, Searching and Confiscation: Advice for Headteachers, School Staff and Governing Bodies,* **London: DfE, viewed 3 July 2018, from www.gov.uk/government/ publications/searching-screening-and-confiscation**
Status: Departmental advice, September 2014.

Appendix 2 lists subject associations and teacher councils and Appendix 3 provides a list of websites.

Capel, S., Leask, M. and Turner, T. (eds.) (2010) *Readings for Learning to Teach in the Secondary School: A Companion to M Level Study,* **Abingdon: Routledge.**
This book brings together essential readings to support you in your critical engagement with key issues raised in this textbook.

Capel, S., Lawrence, J. Leask, M. and Younie, S. (eds.) (2019) *Surviving and Thriving in the Secondary School: The NQT's Essential Companion,* **Abingdon: Routledge.**
This book is designed to support newly qualified teachers in the next phase of development as a teacher. However, you may find it useful as it covers aspects of teaching not included in this book which, nonetheless you experience on your ITE programme.

The subject specific books in the *Learning to Teach (Subject)* series, the *Practical (Subject) Guides, Debates in (Subject)* and *Mentoring (Subject) Teachers* are also very useful.

Any additional resources and an editable version of any relevant tasks/tables in this unit are available on the companion website: www.routledge.com/cw/capel

3.4 Primary-secondary transitions

Divya Jindal-Snape

Introduction

Educational transitions are an ongoing process that involve moving from one educational context and set of interpersonal relationships to another (Jindal-Snape, 2010d; 2016). The change in contexts and relationships can lead to change in identity, and involves ongoing psychological, social and educational adaptation that can be both exciting and worrying, as well as requiring ongoing support (Jindal-Snape, 2018).

It is important to remember that educational transitions are not only about moving from one educational setting to another but also moving from one class to another within the same school or change in staff within the same class. Usually, educational transition signals progression and 'moving up'. It may therefore be assumed that most pupils get positive messages and are happy during transitions. While most do find transitions satisfying and fulfilling, with increases in opportunities and choices (Lucey and Reay, 2000; Jindal-Snape and Foggie, 2008), some pupils find them stressful and challenging, with dips in academic achievement, motivation and self-esteem (Jindal-Snape and Miller, 2008). Also, moving (for instance from primary to secondary school) is not the only transition that pupils may be experiencing. There might be accompanying multiple transitions related to, for example, puberty, moving house, birth of a sibling, starting a club, etc.

This period can also cause anxiety for parents/carers and family while they and their child adjust to, for example, a new system, 'unspoken rules' of schools and changing expectations of their role. Similarly, teachers working with these pupils and families have to learn to implement new strategies according to their varying needs and ways of dealing with transitions. They might also be experiencing their own multiple transitions.

It can be argued that transitions are complex, dynamic, multiple and multi-dimensional (Multiple and Multi-dimensional Transitions (MMT) theory), and, therefore, a holistic approach to understanding them and providing support is required (see Jindal-Snape, 2016 for detail).

This unit introduces you to the concept of transitions and their impact on planning and preparation for primary–secondary transitions. This is important as research suggests a lack of shared understanding about transitions amongst staff (teachers, pupil support worker, guidance staff and senior teachers) even within the same school cluster. This seems to have an impact on planning and preparation even to the extent of when it should start (Jindal-Snape, 2018).

The unit also discusses factors that research has found pupils are excited by and look forward to, as well as what they worry about during this time. Resilience, self-esteem and emotional intelligence theories are used to explore the reasons behind issues faced by pupils, as well as how you, as teachers, can support them.

OBJECTIVES

At the end of this unit, you should be able to:

- explain the concept of educational transition and its impact on planning and preparation for primary-secondary transitions;
- be aware of what pupils are excited and worry about when moving to secondary school;
- consider the best possible ways of supporting pupils during primary-secondary transitions.

Check the requirements for your initial teacher education (ITE) programme to see which relate to this unit.

Conceptualisation of educational transition and its impact on planning and preparation

There are some subtle changes that happen in our lives all the time, some more marked and visible than others. Within these life transitions, there is a distinct type of transition that most individuals go through, that is, educational transitions. To understand what is happening to the pupil during transitions and what can be done to enhance the experience of primary-secondary transitions, it is important to reflect on how you might conceptualise primary-secondary transitions. What does a successful transition look like? Research suggests that this includes pupils having a sense of belongingness; no dips in educational attainment, self-esteem and motivation to learn; and a general sense of wellbeing (Peters, 2010).

In an educational context, transition, also referred to as 'transfer' and 'moving on', has been conceptualised in various ways.

Maturational and interactionist approach

Some literature and practice tends to focus on pupils' skills and how they deal with any change in context and/or setting. This is particularly the case when looking at transition to formal schooling and considering the pupil's readiness to start school, but I believe this applies equally to primary-secondary transitions. This approach to assessing a pupil's readiness to start school is called the maturational approach. It focuses on the pupil's ability to perform at the norm expected at that level, being emotionally and socially ready, as well as the ability to look 'the right age'.

Another approach is an interactionist approach, which looks at the fit between the pupil's readiness and the secondary school's readiness to adapt according to the pupil's needs (Vernon-Feagans et al., 2008). This requires planning so that secondary schools are ready to receive pupils according to their specific and diverse needs. There are several aspects to this, which are addressed below.

One-off event or ongoing process?

Perhaps the biggest problem with planning and preparation comes from transition being seen by some teachers as a one-off event rather than an ongoing process in which pupils have to make sense of everyday changes and relationships. When conceptualised as a one-off event, practice focuses on activities such as meeting secondary school teachers prior to transition, school visits, induction days, residentials, and so on. As a result, the preparation *prior* to the move is the focus of attention. After the pupils have moved to secondary school, there might be a few days of getting to know each other and 'settling-in' activities but little or nothing after that.

However, research shows that there is no single pattern to how long pupils might take to adapt to the move. The results of one longitudinal study showed that some pupils who had reported transition to be difficult immediately after moving to secondary school reported that they had no problems two months later (Jindal-Snape, 2018). You might be thinking, 'Yes, that is to be expected'. Interestingly, though, of those who had not found transition to be a problem immediately after the move, some reported problems by the end of the first year, and, for one, problems emerged at the end of the second year. How many schools would still be looking at any issues with adaptation at that stage?

Galton (2010) suggests that schools need to think longer term, and uses the example of Nicholson's (1987) work-role transition phases from the field of occupational psychology. These four phases are:

- *Preparation.* This is similar to the pre-move programmes put in place by schools, such as induction weeks, open days, and so on.
- *Encounters.* This includes a post-induction programme that, in the context of secondary schools, could include bridging activities. For example, in one project an off-the-shelf computer game was used in some primary schools and their associated secondary schools as a contextual hub to facilitate transitions from primary to secondary school. The project included ongoing work in secondary schools several months after the move.
- *Adjustment.* At the adjustment phase, frequent and immediate feedback is provided on both success and failure. Pupils' reasoning is explored and strategies for identifying and correcting mistakes discussed.
- *Stabilisation.* This involves future goal setting and appraisal of how a pupil might be developing, such as in the end-of-year reviews. These should be more than the typical end-of-year school reports; rather, they should look at those aspects of the pupil's adjustment (whether social, personal or academic) where improvement is required, as well as set future goals for the following year.

Now complete Task 3.4.1.

 Task 3.4.1 Transition practices

Find out the primary–secondary transitions planning and preparation practices of your placement school. Identify the purpose of each of the practices and make notes in your professional development portfolio (PDP) or equivalent. Reflect on where they would fit on Nicholson's (1987) work-role transition phases. Compare your findings with those of another student teacher.

Educational and life transitions

During primary-secondary transitions, pupils and parents tend to focus more on the social aspects of transition, at least before or during the first few months of the move (Jindal-Snape and Foggie, 2008; Galton, 2010). Therefore, any academic transition has to be seen within the daily life experiences of a pupil. It is also important to remember that pupils moving to secondary school are experiencing other changes, including normative developmental and any associated physical and relationship changes. The education and life transitions (ELT) model in Figure 3.4.1 (Jindal-Snape and Ingram, 2013), can be used to understand what might be happening for a pupil.

During the course of the day, even within the school, pupils adapt to their educational environment as well as daily life, such as making friends (see, for example, Pietarinen et al., 2010b). If one aspect of transition is going really well (+ positive experience), it could help the pupil to overcome any problems with other aspects (- negative experience) (Figure 3.4.1). For example, a pupil who might be finding it difficult to cope with studies might still be happy if they have a strong support network of friends around them. This is a dynamic model with continuous fluctuations. However, as a teacher, you could easily tap into and strengthen the positive experiences of transition to overcome any unavoidable negative experiences. For example, your positive interactions with the pupils might lessen their worries about getting lost in school and arriving late to your class or the homework being too difficult. Similarly, group work can be used in class to provide pupils with opportunities to develop friendship and learning networks.

Issues related to primary-secondary transitions

There is a significant change in identity for pupils when moving from being a primary to a secondary school pupil. This may bring happiness, but also some grief at losing the identity they had for the

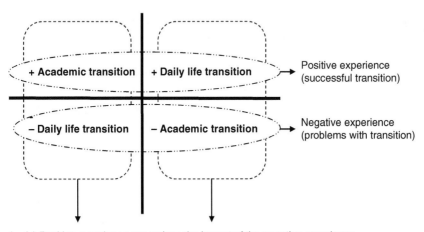

(++/−) Positive experience can reduce the impact of the negative experience
(−−/+) Negative experience can reduce the impact of the positive experience

Figure 3.4.1 Educational and life transitions (ELT) model depicting relationship between academic and daily life transitions

Source: Jindal-Snape and Ingram (2013)

last six to seven years in primary school (which is more than half of their life at the time of moving to secondary school).

We suggest you undertake Task 3.4.2 to remind you of your own experience of transitions.

 Task 3.4.2   Remembering your own experience of transitions

Answer the questions below in relation to transitions you have experienced; for example, when you first started school/secondary school/college/university.

1   How old were you?
2   What is your memory of the first day/first few days?
3   Draw/write how you looked and who was around you?
4   Can you remember any feelings/thoughts from that day?
5   What, if any, support was available to you?

Compare your answers with those of other student teachers to understand a variety of transition experiences. Keep your responses in your PDP.

Numerous international studies have been conducted to understand what is happening during primary–secondary transitions. It seems that despite the variation in educational systems, pupil's age or country, the pedagogical, social and emotional challenges of transitions for pupils from primary–secondary school are quite similar (see, for example, Akos, 2004; Adeyemo, 2005; Jindal-Snape and Foggie, 2008). There is clear evidence of a substantial decline in self-esteem, academic motivation and achievement (Eccles and Midgley, 1989; Wigfield et al., 1991; Jindal-Snape and Miller, 2008). However, as mentioned earlier, this is also a time that many pupils find to be satisfying and use it as a springboard to move on and up.

It is important to understand both what pupils are excited about and what they are worried about at this time. In a study conducted by Jindal-Snape et al. (2011), 10 weeks before their move to secondary school, 139 primary school pupils were asked about their worries as well as things they were looking forward to about moving to secondary school (see Table 3.4.1).

As can be seen from Table 3.4.1, the same aspects were seen as exciting by some and challenging by others, particularly relationships with peers and teachers.

The issue of continuity in curriculum and pedagogical approach has been highlighted both in the educational literature (for example Galton, 2010) and government reports (for example Scottish Executive Education Department (SEED), 1999). Despite developments in practice, such as reciprocal visits of teachers, observations by peer teachers and use of bridging units, there are many challenges to be faced and further work is required to improve this aspect of transition practice. These challenges are, at times, tied to the unspoken values and cultural norms of primary and secondary schools. For example, there seems to be a big gap between primary and secondary schools' expectations of pupils in terms of independence, with some primary schools failing to make pupils independent and secondary schools expecting them to be independent. Similarly, pupils, parents and professionals reported a difference in discipline in primary and secondary schools: 'At Primary, if they are a bit late we comment but say that it's good that they've come, whereas at secondary, if they are late they get a punishment' (professional) (Jindal-Snape and Foggie, 2006, p.69).

Table 3.4.1 Aspects that pupils in final year of primary school were looking forward to or worrying about (*n* = 139) (*Note*: Pupils could tick as many options as relevant)

	Looking forward to	Worried about
Making new friends	111	21
Losing old friends	N/A	88
More choices/opportunities	85	4
More independence	79	12
Several teachers	64	27
Different subjects	117	11
Travelling to school	34	17
Bigger school	64	33
Bigger playground	60	7
Buying school dinners	53	16
Getting a locker	73	8
Variety of sports	2	0
Seeing old friends (already in secondary school)	3	0
Bullied	0	10
Getting lost/late for class	0	2
Too much homework	0	1

Research also suggests that a pupil might find transition to secondary school difficult if there is a big gap in their own expectations and reality. For example, Delamont (1991) found that conceptualisations about secondary school by pupils about to make the transition were influenced by 'horror stories' communicated by their peers. When they reach secondary school, they might find these concerns to be unfounded. However, the stress accompanying their prior perceptions might already have had a detrimental impact on the pupil. Now complete Task 3.4.3.

  Task 3.4.3   Expectations versus reality

You can do this activity on your own or with other student teachers.

1   Note up to five expectations you had when starting your ITE programme or at another transition; for example, going to a different country (expectations can be about everyday life, food, language, culture and so on).
2   Against these expectations, identify what the reality is/was.
3   What are the differences/similarities?
4   For each expectation, add feelings/emotions you experienced at that time.
5   Reflect on the impact of the gap/no gap between expectation and realities on your feelings.

Store your findings in your PDP.

As you can probably see from Task 3.4.3, accurate and detailed information has to be provided to bridge the gap between expectations and reality. Therefore, schools invest a lot of time in giving pupils some knowledge of the new school and familiarisation through first-hand experience on induction days.

Understanding transitions through theoretical perspectives

Researchers have identified different theories to understand what is happening during a transition, as well as how the experience can be improved. Three theories are discussed below: self-esteem, resilience and emotional intelligence.

Resilience

Resilience has been defined as a dynamic process encompassing positive adaptation within the context of significant adversity (Luthar, 2006). Resilience literature looks at risk and protective factors that, at times, might be the same; for example, Newman and Blackburn (2002) identify that a family can be both a chaotic family, a risk factor, and a supportive family, a protective factor (Jindal-Snape and Miller, 2008). Research conducted to look at risk and resilience in the context of preschool–primary school (for example, Griebel and Niesel, 2001) and primary–secondary transitions (for example, Catterall, 1998; Jindal-Snape and Hannah, 2014) emphasises the importance of internal protective factors (for example, self-esteem) and external protective factors (for example, positive relationships at home and school) to help reduce multiple 'risks' or 'stressors' at the time of transitions. Therefore, teachers need to structure a supportive and safe environment for pupils at primary and secondary schools.

Self-esteem

Mruk's (1999) two-dimensional model of self-esteem proposes that self-esteem is dependent not only on feeling competent (self-competence), but also on messages that pupils might receive of their worth and value (self-worth). Primary–secondary transitions involve several instances when a pupil's self-competence and self-worth might be shaken. For example, pupils can worry about their ability to do higher-level work despite there being gradual progression in the difficulty level (self-competence) and about being liked by teachers and peers, sustaining old friendships and making new friends (self-worth).

Further, those pupils with existing low self-esteem might respond more negatively to experiences of failure. On the other hand, those with higher self-esteem are more likely to persist in the face of difficulties (Tafarodi and Vu, 1997). Thus, self-esteem might act as a protective factor, but also the erosion of self-esteem might leave pupils vulnerable. The two-dimensional model of self-esteem emphasises the role of significant others in the environment. Therefore, on the one hand, pupils' high self-esteem can be sustained by careful consideration of curricular progression (self-competence), and, on the other, by ensuring that pupils feel valued and welcome in your classroom (self-worth).

Emotional intelligence

Goleman (1995) identified five 'domains' of emotional intelligence, namely: knowing your emotions; managing your emotions; motivating yourself; recognising and understanding other people's emotions; and managing relationships. Research has suggested that teacher intervention in relation to emotional intelligence can enhance adjustment of pupils (Adeyemo, 2005; 2010). According to Adeyemo, this might be due to the acquisition of emotional intelligence skills, which are the combination of intrapersonal and interpersonal factors that would help individuals cope with their own and others' emotions.

The boundaries are blurred between these three theoretical perspectives; resilience, self-esteem and emotional intelligence There are overlaps, and sometimes cause-and-effect relationships seem obvious and sometimes they are very elusive. This might sit uncomfortably with some. However, it is important for you to generate and engage in this debate. Now complete Tasks 3.4.4 and 3.4.5.

 Task 3.4.4   Exploring theories of transition

Consider useful factors in the three theoretical models. What factors can the school address and what are beyond its reach?

Compare your responses with those of another student teacher and record your responses in your PDP.

  Task 3.4.5   Understanding the theories in the context of your and others' experience

Undertake further reading related to each of these theories. You might want to start with those in 'Further resources' at the end of this unit. Reflect on where they would fit in with your own experiences of transition that you explored in Task 3.4.2 and 3.4.3. Discuss these theories and your view of them with other student teachers. Consider what you can learn from them to improve current transition practices. Store your notes in your PDP.

Examples of planning and preparation for primary-secondary transitions

As mentioned earlier, schools are very aware of issues pupils might face and try to provide support to enhance their experience of transition. Galton (2010) describes *five bridges of transition*, namely: administrative; social/user-friendly; curriculum; teaching and learning; and managing learning. What these might involve is explored below.

Administrative

This involves good communication between schools through exchanging information about pupils, head teachers meeting, and guidance teacher/special educational needs coordinator (SENCO) visiting the primary school. The information exchanged is predominantly academic information, with less emphasis on social and emotional information about each pupil and no information exchanged about a pupil's other experiences of transitions. This applies in an educational context when moving from nursery to primary school, within primary school or primary to secondary school, but also within life transitions such as a major bereavement in the family.

Social/user-friendly

At the very least, this involves familiarisation with the new school and staff, as well as with peers from other primary schools. This can take the form of an open day, induction events and residentials, usually in June/July for the move in August/September. Some schools have been known to organise treasure hunts around the school to help pupils navigate the physical environment and provide opportunities to work with other pupils they do not know. Pupils may be assigned buddies, and, in the age of technology, this can involve online links between pupils in primary and secondary schools.

Curriculum

Several countries around the world, including Scotland and Finland, have changed their national curriculum to enhance its continuity and progression. In England, for example, bridging units and summer schools have been introduced to assist with continuity.

Teaching and learning

This includes a clearer focus on pedagogical continuity, with teachers using similar strategies for teaching and learning in primary and secondary schools. There are examples of reciprocal visits with primary teachers going to secondary school to observe or teach, and vice versa. However, despite these practices, several differences in learning and teaching approaches are still noted within the school systems, including the use of space and layout of the class, use of group work, problem-solving, and so on. However, it must be recognised that there might be differences between subject teachers anyway.

Managing learning

The focus here is on preparing pupils for academic life after they start at secondary school. This might involve developing critical thinking and problem-solving skills. Examples of this might include activities such as critical analysis of a piece of literature or understanding the concept of globalisation where, as a group, pupils need to work on the learning intentions, sources of research, debating and unpacking their and others' understanding, and so on. The idea is to help pupils develop into 'professional learners' (Galton, 2010).

In terms of planning and preparation for the move to secondary school, there are variations in when activities involving pupils start. There is an indication from parents that sometimes the preparation is left until too late. There is also strong evidence that these should start and carry on for at least six months before and six months after the move (Jindal-Snape and Foggie, 2006), if not longer, as part of an ongoing process.

What seems to work for pupils?

A pupil's well-being can be dependent on feeling in control or having a voice (The Children's Society, 2012). All pupils, especially in countries where education is compulsory, go through transition between primary and secondary school, irrespective of the educational system, terminology or age of this transition. For some, it might mean a move to a different school; others might carry on in the same school with some of the same teachers. It might be seen to be a normative transition with no choice in whether the pupil wants to make this move or not. So how can pupils be more in control of this transition?

Voice and opportunities to discuss excitement and concerns

Pupils can feel more in control if they are actively involved in decisions regarding the transition and associated planning and preparation. For example, teachers can involve pupils quite early on in the final year of primary school (or even earlier) in an exploration of what this change might mean to them or what they might be looking forward to or worrying about. Pupils can be given an opportunity to explore in a safe environment any concerns that they might have or 'horror stories' that they might have heard. They can share these with the aim of finding out whether others have similar concerns and how they might be able to resolve them. For example, Jindal-Snape (2010c) created a board game that includes key aspects that pupils have mentioned in the context of primary–secondary transitions (see Table 3.4.1 for some of these themes). Pupils can play this game at home or in school with an adult or a group of peers to explore and discuss transition-related aspects.

Familiarisation and knowledge of the new context

As mentioned earlier, schools are already doing a lot to facilitate familiarisation and knowledge of the new context. These attempts have been found to be most successful when familiarisation happens for a long period; for example, pupils starting to use the swimming pool in the secondary school a couple of years prior to transition.

There is also a clear indication from pupils that they want to move to the new school with pupils they know. However, it is important to remember that moving with friends cannot, alone, guarantee successful transition. Further, the link for some pupils is unclear, as some pupils who move with friends report difficulties and some who do not move with friends report no difficulties with move (Jindal-Snape, 2010b).

Rehearsing in a safe environment

Jindal-Snape and colleagues emphasise the importance of rehearsing in a safe environment. This can be done, for example, through creative drama by constructing a possible real-life scenario in which the actors can depersonalise their actions and responses in the guise of 'playing the character'. This provides them with an opportunity to move from their concerns to 'Sam's concerns', a fictional character on whom everybody is comfortable projecting their own or another's concerns. Task 3.4.6 asks you to be involved in creative drama to experience how this might work.

Task 3.4.6   Using creative drama to construct a real-life scenario

Try this task with other student teachers. You or another student teacher could play the role of the facilitator, as well as the other roles.

Scenario

It is the first day at secondary school. Robert and Mary are among the 80 pupils who are starting today. They were together at primary school. Mary has an older brother at secondary school and is feeling quite confident about starting school. Robert doesn't know anybody older than him in the school and is feeling concerned about the 'horror stories' he has heard from others.

In this scene, they are inside the school gates and have to be in classroom 1L10 to meet their mathematics teacher. They have been given a map but are having problems finding their way around school. They are overwhelmed by the size of the school and number of pupils around them. They had attended the induction event in the school before the summer holidays but everything feels different. They ask Sheila for help, but she mocks them and starts teasing them because...

Characters

- Robert (11 years old) is nervous and under-confident but ends up coming across as overconfident and aggressive.
- Mary (11 years old) is positive, cheerful, very sure of herself and tries to impress others by talking about her older brother in the same school, but this might lead to more teasing and name-calling.
- Sheila (13 years old) enjoys teasing other children, and makes it difficult for Robert and Mary to find their way. *The character has to try to persistently block Robert and Mary in every way possible.*

Creative drama activity

Ask other student teachers to volunteer to play the part of each character. The audience are able to suggest change/come and replace the individual and take over that character. (*The facilitator asks the actors to freeze and then asks questions such as why do you think this is happening, what can be done, how do you think this person is feeling, and so on.*)

The ultimate purpose is to try to resolve the conflict through audience participation and for Robert and Mary to find their way to class.

Note in your PDP how this went and what you learned from it.

We suggest, when ready, that you try this with pupils. You could also create similar scenarios in which you could use themes that might come from the pupils themselves; for example, making friends, bullying. This type of work can lead to a pupil being able to participate actively, as well as feeling in control by resolving any problems. It also gives pupils an armoury of strategies and responses that they can use in similar real-life situations along with feeling more competent. However, it is important that you create a safe environment for pupils before doing this work.

Active learning, learning agency, autonomy and choice

Learning agency, defined as 'a capacity for intentional and responsible management of new learning within and between school transitions' (Pietarinen et al., 2010b, p.144), is crucial for well-being. Research suggests that choice and autonomy can have a positive impact on a pupil's sense of self and ability to manage their environment. Further, there is evidence that this is possible through active learning; for instance, through creative activities and a creative learning environment (Davies et al., 2013) (see Unit 5.2 on active learning). In a project where pupils were actively involved in their preparation for transition and getting to know the school and peers through the use of a computer game, it was found that they benefited from the opportunity to choose the game, as well as supporting their teachers in setting up the games consoles (Jindal-Snape, 2012). Being involved in the game provided an opportunity for active learning and learning agency (Pietarinen et al., 2010a, 2010b). Now complete Task 3.4.7.

 Task 3.4.7   Your support needs in relation to transitions

Reflect on the following:

1 Having read this unit, and more widely around the area, how prepared do you feel about your own transition from student teacher to newly qualified teacher (NQT). Draw up a table, similar to Table 3.4.1, to identify your feelings about working as an NQT in a new school. Identify actions you might take to meet any concerns.

2 What professional development do you need to undertake to enable you to be prepared to support pupils in the context of primary–secondary transitions?

3 How might you meet these professional development needs?

You might want to discuss these questions with other student teachers. It is also advisable to revisit these questions at different times on your journey as student teacher and teacher; hence, we suggest you store your thoughts and answers in your PDP. Also, read about Multiple and Multi-dimensional Transitions Theory by Jindal-Snape (2016).

SUMMARY AND KEY POINTS

■ This unit emphasises that transition is a complex and dynamic process, with individual differences in when and how pupils adapt to their new school.

■ It is best to view transition in the context of the pupil's academic and daily life, with interactions between them.

■ Resilience, self-esteem and emotional intelligence theories provide an insight into the socio-emotional processes that a pupil might be going through, as well as providing a basis for effective transition practices.

■ Effective practices in primary and secondary schools should provide pupils with some opportunities to input into the transition process, giving them a voice, some control over the preparation and a degree of autonomy.

■ Pupils' involvement in planning and preparation for transition should enable them to voice their excitement and concerns in a safe environment, as well as promoting a successful transition.

Check which requirements for your ITE programme you have addressed through this unit.

 ## Further resources

Jindal-Snape, D. (ed.) (2010a) *Educational Transitions: Moving Stories from Around the World*, **Abingdon: Routledge.**
Chapters 2 and 3 provide details on theoretical perspectives of transition. Chapters 7, 8 and 9 cover transition research and practice in England, the United States and Finland. Chapter 13 pulls together international transition research and highlights examples of good practice from different countries.

Jindal-Snape, D. (2016) *A-Z of Transitions*, **Basingstoke: Palgrave.**
This book includes entries on various types of transition and theories and provides clear implications for professionals. It also gives information on some strategies that can be used to support transition.

Jindal-Snape, D. and Hannah, E.F.S. (2014) 'Promoting resilience for primary–secondary transitions: supporting children, parents and professionals', in A.B. Liegmann, I. Mammes and K. Racherbäumer (eds.) *Facetten von übergängen im bildungssystem: nationale und internationale ergebnisse empirischer forschung*, **Munster: Waxmann, pp.265-277.**
This chapter uses resilience theory to understand transition needs and support systems. It also considers the Multiple and Multi-dimensional transitions (MMT) model and how different individuals' transitions interact with each other.

Jindal-Snape, D., Roberts, G. and Venditozzi, D. (2012) 'Parental involvement, participation and home-school partnership: using the Scottish lens to explore parental participation in the context of transitions', in M. Soininen and T. Merisuo-Storm (eds.) *Home-School Partnership in a Multicultural Society*, **Turku, Finland: Turku University Faculty of Education B: 80, pp.73-101.**
This unit did not have space to discuss the role of parents in primary–secondary transition. This chapter will give you an insight into parental participation and how it can be achieved.

Jindal-Snape, D., Douglas, W., Topping, K.J., Kerr, C. and Smith, E.F. (2006) 'Autistic spectrum disorders and primary–secondary transition', *International Journal of Special Education*, **21(2), 18-31.**
This paper provides insight into the transition process for pupils with special educational needs (SEN) and emphasises the importance of early planning for transition.

Miller, D.J. and Moran, T.R. (2012) *Self Esteem: A Guide for Teachers*, **London: Sage.**

This book is based on the two-dimensional model of self-esteem. It looks at what this means for teachers, and provides advice on classroom techniques.

www.dundee.ac.uk/eswce/research/resources/

This website provides you with downloadable resources that you can use to facilitate primary–secondary transition.

Appendix 2 lists subject associations and teacher councils and Appendix 3 provides a list of websites.

Capel, S., Leask, M. and Turner, T. (eds.) (2010) *Readings for Learning to Teach in the Secondary School: A Companion to M Level Study*, **Abingdon: Routledge.**

This book brings together essential readings to support you in your critical engagement with key issues raised in this textbook.

Capel, S., Lawrence, J. Leask, M. and Younie, S. (eds.) (2019) *Surviving and Thriving in the Secondary School: The NQT's Essential Companion*, **Abingdon: Routledge.**

This book is designed to support newly qualified teachers in the next phase of development as a teacher. However, you may find it useful as it covers aspects of teaching not included in this book which, nonetheless you experience on your ITE programme.

The subject specific books in the *Learning to Teach (Subject)* series, the *Practical (Subject) Guides*, *Debates in (Subject)* and *Mentoring (Subject) Teachers* are also very useful.

Any additional resources and an editable version of any relevant tasks/tables in this unit are available on the companion website: www.routledge.com/cw/capel

4 Meeting individual differences

Introduction

Every pupil in your class is unique. A class of same-age pupils is likely to contain individuals at different stages of development owing to the combined differences in physical development, socio-emotional development, cognitive development and background. Significant differences arise in the achievements of members of a class of pupils, including pupils in a class where setting is practised. The cultural, religious and economic backgrounds of your pupils can affect their response to schooling. Some pupils respond to academic challenge while others see no point in such demands. Others are gifted and need special attention, as do many pupils with learning or behavioural difficulties. Some pupils are at ease with adults while others find the experience less comfortable.

This chapter, comprising six units, invites you to consider several aspects of the background and development of your pupils. In practice the features discussed interact, giving rise to the complex and varied behaviours that characterise human beings. For ease of discussion, some factors are discussed separately; we hope this approach helps you subsequently to integrate better your understandings of pupils and their learning and meet their individual needs.

Arguments for and against academic selection, the merits of banding, streaming or setting as opposed to mixed-ability classes, have been voiced ever since the 1944 Education Act (UK Parliament), which advocated the separation of pupils by ability and sending either to a grammar, technical or 'modern' school.

Unit 4.1 addresses pupil grouping for learning and goes on to discuss differentiation and progression, focusing on ways to improve the learning of all pupils in whatever type of grouping they are placed. Central to successful differentiation is the identification of pupil needs; thus, case studies invite you to enquire more deeply into the background and response of individual pupils and ways to plan differentiated work. You may want to return to this unit after dipping into other units.

Unit 4.2 focuses on the physical characteristics of pupils as they approach adolescence and young adulthood and draws attention to the range of 'what is normal'. We address issues of diet and health of young people, and the ways in which schools contribute to healthy eating. We focus a section of this unit on obesity in pupils; we focus, too, on the ways in which schools can address this issue both through the academic curriculum and more widely.

Unit 4.3 addresses the issue of cognition and cognitive development. Logical reasoning is one important aspect of cognitive development, along with others such as problem solving, developing skills and creative thinking. We note the importance placed on logical reasoning by Western societies through tests of ability. The notion of intelligence is introduced, including the 'nature-nurture' debate, and we touch on the theory of 'multiple intelligences'. Examples of teaching material from secondary school curricula are discussed in terms of their cognitive demand on pupils of different ages. Through set tasks there are opportunities for you to work with pupils to see how they respond to different demands. We address, too, the importance of teaching pupils how to learn and to think about their own learning, and the central role of language in the development of cognitive skills is discussed. This unit also has further follow-up information and tasks on the companion website.

In Unit 4.4, 'Responding to diversity', the background of pupils is considered, including class, gender and ethnicity. A significant factor related to class is poverty. These factors are discussed separately while recognising that for every pupil these factors combine in different ways. We highlight some differences in performance of groups of pupils from various backgrounds, using research evidence, and discuss possible causes of those differences.

In Unit 4.5, moral education and values education are introduced and explained, and their development linked to the curriculum for schools in England, including Citizenship and the importance of personal, social and health education (PSHE) courses. The emphasis is on the way that schools contribute to moral education and values education through both the overt and hidden curriculum. While not stressing differences between pupils, the focus of the chapter does acknowledge the range of values and beliefs in our society and how schools not only have to respond to such differences but also contribute to the spiritual, moral and cultural development of pupils in addition to their cognitive and physical development. Opportunities for teachers to address moral and ethical issues are provided through tasks, and ways to introduce discussion between pupils are suggested.

Inclusion and Special Needs education is the focus of Unit 4.6, and it carefully considers the 2014 special educational needs and disability code of practice for schools in England, which has established a framework for the education of children and young people with special educational needs and disabilities (SEND). The unit draws attention to significant changes in recent years in the way in which pupils with SEND are supported, and emphasises the importance of the classroom teacher in the identification of need and response to need. There is reference to sources of support and guidance, including the support of other professionals.

4.1 Pupil grouping, progression and differentiation

Alexandra Titchmarsh

Introduction

In your development as a student teacher, you are required to focus on a number of principles for planning and teaching. These include:

- setting suitable learning challenges;
- responding to pupils' diverse learning needs;
- overcoming potential barriers to learning.

In this unit, we consider how different grouping arrangements have been and are currently used as a means of coping with differences in pupils' performance. There is evidence that pupil grouping may depend on the subject taught and the philosophy of the school (see, for example, the Education Endowment Foundation). We also consider how progression for all pupils across the age and ability range can be achieved through teaching and learning approaches that ensure that account is taken of a range of learning needs. Strategies for developing differentiated units of work are provided, building on your subject specialist focus. See also Units 2.2 and 3.2, which address lesson planning and motivation, respectively.

OBJECTIVES

At the end of this unit, you should be able to:

- understand the links between pupil grouping, progression and differentiation;
- evaluate the implications of learning in a range of pupil grouping arrangements;
- discuss definitions of progression and differentiation and their relationship to effective teaching;
- discuss teaching methods that allow for differentiation;
- begin to apply principles of differentiated approaches to learning in lesson planning.

Check the requirements for your initial teacher education (ITE) programme to see which relate to this unit.

Grouping pupils across the school

There are a range of ways in which schools can cope with differences in pupil performance, i.e. through streaming, banding, setting, or by setting work at the appropriate levels for pupils in wide or mixed-ability classes. Streaming places the best performers in one class for all subjects, the least able performers in another class, with graded classes in between. Banding places pupils in broad performance groups for all subjects and tries to avoid producing classes comprising only pupils of low attainment or those unwilling to learn. Setting describes the allocation of pupils to classes by attainment in each subject, that is, streaming or banding for each subject. Broad streaming and banding support a notion of a general intelligence, whereas setting acknowledges that pupil aptitude and attainment may be different across subjects and contexts. In order to meet the needs of more able or gifted and talented pupils, there is interest both at the policy and school level in acceleration or fast-tracking, that is, moving a pupil or groups of pupils into a class with an older age group for some or all subjects.

There are strong arguments in favour of, and opposing, mixed-ability teaching. Reviews by Hallam (2002) and Kutnick et al. (2005) showed that all pupils gained socially from working in mixed-ability groups. Such groupings allowed pupils from a variety of backgrounds, as well as abilities, to work together, strengthening social cohesion. Another finding was support for some form of setting in mathematics and other subjects where learning is dependent on a more linear acquisition of skills and knowledge, for example, in modern languages and science (Harlen, 1997; Ireson et al., 2002). An earlier comparative study of pupils in two comprehensive schools rigorously documented their differences in knowledge and understanding of mathematics and their motivation and attitude towards the subject (Boaler, 1997). This study identified advantages and disadvantages to both setting and mixed-ability teaching and differences in approach to the teaching of mathematics by the subject staff. One conclusion from the study was that pupils in mixed-ability classes did as well as pupils taught in ability sets. However, the latter were taught in a more traditional way, through rule learning then application, whereas the former linked mathematics to the everyday life of pupils and used more open-ended project work as part of their teaching strategies. From this study, the evidence in favour of grouping pupils one way rather than another is not clear.

Since the introduction of the Education Reform Act (ERA, 1988), successive governments in England have advocated a return to grouping by ability – through streaming, banding or setting, together with increased whole-class teaching. A review of attainment and pupil grouping across schools does not support the contention that setting alone contributes to success or that setting improves the standards of those not achieving adequately (Kutnick et al. 2005, p.6). For example, at KS3, the review identifies:

■ no significant difference between setting and mixed ability teaching in overall attainment outcomes;
■ ability grouping does not contribute much to the raising of standards of all pupils;
■ lower-achieving pupils show more progress in mixed-ability classes;
■ higher-achieving pupils show more progress in set classes.

(Kutnick et al., 2005, p.5)

The advantages of grouping pupils one way rather than another is not clear-cut; the evidence suggests that, in some circumstances, setting may promote the learning for some pupils in some subjects. The downside of setting may be some reduction in positive attitudes by pupils towards their peers, a heightened sense of anxiety of some pupils in higher sets, reduced motivation of those labelled 'not bright' and diminished cross-cultural mixing.

Setting is said to be less demanding on teachers to prepare lessons for setted groups. However, given that top sets are often large groups, top sets may contain not only very able pupils, who may be unchallenged by the work expected of the majority, but may also contain a wide spread of ability and motivation. Organising learning and teaching to maximise the potential of all pupils requires teachers to acknowledge that their classes, however grouped, are mixed ability.

So, the best way to group pupils remains a vexed question. There is debate, for example, as to whether there should be less emphasis on how pupils are grouped and more on strategies that target individual achievement (for example, the use of data, assessment for learning), booster classes, differentiated challenge and, at the same time, approaches to learning that can maximise achievement for all pupils (emphasis on thinking processes, learning to learn, intervention via questioning, collaborative learning and literacy across the curriculum). There is also debate on 'personalised learning', which is intended to allow for greater tailoring of the curriculum to individual needs. Unit 5.5 looks at personalised learning. At the whole-school and class levels, groupings have a very direct link to how we differentiate to meet individual differences in learning and performance. A common theme in the conclusions to the best evidence studies of research into pupil grouping is that what goes on in the classroom, the pedagogic models and the teaching strategies used, is likely to have more impact on achievement than how pupils are grouped.

Task 4.1.1 invites you to investigate pupil grouping in your school.

 Task 4.1.1   How are pupils grouped in your placement school?

Find out the ways in which pupils are grouped in your placement school, the reasoning behind the grouping and how it works in practice. Grouping arrangements often change after pupils have been in the school for a term, or a year. Different policies may apply often at the transition from KS3 to KS4, as well as between subjects.

Are primary school records (for example, their achievement levels) used to group pupils? Or are other tests used, such as the Year 11 Information System (Yellis) or the Cognitive Abilities Test (National Foundation for Educational Research (NFER) – Nelson), to assess pupils and assign them to groups?

Write a summary of your findings and discuss it with your tutor. Revise and file in your professional development portfolio (PDP) or equivalent.

Grouping within the class: jigsawing and rainbowing

The reviews on the effects of particular types of pupil grouping on pupils' achievement point to the positive effects of within-class groupings, which may include grouping by:

■ ability
■ mix of ability
■ gender

- ■ expertise
- ■ friendship
- ■ age

Learning activities that make use of flexible and different forms of grouping include paired tutoring, jigsawing and rainbowing. In jigsawing, the class is split into groups to study a topic. Jigsaw is a cooperative learning strategy that enables each pupil of a 'home' group to specialise in one aspect of a learning unit. Pupils meet with members from other groups who are assigned the same aspect, and, after mastering the material, return to the 'home' group and teach the material to their group members.

Rainbowing is similar to jigsawing. For example, pupils work in groups of four and discuss a problem or task. Each group member has a colour. Only four colours are used. After discussion, new groups are formed, getting together pupils with the same colour. This means that, in a class of 28, new groups of seven members are formed, and the findings or ideas from each group of four can be shared. Pupils can then return to their original groups of four armed with new ideas. You could, of course, begin with four groups of seven, each with a colour of the rainbow, and then form seven groups of four in the same way.

Further information about these learning activities is available (see, for example DfES, 2004d).

Progression and differentiation

By far the greatest challenge to teachers is to ensure progression in the learning of all pupils in their class. Each pupil is different, whether in streamed, banded or wide-ability classes. Each pupil brings to school unique knowledge, skills and attitudes formed by interaction with parents, peers, the media and their everyday experience of their world. Pupils are not blank sheets on which new knowledge is to be written. Many pupils may have skills of which the school is not aware: some pupils care for animals successfully; others play and adapt computer games; yet others may work with parents in the family business. Some pupils may know more arithmetic than we dream of, as the following parody of stock market practice suggests:

> *Teacher:* 'What is two plus two, Jane?'
> *Jane:* 'Am I buying or selling, Sir?'

Your classroom is a reflection of your pupils' diversity of background and culture that interacts with their potential for learning. Each pupil responds to the curriculum in a different way. Some parents and their children may value a vocationally relevant education more highly because it is immediately applicable to earning a living and may not subscribe to the values placed by the school on a broad, largely academic education.

The teacher must take account of personal interest, ability and motivation to design learning that challenges and interests pupils but, at the same time, ensures for each a large measure of success. Planning and teaching for progression in learning is the core business of teachers. It is important that you understand what progression means in your subject. In geography, for example, progression involves:

- ■ an increase in the breadth of studies;
- ■ an increasing depth of study to respond to pupils' growing capacity to deal with complexities and abstractions;

■ an increase in the spatial scale of what is studied;

■ a continuing development of skills to include specific techniques and more general strategies of enquiry, matched to pupils' developing cognitive abilities;

■ increasing opportunity for pupils to examine social, economic, political and environmental issues;

■ awareness and implications of interactions between people and their environments.

Now complete Task 4.1.2.

 Task 4.1.2   Progression in your own and other subjects

This task is in two parts.

In relation to the progression for geography above, consider how these characteristics might relate to teaching in your subject.

Access a copy of the relevant documents for progression in your subject and summarise how they describe progression, similar to the list for geography above.

With another student teacher, discuss:

(i) similarities and differences between subjects; and (ii) what progression means for your teaching in your subject.

Keep your notes in your PDP for later reference.

Facilitating progression: approaches to differentiation and personalised learning

Planning learning for pupils, choosing learning objectives and learning outcomes based on knowledge of the pupils and of what constitutes progression in particular curriculum areas are critical in ensuring pupils' acquisition of the knowledge, skills and understanding underpinning progress (see also Unit 2.2). Progression and differentiation are therefore two sides of the same coin. The use and success of differentiated approaches depends on teachers knowing their pupils, being secure in their own subject content knowledge and having access to a range of teaching strategies. A straightforward way of thinking about planning for progression is the following:

1   What is it you want your pupils to know, understand and be able to do? This might be at the lesson level, the 'unit of work' level or by the end of year.

2   What is it that pupils know, understand and can do at the start of the topic?

3   What sequence of learning activities may help pupils progress from their present state to your objective(s)?

4   How do you know when pupils have reached where you want them to go?

(Levinson, 2005a, p.100)

To this, we would add:

5   Can pupils recognise that they have progressed either through the lesson or over a longer timescale?

6   Do pupils know how they can progress further within their individual subjects?

In planning for progression, you need to start from where the pupils are, not where you would like them to be. Not all pupils are at the same level, so some degree of differentiation must be built into your day-to-day lessons, units of work and the wider scheme of work for most pupils if you expect to achieve points 1-4.

There is no one right way to differentiate for pupils. Effective differentiation is a demanding task and is about raising the standards of all pupils in a school, not just for those underachieving, with learning difficulties or the gifted. The purpose of a differentiated approach is to maximise the potential of each pupil and to improve learning by addressing each pupil's particular needs. But what exactly is meant by differentiation and how is it achieved?

Consider the following definitions. Differentiation is:

- a planned process of intervention by the teacher in the pupil's learning;
- the matching of work to the differing capabilities of individuals or groups in order to extend their learning;
- about entitlement of access to a full curriculum;
- '"shaking up" what goes on in the classroom so that students have multiple options for taking in information, making sense of ideas, and expressing what they learn. In other words, a differentiated classroom provides different avenues to acquiring content, processing or making sense of ideas, and to developing products' (Tomlinson, 2014, p.3).

However differentiation is defined, the challenge begins with its implementation and practice, which in turn is affected by teachers' beliefs about the ability of their pupils, by expectations of particular groups of pupils and by an understanding of how we learn and of optimal learning environments. The nature of the subject itself and the kind of learning it involves may also affect differentiation.

Differentiation has sometimes had bad press because, at its worst, it has implied an unrealistic and daunting demand on teachers to provide consistently different work and different approaches at the level of the individual pupil or has, unwittingly perhaps on the part of teachers, placed a ceiling on achievement for some pupils.

At its best, given what we know about effective approaches to learning, the influence of high expectations and the potential of all pupils, differentiation may be said to combine a variety of learning options that tap into different levels of readiness, interests, ability and learning profiles with more individualised support and challenge at appropriate times and in appropriate contexts. As we know relatively little about the potential of each pupil, differentiation should be used sensitively and judiciously.

A perspective on differentiation as liberating rather than constraining relies on a number of broader principles informing classroom learning and teaching:

- a focus on key concepts and skills;
- opportunities for problem-solving, critical and creative thinking;
- ongoing assessment for learning;
- a balance between flexible groupings and whole-class teaching;
- identifying pupils as active learners with whom learning goals and expectations are shared;
- collaborative and cooperative learning;
- achievable but challenging targets;
- motivating and interesting learning activities;

- supportive and stimulating learning environments;
- effective use of learning support assistants (LSAs) within the classroom.

How would you describe/define differentiation? In Task 4.1.3, an aspect of a curriculum document is interrogated for its implications for differentiation.

 Task 4.1.3   Differentiation in the curriculum

In many curriculum documents there are statements that identify actions that teachers might take to promote inclusion. For example:

- Providing a secure leaning environment for all pupils.
- Using teaching approaches appropriate to different learning needs.
- Using, where appropriate, a range of organisational approaches, such as setting, grouping or individual work, to ensure that learning needs are, for example, properly addressed. (This can be done within an individual classroom through seating plans or groups or differentiated learning outcomes that are shared with the class; however, this requires the class to know their current level.)
- Varying subject content and presentation so that this matches pupil's learning needs.
- Planning work that builds on pupils' interests and cultural experiences.
- Planning appropriately challenging work for those pupils whose ability and understanding are in advance of their language skills.
- Using materials that reflect social and cultural diversity and providing positive images of race, gender and disability.
- Planning and monitoring the pace of work so that all pupils have a chance to learn effectively and achieve success.
- Adapting your lessons to individual classes and being flexible and versatile to the needs of that class on that given day.

(Source: Department for Education and Skills/Qualifications and Curriculum Authority (DfES/QCA), 2004, p.32)

In a group with other subject student teachers, discuss which of these statements are statements of differentiation. To help you, use the definitions of differentiation discussed earlier in this unit.

Write a working definition of differentiation and discuss it with your tutor. Keep a note of this in your PDP.

Managing differentiation

Differentiation starts with a clear view about what you want your pupils to achieve and what individual pupils may need as a particular learning goal as well as using and acting upon what you know about pupils' previous learning and achievement using assessment data from a range of sources. Pupils should know what they are aiming for both in the short and long term. Realistic targets need to be discussed and set through both knowledge of the individual and use of data. Then begins the consideration of appropriate differentiation strategies and how the process can be managed. It is unrealistic to expect one teacher to plan differentiated work separately for each pupil; it is perhaps better to identify groups of pupils who can work to a given set of learning outcomes using methods suitable to those pupils and the topic in question. However, you may find in some classes you do need to differentiate for individuals.

Differentiation always needs to be included as part of your day-to-day lesson planning. Your lesson planning proforma should include a reminder about differentiation (see also lesson planning in Unit 2.2).

It may be helpful to have a framework or steps in which to plan work:

■ *Step 1*: your aims and short-term outcomes must be broad enough to apply to all pupils in your class. There are often a number of ways of achieving the same goal.
■ *Step 2*: consider which activities to give pupils, linking them to what they already know and then identifying outcomes. Achievable outcomes are one way of ensuring motivation, but must set pupils a challenge, that is, not be too easy. By identifying achievable outcomes for different groups of pupils, the process of differentiation is begun.
■ *Step 3*: the selection of one or more activities. As well as factors in Step 2, check the availability of resources, the backup needed, for example, instructions are pupil-friendly, the language is suitable for your pupils, potentially provide samples or examples for pupils to work from, how any LSA is to be deployed.
■ *Step 4*: planning must include assessment. This can be achieved in a number of ways, such as, by question-and-answer sessions, taking part in small group discussions, responding to queries in class, asking questions of pupils working on an activity, listening to pupils discussing their work, as well as marking books or short tests. The information gained helps you identify the next steps for the pupil. Assessment must reflect your objectives and be aligned with your learning outcomes. (See Units 6.1 and 6.3 on assessment.)

Some lesson plans, units of work or schemes of work plan for differentiation by identifying different priorities for activities, such as:

■ must/should/could;
■ core/support/extension.

For example, an activity is selected that all pupils must attempt; it may contain the core idea of the lesson.

However, differentiation models should also recognise that pupils' learning needs may not be fixed or permanent and may relate to the learning context or topic at hand. Differentiation may therefore involve support or challenge being given to different pupils at different times, for example, sometimes to:

■ a whole group;
■ a targeted group;
■ those who work at speed.

Differentiation strategies: stimulus-task-outcome

The outcome of any particular task depends on the way it is presented to the pupil and how they respond. Teaching methods can be restricted by our own imagination; we are inclined to present a task in just one way with one particular learning outcome in mind rather than to look for different ways to achieve the goals you have set for your pupils. One important, but limited, teaching goal is to ensure pupils remember things, which often involves rote learning (see Unit 5.5), for example, learning Mark Antony's speech on the death of Caesar. Very simply, this exercise is:

■ *Stimulus*. Play the role of Mark Antony in a class presentation of excerpts from *Julius Caesar*.
■ *Task*. Learn by heart the relevant text.
■ *Outcome*. Complete oral recall.

Much learning depends on recall methods: learning the names of element symbols in science; preparing vocabulary in a language lesson; recalling formulae or tables from mathematics; learning to spell. Recall is necessary, if unexciting, when compared with creative forms of learning.

If we wish to help pupils recall and use knowledge, then we move up a level, to consolidate and widen understanding. This situation opens opportunities to use a variety of contexts, including ones directly appropriate to pupils' needs, that is, differentiation by choice of stimulus. For example, to consolidate pupils' understanding of punctuation, you could:

1   ask pupils to punctuate a piece of text from which the punctuation has been removed;
2   as 1 above using a written report of an interview;
3   as 1 or 2 above but read it through first with the pupils;
4   engage in a taped discussion with pupils and ask pupils to write a short report of what was said, with verbatim examples;
5   ask pupils to interview other pupils, or staff, about a topic and write a report that includes a record of some interviews;
6   ask pupils to write a scene for a play.

Thus, for different stimuli, all pupils consolidate their understanding of punctuation, but the level of outcome is different according to the difficulty of the task and ability of the pupils, that is, differentiation and progression.

Now complete Task 4.1.4.

By contrast with Task 4.1.4, Task 4.1.5 invites you to discuss and identify ways in which one stimulus might be used for different outcomes.

 Task 4.1.4   Lesson planning for differentiation: different tasks for a similar learning outcome

Choose a specific learning outcome for a topic you have taught or are about to teach. Identify two or three different tasks that allow pupils to achieve the identified learning outcome. In which ways are the tasks the same and different? Use the example above, of developing understanding of punctuation, to help you.

Discuss the tasks with your tutor. If possible, try out the tasks with your class and review the outcomes of the lesson. Keep a copy of the lesson plans and evaluation in your PDP.

   Task 4.1.5   Lesson planning for differentiation: one stimulus with different tasks and outcomes

You have a set of photographs showing the changing landscape of London from 1850 to present. (If you do not like the choice of photographs, choose your own stimulus, for example, an astronaut working in a space lab, a Salvador Dali painting or an environmental activist at work.) Describe two or more ways in which you could use these photographs to teach your subject. Confine your discussion to a class you teach covering one to two lessons. For each example, identify:

■   how you use the photographs;
■   the activities you set your pupils;
■   the objectives and learning outcomes;
■   how you assess outcomes;
■   the ways in which the activities are differentiated.

  Analyse your plan in terms of task and outcome for the differentiated approaches you develop.

  Discuss your plan with your tutor. Identify how differentiation can be achieved for your pupils and why your choice of task, learning outcomes and assessment are appropriate. File your plan and a summary of discussion in your PDP.

Differentiation through teacher input and support

Differentiation also takes place at the point of contact with the group or individual. The level and nature of your response to pupils is itself an act of differentiation, and includes:

■   checking that pupils understand what they are supposed to do;
■   listening to a discussion and prompting or questioning when needed;
■   helping pupils to mind map or spider diagram an idea or problem (see also Unit 5.2);
■   asking questions about procedure or techniques; suggesting further action when difficulties arise or motivation flags;
■   giving pupils supporting worksheets or other written guidance appropriate to the problem in hand; the guidance might explain the topic in simpler terms or simpler language; you may, if appropriate, use word fills or add extra information;
■   checking pupils' notebooks and noting progress;
■   marking pupils' work;
■   encouraging pupils by identifying success;
■   setting achievable and realistic targets for improvement;
■   increasing the demand of an existing task;
■   noting unexpected events or achievements for a plenary session.

Now try Task 4.1.6.

Task 4.1.6   Differentiation: class-teacher interaction

Discuss the above list of teacher support strategies with other student teachers and identify those strategies appropriate to the teaching of your subject. Add to the list of responses for your teaching. Store in your PDP for reference when appropriate.

Knowing how to set differentiated tasks depends on how well you know your pupils. The activity needs to be challenging yet achievable. Other ways in which activities can be differentiated include:

- the task's degree of open-endedness;
- the pupils' familiarity with the type of task (for example, pupils are often used to worksheet-based lessons where the information is given to them and they have to extract the information, and are not necessarily used to enquiry-based lessons);
- the pupils' degree of familiarity with the resources;
- whether the activity is a complete piece of work or a contributory part of a larger exercise;
- the amount of information you give pupils;
- the language level at which it is presented;
- whether the activity is set orally or by means of written guidance;
- degree of familiarity with the concepts needed to tackle the activity;
- the amount of guidance given to pupils, for example, in science lessons, the guidance given on making measurements, recording data or drawing a graph.

The activity suggested in Task 4.1.5 could be discussed in terms of these criteria. Task 4.1.7 invites you to appraise this list for your own subject teaching.

 Task 4.1.7   Differentiation: how the task is presented and supported

Discuss the list above with other student teachers in your subject. In groups, say, of two people, rewrite the list using strategies appropriate to your subject and the context of your teaching. Share your list with the group and go on to revise your own list. Store this in your PDP.

Differentiation by outcome and how the activity is assessed

Differences in outcome may be recognised by the amount of help given to pupils and how the activity was set and supported. This aspect of differentiation was referred to in Task 4.1.6. In addition, your expectations of what counts as a satisfactory response to the activity lies in your assessment criteria. Your assessment strategy reflects your criteria. These criteria might include:

- the extent to which all aspects of the problem have been considered;
- the adoption of a suitable method of approaching the activity;

- the use of more difficult concepts or procedures in planning;
- the recognition of all the factors involved in successful completion of the activity and limiting the choice appropriately;
- thoroughness and accuracy of recording data in a quantitative exercise;
- appropriateness and selection of ways to present information and the thoroughness and depth of analysis;
- use of appropriate ideas (or theory) to discuss the work;
- accuracy and understanding of conclusions drawn from an activity (for example, are statements made appropriate to the content and purpose of the activity?);
- distinction between statements supported by evidence from speculation or opinion;
- the way the activity is written about, such as the selection of appropriate style for the target audience;
- the ability of pupils to express themselves in an increasingly sophisticated language;
- the use of imagination or insight;
- the selection of appropriate diagrams, sketches or pictures;
- sensible use of information and communications technology (ICT) to support a task;
- recognition of the limitations of the approach to a problem and awareness of ways to improve it.

By choice of assessment criteria, you differentiate the work set. Statements such as those listed help you construct your assessment strategy.

Differentiation through curriculum design

Moving from differentiating your teaching in a lesson to one embracing the curriculum, one model of a differentiated curriculum suggests that the curriculum needs to be organised around the following core elements:

- learning environment or context (for example, changes to where learning takes place, open and accepting classroom climate);
- content (for example, greater levels of complexity, abstraction);
- process (for example, promotion of higher-level skills, greater autonomy, creative thinking);
- product (for example, encouraging the solving of real problems, the use of real audiences).

(Maker and Nielson, 1995; DCSF, 2008a)

You might refer back to the ideas in the list above, 'differentiation by outcome'.

Differentiation can therefore include different or enriched learning experiences that take place outside the classroom or beyond the school, providing additional learning opportunities

Differentiation is good teaching and requires that you know your pupils. This knowledge enables you to judge the extent to which pupils have given an activity their best shot or settled for the easy option. Your role is to motivate your pupils and give support. Some pupils may present a greater challenge than others, and examples are given in case studies below. It is important to remember that you are unlikely to be successful with all pupils all the time. Read these case studies and then address Task 4.1.8. See Unit 4.6 on special educational needs (SEN) and Rose (2004) for further discussion of differentiation of pupils with SEN.

Case studies of pupils

Peter

Peter is a popular member of his group and has an appealing sense of humour. He can use this in a disruptive way to disquiet teachers while amusing his peers.

He appears very bright orally but when the work is of a traditional nature (that is, teacher-led), he often avoids the task in hand; it is at such times that he can become disruptive. His disruption is not always overt; he employs a range of elaborate avoidance tactics when asked to settle to work and often produces very little. His written language and numeracy attainments are significantly lower than those he demonstrates orally.

When given responsibility in groups, Peter can sometimes rise to the challenge. He can display sound leadership ability and, when he is motivated and interested in a group project, can encourage his peers to produce a good team effort. His verbal presentations of such work can be lively, creative, humorous and full of lateral thinking. At such times, Peter displays an extensive general knowledge.

Peter's tutor is concerned about Peter's progress. He fears that Peter will soon begin to truant from those subjects in which teaching is traditional in style. He is encouraging Peter's subject teachers to provide him with as much problem-solving work as possible.

Filimon

Filimon arrived a year ago from Ethiopia via the Sudan. He had not been at school for at least a year. He speaks Sunharic at home, as well as some Arabic, but knew no English on arrival. Eight months of the year he has spent at school here have been a 'silent period', during which time he was internalising what he was hearing. Now he is starting to speak with his peers and his teacher. He has a reading partner who reads to him every day, and now Filimon is reading these same stories himself.

Joyce

Joyce is a very high achiever. She always seems to respond to as much extension activity as she can get. She puts in a lot of effort and produces very well-presented work (for example, capably using ICT), and amply demonstrates her ability to understand, evaluate and synthesise. Joyce's achievements are maximised where she is able to work on her own or in a pair with one or a couple of other girls in the class. In other groups, she tends to keep to herself. Some teachers are concerned that she is not developing her social and leadership potential.

Joyce's parents put a lot of pressure on her and are keen for Joyce to follow an accelerated course wherever this is possible. Should she achieve her ambitions for higher education, Joyce will not be the first in her family to make it to Oxbridge.

These case studies were provided by Paul Greenhalgh, adapted by him from Greenhalgh (1994). You may find it instructive to select one of the pupils described above and consider how their presence in your class would modify your lesson planning.

Now address Task 4.1.8.

 Task 4.1.8   Writing your own case study

Prepare a short case study of two pupils in one of your classes. Identify two pupils for whom further information would be helpful to you in lesson planning and use the examples of case studies above to help you identify the information that you need to collect. Do not use the pupil's real name in any report you make or discussion outside the school.

Collect information from the class subject teacher and the form teacher. The form teacher can give you background information about the pupils, as much as is relevant to your study.

After collecting the information and writing your report, ask the class teacher to read it and comment on it. Finally, use the information to amend Task 4.1.7 or plan a new lesson.

If there are other student teachers in your placement school, share your case studies with them. Use the case studies to identify some learning needs of these pupils and plan teaching strategies to take account of these needs. The study can contribute to your PDP.

Finally, we return to the topic of pupil grouping and the use of the teaching strategies of jigsawing and rainbowing (see the section 'Grouping within the class' above). Task 4.1.9 invites you to explore one of these strategies over a small number of lessons and evaluate the experience.

Task 4.1.9   In-class grouping and teaching strategies

Develop a plan to try out either jigsawing or rainbowing with a class you teach. Read the following two papers before embarking on the task:

1   *National Strategies: Grouping Pupils for Success* (DfES, 2006a);
2   *Pedagogy and Practice: Teaching and Learning in Secondary Schools. Unit 10 Group Work* (DfES, 2004d).

Suggested procedure:

▪   Try out one of the strategies identified in 2 above with a class you teach (for example, one that would respond to a new grouping arrangement), or with a class with whom you are not making expected progress.
▪   Select a topic suitable for subgroup working, draft a rough plan for a lesson, including a set of aims and objectives, and discuss the plan with your tutor or class teacher. Redraft and try out the plan on a small scale over one lesson to test out the groupings you can make, the instructions you give, how to move pupils around groups, and how to round off the lesson. Evaluate the lesson and decide whether to continue with this class or choose another.
▪   Develop a set of lesson plans covering three lessons, including learning objectives and learning outcomes for each lesson:
    ▪   Lesson 1: identify the task, provide background for the pupils, including resources and perhaps homework. Brief your class for the second lesson.
    ▪   Lesson 2: introduce the activity, indicate how the groups will form and re-form and what pupils are expected to do in each group. Allow time for pupils to consolidate what

they gained from the activity, for example, by a plenary session and introducing the final lesson.

■ Lesson 3: consolidate the work done, leading to the final product.

Check your plans with your tutor/class teacher and teach the lessons.

You may find it helpful for your evaluation to keep a pocket notebook handy to jot down events that occur, the good things and bad things that happen, including pupil responses and comments. Flesh out these notes after each lesson.

Evaluate your teaching against your aims, including implicit aims such as enjoyment, enthusiasm, greater participation and improved behaviour pattern.

Identify the pupil gains from the strategy, including knowledge and skills both cognitively and affectively, the advantages and drawbacks of the strategies.

Discuss your evaluation report with your tutor and identify how you might develop this report into a piece of coursework. Retain the original report in your PDP.

SUMMARY AND KEY POINTS

■ This unit has discussed the ways in which pupils can be grouped for teaching, from streaming, setting and banding to mixed-ability classes. Relative merits of each strategy are mentioned in the light of research. The advantages of any one way of grouping pupils are not clear-cut and other factors strongly influence the achievement of pupils, such as the expectations of the teacher. The developments of in-class differentiation of work for pupils and personalised learning have moved the discussion away from grouping.

■ Progression and differentiation are addressed and several examples are provided. The ways in which tasks are selected, set, supported and assessed are each susceptible to modification to meet the needs of different pupils. Differentiation is addressed from a number of aspects, starting from a simple model of planning using stimulus, task and outcome. The importance of the role of the teacher in supporting and guiding their pupils is emphasised. Strategies for the management of differentiation are addressed, emphasising that in all classes there are pupils with different needs, irrespective of the way the pupils are grouped for teaching. Differentiating your teaching is a responsibility of all teachers, not just for those teachers addressing pupils with special educational needs.

■ We have suggested that tasks should be related to the experience of the pupil whenever possible and, further, that the outcomes should be achievable. You may find the discussion about Vygotsky and Piaget in Unit 5.1 helpful in developing those ideas. For those wishing to go further, you can explore lesson planning in a different way, using a constructivist approach (see Unit 5.1).

■ The skills of teaching this way are acquired with experience and, importantly, better understanding of your pupils. Whilst acknowledging that many student teachers move schools at least once in their ITE programme, it is important you begin to understand differentiated approaches to teaching and learning.

Check which requirements for your ITE programme you have addressed through this unit.

Further resources

DCSF (Department for Children, Schools and Families) (1997-2011) *Key Stage 3 National Strategy Materials*, viewed 2 July 2018, from http://webarchive.nationalarchives.gov.uk/20110113104120/ http://nationalstrategies.standards.dcsf.gov.uk/
The archive of the National Strategies offers a range of supporting material for teachers and can be explored for materials on ability grouping and differentiation, as well as other teaching resources.

DfES (Department for Education and Skills) (2006a) *National Strategies: Grouping Pupils for Success*, London: DfES, viewed 2 July 2018, from http://webarchive.nationalarchives.gov.uk/20110812191333/ http://nsonline.org.uk/node/84974
This document discusses the arguments for and against different ways of grouping pupils but moves on to explore more flexible ways of grouping beyond rigid streaming and setting models and drawing upon evidence from research. It does not give subject-specific advice about grouping but does identify contexts in which different ways of grouping pupils may be beneficial.

Education Endowment Foundation - Pupil Grouping, viewed 4 February 2019, from: https://educationendow mentfoundation.org.uk/toolkit/toolkit-a-z/ability-grouping/

Imbeau, M.B. and Tomlinson, C.A. (2010) *Leading and Managing a Differentiated Classroom*, Alexandria, VA: Association for Supervision and Curriculum Development (ASCD).
Differentiated instruction recognises that pupils are not the same and that access to equal education necessarily means that, given a certain goal, each pupil should be provided resources, instruction and support to help them meet that objective. This text addresses these factors. See also similar texts on the ASCD website.

Kerry, T. (2002) *Learning Objectives, Task-Setting and Differentiation*, London: Nelson-Thornes.
This book, part of a series addressing professional skills for teachers, clarifies each of these skills, explains their purpose and explores issues around, and the consequences of, the implementation of these skills. Practical application is discussed, supported by examples and activities. It also encourages readers to assess their own implementation and progress by analysing the tasks against standards.

Rose, R. (2004) 'Towards a better understanding of the needs of pupils who have difficulties accessing learning', in S. Capel, R. Heilbronn, M. Leask and T. Turner (eds.) (2004) *Starting to Teach in the Secondary School: A Companion for the Newly Qualified Teacher*, 2nd Edition, London: RoutledgeFalmer.
This chapter addresses lesson planning for pupils who have difficulty learning. The author suggests an enquiry-based approach to teaching alongside cooperative teaching and learning.

Appendix 2 lists subject associations and teacher councils and Appendix 3 provides a list of websites.

Capel, S., Leask, M. and Turner, T. (eds.) (2010) *Readings for Learning to Teach in the Secondary School: A Companion to M Level Study*, Abingdon: Routledge.
This book brings together essential readings to support you in your critical engagement with key issues raised in this textbook.

Capel, S., Lawrence, J. Leask, M. and Younie, S. (eds.) (2019) *Surviving and Thriving in the Secondary School: The NQT's Essential Companion*, Abingdon: Routledge.
This book is designed to support newly qualified teachers in the next phase of development as a teacher. However, you may find it useful as it covers aspects of teaching not included in this book which, nonetheless you experience on your ITE programme.

The subject specific books in the *Learning to Teach (Subject)* series, the *Practical (Subject) Guides*, *Debates in (Subject)* and *Mentoring (Subject) Teachers* are also very useful.

Any additional resources and an editable version of any relevant tasks/tables in this unit are available on the companion website: www.routledge.com/cw/capel

Adolescence, health and well-being

Ceri Magill and Barbara Walsh

Introduction

Adolescence is a transitional stage of growing up that changes a child into an emerging adult and involves biological, social and psychological changes including dramatic changes to the body. The changing nature of family structure and social values play an important part in the adolescent phase of development. The expectation of different cultures and/or families influences young people, especially in the school setting. Important factors that may affect adolescents' self-image and their schooling relate to the family, including the socio-economic status, employment history and family harmony. In an average class of thirty 15-year olds, three could have a mental disorder; 10 are likely to have witnessed their parents separate; one could have experienced the death of a parent; seven are likely to have been bullied and six may be self-harming (Public Health England, 2015).

Student teachers need to be aware of the key factors that cause concern with adolescents. How young people deal with failure, especially around the time of examinations and the pressure put on them by parents and themselves, is an important issue. Bullying, body image, internet/social media, sexual pressures (looking and behaving in a certain way when in a relationship) and employment prospects all impact on young people's well-being (Public Health England, 2015; Department for Education (DfE), 2016f).

Adolescents begin to develop an independence from their parents, which, on its own, can cause many problems, especially because their parents' opinions become less important. This can be reflected in their behaviour in school and this is sometimes seen as them being disrespectful and ignorant. It is important for you as a student teacher to understand these changes; how a pupil is feeling on the inside often affects how they cope and behave in the external environment. There is not always a clear trigger for mental health or emotional well-being issues. Family relationship difficulties, peer relationship difficulties, a family/close friend bereavement, exposure to unhealthy coping mechanisms in other pupils or the media, trouble in school or with the police, exam pressure, transition to a new school or illness in the family can all initiate a change.

One aspect of a good school is how successful it is in promoting the well-being of its young people. During personal, social and health education (PSHE), well-being is taught as a discreet focus during the adolescence phase. This includes sex and relationship education. A social and emotional aspect of learning (SEAL) course normally takes a whole school overview of promoting well-being alongside behaviour, attendance, learning and employability. Promoting emotional well-being and resilience from an early age is important as it can reduce the risk of pupils turning to unhealthy coping mechanisms such as self-harm, eating disorders or substance misuse. These protective factors can be developed through the PSHE education curriculum. They can include:

■ good communication skills;
■ good problem-solving skills;
■ healthy coping skills, including healthy responses to moments of crisis;
■ the knowledge, skills and confidence to seek help;
■ the ability to recognise, name describe and understand a range of emotions;
■ the ability to manage difficult emotions in a healthy way;
■ friends and social engagement and interaction;
■ positive self-esteem and appreciation of difference and uniqueness;
■ experience of, and ability to manage failure.

(PSHE Association, 2016)

Mental health issues

The 21st century has seen a number of changes that could influence young people's mental health (Luthar and Barkin, 2012). They include the rising affluence and worsening income inequality in families. Changes in the family environment including family conflict, parental mental health problems and the emergence of parenting styles that place a lower value on child obedience (DfE, 2016f). There are also the highly publicised links to mental health problems including increased exposure to television, internet and social media and increasing pressure from peers within the school setting (Carli et al., 2014; O'Keeffe and Clarke-Pearson, 2011).

OBJECTIVES

At the end of this unit you should be able to:

■ describe aspects of the physical development of adolescents;
■ describe and understand some of the physical, cognitive, emotional and mental health differences in pupils during adolescence;
■ appreciate the effect of external pressures and influences on pupils' behaviour and identify some implications of these for teaching and learning;
■ discuss healthy eating and the role of the school in promoting pupil well-being.

Check the requirements for your Initial Teacher Education (ITE) programme to see which relate to this unit.

About development and growth

Young people tend to have growth spurts, particularly after puberty, the point at which the sex glands become functional. Most girls mature physically earlier than most boys. There are differences in growth rates between boys and girls at the onset of puberty and, on average, girls show a growth spurt at an earlier age than boys. However, there is little difference, for example, in mean height of boys and girls up to the age of 13, but after the age of 16 boys are, on average, over 13 cm taller than girls. Height increases appear earlier than weight increases, and this has implications for physical activity. The differential rate of height and weight development is the origin of clumsiness and awkwardness of some adolescent pupils. As well as obvious gender differences between pupils in a coeducational context, the differences between individuals within a group of boys, or a group of girls, can be quite large and obvious. These differences in development can be worrying for the individual and may affect pupils' attitudes and performance to academic work. For example, it can happen that some pupils who have developed physically earlier than their peers may dominate activity in a class, causing a number of pupils to reduce their involvement for fear of being ridiculed by more 'grown-up' members of the class. On the other hand, those developing early may feel self-conscious in front of their later developing peers.

Another feature of physical development is the onset of puberty. The age at which this occurs varies quite widely between both individuals and cultures, as does the period of puberty. Adolescence can begin at age 10 for some while for others it may begin much later and may finish around the age of 19. This means that a 12-year-old girl may be in a pre-pubertal, mid-pubertal or post-pubertal state. A 14-year-old boy may be similarly placed. Thus, it is not sensible to talk to a 14-year-old cohort of pupils as though they are a homogeneous group. The onset of puberty is affected, too, by environmental factors, including diet.

There is evidence that environmental factors affect growth (Sawyer et al., 2012).

In England, the up-take of free school meals may be used as a proxy measure of deprivation. Childhood poverty continues to have a significant impact on young people's well-being and education (Bradshaw, 2016; Sawyer et al., 2012; Jackson et al., 2012).

Physical development and managing your classes

The variation in physical development of pupils shown, for example, in any particular class or any year cohort has implications for your management of classes. These differences are particularly apparent in Years 7–9 and may stand out in activities that prosper on physical maturity or physical control. Boys in early adolescence who develop late often cannot compete with their peers in games; and girls who mature earlier than their friends can also be advantaged in physical education and games but at the same time may feel embarrassed. Thus, competitive activities such as running, throwing or physical confrontation games, such as football, hockey and rugby, favour faster-developing pupils. Equally important is physical control, the ability to coordinate hand and eye, and to control tools and equipment properly and safely. In the past, some adolescents have been regarded as clumsy, which may be related to growth spurts. Activity in subjects such as physical education, art and design, technology, science and computing depend, in part, on good coordination and psychomotor skills.

Now try Task 4.2.1 to gain an understanding of the range of backgrounds, abilities and physical development in any one age group.

Task 4.2.1   A profile of a class: background, abilities and physical development

Select a class you teach and find out as much as you can about the background of your pupils. Then shadow the class for a day and try to relate the ways pupils respond to teachers and different subjects. Link this with observation tasks from Unit 2.1. See notes below for guidance on background.

Discuss your plan with your tutor who can direct you to appropriate sources of information, such as the form tutor. There may be special provisions for some pupils in your school that provide additional information, e.g. homework club or other provision for pupils unable to work at home.

When you visit classrooms, get permission from the teachers, tell them what you are doing, what is to happen to the information and what is expected to emerge. Be prepared to share your findings with them.

Write a short report for your tutor. Respect the confidentiality of information you acquire in any written or oral report. Reports should not quote names. The report may contribute to your professional development portfolio (PDP) or equivalent. Record in your PDP your personal response to this work and any implications it has for you.

Pupil background: notes to help with Task 4.2.1
Some of the information you might gather from the form tutor you are working with includes:

- the names and the numbers of boys and girls;
- the ethnicity of pupils; check the way the school reports ethnicity;
- the religious or cultural background of pupils;
- the physical differences in height and weight;
- recent immigrants or children of families seeking asylum;
- patterns of absences and whether absences are supported by notes from parents or guardians;
- the regularity of completing homework and its quality (teachers should have such records);
- the uptake of free school meals.

Gather data about:

- pupils who have individual learning plans and the reason for this;
- the provision of a support teacher and why;
- pupils who do not have a support teacher but need one;
- pupils who have been identified as 'gifted and talented' in the school;
- pupils with specific learning difficulties, e.g. dyslexia.

Some research suggests that pupils physically maturing faster score better on cognitive tests than pupils developing more slowly. On average, girls develop physically and cognitively faster than boys and the results of standard assessment tasks (SATs) and General Certificate of Secondary Education (GCSE) results may be a reflection of this.

Large differences in performance in school subjects, taken together with differences in physical development, have raised the question of whether pupils should be grouped in classes by age, as they are now, or whether some other method should be used to group pupils for teaching purposes, for example by achievement. Some other educational systems require pupils to reach a certain academic standard before proceeding to the next year, leading to mixed-age classes. Thus, underperforming pupils are kept back a year to provide them with an opportunity to improve their performance. Such practice has an impact on friendship, self-confidence and self-esteem. Equally, you may find schemes for extra-curricular support of talented and able pupils.

Healthy self-esteem rather than high or low self-esteem encompasses feelings of actual and perceived competency, self-efficacy and more importantly feelings of being lovable or approved of (Plummer, 2014). When pupils feel good about themselves, they feel confident and ready to experience new things. By contrast, pupils who do not feel good about themselves may have their confidence damaged by every small setback. It is important for you to differentiate your teaching so that every pupil achieves some success; personalised learning helps give pupils belief in their own abilities and the confidence to take on more challenging tasks (see Unit 3.2 on motivating pupils, Unit 5.5 on personalizing learning and 5.6 on Neuroscience).

Everybody has feelings. It is impossible to be human and not have them, and during adolescence, emotions are particularly strong. It is often easy for adolescents to feel helpless and overwhelmed by emotions. During this time, they may say things in anger or act out only to regret it later. It is important for you to gauge the situation if, for example, they shout out, act out of character or tell you some personal details. Some pupils are happy to share their feelings while others hide them. If they are suppressing anger, sadness or bitterness, it might manifest itself in them blowing small situations totally out of proportion. The side effects of this could be headaches, lethargy and disaffection towards their work and, as a teacher, it is important to be aware of these changes. See also Unit 3.3 on behaviour.

We have discussed the physical and cognitive development of pupils and drawn attention to the differences in development both within a gender group and between boys and girls. A large influence on physical development is diet, lifestyle and attitude to exercise. There is concern (Gov.uk, 2016b) about the dietary habits of some young people, in part about risk of disease, the level of fitness of many young people and issues of overweight and obesity. Yet, Scholes (2016) draws attention to the increased use of computers in entertainment and the accompanying sedentary habits this entails. Thus, we turn to consider diet, development and the curriculum. The advent of the concept of 'healthy schools' in England has required teachers to address 'health' issues including health and well-being (including emotional health), healthy eating, physical activity, as well as PSHE. This development has raised the profile of adolescent eating habits and recommendations for physical activity. This is the subject of the next section.

Diet, health and well-being

Background

Nearly a third of children aged two to 15 years are overweight or obese, and younger generations are becoming obese at earlier ages and staying obese for longer. Reducing obesity levels will save lives as obesity doubles the risk of dying prematurely (Gov.uk, 2016b). Obesity is a complex problem with many impacting factors that include our behaviour, environment, genetics and culture. The root of obesity is caused by an energy imbalance: taking in more energy through food than used through activity. Physical activity is associated with numerous health benefits for children, such as muscle and bone strength, health and fitness, improved quality of sleep and maintenance of a healthy weight. There is also evidence that physical activity and participating in a range of organised sports and after school clubs is linked to improved academic performance (Gov.uk, 2016a). Reducing levels of obesity and bringing about long-term change can be achieved through the active engagement of schools, communities, families and individuals (Gov.uk, 2016a).

Why is there an increase in overweight and obesity in childhood?

A simple answer is to do with energy balance. Physical activity (PA), sedentary behaviours and food intake are key variables implicated in childhood due to their influence on energy balance (Rowland, 2004). For example,

Eight per cent of children aged 11 to 18 years met the Five-a-Day recommendation for fruit and vegetable consumption as reported by the Food Standards Agency and Public Health England through a rolling programme survey carried out in 2012, 2013 and 2014 (Public Health England, 2016). The proportion of adults meeting the Five-a-Day recommendation was 27% of those aged 19 to 64 years and 35% of those aged 65 years and over (Public Health England, 2016). These findings highlight the poor intake of fresh fruit and vegetables that are required for a balanced diet.

Today, nearly a third of children aged two to 15 are overweight or obese and younger generations are becoming obese at earlier ages and staying obese for longer (Gov.uk, 2016b). Reducing obesity levels will save lives as obesity doubles the risk of dying prematurely (Gov.uk, 2016b). Increasing the engagement in physical activity levels will support the rise in obesity. However, it has been found that, excluding school-based activities, 22% of children aged between five and 15 met the physical activity guidelines of being at least moderately active for at least 60 minutes every day (23% of boys, 20% of girls), as reported by the Health Survey for England (2015) physical activity in children (Scholes, 2016). The figures have increased since 2012, when 21% of boys and 16% of girls met the guidelines suggest a very little uptake in physical activity. It was also found that time spent being sedentary (excluding time at school) during the week and at weekends increased with age (Scholes, 2016). Similarly, many adolescents in the UK are not eating healthy diets or meeting the recommendations for exercise (Scholes, 2016). The National Diet and Nutrition Surveys carried out over the years by the Department of Health and Food Standards Agency have shown that adolescents eat more than the recommended level of sugar, salt and saturated fats and insufficient dietary fibre. The most frequently consumed foods were cereals and cereal products, i.e. pasta, rice, white bread, savoury snacks, sugar and chocolate confectionery.

Intervention projects have attempted to address the increase in child overweight and obesity levels through a combination of strategies to increase levels of PA, reduce time spent being sedentary and improve nutritional intake (Fairclough et al., 2013). It has been suggested that (Brown and Summerbell, 2009, Fairclough et al., 2013) school-based interventions that combine PA and diet may prevent children becoming overweight in the future. The Public Health England report 'Everybody active, every day' emphasises that the school setting is extremely important when it comes to children's opportunities to be active (Scholes, 2016). In addition, school-based interventions have proven to have more success when PA and dietary behaviours are reinforced at home thorough a family intervention (Brown and Summerbell, 2009; Waters et al., 2011; Scholes, 2015).

The immediate consequences of overweight and obesity in adolescence are social and psychological. Obese children are more likely to suffer from low self-esteem and behavioural problems. Those who are overweight are often seen as an easy target for bullying, with little peer pressure occurring to prevent it. Obesity in adolescence and young adulthood has been found to have adverse effects on social and economic outcomes (for example, income and educational attainment) (National Health Service (NHS), 2010).

The later health consequences are also serious. Increasing fatness is closely correlated with the development of type 2 diabetes that used to be diagnosed in middle to later life but is now increasingly seen in young adults and children (Public Health England, 2016). Childhood obesity that continues into adult life increases the risk of various diseases including cardiovascular disease, cancer and aggravation of rheumatic diseases and respiratory diseases, such as asthma, in later life (Weichselbaum and Buttriss, 2011).

The strategy of the government is to empower individuals through guidance, with information to enable people to make the best possible choices. In England, the NHS support *Change4Life*, an Internet campaign to encourage a healthy lifestyle that includes both healthy eating and exercise activities for children and their families (*Change4Life*: www.nhs.uk/change4life/pages/what-i schange-for-life.aspx). The NHS, through the *Change4Life* programme, also support the 'Five-a-Day' campaign, which encourages the eating of fruit and vegetables. Guidelines for healthy eating including the 'Eatwell Plate' can be found on the Food Standards Agency website www.food.go.uk.

Developing strategies to address obesity

The national curriculum for physical education, which was revised in England from September 2014 (Key stages 1-4), supports the delivery of a high-quality curriculum to inspire all pupils to succeed and excel in competitive sport and other physically demanding activities. In addition, some of the shared aims of the national curriculum at key stages 1-4 include:
That all pupils:

■ are physically active for sustained periods of time;
■ lead healthy, active lives (DfE, 2013).

In support of the aims of the physical education curriculum, the National Institute for Health and Clinical Excellence (NICE) recommends participation in at least 60 minutes of moderate-to-vigorous intensity PA (MVPA) throughout the day for children and young people (five to 18 years) (Public Health England, 2016).

Also addressing strategies to reduce obesity, the scientific advisory committee on nutrition (SACN) reports that sugar consumption increases the risk of consuming too many calories and that consumption of sugar sweetened beverages is associated with increased risk of type 2 diabetes and linked to higher weight in children (Gov.uk, 2016b). Steps outlined by the government to help tackle childhood obesity include the introduction of a soft drinks industry levy across the UK (Gov. uk., 2016b). In England, the revenue from the levy will be invested in programmes to reduce obesity and encourage physical activity and balanced diets for school-age children. This includes doubling the Primary PE and Sport Premium and putting a further £10 million a year into school healthy breakfast clubs to give more children a healthier start to their day (School Sport in England, 2017).

In addition, all sectors of the food and drinks industry will be challenged to reduce overall sugar across a range of products that contribute to children's sugar intakes by at least 20% by 2020, including a 5% reduction in year one. This can be achieved through reduction of sugar levels in products, reducing portion size or shifting purchasing towards lower sugar alternatives (Gov.uk, 2016b).

The next section focuses on the factors relating to food and activity in the obesogenic environment (an environment that promotes weight gain) of schools and how they affect adolescents.

Eating habits

The latest school food standards (England and Wales) were announced in June 2014. From January 2015, all local authority-maintained schools, academies and free schools set up before 2010 and created from June 2014 onwards must meet these new standards for school food (Gov.uk, 2014).

The Government has suggested that all food in schools must meet nutritional standards so that children have healthy, balanced diets. (Gov.uk, 2014).

This means that the following must be available on menus at schools:

■   high-quality meat, poultry or oily fish;
■   at least two portions of fruit and vegetables with every meal;
■   bread, other cereals and potatoes.

There can't be:

1   fizzy drinks, crisps, chocolate or sweets in school meals and vending machines;
2   more than two portions of deep-fried food a week.

To review any changes to school food standards, access the Children's Food Trust website (www. childrensfoodtrust.org.uk).

Ofsted's School Inspection update also requires inspectors to be familiar with the School Food Plan as a means of supporting healthy choices in school food (Ofsted, 2016). Some schools provide voluntary breakfast clubs that are said to improve attendance, punctuality, concentration levels, problem-solving abilities and creativity (Weichselbaum and Buttriss, 2011). Breakfast clubs provide a range of healthy foods and it is reported that this had been a successful first step in engaging pupils on healthy choices. The school lunch may be the first meal of the day for some pupils. The School Food Trust (SFT, 2012; Gov.uk, 2016a) reports that there are at least 1.6 million children in the UK living in poverty. One consequence of this fact is that many of these children arrive at school hungry. This condition affects both their health and their education (Gov.uk, 2016a).

The government, therefore, recognises that schools are central to creating opportunities to support healthier eating, physical activity and to shape healthy habits (Gov.uk, 2016b). Schools also have unique contact with parents and can signpost them to information and advice on keeping their children healthy. As an example, from September 2017, the government introduced a new voluntary healthy rating scheme for primary schools to recognise and encourage their contribution to preventing obesity by helping children to eat better and move more. This scheme will be taken into account during Ofsted inspections (Gov.uk, 2016b). The scheme will help schools to demonstrate to parents that they are taking evidence-based actions to improve their pupils' health. (Gov.uk, 2016b).

Physical activity

It has been mentioned earlier that one strategy for tackling obesity is exercise and that proposals have been made about the nature and extent needed for it to be beneficial. Physical education and school sport form less than 2% of school life but are useful in fostering habits of activity that can last into adult life. In 2012, Ofsted published 'Beyond 2012: Physical education for all' report in order to address the amount of physical activity in physical education. The report particularly found that very few schools had adapted PE programmes to suit the individual needs of overweight or obese pupils. There was little evidence of a coordinated approach to childhood obesity, even though almost three in 10 children between the ages of two and 15 are classed as obese according to NHS Information Centre figures (Gov.uk, 2013). A significant finding from the report, among others that have contributed to the new national curriculum from 2014, suggests that teachers should improve pupils' fitness by keeping them physically active throughout all lessons and engaging them in regular, high-intensity, vigorous activity or sustained periods of time (Gov.uk, 2013).

Household income is also associated with sedentary behaviour, usually watching TV, for more than four hours a day. As the household income decreases, the average number of hours watching TV increases (NHS, 2009; Department of Health (DoH), 2013). This increased sedentary behaviour contributes to obesity and overweight in pupils and affects the 'social gradient of health' as discussed earlier. A study published by Public Health England (Gov.uk, 2015) found that physically active children are happier and more confident. These findings were taken from *Change4life* and Disney's 10-minute shake up campaign. The campaign indicates strong evidence that physical activity and sport have a positive impact on children's social skills and self-esteem. The evidence review also identified further social benefits for children as a result of physical activity, including increased confidence and peer acceptance, alongside a link to friendship (Gov.uk, 2015).

Moving forward

Given the considerable new funding that the soft drinks industry levy will make available for school sports, the government is also keen that schools are supported as much as possible in how they spend the available funds for maximum impact (Gov.uk, 2016b). During inspections, Ofsted assess how effectively leaders use the Primary PE and Sport Premium and measure its impact on outcomes for pupils, and how effectively governors hold them to account for this. Physical activity will be a key part of the new healthy schools rating scheme mentioned earlier, and so schools will have an opportunity to demonstrate what they are doing to make their pupils more physically active (Gov.uk, 2016). County Sports Partnerships are required to work with National Governing Bodies of sport, the Youth Sport Trust and other national and local providers to ensure that, from September 2017, every primary school in England has access to a co-ordinated offer of high-quality sport and physical activity programmes, both local and national (Gov.uk, 2016b).

Now move on to Task 4.2.2.

 Task 4.2.2   Food and health

Access the National Curriculum for England documents (online at www.gov.uk) or related documents in the country where you are learning to teach. Identify those areas of your subject area, and other curriculum areas, that address issues of healthy eating and healthy lifestyles, such as diet, nutrition and exercise. In England, address KS3 first.

Discuss with your tutor whether there is a coordinated approach in your placement school between the subjects and PSHE. Write a summary of your findings and file in your PDP.

Given all the teaching and learning opportunities provided within schools, there continues to be a problem with overweight and obese adolescents, in addition to the declining levels of PA. The effect of advertising on young people, especially through TV advertising, also contributes. Food marketing to children is a global phenomenon and tends to be pluralistic and integrated, using multiple messages in multiple channels. The World Health Organisation (WHO) stated that the primary concern was with products with high fat, sugar or salt (WHO, 2010; NHS, 2014). Over 75% of the websites carrying high fat, sugar and salt products linked to a corresponding product or brand page on a social networking site, with Facebook and Twitter being the most common. Such commercial messages are designed to persuade adolescents to consume unhealthy products. 'If the marketing didn't work, the food industry wouldn't devote multi-million pound budgets to developing slick campaigns to spread their messages' (BHF, 2011).

There is a range of initiatives in schools in England to try to find a means of improving the health of pupils. The National Healthy Schools Strategy is an ongoing project where schools can work with pupils, teachers, families and the local community to actively promote the physical, social and mental well-being of all. It is an attempt by the government in England to bring together a multifaceted approach to the broad problem of improving the obesogenic environment of modern society. Now complete Task 4.2.3 to gain an understanding of the opportunities for exercise for pupils and healthy food choices.

 Task 4.2.3   The school environment

The definition of an obesogenic environment is one that encourages and promotes high-energy intake and inactivity. Use the answers to the following questions and your observations to evaluate the environment of your placement school.

- How many of your pupils walk or cycle to school?
- Is there safe storage for cycles?
- What is the school food policy?
- Is there a breakfast club?
- How would you describe the environment of the dining room at lunchtime?
- What proportion of the school curriculum is given to PE and sports activities?

   In addition, observe:

- the activities of pupils during break and lunchtime on two different weekdays;
- the food availability and food choices made at lunchtimes on one or two days;
- what proportion of pupils have packed lunches compared to school dinners?

   Write a short account of this aspect of the school environment and discuss it with your school tutor. File the account in your PDP.

Now complete Task 4.2.4 to develop your understanding of health and well-being issues for pupils.

M

   **Task 4.2.4   Adolescence, health and well-being:
a whole-school approach**

The task is in two parts.

Part 1

Schools should be supported to adopt a whole-school approach to promoting the social and emotional well-being of young people (Public Health England, 2015). Write a literature review that focuses on the social and emotional well-being of adolescents. You could start by reading the research reports and literature referred to in this unit. Also, see the further reading at the end of this unit. You may need to focus on recent research, say, in the last 10 years, in order to manage the task on what has been published in the three areas. Your purpose is to convey the knowledge and ideas that have been established on these three areas and their strengths and weaknesses (not just a descriptive list of the material available, or a set of summaries).

Part 2

This can be followed by writing a proposal for a small-scale research study in your school. The proposed research should seek to explore the whole-school policy for 'health and well-being' for your pupils in your placement school and to be evaluated in the light of evidence from your literature review.

   We suggest that you discuss your review and the proposed research plan with your tutor as you proceed. The final document may be used as a basis for coursework and a copy placed in your PDP.

SUMMARY AND KEY POINTS

- Adolescence involves physical, mental, social and emotional changes leading towards maturity and presents dramatic changes in young people. These changes may cause nervous introspection: 'Am I growing normally, am I too tall, too short, too fat? Am I physically attractive to others'?
- Personal appearance assumes a growing importance and causes sensitivity. Girls mature physically earlier than boys, but the range of development of both boys and girls is wide. The range of physical differences between pupils means that, at the same age, pupils react quite differently to tasks and situations in school.
- Young people are taller and heavier than previous generations, in part owing to improved diets. But the obesogenic environment of modern society, the more sedentary lifestyle and increased consumption of unhealthy foods can lead to overweight and obesity. There is growing concern about the rising numbers of overweight and obese pupils and adults and the physical, social and psychological effects that this may have on the individual (DoH, 2011).

- The social and emotional effects of obesity on young people can be as damaging as the health risks. A number of other issues affecting the health of adolescents have not been raised including smoking, drinking and drug use, mental health and sexual health. These are discussed further in the report on *Adolescent Health* (Seddon, 2003).

- Schools have a big role to play in helping pupils through adolescence with minimum disruption in understanding the changes in their bodies, being comfortable with themselves as they are and their appearances.

- Schools play an important part in ensuring that pupils have access to a healthy diet and that they understand its importance to them now and in the future. Involving pupils in understanding and learning about themselves through active participation encourages confidence and supports a positive self-image (see also Unit 5.2). The pupil who feels valued for their contribution is a pupil who is likely to have good self-esteem.

- All teachers have the opportunity to contribute to the health and well-being development of their pupils and engender the self-confidence in young people to take control of this aspect of their lives. Self-confidence may help them to resist advertising pressures related to certain foods or, for example, to challenge what is said to be a fashionable appearance.

Check which requirements for your ITE programme you have addressed through this unit.

 Further resources

Department for Education (2016f) *Mental Health and Behaviour in Schools*, London: DfE, viewed 2 July 2018, from https://assets.publishing.service.gov.uk/government/uploads/system/uploads/attachment_data/file/508847/Mental_Health_and_Behaviour_-_advice_for_Schools_160316.pdf
This document offers departmental advice for school staff about the benefits from learning and developing in a well-ordered school environment that fosters and rewards good behaviour and sanctions poor and disruptive behaviour.

Food Standards Agency www.eatwell.gov.uk
Government advice on food is given in this section of the Food Standards Agency site. This site has up-to-date, easy-to-read references with some resources for teachers. The Food Standards Agency main site is www.food.gov.uk.

MindEd https://www.minded.org.uk
A free, educational e-learning resource that supports children's and young people's mental health

**NICE (National Institute for Health and Care Excellence) Guidance
https://www.nice.org.uk/guidance**
This site lists published guidance on and health and care relating to children and adolescents.

PSHE Association https://www.pshe-association.org.uk
Curriculum and resources guidance to prepare for teaching about mental health and emotional well-being.

Public Health England (2015) *Promoting Children and Young People's Emotional Health and Wellbeing: A Whole School and College Approach*, London: Public Health England, viewed 2 July 2018, from https://assets.publishing.service.gov.uk/government/uploads/system/uploads/attachment_data/file/414908/Final_EHWB_draft_20_03_15.pdf
This document links to the Ofsted inspection framework and sets out key actions for a whole school approach to promoting health and well-being.

Steuer, N. and Marks, N. (2008) *Local Wellbeing: Can We Measure It?* **London: The Young Foundation, in collaboration with NEF.**

This is an excellent resource for those interested in statistics and how you can measure well-being quantitatively.

Weichselbaum, E. and Buttriss, J. (2011) 'Nutrition, health and schoolchildren', British Nutrition Foundation, *Nutrition Bulletin***, 36, 295-355.**

This site provides reliable information on diet and health. Particularly useful are the 'Teachers Centre' and 'Pupils Centre', which provide a wide range of resources for teachers, including activities for pupils that are downloadable free of charge. It also has research papers relating to diet and health and is an excellent resource for those teaching about diet and health.

Appendix 2 lists subject associations and teacher councils and Appendix 3 provides a list of websites.

Capel, S., Leask, M. and Turner, T. (eds.) (2010) *Readings for Learning to Teach in the Secondary School: A Companion to M Level Study***, Abingdon: Routledge.**

This book brings together essential readings to support you in your critical engagement with key issues raised in this textbook.

Capel, S., Lawrence, J. Leask, M. and Younie, S. (eds.) (2019) *Surviving and Thriving in the Secondary School: The NQT's Essential Companion***, Abingdon: Routledge.**

This book is designed to support newly qualified teachers in the next phase of development as a teacher. However, you may find it useful as it covers aspects of teaching not included in this book which, nonetheless you experience on your ITE programme.

The subject specific books in the *Learning to Teach (Subject)* series, the *Practical (Subject) Guides*, *Debates in (Subject)* and *Mentoring (Subject) Teachers* are also very useful.

Any additional resources and an editable version of any relevant tasks/tables in this unit are available on the companion website: www.routledge.com/cw/capel

4.3 Cognitive development

Judy Ireson and Paul Davies

Introduction

During the secondary school years, pupils develop their knowledge and understanding of a wide range of subjects and also their ability to perceive, reason and solve problems. All of these skills are aspects of cognition (literally, 'knowing'). A key feature of cognition is that it involves us as learners in making sense of the world around us. As such, it is unlike more basic forms of learning such as memorising a song or rote learning multiplication tables. It includes skills that involve understanding, such as map reading, following instructions to make something, analysing data and solving problems. Making sense, knowing, understanding, thinking and reasoning develop into adulthood and so cognitive development is an important feature of pupils' mental growth during the secondary school years.

Logical reasoning is one important aspect of cognitive development, along with others such as problem solving, developing expertise in a particular field and creative thinking. Many school subjects require us to think and reason logically, e.g. when handling evidence, making judgements, understanding when and how to apply rules, untangling moral dilemmas or applying theories. Most Western societies in their schooling of children privilege logical, mathematical and linguistic abilities over other ways of knowing about the world. The tests of ability used by some schools to select new entrants or to allocate pupils to teaching groups are often problem-solving exercises involving pattern seeking, pattern recognition and pattern using, and the capacity to think logically and quickly.

We consider some of the ways in which pupils' cognitive abilities develop and are identified, particularly logical reasoning, and discuss briefly some ideas about intelligence. We also illustrate some of the cognitive demands made by activities in some curriculum subjects. This unit is a continuation of Unit 4.2, which considered physical development; Unit 5.1 addresses in more detail theories of how children learn and develop. This should be read in conjunction with further material on the companion website (www.routledge.com/cw/capel).

The evidence base for Unit 4.3

Understanding how we make sense of the world around us is a fascinating topic that has occupied many psychologists, educationalists and philosophers for centuries. In this unit, we draw mainly on theories and evidence from psychology in education concerning thinking, reasoning and understanding, including ideas about intelligence. These topics are studied using systematic and rigorous psychological research methods, including observational studies and experiments, and references in the text invite you to delve into sources in more detail. We illustrate ideas through tasks that focus specifically on thinking in different curriculum subjects, logical thinking and reasoning and the variety of naïve conceptions that may exist in pupils' minds. Observing pupils and listening to them as they grapple with learning is a key skill that provides insights into the difficulties they face.

OBJECTIVES

At the end of this unit you should be able to:

■ understand some features of cognitive development and the cognitive demands made by curriculum subjects;
■ explain and evaluate some ideas about the nature of intelligence;
■ identify types of thinking and relate them to learning activities;
■ begin to use tasks as a way of finding out about pupils' cognitive level;
■ identify ways of helping pupils to understand difficult ideas.

Check the requirements for your initial teacher education (ITE) programme to see which relate to this unit.

Differences between pupils

Differences between children are apparent from an early age. Even before they start school, some children pass developmental milestones such as walking and talking more quickly than others. Children may start reading and counting before they begin school or become very confident in their physical skills. When pupils start primary school, some are better than others at school tasks, and those who acquire good language and communication skills tend to be seen as more advanced and may be labelled as brighter than others, something which often leads to pupils being grouped by 'ability' in different subjects, especially Mathematics and Science.

In the secondary school, curriculum subjects call for the development and deployment of a range of cognitive skills. Each learning activity or task set by a teacher makes specific cognitive demands on the pupil, who may be well equipped to meet them or may have gaps in certain areas. At a given point in time, several factors may contribute to the pupil's capability, including their experience of similar tasks, their motivation to learn and cognitive abilities.

Motivational beliefs and learning

One of the reasons that children may be more advanced in certain areas is that they are interested in the kinds of learning valued in school. It can be argued that schoolwork is a game that children have not chosen to play, but that others, teachers and society, have chosen for them. If this assumption is correct, it is likely that some pupils are not highly motivated by the content and focus of lessons, and, therefore, these pupils may be less successful in school. An alternative view is that we all have an intrinsic motivation to acquire competence and a tendency to protect our sense of self-worth, so those pupils who fall behind in their learning and feel they are not competent become demotivated and act in ways to protect their self-image.

Unfortunately, this reaction often involves maladaptive activity such as procrastination, denying interest or playing the class joker. This is challenging for teachers who often resort to extrinsic forms of motivation such as threats or praise. Such encouragement may be effective in the short term, but in the long run you are likely to find that it is beneficial to develop pupils' intrinsic motivation by encouraging them to see the point of their work and emphasizing their growing competence (Ryan and Deci, 2000). It is well documented that pupils work best at activities that they value (Wigfield and Eccles, 2000). See Unit 3.2 on motivation.

Pupils who do well in school subjects are sometimes thought to be 'more intelligent' than others or, more accurately, display more intelligent behaviour. In her research, Dweck (1999) found that some people view intelligence as a fixed capacity or 'entity' that sets a limit on what an individual can achieve, whereas others believe that intelligence is incremental and can grow with learning. Neuroscientists (see Unit 5.6) have also identified intelligence as 'incremental'. An incremental view of intelligence carries with it the potential for change through teaching, whereas an entity view suggests that the effect of teaching is much more limited. Dweck (1999; 2008a, see also Unit 5.5 on personalizing learning) argues that entity beliefs place limits on pupils' achievements whereas young people and adults with incremental beliefs thrive by taking advantage of learning opportunities. These pupils are willing to risk failure, as they believe that challenging tasks offer good opportunities for learning and that making mistakes is a natural part of the learning process.

Before reading on, complete Task 4.3.1 about characteristics of different types of motivation.

 Task 4.3.1   Motivation

Drawing on your experiences as a learner, working with pupils in schools and the readings suggested in the section above, make a list of characteristics that define a 'good' learner and 'poor' learner within a school context.

Do your lists change in a different learning context, for example, a sports or a music club?
Consider what this task tells you about motivation and the context for learning.
Store your lists in your professional development portfolio (PDP) or equivalent and update them as you gain more knowledge about motivation for learning.

As mentioned above, schools commonly group pupils by attainment (see Unit 4.1 on grouping), especially in some core curriculum subjects such as Mathematics and Science. Although common practice, grouping by ability has been shown to make very little difference to overall pupil attainment; Higgins et al. (2013) provide an accessible overview of evidence on this topic and also draw attention to the strength of evidence on which estimates are based. (Note their caution that care is needed when accessing information to ensure that sources of evidence for the ratings are evaluated carefully for relevance.) While ability grouping can make it more straightforward for the teacher to plan for a narrower range of pupils who have similar attainment in the subject, it can be detrimental to pupil progress, particularly for pupils of similar attainment who are placed in low ability groups (Ireson, Hallam and Hurley, 2005). Much research shows that grouping in this way can lead to the teacher not recognizing the range within a group, and teaching as if the pupils are one, supposedly homogenous group of individuals (Coe et al., 2014). This is a potential problem because, as discussed in Unit 4.1, pupils may require individualised support and failing to recognise this impacts on their attainment.

A question of intelligence?

Before reading on, complete Task 4.3.2.

 Task 4.3.2   Intelligent people

Think of two people who you would say are intelligent – they could be adults or children. In what ways are they similar and how do they differ? Share your ideas with other student teachers in your group and make a note of the characteristics in your PDP.

Although a wide variety of abilities are recognised in many cultures, within education the notion of ability generally relates to skills and competence in the performance of tasks that form part of the curriculum. Intelligence may be linked to a pupil's capacity to exercise linguistic and logical mathematical reasoning, though it is important to recognise that concepts of intelligence are complex and there is no simple definition that is universally accepted.

Existing tests of cognitive ability are based on a statistical assumption that if a large number of people are tested, their scores form a bell-shaped distribution, similar to that for height or weight. Statistical methods have been used by researchers aiming to clarify relationships between the various cognitive abilities sampled by the test items, thus uncovering the structure of intelligence. The weight of evidence from these studies suggests that there is a general factor underlying other more specific abilities (see Child, 2006 for a useful introduction). This body of work gives some support to classical theories of intelligence that suggest there is a general factor underlying our performance in a wide range of activities in school and work. However, there are some notable exceptions, too, where a person's intelligence test score may be unrelated to their level of success at particular problems that seem to demand considerable intelligence, such as solving mental arithmetic problems or remembering a very long list of unrelated digits. Thus, the classical position is open to challenge.

Gardner (1993 and updated on his website) criticises classical theories for being concerned with only a very narrow range of human ability, namely language and mathematics. He argues that they fail to take account of many other aspects that are important in the real world. In his 'theory of multiple intelligences' he proposes that there are a number of relatively autonomous intelligences. He describes intelligence as 'the ability to solve problems or fashion products that are of consequence in a particular culture, setting or community' (Gardner, 1993, p.15). He has identified many intelligences, some added later as he developed his theory. They include:

Linguistic: use and understanding of language, including speech sounds, grammar, meaning and the use of language in various settings.

Musical: allows people to create, communicate and understand meanings made with sound.

Logico-mathematical: use and understanding of abstract relationships.

Spatial: perceive visual or spatial information, to be able to transform and modify this information, to re-create visual images even when the visual stimulus is absent.

Bodily kinaesthetic: use all or part of one's body to solve problems or fashion products.

Intrapersonal: knowledge of self and personal feelings. This knowledge enables personal decision making.

Interpersonal: awareness of feelings, intentions and beliefs of others.

Naturalistic: the kind of skill at recognising flora and fauna that one associates with biologists like Darwin.

(Gardner et al., 1996, p.203)

Existential intelligence: concerned with 'big questions about one's place in the cosmos, the significance of life and death, the experience of personal love and of artistic experience'.

(Gardner, quoted in White, 2005, p.8)

Gardner proposes that these relatively autonomous intelligences can be exerted alone or combined in different contexts at different times. A number of intelligences may be needed in order to carry out some tasks, e.g. in the case of art and design both spatial intelligence and bodily kinaesthetic intelligence might contribute to learning.

Look back at the list of characteristics of intelligent people you identified in Task 4.3.2. How well do they map on to Gardner's set of intelligences?

Gardner's 'intrapersonal' and 'interpersonal' intelligences capture much of what has been called 'emotional intelligence' (Salovey and Mayer, 1990). This is the ability to recognise, express and reflect on our own emotional states and those of other people and also to manage these emotions. It is worth noting that, for most people, learning is an emotional experience that may involve confusion, disappointment, apprehension, fascination, absorption, exhilaration and relief. These emotions can disrupt or facilitate learning and it is easy to see that pupils benefit from being able accurately to recognise and manage them effectively. For further reading on emotional factors and learning see Goleman (1995) and Cherniss (2000), and within mathematics learning, Goulding (2005, pp.56-58).

Some of the ideas behind the theory of multiple intelligences have received critical reviews (White, 1998; 2005). It is not yet clear just how autonomous these intelligences are and a common view is that a likely model of intelligence is one that operates through a general underlying intelligence backed up by a small number of special abilities. Thus:

we are bound to look critically at evidence and the evidence of the existence for abilities in different intellectual areas, which are quite independent of each other, is not good... intelligence is not a monolithic unidimensional ability which allows us with one IQ number to define an individual fully. All measures of different aspects of intellectual ability correlate with one another.

(Anderson, 1992)

Any intellectual behaviour is then a product of a general processing ability and a number of special abilities (Adey and Serret, 2010). The use of the word 'ability' above, rather than intelligence, may echo Gardner's early comments: 'nothing much turns on the particular use of this term [intelligences] and

I would be satisfied to substitute such phrases as "intellectual competence", "thought processes", "cognitive capacities", "cognitive skills", "forms of knowledge"' (Gardner, 1983, p.284). In other words, it is not clear whether Gardner is describing an innate faculty, a learned process or a structure of knowledge. However, many teachers find Gardner's ideas helpful as they alert us to a variety of ways in which we might recognise and develop intelligent behaviour. It is important to note that there is little research evidence to support Gardner's theory, with what is reported in classrooms being mostly anecdotal. This raises an important issue in educational research where teachers 'feel' interventions and approaches in the classroom produce reliable, and repeatable, changes while the education research community cannot produce robust evidence to support this. More and more, teachers are being expected to engage with research, both self-generated and published, to inform their practice, and they must be mindful of the persuasive nature of ideas that seem to 'make sense' but are not grounded in reliable research. Having said that, multiple intelligence theory has had an important impact on classroom practice. There is an opportunity to further explore these ideas for yourself in Task 4.3.3.

 Task 4.3.3   Multiple intelligences and design and technology (D&T)

Locate online the D&T curriculum for England (Department for Education (DfE), 2017c). Select teaching D&T at KS3, download the Programme of Study and read the sections 'Aims', 'Attainment targets' and 'Subject content'.

Using this document, identify the skills and intelligences demanded by D&T at KS3. Be sure to consider how pupils with different abilities would access the learning and what support they might need.

These questions may help you.

1   In which ways do the demands of D&T link to the importance attached in school to linguistic and logico-mathematical aptitude?
2   Using Gardner's 'theory of multiple intelligences', discuss the teaching and learning of D&T as the utilisation and development of different intelligences.

For discussion on the place of D&T in the school curriculum, see Owen-Jackson (2008, Chapter 1).

Summarise your findings, including details of what the task has taught you about catering for the needs of all pupils, to discuss with your tutor or the D&T teachers in your school. File the final document in your PDP.

Developing cognitive abilities

Nature and nurture

 In general, pupils' cognitive abilities increase with age, as suggested by the percentage example in Table 4.3.3 on the companion website (www.routledge.com/cw/capel). Older pupils are more capable of abstract, symbolic thinking than younger pupils, who tend to use more concrete representations when solving problems (see the discussion of Piaget's theory of cognitive development in Unit 5.1). It is also clear that in any year group there is considerable diversity, with some pupils able to cope with more demanding work, while others have great difficulty. Several different explanations have been suggested for this diversity and for the general pattern of development during the school years. In the remainder of this section, we briefly outline some of these.

So what might influence the development of cognitive abilities? Most answers to this question emphasise biological and environmental factors, or 'nature' and 'nurture'. 'Nature' refers to our inborn, genetic or inherited characteristics and how these unfold during maturation, while 'nurture' refers to the environment in which we grow and develop. Genetic factors undoubtedly affect development, but the extent of this influence is not entirely clear, as it is difficult to disentangle genetic and environmental processes. The most influential studies compare twins raised together with twins separated at an early age and raised in different families. These studies show that inherited characteristics do have a strong effect, but they do not completely determine measured intelligence; the child's environment also makes an important contribution.

A recent development in the nature–nurture debate is provided by the science of epigenetics. This explores the interactive process between nature and nurture, and argues that development should be viewed as an interactive, dynamic process between the total environment of the genes and the genes themselves, instead of discussing the effects of genes and environment on development each as separate entities (see, for example, Day and Sweatt, 2011).

Turning to the environment, a pupil's attainment on entry to secondary school is influenced by their experiences in the home and in primary school. Evidence has accumulated to suggest that a lack of stimulation in early childhood limits the capacity of children to benefit from school and other learning situations (Sylva, et al., 2004). The researchers followed children from age three to seven years and developed a measure of 'home learning environment' (HLE) to describe activities such as reading with the child, painting and drawing playing with letters, numbers and shapes, teaching songs and nursery rhymes and taking children on visits to the library. A 'good' HLE contained these activities, regardless of the economic status of parents. Children from such homes have a head start when they enter primary school, as they have started to develop many of the cognitive, communicative and social skills needed in school. Later on, their parents may support them directly and indirectly, e.g. explaining homework or enabling them to participate in a wide range of activities. While the majority of parents are able to provide a good HLE, some may find this difficult, perhaps for economic, social or health reasons. Some parents find a high-quality nursery and primary education for their children, while others find this a problem, possibly due in part to more limited high-quality provision in areas of higher socio-economic deprivation. The Child Care Act of 2006 was designed to provide free or affordable childcare for working parents; and, in addition, to provide an integrated education programme for this age group to address some of the inequalities described above.

A pupil's performance in attainment tests is thus a reflection of their innate abilities and the influence of the environment. Attainment tests tell you what a pupil knows, understands and can do at a particular point in time; however, they are not necessarily reliable predictors of future attainment. Pupils who have had less support for their learning in the past, or who do not speak English as their first language, may be more capable than suggested by these tests. For pupils for whom English is an additional language (EAL), their first language is likely to be the one in which they think. The later a child comes to learning in a second language, the more likely is it that their thinking skills use the mother tongue (Lu, 1998). For these reasons it is important to take care not to label pupils in a deterministic way as high, middle or low ability on the basis of attainment tests when they enter the school.

Knowledge base

Another important factor that is easily overlooked is the amount of knowledge an individual has acquired. It is sometimes assumed that the more advanced thinking of adults is due to biological maturation, when in fact it may be owing to increased knowledge. Comparing children who are very knowledgeable about a subject with adults who are not, e.g. children who are very good at chess and adults who are beginners, illustrates the power of knowledge nicely. When shown a chess board with pieces laid out as they might be during a game, the expert children are better than the adult beginners at remembering the positions and, if the board is taken away, expert children are able to place more pieces than adults in the correct position on another, empty board. However, when the pieces are arranged randomly on the board, there is no difference between the adults and the children. This indicates that children who are good at chess build up knowledge of patterns and configurations as they play, and this knowledge helps them remember (see Bransford et al., 1999).

People who are experts are much better at recognising patterns in information and using principles to solve problems. This applies in domains as diverse as medicine, music, physics, computer programming and teaching. Experts build up a strong knowledge base and use it effectively to solve problems. Reading X-ray photographs is one such example (Abercrombie, 1985). For pupils, the development of a strong knowledge base in school subjects is important for remembering and thinking. It also makes learning more enjoyable and satisfying. Good teaching and active learning (see Unit 5.2) should help pupils to build up a well-structured knowledge base, but this may be undermined by pressure to cover the curriculum, leaving insufficient time for understanding and consolidation.

Common-sense beliefs and naïve conceptions

Everyday beliefs and naïve, or intuitive, conceptions are common in science, as shown in aspects of the pendulum task (see Task 4.3.5 on the companion website (www.routledge. com/cw/capel) but they also surface in other subjects. Gardner (1991) gives many examples, including a classic case reported by I. A. Richards many years ago (Richards 1929, cited by Gardner 1991, p.177). Richards asked undergraduates at Cambridge University to read pairs of poems and then to offer their interpretations and evaluations. He found that the students were heavily influenced by the form of the poem, in other words whether it rhymed, had a regular metre or rhythm, and avoided words that were too common or arcane. Many of them failed to understand the meaning of the poems.

Gardner (1991) suggests that many of our everyday understandings take the form of 'scripts' and 'stereotypes' that tend to simplify the world around us and make it more manageable. Unfortunately, pupils use these to interpret information presented in school subjects. For example, intuitive interpretations of historical events tend to be quite simplistic and stereotypical; there is often a good versus evil narrative, with evil leaders taking on great importance and the good usually winning in the end. Even when pupils have learned that events such as the Second World War have complex causes and that war is seldom due to the behaviour of a single evil leader, they may slip back into simplistic ways of thinking.

In art, children's intuitive conceptions of pictorial representation tend to start from an awareness of the relation between the picture and the world, in other words, what the picture represents. As a result, they tend to focus on the picture-world relation and also tend to prefer realistic paintings and drawings. Interestingly, beauty appears to play a significant role in young people's thinking about art, with a beautiful painting considered better than an ugly one. In secondary school, young people may move on to recognise and talk about relations between the picture and the artist, such as understanding that the mood of an artist may affect picture quality. Appreciating relations between the viewer and the picture is a later development (Freeman and Parsons, 2001) and one that may not be realised by all by pupils.

It is worth getting to know about commonly held naïve conceptions in your own subject as this can help you see why pupils have difficulty with some new ideas and ways of thinking. You may be able to plan activities to challenge specific conceptions. We return to this aspect of learning in Task 4.3.6 on the companion website (www.routledge.com/cw/capel).

Curriculum and development

Several ideas have now been introduced to explain pupils' performance in school. It has been suggested that performance is a product of inheritance and environment. Also that, as they grow, develop and learn, pupils become more able to handle complex problems and situations and abstract (formal) thinking. You are not in a position to influence inheritance or the home learning environment, but you can influence classroom learning by providing activities that are aligned with pupils' current knowledge and understanding. To do this requires a careful analysis of the demands made by a piece of work and the current performance of the pupil or group of pupils with reference to relevant knowledge, skills and understanding needed to do the task.

Programmes of study for each of the national curriculum subjects set out aims for all pupils, in terms of their thinking and learning, and even though each subject has different content knowledge and emphasis there are also some similarities in learning and thinking processes across subjects. You should turn to the programme of study for your subject and compare the aims with those for a different subject.

Each subject sets out requirements for pupils to acquire relevant knowledge and skills that form a foundation for that subject at a particular Key Stage. Each subject also specifies thinking and reasoning skills required to draw inferences and make deductions from foundational knowledge, as well as elements of problem solving, reasoning and use of evidence to develop and justify arguments and give explanations. Some subjects place greater emphasis on pupil experience, imagination and creative thinking to generate and extend ideas.

For example, the programme of study for computing (DfE, 2013c) states that it 'aims to ensure that all pupils:

- can understand and apply the fundamental principles and concepts of computer science, including abstraction, logic, algorithms and data representation
- can analyse problems in computational terms, and have repeated practical experience of writing computer programs in order to solve such problems

- can evaluate and apply information technology, including new or unfamiliar technologies, analytically to solve problems
- are responsible, competent, confident and creative users of information and communication technology'.

These aims clearly place emphasis on understanding, application and analysis as well as practice of writing computer programs. Unusually, perhaps, the fourth aim also states personal qualities required for this subject.

You should now turn to your own, specific subject and complete Task 4.3.6 found on the companion website (www.routledge.com/cw/capel). In the task, you will explore the level of challenge for pupils and link this to assessment. The task also introduces different approaches related to cognitive demand in the classroom.

Having identified the aims and subject content for your own subject, pick out statements that mention thinking skills. Which of these are likely to be the most and least challenging for pupils? Then turn to a specific piece of work or topic you are planning to teach and identify the cognitive and other demands for pupils. When you have clarified the task demands, a careful assessment of pupils' current performance may be carried out, through a process that represents an example of assessment for learning (see Unit 6.1; Procter, 2013; Newton and Bowler, 2015). Thus, with evidence from assessment, future learning activities can then be planned so as better to guarantee some success while offering a comfortable level of challenge. This strategy depends on you being able to analyse the cognitive demands of the topic and associated learning activities and the relevant capabilities of pupils. See Units 4.1 and 5.5, which cover processes of differentiating and personalizing learning to meet the diverse needs of pupils.

The Cognitive Acceleration programme offers a somewhat different approach (Shayer and Adey, 2002) that incorporates several key components through what is termed the 'Five Pillar Model'. The emphasis is on helping pupils to understand the context, to 'learn how to learn' and begin to construct meaning for themselves. The first component is 'concrete preparation', which involves you setting activities to ensure that pupils are familiar with the context of a problem and any technical vocabulary. You then give pupils problems to discuss in small groups, designed in such a way that all pupils are able to contribute to the discussion (see jigsawing and rainbowing in Unit 4.1). An important feature of the programme is that pupils are encouraged to think about their own thinking (metacognition). In addition, both you and your pupils are encouraged to think about links between their thinking in other aspects of the curriculum. Results suggest that pupils can be taught to think in generic ways that help them to learn better across a range of subjects and context (Adey and Serret, 2010). Cognitive acceleration started in science but is now being developed in a variety of curriculum subjects (Shayer and Adey, 2002).

Clearly, learning activities that are carefully designed can be very effective in helping pupils to learn and to become aware of their own learning strategies. Both these aspects of learning can also contribute to a pupil's sense of competence, which may be seen as a fundamental human need. Competence is an important aspect of motivation and one that may help to raise pupils' aspirations (see Ryan and Deci, 2000). Task 4.3.4 encourages you to think about how approaches to learning, such as the Cognitive Acceleration Programme, are designed to challenge pupils and move their learning forward.

M **Task 4.3.4   Cognitive challenge and accelerated learning**

Devise a lesson that follows the five-pillar model of Adey and Shayer's Cognitive Acceleration Programme. To help you, follow the steps below that provide information about each stage in designing your lesson:

1   *Concrete preparation*: this involves a series of activities that set the scene about the topic that the pupils are exploring and learning about. Think about the key ideas the pupils need to learn. Is there any specialist vocabulary that they need to access? How will you make the focus of the learning clear to the pupils?

2   *Cognitive conflict*: this part of the lesson should introduce cognitive conflict where the pupils are presented with an idea that challenges their own ideas and misconceptions. You will need to research ideas about what pupils think about the specific learning focus. You may find that resources such as Concept Cartoons help support this stage of the lesson;

3   *Social construction*: in this stage, organise the pupils in small groups and design activities that encourage discussion about the learning focus. Think about how to best group the pupils and the roles they may play in the group that ensures everyone has a chance to contribute. When listening to the groups, it is important to step back and let them talk, so it might helpful to make a list of prompt questions you could ask to encourage deeper discussion;

4   *Metacognition*: in this stage, encourage the pupils to share their ideas with the class. Think about how you will select pupils and help them frame their answers. An important part of this stage is that the pupils need to explain their reasoning. You should ensure that as many pupils as possible contribute to this stage. By doing you this you will hear a greater range of ideas and reasoning;

5   *Bridging*: in this stage you make links between the lesson and other learning. It is helpful to think about how the learning relates to real life contexts as well as learning that the pupils might do in different curriculum areas.

Once you have developed your plan, write 500 words that explain the decisions you made. Use your own learning, ideas from this unit and readings to support your writing. Try to justify the decisions you have made and use evidence from your readings to critically analyse the design of your lesson.

Store your plan and reflection in your PDP and use this to underpin further use of the five-pillar model in your teaching.

Creative problem solving

In this unit we have taken cognition to encompass acquisition, assimilation and application of knowledge and also problem solving and thinking. Earlier in the unit we used an example from design and technology as fostering capability to integrate thought and skills into a holistic exercise, rather than a piecemeal exercise of isolated skills.

A different example of this type of problem solving is shown in a collection of children's responses to problems set by adults. The collection shows the spontaneous work by pupils (upper primary, lower secondary) in response to problems related to everyday events (de Bono, 1972). The tasks include:

- how would you stop a cat and a dog fighting?
- design a machine to weigh an elephant
- invent a sleep machine
- how would you build a house quickly?
- how would you improve the human body?
- design a bicycle for postmen.

(de Bono, 1972)

In this work, pupils need knowledge of the context from which the problem is drawn and also to use knowledge and skills from both inside and outside the classroom. The work of pupils is occasionally unusual and the solutions sometimes impractical. The responses show much imagination and insight into their everyday world.. For more ideas, see Beghetto and Kaufman (2010), or visit https://www.edwdebono.com.

Measuring cognitive development and intelligence tests

Much work has been carried out to help us understand pupils' (and adults') responses to problem situations. For example, Piaget devised many tasks that have been used extensively and adapted by others (see Adey and Serret, 2010; Child, 2007, ch.4; Donaldson, 2013). These tasks provide a window on the type and sequence of thought process adopted by pupils and reveal much about how their thinking develops. Hopefully, if you have tried some of the tasks provided for this unit in the text and on the companion website (www.routledge.com/cw/capel), you are starting to see how you might use problems to help you learn more about your pupils' cognitive processes.

The main purpose of many tests and examinations is to assess, rank, select and make predictions about progress (see Unit 6.1). IQ tests were first developed by Binet to identify pupils who may be in need of special education (Gould, 1981, p.148 *et seq.*). Later, tests of intelligence were designed to assist educational and occupational selection on a fair, meritocratic basis. Most people are familiar with the notion of 'Intelligence Quotient' (IQ), which is reported as a single number. This is derived from test scores and shows the extent to which the pupil is below or above an average score based on a large sample of pupils. The test is norm-referenced and the average score is given an arbitrary value of 100. As indicated above, intelligence tests generally tap a range of cognitive abilities involving language, numerical and non-verbal thinking and reasoning.

Intelligence testing assumed great importance in the UK after the Second World War owing to the 1944 Education Act. Pupils were selected for grammar, technical or 'modern' schools by means of the 11+ examination, a type of intelligence test. Despite being developed into a reliable sophisticated tool, the examination failed to take account of late developers or the effects of pupils' social background. The tests also favoured pupils with good linguistic skills, those who had a good vocabulary and were familiar with middle-class culture, and girls. Girls on average mature faster than boys and the 11+ entry had to be modified to ensure equal access to grammar school for boys and girls. It was shown, too, that performance on the tests could be improved by training, which suggested that, in part, at least, learned skills were being tested rather than purely innate intelligence. Confidence in the whole issue of selection was undermined by research showing that it had negative impacts on pupils from less advantaged backgrounds (see Ireson and Hallam, 2001). In due course, many local authorities abolished grammar schools and moved to a fully comprehensive secondary system on grounds of equity, although some retain selection, e.g. Kent and Buckinghamshire (Ireson and Hallam, 2001). Moreover, concerns about the impact of home background on pupils' achievement in national examinations have led to a call for the use of cognitive abilities tests in selecting young people for gifted and talented programmes and entrance to university.

Standardised testing is a skilled process and many commercially available tests must only be used by approved persons. IQ testing is sometimes used by educational psychologists to assess pupils who, in various ways, find school difficult. This procedure may be necessary for the identification of special educational needs such as dyslexia (see Unit 4.6). Other reasons for standardised assessment may be for research purposes as part of monitoring a population. See Unit 6.1 for further information on assessment.

SUMMARY AND KEY POINTS

Cognitive development is described as a process through which pupils develop their knowledge, understanding, reasoning, problem solving and creative thinking. All these aspects of thinking develop into adulthood and so cognitive development is an important feature of pupils' mental growth through the secondary school years.

In thinking about cognitive development across various secondary school subjects, this unit brings together the following key ideas:

- research reveals that there are differences between pupils in terms of the cognitive processes they use in, and the cognitive demands made by, different curriculum subjects;
- carrying out the practical tasks in this unit encourages you to analyse the cognitive abilities involved in completing them as well as providing you with opportunities for finding out more about your pupils' capabilities;
- key to this is listening to your pupils and finding out about their perspective on learning activities, through this you learn more about their understanding and thinking. This process helps you to design activities to assist their development.

We refer you to Unit 3.2, Unit 5.1 and Unit 5.2 for further discussion of related topics.
Check which requirements for your ITE programme you have addressed through this unit.

 Further resources

Adey, P. and Serret, N. (2010) 'Science teaching and cognitive acceleration', in J. Osborne and J. Dillon (eds.) *Good Practice in Science Teaching: What Research Has to Say*, Buckingham: Open University Press, pp.82-107.
Although written in the context of teaching science, the authors discuss what it might mean to be intelligent, followed by theories about its origin and function. They go on to discuss the implications for learning science in secondary school and for the teaching of other subjects.

Child, D. (2007) *Psychology and the Teacher*, **8th Edition, London: Continuum.**

This is a classic text that provides a useful review of cognitive development, theories of learning and intelligence. It includes research into classrooms, practice, management and special needs. A useful source of references.

Donaldson, M. (2013) *A Study of Children's Thinking*, **Abingdon: Routledge.**

An overview of literature on children's thinking including classic studies by Piaget on cognitive growth.

Gardner, H. (2006a) *Multiple Intelligences: New Horizons*, **New York: Basic Books.**

Gardner provides a summary of his original theory and argues that the concept of intelligence should be broadened, but not so much that it includes every human faculty and value. He also describes how multiple intelligence (MI) theory has evolved and includes a section on educational experiments based on MI theory.

Appendix 2 lists subject associations and teacher councils and Appendix 3 provides a list of websites.

Capel, S., Leask, M. and Turner, T. (eds.) (2010) *Readings for Learning to Teach in the Secondary School: A Companion to M Level Study*, **Abingdon: Routledge.**

This book brings together essential readings to support you in your critical engagement with key issues raised in this textbook.

Capel, S., Lawrence, J. Leask, M. and Younie, S. (eds.) (2019) *Surviving and Thriving in the Secondary School: The NQT's Essential Companion*, **Abingdon: Routledge.**

This book is designed to support newly qualified teachers in the next phase of development as a teacher. However, you may find it useful as it covers aspects of teaching not included in this book which, nonetheless you experience on your ITE programme.

The subject specific books in the *Learning to Teach (Subject)* series, the *Practical (Subject) Guides*, *Debates in (Subject)* and *Mentoring (Subject) Teachers* are also very useful.

Any additional resources and an editable version of any relevant tasks/tables in this unit are available on the companion website: www.routledge.com/cw/capel

4.4 Responding to diversity

Helen Bowhay and Stefanie Sullivan

Introduction

Teaching is a complex process, made interesting by the vast range of educational, social and political contexts and purposes that shape it. Your classroom will be a diverse place. There is likely to be a mix of boys and girls, pupils from different ethnic origins, and pupils from family backgrounds with differing views on the value and purpose of education as well as pupils who have disabilities. In addition, there may be pupils who come from affluent families, pupils from less wealthy backgrounds, or 'looked after' children. Some pupils may live with both of their parents, but some may split their time living in two different homes owing to divorce or separation, and other pupils may not be living with their parents but are looked after in other ways. You may have pupils who have just arrived in this country, some of whom may have had to flee their home countries due to war and conflict.

This unit helps you to understand better the complex make-up of modern UK society, particularly how social diversity, educational opportunity and attainment are interrelated. To develop as a responsive and sensitive teacher, you will need to understand how your pupils are different so that you can adapt your teaching to their particular needs, addressing barriers to learning that may exist for some. This is easy to write but much more difficult to implement. It is important to recognise that your own experiences of education and your perspectives on the educational, social and political contexts of the day have a significant influence on the way in which you respond to diversity. Your own inclusive practices will develop through a critical evaluation of the ways in which you respond to pupil diversity in your own classroom. In this unit we focus on issues around gender, ethnicity and social class, which, although they are examined separately herein, clearly overlap and intertwine.

As you read the unit, keep in mind that intelligence is not fixed, but incremental, depending on learning opportunities. (See Unit 4.3 on cognitive development.) Much of the data relates to England. Government departments in other countries may publish equivalent data.

OBJECTIVES

At the end of this unit you should be able to:

■   access evidence about the relative academic performance of pupils in relation to gender, ethnicity and class;

■   discuss issues of discrimination and bias in relation to gender, ethnicity and class;

■   consider school policies and critique classroom procedures in order to promote better opportunities for learning for all pupils.

Check the requirements of your initial teacher education (ITE) programme to see which relate to this unit.

A history of diversity in the UK

The presence of people originating from other cultures, faiths and backgrounds has been a feature of British society for many centuries. The notion of 'other' suggests that British society is easily described but 'Britishness' is neither a clearly defined nor a fixed concept.

Throughout the last century the population of England and Wales grew steadily, from 35.5 million in 1901 to nearly 49 million in 1991. The 2016 mid-year population estimate suggested that the population of England and Wales was 58 million. According to the Office for National Statistics (ONS), the minority ethnic population in England and Wales reached 14% of the population in 2011 and some studies suggest this may reach around 30% by 2050 (ONS, 2012b). The freedom of movement of EU citizens and the widening of EU membership has added further to the cultural mix. For example, between 2008 and 2013, the estimated number of people resident in the UK born in the EU8 (Czech Republic, Estonia, Poland, Hungary, Latvia, Lithuania, Slovakia and Slovenia) rose from 689,000 to 1,077,000.

The increased diversity of our society does not just come from the range of ethnic and cultural backgrounds it represents. Advancements in health and social care mean more children are surviving with complex needs and the number of people with disabilities in the UK is increasing (Department for Work and Pensions, 2016). The Joseph Rowntree Foundation monitors poverty and social exclusion on an annual basis and highlights that British society is becoming increasingly polarised. In 2014/15, they found 13.5 million people were living in households classified as poor and of that 13.5 million, 55% are in working families. Their 2016 report showed that, in 2014/15, 29% of children were living in poverty (Tinson et al., 2016). The report also highlights that the overall benefit cap introduced by the Government in November 2016 mainly affects households with children.

Equal opportunities and educational equity

By equal opportunities we refer to the lack of discrimination between pupils on the grounds of gender, ethnicity, class and disability. This notion links to the idea of equity in education by which we refer to the achievement of fairness in education, for example, that all pupils should have equal access to state-maintained schools. For many people it is self-evident that the implementation of equal opportunities policies is a reflection of basic human rights, but how does the notion of equality of opportunity relate to a teacher's response to diversity? Should the same curriculum, teaching styles, etc. be used consistently, or does such 'equality' in fact perpetuate inequality? Sociologists of education have argued for many years that if you assume that all pupils come to school equally prepared, and treat them accordingly, then, in reality, you advantage those who have been better prepared in their social milieu to succeed at school (Bernstein, 1977; Bourdieu, 1974; Willis, 1977; Coleman, 1988; Putnam, 2000). Although society has changed in the 40 years since these observations were made, there remain substantial differences between pupils in their educational experiences, i.e. readiness for secondary school; see also Units 4.2 and 4.3, which discuss examples of difference in 'cognitive development' and 'health and well-being'. The notion of the dilemma of difference (Dyson, 2001; Norwich, 1993) is at the heart of this educational debate:

> the dilemma lies in the choice between identifying children's differences in order to secure appropriate provision, with the risk of labeling and discriminating, and accentuating learners' 'sameness' and offering common provision, with the risk of not paying due attention to their needs.
>
> (Terzi, 2008, p.245)

Concerns about educational achievement have shifted between different groups of pupils over the years. In the 1980s and earlier, there was concern about the underachievement of West Indian pupils (Short, 1986). Now there is growing concern about the low performance of many white working-class pupils, with only 26% of white British boys and 35% of white British girls from low income backgrounds achieving five or more GCSEs at A*-C, including English and mathematics, in 2012 (Office for Standards in Education, Children's Services and Skills (Ofsted), 2013). Although much progress has been made in the last three decades as regards equal opportunities for men and women in the workplace and boys and girls at school, the mean gender pay gap for women and men working full time in 2012 was 24.5% for annual earnings, with men still predominating in many of the highest paid occupations (Equality and Human Rights Commission (EHRC), 2013). In 2017, the ONS reported that the gender pay gap had narrowed to 9.1% in favour of men. However, the pay gap varies quite considerably across occupations, with some as high as 26.2% (ONS, 2017).

These issues around gender, ethnicity and class comprise the foci of the remainder of the unit.

In many cases, explanations of pupil underachievement have focused on the shortcomings of the pupil or their families. More recently the focus has shifted to addressing the educational system as one of the factors contributing to underachievement. This focus is not only at the level of government and school policy but also in the classroom where such policies are interpreted and implemented by teachers.

Gender

There remains considerable difference in the ways in which boys and girls/men and women exist and move through our society. Focusing on secondary schooling, both boys and girls have been steadily improving their performance in school examinations over the past 20 years, but there is a clear gender gap. Table 4.4.1 compares the performance of boys and girls at General Certificate of Secondary Education (GCSE) gaining five or more grade A*-C, including mathematics and English over the six-year period from 2009 to 2015. Noticeable from this table is that girls continue to

Table 4.4.1 Percentage of pupils achieving 5+ A*-C grades, including mathematics and English

	2009/10	2010/11	2011/12	2012/13	2013/14	2014/15
Boys	51.5	54.6	54.2	55.7	55.6	53.9
Girls	58.9	61.9	63.7	65.7	65.2	62.5

Source: Department for Education (DfE), 2016h

outperform boys with the widest gap seen in 2012/13 of 10 percentage points. This gap closed to 8.6 percentage points in 2015, which may be a reflection of the change in the examinations through a reduction in coursework, or a reflection of the attention given to boys' underperformance in recent years. Whilst it is understandable that government policy should react to the underperformance of any group of individuals, there needs to be an acknowledgement that there is a far more complex picture with cultural and class differences playing a significant part.

In 2016, a new secondary school accountability system was implemented for English schools. This system has three progress measures: Attainment 8, Progress 8 and Attainment in English and Maths (A*-C). In 2016, as in previous years, girls continue to outperform boys with an average Attainment 8 score of 52.1 compared to 47.5 for boys. The average Progress 8 score for girls was 0.11 compared to -0.17 for boys and Attainment in English and Maths (A*-C) was 66.7% compared to 58.6% (DfE, 2016g).

Following on from the different performance at GCSE level in England, Figure 4.4.1 shows examination entries for General Certificate of Education (GCE) A level courses (Joint Council for Qualifications, 2016). There is clear gender delineation in some areas between what might be considered masculine and feminine subjects (e.g. physics, English, psychology).

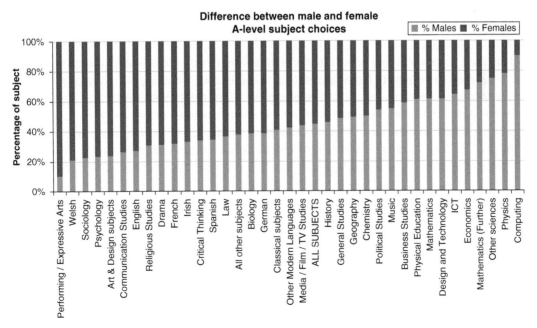

Figure 4.4.1 Differences between male and female A-Level choices, 2016

Source: Joint Council for Qualifications (JCQ)

Pupils often have very stereotyped ideas about the roles of men and women. Hartley and Sutton (2010) found that, by the age of eight, children of both genders believe that boys are less focused, able and successful than girls. There is the potential for such beliefs to lead to a self-fulfilling prophecy with boys accepting this myth as fact and resigning themselves to being unsuccessful (Hartley and Sutton, 2013). Boys' and girls' responses to school are shaped by society's views of how each gender behaves or should behave. In this sense each identity is socially constructed rather than one reflecting the views of individual boys and girls. There is much research on the different ways in which boys and girls are positioned by, and respond to, learning and the curriculum (Paechter, 2000; Smith, 2005), classroom interactions (Myhill, 2002), teachers (Younger et al., 1999; Myhill and Jones, 2006) and moving to a new school (Jackson and Warin, 2000; Noyes 2003). Rudduck (2004) explores the challenges of developing, and possibilities for, gender policies in secondary schools in some detail.

So far in this section we have been looking at the relationship between performance and biological differences between pupils; however, the notion of gender is more nuanced, including different masculinities and femininities. Traditional stereotypes are being broken down and, at the same time, more fragmented. Such differences are increasingly celebrated, and this includes pupils' sexuality. As we said at the outset, teachers' responses to this level of diversity are influenced by their personal views and experiences. Whatever your views, many issues in this area require a thoughtful, professional approach, e.g. towards homophobic bullying (both the Intercom Trust and Stonewall have good websites with useful guidance and resources concerning homophobic behaviour).

Ethnicity

The report, 'How Fair is Britain?' (EHRC, 2010) showed that considerable progress has been made by groups of minority ethnic pupils over recent years and ethnic differences at GCSE are narrowing. In 2011, people from the White Gypsy or Irish Traveller, Pakistani, Bangladeshi and Black Caribbean groups were less likely than White British people to have degree qualifications or equivalent (Lymperopoulou and Parameshwaran, 2014). Two reports from 2000 identified the serious underachievement of Black Caribbean pupils (Fitzgerald et al., 2000; Gillborn and Mirza, 2000). Though this is a group that is still lagging behind, they have shown the largest improvement in recent years; in 2012/13, the percentage of black pupils achieving 5 or more GCSEs at grade A*–C or equivalent, including English and mathematics GCSEs or iGCSEs, was 2.5 percentage points below the national average. This gap has narrowed by 1.7 percentage points since 2011/12, but, over the longer term, this has narrowed by 3.7 percentage points since 2008/09 (DfE, 2014m).

The issues of underachievement of particular groups of pupils is an ongoing concern for government at both a local and central level. There have been various government initiatives over the years designed to address the issues of underachievement of particular groups of pupils; however, there is still a wide gap between the high and low achievers. The under-performance of many white working-class boys serves to emphasise the importance of taking into account how class and gender effects are embedded within the data showing attainments of ethnic groups (see Gillborn and Mirza, 2000; Strand, 2008).

Girls in all ethnic groups continue to score higher than boys in GCSE examinations, although both groups of pupils have improved year on year (DfE, 2014m). Black Caribbean pupils improved their performance in GCSE; about one-third of pupils gained five or more grade A*–Cs at GCSE, including mathematics and English, in 2007, rising to over one-half in 2013. However, the proportion of people with no qualifications in the Black African group was roughly equivalent in 2001 and 2011 (Lymperopoulou and Parameshwaran, 2014).

The evidence accumulated by the Swann Enquiry 30 years ago suggested that many minority ethnic pupils were underachieving (Department of Education and Science (DES), 1985). The data above, and more recent research (e.g. Gillborn and Gipps, 1996; Smith, 2005; Archer and Francis, 2007; Strand, 2014), shows that, although achievement has been raised for most pupils, underachievement still persists and is often linked to particular ethnic groups.

Table 4.4.2 shows the attainment gaps over the last five years between pupils whose first language is English and those who have a different first language. When gaining grades A*-C in mathematics and English is included as an indicator, the data show that pupils whose first language is English are consistently achieving better than their counterparts. Interestingly, however, a higher proportion of pupils whose first language was not English achieved the expected levels of progress in English and mathematics than those whose first language was English. For English, the gap was 7.6 percentage points in 2012/13 and 8.7 percentage points for mathematics (DfE, 2014m).

For teachers working with pupils from a range of ethnic backgrounds, the issue of supporting those for whom English is an additional language (EAL) is important (see, for example, Flynn, Pim and Coles 2015). The issue of language goes far wider than classroom oracy. Many classroom resources are heavily text-based and their use of language requires not only a level of literacy but also cultural awareness. Teachers need to ensure they are adequately challenging pupils whose first language is not English, and they should consider carefully the language requirements that are made by textbooks, classroom talk and homework tasks to identify whether these are creating barriers to learning. There is evidence that giving pupils opportunities and time to use their mother tongue to think about ideas and, where possible, to discuss concepts, allows them to operate at a higher cognitive level.

In 2016, under the new performance measurements, the average Attainment 8 score of pupils with English as an additional language was broadly similar to those with English as a first language (49.9 vs 50.0, respectively), but the average Progress 8 score was higher (0.39 vs −0.09, respectively). Pupils with English as an additional language achieved 60.8% A*-C grades in English and maths compared to 63.5% for non-EAL pupils (DfE, 2016g).

Despite levels of educational attainment improving across ethnic groups, this has not translated to the labour market (Tackey et al., 2011). The 2011 census showed large differences across ethnic groups in rates of employment (Nazroo and Kapadia, 2013). In 2016, the unemployment rate

Table 4.4.2 First language attainment gaps 2009/10 to 2014/15 (English as a first language minus first language other than English expressed as difference between the two percentage scores)

	2009/10	2010/11	2011/12	2012/13	2013/14	2014/15
5 or more A*-C grades at GCSE and equivalent	0.1	−0.5	0.3	−0.5	0.8	unknown
5 or more A*-C grades at GCSE and equivalent including English and mathematics GCSEs	3.1	2.7	2.9	2.5	3.1	2.9

Source: DfE, 2016h

for the Black, Pakistani and Bangladeshi communities was 12, 10 and 11%, respectively, and 5% for white jobseekers (ONS, 2016). Relatively high levels of unemployment have an impact upon the future economic status of groups and, therefore, in a complex way, the chances of their children in school. This is not to say that such inequality of attainment cannot be addressed, or is somehow cyclical, but rather to highlight the limitations of schools' ability to affect social change.

Archer (2008) argues that the dominant educational discourse in Britain contributes to excluding minority ethnic pupils from 'the identity of the "ideal pupil"' (Archer, 2008, p.102), and, as a student teacher, it is important to unpack your own notion of success and ensure it does not favour a particular group of pupils. Recent government initiatives in England have attempted to raise attainment and improve the employment and access to higher education of different pupil groups (explore 'DfE *Raising Attainment*' in 'Useful websites' at the end of this unit).

Class

Class, or social class, is a contested categorisation of people but is usually related to social standing and economic role. The economic role is linked to the person's type of employment, ranging from professional to unskilled. A frequent broad classification is working class, middle class and upper class; for further discussion of class see Savage et al.'s (2013) analysis of the BBC's 2011 Great British Class Survey.

The effect that pupils' economic circumstances have upon their education is very real. Connolly (2006) makes a convincing argument from statistical analyses of performance data that pupils' social class and ethnicity have a far greater effect on GCSE performance than gender. Strand's research from 2011 found that the gap in achievement at age 14 in England due to social class was six times larger than the gap due to gender and three times larger than ethnic gap (Strand, 2011).

Understanding social class goes beyond simply looking at economic capital (e.g. measures such as free school meals) but relates to other 'capitals' that pupils' families possess. This might be social capital or the cultural capital (Bourdieu, 1986) that includes having well-educated parents and ready access to books and digital media; and pupils may be exposed to a wider range of learning and cultural experiences than pupils of less well-educated parents. Although the use of computers and mobile phones is widespread, not all families can afford advanced technological equipment, which affords access to information.

There is much evidence to signal the relationship between culturally rich homes and pupil attainment (see Bourdieu (1986), for an explanation of cultural capital and its potential effects on academic success). When exploring the data referred to in this unit, it is clear that gender, ethnicity and class effects are overlapping and intertwined, as pupils have multiple, overlapping identities. In that sense, data that show the performance of different ethnic groups might have as much to do with class as with gender. Using the rather crude measure of free school meals (FSM) to show how socio-economic status relates to GCSE performance, in 2015/16 the average Attainment 8 score for pupils eligible for Free School Meals was 39.0 compared to 51.6 for all other pupils. FSM pupils also had a lower average Progress 8 score of −0.46 compared to 0.04 for all other pupils (DfE, 2016g). In the same way that our response to gender issues needs to become more nuanced, so here should we include the number of looked-after children and the needs of refugee and asylum seekers' children.

Table 4.4.3 Attainment gap (in percentage points) between pupils resident in the most deprived and least deprived areas (least deprived minus most deprived)

	2010/11	2011/12	2012/13	2013/14	2014/15
5 or more A*–C grades at GCSE or equivalent including English and mathematics GCSEs	33.7	30.6	29.5	27.4	28.0

Source: The *Revised GCSE and equivalent results in England: 2014 to 2015* (DfE, 2016h)

The challenge for teachers is, of course, that we cannot necessarily see who these pupils are, but they might well require different kinds of support. Class works in many subtle ways to disadvantage those already disadvantaged. Through language, manners, cultural awareness, etc., the middle classes have a better sense of the 'rules of the game' and so can capitalise better on their educational opportunities (Scherger and Savage, 2010).

Another aspect of this class discussion is poverty, the effect of which has been described graphically by Davies (2000, pp.3-22) and can be seen in the GCSE attainment data in Table 4.4.3. For some time, there has been evidence of the growing gap between rich and poor (Woodward, 2003, p.8; Reardon, 2011) and the Organisation for Economic Cooperation and Development (OECD) found that inequality in income has risen faster in Britain than in any other country since 1975 (OECD, 2011). An Oxfam report in 2012 further highlighted the impact of the recession on those living in poverty and the rise of inequality (Oxfam, 2012), and, more recently, the Joseph Rowntree Foundation has published a report examining the causes and costs of poverty in the UK (Joseph Rowntree Foundation, 2016).

Typically, more well-educated, middle-class parents have a better understanding of the school system (Power et al., 2003), where to get information from (Hatcher, 1998), how to best support their children's schooling and, so, generally stand a better chance of maximising the opportunities afforded by the new educational markets (Ball, 2003). Class and ethnicity remain the main factors in educational disadvantage and yet class is possibly the most difficult factor to define, identify and respond to in a way that can precipitate meaningful and long-term change.

A key policy development in England in relation to raising the attainment of disadvantaged pupils was the introduction of Pupil Premium funding in April 2011. In an attempt to close the gap between disadvantaged pupils and their peers, additional funding is given to schools for each of their pupils eligible for free school meals or who are classed as a looked-after child. Higgins (2015) gives a good analysis of available data to date and where Pupil Premium may be seen to have impacted on attainment.

The above discussion reminds us that the performance of pupils is related to many factors including gender, ethnicity and class. The variables used here, gender, ethnicity and class, are not causes; these variables hide causative factors, some of which are identified above, which contribute to underachievement.

School policy and classroom practice

In this section we begin to examine both school policies and your classroom practice, in the light of the earlier discussion. If schools play a role in the ongoing structuring of inequality in society, albeit not deliberately, then teachers need to reflect critically upon their practice. This involves examining how your own position and action in a diverse society both help and hinder you from challenging unequal treatment in the classroom. See Task 4.4.1.

 Task 4.4.1   Policies towards equal opportunities (EO)

1   Obtain a copy of the equal opportunities (EO) policy in your school. Read it and try to identify:
   ■   Who was involved in developing and writing the policy.
   ■   How old it is.
   ■   Whether there are any later documents, e.g. working party report.
   ■   What areas of school life it covers. Are any areas of school life omitted from its brief?
   ■   The focus of the policy. Are issues around gender, ethnicity, social class or disabilities part of the policy or are they addressed separately?

2   Who knows about the policy? Devise a way of sampling knowledge, understanding and opinion of pupils and staff about the policy. For example:
   ■   Are copies of the policy displayed in the school?
   ■   How many staff know about it; have read it? How many pupils know about it; have read it?
   ■   Who is responsible for EO in the school? Can you arrange to talk to them about their role?

3   Is the policy treated seriously in the school? For example:
   ■   Has any in-service course been devoted to EO issues?
   ■   Does the school EO policy influence departmental policy or classroom practice?
   ■   Can you identify examples of the policy in action? Within the classroom environment? During the school day?

Summarise your findings to discuss with your tutor then file in your professional development portfolio (PDP) or equivalent.

No matter how concerned the school is to promote equity through good policies, implementing them in the classroom is not an easy matter.

When you first start teaching, your concern is to promote learning through well-ordered lessons. When you feel more confident, ask a colleague to observe one of your lessons, focusing on the questions in Tasks 4.4.2 and 4.4.3. As you develop as a teacher you can consider wider issues of inclusion and diversity. These issues might be regarding language or the textual materials used by pupils who, like us, are influenced by words and pictures, particularly moving pictures. Access to the Internet has opened up all sorts of material to pupils, and not all of this is helpful for their academic or social development. Task 4.4.4 asks you to review teaching materials for their implicit messages.

**Task 4.4.2   Responses to gender and ethnicity:
classroom observation**

Ask a student teacher to do parallel observation with you to find out which pupils participate
in the lesson more than others, and which pupils you invite to answer questions or volunteer
information. Share your findings confidentially with each other.

Keep a tally of the frequency of attention to, and the time given to, boys and girls. Devise a
recording sheet to collect information to explore one or two of the following:

- Who puts their hand up to answer a question?
- Who do you select?
- In class activities, how much time do you spend with boys, with girls?
- How do you respond to a pupil? With praise, criticism or further questioning?
- When pupils are reprimanded, is there any difference (gender, ethnicity) in your actions
  and in what you tolerate, or not.

Consider whether different messages are conveyed to boys or girls by your response to
classroom interactions.

Identify and record the implications for your teaching and file in your PDP.

 Task 4.4.3   Responses to pupils with EAL: classroom observation

Redesign the record sheet you used in Task 4.4.2 to collect data about your response to pupils
with English as an additional language. Use similar questions as listed under Task 4.4.2 and
observe the same protocols about observing classrooms (see Unit 2.1). You may wish to add to
the list of questions:

- How do you support pupils whose first language is not English?
- How do you adapt resources for these pupils?
- How do you adapt their own language for these pupils?

File your notes in your PDP.

 Task 4.4.4   Bias and stereotyping in teaching resources

Select a resource in general use in your subject (for example, a book or DVD) and interrogate it
for bias and stereotyping. Some questions you could use to address this issue include:

- What roles are assigned to males and females?
- Who is shown in a position of authority?
- Are people and jobs stereotyped, e.g. black athletes, male scientists, female social workers,
  male cricketers?

- ■   What assumptions, if any, are made concerning minority ethnic citizens in the UK? How accurate are the images shown of people and of places?
- ■   How are people in the developing world depicted? Is it to illustrate malnutrition, or their living conditions or the technology employed? Are the images positive or negative?
- ■   What assumptions, if any, are made concerning underdevelopment in the developing world?

Identify some issues for discussion with your tutor and other student teachers. File your notes in your PDP.

Responding to diversity in the classroom

Your immediate concerns are focused on the classroom but much of what goes on in the classroom has its origins outside the classroom. These origins include the cultural background of pupils, which includes their class and ethnicity. Yet other pupils may have special educational needs (see Unit 4.6). Other factors to consider when trying to make sense of what goes on in the classroom are the teachers' expectations of pupils, the effect of an externally imposed curriculum and the school's ethos realised through its policies and practices.

Teacher expectations of academic performance are often built upon both evidence of what a pupil has done in the past and their social position: male/female; white/black; working/middle class; stable/unstable family background. A perceived social position is sometimes, if unconsciously, used by teachers to anticipate pupils' progress and their capacity to overcome difficulties (Noyes, 2003). You might have found yourself thinking things, or even making assumptions about pupils from the time you first saw their names on the class register. It is crucial you take time to explore your own beliefs and values in relation to gender, ethnicity and class and explore what prejudices you may be subconsciously harbouring. It is through honest self-reflection that you are able to develop into a teacher committed to inclusive practice.

The interaction of the teacher with pupils in the classroom is often revealing. Some teachers may subconsciously favour asking boys, rather than girls, to answer questions. Once established, the reasons for this behaviour can be explored. Similar questions can arise about the way teachers respond to pupils' answers. Whereas one pupil might make a modest and partly correct response to a question to which the teacher's response is praise and support, to another pupil, offering the same level of response, a more critical attitude may be adopted by the teacher.

Are these different responses justified? Is the pupil who received praise gaining support and encouragement from praise, or is the pupil being sent a message that low-level performance is good enough? It is teacher expectations that direct and control such responses. If, as has been documented in the past about the performance of girls, the praise is implicitly saying, 'You have done as well as can be expected because you are a girl', and the critical response is implying 'Come on now, you're a boy; you can do better than this', then there is cause for concern.

Such interpretations depend very much on the context. A comparison of your behaviours in different lessons might reveal the influences on teaching and learning of the subject and the gender, age, and social and cultural background of teachers and pupils (Pearce, 2005). Tasks 4.4.2 and 4.4.3 addressed this suggestion.

Now complete Task 4.4.5.

M

Task 4.4.5   Diversity and learning

Some schools have much more diverse populations than others; however, the issues of diversity are relevant for all schools and pupils. Question: What has been the impact of legislation and initiatives on the achievement of pupils in your placement school?

Find out from staff, school documents and inspection reports information about the following features of your placement school:

- the mix of the pupil population in terms of gender, ethnicity, socio-economic status;
- the different languages spoken by pupils;
- the number of pupils needing and receiving support because English is not their first language;
- the cultural background of pupils, which includes their ethnicity, class and family religion;
- the academic performance of different groups of pupils, e.g. in-school progress tests, GCSE and GCE A level.

How does the school analyse and use data about their pupils?

Find out to what extent your subject department policy and practice relates to the whole school equal opportunities policies. Focus particularly on the curriculum, for example:

- identify whether there is a commitment to multiculturalism at subject level? If so, identify how this policy influences teaching and learning;
- examine teaching and learning resources to see whether they reflect the school policies;
- explore whether there are different strategies for supporting pupils from different backgrounds.

Is there evidence of positive approaches to diversity in the broader life of the school? (For example, in display material, in assemblies, in the recognition of different cultural and religious practices at different times of the year, in extra-curricular activities.) You may find other examples.

Summarise your findings and analyse the information. Draw out some key issues for discussion with your peers and tutor as a draft document. You could develop this enquiry into a piece of coursework, researching recent equal opportunities legislation, e.g. the 2010 Equality Act, or government policy, e.g. the introduction of Pupil Premium Funding, to provide background for your coursework. Keep a copy in your PDP.

Some schools have much more diverse populations than others; however, the issues of diversity are relevant for all schools and pupils. See the companion text 'Surviving and Thriving' by Capel, Lawrence, Leask and Younie (2019) for advice about understanding your school and community.

SUMMARY AND KEY POINTS

- In order to promote equity in educational contexts you need to 'have a secure understanding of how a range of factors can inhibit pupils' ability to learn, and how best to overcome these' (DfE 2011d).

- Beyond 'understanding', there needs to come action, which involves noticing, critiquing and changing your own practices if necessary, in order to create learning environments in which all pupils can thrive and succeed, and where prejudice is rooted out.

- You might develop your practice by changing resources, adopting different approaches to grouping procedures and developing other teaching styles. Through such actions, you can begin to challenge some of the inequalities in our society. Alternatively, you can simply maintain the status quo and, although your discourses might welcome diversity, your practices might be maintaining inequity.

- Sometimes you hear a teacher say, 'I didn't notice their colour, I treat them all the same'. Learning opportunities are enhanced by not being 'gender blind' or 'colour blind' or 'class blind'. We suggest that not recognising pupil differences is just as inadequate a response to teaching demands as is the stereotyping of pupils. Teachers need to recognise those differences without placing limits on what can be achieved.

- You need to reflect on their expectations, preconceptions and even prejudices (however unintended). If you expect most Asian girls to be quiet and passive and good at written work, then that is not only what they do, but also perhaps all they do. Individuals respond in different ways to teachers; you should try to treat each person as an individual and respond to what they do and say, making positive use of your knowledge of the pupils' culture and background.

- A *deficit* view of education will see difference as a problem. It will focus on what an individual cannot do rather than what they can. As responsive teachers, we need to move from a position of *integration* to one of *inclusion*.

- An inclusive school, or society, is based on an appreciation, acceptance and, indeed, celebration of diversity. It welcomes into its cultures, policies and practices, the fresh input from diverse persons as full members within it. It does not try to make every person 'normal' (Bartolo et al., 2007 p.49).

Check which requirements for your ITE programme you have addressed through this unit.

 Further resources

Diversity and social justice

Adams, M. and Bell, L. A. (eds.) (2016) *Teaching for Diversity and Social Justice*, **Abingdon: Routledge.**

Ajegbo, K. (2007) *Diversity and Citizenship Curriculum Review*, **London: DfES.**

EHRC (Equality and Human Rights Commission), viewed 6 June 2017, from www.equalityhumanrights. com/en
This site provides a wealth of information and includes many easily downloadable statistical summaries of social life in Britain. 'How Fair is Britain?' is a triennial review that monitors the progress that society makes towards becoming one that is more equal.

Intercom Trust: viewed 20 December 2017, from https://www.intercomtrust.org.uk/
Intercom Trust is a lesbian, gay, bisexual and trans community resource. They provide help against homophobic and transphobic prejudice, crime and discrimination (including bullying, harassment, abuse, attacks, and threatening behaviour), helping to develop the LGBT communities, providing professional training and consultancy, and working in partnership with local government, the police, health and other organisations.

Joseph Rowntree Foundation: viewed 6 August 2017, from https://www.jrf.org.uk/
The Joseph Rowntree Foundation aims to identify the root causes of poverty and injustice. The website provides a wealth of information and research on the barriers to educational achievement and the impact of gender, ethnicity, social class and poverty.

Stonewall: viewed 20 January 2017, from http://www.stonewall.org.uk/
Stonewall is a lesbian, gay, bisexual and transgender (LGBT) rights charity in the United Kingdom. It was founded by a small group of people in 1989 who had been active in the struggle against section 28 of the Local Government Act.

Poverty and low achievement

DfE (Department for Education) (2014c) *Child Poverty Strategy 2014-17*, London: HMSO.

DfE (Department for Education) (various) *Raising Attainment*, viewed 2 July 2018, from https://www.gov.uk/government/publications/supporting-the-attainment-of-disadvantaged-pupils
The section of the Department for Education's site includes reports and advice on how schools may raise achievement, addressing a variety of different circumstances in which schools are placed and the particular factors affecting achievement in their geographical area. It includes, as well, information on how the Pupil Premium might be used.

DfE (Department for Education) (various) Statistical Data, viewed 2 July 2018, from www.gov.uk/search?q=gcse+and+equivalent+attainment
The GCSE and 'Equivalent Attainment' section of the DfE website contain extensive information that helps you to consider the performance and characteristics of pupils from different backgrounds. The GCSE and Equivalent Attainment by Pupil Characteristics reports on the number and percentages of pupils achieving various outcomes at the end of KS4.

Kingdon, G. and Cassen, C. (2007) *Understanding Low Achievement in English Schools.* **London: Centre for the Economics of Education, LSE.**

Ofsted (Office for Standards in Education) (2013) *Unseen Children: Access and Achievement 20 Years On*, **London: Ofsted.**

Appendix 2 lists subject associations and teacher councils and Appendix 3 provides a list of websites.

Capel, S., Leask, M. and Turner, T. (eds.) (2010) *Readings for Learning to Teach in the Secondary School: A Companion to M Level Study*, **Abingdon: Routledge.**
This book brings together essential readings to support you in your critical engagement with key issues raised in this textbook.

Capel, S., Lawrence, J. Leask, M. and Younie, S. (eds.) (2019) *Surviving and Thriving in the Secondary School: The NQT's Essential Companion*, **Abingdon: Routledge.**
This book is designed to support newly qualified teachers in the next phase of development as a teacher. However, you may find it useful as it covers aspects of teaching not included in this book which, nonetheless you experience on your ITE programme.

The subject specific books in the *Learning to Teach (Subject)* series, the *Practical (Subject) Guides, Debates in (Subject)* and *Mentoring (Subject) Teachers* are also very useful.

Any additional resources and an editable version of any relevant tasks/tables in this unit are available on the companion website: www.routledge.com/cw/capel

4.5 Values education

Discussion and deliberation

Ruth Heilbronn

Introduction

Values education takes place in formal and informal settings. There are many factors that make such education effective, some in the control of the school and some not. This unit draws on evidence from research on character education and moral development education to point to sources of reference in drawing up a programme. Other evidence of what is included under the umbrella of values education is cited from policy sources, such as the Department for Education.

This unit first focuses on you as a practitioner; second, on your pupils and their development; and, lastly, on classroom discussions relating to values. As a member of a profession, a teacher should behave with integrity and uphold professional values; these may be expressed in a code of conduct or in competency statements, such as the Teachers' Standards in England (Department for Education (DfE), 2011d) with its explicit *Preamble* about behaving with 'honesty and integrity' and the emphasis on teaching 'British Values'.

Teachers are also concerned with pupils' behaviour and must intervene if needed to guide the way pupils behave. This guidance is underpinned with value judgements about maintaining positive relationships with pupils, being fair, respectful and supportive. Teaching can be considered a practice in which the good teacher exemplifies both the skills and the values of the practice (Dunne, 2003, pp.353-371). We expect teachers to be exemplary figures in the course of their work (McLaughlin, 2004, pp.339-353). When teachers stop a class because they have overheard a racist remark, which they tackle sensitively, knowledgeably, successfully, while upholding the value of tolerance, we would say they dealt competently with the situation, drawing on their own values and their experience, in a 'deliberate exercise of principled judgement in the light of rational knowledge and understanding' (Carr, 1993, pp.253-271). Importantly,

> morality is the area of values which affects how we treat each other and hence the area of values which in an important sense is not optional. It is about what we owe to each other, what we may blame others for not living up to.
>
> (Haydon and Hayward, 2004, p.165)

OBJECTIVES

At the end of this unit you should:

- understand the place of values education and ethical deliberation in a subject and school context;
- understand the various legal responsibilities of schools in the area of moral, social and cultural development, including civic responsibility;
- identify core values for yourself and those of the school in which you are teaching;
- identify opportunities to promote understanding and practice of these core common values in school;
- try out some methods of leading discussion and promoting ethical deliberation.

Check the requirements of your initial teacher education (ITE) programme to see which relate to this unit.

Values education

The terms 'values education' and 'moral education' are often used interchangeably, but 'morality' involves wider notions of 'goodness' and particular views on the nature of right and wrong, than the term 'values'. Any adult in a relationship with a child is in some sense teaching about values, and such teaching takes place in various situations, such as in one-to-one conversations, classroom teaching, parent or carer interactions. 'Values' might be defined as:

> the principles and fundamental convictions which act as general guides to behaviour, the standards by which particular actions are judged to be good or desirable. Examples of values are love, equality, freedom, justice, happiness, security, peace of mind and truth
>
> (Halstead and Taylor, 2000, pp.169–202)

In 2011 the DfE had some general comments to make about values education, stating that it is

> a broad term and may carry a particular emphasis on education in civic and wider moral values, or 'character education' and be closely related to other terms in current use, including spiritual, moral, social and cultural development, for example in some of the formulations of the English National Curriculum.
>
> (DfE, 2013b)

Our values determine how we choose a course of action or a belief in situations where different views are held. This is important because sometimes our values might be conflicted. Value judgements on controversial issues differ from judgements of fact, where evidence can help us to make decisions. When teacher or pupil is unable to decide what to do and when more facts about a situation cannot help, because the particular dilemma is an ethical one, it is useful to have skills in ethical deliberation, the kind of moral reasoning that goes on when making ethical judgements. At the end of the unit, some support is provided on a way of developing this form of discursive reasoning, which can be adopted in a classroom, for pupils dealing with difficult issues or choices, or in a community of practitioners similarly searching for guidance on a difficult choice of action (see Orchard et al., 2016).

In many countries some form of civic education is a vehicle for promoting values and encouraging pupils to develop their ability to deliberate on moral matters. This is particularly relevant to today's context – See the Council of Europe's Report on Citizenship and Human Rights Education Council of Europe (2017) for a fuller discussion.

Schools, as well as individual teachers, uphold values and express these in their policies and practices, which often makes for differences in ethos between schools. Research shows that these differences are important to the individual teachers' ability to thrive and develop in school (Heilbronn et al., 2002, pp.371-389) and to the pupils' expressions of respect for one another and their socially responsible behaviour in the classroom (Hansen, 1995, pp.59-74). School ethos is largely created through the leadership. Some tangible expressions of a school's ethos might be found in the way parents are welcomed, the relationships between adults and young people outside as well as inside the classroom, staff sensitivity to cultural and faith differences in the school, or how the school celebrates the success of its pupils. The ethos of a school contributes as much to values education as does the prescribed curriculum.

Values underlie all aspects of school life. In some schools, there is a common understanding about the basis of these values in definable moral codes, such as in a faith school where there is accepted tradition and 'scripture'. In a secular school, a common understanding is not so tightly defined. Nevertheless, even in a faith school, there are many areas where value judgements are made, which are not clearly indicated by the underlying faith ethic, such as judgements about what is 'fair' in a particular situation, which may involve judgement in choosing one claim over another. Teachers frequently have to make such judgements in particular situations. School policies, rules and regulations may provide guidelines, for example, when dealing with racist or bullying incidents, often based on the core value of 'respect', but this guidance cannot tell us what we *ought* to say and to do in response to a particular situation. As a teacher, it is a matter of judgement how to mediate the policy. So, in acting and being in the classroom, a teacher stands as a moral example. For example, a teacher might punish a pupil who steals from another pupil without much discussion; or the teacher might decide to talk to the pupil, to get them to understand that what they had done was wrong. Choosing how and when to have this discussion is also a matter of judgement (see Heilbronn, 2008).

Talking with pupils about the rights and wrongs of their behaviour is important, as it acknowledges and respects the pupils' ability to develop an understanding of the consequences of their actions, which encourages a sense of responsibility and agency and, so, helps pupils to develop moral understanding. School policies are in some sense a formal interface between the individual pupil and teacher. The teacher in the example could relate the discussion about why stealing is wrong to the school's formal statement or rule relating to respect. In fact, 'everyday classroom life is saturated with moral meaning. Even the most routine aspects of teaching convey moral messages to students' (Hansen, 1995, para.2).

Pupils judge their teachers on the way they develop good relations with them and believe that without good relationships they do not learn effectively (Wiedmaier et al., 2007; Liu and Meng, 2009; Wang and Holcombe, 2010; Morgan, 2011). Pupils tend to have good relationships with teachers who are good at engaging in reasoned discussion and are able to articulate the values underlying the rules about what is acceptable and non-acceptable behaviour (Lickona, 1983). Although written over 30 years ago, the nature of Lickona's enquiry means that the research is still as relevant today, as is Nucci's corroboration that:

> students rated highest those teachers who responded to moral transgressions with statements focusing on the effects of acts ('Joe, that really hurt Mike'). Rated lower were teachers who responded with statements of school rules or normative expectations ('That's not the way for a Hawthorne student to act'). Rated lowest were teachers who used simple commands ('Stop it!' or 'Don't hit').

> (Nucci, 1987, pp.86–92)

It may not be possible to take all the time necessary to deal in-depth with particular issues as they arise, but this too can be acknowledged with the pupils. What is important is to reflect back to them an example of the kind of behaviour that is acceptable and the reasons behind the values expressed, rather than ignoring or suppressing the unacceptable. It is important to attend to issues of values in any particular classroom situation since pupils experience lessons as individual young people and not as disembodied 'learners' of a particular curriculum area. As participants in the classroom, their experiences need to be attended to. Van Manen has written of 'the tact of teaching' and how good, trustful relationships rely on the teacher's 'pedagogical thoughtfulness' (van Manen, 1991). This is not always easy to achieve, of course. Judgement over the right thing to do can be difficult, for example, being fair to all whilst also taking individual needs into account.

Cultural diversity and common values

Quite young children can distinguish moral judgements related to justice and fairness from judgements about social conventions, such as how to address people politely or follow dress codes (Nucci, 1987, pp.86–92). It is important in a pluralistic society to be able to distinguish a number of fundamental common values that do not rely on any specific cultural or religious foundations. In England, subsequent revisions of the NC contained clearly stated underlying aims, to promote 'the spiritual, moral, cultural, mental and physical development of pupils at the school and of society' (DfE, 2013b). Currently, in England, the government has required schools to promote 'fundamental British values', a term which is taken from the definition of extremism as articulated in the new Prevent Strategy, launched in June 2011. It includes 'democracy, the rule of law, individual liberty and mutual respect and tolerance of different faiths and beliefs' (DfE, 2011d, p.9). These values are fundamental to all liberal democracies so there is considerable debate about why they are classed as 'British' values (Lander et al., 2016; Both, 2017; Elton-Chalcraft et al., 2017).

Successive Education Acts since 1988 have required the Office for Standards in Education (Ofsted) to inspect the contributions that English schools make to pupils' spiritual, moral, social and cultural education and how well pupils' attitudes, values and other personal qualities are developed. Ofsted (2004) published guidance entitled *Promoting and Evaluating Pupils' Spiritual, Moral, Social and Cultural Development,* subsequently updated in school inspection guidance (Ofsted 2014b). However, there is considerable debate about how the term 'spiritual' is to be defined and whether it is the job of schools to promote spirituality, and, more than any other area of the curriculum, it is difficult to see how the development of spirituality could be measured, assuming an acceptable definition of what it is could be agreed (Hand, 2003). So, it seems sensible to concentrate on schools as ethical places, and teachers as ethical people, with responsibilities to develop pupils' sense of values and their ability to act ethically.

Settings and opportunities for values education

A question of continuing interest and research concerns how a child develops moral reasoning (MR). Building on Piaget's 1932 foundational work, Kohlberg developed his own theory of how MR develops. Both writers stressed maturation factors, arguing that mature MR depends on the development of the capacity for logical reasoning (Kohlberg, 1985, pp.27-87). In discussing the development of children's ability to use increasingly nuanced MR, the term 'moral development' is frequently used, particularly in policy and curriculum documents. See Units 4.3 and 5.1 on maturation of reasoning and cognitive development.

The structured nature of both Piaget's stage theory and the Kohlberg framework is a contested matter (see Stern, 1985; Donaldson, 1978; Weiten, 2010). The following articles provide an introduction to their work: Huitt and Hummel (2003); Nucci (2007).

Arguably, pupils' understanding of the school's values, and more widely of right and wrong, is 'caught', rather than 'taught'. Many argue that the only way for values and moral reasoning to develop is through experience (Dewey, 1909; 1916; Van Manem, 1991; Campbell, 2008). In particular, experiences that arise from a real situation and subsequent discussion of that experience with peers or adults. Research has shown that there *are* common features of schools that seem to have a positive impact on the development of pupil values, such as participation in the communal life of the school and the classroom; encouragement to behave responsibly; provision of an orderly school environment, and clear rules that are fairly enforced (Battisch et al., 1998). A school's explicitness about its values and the extent to which teachers practice shared values also has an important influence on the pupils' own development of moral understanding and responsibility. The home influence in values' formation is of course far more significant than that of the school, given the early nurture period and the time spent in the family. This reinforces the importance of a partnership approach between schools and their local communities (Nucci, 1987, pp.86-92).

The curriculum is one vehicle through which 'moral development' can be channelled, for example in subjects, such as religious education (RE). Citizenship education is also inherently related to values since political and social issues concern the question of how we should collectively live, which is at root an extension of the basic moral question 'How should I live my life?' (Haydon and Hayward, 2004, pp.161-175). Although many areas of public life can be an occasion for teaching and discussing in a fairly descriptive manner, they remain value-laden in nature and may often call for sensitive handling.

The curriculum can also outline courses of study for matters relating to pupils' personal life under the auspices of a personal, social and health education course (PSHE). There are also curriculum initiatives to foster the development of moral reasoning through specific learning activities, such as various courses of 'character education'. In England, the Jubilee Centre for Character and Virtues is involved in this work; see http://www.jubileecentre.ac.uk. There are many resources for 'character education' (e.g. Freakley et al., 2008) and arguments in its favour (Curren, 2017); although, some have challenged the difficulty in such programmes. This is because such programmes are built on choices of values, and there can be debate about which values should be promoted to children as 'good character'.

There remains a fundamental question in relation to values education as to whether values can be *taught* or only *caught*. Kohlberg (1985) commented on the artificiality of creating a specific curriculum area purely to foster moral development. In an evaluation of one of his own early projects in school he stated: 'While the intervention operation was a success, the patient died. When we went back a year later, we found not a single teacher had continued to engage in moral discussion after the commitment to the research had ended' (Kohlberg, 1985, p.80). This underlines the importance of personal experience and continued commitment to engaging with discussion about values in context and when occasion arises. When we talk to a pupil about something that we have both experienced, we engage in a process of talking about values in a direct and practical way.

Ethical deliberation through discussion

Discussion is a common means of raising moral and ethical issues. Young people can be taught some deliberative rules and practices for grappling with ethical dilemmas and difficult moral choices. The ability to make moral judgements wisely depends on weighing up fine balances of possible actions, within an understanding of context, and we expect this ability to develop as children mature. In their discussions, pupils may not reach agreement, but the discussions can lead to a deeper understanding of the issues and the positions of others. Evidently underlying all these discussions are the values that participants hold; although, they may not be able to articulate them fully. Taking part in well-managed and well-conceived deliberation on ethical matters enhances pupils' social interaction, because they need to listen to each other and respect each other's opinions (see Hand and Levison, 2011).

It is clear that engaging in ethical deliberation through discussion involves respect for the opinions of others, sincerity in seeking to clarify what is said by others and skill in relating what is said to one's own situation and choices. Managing such discussions or explorations requires skill, to avoid them becoming merely ritualistic or worse, a confirmation of prejudices and an opportunity for the strongest characters to dominate. Discussions need to be appropriately related to the pupils' own experience or imaginative capacities. (See Appendix 4.5.1 for advice on classroom discussion.) At any given time, there are likely to be 'hot topics' that concern young people in their lives outside the classroom, e.g. social networking is a key issue for young people since it can raise questions about relationships, trust and privacy that draw on the ethics of a responsible online community (Bradshaw and Younie, 2018). In the public domain, the debates and dilemmas are often age related and may involve concerns for the environment, endangered species, fair trade, equality of opportunity, sexual harassment or legal and medical decisions, such as the case of conjoined twins, where the operation to separate them would lead to the survival of only one of the babies. (Wasserman, 2001). The debate about conflicts on moral issues continues to be relevant as medicine's technical possibilities grow.

> As medicine drives us past the limits of our settled moral deliberations, it becomes increasingly important to take stock of the rules and principles by which our lives, and those of others, are ordered. We should be painstaking in our attempts to resolve moral and legal dilemmas that threaten the most basic rights of individuals.
>
> (Clucas and O'Donnell, 2002, p.?)

Some worked-through discussion of examples of controversial issues can be found in Levinson (2005b, pp.258-268).

As well as discussion as a pedagogic technique, there are also educational games that foster moral development, including digital computer games. Some have been specifically designed to increase values awareness, such as the *RealLives* simulation that enablers players to learn more about different cultures and develop inter-cultural competence (Struppert, 2010). In a critical consideration of digital games-based learning, Younie and Leask (2013) argue that gaming can help engender values and resilience in young people through learning to manage emotions (from frustration of losing to elation at winning) by following rules, and, in team-based games, through co-operation to achieve shared goals. Citing Piaget (1932), they outline how games can help pupils' emerging social and cognitive capabilities, especially boys (Hromek and Roffey, 2009). Games particularly aid working with rules and the development of self-discipline, which underpins society and social order. Similarly, Mead (1934) outlined how role-playing fosters empathy in children, which is essential for developing a sense of morality. Game-playing can then aid the socio-emotional, moral and cognitive development of pupils (Younie and Leask, 2013, pp.37-83).

The following section of the unit identifies some generic, rather than subject-based, areas for reflection about values with suggestions for tasks from which you can select the most appropriate for you. They are intended to be discussed with other students, teachers and tutors.

Reflecting on teacher values

Task 4.5.1 asks you to reflect on the values stated in the Teachers' Standards in England, in relation to your ITE programme and the country in which you wish to teach.

 Task 4.5.1   Reflecting on teachers' values

This task draws on the Teachers' Standards in England (DfE, 2011d), available on the Internet. To understand the full context, you particularly need to look at the 'Preamble'. It is available at: www.education.gov.uk/publications/eOrderingDownload/teachers%20standards.pdf

Refer to Figure 4.5.1 and read the statement of values defined there, which teachers should uphold.

- Do you believe that these should be your core values as a teacher? Are there any you do not agree with?
- Are there any aspects that may be more difficult to apply than others?
- Are there any issues that you think you might experience in putting these values into place?
- Are there any aspects of the values relating to teaching that you think are missing here?

Summarise your views identifying the values you currently hold. Store in your professional development portfolio (PDP) or equivalent.

Teachers' Standards in England part 2

Personal and professional conduct

A teacher is expected to demonstrate consistently high standards of personal and professional conduct. The following statements define the behaviour and attitudes which set the required standard for conduct throughout a teacher's career.

- Teachers uphold public trust in the profession and maintain high standards of ethics and behaviour, within and outside school, by:

  - treating pupils with dignity, building relationships rooted in mutual respect, and at all times observing proper boundaries appropriate to a teacher's professional position
  - having regard for the need to safeguard pupils' well-being, in accordance with statutory provisions
  - showing tolerance of and respect for the rights of others
  - not undermining fundamental British values, including democracy, the rule of law, individual liberty and mutual respect, and tolerance of those with different faiths and beliefs
  - ensuring that personal beliefs are not expressed in ways which exploit pupils' vulnerability or might lead them to break the law.

- Teachers must have proper and professional regard for the ethos, policies and practices of the school in which they teach, and maintain high standards in their own attendance and punctuality.
- Teachers must have an understanding of, and always act within, the statutory frameworks which set out their professional duties and responsibilities.

Figure 4.5.1 Teachers' standards in England, part 2
Source: DfE, 2011d

Aims of schools

Task 4.5.2 focuses on the aims of a school and how these are interpreted.

 Task 4.5.2   Aims of the school and how they are interpreted

For discussion with other students, teachers and tutors:

1   Find the aims of your placement school and of another school and compare them:
   ▪   Do the aims express responsibility for the moral development of pupils?
   ▪   How do the school statements differ?
2   Many school curricular statements are prefaced with some broad aims, relating to fostering pupils' self-esteem, valuing their contribution and helping them to develop independently. How might these aims become teaching opportunities?
3   Select a topic from the PSHE syllabus and reflect on the underlying values promoted, Topics might for example cover inclusion, environmental, relationship issues;
4   Assemblies can contribute to moral and values education. To reflect on these, you could:
   ▪   Attend assembly; record its purpose and what and how any 'message' was conveyed and then interview some pupils. Did they understand any 'message'? If so, did they agree with it. Is it relevant to them?
   ▪   Help plan an assembly and find out:
      ▪   if there is a school programme for assemblies and how the content and approach is agreed;
      ▪   how the content and messages relate to the cultural mix of the school;
      ▪   if you think the assembly develops a sense of community or is more ritualistic;
      ▪   how is success celebrated and whose success is mostly recognised?
5   In the school's in-service education and training (INSET), is there any provision relating to moral, ethical and values education? If so, investigate how and by whom.

Write a short report on one of the five exercises above to discuss with your tutor. Record your discussion in your PDP.

Subject teaching

Task 4.5.3 relates to subject teaching.

 Task 4.5.3   The place of subject work in promoting moral development and values education

Identify and evaluate a social, ethical or moral issue that forms part of teaching your subject. Include:

- a statement of the subject matter and its place in the curriculum;
- the ethical focus for pupils;
- a sample of teaching material;
- an outline teaching strategy, e.g. a draft lesson plan;
- any problems that you anticipate teaching the issue;
- any questions that other student teachers might help you resolve;
- resources to support the ethical focus.

Record your evaluations in your PDP.

Class management

Task 4.5.4 relates to class management.

 Task 4.5.4   Classroom management

Class detention

Consider the following scenario:

A class is reading from a set text and periodically stopping to discuss points. Some pupils start flicking pellets at others. The teacher sees it happening but cannot identify the culprits. Some pupils start complaining. The noise level rises and the whole class gets involved. The teacher says that the person who started the flicking should own up. No one does and the class is given time to sort it out among themselves. No one owns up and the teacher keeps the whole class in after school for 15 minutes. This causes resentment and some walk out and refuse to stay.

How might the teacher have dealt differently with:

- the whole incident?
- those left in detention?
- those who walked out?
- complaints about unfair practice/injustice?

What larger themes does this incident raise (e.g. the justice of collective punishment)? Record your reflections in your PDP.

Critical incidents

Many classroom incidents have an ethical dimension. How we respond to them is largely a function of our own ethical beliefs, and what we do models our underlying values. Whether we act judiciously, for example, or react inappropriately in haste may determine whether we are just and fair or not, and pupils quickly pick up which is the case. Task 4.5.5 has two incidents of this kind. In the first, a pupil has to decide what to do and a teacher has to act accordingly. In the second, the teacher faces a conflict of responsibilities towards the parents on one hand and the pupils on the other, and has to take a stand.

 Task 4.5.5   Critical incidents for discussion

1   Wayne is in school during break to keep an appointment with a teacher. Passing his form room, he sees a pupil going through the teacher's desk drawer, taking things out and putting them in his pocket. Wayne walks away unseen by the other pupil and decides to tell his class teacher.

2   A 14-year-old girl attends a local girls' school. Her parents do not allow her to mix socially with young people they do not know, and they expect her to return home immediately after school. She often goes home with other girls and part of the way with boys from the nearby boys' school. One day she arranges to meet a boy after school and that morning she asks her friend Serena to give her an alibi. But Serena refuses as she does not want to lie to her friend's parents. The two girls argue in class and the teacher keeps them back after school, and then learns why the girls were quarrelling.

■   What would you do in each of these cases if you were the teacher?

■   What advice would you give to the pupils?

■   Can you imagine any difficult decisions you might have to take? If so, explain the considerations.

■   If you didn't know what to do, do you know where to get the advice and support you need to help you manage challenging situations?

■   How do the situations relate to the particular formulation of the ethical responsibilities of teachers as stated in your ITE programme requirements or accreditation standards?

Store this in your PDP.

Now complete Task 4.5.6.

M

✎ Task 4.5.6   Teaching right and wrong

Consider the following questions and draft a response to them before reading the extracts from Smith and Standish (1997), then review your responses.

1   In your opinion can values be explicitly 'taught' or only 'caught' by example and through experience? Draft a response to this question before reading the text: see Smith and Standish (1997, pp.75–91).

2   'If we are supposed to instil values in the young, whose values are these?' Where do values come from?

3   Investigate the Kohlberg stages of moral development, e.g. through the paper by Nucci (2007). What is your view of these stages? Do they tally with your views on how a moral sense develops? Do people pass through various stages of moral development as they grow up? See Smith and Standish (1997, pp.93–104).

Summarise your thoughts and discuss them with other student teachers before finalising your response. This topic could be written up as an essay (5,000 words) with a title such as 'Teaching right from wrong'.

Store this in your PDP.

SUMMARY AND KEY POINTS

■   Moral judgement and behaviour derive from personal, social, cultural, religious and political viewpoints and conventions.

■   Societies with diverse groups have a potential for enrichment or friction.

■   Young people develop an ability to reason about values and to make ethical choices. They are helped towards maturity in this respect by parents and carers, teachers and peers. This mature stage of development may lead to questioning the values they have grown up with.

■   Some moral and ethical matters can arise naturally in dealing with children but subject work may afford opportunities for approaching them (Task 4.5.3). While some subjects lend themselves more easily than others to these matters – such as English, religious education, citizenship and civic education – all subjects can provide an opportunity. The use of simulations and discussion are good ways of introducing moral and ethical matters (see advice in Appendix 4.5.1 at the end of this unit).

■   Teachers have a particular responsibility to promote pupils' development as ethically responsible people. In some countries there is a legal responsibility.

■   Ethical dilemmas continually arise in practice and need good judgement. It is important to know the school policy about the issue that confronts you and the expected response in your school.

■   When you find it difficult to respond by yourself you should refer to experienced and qualified staff for help. These dilemmas are part of being a teacher with responsibility for others.

Check which requirements for your ITE programme you have addressed through this unit.

APPENDIX 4.5.1

The following notes may help you develop your strategies for conducting discussion. They adopt the neutral chairperson approach.

A useful model for discussion is to engage with the following four principles:

1   There should be rules and procedures for discussion that all understand.
2   Speakers should provide evidence and information to back up their comments.
3   A neutral chairperson should have overview of the discussion.
4   The expected outcomes should be understood and communicated to everyone.

1   Rules and procedures

You need to consider:

■   choice of subject and length of discussion (young pupils without experience may not sustain lengthy discussion);
■   physical seating; room size; arrangement of furniture so that most pupils have eye contact;
■   protocols for discourse; taking turns; length of contribution; abusive language;
■   procedures for violation of protocols, e.g. racist or sexist behaviour;
■   how to protect the sensitivity of individuals; pupils may reveal unexpected personal information in the course of a discussion;
■   stance of the chairperson.

2   Provision of evidence

In order to stimulate discussion and provide a clear basis for argument, you need to:

■   know the age, ability and mix of abilities of the pupils;
■   know what information is needed;
■   know sources of information;
■   decide at what point the information is introduced (before, during).

3   Neutral chairperson

A neutral stance may be essential because:

■   the authority of the opinions of the chair should not influence the outcome;
■   the opinions of pupils are to be exposed, not those of the teachers;
■   the chairperson can be free to influence the quality of understanding, the rigour of debate and appropriate exploration of the issues;
■   pupils will understand the teacher's stance if it is made clear at the start.

4   Possible outcomes

The strategy is discussion not instruction. Pupils should:

- learn by sharing and understand the opinion of others;
- be exposed to the nature and role of evidence;
- realise that objective evidence is often an inadequate basis for decision making;
- come to know that decisions often rely on subjective value judgements;
- realise that many decisions are compromises.

Action

Try out these rules by setting up a discussion with other student teachers on the topic of: 'Equal opportunities for girls enable them to join the power structure rather than challenge it' (Levinson, 2005b, pp.258-268). A fuller description of simulations is given in Turner, S. (1995) 'Simulations', in J. Frost (ed.) *Teaching Science*, London: Woburn Press. See also, Frost (2010) and Unit 5.4.

Further resources

There are many resources on values education in schools. The following websites are helpful:

British Humanist Association: http://www.humanism.org.uk/education/education-policy
Citizenship Foundation: http://www.citizenshipfoundation.org.uk
CitizED subject resource bank: http://www.citized.info

Several of the books below are recommended as the latest edition of the work. Philosophy books remain current because philosophical deliberation deals with conceptual matters and whilst the content/context may change, the arguments and debates do not.

Haydon, G. (2006a) *Values in Education*, **London: Continuum.**
Addresses the issues of 'what are the fundamental aims and values underlying education'? And how can education promote values in a world of value pluralism? The text also discusses morality and if schools should teach it. And, in a secular society, how should schools treat the links between morality and religion? This is an updated version of an earlier text *Teaching about Values* (1997).

Haydon, G. (2006b) *Education, Philosophy and the Ethical Environment*, **London: Faber and Faber.**
This book offers a critical analysis of some of the fundamental questions about the nature and purpose of education, using the concept of 'ethical environment'. It addresses many ideas about values education including the contrasting ideas of relativism and universal values, indoctrination, the relationship between values and sense of identity and the demands of pluralism.

Nucci, L., Narvaez, D. and Krettenauer, T. (2014) *Handbook of Moral and Character Education*, **2nd Edition, New York: Routledge.**
The book has a wide range of articles across the whole field of values and moral education. The second edition includes updated applications from mental and cognitive psychology and moral and character education relevant to various educational settings.

Smith, R., and Standish, P. (eds.) (1997) *Teaching Right and Wrong: Moral Education in the Balance*, **Stoke on Trent: Trentham.**
This discusses the work of the National Forum on Values Education and also argues for alternative approaches to values education.

Appendix 2 lists subject associations and teacher councils and Appendix 3 provides a list of websites.

Capel, S., Leask, M. and Turner, T. (eds.) (2010) *Readings for Learning to Teach in the Secondary School: A Companion to M Level Study*, **Abingdon: Routledge.**
This book brings together essential readings to support you in your critical engagement with key issues raised in this textbook.

Capel, S., Lawrence, J. Leask, M. and Younie, S. (eds.) (2019) *Surviving and Thriving in the Secondary School: The NQT's Essential Companion*, Abingdon: Routledge.
This book is designed to support newly qualified teachers in the next phase of development as a teacher. However, you may find it useful as it covers aspects of teaching not included in this book which, nonetheless you experience on your ITE programme.

The subject specific books in the *Learning to Teach (Subject)* series, the *Practical (Subject) Guides, Debates in (Subject)* and *Mentoring (Subject) Teachers* are also very useful.

Any additional resources and an editable version of any relevant tasks/tables in this unit are available on the companion website: www.routledge.com/cw/capel

4.6 An introduction to inclusion, special educational needs and disability

Nick Peacey

Introduction

The UK 2014 Children and Families Act (the 2014 Act, in this unit) and the 2014 special educational needs and disability code of practice (referred to as the '2014 code') form the framework in England for the education of children and young people with special educational needs and disabilities (SEND). The framework in England is used throughout this unit.

The framework:

- covers provision for children and young people between 0-25 years of age;
- makes collaboration between services and all types of educational institution mandatory;
- provides for local authorities (LAs) to publish a 'local offer' explaining exactly what is available in their area and 'to make provision more responsive to local needs and aspirations' (the 2014 code, para 4.2);
- emphasises schools' duty to optimise 'ordinary differentiation' before intervention;
- introduced an 'Education, Health and Care Plan (EHCP)' to replace the 'statement of special educational needs' and 'learning difficulties assessment (LDA - these were assessments used in post-16 education);
- strengthened the rights of pupils with SEND and their parents (referring to both parents and carers).

Article 24 of the UN Convention on the Rights of Persons with Disabilities (UNCRPD) guarantees all disabled learners a right to participate in all forms of mainstream education with appropriate support (see also Unit 4.4).

OBJECTIVES

At the end of this unit you should be able to:

- explain how the terms inclusion, special educational needs, disability and inclusive pedagogy are used;
- understand recent legislation and regulation in this area, in particular teachers' responsibilities for what is known as SEN[1] Support in the 2014 code, and the disability discrimination requirements in the Equality Act 2010 (if you are outside England, ask your tutor about legislation relevant to you);
- start developing your knowledge of teaching strategies, which may be used with pupils with different SEND[2] within the whole-class inclusion approach.

Check the requirements for your initial teacher education (ITE) programme to see which relate to this unit

---

The background

Some definitions

The publication *Index for Inclusion,* which was sent with government support to every school in England, describes inclusion in these terms:

> Inclusion in education involves the processes of increasing the participation of students in, and reducing their exclusion from, the cultures, curricula and communities of local schools. Inclusion is concerned with the learning participation of all students vulnerable to exclusionary pressures, not only those with impairments or categorised as having special educational needs. Inclusion is concerned with improving schools for staff as well as for students.
>
> (Centre for Studies on Inclusive Education (CSIE), 2011)

The authors of *Index for Inclusion* noted that schools cannot remove all barriers to inclusion, such as those created by poverty.

The CSIE definition of inclusion is comprehensive. You will also find the term used to mean the process by which pupils with SEND are placed in mainstream schools as opposed to specialist provision like special schools.

Defining SEN and disability

The 2014 Act and 2014 code use this definition of SEN: 'A child or young person has SEN if they have a learning difficulty or disability which calls for special educational provision to be made for them'.

A disabled person has 'a physical or mental disability which has an effect on their ability to carry out normal day-to-day activities'. That effect must be substantial (i.e. more than minor or trivial), adverse and long term (has lasted or is likely to last at least a year or for the rest of the life of the person affected).

The disability discrimination legislation in the Equality Act (EA) (2010) includes a wider group of pupils than those defined as having SEN. For example, it covers those with medical or physical impairments for whom there may be no educational barriers to learning. The EA applies across the United Kingdom and to all educational establishments, public or private, whereas the 2014 code only applies to publicly funded English schools. Its duties are 'anticipatory – they require schools to give thought in advance to what disabled young people may require and what adjustments might need to be made to prevent that disadvantage' (ibid, p.17).

Much English, Northern Irish and Welsh government statute and regulation still use SEN, but Scottish law prefers the broader concept 'additional support needs' (ASN). 'Additional support needs can be both long- and short-term, or can simply refer to the help a child or young person needs in getting through a difficult period. Additional support needs can be due to: disability or health; the learning environment; family circumstances; social and emotional factors' (Scottish Government, 2017, p.1)

The term 'SEN' has long attracted criticism for reinforcing a 'medical' model of disability that emphasises within-individual difficulties, rather than tackling the cultures and practices that can create barrier. These authors prefer a 'social model' (e.g. Oliver, 1990) that addresses the role of attitudes and environments in creating disability. Shakespeare and Watson (2002) brought the 'medical' and 'social' viewpoints together into an 'interactionist' approach that recognises factors within the individual and those within their environment. More recently, Degener (2016) has suggested that another integrating approach, the 'human rights' model, offers the best chance of finding innovative ways forward. Now complete Task 4.6.1.

 Task 4.6.1   Identifying pupils with SEND

- List the ways in which schools you know identified/identify pupils as having special educational needs.
- Look critically through the articles referenced in the paragraph above and note any insights they give you into SEND identification in schools you know.
- Read the Joseph Rowntree Foundation (JRF, 2016) review of SEND identification across UK populations and consider what it tells you about on poverty, ethnicity and the identification of SEND.

Note your reflections in your professional development portfolio (PDP) or equivalent.

The developing legislative framework

1971	Legislation in England and Wales brought those considered 'ineducable' into education
1981	The 1981 Education Act placed duties on local education authorities (LEAs) and school governors to make provision for SEN
1994	The first SEN *Code of Practice* (DfE, 1994a) came into effect
2001	Part 4 of the Disability Discrimination Act (DDA) placed duties on schools and educational institutions not to treat disabled pupils less favourably and to make 'reasonable adjustments' to ensure that disabled pupils are not put at a substantial disadvantage. Disabled school staff have rights under Part 2 of the Act
2005	The DDA 2005 gave disability equality the same legislative status as gender equality and race equality
2009	The *Achievement for All (AfA)* programme (see Knowles, 2015, p.2) involved: ■ tracking children's progress in English and mathematics with intervention when pupils fall behind; ■ a termly 'structured conversation' on progress between the teacher that knows the pupil best and the parent; and ■ a common sense approach to barriers to learning, such as bullying, persistent absence or poor social skills. Evaluation by DfE (2011b) concluded that AfA schools 'really listened' to parent views and translated what they heard into changes that made a real difference
2009	The UK ratified the UN Convention on the Rights of Disabled Persons
2010	An Office for Standards in Education (Ofsted) review found that pupils were often identified as having SEN when they just needed 'good ordinary teaching' and that those identified as having SEN often did not receive effective support. Ofsted revised its SEND inspection framework (http://www.ofsted.gov.uk) to concentrate on 'ordinary' learning and teaching rather than specialist SEN provision
2010	The Equality Act brought together equality legislation on disability; race; gender, pregnancy, maternity; sexuality; age; religion and belief. These 'protected characteristics' can be cited in discrimination claims
2014	Both Houses of Parliament approved the 2014 Act and 2014 code of practice. All institutions and services to which the code applies must 'have regard' to its provisions; they can implement them with some flexibility, but must be able to justify their changes if challenged. The Act and code: ■ introduced a single Education, Health and Care Plan (ECHP) running from 0-25 years of age; ■ mandated all parties across education, health and social care, and all types of government-funded schools, including academies and free schools, to work together for SEND. This includes the duty to provide health services in EHCPs (section 42); ■ set down that the duty applies to helping the child or young person achieve the best possible 'educational and other outcomes' (section 19). Section 19 states that local authorities 'must have regard to' the views, wishes and feelings of the child or young person and the children's parents and support them through joint decision-making processes'
2014	The revised national curriculum maintained the statutory principles, known as the 'general inclusion statement', that give teachers freedom to adapt the national curriculum for SEND so they can respond to set 'suitable learning challenges' and ensure high expectations for all learners and meet pupils' diverse learning needs: 'lessons should be planned to ensure there are no barriers to *every* pupil achieving' (DfE, 2014i; 2014n)

| 2017 | The Review Committee established to consider the United Kingdom's fulfilment of its commitment to the UN Convention on the Rights of Disabled Persons (UNCRDP, 2017) criticised the UK government for 'the persistence of a dual education system that segregates children with disabilities to special schools', noting that numbers in segregated education were increasing, and expressing concern about the quality of ITE in 'inclusion competences'. The percentage of pupils with a statement or EHC plan attending maintained special schools has increased by 5% since January 2010 (DfE/ONS, 2017). |

The first step: high quality differentiated teaching

As a student teacher, the background to SEND provision in secondary schools sketched above has implications for the way you need to develop your practice.

The SEN Code supports the Ofsted framework in emphasising the foundation of 'high quality ordinary teaching':

> High quality teaching, differentiated for individual pupils, is the first step in responding to pupils who have or may not have SEN. Additional intervention and support cannot compensate for a lack of good quality teaching. Schools should regularly and carefully review the quality of teaching for all pupils, including those at risk of underachievement. This includes reviewing and, where necessary, improving, teachers' understanding of strategies to identify and support vulnerable pupils and their knowledge of the SEN most frequently encountered.
>
> (DfE/DoH, 2014, 6.37)

Inclusive pedagogy

Even before the 2010 Ofsted Review, the literature on learning and teaching in relation to pupils with SEND had moved decisively to emphasise quality teaching approaches, often known as 'inclusive pedagogy' (e.g. Lewis and Norwich, 2004). It was noted that:

■ advice on teaching pupils with particular SEND frequently recommends methods that could support individuals in all sorts of diagnostic categories;
■ many 'SEND methods' are not qualitatively different from those used in ordinary teaching but simply extend or emphasise 'ordinary' approaches.

So, it makes sense to prioritise development of 'ordinary' teaching methods before assuming anything different will be needed for individuals. This is not to devalue knowledge of specific impairments: for example, when teaching English literature to autistic pupils, you should know that care with metaphor and simile will often be important (and will support many other pupils as well). But such knowledge can only be a part of your planning.

Of course, the good news that comes with this approach is that you do not need to develop an infinite number of 'SEN pedagogies' for each impairment but can build a broad repertoire, a toolkit, to extend or intensify for particular individuals or groups.

So what approaches go into your toolkit?

1   You need teaching approaches that benefit all pupils and can be modified to remove barriers for those with SEND.

2   You need subject-specific ideas relating to SEND. This is the weak point in much SEND advice, because little funded research explores this aspect of 'ordinary' teaching. For example, DfE (2017f) says: 'There is limited research evidence on the development and support of maths skills in pupils and students with SEN'. Your teaching will benefit from a knowledge of the strengths of a subject for supporting learners with SEND as well as insights into the barriers some areas of curriculum can create if you do not anticipate them.

3   You need to know about the special educational needs and disabilities you are most likely to meet in your teaching.

This unit covers each of the three areas above. The first two are explored through Task 4.6.2, an exercise that brings together the implications of specific subjects and a range of teaching approaches. The third is considered once the elements of the structure within which SEN support and EHCPs are intended to function have been established.

The Pillars of Inclusion

To help the student teacher, the Training and Development Agency for Schools (TDA, nd) disseminated resources on 'inclusive pedagogy', including adaptable planning approaches and subject learning booklets in a well-evaluated programme (Lindsay et al., 2011).

Planning to help everyone learn and participate

The TDA documentation identified eight aspects of planning as 'The Pillars of Inclusion' (The Pillars):

■   inclusive learning environments;
■   multi-sensory approaches including the use of information technology;
■   working with additional adults;
■   managing peer relationships;
■   adult–pupil communication;
■   formative assessment/assessment for learning;
■   motivation;
■   memory/consolidation of learning.

The model is not the only way of demarcating areas of planning. The point is that if teachers are not to create barriers to access before they walk into the classroom, they need some such checklist for differentiation in their minds.

Now complete Task 4.6.2

Task 4.6.2   The pillars of inclusion applied to the teaching of English and other subjects

The TDA materials explored the possibilities and potential barriers of all subjects within the model of pedagogy outlined above.

Download the English booklet, viewed 6 February 2019, from

http://webarchive.nationalarchives.gov.uk/20111218081624/http://tda.gov.uk/teacher/developing-career/sen-and-disability/sen-training-resources/one-year-itt-programmes/~/media/resources/teacher/sen/secondary/english.pdf

and the booklet for your own subject from the series developed to show how the pillars apply to subject teaching.

Find ideas in the tables in the English booklet, or that of your own subject, to discuss with your tutor or other student teachers and note conclusions in your PDP.

The code's two stage approach to meeting needs

The two stages are:

- **SEN support**: intervention planned and delivered by the school within its own resources, sometimes using external specialist help. If SEN support does not result in appropriate progress, moves may be made towards assessment for:
- **The Education, Health and Care Plan (EHCP)**: a multi-professional agreement, overseen by the LA, detailing, with statutory force, interventions and resources to enable the pupil to make appropriate academic and social progress. Schools are normally expected to use delegated budgets to make the provision specified but can seek local authority help if interventions are expensive.

The 2017 'SEN population' (DfE/ONS, 2017)

- 1,002,070 pupils are on SEN support, equal to 11.6% of the total pupil population.
- 242,185 pupils, equal to 2.8% of the school population, have a statement of SEN or an EHCP.
- The percentage of pupils identified with SEN fell from over 20% in 2010 to 14.4% in 2017 (DfE/ONS, 2017). It seems likely that the reduction dates from, and largely relates to, the revision of the Ofsted SEND framework to concentrate on inspection of 'ordinary' teaching.

Implementing SEN support

If concern about a pupil's progress relates to SEND, the school may design a package of 'SEN support'. The code (para 6.44) expects this to be set within the model: 'Assess, Plan, Do, Review'. The SENDCo and others, in consultation with the parents and pupil, complete *assessments* and design a support *plan*, including setting expected outcomes and *review* dates. Subject teachers remain responsible for '*do*', day-to-day implementation.

The review process

The effectiveness of the support and interventions and their impact on the pupil's progress should be reviewed at the date agreed in the support plan and appropriate changes made to provision based on the findings (DfE/DoH, 2014, 6.53–6.55). Now complete Task 4.6.3.

 Task 4.6.3   Measuring outcomes

The 'Assess, Plan, Do, Review' model emphasises measurement of outcomes of SEN support. The exercise below will help you learn how your school tackles this.

Meet the SENDCo or inclusion manager and briefly note your school's systems for:

1   tracking the attainment of all pupils and, within that, monitoring the progress of pupils with SEND (academic progress and social inclusion);
2   monitoring the outcomes of plans and interventions to support pupils with SEND across the school (e.g. provision mapping and management, data on specific interventions, pupils and parent views, input from external professionals, reviews of pupils' progress, attendance data).

Store your notes in your PDP.

The EHCP: the second stage of assessment in the SEN code of practice

If a review reflects continuing lack of progress, the school or parent(s) may seek a local authority assessment on whether an EHCP should be prepared. Schools must implement SEN support and review it before thinking about that step.

The EHCP process is expensive, as assessment can cost several thousand pounds, so local authorities (LAs) must also consider carefully whether to embark on it. Because an EHCP guarantees additional resources, everything about it is 'high stakes'; unlike the flexibility of SEN Support, the whole EHCP process is embedded in statute.

Your head of department or faculty and the SENDCo should help you plan for pupils who have an EHCP.

Find out more about how pupils with an EHCP experience school through Task 4.6.4.

 Task 4.6.4   How does an EHCP come about in your school?

Arrange a time with the SENDCo to discuss how an EHCP is drawn up and reviewed. Has local authority/school practice changed recently? Summarise your findings and arrange to have them checked by your tutor or the SENDCo. Store the final version in your PDP.

You can prepare for the conversation by exploring examples of EHCPs (Council for Disabled Children (CDC), 2017) and the case law that affects them (IPSEA, 2017).

English as an additional language (EAL) and SEN

Never assume without good reason that a pupil whose first language is not English has SEND.
The 2014 code says:

> Identifying and assessing SEN for children or young people whose first language is not English requires particular care. Schools should look carefully at all aspects of a child or young person's performance in different areas of learning and development or subjects to establish whether lack of progress is due to limitations in their command of English or if it arises from SEN or a disability. Difficulties related solely to limitations in English as an additional language are not SEN.

> (DfE/DoH, 2014, 6.24)

- Pupils learning English go through well-researched stages: they may for instance say little or nothing for some time after arriving in a new country, but are learning nonetheless.
- Pupils learning English benefit from high-quality learning environments: they do not, as a rule, need individual programmes; see, for example, Unit 3.2, which discusses motivation.
- If the English learning stages are not proceeding as they should, the possibility of a learning difficulty may be considered. This is the time for teachers to consult specialist help, such as the SENDCo.

Access arrangements for examinations and assessments

Awarding bodies for public examinations, such as GCSE and GCE A level, make 'access arrangements' for pupils with SEND. If you feel a pupil needs such arrangements and they are not in place, contact the SENDCo or the schools examination co-ordinator to find out what can be done.

Concerns about a pupil not recognised by the school as having SEND

If observation of a pupil's progress makes you wonder if they have unrecognised SEND, try comparing notes with another teacher on how the pupil responds with them. If your concerns are shared, you can take them to the SENDCo together.

Concerns raised by pupils

Pupils may raise concerns about their own progress. As issues brought to you can be the tip of the iceberg, try to reflect back on what you have been told to clarify the extent of the concerns before moving to possible solutions. Once you have listened carefully, you will be better able to decide if this is a situation you can help with or one where you need colleagues' advice.

A red flag: eating disorders

You should be particularly alert for signs of eating disorders, particularly anorexia, whether they emerge through observation, written work or conversation. Such signs should always be reported for urgent consideration.
    Now complete task 4.6.5.

Task 4.6.5   Implementing the SEN code in school

- Read the SEND policy in your placement school.
- Discuss with your tutor and the SENDCo how your placement school implements the policy and the SEN code. You could ask: how does your school ensure that the requirements of the SEN code are met? How are all staff, and how are parents/carers, involved?
- Discuss your findings with another student teacher who has undertaken the task in another school. Summarise the similarities and differences you find in your PDP.

Helping pupils with SEN support to learn: specific impairments

This section provides some guidance on working with pupils with SEND in mainstream classrooms.

Planning should involve (at a tactful moment) asking pupils with SEND how they like to be taught. As an example, the British Stammering Association has excellent materials on consulting youngsters worried about speaking up in class, viewed 6 February 2019, from http://www.stammeringineducati on.net/england/secondary/

With advice from your tutor, you should:

- use the SEN support plan, the knowledge of others in the school and books and websites to build your awareness of pupil strengths and the barriers they may face; do not assume that you need to teach that pupil differently or separately;
- see what aspects of the toolkit in Section 2 you will use to extend or emphasise to create the best possible learning environments for the pupil;
- explore broad-based summaries of research into 'what works in the classroom', such as that in DfE (2017f);
- remember that motivation is a key part of learning, whatever the SEN: special treatment can 'turn off' adolescents (see Unit 3.2);
- remember that the timing and intensity of interventions often makes the difference rather than the pedagogy;
- have high expectations of homework and classwork.

Using information and communications technology (ICT) is an important way of helping some pupils with SEN (see Unit 5.5. and Leask, 2013). To check that you are covering all aspects of preparation for SEND in planning lessons, have a look at the TDA Pillars of Inclusion (above) and the associated subject booklets.

Categories of the SEN Code

The next section looks at the way groups of pupils with SEN are discussed in the 2014 code.

The code separates SEN into four areas, but it points out that pupils often have needs that cut across all these areas and their needs may change over time.

> These four broad areas give an overview of the range of needs that should be planned for...
> The support provided to an individual should always be based on a full understanding of their

particular strengths and needs and seek to address them all using well-evidenced interventions targeted at their areas of difficulty and where necessary specialist equipment or software.

(DfE/DoH, 2014, 6.27)

Similarly, the teaching ideas below are helpful with many groups of pupils.

The four areas

Area one: communication and interaction

'This area covers pupils with speech and language delay, impairments or disorders, specific learning difficulties, such as dyslexia and dyspraxia, hearing impairment and those who demonstrate features within the autistic spectrum'.

While *expressive* communication impairments, such as stammering, are readily recognisable, *receptive* language impairments, when someone finds it hard to listen or to understand oral communication (not the same as deafness), can be easily overlooked.

When teaching these pupils be sure to:

- check understanding;
- use visual aids and cues to the topics being discussed;
- place the pupil so that they can hear and see;
- explain something in different ways if you have not been understood the first time;
- repeat what pupils say in discussion or question and answer sessions (in any case, others in the class may not have heard);
- allow time for pupils to respond in question and answer sessions and, if necessary, ensure that they are pre-prepared for responding, perhaps by a TA. See Unit 3.1 on questioning.

For further information see: The Communication Trust (www.thecommunicationtrust.org. uk) (including their 'What Works' pages); ICAN (www.ican.org.uk) (this charity supports speech, language and communication development in schools and elsewhere); British Stammering Association (http://stammeringineducation.net/)

Deafness and hearing impairment

- Specialist advice on deafness is usually not difficult to come by: ask the SENDCo.
- Deaf pupils have individual communication needs: you should check what they are.

For further information see: Action on Hearing Loss (formerly Royal National Institute for the Deaf, RNID) (www.actiononhearingloss.org.uk) (useful teaching booklets); the National Deaf Children's Society (www.ndcs.org.uk)

Autism

While autism presents in many ways, autistic people typically lack 'mentalisation', the ability to picture what another person is thinking. Any social context can create barriers for them.

- Autistic pupils' absorbing interests (such as train timetables), lack of social focus and anxiety over unexpected change mean coordinated planning is essential.
- Observe autistic pupils' behaviour carefully. Even if it is unusual, there will usually be a reason for it: it can be an attempt to communicate, or a way of coping with a situation that feels challenging.
- Autistic people can learn 'intellectually' how to act socially, e.g. in the matter of eye contact.
- Suggestions on approaches to autism vary widely; you need to be clear what strategies are agreed by school and home and work within them.

For further information see: the National Autistic Society (www.nas.org.uk); the Autism Education Trust (www.autismeducationtrust.org.uk)

Area two: cognition and learning

Learning difficulties cover a wide range of needs, including moderate learning difficulties (MLD), severe learning difficulties (SLD), where children are likely to need support in all areas of the curriculum and associated difficulties with mobility and communication, through to profound and multiple learning difficulties (PMLD), where children are likely to have severe and complex learning difficulties as well as a physical disability or sensory impairment. (DfE/DoH, 2014).

Learning difficulties

Pupils identified in this group will typically attain well below others of their age in a range of areas. Such pupils do not necessarily need different teaching approaches from those used with typically developing pupils, but they benefit from planning that sets appropriate objectives at appropriate levels (Fletcher-Campbell, 2004).

Pupils with more severe impairments are likely to have a range of co-occurring conditions that create a complex profile of potential barriers. They should have a personalised learning pathway, designed with their input through their preferred communication medium.

You should check exactly what the pupil's support plan advises and seek advice from the SENDCo. Advice from the agencies mentioned under 'Communication' (above) and a basic knowledge of 'Working memory' (below) will also help you plan for learning difficulties.

Working memory

Working memory is the system that allows us, for example, to do mental arithmetic or transfer information accurately from a screen to a writing book. Gathercole (2008) has suggested principles to support working memory. See Table 4.6.1.

For further information see: Downs Syndrome Association (https://www.downs-syndrome.org.uk/); The Communication Trust (www.thecommunicationtrust.org.uk) advice on augmentative and alternative communication (AAC).

Dyslexia

The term 'dyslexia' covers a wide range of needs.

Table 4.6.1 Principles to support working memory (adapted from Gathercole, 2008)

Principle	Watch out for
Recognise working memory failures	Warning signs include incomplete recall, failure to follow instructions, place-keeping errors, abandoning tasks or guessing at answers
Monitor pupils	Look out for the warning signs and ask pupils to let you or a buddy know if something is going too fast for them
Evaluate working memory loads	Think about the load on working memory caused by lengthy sequences, unfamiliar and meaningless content and demanding mental processing activities
Reduce working memory loads	Reduce the material to be remembered, use shorter sentences, make the material more meaningful and familiar, simplify mental processing required and restructure explanations of complex tasks
Structure activities so that the pupil can use available resources, such as word banks	Check that new learning fits into the framework of what the pupil already knows
Repeat important information	Repetition supplied by teachers, TAs or fellow pupils nominated as 'memory guides'
Encourage the pupil to use memory aids	Include wallcharts and posters, personalised dictionaries, cubes, counters, abacus, number lines, multiplication grids, calculators, memory cards, audio recording and computer/phone software
Support memory through motivating approaches	Visual or concrete ('real') materials, or activities involving movement, reinforce learning through a range of sensory channels. New knowledge can be tried in a range of enjoyable applications, such as computer software or simulations
Develop the pupil's own strategies	Agree an approach to the pupil's own strategies in seeking help, rehearsing, note-taking, and place-keeping and organisation

The current emphasis is on examining the individual's skills, such as phonological awareness, and working on them as a way forward.

Phonological awareness is conscious sensitivity to the sound structure of language. It includes the auditory ability to distinguish units of speech, such as a word's syllables and a syllable's individual phonemes (the smallest functional unit of sound such as 'c' in *cat* or 'th' in *that*).

Most schools have access to specialists in this area.

For further information see: the British Dyslexia Association www.bdadyslexia.org.uk/ ; the Professional Association of Teachers of Students with specific learning difficulties (PATOSS) (www.patoss-dyslexia.org).

Dyspraxia

Dyspraxia often shows as clumsiness and or a lack of co-ordination. It may be defined as difficulty in planning and carrying out skilled, non-habitual motor acts in the correct sequence. Pupils with dyspraxia need the support of whole-school systems, particularly in terms of making exercises fun, so advice should be sought from physical education staff as well as the SENDCo.

Dyspraxia and handwriting

Difficulties with handwriting are a specific co-ordination issue. For further information see: the National Handwriting Association (www.nha-handwriting.org.uk); the Dyspraxia Foundation (www. dyspraxiafoundation.org.uk/).

Area three: social, emotional and mental health difficulties

The term 'social, emotional and mental health difficulties' reflects the understanding that behaviour concerns may be associated with every form of learning difficulty or disability.

The 2014 code says:

> 6.32 Children and young people may experience a wide range of social and emotional difficulties which manifest themselves in many ways. These may include becoming withdrawn or isolated, as well as displaying challenging, disruptive or disturbing behaviour. These behaviours may reflect underlying mental health difficulties such as anxiety or depression, self-harming, substance misuse, eating disorders or physical symptoms that are medically unexplained.

Behavioural concerns

Behavioural problems are discussed in Units 3.1, 3.2, 3.3 and 4.1, and tasks are set there to develop your skills in this area. The differentiation case studies in Unit 4.1 are also relevant.

Pupils whose behaviour is often a concern may:

■ have special needs: a language impairment or an autistic spectrum disorder;
■ have mental health needs: may be depressed, for instance;
■ be responding to an unsatisfactory school environment: for instance, bullying in the playground, or an irrelevant curriculum.

The 2014 code does not discuss the possibility that the behaviour is a response to something in the school environment.

In your response to worrying behaviour, bear in mind that:

■ learning, the 'therapy of achievement', not counselling, is the teacher's contribution to resolving behaviour concerns;
■ many whose behaviour is a concern have communication impairments and benefit from teaching that recognises those needs;
■ 'scaffolding' success for such pupils can be demanding. You should expect support with your planning (and lessons learnt) from experienced colleagues. Scaffolding is discussed in Unit 5.1.

Good working within school management is critical to success with emotional, social and mental health difficulties.

Lesson preparation should address:

■ pupils' strengths and interests;
■ levels of language and literacy;
■ alternatives within plans in case your first approach does not work.

Attention deficit hyperactivity disorder (ADHD)

All the approaches above are relevant to ADHD.

Remember it is a medical diagnosis which, in itself, tells you nothing about teaching pupils with the condition and you need advice (including from the pupil) on what will help. While stimulant medication, such as Ritalin, is widely known as a treatment, National Institute for Health and Care Excellence (NICE) guidance recommends that children and young people with moderate forms of ADHD should be offered psychological group treatment, while their parents are offered a parent training programme (NICE, 2013). For further information see: Attention Deficit Disorder Information Service (ADDIS) (http://www.addiss.co.uk/); Young Minds (https://youngminds.org.uk/).

Area four: sensory and/or physical needs

The 2014 code advises that:

Some children and young people require special educational provision because they have a disability which prevents or hinders them from making use of the educational facilities generally provided. These difficulties can be age related and may fluctuate over time. Many children and young people with vision impairment (VI), hearing impairment (HI) or a multi-sensory impairment (MSI) will require specialist support and/or equipment to access their learning or rehabilitation support. Children and young people with an MSI have a combination of vision and hearing difficulties. Information on how to provide services for deafblind children and young people is available through the Social Care for Deafblind Children and Adults guidance published by the Department of Health. 'Some children and young people with a physical disability (PD) require additional ongoing support and equipment to access all the opportunities available to their peers' (DfE/DoH, 2014, 6.34/5).

Visual impairment

The SENDCo in your school and the individual plan for the pupil concerned will be helpful. It is also particularly important to talk to the pupil concerned because the range of possible communication media is significant: some will find enlarged texts helpful, others will be Braille users and others (increasingly) will favour audio recorded resources. For further information see: the Royal National Institute for the Blind (RNIB) (www.rnib.org.uk).

Physical disability

Guidance on any barriers to learning that a pupil's physical disability may present should normally be sought from school records, from the pupil and their parents and from any staff, such as TAs, who have worked with them. The core message should be the same as that for dyspraxia above: engagement, fun and building on strengths will be central to any learning plans.

Medical conditions

The 2014 code notes that:

The Children and Families Act 2014 places a duty on maintained schools and academies to make arrangements to support pupils with medical conditions. Individual healthcare plans will normally specify the type and level of support required to meet the medical needs of such pupils.

Where children and young people also have SEN, their provision should be PLANNED and delivered in a co-ordinated way with the healthcare plan. Schools are required to have regard to the statutory guidance *Supporting pupils at school with medical conditions*.

(DfE/DoH, 2014, 6.11)

A medical condition can affect a child's learning and behaviour. The effect may also be indirect: time in education can be disrupted, or there may be unwanted effects of treatment. Additional disruption can occur through the psychological effects that serious or chronic illness or disability can have on a child and their family. Schools and the pupil's carers and the medical services should collaborate so that pupils are not unnecessarily excluded from any part of the curriculum or school activity because of anxiety about their care and treatment. Task 4.6.6 asks you to focus on individual pupils with SEND.

M

Task 4.6.6   Thinking about individual pupils

This task asks you to investigate, in-depth, the experience of some pupils with SEND in your classes.

Identify, with the help of your tutor, pupils with whom you have contact who have SEND of different types. Draw up a table similar to Table 4.6.2 in your PDP and complete it, drawing on the expertise of different staff as necessary. Use fictional names to preserve confidentiality and compare practice in your school with student teachers from different schools.

For one or more of your pupils identify:

■   the implications of your findings for lesson planning;
■   how you can work with the support teacher/TA.

Share your ideas with your tutor and/or the SENDCo or school-based mentor. Store these in your PDP.

Table 4.6.2 Experience of pupils with SEND

Description of pupil's SEND	Paul has severe hearing loss. He can lip read reasonably well and his speech is fairly clear.
Pupil's strengths and interests	
Interaction with classroom work and environment in my subject	
General interaction with school environment	
The role of the school/SENDCo	
The role of outside agencies (LA services, educational psychologists, educational welfare officers)	

SUMMARY AND KEY POINTS

This unit has introduced you to a range of issues and responses relating to pupils with special needs and/or disabilities and set those issues and possible responses in the context of the special educational needs and disability *code of practice: 0-25 years* (DfE/DoH, 2014).

- In your work as a student teacher, you are expected to develop your understanding of the teacher's responsibilities for pupils' SEND so that, when you are in your first post, you are sufficiently aware of your responsibilities, including those set out in the code of practice, and that you ensure that your pupils' SEND are met.
- You cannot expect to solve all pupils' learning problems on your own. You must seek advice from experienced staff. And never forget to listen to the pupils on what works for them.
- Every child is special. Every child has individual educational needs. A major problem experienced by pupils with SEND is the attitudes of others to them. For example, pupils who have obvious physical disabilities, such as cerebral palsy, often find they are treated as though their mental abilities match their physical abilities when this is not the case. How will pupils with SEN find you as their teacher?
- Teachers need to ensure that all their pupils learn to the best of their abilities and that pupils with SEND are not further disabled by the lack of appropriate resources to support their learning, including software (Leask and Pachler, 2013).

Check which requirements for your ITE programme have been addressed through this unit.

Further resources

The web pages listed throughout the text are very useful. The following websites and texts should also be useful.

Alloway, T.P. and Alloway R.G. (2015) *Understanding Working Memory*, 2nd Edition, London: Sage Publications.

Blatchford, P., Bassett, P., Brown, P., Koutsoubou, M., Martin, P., Russell, A. and Webster, R. with Rubie-Davies, C. (2009) *Deployment and Impact of Support Staff in Schools: The Impact of Support Staff in Schools. Results from Strand 2, Wave 2. DCSF Research Report DCSF RR148* https://www.ioe.ac.uk/DISS_Strand_2_Wave_2_Report.pdf

CSIE (Centre for Studies on Inclusive Education) (2011) *Index for Inclusion: Developing Learning and Participation in Schools*, viewed 3 July 2018, from www.csie.org.uk/resources/inclusion-index-explained.shtml

Farrell, M. (2009) *The Special Education Handbook: An A-Z Guide for Students and Professionals*, 4th Edition, Abingdon: Routledge.

Lindsay G., Cullen, M.A., Cullen, S., Dockrell, J., Strand, S., Arweck, E., Hegarty, S. and Goodlad, S. (2011) *Evaluation of impact of DfE investment in Initiatives Designed to Improve Teacher Workforce Skills in Relation to SEN and Disabilities*, London: DfE RR115.

MESHGUIDES (Mapping Educational Specialist knowHow)
This website hosts a growing number of research informed guides for teachers including specific guides on SEND, including 'Achievement for All'; 'EAL'; 'Hearing Impaired'; 'Reluctant Writers' (see https://www.meshguides.org)

NASEN (National Association for Special Educational Needs): www.nasen.org.uk/.
The NASEN site hosts a number of valuable resources produced by the Department for Education (www.nasen.org.uk/onlinesendcpd/)

Sharples, J., Webster, R. and Blatchford, P. (2015) *Making Best Use of Teaching Assistants,* **London: Education Endowment Foundation.**

Appendix 2 lists subject associations and teacher councils and Appendix 3 provides a list of websites.

Capel, S., Leask, M. and Turner, T. (eds.) (2010) *Readings for Learning to Teach in the Secondary School: A Companion to M Level Study,* **Abingdon: Routledge.**
This book brings together essential readings to support you in your critical engagement with key issues raised in this textbook.

Capel, S., Lawrence, J., Leask, M. and Younie, S. (eds.) (2019) *Surviving and Thriving in the Secondary School: The NQT's Essential Companion,* **Abingdon: Routledge.**
This book is designed to support newly qualified teachers in the next phase of development as a teacher. However, you may find it useful as it covers aspects of teaching not included in this book which, nonetheless you experience on your ITE programme.

The subject specific books in the *Learning to Teach (Subject)* series, the *Practical (Subject) Guides, Debates in (Subject)* and *Mentoring (Subject) Teachers* are also very useful.

Any additional resources and an editable version of any relevant tasks/tables in this unit are available on the companion website: www.routledge.com/cw/capel

Notes

1 The abbreviation SEN is used throughout the unit to refer to special educational needs as set down in English law governing the 2014 code; the abbreviation SEND refers to special educational needs and/or disability.

2 Pupils learning English as an additional language (EAL) and 'gifted and talented' pupils are not *per se* regarded in law as having special educational needs, though they may be so identified if they are also assessed as having an impairment or learning difficulty.

5 Helping pupils learn

This chapter is about teaching and learning. As you work through these units, we hope that your knowledge about teaching and learning increases and that you feel confident to try out and evaluate different approaches.

Unit 5.1 introduces you to a number of theories of learning. Theories about teaching and learning provide frameworks for the analysis of learning situations and a language to describe the learning taking place. As you become more experienced, you develop your own theories of how the pupils you teach learn and you can place theories in the wider context.

In Unit 5.2, teaching methods that promote learning are examined. How you use these methods reveals something of your personal theory of how pupils learn. At this point in your development we suggest that you gain experience with a range of teaching methods so that you are easily able to select the method most appropriate to the material being taught.

Unit 5.3 provides you with details about teaching styles. Again, we suggest that as you gain confidence with basic classroom management skills you try out different styles so that you develop a repertoire of teaching styles from which you can select as appropriate.

We have talked at various points in this book about the characteristics of effective teaching.

Unit 5.4 is designed to provide you with information about methods for finding out about the quality of your own teaching and that of others through the use of reflection using action research techniques and drawing on the evidence base underpinning educational practice. During your initial teacher education course, you are using action research skills in a simple way when you observe classes. In this unit, we explain the key aspects of action research and reflective and evidence-informed practice.

Unit 5.5 focuses on the concept of personalising learning. Digital technologies or information and communications technologies (ICTs) have made it possible to monitor pupils' actual attainment in tests against their expected grades across all subjects and this means that teachers can be sent alerts automatically when pupils are not achieving what is expected. This allows for teachers to intervene more quickly to help pupils falling behind and provide a more 'personalised' learning experience. The concept of 'personalised learning' has many other features and these are discussed in this unit.

Unit 5.6 introduces you to research in neuroscience that is yielding knowledge about brain function and how teachers can maximise pupil learning. This area of work is possible because activity of the brain can be monitored more easily than before using the latest MRI scanners and other techniques.

Unit 5.7 builds on the focus on personalising learning. It invites you to develop your own critical thinking skills and those of the pupils.

Unit 5.8 focuses on the use of language in the classroom so as to improve the learning of pupils.

5.1 Ways pupils learn

Diana Burton

Introduction

As a good teacher you do not simply concentrate on subject content; instead, you ensure that your pupils learn *how*, *what*, *whether* and so on in relation to your subject. The interaction between the activities of teaching and the outcomes of learning is critical. In order to develop presentation and communication techniques that facilitate effective learning, a teacher must have some understanding of how pupils learn. ITE lectures and school placements add to and refine the ideas you already have about learning and reveal differences in how individuals learn. Psychological research is concerned with this individuality of *cognition:* knowing, understanding, remembering and problem solving. Research reveals information about human behaviour, motivation, achievement, personality and self-esteem, all of which impact on the activity of learning.

Several theoretical perspectives contribute to our understanding of how learning happens, e.g.:

■ behaviourism, which emphasises external stimuli for learning;
■ gestalt theory, which expounds principles of perception predicated on the brain's search for 'wholeness';
■ personality theories, which are located in psycho-analytic, psycho-metric and humanist research traditions.

Discussion of such work can be accessed quite easily in libraries and journals (see Rudman, 2018 or Long et al., 2013 for very good overviews), so this unit is organised around theories that have been particularly influential on pedagogic strategy. These theories include:

■ Piaget's cognitive-developmental theory of maturation;
■ metacognition, the way in which learners understand and control their learning strategies;
■ social constructivist theories that emphasise social interaction and scaffolded support for learning;
■ information processing explanations of concept development and retrieval;
■ learning style theories, which question qualitative distinctions between ways of learning, stressing instead the matching of learning tasks to a preferred processing style.

OBJECTIVES

At the end of this unit you should be able to:

- appreciate the interaction between ideas about learning and pedagogic strategies;
- explain and differentiate between some psychological perspectives on learning;
- appreciate more about your own approach to learning.

Check the requirements of your initial teacher education (ITE) programme to see which relate to this unit.

How ideas about teaching and learning interact

Decisions you make about how to approach a particular lesson with a particular pupil or group of pupils depend on the interplay between your subject knowledge and pedagogic knowledge, your knowledge of the pupils and your understanding about how learning happens. Let us imagine that you have spent ten minutes carefully introducing a new concept to your class, but a few pupils unexpectedly fail to grasp it.

You test the reasons for their lack of understanding against what you know about the pupils and their:

- prior knowledge of the topic;
- levels of attention;
- interest and motivation;
- physical and emotional state of readiness to learn, etc.

You consider also factors relating to the topic and the way you explained it, for example:

- the relevance of the new material to the pupils;
- how well the new concept fits into the structure of the topic;
- the level of difficulty of the concept;
- your clarity of speech and explanation;
- the accessibility of any new terminology;
- the questioning and summaries you gave at intervals during your explanation.

Finally, you draw on explanations from educational psychology that have informed your understanding of how pupils learn and provided you with questions such as:

- Does the mode of presentation suit these pupils' learning styles?
- Has sufficient time been allowed for pupils to process the new information?
- Does the structure of the explanation reflect the inherent conceptual structure of the topic?
- Do these pupils need to talk to each other to help them understand the new concept?

Table 5.1.1 Different types of learning

Activity	Intellectual skills	Verbal skills	Cognitive	Attitudes strategy	Motor skills
Science: a group activity using particle theory of matter	Discussing how to set up the activity to test a hypothesis	Defining solids, liquids and gases	Recalling previous knowledge about particles	Listening to and sharing ideas	Manipulating equipment

Your ideas about learning usually derive from a number of theories rather than from one specific theory, which allows you to continually revise them as you gain more experience. This process is known as 'reflecting on theory in practice'. Some of the theories from which your ideas may be drawn are reviewed in this unit. In order to contextualise that review it may be helpful to think about the types of learning activities you engage your pupils in.

Fifty years ago, Gagné (1977) identified five factors that contribute to effective learning. Each of these factors is still used today across the curriculum and they interact in complex ways. It is helpful to consider them separately so that a particular pupil's learning progress and needs can be monitored and so that you can plan lessons that foster all types of learning and employ different pedagogical strategies depending on the type of learning planned. Task 5.1.1 invites you to analyse the demands on pupils in a lesson using the factors identified by Gagné.

M

Task 5.1.1   Analysing learning activities: for demands on pupils

Select a learning activity from a lesson you have taught or observed. Describe the types of learning involved using Table 5.1.1 for each of the five factors. An example from science has been provided to guide you.

Share your findings with other student teachers, your tutor or class teacher. Identify the implications for planning future lessons and record these in your professional development portfolio (PDP) or equivalent.

Psychological perspectives on learning

A determining factor in lesson preparation is the knowledge that pupils already possess. Unfortunately, identifying this knowledge is not as simple as recalling what you taught the pupils last time, for knowledge is, by definition, individualised. Each pupil's experiences of, attitudes towards, and methods of processing prior knowledge are distinct. Psychologists are interested in how learners actively construct this individualised knowledge or 'meaning', and different theories offer different notions about what constitutes knowledge. *Cognitive developmental theory* depicts knowledge as being generated through the learners' active exploration of their world (Piaget, 1932, 1954). More complex ways of thinking about things are developed as the individual matures. *Social constructivism* explains knowledge acquisition by suggesting that learners actively construct their individual meanings (or knowledge) as their experiences and interactions with others help develop the theories they hold (Brown, 1994; Rogoff, 1990). *Information processing theories* view knowledge as pieces of information that the learner's brain processes systematically and that are stored as abstractions of experiences.

These theories have been particularly influential in shaping pedagogy and are outlined briefly below.

Cognitive developmental theory

Piaget

Jean Piaget was a Swiss psychologist who applied Gessell's (1925) concept of maturation (genetically programmed sequential pattern of changing physical characteristics) to cognitive growth. He saw intellectual and moral development as sequential, with the child moving through stages of thinking driven by an internal need to understand the world. His theory implied an investigative, experiential approach to learning.

According to Piaget, the stages through which the child's thinking moves and develops is linked to age. Piaget thus provides a criterion-referenced, rather than norm-referenced, explanation of cognitive development (Shayer, 2008). From birth to about two years, children understand the world through feeling, seeing, tasting and so on. Piaget called this the *sensory-motor* stage. As children grow older and mature, from about two to six years, they begin to understand that others have a viewpoint. They are increasingly able to classify objects into groups and to use symbols. Piaget termed this the *preoperational* stage.

The third stage identified by Piaget, from six to about 12 years, is the *concrete operational* stage. Children are still tied to specific experience but can do mental manipulations as well as physical ones. Powerful new internal mental operations become available, such as addition, subtraction and class inclusion. Logical thinking develops.

The final stage of development sees children manipulating ideas in their heads and able to consider events that haven't yet happened or think about things never seen. Children can now organise ideas and events systematically and can examine all possibilities. Deductive thinking becomes possible. Piaget suggested that this final stage, called the *formal operational* stage, begins at about 12 years of age.

The learner's stage of thinking interacts with experience of the world in a process called *adaptation*. The term *operations* is used to describe the strategies, skills and mental activities that children use in interacting with new experience. Thus, adding 2 and 2 together, whether mentally or on paper, is an operation. It is thought that discoveries are made sequentially, so, for example, adding and subtracting cannot be learned until objects are seen to be constant. Progress through the sequence of discoveries occurs slowly and at any one age children have a particular general view of the world, a logic or structure that dominates the way they explore the world. The logic changes as events are encountered that do not fit with their *schemata* (sets of ideas about objects or events). When major shifts in the structure of children's thinking occur, a new stage is reached. Central to Piaget's theory are the concepts of *assimilation*, taking in and adapting experience or objects to existing strategies or concepts, and *accommodation*, modifying and adjusting strategies or concepts as a result of new experiences or information (see Bee and Boyd, 2013, for a full description of Piaget's theory).

The influence of stage theory

Piaget's work influenced the way in which some other psychologists developed their views. Kohlberg (1976) saw links between children's cognitive development and their moral reasoning, proposing a stage model of moral development (see also Unit 4.5). Selman (1980) was interested in the way children make relationships, describing a set of stages or levels they go through in forming friendships. Stage models of development were also posited in relation to personality growth, quite independently of Piaget's work. Influenced by Freud's (1901) psychoanalytic approach, Erikson's (1980) stages of psychosocial development explain the way in which an individual's self-concept develops, providing important insights into adolescent identity issues, such as role confusion. You may be aware of the fragility of an adolescent's self-concept, of the fundamental but often volatile nature of adolescent friendships and of the increased interest adolescents show in ethical issues. It is essential to consider these factors when planning for learning since they impact so heavily on pupils' motivation for, and capacity to engage with, lesson content. Research has identified the significance of teacher–pupil relationships for pupils' feelings of self-worth in relation to learning competence (see Bartlett and Burton, 2016).

Jerome Bruner, a prolific American cognitive psychologist, also developed a stage model of the way people think about the world. He described three stages in learning: the enactive, iconic and symbolic. Unlike Piaget's stages, learners do not pass through and beyond Bruner's different stages of thinking. Instead, the stage or type of representation used depends on the type of thinking required of the situation. It is expected, however, that, as pupils grow up, they make progressively greater use of symbolic representation (Bruner, 1966).

The stress on the idea of 'stages' in Piaget's theory was far-reaching, especially the implication that pupils need to be at a particular developmental level in order to cope with certain learning tasks. However, research studies have substantially refuted such limitations on a pupil's thinking (Donaldson, 1978). Thus, the construct of a staged model of cognitive maturation probably has less currency than the features of development described *within* the various stages. Flavell (1982), a former student of Piaget, argued that, while stage notions of development are unhelpful, Piaget's ideas about the sequences that learners go through are still valid. They can help teachers to examine the level of difficulty of topics and curriculum material as a way of deciding how appropriate they are for particular age groups and ability levels. The key task for teachers is to examine the progress of individuals in order to determine when to increase the intellectual demand on them. Bruner (1966) argued that difficult ideas should be seen as a challenge that, if properly presented, can be learned by most pupils.

Metacognitive awareness

Philip Adey and Michael Shayer have demonstrated that learning potential is increased if pupils are metacognitively aware, i.e. if they understand and can control their own learning strategies (Adey and Shayer, 2002; Adey, 2008; Adey and Shayer., 2013). These strategies include techniques for remembering, ways of presenting information when thinking, approaches to problems and so on. So, if you cue pupils into the specific skill being learned and encourage them to reflect on its transfer potential, this will extend their strategies to other tasks and subjects. It was Flavell who first proposed the notion of metacognition, arguing that becoming 'aware of one's own "cognitive machinery" is a vital component of intelligence' (1979, p.907). It has become fashionable to refer to metacognition as 'learning to learn', and whole systems explaining how to achieve it are available (see, for example, the long established 'learning power' approach in Claxton et al., 2011, or a scheme for secondary schools by Best and O'Donnell, 2011).

Being metacognitively aware can be likened to having a commentator in the learner's mind who analyses and comments upon the methods they are using to learn a new concept or skill while the learning is happening. Hattie (2012a) claims it enables learners to attain better outcomes.

It seems, then, that the higher-order cognitive skills of Piaget's stage of formal operations can be promoted and encouraged through a focus on metacognition. Learners need, above all, to learn to learn, and it is your job to help them (Claxton and Lucas, 2015). The ready availability of instant information via the Internet requires pupils to have the confidence and skills to sift through it and judge its utility and relevance to their work. See Gallard and Cartmell (2015) or Wegerif, Li and Kaufman's (2015) handbook for a number of chapters on metacognition and teaching creative thinking. Now complete task 5.1.2.

 Task 5.1.2   Analysing learning activities: learning how to learn

Consider how you can give pupils at least one opportunity during each lesson to think about the strategies they are using in their learning. Ask them, for instance, how they reached a particular conclusion, how they tackled the drawing of a 3D shape or how they would undertake a journey from point A to point B. Summarise your findings and file in your PDP.

Social constructivist theory

The ideas of Russian psychologist Lev Vygotsky and of Jerome Bruner in the USA have increasingly influenced educators in recent years. Vygotsky's work dates from between the 1920s and 1930s (he died in 1934). His most influential work, *Thought and Language*, was not available in English until 1962 (Vygotsky and Kozulin, 2012).

Vygotsky

Both Piaget's and Vygotsky's theories reveal a child-centred position and an emphasis on action in the formation of thought but, for Vygotsky (1978), psychological activity has sociocultural characteristics from the very beginning of development (see Keenan et al., 2016). Conceptual understanding can be generated from a range of different stimuli, implying a problem-solving approach for pupils and a facilitator role for the teacher. Whereas Piaget considered language a tool of thought in the child's developing mind, for Vygotsky language was generated from the need to communicate and was central to the development of thinking. He emphasised the functional value of egocentric speech to verbal reasoning and self-regulation, and the importance of sociocultural factors in its development. His work has spawned much interest in sociocultural theory (Mercer and Littleton, 2007) wherein thinking and learning are shaped by culture, and human development is understood by reference to its social and communicative form. In communicative talk, the development is not just in the language contrived to formulate the sentence but also through the process of combining the words to shape the sentence because this shapes the thought itself.

Vygotsky's emphasis on the importance of talk as a learning tool has long been absorbed into UK teaching practices, with seminal reports reinforcing the status of talk in the classroom (Bullock Report, 1975; Norman, 1992). Vygotsky believed that such communicative instruction could reduce a pupil's 'zone of proximal development' (ZPD), i.e. the gap between their current level of learning and the level they could be functioning at with adult or peer support: 'What a child can do today in cooperation, tomorrow he will be able to do on his own' (Vygotsky, 1962, p.67, see Vygotsky and Kozulin, 2012). Social constructivism thus stresses the necessity for group interaction and adult intervention in consolidating learning and extending thinking. Myhill (2006) found that teacher discourse can variously support or impede pupil learning, so it is vital that your own discourse assists cognitive and conceptual connections in pupils' learning. Task 5.1.3 asks you to analyse pupil talk.

 Task 5.1.3   Analysing learning activities: pupil talk

Review the advice for teachers on the University of Cambridge Thinking Together website. Consider how often you make opportunities for your pupils to talk in lessons, to each other, to you, to a digital or video recorder or via a CD-ROM. Listen to how the talk develops the thinking of each member of a small group of pupils. Notice how well-timed and focused intervention from you moves the thinking on. Write up examples, showing the advantages of promoting pupil talk with your pupils; file the report in your PDP.

Bruner

Bruner also placed an emphasis on structured intervention within communicative learning models. He formulated a theory of instruction, central to which is the notion of systematic, structured pupil experience via a spiral curriculum where the pupil returns to address increasingly complex components of a topic. Current and past knowledge is deployed as the pupil constructs new ideas or concepts. Thus, the problem of fractions in Year 5 may be tackled via many more concrete examples than when it is returned to in Year 7. Learning involves the active restructuring of knowledge through experience; the pupil selects and transforms information, constructs hypotheses and makes decisions, relying on a developing cognitive structure to do so.

You should try to encourage pupils to discover principles by themselves through active dialogue with yourself. Bruner said the teacher's job is to guide this discovery through structured support, e.g. by asking focused questions or providing appropriate materials; he called this process 'scaffolding' (Bruner, 1983). The ideas of pupils emerging through their talk are scaffolded or framed by the teacher putting in 'steps' or questions at appropriate junctures. When hearing an idea emerge you can intervene by asking a question that requires the pupils to address that idea explicitly, which may help them find the solution.

Bruner argued that the scaffolding provided by the teacher should decrease in direct correspondence to the progress of the learner. Wood (1988) developed Bruner's ideas, describing five levels of support, which become increasingly specific and supportive in relation to the help needed by the pupil. See Table 5.1.2.

Having established the task that the pupils are to complete, you might give general verbal encouragement to the whole class, follow this up with specific verbal instruction to groups who need it, perhaps targeting individuals with guidance on strategies for approaching the task. Some pupils need physical help in performing the task and yet others need to be shown exactly what to do, probably in small stages. This approach can help you to think systematically about the nature of the support you should prepare for particular pupils, and to keep a check on whether the level is becoming more or less supportive. This has obvious relevance for differentiation in your classroom, workshop or gym. Task 5.1.4 looks at scaffolding learning.

Task 5.1.4   Analysing learning activities: scaffolding learning

Try scaffolding a pupil activity during a school placement:

- How easy or difficult was it to work out when to intervene?
- How far did the influence of an idea reflect the strength of the pupil's personality or the validity of the idea?
- How did you as the teacher handle this without demotivating the pupil/pupils?

File your comments in your PDP.

Studies have warned of the dangers of casually incorporating 'scaffolding' into the professional lexicon as a proxy for generalised help or support rather than, as was originally intended, a very precise means of helping pupils master a specific task (Mercer and Littleton, 2007). Furthermore, Russian neo-Vygotskians have argued that there has been considerable misunderstanding in educational circles of what Vygotsky said about ZPDs and about meaning being socially constructed (Goswami, 2008). Similarly, Bartlett and Burton (2016) suggest that advances in communication technologies have led to the global popularisation of some psycho-pedagogical ideas that may not have been fully researched, so you should beware over-interpreting their impact within your classroom.

Table 5.1.2 Scaffolding: Bruner's levels of support

Five levels of support a teacher may use in scaffolding learning:

- general verbal encouragement
- specific verbal instruction
- assistance with pupil's choice of material or strategies
- preparation of material for pupil assembly
- demonstration of task

Information processing theory (IP theory)

This approach to learning originated within explanations of perception and memory processes and was influenced by the growth of computer technology. The basic idea is that the brain attends to sensory information as it is experienced, analyses it within the short-term memory (STM) and stores it with other related concepts in the long-term memory (LTM).

Psychologists saw the functioning of computers as replicating the behaviour of the brain in relation to the processing of information. Information is analysed in the STM and stored with existing related information in the LTM. This process is more efficient if material can be stored as abstractions of experience rather than as verbatim events. If I ask you to tell me the six times table, you recite, 'one six is six, two sixes are twelve', and so on. You do not explain to me the mathematical principle of multiplication by a factor of six. On the other hand, if I ask you the meaning of the term 'economic enterprise', it is unlikely that you will recite a verbatim answer. Instead, your STM searches your LTM for your 'schema' or idea of enterprise. You then articulate your abstracted understanding of the term, which may well be different from that of the person next to you. In terms of intellectual challenge, articulating the second answer requires greater mental effort, although knowing one's multiplication tables is a very useful tool.

You always need to be absolutely clear that there is a good reason for requiring pupils to learn something by rote because rote learning is not inherently meaningful so cannot be stored in LTM with other related information. Rather, it must be stored in its full form, taking up a lot of 'disk' space in the memory. Information stored in this way is analysed only superficially in STM; the pupil does not have to think hard to make connections with other pieces of information.

It can often be difficult in secondary schools for teachers to determine precisely the prior knowledge of their pupils. You will observe that good teachers cue pupils in to their prior knowledge by asking questions about what was learned the lesson before or giving a brief resume of the point reached in a topic. Such strategies are very important because, if previous learning has been effective, information is stored by pupils in their LTMs and needs to be retrieved. Seminal psychological work established that learning is more effective, i.e. more likely to be understood and retained, if material is introduced to pupils according to the inherent conceptual structure of the topic (Ausubel, 1968; Gagné, 1977). Concept maps reflect the conceptual structure of a topic. When preparing a scheme of work, you should identify the over-arching broad concepts that encapsulate the topic, then think about how these break down into more specific ideas and how they apply within different contexts. To understand, for example, momentum, you need to understand mass and velocity (which in turn requires an understanding of speed and direction), and so on. Information that is stored using a logical structure is easier to recall because the brain can process it more easily in the first instance, linking the new ideas to ones that already exist in the memory. As a teacher, this requires you to have thought through the structure in advance, and to know how the concepts fit together; hence the importance of spending time on schemes of work even where these are already produced for you.

This emphasis on structure and sequence can be found perhaps most readily in the teaching of modern foreign languages (MFL) and mathematics. In MFL, for instance, teachers encourage recognition and acquisition of vocabulary first, followed by the construction of spoken and written sentences. This approach might be described as moving from the general to the specific. Thus, in mathematics, we start with number recognition, moving to the general concepts of addition, subtraction and multiplication, and on to more specific computations such as calculating area, solving equations or estimating probabilities. In Task 5.1.5, you are asked to structure a topic for effective learning.

 Task 5.1.5   Structuring a topic for effective learning

Choose a topic from your subject area that you are expecting to teach. Think freely about some of the ideas contained within it, jotting them down haphazardly on paper. Now think about how those ideas fit together and whether, in teaching the topic, you would start with the general overarching ideas and then move to the specific ones or vice versa.

You can organise your topic by drawing up a conceptual hierarchy of it like the one started below for a Personal and Social Education (PSE) topic. This hierarchy moves from the general to the specific.

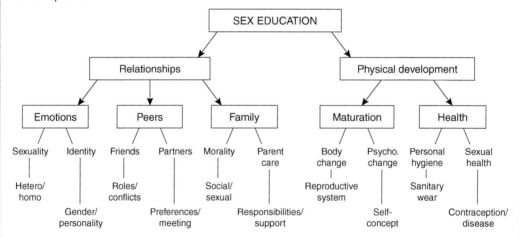

Discuss your hierarchy with other student teachers and your tutor, using their responses to finalise your hierarchy. Compare the sequencing of ideas in your hierarchy with that in the Department's Scheme of Work.

If there are differences, are they to do with interpretations of the topic or are they related to the ways pupils respond to the topic or perhaps there is a practical issue to do with resources?

Write an account of the study, including implications for the way you approach teaching this topic. File in your PDP.

Concept development

It is helpful to consider briefly how information processing relates to concept development. The material held in the LTM is stored as sets of ideas known as 'schemata' ('schema' is the singular). A schema is a mental structure abstracted from experience. It consists of a set of expectations with which to categorise and understand new stimuli. For example, our schema of 'school' consists of expectations of pupils, teachers, classrooms, etc. As teachers, our school schema has been refined and developed as more and more information has been added and categorised. Thus, it includes expectations about hierarchies, pupil culture, staff room behaviour and so on. It is probable that our school schema is different from, and more complex than, the school schema held by a parent, simply because of our involvement in schools.

When children are young, their schemata do not allow them to differentiate between pieces of information in the way that those of older pupils do. A one-year-old's schema of dog might include expectations about cats too because they have insufficient experience of the two animals to tell them apart. As they experience cats as furry, dogs as hairy, cats meowing, dogs barking, etc., greater differentiation is possible. Since the object of school learning is to promote pupils' concept differentiation in a range of different subjects, you should encourage comparison between objects or ideas and introduce new ideas by reference to concrete examples. Even as adults, while we *can* think abstractly, we find new ideas easier to grasp if we can be given concrete examples of them. Teaching in the context of IP theories stresses the application of knowledge and skills to new situations. Your role is to help pupils find new ways of recalling previous knowledge, solving problems, formulating hypotheses and so on. Critical thinking tasks in which pupils have to wrestle with new ideas and issues encourage connections between areas of subject knowledge or experience. Rote learning, copying information from a book or taking dictated notes from the teacher are very unsuitable for promoting concept development.

We have discussed cognitive development theories, social constructivist theories and information processing theories. In each of these theories about how learning occurs, there has been an emphasis on the individual and the differences between them. Looking at what is known about how pupils' styles and strategies differ equips us further to understand individual differences.

Learning styles, strategies and approaches

You may encounter popular systems for categorizing pupils' 'learning styles'; there are a number of classifications based on different constructs and using a range of measurement tools. Such approaches were readily embraced at first but have since been heavily critiqued (see, for example, Bartlett and Burton, 2016). See also Unit 5.6 for a perspective from neuroscientists.

It is clear to see why categorising pupils into fixed learning approaches or styles and then teaching to a formula that such a categorisation suggests might be attractive. However, we know that learning is complex and context-dependent with pupils employing different approaches in different settings. It is important to take an eclectic approach to learning style classification and measurement lest you too readily pigeonhole pupils and fail to provide a range of approaches to learning, including choice of activities and resources to maximise access for all to the curriculum. In this section, you are introduced briefly to some categorisations that have been researched over a considerable number of years but for a systematic review of 71 different constructs see Coffield et al. (2004a and 2004b).

> The learning styles movement has muddied the waters by producing endless dichotomies such as 'pragmatists' v 'theorists', 'field independent' v 'field dependent' learners, and 'left' v 'right brainers'. Most of these terms have no scientific justification whatsoever; nevertheless too many tutors succumb to the intuitive appeal of these pseudo-scientific concepts.
>
> (Coffield, 2008, p.33)

There is often confusion about what constitutes learning style as distinct from learning strategy. The *cognitive* or *learning style* may be a fairly fixed characteristic of an individual, is static and a relatively in-built feature of them. In contrast, *learning strategies* are the ways learners cope with situations and tasks. Strategies may vary from time to time and may be learned and developed.

Learning style

Riding and Cheema (1991) studied a huge number of cognitive and learning style constructs developed by a range of established psychological researchers, concluding that learning styles may be grouped into two principal cognitive styles. The first, the *Wholist-analytic style*, identifies whether an individual tends to process information in wholes (wholist) or in parts (analytics). The second, known as *Verbal-imagery style*, describes whether an individual is inclined to represent information during thinking verbally (verbalist) or in mental pictures (imagers) (Riding and Burton, 1997).

The two styles operate as dimensions so that a person may be at either end of the dimension or somewhere along it. You are asked to consider your own learning style in Task 5.1.6.

 Task 5.1.6   Considering your own learning style

Do you:

■ Approach essay writing incrementally, step by step, piecing together the various parts, or do you like to have a broad idea of the whole essay before you start writing?
■ Experience lots of imagery when you are thinking about something or do you find yourself thinking in words?

Discuss your style with other student teachers. In doing so you are developing your metacognitive knowledge about your own way of learning.

Store in your PDP and add any examples which were effective.

These styles are involuntary, so it is important to be aware that your classes contain pupils whose habitual learning styles vary. You need to ensure that you provide a variety of ways in which pupils can work and be assessed. It would not be sensible to present information only in written form; if illustrations are added, this allows both 'Verbalisers' and 'Imagers' easier access to it. Similarly, 'Wholist' pupils are assisted by having an overview of the topic before starting while 'Analytics' benefit from summaries after they have been working on information.

This is not to suggest that you must determine the style of each pupil, but that there must be opportunities for all pupils to work in the way that is most profitable for them. Unlike the way in which intelligence quotient (IQ) is used (the higher the IQ score the better the performance is expected), the determination of learning style does not imply that one way of processing is better than the other. The key to success is in allowing learners to use their natural processing style. It is important for you to be aware of your own style because teachers have been found to promote the use of approaches that fit most easily with their own styles.

Learning strategy

Learning strategy describes the ways in which learners cope with tasks or situations. These strategies develop and change as the pupil becomes more experienced. Kolb's work is the most widely known (Kolb, 1976; 2015). Kolb envisaged a cyclical sequence through four 'stages' of learning (concrete experience, reflective observation, abstract conceptualisation, active experimentation) arising from the interaction of two dimensions. The east–west dimension represents 'processing' (how we approach a task) and the north–south dimension 'perceiving' (our emotional response, or how we think or feel about it). Kolb argued that these two dimensions interact and that, although learners use preferred strategies, they could be trained to develop aspects of other strategies through experiential learning. Pupils may have a predilection for one of the stages, so, when planning a sequence of lessons around a topic, you should provide pupils with experiences that ensure that they use each of the stages in the cycle at some time, in addition to their preferred one.

Learning approaches

Other researchers are interested in the motivations and attitudes pupils and students bring to their learning, described as 'approaches to learning'. They have investigated learners' approaches to study and how learning approaches interact with learning strategies (Biggs, 2001; Entwistle, 2009; Schmeck, 2015).

Entwistle described different orientations to learning, such as being oriented towards discovering the meaning of a topic or being oriented simply to scratch the surface. Combinations of these orientations with extrinsic factors, such as the need to pass examinations or the love of a subject, were thought to lead to learning strategies that characterised certain approaches to study, from 'deep' to 'surface' levels of thinking.

A pupil's approach is a function of both motive and strategy: thus, a pupil with an instrumental (surface) motive is likely to adopt reproducing or rote-learning (surface) strategies. Deep motive results from an intrinsic desire to learn and can inspire the use of deep strategies, emphasising understanding and meaning. An achieving motive might be an egotistical need to pass examinations; from this perspective the learner can derive achieving strategies that stress time management, well-ordered resources and efficiency.

Pupils whose motives and strategies are compatible with the demands made by learning tasks are likely to perform well. Pupils are likely to be less successful where motives and strategy are incompatible with task demand. For example, a pupil with a deep approach to learning is constrained by superficial task design such as a requirement for short answers, whereas a pupil with an achieving motive may be deterred if set very long-term objectives or vague objectives. Successful learning, if defined in terms of understanding and permanence, is linked with deep approaches that achieve higher-order thinking, which can be taught. A number of researchers have stressed the impact of social and cultural environment on learning approaches. Thus, the achievement-driven context within which secondary school pupils in England currently learn, for instance, could combat the possibility of teaching deep approaches because of time constraints. Greater use of individualised learning, facilitated by technology, may encourage the use of deep approaches to learning if pupils have the time and autonomy to pursue a topic in depth. Currently there are worries that the use of the internet develops a surface approach, with learners simply cutting and pasting from unregulated information sites. Task 5.1.7 asks you to analyse your own approaches to learning.

 Task 5.1.7   Analysing your own approaches to learning

Do you recognise any of the learning approaches described above in relation to your own learning? Do your motives and associated learning strategies stay the same over time or do they depend on the task and the reason you are completing it? In your PDP, record some notes on your own ways of learning for discussion with your tutor.

What the vast array of research into styles, strategies and approaches tells us is NOT that you need to identify every pupil's distinctive profile but that you should endeavour to maintain variety in the learning experiences you design for pupils, in the ways you present information, in the resources pupils use and the tasks they undertake, and in the ways you assess their progress.

SUMMARY AND KEY POINTS

▪ It is important to develop and refine your own models of learning as you gain more experience of your pupils, your subject and how learning contexts interact with teaching processes.

▪ The symbiosis between theoretical positions and pedagogic practices has been emphasised. For instance, concept development is enhanced when pupils are introduced to new ideas via concrete examples and retention is aided if topics are taught according to their inherent conceptual structure.

▪ The key features of cognitive development, social constructivism and information processing theories, as they apply to pupil learning, have been outlined and your attention has been drawn to the implications of learning style and strategy for teaching techniques.

▪ The benefits of adopting a facilitative, interventionist approach and of aiming for a variety of approaches in presentation, resource, task and assessment can be extrapolated from all the theories that have been discussed.

▪ Learning is likely to be most effective when pupils are actively involved with the material through critical thinking, discussion with others and metacognitive awareness of their own learning strategies.

Check which requirements for your ITE programme you have addressed through this unit.

 Further Resources

Bartlett, S.J. and Burton, D.M. (2016) *Introduction to Education Studies*, **4th Edition, London: Sage.**
Chapters 8 and 9 provide a full outline of major psychological theories and contemporary psychological research into how pupils learn.

Bee, H. and Boyd, D. (2013) *The Developing Child*, **13th Edition, Boston, MA: Pearson Education.**
This fascinating text covers all aspects of human development, using the very latest research studies.

Claxton, G (2017) *Building Learning Power*, viewed 10 November 2107, from https://www.buildinglearning power.com
Offers extensive practical strategies for helping pupils to learn how to learn.

Goswami, U. (2017) *Centre for Neuroscience in Education*, viewed 10 November 2017, from http://www.cne.psychol.cam.ac.uk/people/ucg10@cam.ac.uk
The Centre aims to establish the basic parameters of brain development in the cognitive skills critical for education, e.g. to understand how the brain functions and changes during the development of reading and maths.

Keenan, T., Evans, S. and Crowley, K. (2016) *An Introduction to Child Development*, London and New York: Sage.
A comprehensive text covering cognitive, social and emotional development, which has a very useful companion website with further information and exercises to test your understanding.

Let's Think: Cognitive Acceleration http://www.letsthink.org.uk/about-us/
Draws on Shayer's and Adey's metacognition research into developing the intelligence of pupils by improving their thinking processes. Includes audio-visual content.

Long, M., Wood, C., Littleton, K., Passenger, T. and Sheehy, K. (2011) *Psychology of Education*, Abingdon and New York: Routledge.
Written in an accessible and engaging style, key concepts from psychology that relate to education are addressed together with practical suggestions to improve learning outcomes and opportunities to apply your theoretical knowledge to real-world contexts.

Rudman, D. (2018) *Learning and Memory*, London and New York: Sage.
Uses an engaging personal writing style appropriate for pupils with little or no previous background in psychology to discuss topics including the major behaviourist theories of learning, cognitive theories of memory, social learning theories, the roles of emotion and motivation in learning and the neurological underpinnings of these perspectives.

Schmeck, R. (ed.) (2015) *Learning Strategies and Learning Styles*, New York: Springer Science and Business Media.
Comprehensive overview of style and strategy research across three continents.

University of Cambridge (2017) Thinking Together, viewed 10 November 2017, from http://thinkingtoget her.educ.cam.ac.uk/resources/
Offers practical advice on developing intellectual development through talk.

Wegerif, R., Li, L. and Kaufman, J.C. (eds.) (2015) *The Routledge International Handbook of Research on Teaching Thinking*, London and New York: Routledge.
A comprehensive guide to research on teaching thinking in a range of contexts, including approaches for teaching thinking; developing creative thinking; metacognition; and neuro-educational research on teaching thinking.

Appendix 2 lists subject associations and teacher councils and Appendix 3 provides a list of websites.

Capel, S., Leask, M. and Turner, T. (eds.) (2010) *Readings for Learning to Teach in the Secondary School: A Companion to M Level Study*, Abingdon: Routledge.
This book brings together essential readings to support you in your critical engagement with key issues raised in this textbook.

Capel, S., Lawrence, J. Leask, M. and Younie, S. (eds.) (2019) *Surviving and Thriving in the Secondary School: The NQT's Essential Companion,* Abingdon: Routledge.
This book is designed to support newly qualified teachers in the next phase of development as a teacher. However, you may find it useful as it covers aspects of teaching not included in this book which, nonetheless you experience on your ITE programme.

The subject specific books in the *Learning to Teach (Subject)* series, the *Practical (Subject) Guides*, *Debates in (Subject)* and *Mentoring (Subject) Teachers* are also very useful.

Any additional resources and an editable version of any relevant tasks/tables in this unit are available on the companion website: www.routledge.com/cw/capel

5.2 Active learning

Michelle Shaw

Introduction

As a teacher, one of your most important tasks is to encourage the development of pupils' understandings of key curriculum 'concepts'. Vygotsky (1986) provided a definition of a concept that can help us understand the role teachers must play in the process:

> A concept is more than the sum of certain associative bonds formed by memory, more than a mere mental habit; it is a complex and genuine act of thought that cannot be taught by drilling but can be accomplished only when the child's mental development itself has reached the requisite level.
>
> Practical experience also shows that direct teaching of concepts is impossible and fruitless. A teacher who tries to do this usually accomplishes nothing but empty verbalisation, a parrot like repetition of words by the child, simulating knowledge of the corresponding concepts but actually covering up a vacuum.
>
> (Vygotsky, 1986, pp.149-150)

The quotation suggests that a teacher cannot do the learning for the pupil and that in order for understanding to occur the pupil has to be active in the learning process.

This unit addresses ways in which you can help pupils to become active learners through providing active learning in your classroom. Some writers argue that active learning underpins 'deep learning', as opposed to 'surface learning', which is learning with little understanding. They argue that 'deep learning' is the only meaningful learning (see Unit 5.1 for detailed references). Active learning underpins meaningful learning because it enables pupils to develop knowledge of the subject taught, and skills for learning including the ability to reflect on the processes involved in that learning.

In this unit, learning is defined in the first section, then active learning and then there is a discussion of different forms of learning that can be related to active learning: lifelong learning, deep learning, learning to learn, discovery learning, rote learning and aids to recall. The unit concludes with a section on Directed Activities Relating to Texts (DART).

OBJECTIVES

At the end of this unit you should be able to:

■ explain the term 'active learning' and discuss the advantages of active learning to the teacher and the pupil;

■ be aware of ways of embedding active learning in the classroom;

■ consider the use of resources to support active learning in your lessons.

Check the requirements for your initial teacher education (ITE) programme to see which relate to this unit.

What do we mean by 'learning'?

Before we can begin to understand what active learning might be and why we should want to encourage it, we need to think about what 'learning' is.

Säljö (1979) carried out an interview study in which he asked a group of adults what learning meant to them. Analyses of the transcripts produced five qualitatively different conceptions and a sixth has been added subsequently by Mezirow (1997). The text box below lists these six characteristics of learning.

Aspects of Learning (adapted from Säljö, 1979; and Mezirow, 1997)

Learning can be defined as:

1 a quantitative increase in knowledge;
2 memorising;
3 acquisition of facts, methods, etc. that can be retained and used;
4 the abstraction of meaning;
5 an interpretative process aimed at understanding reality;
6 changing a person's perceptions, i.e. transformational.

In general terms, the first three types of learning can be described as *surface* learning or *atomistic* learning in which learning focuses on specifics, on details, and on memorising facts without necessarily understanding the whole message or concept. This type of learning is essentially passive, and is often associated with learning environments where the pupils see the aim of learning as fulfilling requirements of the course, in order to pass the exam or in order to please the teacher (see Unit 5.1).

The next two types of learning can broadly be described as *deep* or *holistic* learning that is characterised by a search for meaning that demands an active engagement with the learning and leads to a broader understanding of the whole topic (see Unit 5.1 for detail). It involves the pupil in realising that the study deals with some aspect of the real world that they are trying to understand more fully.

The last type, which a number of writers, e.g. Mezirow (1997), have since added to Säljö's definitions is transformational, i.e. changing as a person, which reflects the fact that learning at its deepest level changes the pupil's perception of reality, and therefore changes them as a person.

Case studies: two pupils learning mathematics

Manjeet and Robert are two pupils in Year 9. They are taught the same syllabus at the same school and complete the same activities and assignments but with different teachers. They had similar scores on entry from primary school. Here's what they have to say about one of the subjects they take.

Robert: I enjoy maths because I can think, which is not something I always do in other subjects. I try to see the maths that is being taught in other areas as well. For example, I use it at home to help my younger brother and when I go to town with my friends. I'm the one who always manages to save money and get deals! I like watching TV programmes too, there are quite a few now about maths . . .it's really interesting to find out where our maths comes from. All the time I like to think about how it links to what we've been doing in class. It's funny because I never liked maths in my primary school, but I do now. I even do the homework, and ask the teacher for extra work. I also try to make up sums and problems of my own. The way I work is to try to understand the information first, then try it out. If I don't understand I will ask the teacher, or a friend, or my mum, she's good with maths! I think that someone who is not so good at maths would struggle a bit. You know, to get interested in it. To find different ways to understand it. In our class we do a lot of group discussions and pair work and the teacher really makes us think by asking some very difficult questions. She also lets us work on our own by getting us to do investigations and surveys and looking on the Internet. It must work because I passed the latest tests and I'm predicted to get a good grade in General Certificate of Secondary Education (GCSE).

Manjeet: The way I do it is to keep trying the same activity until I get it right, you know, trying different techniques to solve the same problem. I know I have to get the maths right because my parents say it will be useful for me in the future to get a good job. I usually try to write down formulas and learn them by heart. I always do the class work and homework the teacher has given me so I can get a good enough mark but I only spend a short time on it as I like to go out with my friends. The lessons are usually the same. The teacher explains something to us, then shows us some examples on the board. Then we usually have to do some exercises from a textbook or worksheet. We usually work on our own. Sometimes we do past test papers as practices, but I didn't do well on the last one!

Task 5.2.1 helps you to reflect further on the different perceptions of learning that Robert and Manjeet have.

 Task 5.2.1   Two pupils' experiences of mathematics

Discuss with other student teachers the observations made by these pupils from the standpoint of (1) their response to the tasks set and possible reasons for these responses; (2) the way the tasks may have been set by their teachers.
   Record your findings in yourprofessional development portfolio (PDP) or equivalent.

The responses of Robert and Manjeet suggest two important things. The first of these is that they experience mathematics differently. They appear to approach their learning in two qualitatively different ways. Robert appears to take a deep approach to his work, while Manjeet appears to adopt a shallow (surface) approach. Nevertheless, Manjeet's willingness to try different ways of solving problems is a positive feature of his attitude to work. Those who take a deep approach tend to have an intrinsic interest in the topic and the tasks and aim to understand and seek meaning. They adopt strategies that help them to satisfy their curiosity and to look for patterns and connections in other areas. They think about the task. Those who adopt a surface approach see tasks as work given to them by others. They are pragmatically motivated and seek to meet the demands of the task with the minimum of effort (Entwistle, 1990; Prosser and Trigwell, 1999).

We suggest that Robert is engaged mainly in active learning and Manjeet is engaged more in passive learning. This may mean that Robert is able to think abstractly and is actively involved in the process of learning. This may involve, for example, learning through doing, trying things out, getting it wrong and knowing why. It is not just the pupil's attitude but the way the task is set. Active learning has to be encouraged. Perhaps the way Manjeet engages with the subject is as much to do with the way the lessons are taught and the learning structured as it is with Manjeet's own approach to learning.

What is active learning

Active learning draws from the theories of learning that were outlined in Unit 5.1, perhaps taking the best from each!

Active learning occurs when a learner takes some responsibility for the development of the activity, emphasising that a sense of ownership and personal involvement is the key to successful learning.

Unless the work that pupils do is seen to be important to them and to have purpose and unless their ideas, contributions and findings are valued, little of benefit is learned.

Active learning can also be defined as purposeful interaction with ideas, concepts and phenomena and can involve reading, writing, listening, talking or working with tools, equipment and materials, such as paint, wood, chemicals, etc. In a simple sense, it is learning by doing, by contrast with being told.

Active learning may be linked to experiential learning. Experiential learning is also learning by doing but with the additional feature of reflection upon both action and the results of action; only where pupils are 'engaged actively and purposively in their own learning is the term experiential appropriate' (Addison and Burgess, 2007, pp.35-36). Both active and experiential learning contribute to meaningful learning.

Active learning strategies benefit both teachers and pupils. As a teacher, they enable you to spend more time with groups or individuals, which allows better-quality formative assessment and feedback to take place (both of these are key features of 'Assessment for learning', see Unit 6.1; Procter, 2013). Active learning can also enhance your support for pupils with special educational needs (see Unit 4.6 on special educational needs and Blamires, 2014). Activity methods encourage autonomous learning and problem-solving skills, important to both academic and vocationally based work. There is, of course, an extra demand on you in the planning and preparation of lessons. The advantages of active learning to pupils include greater personal satisfaction, more interaction with peers, promotion of shared activity and team work, greater opportunities to work with a range of pupils and opportunities for all members of the class to contribute and respond. It can encourage mutual respect and appreciation of the viewpoint of others (see also Unit 5.5 on personalising learning).

It is important to realise that learning by doing, by itself, is not enough to ensure learning. The proverb 'Tell me, I will forget. Show me, I may remember. Involve me and I will understand' at the beginning of Unit 1.1 was reformulated by a prominent educationalist as 'I do and I am even more confused' (Driver, 1983, p.9). The essential step to learning and understanding is reflection through discussion with others, especially the teacher; such discussions involve 'thinking' as well as recalling, i.e. experiential learning.

Matt, a newly qualified teacher, articulates his experience of trying to embed active learning in his classroom:

A newly qualified teacher's view on implementing active learning:

It was difficult to understand this aspect when I began teaching. Of course you want to plan lessons that engage pupils but the English National Curriculum almost implies that as a teacher you have to "put on a show" in order to have exciting and stimulating lessons. What I realised very soon was that entertainment isn't the focus. If you take that approach you cannot do it for every lesson you teach. Using the principles of active learning made a real difference. When I started to think about how I structure activities to maximise each pupil's engagement and activity in the learning I noticed that their attainment and achievement also improved. It takes time to become familiar with all of the different active learning strategies and I think you need to introduce them carefully and build them up over time in the classroom. Now I have a range of strategies I can use and nothing beats the buzz of seeing pupils actively engaged in their own learning.

Lifelong learning

Some writers believe that building the individual's capacity to learn should be the main focus of education in our schools. Guy Claxton (2002; 2015) argues that in order for this to happen the following principles should be taken into account:

- The focus for learning should move from predominance on content to predominance on the learning process itself.
- Pupils should be given the skills needed to learn under any conditions.

- Pupils should be equipped with a range of learning methods, some rational and precise, some experimental or even unconscious.
- Pupils must be made aware of their own learning process.

(Teaching and Learning Research Programme (TLRP), 2006)

In his work, Claxton has described four characteristics of expert, lifelong learners, commonly referred to as the 'four Rs'.

Claxton's four Rs: Resilience, Resourcefulness, Reflectiveness, Reciprocity

- **Resilience** describes the learners' enjoyment of learning and their ability to resist distraction and persevere with their learning, despite setbacks.
- **Resourcefulness** refers to the learners' ability to look more deeply into issues and question taken for granted assumptions.
- **Reflectiveness** is about the learners' ability to consider and adjust approaches and concepts in the light of changing understandings and information.
- **Reciprocity** encompasses the learners' ability to contribute to and learn from others' understandings and approaches.

Task 5.2.2 asks you to apply these ideas.

 Task 5.2.2   The four Rs

Think of a lesson you have taught recently and answer the following questions on it:

1   What opportunities were there in the lesson for the pupils to display or develop skills in the four Rs?
2   How could you adapt the lesson, or series of lessons, to enable pupils to develop or improve one or two of these characteristics as appropriate?

Record your notes in your PDP.

Active learning encourages the development of the four Rs in learners. A similar approach has been taken by Hargreaves (2005), who has argued that the best schools personalise learning to ensure that 'deep learning' happens. Most schools recognise that enabling pupils to perform well in exams is only a part of their wider educational purpose (see Unit 7.1 on Aims of Education). Schools are increasingly seeking to support the development of their pupils as learners equipped for the 21st century world in which being a lifelong learner is paramount. 'Deep learning' is best developed through encouraging pupil voice, assessment for learning (Procter, 2013) and learning to learn (TLRP, 2006). See also Unit 5.1. In addition, Hargreaves identified the importance of 'deep experience', arguing that pupil engagement was the key to better relationships between staff and pupils and was a prerequisite for the development of good learners who possess independence, responsibility, confidence and maturity.

Learning how to learn (see also metacognition in Units 4.3, 5.1, 5.5, 6.1)

Learning how to learn is a feature of active learning (TLRP, 2006). By promoting activities that engage pupils and require them to participate in the task from the outset, teachers encourage an approach to learning that is both skills-based and attitude based. Active learning methods promote habits of learning that, it is hoped, are valuable in the workplace, the home, and generally enhance pupils' capacity to cope with everyday life. School can be a place where pupils learn to do things well and in certain ways, thereby developing skills that are used throughout life. For example, pupils learn to consult a dictionary or a thesaurus in book form, as part of a word processing program or online in order to find meanings or to check their spelling and grammar. These skills become habits, capable of reinforcement and development. Reinforcement leads to improved performance. However, unless teachers can engage pupils with their need to know, learning is done under sufferance, leading to problems. Such problems may include poor recall of anything learned or rejection of learning tasks, which in turn may lead to behaviour problems.

Active learning, discovery learning and rote learning

Discovery learning

Discovery learning at its simplest occurs when pupils are left to discover things for themselves. This is a common approach taken with younger pupils, but, in the secondary school, a more structured framework is often used to facilitate learning. This is called 'guided discovery'.

But is the intention of guided discovery that pupils come to some predetermined conclusion, or is it that learning should take place but the outcomes vary from pupil to pupil? You need to be clear about your reason for adopting guided discovery methods. If the intention in discovery learning is to move pupils to a specific end point, then as discovery it could be challenged. This approach might preclude, for example, considering other knowledge that surfaced in the enquiry. If discovery learning focuses on how the knowledge was gained, then the activity is concerned with processes, i.e. how to discover and how to learn. The question is one of means and ends. Are discovery methods then concerned with discovery as 'process', learning how to learn? Or discovery as 'motivation', a better way to learn predetermined knowledge and skills and to support personalised learning with pupil and teacher working together to set the direction of open-ended work? Or is it discovery as 'change in self', learning something about yourself as a teacher and using this knowledge to deal with pupils' learning differently? This is also called reflection and is a key component of professional learning (Schon, 1983).

Rote learning

It is a fallacy, we suggest, to assume that pupils can learn everything for themselves by discovery methods. Teachers are specialists in their fields of study; they usually know more than pupils and one, but not all, of their functions is to tell pupils things they otherwise might not know but need to know. You need to consider what you want to achieve and match the teaching style with the purpose (see Unit 5.3 on teaching styles). Pupils need to be told when they are right; their work needs supporting. On occasions you need to tell pupils when they are wrong and how to correct their error. How this is done is important, but teachers should not shirk telling pupils when they underperform or make mistakes. See Unit 3.2 on motivating pupils, which includes a section on giving feedback. The Education Endowment Foundation (2015) reports research on the importance of feedback, as well as on many other issues affecting pupil attainment (viewed 3 July 2018, from https://education endowmentfoundation.org.uk/toolkit/toolkit-a-z/feedback/).

Rote learning may occur when pupils are required to listen to the teacher. There are occasions when you need to talk directly to pupils, e.g. to give facts about language, of spelling or grammar, formulae in science or health matters such as facts about drug abuse or safe practice in the gymnasium. Other facts necessary for successful learning in school include recalling multiplication tables, remembering vocabulary, learning the reactivity series of metals or recalling a piece of prose or poetry. Some facts need to be learned by heart, by rote methods. There is nothing wrong with you requiring pupils to do this from time to time, provided that all their learning is not like that. Such facts are necessary for advanced work; they contribute to the sub-routines that allow us to function at a higher level. Habits of spelling, of adding up, of recalling the alphabet are vital to our ability to function in all areas of the curriculum and in daily life.

Sometimes pupils need to use a routine as part of a more important task but which they may not fully understand. You may decide that the end justifies the means and that, through the experience of using the routine in different contexts, understanding of that routine develops. Many of us learn that way.

Learning facts by heart usually involves a coding process. For example, recalling a telephone number is easier if it is broken into blocks such as 0271 612 6780 and not as 02716126780. Another strategy is the use of a mnemonic to aid recall, such as recalling the musical scale E G B D F by the phrase 'Every Good Boy Deserves Fun'. Do you know any other mnemonics? What other ways are there of helping pupils to learn by rote?

Use Task 5.2.3 as a starting point to evaluate the different types of learning your teaching provides.

 Task 5.2.3   Identifying types of learning

Review a selection of lessons that you have taught and identify where you have used active learning, guided discovery and rote learning. Critically reflect on the reasons for your choices and whether these were appropriate. If you have not given the pupils opportunities to learn in these ways, try to work out some lesson plans where you build them in. Record your reflections in your PDP.

Active learning in the classroom: aids to recall and understanding

Sometimes information cannot easily be committed to memory unless a structure is developed around it to help recall. That structure may involve other information that allows you to build a picture. In other words, recall is constructed. Structures may include other words, but often tables, diagrams, flow charts or other visual models are used. Another way of helping pupils to remember ideas or facts is to construct summaries in various forms. Both the act of compiling the summary and the product contribute to remembering and learning. Figure 5.2.1 shows a model of learning based on the idea that personal development proceeds best by reflection on your own actions. Reflection in the model is incorporated in the terms 'review' and 'learn'. This model is presented as a cyclic flow diagram that enables you to keep in mind the essential steps.

This model can be applied to pupils' learning as well as your own. You might also want to develop a more sophisticated model of active learning in relation to your own practice. We recommend you consider carrying out research in your own classroom. See Unit 5.4.

Mapping tools: spider diagrams and mind maps

It is often helpful to pupils and teachers to 'brainstorm' as a way of exploring their understanding of an idea. One way to record that event is by a spider diagram (or burr diagram) or mind map in which the 'legs' identify the ideas related to the topic. Figure 5.2.2 shows a spider diagram constructed by a pupil of some ideas associated with 'fruit'.

Concept maps, more commonly called 'mind maps', are developments from spider diagrams and are used to display important ideas or concepts that are involved in a topic or unit of work and, by annotation, show the links between them. An example is shown in Figure 5.2.3. Concept maps can be made by pupils as a way of summarising their knowledge of a unit of work. The individual map reveals some of the pupil's understanding and misunderstandings of the topic. Making a concept map at the start of a unit helps to probe pupils' prior knowledge of the subject. In either case, you may need to provide a list of ideas with which pupils can work and to which they can add their own ideas, as illustrated in Figures 5.2.2 and 5.2.3.

Concept mapping is useful as part of your lesson preparation, particularly when beginning a new unit of work. See also Task 5.1.5 in Unit 5.1. Concept maps have their origin in the learning movement called constructivism. In particular, constructivists hold that prior knowledge is used as a framework to learn new knowledge. In essence, how we think influences how and what we learn. Concept maps identify the way we think and, more importantly, the way we see relationships between knowledge. Concept mapping enables you to gain an overview of the unit, to consolidate links between several

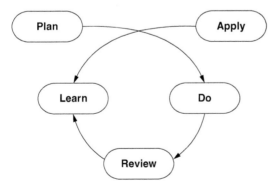

Figure 5.2.1 An active learning model: plan, do, review, learn, apply

Source: Watkins et al. (2007, p.77)

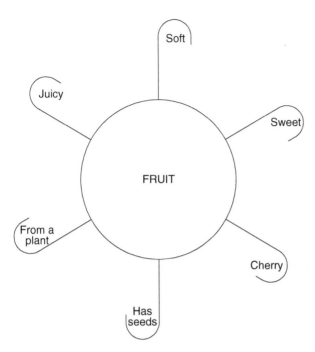

Figure 5.2.2 A pupil's meaning of fruit or a pupil's understanding of the concept of fruit

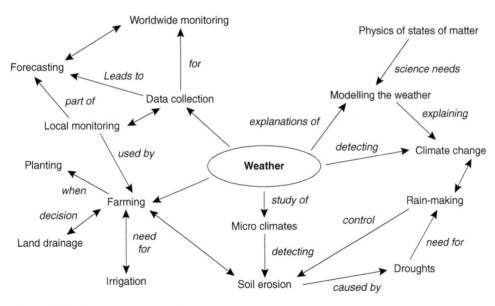

Figure 5.2.3 Concept map: weather

ideas and may reveal weaknesses or gaps in your own understanding. Concept mapping is a useful way of linking topics in the curriculum so as to promote continuity and breadth of understanding in your teaching (see, for instance, concept maps in science in Frost and Turner, 2005, Chapter 5.2). Concept maps are difficult to construct but the process of drafting one is a valuable exercise. Task 5.2.4 asks you to prepare a concept map.

Task 5.2.4   Using concept mapping

Prepare a concept map for a unit of work that you are going to teach. Discuss this map with other student teachers, your tutor and reflect on its value to enhance active learning in the lesson. Record in your PDP ideas for the use of concept maps in your lessons.

Directed activities related to text (DART)

DART are ways of engaging pupils in active reading, writing and listening in order to foster their understanding of a text and their ability to reflect. These are long-standing classroom teaching strategies (see, for instance, Davies and Greene, 1984; Gilham, 1986, p.164), which continue to be widely used (e.g. Davison and Dowson, 2003, p.69, 79, 254). DART can involve the use of textbooks, but they use a variety of written and other visual materials, including resources downloaded from the web. DART are devised to ensure that pupils interact with a text. Interaction includes, for example, underlining certain types of word, listing important words, drawing diagrams or reformulating a labelled diagram into continuous prose. The level of demand, i.e. differentiation, is adjusted by you to meet the needs of the pupils. A listening activity may be designed to help pupils understand instructions given by the teacher. DART and related types of learning activities emphasise the importance of language in learning and in assessing learning. For further discussion on the role of language in learning, see, for instance, Burgess (2004). Some examples of DART in the classroom are discussed below. See also Unit 5.5.

DART: giving instructions

This includes activities as diverse as making bread, carrying out a traffic survey or gathering information on the effects of the Black Death. A common complaint by teachers is that pupils do not read instructions or, if they do, are unable to comprehend them. Sometimes the language level is too high; or pupils may understand each step but not the whole or just lack confidence to act. Sometimes it is because pupils do not have any investment in the project; it is not theirs. Ways of alleviating such problems depend on the ability and attentiveness of your pupils but can include:

- co-writing the instructions for an activity. Pupils then use their own checklist as they complete each stage of the task;
- writing instructions on numbered cards. A set of cards can be given to a group who are instructed to put the cards into a working order. Discrepancies are discussed and the order checked against the purpose in order to agree on the acceptable sequence, which can then be written or pasted in pupils' books;
- matching instructions to sketches of events: ask pupils to read instructions and select the matching sketch and so build a sequence;
- discussing the task first and then asking pupils to draft their own set of instructions. After checking by the teacher, the pupils can begin.

The same approach can be applied to how to do something or explain a process, for example helping pupils explain how ice erodes rock or how to interrogate a database.

DART: listening to the teacher

Sometimes you want pupils to listen and enjoy what is being said to them. There are other occasions when you want pupils to listen and interact with the material and keep some sort of record. It may be to:

- explain a phenomenon, e.g. a riot;
- describe an event, e.g. a bore in a river;
- describe a process, e.g. making pastry;
- demonstrate a process, e.g. distillation;
- design an artefact, e.g. a desk lamp;
- give an account, e.g. of work experience or a visit to a gallery.

There are a number of ways you can help pupils in their work. For example:

- identifying key words and ideas as you proceed, signalling to pupils when you expect them to record them;
- identifying, or getting pupils to identify, key words and ideas in advance on a worksheet and asking pupils to note them, tick, underline or highlight as they are discussed. These words can be written on the board;
- using a diagram that pupils annotate as the lesson proceeds. This diagram might be used to: label parts, describe functions or identify where things happen. Pupils could keep their own notes and then be asked to make a summary and presentation to the class. Some pupils may need a word list to help them.

A possible way to support pupils in preparing a summary could be to give them a depleted summary and ask them to complete it. The degree of help is a matter of judgement. For example:

- give the summary with some key words missing and ask pupils to add the missing words;
- give the depleted summary with an additional list of words. Pupils select words and put them in the appropriate place. The selection could include surplus words;
- vary the focus of the omitted words. It could be on key words, or concepts, or focused on meanings of non-technical words, e.g. on connecting words or verbs, etc. (Sutton, 1981, p.119; Frost and Turner, 2005, pp.181-184).

Another possibility could be to provide pupils with a writing frame. A writing frame consists of 'visual guidance on the construction of each paragraph or section of a piece of writing, which includes all or part of a topic sentence and bullet points identifying items which pupils should include' (see Moss in Davison and Dowson, 2003, p.151). So, in the example given above of writing an account of a visit to a gallery, a possible frame might look like this:

- give details of the journey to the gallery (e.g. times of departure and arrival, mode of transport, route);
- describe the gallery (e.g. size, age of the building);

- list three artists whose work is exhibited there and give some information about what you have learned about them;
- say whether you would recommend this gallery to friends and give at least two reasons.

DART: characterising events

You may wish to help pupils associate certain ideas, events or properties with a phenomenon, for example, what were the features of the colonisation of the West Indies; or what are the characteristics of a Mediterranean-type climate? As well as reading and making notes:

- list ideas on separate cards, some of which are relevant to the topic and others not relevant. Ask pupils to sort the cards into two piles, those events relevant to the phenomenon and those not directly related. Pupils compare sorting and justify their choice to each other;
- mix up cards describing criteria related to two phenomena. Ask pupils to select those criteria appropriate to each event. A more complex task would be to compare, for example, the characteristics of the Industrial Revolutions of the 18th and 20th centuries.

DART: interrogating texts or reading for meaning

Pupils often feel that, if they read a text (a book, an online source), they are learning and don't always appreciate that they have to work to gain understanding. Pupils need to do something with the material in order to understand it. There are a number of ways of interrogating the material in order to assist with learning and understanding. There are some general points to be considered. It is important that pupils:

- are asked to read selectively - the length of the reading should be appropriate;
- understand why they are reading and what they are expected to get out of it;
- know what they are supposed to be doing while they read, what to focus on, what to write down or record;
- know what they are going to do with the results of their reading; e.g. write, draw, summarise, reformulate, précis, tell others, tell the teacher, carry out an investigation.

To help pupils read for meaning you could try the following activities.

DART: getting an overview

Using photocopies of written material is helpful; pupils annotate or mark the text to aid understanding. Pupils read the entire text quickly, to get an overview and to identify any words they cannot understand and to get help from an adult or a dictionary. Ask pupils to read it again, this time with a purpose, such as to list or underline, or group key words or ideas.

DART: reformulating ideas

To develop understanding further, pupils need to do something with what they have read. They could:

- make a list of key words or ideas;
- collect similar ideas together, creating patterns of broader concepts;

- summarise the text to a given length;
- turn prose into a diagram, sketch or chart;
- make a spider diagram;
- design a flow chart, identifying sequence of events, ideas, etc.;
- construct a diagram, e.g. of a process or of equipment with labels;
- turn a diagram into prose, by telling a story or interpreting meanings;
- summarise using tables, e.g. relating structure to function (e.g. organs of the body), historical figures' contribution to society (e.g. emancipation of women), form to origin (e.g. landscapes and erosion).

Where appropriate, pupils could be given a skeleton flow chart, spider diagram, etc., with the starting idea provided and asked to come up with further ideas.

DART: reporting back

A productive way of gaining interest and involvement is to ask pupils to report their findings, summaries or interpretation of the text to the class. The summary could take one of the forms mentioned above. In addition, of course, a pupil could use the board, overhead projector, poster or a computer-assisted presentation such as PowerPoint. Pupils need to be prepared for this task and need to be given sufficient time. Public reporting is demanding on pupils and it is helpful if a group of pupils draft the presentation and support the reporter. The presentation could be narrative, a poem, a simulation, diagram, play, etc. A suggested sequence of events is shown in the feedback loop, from 'Class discussion' to 'Task' in Figure 5.2.4, which can be introduced depending on the time available and the interest and ability of the class.

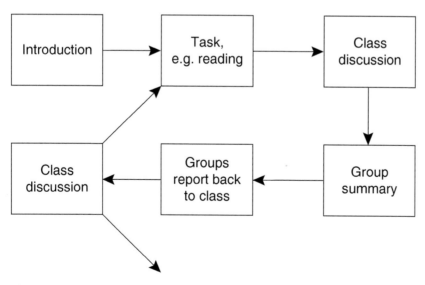

Figure 5.2.4 Reporting back

Lesson planning for active learning

It is important to distinguish between 'activities' and 'active learning'. It is relatively easy to fill a lesson with a series of activities that keep pupils busy and apparently enjoying it, yet these may provide an insufficient learning challenge. Such work may be well within the pupils' grasp and so they do not have to think much about what they are doing or why. Many pupils take seriously copying from the board, book or worksheet but such activities are often superficial and should be used very sparingly, even though they can keep a noisy class quiet.

Some lesson planning in the early stages of learning to teach may be to ensure that all your learning outcomes are addressed, or that your discipline is effective; this requirement may lead to a lesson that is teacher dominated. For example, you may have explained orally the lesson and its purpose and have asked some bridging questions; you may have then used a video and asked the pupils to complete a worksheet in response to watching the video; finally, you may have given out homework based on the class work. You, as the teacher, have been very active in the lesson and may well feel exhausted at the end of it! From the pupils' point of view, however, the lesson may have been quite passive because they were told what to do at every step, with little or no input into what they were to do and learn. In these circumstances many pupils may not fully engage in learning except in a superficial sense.

Task 5.2.5 provides a springboard to explore these issues.

 Task 5.2.5   Active classroom or active learning?

You may find this task best discussed in a tutor group.

A structured sequence for the learning of new vocabulary in a modern foreign language lesson is presented in Table 5.2.1.

The pupils seem to be busy but to what extent do you think the pupils are actively engaged in learning?

Identify any changes you would make to the lesson and explain why.

Record your notes in your PDP. After you have carried out this task compare your response to that of an experienced teacher.

This short lesson sequence illustrates how to scaffold the learning at the initial stage (see references to scaffolding in Units 3.1 and 5.1). It provides ample opportunities for pupils to take part, but the cognitive demands remain mostly at word or phrasal level and the activities are tightly controlled by the teacher. For pupils to progress further, they would need to be led gradually towards the challenge of identifying patterns, generating sentences of their own and integrating this vocabulary into new structures and contexts. Furthermore, the memorisation techniques illustrated here may well be helpful in the short term but are unlikely to be sufficient to secure deep learning by way of retaining the newly acquired words in the longer term.

To begin to use active learning, you need to have a clear idea about what you want to achieve. Monk and Silman (2011) suggest that the way to begin is to visualise the learning atmosphere you are aiming to achieve by the end of the term and then to plan the steps that get you there. You need to consider your knowledge of the pupils, the curriculum, the learning space available (your

Table 5.2.1 An example of a structured sequence for the oral introduction of new vocabulary for beginners in a modern foreign languages lesson

Activity	Pupils' physical involvement	Pupils' mental involvement
Teacher presents new vocabulary items with visuals (e.g. downloaded pictures, flash cards, etc.)	Pupils repeat each word at a time, in chorus and individually at random	Pupils try to work out the meaning of the word. The repetition helps them to start to commit the new vocabulary to their short-term memory
Teacher numbers visuals on the board, then calls out the words at random (or this could be done with the use of a list on tape)	Pupils write the number that corresponds to the word they have heard	Pupils draw upon their short-term memory to identify the correct item.
Teacher asks question: 'What is this' in the target language	Pupils put their hands up, selected individuals speak	Pupils draw upon their short-term memory to produce the words
Teacher asks pupils to work in pairs and ask each other what the new words are. Teacher encourages the class to answer in short sentences, e.g.: this is a...	All pupils involved in speaking	Pupils recall the words as well as the question. They begin to formulate a simple sentence

classroom or perhaps somewhere else in the school) and then begin to plan activities that signal to the pupils that your classroom is an active not passive one, where their views, interest and opinions are central to their learning experience.

These issues suggest some key questions to keep in mind when planning for active learning:

What will the pupils actually do that enhances their learning?
How will I ensure that, as I am talking, the pupils are processing what I am saying?
Does the majority of the class have the life experiences to understand what I am trying to teach?
Am I planning my teaching to cover the curriculum or am I planning the teaching of the curriculum to ensure the pupils are actively learning?

(Monk and Silman, 2011, p.189)

Some teachers might use the word *hook* to describe an activity planned at the start of a sequence of lessons that engages pupils in their learning. 'Hooks' can involve:

- challenges;
- problems to solve;
- role play to bring an experience to life;
- visits and visitors;
- visual and auditory stimuli.

A multisensory classroom experience can contribute towards active learning. Visual aids can generate interest, bring 'reality' into the classroom and enable an interactive approach to be adopted. Visual aids may take the form of a simple prompt, e.g. a picture, a poster, an object, an overhead projector transparency, a PowerPoint presentation or an interactive whiteboard.

Visual aids are a powerful tool for focusing attention, stimulating memorisation and conveying meaning, all of which contribute to active learning. They enable the teacher not only to present information but also to clarify concepts and meanings and build ideas, models, diagrams and sequences with the class. For example, you can hide definitions that the pupils then complete. Pupils can hypothesise from partly revealed screens, share their ideas and complete some creative writing from these ideas as a class activity. Equally importantly, the pupils can use these aids to display their own understanding.

Increasingly, pupils have access to iPads or tablets (Burden and Younie, 2014) and the teacher often has an interactive whiteboard (a touch-sensitive projection screen that is connected to a computer and a projector that allows you or your pupils, using a pen or finger, to highlight or move what is displayed on the board). Text can be written on the whiteboard, for instance a whole-class correction of an exercise, and then saved for further use at a later date. You and your class can also interface with downloaded interactive materials from the Internet, or simply use downloaded images, graphs, texts, etc. These added advantages make the interactive whiteboard and tablets/iPads or other digital devices powerful tools for engaging pupils in learning. Although this way of working requires a fair amount of preparation time, it helps to make smooth transitions between activities and there is an increasing range of time-saving resources being developed for use in the classroom

Task 5.2.6 invites you to consider the use of 'hooks' in one of your units of work.

 Task 5.2.6   Using hooks

In one of your units of work, plan how you can involve pupils through the use of a 'hook' (see examples in the list earlier in this unit) to promote active learning. Teach the lessons incorporating this 'hook' and then evaluate the effectiveness of this approach and how you might improve their use in future lessons. Record the outcomes in your PDP focusing on analysing the learning outcomes (using guidance in Units 5.1, 5.3 and 5.5).

Whatever visual aids you choose to use, it is worth bearing in mind that they require management. There are practical implications for maximising the impact of visual aids, including their clarity, lack of ambiguity and appropriateness of the language level to your class. Another practical implication is to make sure all pupils can see and, if appropriate, read your visual prompts. It is useful, for example, when using visual aids to practise where to stand so as not to obstruct pupils' vision. You do need to be careful that your 'hook' doesn't become the main focus for your planning. Planning for learning requires you to focus on what the pupil is doing as well as what you are doing. To encourage pupils to participate fully in the lesson and, hence, promote meaningful learning, there are some important features to bear in mind when planning your lesson. As well as planning strategies that include an input from pupils into the development of the lesson, you should:

■ share the learning outcomes with your pupils and give an example of what your pupils' finished work should look like, i.e. what counts as a successful piece of work;
■ focus some learning outcomes on process rather than content, i.e. on pupil action and contribution to their own learning;
■ illustrate your criteria for assessment;
■ link the lesson to the pupils' prior knowledge and include your strategies for eliciting it;

- prepare contingency plans for differentiating for both faster and slower pupils;
- think about ways to help pupils in difficulties, i.e. give support (see Units 4.1 and 5.1).

Task 5.2.7 helps you to consider strategies to activate pupils' prior knowledge.

 Task 5.2.7   Activating pupils' prior knowledge

(See also short-term and long-term memory in Unit 5.1)

Select a strategy for probing pupils' prior knowledge of a topic and use it in a lesson in which you are being observed. Evaluate the effectiveness of the activity yourself and also ask your tutor or class teacher to give you feedback on its effectiveness. Strategies you could use include a question and answer session, brainstorming in small groups (i.e. eliciting spontaneous recall of relevant information or randomly listing ideas/suggestions in relation to a particular topic or question) followed by a plenary session, asking pupils to prepare a spider diagram summarising what they know. You then use these to plan the next lesson. File feedback in your PDP.

Active learning goes hand in hand with an approach to teaching that encourages pupils to develop and progress as individuals and not merely to receive information from the teacher. Active learning, therefore, is a process that is:

- structured and organised, a purposeful activity through which pupils can achieve the intended learning outcome as you have planned it;
- transformational, enables pupils to consider alternatives, to think differently and develop attitudes and values;
- communicative, involves engagement with others within and beyond the classroom and develops higher-order skills such as analysis, communication, investigation, listening;
- generative, pupils are engaged in the process of their own learning and generates deeper understanding by challenging pupils' understanding;
- supportive of meaningful learning.

If this description is correct, then a lesson must invite pupils to participate in the work, contribute to its development and, consequently, begin to shape their own learning. The demands on the pupil in such a situation move learning to higher-order skills to which we now turn.

Developing pupils' higher-order thinking skills

It is now generally acknowledged that the explicit development of thinking skills needs to take place alongside teaching of factual content and that the emphasis in learning is not just on the outcomes, but also on the processes. Teaching, therefore, needs to be designed to enable pupils to:

- develop logical reasoning in order to apply it to new contexts (formal thinking approach);
- deconstruct problems in order to find solutions to them (heuristic approach);
- reflect on, and evaluate, their own learning (metacognitive approach) (Muijs and Reynolds, 2005).

These three approaches are at the heart of active learning because they promote the learners' engagement with the task and encourage pupils to make sense of their learning (see also Unit 5.1). Bloom identified six levels of thinking of gradually increasing complexity, which make increasing demands on the cognitive processes of learners (Bloom, 1956; see also Unit 3.1). These six levels are listed in column one of Table 3.1.2 in Unit 3.1. While there is the potential for active learning at every level, the last three levels can be linked to the higher-order thinking skills mentioned above.

Providing suitable challenges is fundamental to active learning. One strategy used extensively by teachers is questioning (see also Unit 3.1). The importance of questioning as a teaching and learning strategy is long established and well documented in educational research, e.g. Wragg and Brown (2001), Kerry (2004). Many studies show how questions can take various forms and how they can be adapted to serve a variety of purposes to promote active learning.

Purposes of questioning:

- capturing pupils' attention and interest;
- recalling and checking on prior knowledge;
- focusing pupils' attention on a specific issue or concept;
- checking and probing pupils' understanding;
- developing pupils' thinking and reasoning;
- differentiating learning;
- extending pupils' power of analysis and evaluation;
- helping pupils to reflect on how they learn.

To the student teacher, questions asked by experienced teachers may appear intuitive and instinctive whereas, in reality, good questioning develops by reflection on experience. Questions should not just be 'off the cuff' but prepared in advance and related to the learning outcomes, so that pupils' learning is structured. Good and Brophy, (2000, p.412) provide a useful observation schedule identifying good principles for effective questioning. Morgan and Saxton (1991) identify six different types of questions that stimulate thinking.

Six different types of questions (adapted from Morgan and Saxton 1991):

1   questions that draw upon knowledge (Remembering);
2   questions that test comprehension (Understanding);
3   questions that require application (Solving);
4   questions that encourage analysis (Reasoning);
5   questions that invite synthesis (Creating);
6   questions that promote evaluation (Judging).

Experienced teachers have the skill of asking questions beyond those planned in response to pupils' replies. Experience here depends largely on knowing your subject and how to use this knowledge, that is, how to put across your knowledge of the subject to the pupils in a way that enables them to learn, and on knowing your pupils and how they respond to your subject and your teaching. You also need to know the ideas/concepts that pupils find difficult and, therefore, need to probe their understanding/misunderstandings.

Effective questioning is central to the teaching and learning process. How Bloom's taxonomy relates to the use of questions by the teacher is shown in Table 3.1.2 in Unit 3.1. This table identifies the purposes of questioning at the various levels and gives examples of the sort of question that may be asked.

Finally, complete Tasks 5.2.8 and 5.2.9.

 Task 5.2.8   Developing higher-order thinking skills through the use of questioning

Observe a lesson and script the questions used by the teacher to promote learning. Try to classify against Bloom's (1956) taxonomy of educational objectives (Stanford University, 2015). How does the type and frequency of question used impact upon active learning? Discuss your observations with the teacher or your tutor and record them in your PDP.

  Task 5.2.9   Reflecting on your use of active learning

Read the article: Powell (2005) 'Conceptualising and facilitating active learning: Teachers' video-stimulated reflective dialogues', Reflective Practice, 6 (3): 407-18.

Make notes in your PDP. Arrange to video-tape a lesson, or a part of a lesson that aims to promote active learning. If possible, discuss the video extract with other student teachers or your tutor, using Moyle's reflective framework (see Appendix 1(b) of Powell's article). Alternatively analyse your questioning technique using the information in the textboxes and other research literature on questioning that you have selected. Write a critical analysis of your teaching, drawing upon the research literature that you have read, and store this in your PDP.

SUMMARY AND KEY POINTS

- Teaching is an enabling process; teachers can guide pupils' learning but cannot do the learning for them.
- Pupils need to engage mentally with a task if learning is to take place; thus, you need to enthuse and motivate pupils, give purpose to their learning tasks, and to provide active learning experiences. Some of these activities, e.g. DART, introduced study skills, are important for pupils preparing for public examinations.
- This unit has used examples of reading, writing, listening and talking activities designed to improve learning and learning skills.
- There is hands-on activity in practically based subjects, such as art and design, science and technology. Working with your hands does not guarantee that learning takes place; both hand and brain need to be involved.
- Pupils need to have a say in the design, execution and evaluation of practical work in the same way as we have stressed the need for their active involvement in reading and listening.

The advantages claimed for active learning include an emphasis on cooperative learning, which can provide opportunities for pupils to take some responsibility for their own learning by, for example, active participation in the development of the task. This approach requires pupil self-discipline and may contribute to that wider goal of education. For the teacher, it opens up a wider range of teaching methods to develop personalised learning, allows the growth of resource-based learning and provides space for monitoring pupil progress and giving formative feedback. Aims can be widened. Active learning can be used to promote process skills and higher-order skills, as well as encouraging acquisition of knowledge and understanding.

The key to good teaching is preparation. This is particularly important if you select active learning strategies. These strategies are a major part of your teaching repertoire and, as such, contribute significantly to the professional standards required of an NQT. Further advice and guidance on active learning is available in the 'Further resources' section.

Check which requirements for your ITE programme you have addressed through this unit.

Further resources

A wide range of literature is available on developing memory and thinking skills, e.g. Edward de Bono's work. The resources below provide specialist information relating to this unit.

Burden, K. and Younie, S. (2014) *Using iPads Effectively to Enhance Learning in Schools MESHGuide*, viewed 30 November 2017, from http://www.meshguides.org/category/icttechnology/tablets ipad-pedagogy/

Claxton, G. (2015) *Building Learning Power*, viewed 30 November 2017, from http://www. buildinglearningpower.co.uk/

Education-line, viewed 30 November 2017, from www.leeds.ac.uk/bei/COLN/COLN_default.html holds a repository of papers presented at the British Education Research Association conferences (BERA): www.bera.ac.uk
These provide a useful starting point to find out about recent research projects on active learning and thinking skills.

'Google Scholar' also provides open access to a wide variety of research papers
University libraries subscribe to online journals so that members of libraries can gain access to the world-wide body of research literature. In the UK, local neighbourhood libraries are usually able to borrow copies of the wide range of literature held by the British Library.

Kagan: http://www.kagan-uk.co.uk/
Kagan UK trains teachers to use Kagan Structures, a set of research-based instructional strategies that have been created to teach pupils cooperation and learning strategies to enhance achievement.

Muijs, D. and Reynolds, D. (2005) *Effective Teaching: Evidence and Practice*, 2nd Edition, London: Paul Chapman.
This book provides a comprehensive introduction to what are considered to be key elements of effective teaching, as evidenced by recent research on practice. The chapters on interactive teaching, collaborative small group work, constructivism and problem-solving and higher-order thinking skills are particularly useful for deepening your understanding of what active learning involves and how you can bring it about in your own teaching.

Stanford University (2015) *Teaching Commons: Blooms Taxonomy of Educational Objectives*, viewed 30 November 2017, from https://teachingcommons.stanford.edu/resources/course-preparation-reso urces/course-design-aids/bloom%E2%80%99s-taxonomy-educational-objectives

The Education Endowment Foundation (2015) *Feedback*, viewed 3 July 2018, from https://educationend owmentfoundation.org.uk/evidence-summaries/teaching-learning toolkit/feedback/

University of Cambridge/Professor Neil Mercer (2015) *Thinking Together*, viewed 30 November 2017, from http://thinkingtogether.educ.cam.ac.uk/resources/

Watkins, C., Carnell, E. and Lodge, C. (2007) *Effective Learning in Classrooms*, London: Paul Chapman.
This book focuses on learning, what makes it effective and how to promote it in classrooms. The authors identify active learning as a core process for promoting effective learning in classrooms. Drawing upon international research as well as case studies involving practicing teachers, they provide you with useful ideas and frameworks for developing your own conception of active learning.

Appendix 2 lists subject associations and teacher councils and Appendix 3 provides a list of websites.

Capel, S., Leask, M. and Turner, T. (eds.) (2010) *Readings for Learning to Teach in the Secondary School: A Companion to M Level Study*, Abingdon: Routledge.
This book brings together essential readings to support you in your critical engagement with key issues raised in this textbook.

Capel, S., Lawrence, J. Leask, M. and Younie, S. (eds.) (2019) *Surviving and Thriving in the Secondary School: The NQT's Essential Companion*, Abingdon: Routledge.
This book is designed to support newly qualified teachers in the next phase of development as a teacher. However, you may find it useful as it covers aspects of teaching not included in this book which, nonetheless you experience on your ITE programme.

The subject specific books in the *Learning to Teach (Subject)* series, the *Practical (Subject) Guides*, *Debates in (Subject)* and *Mentoring (Subject) Teachers* are also very useful.

Any additional resources and an editable version of any relevant tasks/tables in this unit are available on the companion website: www.routledge.com/cw/capel

Acknowledgements

The author would like to thank Matthew Lowe for his willingness to try the strategies advocated in this unit.

5.3 Teaching styles

Chris Carpenter and Hazel Bryan

Introduction

This unit is concerned with *individual teaching styles*. In the same way that assessment, curriculum and pedagogy are closely interrelated, we suggest that while teaching style is a topic worthy of study in its own right it is informed by other aspects of teaching. We take the position that, in terms of teaching style, there is no one 'perfect' way to teach because classroom interactions are subject to many influences. Indeed, Hattie (2012a,b) argues that too much time is spent talking about particular methods of teaching whereas our attention should have been on the effect we have on pupil's learning. Therefore, while teaching style will be at the heart of the unit, we draw on aspects such as learning theory, pedagogy and the activities that teachers employ in helping pupils to learn to shed light on teaching styles. In this way you will be supported in building knowledge about teaching styles and in considering how the styles that teachers use are related to other aspects of teacher knowledge that you will be developing as a part of your initial teacher education (ITE) programme. The section 'Classroom approaches: teaching/pedagogical strategies' in Unit 5.5 provides a list of strategies to consider together with the styles outlined in this unit.

OBJECTIVES

By the end of this unit you should:

- understand the possibilities for a repertoire of teaching styles that you can draw upon to enable pupils to learn in various situations;
- have thought about the relationship between the teaching styles that you employ in the classroom and what you intend pupils to learn;
- have developed an understanding that learning is concerned with helping *particular* pupils learning *something*, and, therefore, teaching styles need to be specific to what is learned, the pupils and the teacher;

■ be able to apply knowledge that you have about how pupils learn to underpin the teaching styles that you employ;

■ map your developing style to the requirements of your ITE programme and use your mapping to set targets for further development.

Check the requirements of your ITE programme to see which relate to this unit.

Developing a repertoire of teaching styles

First, look at developing a repertoire of teaching styles in Figure 5.3.1.

Anyone who has been to school will be familiar with the kinds of things that teachers do. Indeed, the modes of teaching that teachers employ are often a feature of film, television series and novels, which use schools as a place to situate the drama. You might reflect for a moment on memorable scenes from film or book: in what way would you describe the teaching style of that teacher? There is a vast array of approaches that teachers use in classrooms that range from telling, describing, setting tasks, assessing learning and modelling various learning activities. If we do not understand the underpinning principles of teacher activities and develop a growing appreciation of why teachers do what they do, then we can focus merely on 'procedural display' aspects. In other words, that as a student teacher you might carry out certain tasks but are not necessarily clear why you might be doing them, other than because we know that those are the kinds of things that teachers do. This unit introduces ideas about teaching styles and provides opportunities for you to use theories encountered in other units in this book to widen your range of teaching styles and their associated strategies so that your actions as a teacher are informed.

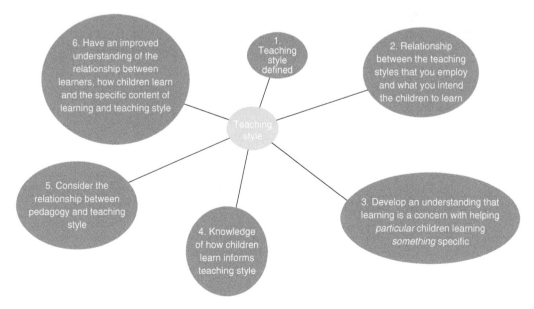

Figure 5.3.1 Developing a repertoire of teaching styles

The teaching styles we introduce in this unit include the following:

■ closed, framed and negotiated strategies (see Table 5.3.1);
■ command, practice/task, reciprocal, self-check, inclusion, guided discovery, convergent discovery, divergent discovery, learner-initiated, self-teaching strategies (see Table 5.3.2);
■ peer tutoring (see Table 5.3.3).

In developing this idea of teaching styles, we draw upon a model developed by Barnes (1987) that can be used to identify the basic elements of different teaching styles. This model works on a continuum of 'closed' to 'negotiated' styles.

In the 'closed' teaching style, the teacher assumes a high degree of control in relation to all decisions. This is a most authoritative teaching style: in this mode, the role of the pupil is to learn from the teacher and from the activities the teacher provides. This is a highly interventionist style of teaching where the teacher may even demonstrate what is to be achieved. In the more 'negotiated' teaching style, the teacher foregrounds the pupils more explicitly in the process. That is, the teacher creates a context where pupils are actively involved in planning and evaluating. Between these two poles is the 'framed' approach where the teacher still controls the overall topic, but pupils are invited to play an active role.

In order to illustrate the ideas behind the teaching styles suggested by Barnes, we have used the example of a secondary maths lesson, where the teacher is teaching algebra:

Now undertake Task 5.3.1.

Table 5.3.1 Teaching styles adapted from (Barnes, 1987, p.25)

	Closed	Framed	Negotiated
Content	Tightly controlled by the teacher. Not negotiable.	Teacher controls the topic, frames of reference and tasks; criteria made explicit.	Discussed at each point: joint decisions.
Focus	Authoritative knowledge and skills; simplified monolithic.	Stress on empirical testing processes chosen by teacher; some legitimation of pupils' ideas.	Search for justifications and principles; strong legitimation of pupils' ideas.
Pupils' role	Acceptance; routine performance; little access to principles.	Join in teachers' thinking; make hypothesis, set up tests.	Discuss goals and methods critically; share responsibility for frame and criteria.
Key concepts	'authority; the proper procedures and the right answers.	'Access'; to skills, processes criteria.	'Relevance'; critical discussion of pupils' priorities.
Methods	Exposition; worksheets (closed); note giving; individual exercises; routine practical work. Teacher evaluates.	Exposition; with discussions eliciting suggestions; individual/ group problem solving; lists of tasks given; discussion of outcomes; teacher adjudicates.	Group and class discussion and decision making about goals and criteria. Pupils plan and carry out work, make presentations, evaluate success.

Table 5.3.2 Examples of Barnes' teaching styles in the teaching of algebra

Closed	Framed	Negotiated
■ Pupils learning to solve equations in a maths lesson; ■ teacher models the process; ■ teacher gives pupils the sums to complete; ■ teacher insists on the pupils using the method they demonstrated; ■ teacher marks the sums.	■ Teacher sets the tasks; ■ pupils shown a method; ■ pupils are encouraged to try the method and reflect on the efficacy of it for them.	■ Teacher presents the 'unknown' as a problem to be solved; ■ pupils suggest ways this might be solved. They must test their methods on other pupils; ■ pupils are encouraged to try their methods and then reflect on what happened; ■ new methods proposed; ■ teacher models 'correct' solution; ■ when pupils are 'stuck' they ask.

Table 5.3.3 Examples of activities that teacher might use in the classroom

■ Mind maps	■ Formal presentations
■ Case studies	■ Games
■ Computer assisted learning	■ Interviewing
■ Creative writing	■ Problem solving
■ Directed Activities Related to use of texts (DARTS)	■ Reports
■ Debating	■ Reciprocal teaching
■ Designing	■ Role play
■ Developing multimedia presentations	■ Simulations
■ Podcasts	■ Small group discussion.
■ Animations	■ Surveys
■ Videos	■ Teacher demonstration
■ Diaries	■ Visitors
■ Drama/role play	

 Task 5.3.1   Closed, framed and negotiated teaching styles

Consider a lesson that you have either taught or have observed, map the key components of the lesson from a closed teaching style:

■   How would the topic be introduced?
■   What resources will you need?
■   How will the pupils work?
■   What will your role be?
■   How will the work be assessed?

Now repeat this task from a framed and then negotiated teaching style perspective and reflect upon the following questions:

- What was the learning experience like for pupils in each mode?
- How effective were the assessment methods in each mode?
- What implications are there for resources in each mode?

Record your reflections in your professional development portfolio (PDP) or equivalent.

You will notice that we have invited you to reflect upon this activity from the point of view of the pupil in terms of their overall experiences in each of the modes. The reason for this is because the 'processes' that pupils go through necessarily colour what it is that they learn about the task. This is because we know that cognitive and emotional processes are not separate. Therefore, the more control over the processes the learner has, the more likely they are to feel empowered and the more likely they are to have positive feelings about the task. It then follows that if they have positive feelings, they are more likely to persist and, even more importantly, the more likely they are to care about getting to a point of some level of mastery. There is a relationship, then, between the teaching style that is adopted and the learning experiences of the pupils. While we are a long way from having a definite theory about how it is that pupils learn, it seems probable that meaningful learning happens best where there is social interaction between the learner and a more knowledgeable other and where there is a cooperative and supportive ethos. It is also important that, to some extent, the pupil cares about the content under consideration (Winch, 1998) and that they feel that they are active agents in the process (Nixon, et al., 1996).

Teaching styles therefore need to take account of the need for negotiation both between pupils and between pupils and teacher; this aligns with a constructivist model of learning and teaching (see Unit 5.1). Your teaching style should not only promote discussion but encourage pupils to challenge their own and others' ideas and to go back and forth in a non-linear way. In this process, 'wrong' responses are to be welcomed as they give the teacher clues to the pupil's construing. In addition, the process of the pupil themselves identifying 'less good' responses is a powerful part of being able to identify the better responses. To do this you may need to move from *closed* strategies (Barnes, 1987) where the teacher tightly controls the content of the lesson, the learning environment and the outcomes of the lesson, through *framed* strategies, where the teacher controls the topics and has clear expectations of outcomes but encourages the pupils to propose and test alternatives, to *negotiated* strategies, where the pupils have much more freedom in determining the area of investigation and the way in which work is reported, with, possibly, variable outcomes. Table 5.3.1 describes the main differences between these strategies.

As you progress through your school experiences, you should refine your practice to develop teaching styles that suit different circumstances and achieve diverse learning outcomes. *Usually you need to adopt a range of styles within a single lesson in order to ensure all pupils are deepening their understandings about the topic being considered.* Of course, there may be an element of habituation here; pupils may become used to being taught in a particular way and to some extent become 'conditioned' so that even if they subsequently get something potentially richer, they may find it initially unsettling. It is worth bearing in mind that teachers may prefer to adopt styles of teaching that are actually best suited to themselves and not necessarily to their pupils. The position may be even worse for student teachers; Calderhead and Shorrock (1997) suggest teachers, especially student teachers, are initially more comfortable with structures and styles they experienced as pupils than with new ideas, and Evans (2004) reports 41% of a sample of student teachers felt they taught in the way that

Table 5.3.4 Water aid project Ghana

Water Aid project in Ghana http://www.wateraid.org/uk/where-we-work/page/ghana	Closed style	Read the piece together. Pupils answer the questions set by the teacher (for example, on the work of a cocoa plantation).
	Framed style	Read the piece together. Take one aspect of the project (for example, the work on a cocoa plantation). Teacher explains what is to be learned and sets activities for pupils to undertake.
	Negotiated style	Read the piece together. Ask the pupils what they might do next if they are to learn more about the issues of running a cocoa plantation. What do they know? What do they want to know? Where might this information be held? How will the information be collected?

they had been taught. Therefore, it is important that when you reflect critically on your teaching, you take steps to incorporate effective practice, including ideas gained from discussion, observation of other teachers and reading, to become comfortable and confident with a wide repertoire of strategies.

At this point, we would wish to draw a clear distinction between the *'style'* of teaching and the *activities* that that teacher employs. We feel that they are clearly related but not the same. We would argue that there are a multitude of activities that teachers may use in the classroom, such as those shown in Table 5.3.3.

We argue that the *activities* that teachers employ are a *part* of teaching style but not the same thing. For example, a secondary geography teacher might employ a directed activity related to texts (DARTS) (see Units 5.2 and 5.7); however, they might do this using different teaching styles. The teacher might give pupils a 'Water Aid Report' on developing irrigation projects in Ghana (http://www.wateraid.org/uk/where-we-work/page/ghana) but might approach this using different teaching styles. The decision the teacher makes in determining which teaching style to adopt is influenced by a range of complex factors. It might be that a particular teaching style is used because it is expected in that department. On the other hand, it might be shaped by what the teacher wants his or her pupils to learn through the process of addressing the task. That is, not simply the facts of the Water Aid project, but the experience of working together, developing an inquisitive mind-set and research skills. It may be that the teacher's own values about the purpose of the activity, and indeed, the teacher's views on the purpose of schooling itself influences the teaching style adopted (see Table 5.3.4).

The relationship between learning activities and teaching styles can be thought of like the cover version of a song. To give an example, in 2011 Amy Winehouse covered 'The Girl from Ipanema', a song originally released in 1964 by Joao Gilberto and Stan Getz, (https://www.youtube.com/watch?v=UJkxFhFRFDA) featuring Astrud Gilberto.

As you would expect, Winehouse's version was a very different interpretation from the 1964 version. In our analogy the song represents the activity and the style is the artist's interpretation of the song.

Mosston and Ashworth's continuum of teaching styles (2002)

A helpful way to frame the styles that teachers employ is to look at it from the point of view of how much 'say' the learner has and how much 'say' the teacher has in terms of the decisions being made

Figure 5.3.2 Mosston and Ashworth teaching styles

in the learning context. In a Physical Education setting, Mosston and Ashworth (2002) describe this as a continuum that is illustrated graphically in Figure 5.3.2.

In the Mosston and Ashworth continuum, the left-hand side (closed style) shows the teacher making all the decisions about what is to be learned, how it will be learned and how this will be achieved. In this sense the teaching style is formal and authoritative. An example of this is an aerobics class where the teacher models what is to be done and then the class members copy the teacher. Towards the right-hand side (negotiated style) the learner has increasing amounts of control to the point where, at the extreme right-hand side, they decide what they will learn and how they will go about it: this learner-initiated approach affords pupils a greater amount of intellectual freedom, creativity and enquiry. This negotiated style is commonly found in early years settings where a belief in the importance of pupils constructing their own understandings of the world frame the style the teacher adopts. Linking the 'closed' teaching style and the highly negotiated teaching style is a *continuum* of teaching styles: thinking about teaching styles on a continuum is helpful as it allows you to understand that having a range of teaching styles – a repertoire – at your fingertips will enable you to employ the most appropriate style for any given context. In the famous scene of the football lesson in the film *Kes*, Mr Sugden, the PE teacher, adopts a predominantly closed style.

By contrast, the most skilful and creative teachers are able to tap into their repertoire of teaching styles according to the given context.

At this point, is it helpful to acknowledge the ways in which different teaching styles shape the balance of pupil talk to teacher talk. This is not simply a matter of balance but of understanding the demand that particular teaching styles make of the learner.

Mosston and Ashworth's continuum of teaching styles offers a nuanced means by which teaching styles can be understood (see Table 5.3.5).

Now undertake Task 5.3.2.

 Task 5.3.2   Teaching style observation

Observe a lesson in your placement school

■   How might you describe the teaching styles that the teacher employs?
■   How involved were the pupils in making decisions?
■   What were they able to make decisions about?
■   Why did the teacher employ that style?
■   What were the issues that emerged?

Record your observations in your PDP.

Table 5.3.5 Mosston and Ashworth's 'Continuum of teaching styles' (2002 version)

Note: You will see that they have structured these in a particular order ranging from the command style to the learner designed individual programme.

The command style
This style is often described as autocratic or teacher centred. It is appropriate in certain contexts, e.g. teaching safe use of equipment, learning particular routines in dance.

The practice style
Whilst similar to the command style, there is a shift in decision-making to pupils and there is more scope with this style for the teacher to work with individuals whilst the group is occupied with practice tasks.

The reciprocal style
The pupils learn by working in pairs. Each partner is actively involved – one as the 'doer' and one as the 'teacher partner'. The class teacher works with the 'teacher partner' to not only improve mastery of the topic under consideration but also to help develop their capacity to evaluate and provide feedback. This style provides rich possibilities for interaction and communication among pupils. Pupils can also learn to judge performance against criteria.

The self-check style
This style is designed to develop the learner's ability to evaluate their own performance. The teacher sets the task and the pupils evaluate their own performance against set criteria and agree goals in collaboration with the teacher.

The inclusion style
In this style, differentiated tasks are presented to ensure that all pupils gain some feeling of success and so develop positive self-concepts, e.g. if an angled bar is provided for high jump practice, all pupils can succeed as they choose the height over which to jump. They decide at what level to start.

Guided discovery style
The teacher plans the programme on the basis of the learners' competence. The teacher then guides the pupil to find the solution – reframing the question and task if necessary but always controlling the teaching agenda. Pupils with special educational needs are often taught in small groups and this approach might be used by the teacher to develop an individualised learning programme for each pupil.

Convergent discovery style
In this style there is a single desired outcome to the learning episode, but the learners have autonomy over processes and presentation. The teacher provides feedback and clues (if necessary) to help them reach the correct outcome.

Divergent discovery style
Learners are encouraged to find alternative solutions to a question, e.g. in approaching a design problem in art. Multiple solutions are possible and the learners assess their validity, with support from the teacher if necessary.

The learner designed individual programme
A pupil designs and carries out a programme of work within a framework agreed and monitored by the teacher. Pupils carrying out open-ended investigations to answer a particular question in science provide an example of this style. The knowledge and skills needed to participate in this method of learning depend on the building up of skills and self-knowledge in earlier learning experiences.

Learner-initiated style
At this point on the continuum, the stimulus for learning comes primarily from the pupil, who provides the question to investigate as well as the method of investigation. Thus, the pupil actively initiates the learning experience and the teacher provides support. Giving homework that allows pupils freedom to work on their own areas of interest in their own way might fall into this category. However, Mosston and Ashworth make the point that this kind of learning arises 'only when an individual approaches the teacher and initiates a request to design his/her own learning experiences'. When teachers ask pupils to *do a project* it cannot be construed to be an example of this style' (Mosston and Ashworth, 2002, p.284-285).

Self-teaching style
This style describes independent learning without external support. For example, it is the type of learning that adults undergo as they learn from their own experiences.

Source: Adapted from Mosston and Ashworth, 2002

Teaching style as an element of constructive alignment

So far, we have suggested that teaching styles might best be considered on a continuum, and that the most skilful teachers have a repertoire of teaching styles that they use for different learning contexts. We have considered also the relationship between the teaching style, what is to be learned, activities that teachers might use in learning contexts and the learning experiences of the pupils. In this section we will locate teaching style in the slightly wider context of learning intentions and the assessment of learning. This leads into what Biggs (1996) refers to as 'constructive alignment' (see Figure 5.3.3). In other words, what the teacher intends the pupils to learn, the activities that enable the pupils to build deeper understanding and the way this is assessed should all 'line up' or be coherent and mutually supporting. That is, constructively aligned. There are implications for teaching styles here: the teacher will need to adopt a teaching style that enables the pupils to have plenty of opportunities to be able to practice the thing to be learned. The teacher needs to have the opportunity to make judgements about how well the pupil is mastering the thing under consideration as they progress and to be able to make helpful suggestions about the next steps:

For example, if a history teacher wants the pupils in their class to learn to make interpretations about historical events, they might show the pupils a picture of a Victorian street scene and then ask questions such as:

■ What do you notice?
■ What can we say about the times from this?
■ What do you think it might have been like to live in those times and why?

Pupils might then discuss their ideas in pairs, engage in some further joint reading - either on line or from texts provided by the teacher - and carry out a brief piece of joint writing. Pupils might then present their writing to the rest of the class.

Bigg's model of constructive alignment makes visible the connections between the learning the teacher wishes the pupils to achieve, the teaching style adopted and assessment. See Table 5.3.6, then undertake Task 5.3.3.

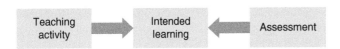

Figure 5.3.3 Biggs' (1996) model of constructive alignment

Table 5.3.6 Example of constructive alignment

Learning intention	Teaching style	Assessment
To understand what it was like to live in Victorian times.	Framed style: ■ teacher provides the picture; ■ teacher generates initial questions engaging in whole class discussion; ■ teacher sets up the sequence of activities.	■ teacher listens to pupil's discussions; ■ teacher reads the written work; ■ teacher monitors the presentations.

✏ Task 5.3.3   Constructive alignment

Learning intention	Teaching style	Teaching style	Assessment

Think about your own subject. Work through some examples of 'constructive' alignment. Discuss with a fellow student teacher and store your thoughts in your PDP.

Information processing models and teaching style

As well as constructivist models of learning (see Unit 5.1), there are models that represent learners as information processing systems (see Figure 5.3.4). This model assumes that learners process a certain amount of information in a set time. There may be limitation of capacity, and bottlenecks can occur when a lot of information is transmitted. When bottlenecks occur, not all of the transmitted information is received in the memory. Therefore, the teacher should be wary of offering too much information too quickly or introducing digressions. Reflect on whether using closed or framed strategies will enable you to get your key points across with most effect. At the start of the lesson, when objectives and activities are outlined or, for example, when demonstrating a technique or ensuring safety, a very focused, closed, instructional style might be required.

After information is received, short- and long-term memory work together dynamically. Information is processed in short-term memory, where fresh information and retrieved existing knowledge are used together to make meaning of new situations. This meaningful learning can then be stored in long-term memory. A teaching style that incorporates a range of teaching strategies to present information in different ways and provides a variety of perspectives matches a range of preferred learning styles.

Once you have considered the teaching styles most likely to support the achievement of your lesson objectives, consider your strategies. Because pupils learn in different ways, you might use talk in conjunction with, for example, a visual presentation of key themes. You might also think about your strategy for grouping. Kutnick et al. (2006) suggest no one form of grouping benefits all pupils.

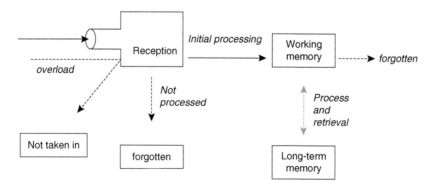

Figure 5.3.4 A flowchart for an information processing model. The flowchart shows the typical pattern of information flow and processing suggested by a multi-store model of memory proposed by Atkinson and Shiffrin (1968)

Grouping by ability can benefit the most able but demotivate the less able; friendship groups can sometimes provide a non-threatening environment that promotes learning, at other times they can reinforce cultural stereotypes that prevent progress. Be prepared, therefore, to seek advice about the organisational strategies you employ within the classroom and how best to exploit the different opportunities they present.

Personalised learning and independent learners

Personalised learning requires that you 'shape teaching and learning around the different ways children learn' (after Barnes and Harris, 2006, p.1). In some circumstances, such as using resistant materials workshops, science labs or working with javelins, your choice of actions is quite constrained. Nevertheless, it is unlikely that you adopt a complete command style during your school experience. It is even less likely that you have the confidence or desire to adopt a discovery style, and hand over the majority of the decisions to the pupils. However, it is important that you encourage pupils' independence in order to further the personalisation of their learning. Mosston and Ashworth (2002) argue that there is a 'discovery threshold', and independent learning is not possible if teachers do not use discovery or divergent styles. Therefore, your repertoire should provide pupils with challenging opportunities for independent learning. In a project to investigate personalised learning, Rudduck et al. (2006) identified two strategies that were preferred by pupils, namely, oral praise and feedback, both of which provided immediate support and helped clarify misunderstandings. Task 5.3.4 asks you to consider how you might develop independent learners.

Unit 5.5 provides further advice on personalising learning.

 Task 5.3.4   Developing independent learners

Consider the following advice from what was the Qualifications and Curriculum Agency in England (viewed 3 July 2018, from www.qca.org.uk/14-19/6th-form-schools/index_s3-3-learning-teaching. htm):

■ When you set and clarify learning objectives, expectations and boundaries, how do you share these with pupils? Do you instruct or allow pupils to construct their own understanding?

■ How do you help pupils to acquire knowledge, skills and understanding? Do you tell them or do you ask them open-ended questions? Do you accept different answers as being of equal value?

■ How structured are the opportunities you provide for pupils to demonstrate, practise and apply what they have learned? Who decides the format for demonstrating learning?

■ How do you support pupils in becoming independent? Is it by helping them to reflect and build on their existing learning through open-ended questions or allowing trial and error? Alternatively, do you have a 'this is how to do it' approach?

The questions above are open ended. They do not all have hard and fast answers. If your answers are of the 'usually I would but sometimes...' or 'when I started I would but now I...', then you are beginning to adjust your style in response to your experience and to develop as a teacher.

You are beginning to widen your repertoire and developing *mobility ability* in order to develop independent learners. Record your observations in your PDP.

Pedagogy and teaching styles

Student teachers sometimes talk about 'teaching styles' and pedagogy' as if they are the same thing. We suggest that 'pedagogy' needs to be understood as something far wider than merely the acts of teaching and the styles that teachers employ. We feel that teaching is an act that is deeply embedded in cultural norms and, as such, is saturated with the values and customs of particular communities:

> Pedagogy is the act of teaching together with its attendant discourse. It is what one needs to know, and the skills one needs to command, in order to make and justify the many kinds of decisions of which teaching is constituted.
>
> (Alexander 2004, p. 11)

In this way we argue that teaching is never 'innocent'. By that we mean that when a teacher is teaching a class, pupils are 'making sense' not only of the explicit content of the lesson but also the teacher themselves and the teaching styles that they use. Salmon (1988) describes how pupils inevitably get an impression of their teacher not only from what they do but the *way* that they do it. Now complete Task 5.3.5.

 Task 5.3.5   Memorable teachers

Ask anyone about their most significant experiences in learning and they will almost certainly start talking about the people who taught them. That awkward, memorable, young man whose own ardent passion for mathematics created from a dry-as-dust subject a distinctive, fascinating world. The woman English teacher, who with her undaunted faith in you, finally allowed you to break through your writing block.

Salmon (1988)

When you think about memorable teachers who taught you:

- Whom do you remember?
- What do you remember?
- What activities did they employ with you?
- How would you describe their style?

Record your responses in your PDP.

There will no doubt be times when you feel pressure to inhabit a teacher identity that you feel uncomfortable with or to employ teaching styles that may not feel right to you. However, by developing a deep understanding of the potential of different teaching styles, the uses and limitations of such teaching styles and the constructive alignment needed between learning, teaching style and assessment, you will develop as a skilful, responsive teacher.

The 'hidden curriculum'

In Unit 5.1 you were introduced to the idea that we can use theory to explain how children learn. If we adopt a constructivist theory of learning it can be seen that no matter what teaching styles the teacher uses the pupils will make sense of classrooms and the activities, they undertake in their own way. In other words, they will 'construct' their own understandings. The way in which the teacher carries out the teaching style will convey messages about other aspects such as their enthusiasm for the subject, how much they are enjoying being with the pupils and how confident they are in their subject. It follows then that there can often be unexpected learning that is not visible to the teacher or the pupils. This is sometimes referred to as the 'hidden curriculum' (see also Unit 7.2). There are a number of ways that this can be conceptualised. For example, Jackson (1968) describes it as 'unofficial expectations of the school conveyed by implicit messages'. Martin (1976) talks in terms of 'some of the outcomes or by-products of learning…particularly those states which are learned but are not openly intended'. In this way it is important for student teachers and teachers to bear in mind that the lack of 'innocence' can result in 'hidden' learning. The hidden curriculum is the focus of Task 5.3.6.

 Task 5.3.6   Hidden curriculum

Example of 'hidden' learning

A Year 8 class are asked to write a creative poem about a memorable experience. Josh gets very excited about this and writes a long descriptive piece about the time he went to the park and helped a child retrieve their football from a tree.

The teacher sees this and their first comments are to point out transcriptional features of the text rather than authorial features (can you explain these two terms briefly – transcriptional and authorial):

■ What might be the explicit and 'hidden' messages about what the teacher values being transmitted?

Record your observations in your PDP.

It is important therefore to remember that, although you may have thought carefully about what you will teach and how you will go about it, there is always likely to be 'unexpected' or 'hidden' learning.

SUMMARY AND KEY POINTS

Although any teaching style is individual, it tends to be identifiable within a continuum of styles and associated strategies. In this unit, we have explored:

■ the nature of pedagogy and how it relates to teaching style;
■ Mosston and Ashworth's (2002) spectrum of teaching styles (in order to empower you to make informed choices in relation to teaching styles);
■ the way in which both the topic under consideration and the pupils should influence the teaching styles to be adopted;

- the fact that inevitably there will be 'noise' in the communication between the teacher and the pupils. This 'unintended' learning is called the 'hidden curriculum';
- the notion that if independent learning is to take place, teaching styles that provide pupils with optimum conditions should be employed.

Check which requirements for your ITE programme you have addressed through this unit.

Further resources

British Council/British Broadcasting Corporation Learning Styles and Teaching, viewed 20 June 2018, from https://www.teachingenglish.org.uk/teaching-teens/articles
This site has useful information about different approaches to teaching.

Geoff Barton's website: www.geoffbarton.co.uk
Geoff Barton has been an English teacher for years. His website is well worth a visit.

Jensen, E. (2009) *Super Teaching*, 4th Edition, San Diego, CA: The Brain Store.
This is an easy-to-read book that contains many ideas that help the development of teaching strategies and styles.

Joyce, B., Weil, M. and Cahoun, E. (2009) *Models of Teaching*, 8th Edition, Boston, MA: Allyn and Bacon.
The authors identify models of teaching and group them into four 'families' that represent different philosophies about how humans learn. This is a comprehensive text designed for those who wish to deepen their knowledge of teaching and learning issues.

Mosston, M. and Ashworth, S. (2002) *Teaching Physical Education*, 5th Edition. New York: Maxwell Macmillan International.

Appendix 2 lists subject associations and teacher councils and Appendix 3 provides a list of websites.

Capel, S., Leask, M. and Turner, T. (eds.) (2010) *Readings for Learning to Teach in the Secondary School: A Companion to M Level Study*, Abingdon: Routledge.
This book brings together essential readings to support you in your critical engagement with key issues raised in this textbook.

Capel, S., Lawrence, J. Leask, M. and Younie, S. (eds.) (2019) *Surviving and Thriving in the Secondary School: The NQT's Essential Companion*, Abingdon: Routledge.
This book is designed to support newly qualified teachers in the next phase of development as a teacher. However, you may find it useful as it covers aspects of teaching not included in this book which, nonetheless you experience on your ITE programme.

The subject specific books in the *Learning to Teach (Subject)* series, the *Practical (Subject) Guides*, *Debates in (Subject)* and *Mentoring (Subject) Teachers* are also very useful.

Any additional resources and an editable version of any relevant tasks/tables in this unit are available on the companion website: www.routledge.com/cw/capel

Note

'The discrepancy between a child's actual mental age and the level he reaches in solving problems with assistance indicates the zone of his proximal development' (Vygotsky, 1986, p.187). See Unit 5.1 for detail on learning theories.

5.4

Improving your teaching

An introduction to practitioner research, reflective practice and evidence-informed practice

Marilyn Leask and Tony Liversidge

Introduction

As a student teacher, you might ask yourself why there is such an emphasis placed on reflective practice and the use of evidence to underpin your professional judgement in your initial teacher education (ITE) programme (see Unit 1.1 and 8.4). The analysis of your practice is one of many activities that you are asked to do, such as lesson evaluations, lesson debriefs with tutors, critical reflection on aspects of school-based experience and taking part in lecture and seminar discussions.

Developing your professional judgement through analysing what you are doing, why you are doing it and how to do it effectively as well as systematically evaluating what you have done, particularly in terms of improving pupils' learning experiences, is a central part of your practice. This reflective practice is undertaken to ensure your teaching produces new learning. Using data from the sources above helps provide evidence for your answer to the question, 'How do you know that your lesson went well?' Observing that pupils are quiet, busy, happy or good, and look as if they are working industriously is no guarantee that the learning you have intended is taking place. Detailed advice about evaluation of your lessons is provided in Units 2.1 and 2.2.

OBJECTIVES

At the end of this unit you should be able to:

- demonstrate an understanding of the terms: practitioner research, action research, reflective practice and evidence-informed practice;
- identify different forms of evidence on which you can draw to enable you to make an informed decision concerning an aspect of practice;
- apply research strategies to evaluate and improve aspects of your teaching;
- develop your ability to reflect on practice based on evidence from research to acquire higher levels of professional knowledge and judgement.

Check the requirements of your ITE programme to see which relate to this unit.

Reflective practice and evidence-informed practice

Wright (2008) argues that developing the habit of reflecting on your work is perhaps the most significant driver of your learning to teach, and your tutors will push you on this aspect from the very start so that you will develop these good habits. However, they will recognise that you will need constructive guidance on reflective practice and they will give feedback on your teaching, suggest new strategies to try out, and encourage you to spend time and energy thinking about how to develop your teaching. The time that you spend thinking about your practice (e.g. personal reflections or reflection in discussion with your mentor or other teaching colleague after teaching a lesson or thinking about planning lessons for particular classes) will help you to develop your ability to reflect effectively. One useful way of going about this is to first focus on positive aspects of your practice, then areas for further development and then, third, think about specific targets that you want to achieve over the next period of your practice.

Casting a critical eye over what you do, including carrying out the tasks throughout this book, and sharing and discussing your 'findings' with fellow professionals, will bring new insights and new levels of understanding and enable you to refine your teaching methods, discover new approaches and compare how others have tackled similar situations. Rather than relying on your own opinions or superficial anecdotal observations, this reflective practice will allow you to gather evidence that can be examined critically. In this way, your evaluation of practice becomes more rigorous and can be regarded as being practical research into teaching with a view to enhancing the quality of learning and teaching at the same time. You become what Handscomb (2013) calls a 'teacher enquirer'.

In this unit, we introduce you to simple techniques that may help you find more systematic answers to questions about your teaching and other school activities and provide a brief introduction to practitioner research, more generally. This type of research is undertaken in many schools to support school improvement, and the approach stems from a long-standing research into how professionals can work to improve practice (Stenhouse, 1975). We also suggest that, once you gain qualified teacher status, you extend your knowledge and understanding of the tools of practitioner research. Here, as Biggam (2015) notes, the incorporation of information skills (or i-skills) plays a crucial role: you need to establish what information you need; where to get that information; how to access, retrieve and organise it; assess its relevance and worth; exploit it and communicate it to your advantage. In addition, you should aim to develop techniques for reflective thinking and reviewing evidence of effective practice as part of your continuing professional development (CPD).

Increasingly, teachers are able to access research and evidence to inform their decisions. This approach gives rise to the phrase 'evidence-informed' practice. Oversby (2012) (in quoting from Morris, 2004) offers that such practice involves the *conscientious, explicit and judicious use of current best evidence in making decisions about the learning and learning experience offered to students*. It is no coincidence that recent governmental championing of evidence-based teaching has recognised the importance of teachers taking an evidence-informed approach and that there needs to be a strong evidence base to build arguments about effective practice.

We use the term 'evidence-informed' rather than 'evidence-based' as educational contexts and pupils backgrounds vary, so we define *evidence-informed practice as coming from the exercise of your professional judgement in the light of evidence from a range of sources*.

You may at some point find that you have the opportunity to join teacher–researcher networks, which have the goal of building the evidence base for practice. Schools may be part of networks, and you may be part of a subject specialist network. There are networks on LinkedIn, groups on Facebook and one such set of professional networks is developing through the MESH (Mapping Educational Specialist KnowHow) Initiative, an educational charity which aims to provide a sustainable system using resources already in the education system to generate, quality assure and update evidence-based summaries written for educators (www.meshguides.org).

Processes of reflective practice and practitioner research

Schön (1983) used the phrase 'reflective practitioners' to explain how enlightened professionals work in modern society. Within his description, he distinguished between 'reflection *in* action' and 'reflection *on* action'. Reflection in action involves reflecting on an incident whilst it can still benefit the situation and can be a particularly useful tool for a teacher who might have to react to a classroom event at the time it occurs. Alternatively, reflection on action involves reflecting on how practice can be developed after the event using our knowledge of previous similar events, and how our actions might have contributed to the successful outcome (or otherwise).

Further, Dewey (1933) introduced the notion of 'reflective thinking'. These concepts signify how professionals, such as teachers, are able to analyse the effectiveness of their actions and to develop different ways of working as a result. Thus, professionals are constantly learning about what they do and so improve their practice. Drawing upon the concepts advanced by Schön and Dewey, in addition to those proposed by Stenhouse (1975; 1983) of the 'teacher as researcher' and Hoyle and John's (1995) distinctions between 'extended and restricted' professionals, Zwozdiak-Myers (2009) identifies nine dimensions of reflective practice. You may find it helpful to keep these in mind as you work through this unit and consider how you might collect data on your own practice to provide a foundation for improvement. Figure 5.4.1 sets out these dimensions.

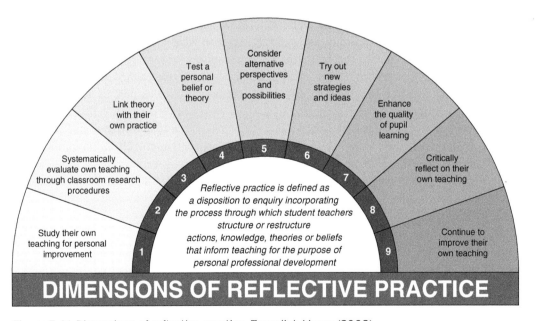

Figure 5.4.1 Dimensions of reflective practice, Zwozdiak-Myers (2009)

However, merely thinking about what you do is not the same as researching it. A teacher researcher, whilst also being a reflective practitioner, adds to this by using research techniques to enhance and systematise that reflection to justify their actions and, thus, to improve their practice and continue to develop professionally. Such investigation into their own practice by professionals themselves has come to be known as 'action research'. 'practitioner research', 'teacher enquiry' or, more recently, 'lesson study'. The last is a form of professional learning that is centred on the classroom, is designed to change practice and is a collaborative endeavour (a type of action research in effect).

In practitioner and action research, the aim is to look at some aspect of your own or the school's practice that is giving rise to some concern, identify the precise nature of the problem, collect some data concerning the problem and then devise a solution. In this respect, McNiff and Whitehead note that:

> Action research involves learning in and through action and reflection...Because action research is always to do with learning and learning is to do with education and growth, many people regard it as a form of educational research.
>
> (McNiff and Whitehead, 2002, p.15)

For a beginning practitioner researcher, a more 'manageable' type of action research might be that termed by Cain et al. (2007) as 'literature-informed, one-turn action research', where 'literature-informed' indicates the guiding role played by relevant literature and where 'one-turn' indicates one turn of the planning, acting, observing and reflecting cycle is sufficient to effect significant improvement in practice.

The additional aspects of true action research are that the devised solution is then implemented and evaluated, which may then lead a series of cycles of research and to further reflection on the problem, additional data collection and another solution being devised, implemented and evaluated. It is the link between action and research that Hopkins (2008) suggests has a powerful appeal for teachers, and in this 'living theory' action research methodology (McNiff and Whitehead, 2009), which is something of an on-going, formative, proactive and evolutionary process, the teacher can be 'at the heart of the action and at the heart of the research' (McDonagh, et al., 2012, p.112).

In theory, an action research cycle may be repeated a number of times before suitable solutions are found. Thus, evaluation, reflective teaching and practitioner (action) research are closely bound together, sharing a similar concept of cyclical or spiral development, often going through several iterations (see the action research models of Kemmis and McTaggart, 1988, p.14; Elliott, 1991, p.71).

In addition, Menter et al. (2010) note that practitioner research can be collaborative and involve a group of teacher researchers working together, investigating the practice of others as well as their own across a school or college or other educational setting, scaling up small scale research. They also add that this research is often classroom-based, but could include activities in staff rooms, or enquiries with parents or other community members, or indeed to look into the practice of education policy-making, perhaps in local authorities or in government departments, and, hence, the outcomes might be shared with other practitioners beyond the individual researcher or collaborative group. For example, teachers researching into an issue that they have noticed, such as pupil achievement in a particular subject or the school monitoring process, may have identified areas such as pupil behaviour at lunchtime, truancy or pupil preparation for assessment at Key Stage 3 (KS3) as being in need of investigation.

Table 5.4.1 outlines points to consider in planning a practitioner research project. Schools have access to benchmarking data and pupil data, which can provide a useful foundation for researching the impact of different forms of teaching on different types of pupils e.g. data from the Centre for Evaluation and Management (Durham University) pupil tests (ALIS and YELLIS, MidYS, SOSCA as described on http://www.cemcentre.org/) or the GL Assessment Cognitive Abilities Tests (previously called National Foundation for Educational Research (NFER) CATS tests).

Before embarking on practitioner research, you, along with other colleagues involved, need to have thought through and discussed the purpose of the enquiry. This enables you to construct a plan that identifies what is going to be investigated, what questions you want to try and answer, how the research will be carried out and what will be the expected outcomes in terms of data and analysis. These factors can then be put in a time frame that offers targets to work towards. Whilst it is important to have a clear plan, as a researcher you must be prepared to adapt and change according to altering circumstances. In this way, planning and conducting classroom research mirrors the teaching process itself. The research encompasses some of the methods you have already been using, such as observation, keeping a diary, obtaining the perspective of different interested parties (pupils, staff, parents) by the use of interview and questionnaire, and examining documents (Patterson, 2016). Table 5.4.1 provides you with guidance for planning a practitioner research project. Evaluating evidence from practice and research is a professional skill. Task 5.4.1 is designed to give you practice in this.

Table 5.4.1 Planning a practitioner research project

Research Focus
You need to be clear about the focus of the research. It is a useful exercise to write a paragraph at the outset explaining what is going to be investigated and why this is worth doing. When the focus is decided, a number of research questions need to be devised in order to identify precisely what it is you wish to find out. These are the central questions of the research and are important as they provide you with a clear trail to follow.
Data Sources
It is important to consider current research findings and what has already been written about your focus. (Many schools have links with universities and so can access university libraries, increasingly there are open online resources – see the websites at the end of this unit as well as the further reading. Alternatively, local libraries can usually order in articles and books from the national libraries.) This will add to your professional knowledge and inform your research. You then need to decide what data you need to collect and where that data might be held. The most likely sources of data for teacher researchers include pupils, teachers from the same or different schools, parents, other adults working with pupils, documents such as pupil reports, school records and written policies, inspection reports, government or similar publications. Please make yourself aware of the ethical guidelines governing educational research (see Patterson, 2016 and BERA, 2018).
Research Methods
After identifying the sources, you can now decide upon appropriate methods of data collection. Designing the 'tools' to gather information may at first seem daunting but this should not be the case. In your teaching you are continually using data collection skills through questioning pupils, scanning your classroom, marking pupils' work and analysing curriculum documents. Carrying out practitioner research enables you to use and further develop these skills. Basic tools for collecting data are through interviews, questionnaires, observation and through analysis of documents.

Table 5.4.1 continued

Timeline

Now that you have a clear research focus and research questions, the sources of data have been identified and the methods have been decided upon, you can develop a timeline for the collection and analysis of data. A clear plan helps ensure that nothing important has been missed out and gives you more control over the process by fitting the research into your existing work commitments. It is particularly important to have a clear timeline when evaluating initiatives where data has to be collected at specific points. For instance, the evaluation of a curriculum initiative on the teaching of a history module, using drama techniques, to a Year 7 class, would have to be carefully planned beforehand as data could only be collected during the teaching and immediately after.

 Task 5.4.1   Evaluating research and evidence

You need to understand data collection methods not just so that you can conduct research yourself but also to evaluate evidence from other larger-scale research projects that may be used to make informed judgements on your own practice. In this way teaching becomes an evidence-based profession.

Choose a research article from an education research journal, the *Online Educational Resources Journal* or the Education Resource Information Center (ERIC) or a systematic review from the Evidence for Policy and Practice Information Centre (EPPI) on an area of teaching that particularly interests you. How were the data in the article collected? What are the key findings and do they add to your knowledge or understanding in any way?

Record your reflections in your professional development portfolio (PDP) or equivalent.

Research techniques for use in the classroom

Methods of collecting data used often are interviews (group or one-to-one), questionnaires, observations, diaries and analysis of documents (the texts in the further resources provide more detail). When used, these methods need to be carefully designed to ensure the information you want is obtained while also considering the feelings of those from whom it is being collected.

Ethical issues

An ethical approach is a key aspect of any educational research. Teachers and other professionals working in classrooms have a duty of care for their pupils and colleagues. Within this professional way of working, there is a need to respect others and share information as appropriate yet also maintain trust and individual confidentiality.

You must be open about the purposes of your research and obtain agreement from those who are in a position to give it; your tutor may advise you to get the permission of the headteacher and others involved. You should consider the role of the pupils in your research and how much to involve them. Pupils are invariably as interested as teachers in educational improvements and the positive developments in school life that can result from such research. You need to take your responsibility in the area of ethics seriously. It is worth consulting the British Educational Research Association ethical guidelines (http://www.bera.ac.uk) for a more detailed consideration of ethical issues. Table 5.4.2 outlines the key areas to consider.

Table 5.4.2 An ethical approach to practitioner research

You must take responsibility for the ethical use of any data collected and for maintaining confidentiality. Before starting, check the ethical requirements at your university and/or school, we suggest that you should as a matter of course:

1 Ask a senior member of staff as well as teachers directly involved with your classes for permission to carry out your project. Get ethics approval from your ITE provider. They will have a formal process for this.
2 Before you start, provide staff involved with a copy of the outline of your project which should include:

    a. The area you are investigating.
    b. How you are going to collect any evidence.
    c. Who you are going to collect evidence from.
    d. What you intend to do with the data collected e.g. whether it is confidential and whether it will be written up anonymously or not.
    e. Who the audience for your report will be.
    f. Any other factors relevant to the particular situation.

3 Consider if you need to ask for pupil and/or parental consent.

4 Think about how you want the pupils to be involved in the research.

5 Check whether staff expect to be given a copy of your work.

6 If you store data electronically, then you should check that you conform to the requirements of the Data Protection Act. For example, you should not store personal data on computers without the explicit authorisation of the individual.

Interviewing

Interviews can take many forms depending upon whom you are interviewing, where the interview is being held and what the focus is. Different types of interview are a normal part of a school day and teachers can become very skilled at gathering information from pupils by such methods. Consider, for instance, how you might 'interview' a pupil about an incident on the corridor between lessons, or a pupil who is finding work in a particular subject difficult. These are both instances where you employ your professional judgement and skills to find out what has been going on and what the issues are. You are then in a position to act appropriately. Teachers are also used to 'interviewing' or talking with parents when working together to aid the progress of their children. It is also helpful to ask small groups of pupils about particular issues in what can be termed 'focus group interviews'.

When conducting interviews as part of practitioner research, it is important to consider beforehand what questions need to be asked, how they will be asked and how the data will be recorded. You may wish to record them; however, it may be easier to make brief notes under key headings during or immediately after the interviews.

Questionnaires

A questionnaire is useful for surveying pupil, teacher or parental views. Questionnaires can enable the collection of information from a large number of people comparatively quickly and anonymously, if appropriate. Here you might want to consider the use of an online survey tool such as Survey Monkey or Bristol Online Surveys (BOS), which can also do some analysis of the data for you. In a questionnaire, the wording and layout of the questions is very significant. They need to be framed so that those being asked, Year 7 pupils, for instance, can understand and answer appropriately. How the completed questionnaires are collected in also needs to be considered. If they are given to whole groups of pupils, it is possible to explain the purpose of the questionnaire, read out the questions and then collect them all in at the end of a lesson. Always test out the questions with a small group to check the questions are understood and that the answers are likely to be relevant to the topics being researched.

Observation schedules

An observation schedule provides a structured framework for recording classroom behaviours. Observations should be carefully planned so as to cause the least disruption to the lesson. Unit 2.1 provides information about observation schedules, as does Unit 5.3. You should by now have used forms of observation schedules to observe classroom routines. It is not possible to record everything that happens in a classroom, so you need to focus on, for example, a particular group or pupil or aspect of the teacher's work and record behaviour over time. It is important that you devise your own observation schedules to suit your particular purpose. Video recordings provide an additional way of recording data about classroom activities.

Paired observation

This is a streamlined procedure that enables you to obtain feedback on aspects of your work that are difficult for you to monitor. The example in Unit 5.3, of two student teachers working together with one providing feedback on the topic chosen by the other, is an example of paired observation in practice. Paired observation works in the following way: Two colleagues pair up with the purpose of observing one lesson each and then giving feedback about particular aspects of the lesson or the teaching of the person observed. The person giving the lesson decides the focus of the observation. The three stages of a paired observation are:

Step 1: You both agree the focus of the observation and what notes, if any, are to be made;
Step 2: You each observe one lesson given by the other. Your observations and notes are restricted to the area requested;
Step 3: You give each other feedback on the issue under consideration.

The cycle can be repeated as often as you wish.

Research diaries and other documents

Diaries can provide valuable data and useful records over a period of time. The researcher and also those involved in the research, such as pupils or teaching colleagues, could keep them. They can be designed in different ways, for instance, a decision may be made to write under specific headings giving short, relevant pieces of information such as the subjects that give homework each night, the particular tasks set and the length of time spent on each. Alternatively, the diarists could be allowed to express themselves more freely, for example explaining how they feel each day's lessons have gone and the reasons why they think this. The structure chosen depends upon the nature of the research project and is a decision to be made by the researcher often in conjunction with the participants. All sorts of documents can provide useful information to the practitioner researcher, e.g. government, local authority (LA) and school policies, pupil work and curriculum documents. In addition, analysis of pupil work, asking pupils to write about or draw images of a topic/issue being researched, biographical accounts written by participants, all provide useful insights into life in school and the learning that is taking place.

You need to be aware that there are, in fact, many ways of collecting information and it is important to be creative as well as adaptable in considering data collection. For instance, the use of social media, such as Facebook, Twitter, LinkedIn, blogs, crowdsourcing and open community research sites, can be a source of data or information and enable you to network with other researchers (Bell and Waters, 2014), but again, be aware of ethical issues. In addition, YouTube has a huge number of videos about aspects of research that are accessible and informative for teacher researchers. Note that some of the texts and web sources in the recommended reading give more detailed advice on how to design and use the methods mentioned above.

Task 5.4.2 is designed to give you practice in planning the kind of research project that student teachers are likely to undertake.

 Task 5.4.2 Planning your research project

Your ITE programme will normally include a small research project as an assignment. Check your programme requirements with your tutor. The process is as follows:

- identify an issue or problem associated with your teaching for further investigation (e.g. challenging the more able pupils or the development of active learning techniques);
- outline the focus of the research and explain why this is an important area for you to investigate;
- write a number of key research questions (about three) that identify what you need to find out;
- undertake a literature review to check what has been done before (use the websites at the end);
- list the likely sources of data;
- identify methods to collect the data;
- if they are available, have a look at some of the projects that have been done previously by people on your programme.

We suggest you discuss your findings with your tutor and other student teachers. Store your findings in your PDP.

Analysing evidence about teaching and learning

As a practitioner-researcher you need to develop a strategy for data collection that is most appropriate for the chosen research focus. This strategy often involves the use of both quantitative and qualitative data. Decisions that you make have implications for the type of data analysis that will be appropriate for you to use. However, whatever types you use, the onus will be on you to present your analysis in a way that can be understood, so that, for instance, patterns can be more easily identified.

The evidence available for drawing conclusions about teaching and learning can take different forms. This evidence includes:

Quantitative data in numerical form that can be collected from a range of sources, e.g. statistical returns, questionnaires and school management information systems. League tables of school performance are a good example of how quantitative data can be presented and used. This type of data is useful for measurement and comparison on a large scale but often lacks explanation for individual differences and can feel very impersonal.

Qualitative data, which are more descriptive and often include detailed personal explanations. These data are 'richer' and give a feel for particular cases but are sometimes harder to analyse and do not lend themselves easily to measurement. Such data are collected through observation, interview, analysis of documents, diaries, video, photographs, discussions and focus group brainstorming.

For instance, if you were investigating a problem of pupil truancy at your school, you would be likely to require quantitative data showing the extent of truancy and any relationship this has to factors such as age, gender, pupil performance, the time of day or particular lessons. You may also want qualitative data that gives a more in-depth and personal explanation of truancy from the perspectives of truants, their teachers and parents. Using both types of data helps to give a fuller understanding of the issues.

Task 5.4.3 is designed to give you an overview of the performance data available in your school.

 Task 5.4.3   Reviewing performance data at your school

Schools have information systems that provide data showing how pupils are performing. Subject departments collect such data as part of the annual reviewing process and to inform future development plans. Find out about the different types of evidence and the process used in your school to evaluate the effectiveness of teaching, pupil's learning and the monitoring of individual pupil progress. Consider how this data informs the setting of future targets for pupils, teachers, subject departments and the school. Store your findings in your PDP.

As part of any previous school experience, you may have been set assignments that involved the collection of a range of information to support your analysis. These tasks will have started with a clear focus or a question to answer, such as what routines does the teacher use in managing the work of the class. You may have collected evidence from various literature sources to help you to answer that question initially. In addition, you may have observed and made notes about what the pupils and the teacher actually did during a variety of lessons; you may have looked at the pupils' work and the teacher's lesson plans; you may have cross-checked your perceptions with those of the teacher as a way of eliminating bias, improving accuracy and identifying alternative explanations. In doing such assignments, you have been involved in basic classroom research. In such research, data are gathered from different sources, checked for alternative perceptions/ explanations, as exemplified in the fifth dimension of Zwozdiak-Myers' (2008) model of reflective practice, and conclusions are drawn from this information so as to develop teaching in the future. This process, whereby you approach the topic of the research from as many different angles and perspectives as possible, gathering a wide range of data in order to gain a greater understanding, is called triangulation. Miles and Huberman (1994) have suggested that the constant checking and double-checking involved means that triangulation becomes a way of life in such research. Burton et al. (2008) provide a more detailed discussion of how to improve the validity of your research project in this way.

In conclusion, the aspects that will enable you to produce an effective and reflective research assignment (which on PGCE programmes will be marked using postgraduate level 7 criteria) will be the relevance of your writing to the topic chosen and an appropriate methodology and method(s) that enable you to answer your research question(s). The key to this is to demonstrate your critical understanding of, reflection on, and analysis of, the literature that you have sourced in relation to your own results and findings. In addition, you should have a clear structure for the work that is written in a good academic style and is correctly referenced in both the text and the bibliography.

SUMMARY AND KEY POINTS

In this unit, we have provided simply a brief introduction into an important area of professional practice and accountability.

- Evidence-informed practice = professional judgement + evidence. Critical reflection aided by practitioner research, by individuals or by teams, provides the means by which the quality of teaching and learning in the classroom can be evaluated as a prelude to improvement.
- Developing your teaching skills is one important aspect of your professional development. But other important attributes of the effective teacher that we stress in this book are developing the quality and extent of your professional knowledge and judgement through reflective practice.
- Building your professional knowledge and judgement are longer-term goals, which are developed through reflection and further professional development.
- In this unit, we have opened a door on information and strategies that you can use to reflect on the quality of your teaching.
- We suggest that you come back to this work during the year and again later in your career because increasingly as a professional you can expect to be asked to provide evidence to underpin your approach to education. The application of practitioner research to your work at that later stage opens your eyes to factors influencing your teaching and learning that you may not have known existed.
- You should now have ideas about practitioner research and how to evaluate the quality of your teaching through using a continuous cycle of critical reflection so that you can plan improvement based on evidence. If you intend to develop your research skills, then we suggest that you join relevant communities of practice through a professional association or school network, read texts and materials on the websites referenced below and in Appendix 3, and consult with experienced colleagues.

Check which requirements for your ITE programme you have addressed through this unit.

 Further resources

Bell, J. and Waters, S. (2014) *Doing Your Research Project: A Guide for First-Time Researchers*, **6th Edition, Maidenhead: Open University Press.**
This is an excellent text that gives step-by-step advice.

British Educational Research Association http://www.bera.ac.uk
Professional association for educational researchers.

Costello, P.J.M. (2011) *Effective Action Research. Developing Reflective Thinking and Practice*, **London: Continuum.**
This title provides clear and accessible advice.

Education Endowment Foundation toolkits

https://educationendowmentfoundation.org.uk

ERIC (the Education Resources Information Center) http://www.eric.ed.gov/ERICWebPortal/resources/html/about/about_eric.html
This is the US government-sponsored online digital library for education.

Evidence for Policy and Practice Information Centre http://www.eppi.ioe.ac.uk
This has a list of systematic reviews of practice in education.

Hopkins, D. (2014) *A Teacher's Guide to Classroom Research*, **5th Edition, Maidenhead: Open University Press.**
This provides very useful guidance for new researchers.
Patterson, E.W. (2016a) Research Methods 1: Doing a literature review: How to find and make sense of published research; (2016b) Research Methods 2: Developing your research design; (2016f) Research Methods 3: Considering ethics in your research, available at www.MESHGuides.org
These MESHGuides are written specifically for teachers interested in research.

Schon, D. (1983) *The Reflective Practitioner: How Professionals Think in Action*, **London: Temple Smith.**

Wilson, E. (2009) *School-Based Research: A Guide for Education Students*, **London, Sage.**
Has ideas on how to research issues such as ability grouping, pupil behaviour, teaching approaches and pupil motivation.

Appendix 2 lists subject associations and teacher councils and Appendix 3 provides a list of websites.

Capel, S., Leask, M. and Turner, T. (eds.) (2010) *Readings for Learning to Teach in the Secondary School: A Companion to M Level Study*, **Abingdon: Routledge.**
This book brings together essential readings to support you in your critical engagement with key issues raised in this textbook.

Capel, S., Lawrence, J. Leask, M. and Younie, S. (eds.) (2019) *Surviving and Thriving in the Secondary School: The NQT's Essential Companion,* **Abingdon: Routledge.**
This book is designed to support newly qualified teachers in the next phase of development as a teacher. However, you may find it useful as it covers aspects of teaching not included in this book which, nonetheless you experience on your ITE programme.

The subject specific books in the *Learning to Teach (Subject)* series, the *Practical (Subject) Guides*, *Debates in (Subject)* and *Mentoring (Subject) Teachers* are also very useful.

> **Any additional resources and an editable version of any relevant tasks/tables in this unit are available on the companion website: www.routledge.com/cw/capel**

Acknowledgements

Research underpinning the advice in this unit stems from a number of research and development projects funded by the Local Government Association, Becta, the European Union, the Manpower Services Commission, the Department for Education/Department for Education and Skills (DFE/DFES) and what was the Training and Development Agency for schools (TDA) over a 25-year period. Further information on these initiatives is provided in the following:

Leask, M. and Younie, S. (2014) 'National models for CPD: the challenges of twenty-first century knowledge management', Special Edition, *Journal for Professional Development in Education (PDiE)*, Vol. 39, No. 2, pp 273-287. doi:10.1080/19415257.2012.749801.

Leask, M. (2011) Improving the Professional Knowledge Base for Education: Using Knowledge Management and Web 2.0 tools. *Policy Futures in Education*, 9(5), pp. 644-660 http://dx.doi.org/10.2304/pfie.2011.9.5.644

Leask, M. (1988) 'Teachers as evaluators: a grounded approach to project evaluation', This work researched reliability and validity of the Teacher Evaluator approach building on Lawrence Stenhouse's seminal work. MPhil thesis, University of Cambridge library also available on http://library.beds.ac.uk/record=b1468955~S20

5.5 Closing the achievement gap

Self-regulation and personalising learning

Carrie Winstanley

Introduction

Successive English governments have focused particularly on closing the achievement gap through different approaches to school improvement, general education policy and social initiatives. Early secondary school education has been identified as a key stage for the introduction of 'intensive catch-up programmes' to address problems persisting from early years and primary school contexts (Wellings and Wood, 2012, p.7:D.2). Units in Chapter 7 consider issues around social initiatives and education policy. This unit is concerned more with pedagogic practices that can help in the struggle to raise achievement through matching learning tasks to pupils' strengths and supporting them effectively where necessary. Primarily the unit focuses on personalising tasks and feedback, and on helping pupils to improve how they understand their own learning through self-regulation. These pedagogic strategies are effective for all kinds of pupils, not only for groups of pupils who persistently tend to have low attainment, including, but not limited to, pupils with English as an Additional Language (EAL), pupils eligible for Free School Meals (FSM), those with Special Educational Needs and Disability, and Looked After Children (LAC). For these particular target groups, specific Catch-up Pupil Premium projects are used, generally targeting literacy and numeracy. See DfE (2017b) for details and also the Education Endowment Foundation (EEF) for a number of evaluations of these projects. Whilst these are effective (usually more so if implemented early on, in Year 7 for pupils who have not reached KS2 standards), personalising and self-regulation approaches are more general pedagogic techniques that benefit all pupils through providing positive and generalisable work habits.

Personalised learning occurs when learning is tailored to individual needs, interests and aptitudes. The aim is to ensure that each pupil achieves the highest standards possible for their abilities, regardless of their background and circumstances. A further emphasis is on equipping pupils for more autonomy in their learning, which is considered vital to cope in the rapidly changing world of work. Closely related to this is the notion of self-regulated learning; pupils can be helped to learn about how they learn and to control and improve their learning.

This unit first explains the concepts of personalising learning. It then places these ideas in a classroom context. The next section discusses self-regulation, with a focus on helping pupils become independent learners. All of the concepts in this unit are linked to aspects of good practice in learning and teaching, such as the importance of knowing pupils' interests, motivations, strengths and problems. The role of the teacher in ensuring consistent best practice, meeting pupils' needs and facilitating acceptable levels of achievement is therefore very important.

OBJECTIVES

At the end of this unit you should be able to:

■ show awareness of the issues surrounding the aim of closing the achievement gap;
■ understand what is meant by self-regulated learning and by personalising learning;
■ recognise instances of good practice in self-regulation and in personalising learning;
■ be better equipped to support pupils developing self-regulation and to embed personalising learning in your own teaching.

Check the requirements of your initial teacher education (ITE) programme to see which relate to this unit.

Closing the achievement gap

Raising achievement is a vital part of education and so the means and commitment required to close the gap extend beyond the teacher in the classroom. Through effective systems and organisation, school structures need to help with the development of a supportive ethos. A positive school culture promotes teachers and school leaders with high aspirations for all pupils and facilitates significant levels of engagement. This in turn helps to maximise achievement for all. In England, the Catch-up Pupil Premium is a funding allocation to support pupils who need additional support when entering Year 7, and schools are able to use this in ways that meet their pupils' needs. As well as transition visits and collaboration with feeder primary schools and other settings, common uses of funding include small-group teaching, progress coaching, breakfast clubs, literacy and mathematics support and increased staffing for support and progress tracking (see various projects as reported by the EEF, 2012-2016). Schools are required to publish their pupils' premium strategy on their website and so you can easily access this information, which should help you see the approach and priorities of any school.

Schools do not operate in a vacuum. It is incumbent on Local Authorities (LAs) and government agencies to provide a supportive and flexible environment to help schools achieve their learning aims. Similarly, pupils' parents and carers should be encouraged to develop active partnerships with schools in order to help them understand, value and contribute to their children's education. By involving families and communities with their pupils' education, the high aspirations and support are not restricted to the hours in a day when the child is in school. Since the first priority for you as you learn to teach is how to manage general classroom learning, however, this unit focuses on personalising learning in practice and on self-regulation. A range of teaching and learning techniques and strategies that will help close the achievement gap if harnessed effectively are introduced, including many that are part of personalised learning and self-regulation such as meta-cognitive strategies and subject-specific ideas and ways of fostering positive attitudes to learning. The English Department for Education (DFE, 2017b) suggest some '[g]eneric strategies which are beneficial for low attainers' but many of these are generally good practice for all pupils and as such they overlap with the ideas in this unit:

> Early intervention; monitoring of pupils' progress; tailoring teaching to the appropriate needs of individual pupils; coaching teachers/teaching assistants in specific teaching strategies such as cooperative learning; cognitive approaches, based on mental processes; one-to-one tuition; peer-to-peer support; aspects of the home-school relationship; and study support.
>
> (DfE, 2017b, p.6)

Task 5.5.1 asks you to reflect on issues around closing the achievement gap for your pupils.

 Task 5.5.1   Considering the Catch-up Pupil Premium

Find two or three schools in contrasting settings and review the information published on their websites about their Catch-up strategies. Try and find schools that have used the DfE-recommended Teaching Schools Council template since the information is very comprehensive (https://www.tscouncil.org.uk/resources/guide-to-effective-pupil-premium-review/). Cross-reference the schools' strategies with evidence-based recommendations from the EEF, DfE or other research papers. Consider to what extent the schools' ideas have empirical support and how the school seems to be focused on the specific needs of its pupils' demographic. Record your responses in your professional development portfolio (PDP) or equivalent and discuss with other student teachers.

Task 5.5.2 asks you to put together and then compare resources to support personalising learning in your classroom with those of other student teachers. Collegial support and collaborative working are important features of teaching where the goal is for every pupil to succeed.

 Task 5.5.2   Resources to support closing the achievement gap

If you are learning to teach in Northern Ireland, Scotland or Wales, there are considerable resources available online to support the curriculum and teaching in each country. We suggest that you become familiar with the specific resources developed by the department for education in your country. The links below provide a starting point.

Department for Education Northern Ireland: raising standards and school improvement: http://www.deni.gov.uk/index/curriculum-and-learningt-new/standards-and-school-improvements.htm

Education Scotland: http://www.educationsscotland.gov.uk/

Learning Wales: raising standards together http://learning.gov.wales/?skip=1&lang=en

The Education Endowment Foundation: https://educationendowmentfoundation.org.uk/ has been funded by the UK government specifically to support closing the gap in attainment. Research-informed Toolkits for many areas of education are available.

Also ensure that you are familiar with the pupil progress tracking tools used in your placement school. Compare what you have found with other student teachers.

Record your findings and responses in your PDP.

Raising achievement for all pupils through self-regulation and personalised learning

When researching theory and ideas about how to support pupils' achievement, it is worth searching for the terms 'underachievement' and 'underachiever'. These terms, now replaced by 'raising achievement', are less frequently used in current literature. This shift towards positive reframing is helpful, but you may still find some very relevant and interesting research that has been published under the auspices of 'underachievement'.

The concept of 'achievement' is less straightforward than it might first appear. Of course, we can measure it through examination and test results, but, taken out of context, these results do not give us the whole picture of a child's development and learning. Remember that achievement and ability can be easily confused; see Dweck's work for a contemporary take on how we think about ability. Different types of underachievement can be identified, and for some interesting work on various typologies of underachieving pupils see Wallace et al. (2009). It is worth considering the characteristics of high and low achievers when thinking about how to improve performance in all pupils. As you review these in Table 5.5.1, consider which characteristics could be described as 'self-regulation'.

Table 5.5.1 Characteristics of high and low achievers

Characteristics of low achieving pupils	*Characteristics of high achieving pupils*
Rarely monitor their performance	Continually self-monitor
Stick to the same strategies	Adapt their strategies to contexts and tasks
Vague learning goals	Set specific learning goals
Tend to have static learning goals	Willing to adapt their learning goals
Have a narrow range of learning strategies	Use a wide range of learning strategies
Focus on performance goals (comparing with others)	Mastery goals (focusing on self-improvement)
Give up readily in the face of failure	Demonstrate persistence in the face of failure

Self-regulated learning

Self-regulated learning, also called 'self-regulation', refers to the use of strategies and techniques that helps pupils to reflect actively on their attitudes and to adapt behaviours to improve the achievement of suitable goals to improve learning. Pupils need to be taught techniques and strategies for self-regulation that work for them; it is an individualised process. It requires careful consideration of activities and behaviours in which pupils evaluate what they have done and how well they achieved their goals. Through repeatedly asking themselves if the strategy they have used really works well for them, they can try to reduce negative behaviours and increase the use of positive behaviours. Through this active process of reflection, pupils learn to take more responsibility for their own learning and focus on improving and developing their own performance and learning.

Zimmerman (2002) describes self-regulation as a self-directive process. Learning becomes a proactive pursuit that pupils do for themselves. Zimmerman and Schunk (1989) identify three aspects of learning that pupils can be taught to self-regulate in order to improve performance:

- behaviour – actively controlling resources for study (such as time, place of study and use of staff and peer support);
- motivation and affect – controlling feelings about work (such as reducing anxiety) and setting reasonable goals;
- cognitive strategies – aiming for deep learning by using effective processing strategies.

Among other researchers, Bjork et al. reviewed the value of self-regulation, concluding that, despite the increased recognition that the skills are important, 'research on learning, memory, and metacognitive processes has provided evidence that people often have a faulty mental model of how they learn and remember' (2013, p.417). This reinforces the need for teachers to guide pupils in their reflective strategies. In addition to not carefully scrutinising how they learn, pupils are prone to lapse into making assumptions that can be counter-productive, such as 'over-attributing differences in performance to innate ability' and 'assuming that learning should be easy' (p.436). This links closely to the notion of a flexible, growth mindset (Dweck, 2012) in which pupils believe that their effort can reap rewards, and that success is achievable as a result of hard work.

Now complete Task 5.5.3, which serves as your own self-regulation activity as well as one you can use with pupils.

 Task 5.5.3   Self-regulating how you study and approach homework

Study time: How long do you study for each day? Does this depend on the tasks you have been set, or do you have a fixed amount of time for working each day? How often do you take breaks and what do you do when you have a break?

Study space: Have you access to a dedicated study space? Is it always the same space? Shared? Personal? How is it laid out? Do you enjoy studying there? What would make it even more comfortable?

Personal timetables: Do you study best in the morning or evening? What other activities do you do during the week and are there days when it is better or worse for you to study? What about the weekends?

Keeping on track: What distracts you when you are supposed to be studying? How do you manage the distractions? How do you record what you have done and what is left to do? Have you made a study plan or timetable? Do you stick to it?

Planning: Are you able to accurately plan how long tasks will take? Have you tried timing yourself? How do you manage your deadlines? Do you ever find yourself working right up to a deadline? How does this make you feel? How good are you at prioritising and ordering your work?

You should complete this task individually and then come together with other student teachers to discuss your responses to the questions as well as thinking about your emotional response to the task. You may find that you were making excuses to yourself or being harsh and chastising yourself for poor work habits. Consider how this task might work with pupils and adjust the questions to meet your group's needs and interests. Consider which of the questions relate to the different areas identified by Zimmerman and Schunk (1989), i.e. behaviour, motivation and affect, and cognitive strategies.

Try some of the questions with a group of pupils in your teaching and evaluate their effectiveness. Present the findings to the rest of the group. Record the outcomes in your PDP.

Goal setting and self-regulation of tasks (see also Units 3.2, 6.1)

Goal setting is a vital aspect of self-regulation that pupils can actively be taught to develop. Teachers should support pupils to develop strategies for reviewing their own performance. Once these have been cultivated, pupils can be more involved in setting their own realistic and negotiated learning goals in collaboration with their teachers. This provides vital clarity and transparency, and making the next steps explicit helps keep pupils and teachers on target. Where pupils are progressing particularly well, there is also potential to compact curricula, allowing pupils to skip tasks that do not provide them with adequate challenge.

Self-regulation can be approached in different ways, commonly including: self-evaluation, goal-setting, completing the activity, and monitoring and evaluation.

All of these steps are best undertaken with the help of the teacher until the pupil is able to take responsibility for their own learning. So, pupils can be helped to evaluate where they are at the start of a task by thinking about how much they already know about a topic and through linking new experiences to their existing understanding. They then analyse the set task and break it down into manageable learning goals, thinking about the sequence of tasks, timing and the pace of work. The next step is to choose appropriate strategies from a wide range of strategies that have been used in previous tasks. Some teachers help by providing a list of ways to engage in active study such as:

Recording my ideas / understanding; explaining the information to another person; transferring key ideas to electronic or paper index cards; creating quiz questions for a friend to answer; translating the information into a diagram etc.

Self-regulation is more than just effective study skills, however; it requires careful and thorough self-monitoring of pupils' own performance once they have attempted the task and received feedback. Pupils benefit from explicitly noting what could be improved and reviewing their progress.

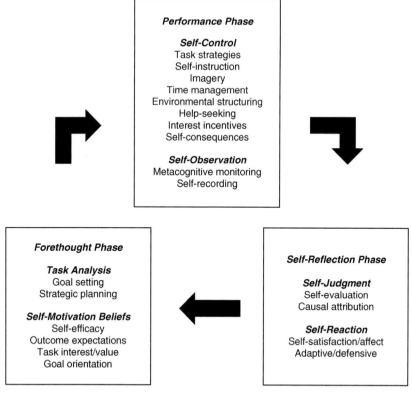

Figure 5.5.1 Panadero (2017)'s cyclical phases model of self-regulated learning

Source: adapted from Zimmerman and Moylan (2009)

Feedback

Pupils learn to develop their self-regulation through the feedback they receive. When assessing pupils' work, you should emphasise progress and achievement, rather than failure, and avoid making unhelpful comparisons between pupils. Feedback must be constructive and should nurture pupils' strategies to help them manage their work. The aim is to involve both teachers and pupils in reflection and dialogue, enabling all to have learning opportunities and ensuring that pupils are recognised for their efforts. The feedback should be about the task rather than the pupil and should be linked to attainable standards expressed clearly.

Actively helping pupils learn how to self-regulate can be done by teachers modelling reflection, through thinking aloud and encouraging pupils to practice the same processes together with the teacher and with peers. This can be done in groups, as collaborative learning. Feedback can also be used to help deepen pupils' learning as well as correcting the mechanics of presentation, writing and accuracy of information, and teachers can help pupils make links between concepts. They can be directed to relevant information and helped to focus their attention on relevant ideas and shown how to develop an analytical approach.

Sometimes it is possible to incorporate a grade for how well pupils have responded to feedback and this is known as ipsative assessment (see the Appendix for a definition). Here, teachers can provide a few points of actionable feedback and then evaluate how well the pupil has taken the suggestions on board and incorporated the improvements into the next task, or the next draft of the work. This has the advantage of directly feeding back to the pupil on their understanding and implementation of feedback, which can help them see their own development, making it easier to generalise their progress to other aspects of their work.

Teaching for self-regulation

As you will have noted, there are implications for the teacher's role in supporting pupils to develop effective self-regulation. In order to help with goal-setting, teachers can help to tease apart the components of tasks so that they can be tackled effectively. This can be done very clearly at first and then phased out as the pupils see how to break down the tasks themselves. The intention is to shift the responsibility for learning from the teacher to the pupils. Teachers should also encourage a wide range of learning strategies through allowing different responses to tasks where appropriate so that pupils can provide audio and visual answers and not be confined to writing.

The key point to remember is that pupils require direct and explicit teaching if they are to develop effective self-regulation and that these strategies have been shown to improve learning (Bjork et al., 2014). How can you manage, however, to provide direct and personally relevant teaching for a class of pupils? The rest of this unit considers how you can match your teaching to your pupils' learning.

What is meant by personalising learning?

There are no widely agreed definitions of personalised learning and so there can be some confusion about what is meant by the term, in particular as it relates closely to individualised learning. You might find slightly different interpretations in official documents and in general education publications, and even see diverse definitions in policy documents in different schools. Generally, however, both terms refer to matching learning tasks to pupils' needs wherever possible.

Individualising learning usually suggests pupils working alone, following solo agendas, essentially working in isolation. There may be several pupils working individually, yet all aiming to achieve the same intended learning outcomes, perhaps working through a planned programme at their own individual pace, but essentially completing the same tasks. This is usually led or constructed by the teacher.

Personalising learning differs as it generally incorporates whole-class work and, in particular, interactive group work with interventions for pupils who need additional support. Personalising learning means shaping teaching and learning around the different ways that pupils learn. The onus is on schools and teachers to ensure that what they provide in terms of the teaching, curriculum and school organisation is designed to reach as many pupils as possible by providing a wide range of learning experiences for diverse pupil needs across a unit of work. Thus, every pupil's learning is maximised in the context of the current curriculum; it does not mean that each pupil has a personalised curriculum.

Personalised learning is suitable for all pupils and does differ from the kind of tailored learning or personal curriculum as designed for a pupil with additional learning needs. These plans are often referred to as Individual Education Plans (IEPs), created as part of an Education and Health Care Plan (EHCP). Pupils in receipt of these plans generally have additional learning needs, having been assessed by a psychologist or other specialist. In these instances, pupils can be provided with a very detailed modified curriculum for each and every subject that goes well beyond the more straightforward personalising and individualising learning discussed here. For more details on this type of work, see Unit 4.6 on inclusion and special educational needs.

As the personalisation of learning is such a broad concept, many of these approaches are already discussed in other units; you should therefore also refer to these other units. (See for example, Units 2.3, 3.1, 4.1, 4.3, 5.3, 6.1.)

The principles and practices of personalising learning

The principles of personalising learning in the classroom are a reflection of existing good practice. Pupils' individual needs must be assessed and the curriculum and work being set should be responsive to these needs, creating an inclusive approach to teaching. Useful assessment supports learning and is linked to personal targets, making use of effective feedback primarily from teachers, but also including peer and self-assessment. Peer support should be harnessed, including the use of mentoring for learning matters as well as social and emotional concerns. Learning strategies should be directly taught and this links directly to self-regulation.

So, what should personalised learning be like in the classroom? Effective ways to personalise learning include:

■ using Assessment for Learning, i.e. focusing assessment on its value for learning rather than merely for measuring; making use of assessments and the associated data in order to plan pupils' targets;

■ preventing pupils from falling behind through early interventions; pupils taught in smaller groups to meet their needs better (accomplished by using teaching assistants and by extending the school day);

■ focusing on developing learning strategies and independent learning skills; dynamic approaches to grouping pupils; matching tasks to ability and providing appropriate challenge; negotiated and realistic targets;

■ information and communications technologies (ICT) used more often and with creative approaches; making good use of pupil-friendly virtual learning environments with off-site accessibility;

■ providing additional support for pupils when needed to facilitate achievement; a focus on safe school environments where hindrances to learning and teaching (e.g. bullying, poor behaviour) are tackled promptly and decisively; ensuring that all pupils have increased opportunities to study safely, particularly pupils from disadvantaged backgrounds (achieved through opening libraries in the evening, running supervised homework sessions etc.);

■ teachers and managers celebrating achievement and keeping expectations of pupil performance high; relaxing the timetable to increase choice and opportunities; oral praise and prompt feedback to clarify misunderstandings;

■ augmenting or replacing parents' evenings with 'pupil review days' that allow personal meetings for pupils to discuss targets and progress with teachers; shifting the way that parents and carers are involved in their child's education so that they have a more active role rather than merely receiving reports of progress or problems reorganising school staffing to create different approaches to leadership and teaching.

The benefits for pupils

Some of the main potential advantages for pupils in terms of the skills developed through more personalised and individual learning are listed below (assembled from a range of teaching and government web sources). Note the repeated emphasis on increasing independence and the account taken of pupils' emotional development. Pupils should:

■ become more independent workers, requiring less supervision as they build project management techniques;
■ develop team work skills through varied small group work;
■ learn about the importance of being a reliable, consistent team member;
■ become increasingly confident in their approach to problems, building resilience and demonstrating persistence in resolving difficulties through expanded opportunities to control their own work;
■ improve their written and oral communication skills owing to increased small group work and more contact with teachers in deeper-level conversations (rather than short answers in a class context);
■ increase the responsibility for their own actions by planning their own work, not just responding to short in-class tasks and homework;
■ respond to resources with an evaluative and critical mindset, questioning new ideas effectively;
■ become more motivated, engaged and excited by their work, encouraging creative responses and deeper learning.

   As a student teacher, your major concern is what this means you might do in the classroom. We now turn to some commonly recommended approaches closely associated with personalising learning that you can adopt in your classroom, with short explanations and some suggestions for further developments.

Classroom approaches: teaching/pedagogical strategies

Various factors in approaches to teaching and learning will impact on the personalisation of learning, and in this unit, those that link to self-regulation are considered in detail. Other concerns are noted here below; each one is covered in more depth in other units in this volume:

Grouping pupils and group work (see also Unit 2.3 and 4.1)

Collaborative group work is central to personalising learning and differs from individual learning in this respect, so it is well worth spending some time considering different options for grouping pupils. Flexibility is the key to ensuring that pupils have a range of experiences, and you must be willing to move groups around for different tasks and sometimes even just for a refreshing change.

Assessment for Learning (see also Units 6.1 and 6.2)

Assessment for Learning (AfL) is central to personalising learning, 'as a means of tracking how a child is progressing against national and personal targets, and the subsequent use of this data to inform lesson planning and interventions' (Rose, 2009, p.12, note7).

The importance of questioning techniques (see also Unit 3.1)

The quality of questions both to pupils and from pupils is important, and the 1956 work of Bloom is a still much-used (often adapted) way of thinking about higher-order questioning. Numerous different versions of Bloom's taxonomy exist (Stanford University, 2015), but a useful rule of thumb is to ensure that the higher-level aspects or types of thinking – analysis, evaluation and synthesis – are incorporated into all lessons.

Task setting, problem-solving and investigations (see also Unit 5.2, 5.3)

Real-life problems, interesting investigations and meaty projects in which pupils can be involved in depth are preferable to isolated, disconnected tasks and activities. One useful technique for helping pupils plan and execute projects is 'Thinking Actively in a Social Context' (TASC) (Wallace, 2000), a model that can be used by pupils to plan long-term project work or short-term activities. It is a flexible tool for thinking and discussing ideas and tasks. The elements are below. There is no prescribed order; the model is usually presented in a circle with no specified start or end point and there are verbs to explain what is being done with a linked trigger question.

- Gather/organise – What do I know about this?
- Identify – What is the task?
- Generate – How many ideas can I think of?
- Decide – Which is the best idea?
- Implement – Let's do it!
- Evaluate – How well did I do?
- Communicate – Let's tell someone!
- Learn from experience – What have I learned?

The model works well for a variety of ages and there is plenty of guidance on its use on the National Association for Able Children in Education website (www.nace.co.uk/).

Cognitive issues: accelerated learning, learning styles and metacognition (see also Units 4.3, 5.1)

Many contemporary ideas about how children's cognitive processes should be harnessed have been controversial. There is little empirical evidence to support the notion of 'accelerated learning' and there is some suggestion that relying on 'learning styles' can even be detrimental (Bjork et al., 2013). The idea of metacognition, however, is to focus on how we learn and how we can improve our learning. Much like self-regulation, useful metacognitive techniques aim to help pupils analyse their own strengths and weakness and develop their self-understanding in relation to their work (see Units 4.3 and 5.1 for more on multiple intelligences and metacognition).

Emotional intelligence and motivation

Together with understanding your pupils' metacognition and learning styles, knowledge of their emotional intelligence allows insights to their responses to tasks and assists you with pupil groupings (see Units 4.1 and 4.3). Personalising learning should make it easier to keep pupils motivated as they have been involved in choosing much of their learning (see Unit 3.2).

Differentiation (see also Unit 4.1)

Central to personalising learning is differentiation in order to meet pupils' individual needs. There are many varied ways to differentiate and you need to choose what is most appropriate in relation to the required learning outcomes. Options include differentiating by adjusting for example, the content, pace, outcome, assessment, way of recording ideas, level of support or resources.

SUMMARY AND KEY POINTS

Personalising learning involves shaping teaching and learning around the different ways that pupils learn. This has implications for teaching methods, curricula structure and school organisation. Self-regulating learning has been shown to be an effective way to improve motivation and achievement.

You are likely to find that many of the elements of these aspects of learning are already part of what you plan to do in the classroom as they emphasise ideas widely recognised as best practice. These include really getting to know your pupils, varying pedagogies in the classroom, encouraging pupils to understand their own learning strategies in order to raise their achievement and using assessment to help with learning.

Check which requirements for your ITE programme you have addressed through this unit.

Further resources

BBC Assessment for Learning, viewed 3 July 2018, from http://www.bbc.co.uk/northernireland/forteach ers/curriculum_in_action/assessment_for_learning.shtml

Cash, R.M. (2016) *Self-Regulation in the Classroom: Helping Students Learn How to Learn*, Golden Valley, MN: Free Spirit.
Despite its American context, this book has ideas that are relevant for every classroom. It covers theoretical and practical issues around self-regulation and self-efficacy and some of the ideas on reflection, goal-setting and procrastination are helpful for readers in their identities not just as teachers, but also as lifelong learners.

Dweck, C. S. (2012) *Mindset: How You Can Fulfil Your Potential*, London: Constable and Robinson Limited.
This book addresses what is one of the principal barriers to learning pupils experience – the belief their abilities are fixed. It raised the importance of pupils being helped to adopt a 'growth mindset'. Further references to Dweck's work can be found through her Wikipedia entry or the Mindset website http://www.mindsetonline.com/.

Education Endowment Foundation (EEF), viewed 3 July 2018, from https://educationendowment foundation.org.uk/
Runs various education projects and has many evaluations and case studies to explore.

Lee, C. (2013) Mathematics: Assessment for Learning: The Four Operations, MESHGuide, viewed 3 July 2018, from http://www.meshguides.org/

National Association for Able Children in Education website, viewed 3 July 2018, from https://www.nace. co.uk

National College of School Leadership Personalising Learning, viewed 3 July 2018, from https://www.nat ionalcollege.org.uk/transfer/open/adsbm-phase-3-module-1-enabling-learning/adsbm-p3m1s2/ad sbm-p3m1s2t4.html
This website has links to some of the archived documents from the personal learning strategy, containing practical ideas.

Open University, Open Learn Self-Regulated Learning, viewed 3 July 2018, from http://www.open.edu/ openlearnworks/course/view.php?id=1490%3F
This is an open access Open University supported course focusing on self-regulated learning and on creating personalised technology-enhanced learning environments.

Stanford University (2015) Teaching Commons: Blooms Taxonomy of Educational Objectives, viewed 3 July 2018, from https://teachingcommons.stanford.edu/resources/course-preparation-resources/ course-design-aids/bloom%E2%80%99s-taxonomy-educational-objectives

Teaching Schools Council (TSC), viewed 3 July 2018, from https://www.tscouncil.org.uk/
This organisation aims to develop education 'in English schools through a self-improving school-led system, so that all children attend a good school' and the case studies are of particular interest.

Wallace, B., Leyden, S., Montgomery, D., Winstanley, C., Pomerantz, M. and Fitton, S. (2009) *Raising the Achievement of All Pupils within an Inclusive Setting: Practical Strategies for Developing Best Practice***, Abingdon: Routledge.**
For some really practical examples of proven effective classroom and whole-school practices, this book is extremely useful. Based on case studies of schools, each chapter combines theory with illustrative examples and covers areas including multiple exceptionalities and social and emotional issues as well as leadership and inclusion.

Winstanley, C. (2010) *The Ingredients of Challenge***, Staffs: Trentham Books.**
This book is an exploration of the provision of an appropriate challenge for pupils and provides practical suggestions as well as a theoretical grounding. Understanding pupils as learners is central to the book and many aspects relate closely to individual and personal learning.

Appendix 2 lists subject associations and teacher councils and Appendix 3 provides a list of websites.

Capel, S., Leask, M. and Turner, T. (eds.) (2010) *Readings for Learning to Teach in the Secondary School: A Companion to M Level Study***, Abingdon: Routledge.**
This book brings together essential readings to support you in your critical engagement with key issues raised in this textbook.

Capel, S., Lawrence, J., Leask, M. and Younie, S. (eds.) (2019) *Surviving and Thriving in the Secondary School: The NQT's Essential Companion***, Abingdon: Routledge.**
This book is designed to support newly qualified teachers in the next phase of development as a teacher. However, you may find it useful as it covers aspects of teaching not included in this book which, nonetheless you experience on your ITE programme.

The subject specific books in the *Learning to Teach (Subject)* series, the *Practical (Subject) Guides*, *Debates in (Subject)* and *Mentoring (Subject) Teachers* are also very useful.

Any additional resources and an editable version of any relevant tasks/tables in this unit are available on the companion website: www.routledge.com/cw/capel

5.6 Neuroeducation

Classroom practice and the brain

Paul Howard-Jones

Introduction

> *Education is about enhancing learning, and neuroscience is about understanding the mental processes involved in learning. This common ground suggests a future in which educational practice can be transformed by science, just as medical practice was transformed by science about a century ago.*
>
> (Opening lines of the Royal Society report 'Neuroscience: Implications for education and lifelong learning', 2011, p.1)

In recent years, there has been a step change in efforts to bring neuroscience and education together in dialogue. Excitingly, our scientific understanding of learning is now allowing us to consider everyday learning in the classroom in terms of the underlying brain processes involved.

OBJECTIVES

At the end of this unit you should be able to:

- avoid some popular neuromyths;
- think about classroom practice in terms of three categories of learning process (engage, build, consolidate);
- draw on insights from cognitive neuroscience when planning your lessons;
- draw on insights from cognitive neuroscience to evaluate your lessons.

Check the requirements of your initial teacher education (ITE) programme to see which relate to this unit.

Neuromyths to avoid

Most teachers consider a knowledge of the brain is important when developing their practice and, given the brain's central role in learning, this belief appears justified. However, a lack of valid information about neuroscience in initial teacher education has helped create a parallel world of pseudo-neuroscience within schools. Many concepts that claim a brain-basis are unscientific and educationally unhelpful, so let's first identify some of the most popular but unscientific beliefs about the brain (so-called 'neuromyths'). These often originate from authentic science that has then become misinterpreted or overinterpreted. That makes it difficult, but also important, to separate the fact from the fiction. Task 5.6.1 introduces some neuromyths.

 Task 5.6.1   Neuromyths: true or false?

Carry out this quick TRUE/FALSE survey on some teachers, learners and friends. You may be surprised how common neuromyths are. The answers are in brackets.

1 We mostly only use 10% of our brains (FALSE – we use all our brains all the time).
2 Exercise can improve mental function (TRUE – see main text).
3 Coordination exercises can improve integration of left and right hemispheric brain function (FALSE – see main text).
4 Pupils are more attentive after sugary drinks and snacks (TRUE – although not healthy in other ways, sugary snacks actually increase attention (Busch et al., 2002)).
5 Regular drinking of caffeinated drinks reduces alertness (TRUE – regular caffeine, e.g. two cans of caffeinated soft drink a day, reduces children's cognitive function by initiating counter-regulatory changes in the brain (Heatherley et al., 2006)).
6 Individuals learn better when they receive information in their preferred learning style (FALSE – see main text).

Record the outcomes in your professional development portfolio (PDP) or equivalent.

Surveys of teachers in countries as diverse as the United Kingdom (UK), Turkey and China show over 90% of teachers believe teaching to pupils' preferred learning styles can improve outcomes (Howard-Jones, 2014). Learning preferences do exist, in the sense that different individuals may prefer to receive information in different ways. For example, it is possible to categorise learners' preferences in terms of visual, kinaesthetic or auditory (VAK). However, there seems little educational value in doing so, despite the references to neuroscience by those promoting learning style theory. Different regions of the brain are more involved than others in processing visual, auditory and somatosensory (touch) information. But performance in most everyday tasks, including learning of information provided in just one modality (e.g. visual), prompts many regions in both hemispheres to work together in a sophisticated parallel fashion.

In reality, the brain is so massively interconnected that sensory experience is always cross-modal in nature. This means, for example, that visual experience can result in activity in parts of the brain often referred to as auditory. As Kayser (2007) puts it, 'the brain sees with its ears and touch, and hears with its eyes'. (This interconnectedness of the brain also means that neuroscience cannot be used to support multiple intelligences theories since the distributed nature of neural function suggests that we should not characterise individual differences in terms of some limited number of capabilities.) Scientific evidence from laboratory experiments shows that providing information in a learner's preferred VAK style is 'wasted effort' (Kratzig and Arbuthnott, 2006). At the end of their extensive educational review, Coffield et al. (2004) concluded there were no clear implications for pedagogy arising from any existing models of learning styles. However, the effectiveness of multimodal teaching is supported by both educational and scientific research. That is, using a wide variety of modalities (visual, auditory, touch, taste, smell, etc.) to teach *every* child really can support their learning.

Educational kinesiology (or Edu-K, also often sold under the brand name of Brain Gym®) draws on ideas about perceptual-motor training, i.e. that learning problems arise from inefficient integration of visual, auditory and motor skills. This idea spawned several training programmes to remediate learning difficulties through exercises, but these were shown to be ineffective by numerous studies in the 1970s and 1980s (Arter and Jenkins, 1979; Bochner, 1978; Cohen, 1969; Hammill et al., 1974; Kavale and Forness, 1987; Sullivan, 1972). A major review of the theoretical foundations of Brain Gym® and the associated peer-reviewed research studies failed to support the contentions of its promoters (Hyatt, 2007). Despite this, many teachers remain enthusiastic about Brain Gym® and convinced that it supports learning, with reports of increased reaction times following its exercises suggestive of some positive effect on cognition (Sifft and Khalsa, 1991). If Brain Gym® can contribute to learning, it may be for entirely different reasons than those used to promote it.

There is an emerging body of multidisciplinary research showing the beneficial effect of aerobic exercise on selective aspects of brain function, and some of these aspects happen to be particularly important for education (Hillman et al., 2008). For example, a study of adults revealed increased levels of brain-derived neurotrophic factor (BDNF) after two three-minute sprints (Winter et al., 2007). When compared to sedentary or moderate exercise conditions, participants showed a 20% increase in the speed of recall for words they learned immediately following their intense exercise. BDNF plays an important role in synaptic plasticity, the making of connections between neurons, which is thought to underlie our ability to learn. Neuroscience is shedding light on how exercise and fitness can promote learning. But, it seems that aerobic exercise is what's needed, rather than the rehearsal of motor-perception skills.

Drinking water is often promoted as a way to improve learning and it is true that even mild dehydration can reduce our ability to think (Cian et al., 2000). However, a recent adult study has shown that drinking water when not thirsty can also diminish cognitive ability (Rogers et al., 2001). Luckily, forgetting to drink water is not usually a problem, because our brains have evolved a sophisticated system that makes us thirsty when our bodies (and brains) need more fluid. So, encouraging and enabling children to drink water when they feel thirsty may be a more sensible approach than constantly monitoring the amount of water they consume. Exercise and unusually hot weather are the exception to this rule, when there is evidence that the body's own monitoring system becomes less reliable, suggesting children might then need encouragement to drink in order to avoid dehydration (Bar-David et al., 2005; Bar-Or et al., 1980). Apart from these special circumstances, there is no evidence to suggest that normally functioning children are generally prone to voluntary dehydration. Indeed, the only study showing voluntary dehydration in the classroom comes from the Dead Sea region – the lowest point on the planet and notoriously hot (Bar-David et al., 2005). Our survey also revealed 20% of student teachers thought their brain would shrink if they failed to drink 6–8 glasses of water a day. Very serious dehydration can do this, as graphically illustrated when a man in Japan tried to commit suicide by overdosing on soy sauce (Machino and Yoshizawa, 2006). Three weeks later, after appropriate treatment, the man's brain was shown to have returned (mostly) to its original dimensions. However, this was a rare case and one caused by vast amounts of soy sauce, not by forgetting to drink water.

Brain plasticity and learning

Whatever your age and stage of development, the brain remains plastic. That means that our experience, including our educational experience, can change the way our brain functions, the way its neurons connect with each other and even the shape and size of its various parts. Of course, the brain is more plastic during childhood but, as adults, it remains plastic and always able to learn. It is important that teachers and their pupils understand about brain plasticity, because many learners feel their brains limit their potential and prevent them from learning. However, when we decide we want to learn we are choosing to change our brain's function, connectivity and structure. Research has shown that simply knowing this can improve the self-concept and academic potential of learners. So, tell your pupils: their brain isn't something they're stuck with – they can change their brains – and the best way to change them is through learning!

Three broad categories of learning processes provide a convenient starting point for analysing classroom practice in terms of underlying brain function. Recent research offers an understanding of how a pupil becomes *engaged* with a source of new knowledge prior to the building of new knowledge, how he/she first comes to *build* new knowledge, and how this new knowledge later undergoes *consolidation*, causing it to become more permanent, accessible and useful. These three categories are broad headings that are helpful for breaking down learning into component processes. They are introduced in this order for the sake of convenience; in reality, they may be sequenced differently and even simultaneously.

Engagement of the learner

Every learner's brain is unique, and pupils differ in what most engages their attention and the extent to which they can control it, making it important for the teacher to monitor engagement and vary approach accordingly. Scientific studies have revealed the role of *subcortical* structures deep below the cortex in the emotional states that encourage us to attend and learn. For example, praise is commonly used as an effective means to reinforce classroom behaviours conducive to learning (Becker, Madsen, Arnold and Thomas, 1967; Dufrene, Lestremau and Zoder-Martell, 2014; Reinke, Lewis-Palmer and Merrell, 2008; Sutherland, Wehby and Copeland, 2000). Praise is a social reward and social reward appears to recruit similar subcortical regions of the brain's reward system as receiving money (Izuma, Saito and Sadato, 2008; Knutson, Adams, Fong and Hommer, 2001) or anticipating food (Farooqi et al., 2007). A recent study has shown increases in reward system activity during the answering of educational questions, in conditions that favoured engagement and educational learning (Howard-Jones, Jay, Mason and Jones, 2016). The anticipation and receipt of rewards can release neuromodulators capable of improving attention and memory. Teachers employ many other strategies known to stimulate this "approach" response in the brain's reward system. These include novelty, the provision of choice and activities such as group work and presentation to peers that involve the sharing of attention.

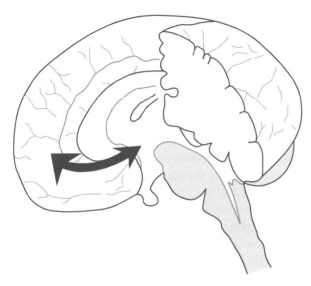

Figure 5.6.1 Engagement with a learning opportunity is influenced by interaction between subcortical structures (that are important for processing emotion) and frontal regions of the cortex (that are involved with attention and working memory).

Other types of subcortical activity, including activations within the amygdala, are implicated in the development of maths anxiety and negative emotions towards learning (Young, Wu and Menon, 2012). In positive and negative ways, our engagement is influenced by two-way interaction between our subcortical structures and the cortical processes required for learning (Figure 5.6.1).

Building of knowledge and understanding

Once a pupil is engaged with a source of new knowledge, such as an explanation or other stimulus provided by the teacher, a channel of communication can open to enable new learning to occur – although much depends on the quality of this communication. Effective teachers (and the resources they use) communicate clearly and concisely, with minimal opportunities for minimise distraction. The brain is organised around our senses and movement, and instruction that encourages the making of links between different representations of concepts, using our different senses and our ability to enact ideas, can enhance our learning new knowledge and understanding. It may be helpful to remember that some communication is unconscious. When we move, or express emotion in in our faces, the brains of those observing us activate as if they were moving similarly or experiencing similar emotions. (The brain networks involved have been referred to as the 'Mirror Neuron System'.) If gestures and faces communicate knowledge and emotions both consciously and unconsciously, this emphasises the importance of feeling genuinely confident and enthusiastic about what you are teaching – if you want your pupils to feel the same.

It is important for a teacher to be aware of their pupils' prior knowledge, since this is the foundation upon which the pupils' new knowledge will be built. However, your role goes beyond just ensuring that the pupil has the required prior knowledge before progressing to new learning content. Making these connections with prior knowledge involves prefrontal brain regions (just behind the front of the brain) and in school children these are known to be relatively immature

(Brod, Werkle-Bergner and Shing, 2013). This means that young pupils, compared with adults, are at a disadvantage in making use of prior knowledge, even when they possess it (Shing and Brod, 2016). Therefore, you can help your pupils to think meaningfully about new ideas by supporting them in connecting the new knowledge to what they already know. For example, it can be helpful to prompt pupils to reactivate appropriate prior knowledge through a revision question-and-answer before new information is presented, and then encourage them to make explicit connections between the new information and their existing knowledge.

As well as learning new information, a pupil must also learn how to apply it. Applying new information requires using prior knowledge to transform, organise and elaborate the new input. This type of effortful processing also recruits circuitry in the prefrontal cortex. Much educational learning, therefore, requires this type of effortful, conscious processing that activates the so-called 'working memory' network in the brain, as pupils attempt to control their attention and manipulate the information they are trying to hold in their working memory (Kane and Engle, 2002). For these reasons, the building of new knowledge is often accompanied by increased activation of the prefrontal regions of the brain (Figure 5.6.2).

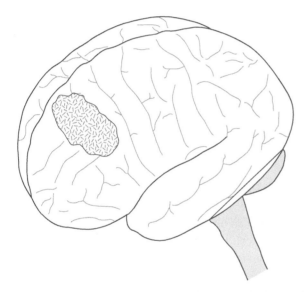

Figure 5.6.2 Building new knowledge and understanding requires effortful conscious processing and activation of a working memory network that includes prefrontal regions of the cortex.

Differences in prior learning but also in the development of this working memory network are two major factors that result in diverse individual differences in terms of children's capacity to build new knowledge.

Consolidation of learning

New learning is more vulnerable to loss, and recalling and applying freshly learnt knowledge occupies the limited working memory capacity we have available. This is a capacity that needs freeing up if we are to learn more. Fortunately, when we consolidate our learning, it not only becomes more

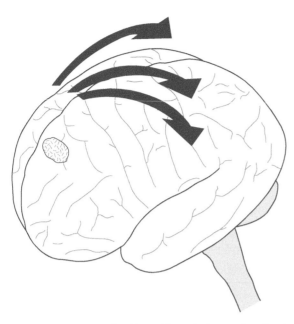

Figure 5.6.3 Consolidation of knowledge and understanding results in a shift in activation away from frontal regions – freeing up working memory for more learning.

permanent, but accessing it also becomes easier and quicker, demanding less conscious effort (Tham, Lindsay and Gaskell, 2015). Practice tends to shift activity away from working memory regions to regions more involved with automatic unconscious processing (i.e. away from the front of the brain – represented schematically in Figure 5.6.3).

   This was demonstrated neatly in a study of adults undertaking mathematics training. Figure 5.6.4 shows how their brain activity when doing mathematical problems shifted after training from the front to the back of the brain. This left image (Scan 1) shows where activity reduced after training, and the image on the right (Scan 2) shows where activity increased. This shift arises from a decrease in working memory load (i.e. a reduced amount of information to hold in one's immediate attention –

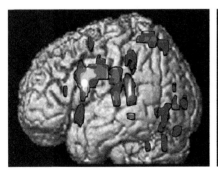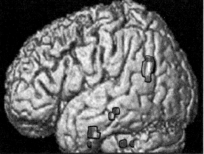

Figure 5.6.4 Changes in brain activity following training. Scan 1: activity decrease; Scan 2: activity increase

Source: Delazer et al., 2003, pp.82-83

such as the steps that must be followed) and an increase in more automatic processing (i.e. doing some parts of the mathematical processes without thinking about them).

Reducing the burden of fresh learning on working memory is important, because our limited working memory needs liberating before it can be occupied by new information, enabling us to learn more. Consolidation can be helped by practising the recall and application of our new knowledge in different ways. Questioning is often used to assess what learning has been achieved, but it is also an effective means to ensure that this deeper processing occurs, and to accelerate the rate at which learning becomes consolidated. This emphasises the need for pupils to be provided with interesting opportunities to apply and test their knowledge, but in low-risk tasks that are free of anxiety (unlike exams or formal assessments). Recent neuroimaging research suggests that repeatedly retrieving information causes it to become represented in the brain in different ways – essentially connecting it with different meanings and making it easier to retrieve in the future (Wirebring et al., 2015). Sleep also plays an important role in the processes that consolidate our learning. A good night's sleep helps attend to today's learning but also makes yesterday's learning more permanent.

Applying scientific insights when planning activities

The learning processes underlying a particular classroom activity can be broken down into those supporting engagement, the building of knowledge and the consolidation of learning (Figure 5.6.5)

However, it should be made clear that the categories 'engage', 'build' and 'consolidate' should not be used to partition a lesson. This would over-simplify many learning experiences encountered in a real classroom. In everyday teaching and learning, all three types of process might occur simultaneously, or at least in such quick succession that allocating one type of process to any single stage in a classroom activity is unhelpful. For example, consider the situation in which you use a quiz activity to introduce a new topic and link it to yesterday's learning. Based on a scientific understanding of the brain, you might use a reward schedule that promotes engagement, verbally scaffolding the

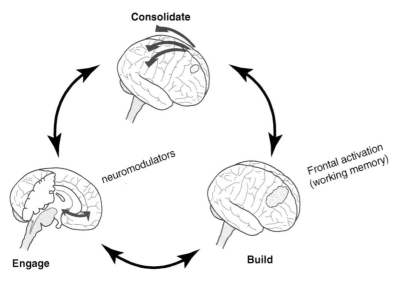

Figure 5.6.5 Engage, build, consolidate: the learning underlying classroom learning can be categorised into 3 types of process

Table 5.6.1 Questions to help you reflect on learning

Activity (referenced to concepts above)	Questions that might be prompted by the scientific concepts...
Q and A on content from last lesson using images	What difficulties did the pupils have when responding to your questions – was more support needed for some pupils? Did you spot individual differences in engagement – why might this be and what could you have done differently? Were contexts sufficiently novel, were there signs of anxiety, should it have been more collaborative requiring more shared attention, allowed for more choice? Where was support needed, e.g. were pupils having difficulties linking your verbal questions to your visual images? Did their responses suggest they had had sufficient practise on this topic using questions, applying knowledge in new situations, discussing, expressing in new forms?
Introduce new topic, discussion linking to prior knowledge	Did some pupils show lack of willingness to engage with the discussion – why might this be – and what could you do differently? Did pupils demonstrate that you had communicated the new concepts clearly? Did you make sufficient use of their senses, embodiment and action and encourage links across different representations of the concepts? Would the pupils have benefited from encouragement and support to connect the new concepts to their prior understanding?
Pair work: investigating new topic...	Did the pupils share attention to the stimulus and tasks you provided them with?

pupils' efforts to build their knowledge and link the new learning to old, using questions that require application of the prior knowledge in a range of different ways. This simple activity would, therefore, involve concepts from all three categories of engage, build and consolidate.

Also, the science does not provide a list of 'top tips' or list of good practices. Rather, it offers principles and a scientifically-determined understanding of how learning generally works, based on concrete measurement of behaviour and brain function. This cannot tell you exactly what to do but it can valuably inform your decisions and help you think more carefully about planning and evaluation. Now complete Task 5.6.2.

   Task 5.6.2   Discovering the science behind your lesson plans

Choose a typical lesson plan in which you will carry out a range of different activities. Which of the concepts discussed in this unit provide insight about why or how each activity might support learning? One way of approaching this task is to summarise and number the concepts above and then use this as a key to map concepts onto activities:

ENGAGE

1   Every learner's brain is unique, and pupils differ in what most engages their attention and the extent to which they can control their attention, making it important for teachers to monitor engagement and vary approach accordingly.

2   Teachers employ many strategies known to stimulate an "approach" response in the brain. These include rewards such as praise and tokens acknowledging achievement, novelty,

provision of choice and shared attention. The anticipation and receipt of rewards can release neuromodulators capable of improving attention and memory.

3 In contrast, fearfulness can avert attention, and anxiety can diminish a pupil's learning by reducing the brain's ability to process information.

Etc.

BUILD

4 Being aware of pupils' prior knowledge is important for a teacher because this is the foundation on which the pupils' new knowledge will build.

5 Teachers can help pupils think meaningfully about new ideas by encouraging them to make connections with their prior knowledge. This is important for children, whose neural circuitry for this connection-making process is still developing. Differences in learning and development result in diverse individual differences.

6 The brain is multisensory, and understanding of new knowledge is helped by clear, concise instruction using all the senses, embodiment and action to encourage links between different representations.

Etc.

CONSOLIDATE

7 Practice and rehearsal of freshly learnt knowledge causes it to become automatically accessible. This frees up the brain's limited capacity to pay conscious attention, and so be ready for further learning.

8 Answering questions, applying knowledge in new situations, discussing it with others or expressing it in new forms consolidate our learning through helping us to store it in different ways – making it easier to recall and apply it.

Etc.

Discuss your analysis with others and record your notes in your PDP.

The science of learning and the reflective practitioner

Effective teachers tend to employ 'good' practices that have, in general terms, been identified by educational researchers as effective. However, simply applying good practices cannot, in itself, assure the best possible levels of learning are achieved. This may be because teachers require an understanding of why, when and how each practice can be effective, in order to adapt it optimally for their pupils (Coe, Aloisi, Higgins and Major, 2014). Lesson evaluation is an important part of gaining this understanding. Ensuring your evaluation is informed by the science of learning can not only be helpful in terms of providing insight into a specific lesson, it can also help build your general understanding of classroom learning practices, and so improve your ability to adapt these practices to different classes, individuals and contexts. Task 5.6.3 asks you to reflect on learning in your lesson evaluations.

 Task 5.6.3   Reflecting on learning in your lesson evaluations

When evaluating the lesson you planned in Task 5.6.2, look back at the concepts you linked to each activity. Use these when reflecting on how the lesson went, and to prompt questions for thinking more deeply about learning processes and why learning may, or may not have occurred. For example, see Table 5.6.1.

Store this in your PDP.

We are still at the beginning of a long journey when it comes to introducing cognitive neuroscience into classroom practice. There remain significant theoretical and cultural gaps between education and the sciences of mind and brain that will require investment, research and time to fill. However, even while such work continues, this short introduction should allow you to begin introducing the science of learning into your planning and evaluation in a meaningful and insightful way.

SUMMARY AND KEY POINTS

■ There is a lack of evidence for many supposedly brain-based ideas meant to improve learning, e.g. teaching to learning styles, through rehearsing perceptual-motor exercises or by increasing water intake.

■ In contrast, a genuine understanding of learning from the sciences of mind and brain can provide insight into everyday classroom learning processes.

■ Such understanding is helpful for developing a more secure rationale when planning your approaches to teaching in the classroom and, when evaluating, for critically reflecting on the effectiveness, or otherwise, of these approaches.

Check which requirements for your ITE programme you have addressed through this unit.

 Further resources

Churches, R., Dommett, E. and Devonshire, I.]. (2017) *Neuroscience for Teachers: Applying Research Evidence from Brain Science*. **Williston, US: Crown House.**
A very readable exploration of concepts from neuroscience that are relevant for teachers.

Geake, J. G. (2009) *The Brain at School*, **Milton Keynes: Open University Press.**
An expertly-written guide for teachers who want to know whether and how neuroscience can be applied in the classroom.

Howard-Jones, P.A. (2010b) *Introducing Neuroeducational Research*, **Abingdon: Routledge.**

An in-depth text on the issues, opportunities and methods by which neuroscience may be used to inform educational practice.

Howard-Jones, P.A. (2018) *Evolution of the Learning Brain: Or How You Got to Be so Smart*, **Abingdon: Routledge.**
Written for non-specialists, this is an accessible journey through the most important brain processes for learning, explained through the engaging narrative of evolution.

Howard-Jones, P.A. (2013) *Neuroscience and Education: A Review of Educational Interventions and Approaches Informed by Neuroscience*, **London: Educational Endowment Foundation, viewed 3 July 2018, from http://educationendowmentfoundation.org.uk**

Neuroscience for Kids, **viewed 3 July 2018, from http://faculty.washington.edu/chudler/neurok.html**
There are very few sites that translate neuroscience into something understandable. Don't be put off by the title, it's a useful site for grown-up neuroscientists too!

Royal Society (2011) *Brain Waves Module 2: Neuroscience: Implications for Education and Lifelong Learning*, **viewed 3 July 2018, from http://royalsociety.org/policy/projects/brain-waves/education-lifelong-learning/**
A free and forward-looking review of how neuroscience may inform education in the future.

Royal Society, viewed 3 July 2018, from http://royalsociety.org/policy/projects/brain-waves/education-lifelong-learning
The full report and further details about the work by the Royal Society on the implications of neuroscience for education are available on this site.

The International Mind, Brain and Education Society, viewed 3 July 2018, from www.imbes.org
You can also find out here about the journal associated with this society.

Appendix 2 lists subject associations and teacher councils and Appendix 3 provides a list of websites.

Capel, S., Leask, M. and Turner, T. (eds.) (2010) *Readings for Learning to Teach in the Secondary School: A Companion to M Level Study*, **Abingdon: Routledge.**
This book brings together essential readings to support you in your critical engagement with key issues raised in this textbook.

Capel, S., Lawrence, J., Leask, M. and Younie, S. (eds.) (2019) *Surviving and Thriving in the Secondary School: The NQT's Essential Companion*, **Abingdon: Routledge.**
This book is designed to support newly qualified teachers in the next phase of development as a teacher. However, you may find it useful as it covers aspects of teaching not included in this book which, nonetheless you experience on your ITE programme.

The subject specific books in the *Learning to Teach (Subject)* series, the *Practical (Subject) Guides*, *Debates in (Subject)* and *Mentoring (Subject) Teachers* are also very useful.

Any additional resources and an editable version of any relevant tasks/tables in this unit are available on the companion website: www.routledge.com/cw/capel

5.7 Developing critical thinking

Hazel Bryan and Chris Carpenter

Introduction

When you first go into school you may be dazzled by the sheer volume of activity that you encounter. Secondary schools are large, complex organisations that take time to understand, as there are multiple systems operating at any given time. The core business of teaching pupils is at the heart of the organisation. As a developing professional, you bring with you your graduate subject knowledge and pedagogical values: you have an increasing amount of 'professional capital' (Hargreaves and Fullan, 2012) as a student teacher. However, as an 'extended professional' (Hoyle, 1974) you also need to develop critical thinking skills that enable you to adopt an objective, questioning perspective. Critical thinking skills enable you to take a step back from any immediate situation (Barnett, 1994; Education Scotland, 2015) and 'read' it from an objective position, whether this is in relation to teaching, learning or the introduction of, for example, a new curriculum specification document. The development of a critical perspective provides you with the skills to read any given text (for example, a government policy document or a more localised school policy) from an informed position. Such a perspective also supports you in the development of problem-solving skills (King and Kitchener, 1994). Well-honed critical thinking skills empower you to ask questions of any given context and text and, by having this model of enquiry at the core of your professional self, you develop as an inquisitive practitioner, seeking to enhance your practice by understanding better any given context. However, 'critical thinking' should not be reduced simply to a set of skills. Rather, it should be regarded as an 'attitude, underpinned by curiosity...the motivation to understand at deeper levels' (Bryan et al., 2010, p.62). Indeed, Brookfield (1993) uses the rather beautiful analogy of a conversation about learning to describe critical thinking. You adopt this approach in evaluating your lessons (see Unit 2.2 on planning and evaluating) and in undertaking reflective practice and action research (see Unit 5.4 on action research).

Poulson and Wallace (2004) suggest the following as indicators of a critical perspective:

- adopting an attitude of scepticism;
- habitually questioning the quality of your and other's claims to knowledge;
- scrutinising claims to see how convincing they are;
- respecting others as people;
- being open-minded to other perspectives;
- being constructive by using your scepticism to find better ways or interpretations.

Similarly, Scott (2000) offers the following four indicators:

■ identifying and challenging assumptions;
■ challenging the importance of context;
■ imagining and exploring alternatives;
■ developing reflective scepticism.

The model outlined in this unit, the linden tree, supports your pedagogy in two ways. Firstly, it provides you with a simple, elegant tool to develop your critical thinking capacity from the first time you enter a school. It supports you in understanding the school as an organisation, the learning spaces within school and learning as a concept. Throughout the process, the models offered above by Poulson and Wallace (2004) and Scott (2000) are drawn upon to illuminate critical issues. Secondly, this unit supports you in developing critical thinking, a critical disposition in your pupils.

OBJECTIVES

At the end of this unit you should be able to:

■ read the physical environment of your school (the architecture and icons) with a critical eye;
■ understand the learning spaces you construct from a critical perspective;
■ approach the interactions and pedagogical encounters you have with your pupils from a critical perspective;
■ develop critical thinking in your pupils.

Check the requirements of your initial teacher education (ITE) programme to see which relate to this unit.

The linden tree

As a starting point, consider a cross-section of the tree, and the concentric layers revealed in this cross section (Figure 5.7.1).

Each concentric circle represents that which is visible as you approach, enter and spend time in school. Within each concentric circle you are introduced to theory and practice from a national and international perspective and offered tasks that develop your critical thinking.

Architecture

The outer layer, the bark, is what you see as you walk up to the tree. If you apply this model to the school, the outer layer is that which is visible from the outside. What is there to see as you approach the building? The design of the school represents the intentions of the architects, and those who

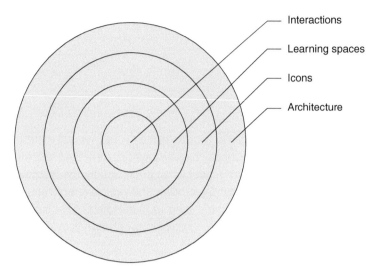

Interactions

Learning spaces

Icons

Architecture

Figure 5.7.1 Critically evaluating the learning environment

commissioned the building of the school. It is common practice today for architectural design teams to work with stakeholders (community representatives, governors, parents, teachers and pupils) in discussions around school design, but of course, this was not always the case. The school architect, Mark Dudek, discusses his work in terms of the psychological and spatial requirements needed in school design to accommodate and respond to theories of learning and cognitive development that inform pedagogy today: 'More esoteric factors such as the effects on behaviour of colour, light, surface texture and imagery are considered in addition to the more practical aspects of designing for comfort and health' (Dudek, 2000). So, as you might expect, a boys' grammar school built in the 1930s has a different provenance from, for example, an academy commissioned and built in 2017. And yet, embodied within the obviously visible, the design of the school represents a range of values in relation to beliefs about learning, teaching and the place of the school in any given community.

At the award-winning Rumi Jiya School in Hyderabad, India, the architects sought to design a school that would challenge assumptions about traditional models of rote learning. The design principles include:

■ building a learning community;
■ treating stakeholders as partners;
■ making nothing rote;
■ extending the spirit of entrepreneurship;
■ celebrating constraints.

(http://architecture.about.com/od/schooldesign/ig/Winning-Sc
hool-Designs/Rumi-School-of-Excellence.htm)

Similarly, in the Building Tomorrow Academy, Kiboga, Uganda, the design principles included the importance of community use, as the community had invested so much in the building. The design principles also included a requirement for the teacher to be able to see all the pupils in her classroom at any one time, as, in Uganda, teachers are scarce and numbers of pupils in each classroom are relatively high (http://architecture.about.com/od/schooldesign/ig/Winning-School-Designs/Rumi-School-of-Excellence.htm).

There are, of course, other design features in each of these schools that focus upon green initiatives and safety requirements, but the design principles outlined above relate to the ways in which the buildings have been conceived in relation to learning and teaching.

In Reggio Emilia in Northern Italy, the Reggio schools are designed in partnership with the famous Domus Academy, Milan. The resident Reggio architect, Professor Andrea Branzi, refers to the concept of 'liquid modernity' when articulating his vision for the school buildings (Branzi, 2004). That is, buildings within which everything is moveable, including walls and floors, in order to respond to the changing needs of pupils. Task 5.7.1 invites you to critically evaluate the external features of your placement school.

✏️ Task 5.7.1   Consider your placement school from the outside

Questions	Critical thinking indicators
What, in your opinion, were the design principles upon which the school was constructed?	Being open-minded to other perspectives (Poulson and Wallace, 2004).
In what way is this a community school?	Challenging the importance of context (Scott, 2000).
How well does this design work for the purpose of educating young people today?	Imagining and exploring alternatives (Scott, 2000).

In this task and the following tasks in this unit, record your notes in your professional development portfolio (PDP) or equivalent and reconsider your observations when you know the school better. Then make notes about what you would like to see in the school in which you are working when qualified and consider these points when you are being shown around the school prior to interview.

Icons

The second concentric circle of the cross-section of the tree relates to the things that are visible as you enter the school. These are referred to here as 'icons'. Icons were traditionally Christian images represented in art form, but today are used widely in marketing and fashion to depict values through well-known symbols.

It is likely that you enter your placement school via the school Reception, in order that you can sign in. Reception in secondary schools in the UK today is likely to be used by visitors and parents, rather than the main entrance for pupils. By learning to read the messages relayed by these icons, you are developing a critical perspective on what the school is saying to visitors. As such, the Reception area is a space where values about the school are expressed, and a critical reading of the icons in this area provides you with a sense of how the school wishes to be understood by visitors.

If your school is a faith school, there may be religious artefacts in the Reception area, if this is appropriate to the faith. What can you see? Are these artefacts what you would also see in, for example, a church? If so, what does this say about the relationship between the school and the church?

Secondary schools welcome visitors every day, including prospective parents and Office for Standards in Education, Children's Services and Skills (Ofsted) inspectors. There is likely to be a Mission Statement in the Reception area. Similarly, there are likely to be badges of school success or school validation by external bodies such as Healthy Schools or Investors in People. Schools increasingly provide visitors with a file containing newspaper clippings of events and pupils' success, promoting the positive image of the school. There might be a notice board for parents and school prospectuses. Finally, there might be work by the pupils on display in the Reception area. Task 5.7.2 invites you to critically evaluate the reception area of your placement school.

Task 5.7.2   Consider the reception area

Questions	Critical thinking indicators
What artefacts are in the Reception area? What is the relationship between these and the Mission Statement?	Being open-minded to other perspectives (Poulson and Wallace, 2004).
What are the badges of school success or sponsorship? What does this suggest to you in terms of the way the school values external validation?	Identify and challenge assumptions (Scott, 2000). Adopting an attitude of scepticism (Poulson and Wallace, 2004).
Is pupil work on display in Reception? If yes, is it written work or only art work? How long has the work been on display?	Adopting an attitude of scepticism (Poulson and Wallace, 2004).
What would you expect to see in this school's Reception area?	Being constructive by using your scepticism to find better ways or interpretations (Poulson and Wallace, 2004).

As suggested in Task 5.7.1, record your notes in your PDP and reconsider your observations when you know the school better.

The learning space

As you leave the Reception area and walk to your classroom, pause. On entry into your classroom, take a moment to consider the learning space. If you are in a traditional classroom, start by looking at the layout of the classroom furniture. How have the desks and chairs been arranged? In what ways has the furniture been organised to accommodate or reflect what you know about effective learning? Is there flexibility for the teacher to rearrange the furniture to create specific learning environments for specific purposes?

From a behaviourist perspective (see Unit 5.1 on how pupils learn and Unit 5.3 on teaching styles) the teacher is placed at the centre of the learning process. The role of the teacher in a predominantly behaviourist-influenced classroom would be as director, instructor and transmitter. The role of the pupil in such a classroom would be as passive recipient of a predetermined, tightly structured, linear curriculum. Knowledge in such an environment is conceived as residing with the teacher or within selected texts, and pupils are rewarded for correct answers or behaviours. Task 5.7.3 invites you to critically evaluate learning spaces from a behaviourist perspective.

 Task 5.7.3   Consider the learning space – from a behaviourist perspective

Questions	Critical thinking indicators
Does the layout of the furniture suggest a behaviourist approach to learning? If yes, why do you think the classroom is laid out in this way? What has been the guiding principle for the teacher whose layout this is?	Being open-minded to other perspectives (Poulson and Wallace, 2004). Imagining and exploring alternatives (Scott, 2000).
Does the layout suggest the teacher plays a dominant role in addressing the class?	Identifying and challenging assumptions (Scott, 2000).
Does the furniture dictate a passive role for the pupils?	Imagining and exploring alternatives (Scott, 2000).

Discuss your responses with another student teacher and store your findings in your PDP.

Within a classroom organised upon constructivist principles of learning (see Unit 5.1, 'Ways pupils learn' and Unit 5.2, 'Active learning'), the pupil is regarded as an active agent in their own cognitive development. They are viewed as meaning makers, motivated to construct their own understandings of the world, rather than passive recipient sponges, if you like, of knowledge. Of course, meaning-making is a complex concept, 'whether learning is meaningful can only be judged by the learner because meaningfulness is an expression of the relationship between the material of learning and the learner's existing understandings' (Moon, 2005, p.106).

Within the constructivist classroom, the role of the teacher is to scaffold the individual pupil's learning, to provide appropriate learning experiences and opportunities so that the pupil can actively make sense of their world, and create understanding themselves. As such, the place of knowledge shifts from residing with the teacher or text, to the pupil, who, given the right conditions, naturally moves through stages of learning. Vygotsky built upon Piaget's constructivist theory by making the case for language within learning. Vygotsky's model of social constructivist learning emphasised the centrality of language in cognitive development (see Unit 5.1). Other modes of learning (imitation and learning from observation) come to the fore within this approach (Bandura, 1969). Task 5.7.4 invites you to critically evaluate learning spaces from a constructivist perspective.

Task 5.7.4   Consider the learning space – from a constructivist perspective

Questions	Critical thinking indicators
Does the layout of the furniture facilitate group learning? If yes, why do you think the classroom is laid out in this way? What has been the guiding theory of learning or pedagogical principle for the teacher whose layout this is?	Being open-minded to other perspectives (Poulson and Wallace, 2004). Imagining and exploring alternatives (Scott, 2000).
Does the layout of the furniture facilitate an active role for the pupil?	Developing reflective scepticism (Scott, 2000).
Does the furniture suggest a scaffolding role for the teacher?	Identifying and challenging assumptions (Scott, 2000).

Discuss your responses with another student teacher and store your findings in your PDP.

Within a classroom organised around a belief in experiential learning (see Unit 5.1), experience is the starting point for learning (Miller and Boud, 1996). Kolb's four point model of experiential learning suggests that concrete experiences, followed by reflection, enable the learner to theorise what they have learned in order to use it in future (Kolb, 1984). As learning is viewed in this model as subjective, when it does happen it is transformative as it occurs through a process of reflection. Task 5.7.5 invites you to critically evaluate learning spaces from an experiential learning perspective.

 Task 5.7.5   Consider the learning space – from an experiential learning perspective

Questions	Critical thinking indicators
How might first-hand experiences occur in this classroom?	Developing reflective scepticism (Scott, 2000).
In what ways are pupils supported in reflecting on their experiences in this classroom?	Being open-minded (Poulson and Wallace, 2004).
What would it take to enable pupils to reflect upon their learning?	Imagining and exploring alternatives (Scott, 2000).

Discuss your responses with another student teacher and store your findings in your PDP.

Interactions

Teachers create the conditions within which learning opportunities occur. In addition to the concrete structures of classroom organisation considered above, teachers also construct opportunities for pupils to interact with each other and with texts, with the teacher herself or other adults. For example, within the behaviourist classroom considered above, the pupil interacts mainly with the teacher and selected texts. On the other hand, the principles that underpin a constructivist classroom would give rise to interactions between the pupil, teacher and first-hand resources. The social constructivist classroom brings into play interactions between pupils, resources, texts and the teacher or knowledgeable other, and within the experiential classroom, pupils are interacting with first-hand resources including texts, other pupils, the teacher and other adults.

It is possible, then, to map visible interactions against learning theories. Interactions, though, can be understood differently, as pedagogical actions within consciously created contexts. The term pedagogy is used to describe the 'artistry' of teaching (Moon, 2005), collaborative practices (Pickering et al., 2007) and the 'science of teaching' (Bryan et al., 2010). Pedagogy, though, is far more than practices undertaken by teachers to bring about specific learning outcomes. Pedagogical practices have the potential to oppress or liberate the learner and, as such, can be understood to be political actions (see Giroux's notion of 'Critical pedagogy', 2011). Critical pedagogy locates learning within the wider context of society, and, as such, positions the teacher as a significant agent in this endeavour. This is in line with Freire's (1992) belief that pedagogies create social justice or injustice, thereby creating or denying the 'humanising' potential of education. Task 5.7.6 invites you to critically evaluate interactions within your placement school.

✎ Task 5.7.6   Consider the interactions

Questions	Critical thinking indicators
In what way do you construct your role in relation to your pupils and talk about your role to other student teachers in relation to pupils?	Scrutinising claims to see how convincing they are (Poulson and Wallace, 2004).
What are your expectations of pupil relationships?	Scrutinising claims to see how convincing they are (Poulson and Wallace, 2004).
Do the learning opportunities draw from a range of disciplines?	Imagining and exploring alternatives (Scott, 2000).
	Habitually questioning the quality of others' specific claims (Poulson and Wallace, 2004).
What would you do differently?	Being constructive by using your scepticism to find better ways or interpretations (Poulson and Wallace, 2004).

Discuss your responses with another student teacher and store your findings in your PDP.

By now you have begun to develop an inquisitive, consciously questioning state of mind in relation to the school. That is, the start of a disposition of criticality. By working through the concentric circles of the tree, you have looked at that which is visible from the initial impressions given by the architecture, and then applied the linden tree model to take you step by step through the school into the heart of classroom practice. The activities you have undertaken using the concentric circles lead you towards a 'critical stance…[which] has the connotation of sharpness and precision' (Moon, 2005). That is, a disposition that enables you to analyse, question, interrogate to engage in different 'ways of seeing' (Berger, 1972). This approach emerges in some methodological approaches. Clough and Nutbrown (2007) refer to 'radical looking' and 'radical listening' when introducing pupils to data analysis. That is, they encourage pupils to actively seek information. Similarly, Holliday (2007) encourages pupils when considering research in familiar settings or with colleagues, to make the 'known strange'. That is, to step back, remain objective, look for details and resist complacency. The section that follows supports you in developing a critical disposition in your pupils in school.

Fruits of the tree: creating a critical disposition in your pupils

Carol Dweck (2000) has explored the ways in which teachers understand children's capacity to learn and develop. She proposes that teachers often see children's state of competence as 'fixed', and by this she means that their ability dwells in them as an 'entity', and, as such, they are not capable of change. In contrast to this, Dweck (2000) argues that we can see children as capable of change, which she refers to as taking an 'incremental' perspective in relation to learning. In other words, learners *are* capable of growth and development. Based on this idea, Dweck (2017) developed the idea of 'growth mindset' where she proposes that growth mindset leads to a desire to learn and therefore there is "a tendency to embrace challenges, persist in the fact of setbacks, see effort as the path to mastery, learn from criticism, find lessons and inspiration in the success of others" (Dweck, 2017, p.263).

Dweck's work brings to the fore the importance of teachers viewing their pupils' learning potential as organic and capable of growth. This situates the teacher at the heart of the pupils' learning processes, and we argue that the capacity to think critically is an invaluable disposition.

The development of critical thinking in your pupils requires you to focus first upon the word 'thinking'. Guy Claxton, in his very accessible book *Wise Up* (Claxton, 2001; see also Claxton, 2015), draws upon the work of Diane Halpern (1998) in promoting a four-fold model of critical thinking that you might develop in your pupils. Halpern's model is as follows:

Part 1: develop the right disposition

Halpern argues that pupils should expect thinking to sometimes be hard, and that they should not be dispirited in this possibility. Developing the right disposition involves your pupils in persisting with complex tasks. In a sense, this is about developing 'learning resilience' and 'thinking resilience' (Johnston-Wilder and Lee, 2010). A task for you in relation to developing the right disposition in your pupils is to reflect upon the opportunities you provide for your pupils: do you include complex thinking tasks as part of your pedagogical menu? When do your pupils have good opportunities to discuss, rationalise and problematise in their work?

Part 2: skills training

Halpern suggests that in order for critical thinking to be able to be engaged in successfully, certain skills need to be developed in young people. For example, Halpern advances the case for a focus upon the use of language in learning. Ask yourself, when do your pupils have opportunity to think about developing a precise language; a sound, persuasive argument; a questioning mind that interrogates arguments and claims. In addressing these areas, your pupils are engaging with issues of validity and reliability.

Part 3: recognising when to activate critical thinking

Halpern argues that the teaching of thinking skills involves you in supporting your pupils in finding out for themselves how to approach complex problems, and having opportunities to reflect with others upon the success or otherwise of the approach.

Part 4: metacognition

Developing in your pupils an awareness of the process of critical thinking brings about a state of self-awareness, and this, Halpern suggests, is crucial to the teaching of thinking. In this way, your pupils develop an ability to use critical thinking with 'conscious intent in a variety of settings' (Claxton, 2001, p.130).

Halpern's four-fold model is a useful starting point for focussing the mind on developing critical thinking in pupils in school.

Thinking

Your pupils need time to think. Moon (2008) suggests that you introduce your pupils to the concept of 'think time' or 'quick think'. This has the potential to be valuable to your pupils, but there are implications for you to consider to ensure that your practice is appropriate. The following approach set out in Tables 5.7.1–5.7.4 are based upon Moon's (2008) 'pedagogy of critical thinking'.

The suggestions in Tables 5.7.1–5.7.4 provide you with approaches to the development of critical thinking in class. They offer the opportunity for pupils to work collectively in the development of critical reading, the development of a critical perspective and the start of critical writing.

Table 5.7.1 Introducing 'think time' and 'quick think'

Concept	Pupil activity	Implications for your practice
Pupils are invited to 'stop and think' or take part in 'think-time' at appropriate times in the lesson	Pupils might reflect upon the task independently or discuss with other pupils	You should ensure that pupils have adequate time to engage in deep thinking and discussion
Pupils are invited to 'quick think'	Pupils write down notes based upon their deep thinking and discussions with fellow pupils	Moon (2008) reminds us of Tobin's (1987) concept of 'wait time'. Thinking takes time: do not be tempted to fill the pauses with teacher talk

Table 5.7.2 Developing critical thinking through real life scenarios

Activity	Pupil activity	Implications for your practice
Provide pupils with extracts from current newspapers of issues that are controversial (e.g. global warming; legal rulings).	Pupils should work in small groups to discuss the issues and: ■ list the further questions they have; ■ offer a range of possible solutions in bullet point format; ■ consider the consequences of each solution, possibly written in short paragraph.	You need to find current events that are well written in newspapers. Pupils need plenty of time to engage in this activity.
Provide pupils with the same current story, but presented in a range of newspapers.	Pupils should read the same story in each newspaper and consider the ways in which each newspaper has presented the same event. What are the features of text in each paper that are effective? What is the overall impression of the event from each newspaper? Thoughts can be presented as a concept map or bullet points.	As above, but you need a range of newspapers offering the same event/ storyline.

Table 5.7.3 Developing critical thinking through personal critical incidents

Activity	Pupil activity	Implications for your practice
Invite pupils to consider a personal critical incident at a time when they were faced with a dilemma that they are happy to discuss and explore.	Pupils work in small groups to first describe the dilemma. Pupils then move on to explain how the actions they took/the dilemma made them feel. Finally, other pupils ask *questions* to encourage the pupil to explore other ways in which they might have acted. This activity lends itself best to discussion rather than writing.	This activity must be set up in a sensitive manner, and only involve pupils who wish to discuss a critical incident. You should ensure that the 'rules' are followed in terms of the supportive nature of this activity.

Table 5.7.4 Developing critical thinking through creative scenarios

Activity	Pupil activity	Implications for your practice
Watch an extract from a film that provides opportunity for robust debate and differing perspectives, e.g. *Titanic*, *Jumanji*, Baz Luhrman's *Romeo and Juliet*...	Consider options from various characters' perspectives – what could have been done differently? Invite pupils to consider a different storyline/different ending based on characters acting differently.	You need to find films that lend themselves to robust debate.
Watch an extract from, for example, *Dr Who*, *Star Wars*, *Men in Black* that provides complex ethical dilemmas for the characters.	Invite your pupils to consider all the options open to the characters, setting out the pros and cons, and seeking a resolution.	Pupils need time to watch the extracts, and maybe re-watch them. Pupils need to have been introduced to the notion of pros and cons in action.
Offer pupils dilemmas from literature, for example, Goldilocks's hunger and exhaustion. Present it as a critical incident. Pupils in the secondary school will appreciate the irony in this activity and enjoy the playful nature of the activity. Of course, any character (with imaginary related relatives/friends) can be hot-seated, such as the key characters from poetry (e.g. *The Charge of the Light Brigade*) or literature (Anne Fine's *Tulip Touch*).	Hot-seat the following characters: Goldilocks; Goldilock's parents; the three bears: invite the hot-seated pupils to work collaboratively to create their storylines. The rest of the pupils should work together to construct questions for the hotseated characters.	Pupils need time to construct their storylines and time to engage in the hot-seating activity.

SUMMARY AND KEY POINTS

This unit has introduced you to the concept of critical thinking as an empowering, creative disposition.

- You have been offered a thinking tool in the shape of the linden tree to develop your skills of interrogation and analysis.
- You have begun to understand the benefits of stepping back from any immediate situation, asking questions and looking for details. In developing a critical mindset in relation to education, you are enhancing your ability to engage in a 'critical confrontation with your problems' (Smyth, 1989).
- Developing such a critical disposition in relation to education is in line with Habermas' notion that 'empowerment and political emancipation' result from critical and evaluative engagement (Moon, 2008: 15).
- You may have begun to notice throughout this unit that critical thinking and reflective practice are closely linked (Smyth, 1989). In essence, reflective thinking, developed by Dewey

in 1933, seeks to *understand* phenomena, whereas critical thinking results in a 'critical being' (Barnett, 1997), who is both creative and *empowered* in practice (Habermas, 1971).

■ This unit has also introduced you to the possibility of developing a *critical disposition* in the minds of your pupils and this is demonstrated in the classroom activities suggested above, where pupils are encouraged to arrive at solutions, rather than simply debate issues.

■ And why the linden tree? Known as a sacred tree in Slavic tradition, the linden tree is also known as the Holy Lime in Poland. Pre-Christian Germanic tradition held that the linden tree had such properties that it would reveal truths; judicial meetings were held beneath the linden tree as it was believed the tree would help to restore justice. The linden tree is associated with cultural and spiritual significance in Greek and Roman mythology – in both it is regarded as a tree symbolising the virtues. The linden or lime tree can live for centuries, and is revered for its medicinal lime blossom and practical versatility. In all these societies, the linden tree has symbolised justice, the virtues and practical applicability. As such, the linden tree has provided a fitting metaphor upon which a model to develop critical thinking in teachers and pupils has been constructed.

Check which requirements for your ITE programme you have addressed through this unit.

Further resources

Bryan, H., Carpenter, C. and Hoult, S. (2010) *Learning and Teaching at M Level: A Guide for Student Teachers*, London: Sage.
This text is designed for all student teachers. It promotes the importance of enquiry in professional practice and, as such, makes explicit links between theory and practice. Starting with a belief in the importance of teachers having a deep understanding of learning, the book immerses the reader in issues relating to pupil learning. There is a chapter dedicated to the development of critical thinking, reading and writing.

Claxton, G. (2015) *Building Learning Power*, viewed 18 June 2918, from http://www.buildinglearningpower.co.uk/

Education Scotland (2015) *Thinking Skills*, viewed 18 June 2918, from https://education.gov.scot/improvement/practice-exemplars/Carol%20McGuiness%20-%20Teaching%20thinking%20skills

Johnston-Wilder, S. and Lee, C. (2010) *Developing Mathematical Resilience*, in: BERA Annual Conference 2010, 1-4 Sep 2010, University of Warwick, viewed 18 June 2918, from http://oro.open.ac.uk/24261/2/3C23606C.pdf

Moon, J. (2008) *Critical Thinking: An Exploration of Theory and Practice*, Abingdon: Routledge.
This comprehensive text introduces the reader to theory underpinning critical thinking. The book sets out for the reader the conceptual issues surrounding the notion of critical thinking. It introduces the individual as a critical thinker, exploring emotions, language and curiosity in thinking. The text engages well with the concept of knowledge, setting complex ideas out with a lightness of touch. Finally, Moon offers practical suggestions for the development of critical thinking in educational settings.

Appendix 2 lists subject associations and teacher councils and Appendix 3 provides a list of websites.

Capel, S., Leask, M. and Turner, T. (eds.) (2010) *Readings for Learning to Teach in the Secondary School: A Companion to M Level Study*, Abingdon: Routledge.
This book brings together essential readings to support you in your critical engagement with key issues raised in this textbook.

Capel, S., Lawrence, J., Leask, M. and Younie, S. (eds.) (2019) *Surviving and Thriving in the Secondary School: The NQT's Essential Companion*, **Abingdon: Routledge.**
This book is designed to support newly qualified teachers in the next phase of development as a teacher. However, you may find it useful as it covers aspects of teaching not included in this book which, nonetheless you experience on your ITE programme.

The subject specific books in the *Learning to Teach (Subject)* series, the *Practical (Subject) Guides*, *Debates in (Subject)* and *Mentoring (Subject) Teachers* are also very useful.

Any additional resources and an editable version of any relevant tasks/tables in this unit are available on the companion website: www.routledge.com/cw/capel

5.8 Creating a language-rich classroom

Annabel Watson and Debra Myhill

Introduction

The importance of language for learning

Language is fundamental to learning and fundamental to being human: it is language that distinguishes us from animals. Although animals can communicate, only humans can use language to reflect on the past, to communicate complex abstract ideas or emotions, and to shape or imagine new futures. And language shapes how we see and interpret the world. As Wittgenstein famously proposed, 'The limits of my language are the limits of my world. All I know is what I have words for' (Wittgenstein, 1961, pp.5-6).

What we can articulate and express is influenced by the language we have to express it, and language itself influences how we think. Think, for example, of the common metaphor of the sun setting over the horizon, creating a conceptual image of the sun moving rather than the correct scientific understanding that it is the earth rotating that causes the sun to disappear. Or consider the fact that in English we can discriminate between a foreigner and a stranger, whereas in French there is only one word (*étranger*) to cover both these ideas. When new learning or discoveries occur, we have to create new words to express them. Language is the most powerful tool we have as learning beings.

The relationship between thinking and language has been explored most comprehensively by Vygotsky, who highlights the symbiotic relationship between the two: thoughts are not mentally 'translated' into words, rather thought and language interact together to generate new knowledge and understanding. It is a dynamic, constructive process:

> The relation of thought to word is not a thing but a process, a continual movement back and forth from thought to word and from word to thought. In that process the relation of thought to word undergoes changes which themselves may be regarded as development in the functional sense. Thought is not merely expressed in words; it comes into existence through them.
>
> (Vygotsky, 1986, p.218)

Although this might seem an abstract philosophical idea, it is one we all experience many times in our own social interactions with others. Most of us have had the experience of beginning a sentence and being surprised at where we end up, or of trying to articulate a half-formed idea and getting tangled up in our own words as we struggle to bring thoughts and words together. In the classroom, then, it is important that we see opportunities to use language to talk, read and write not as reductivist representations of thought but as the very processes that facilitate thinking and learning. This unit sets out to encourage you to think how you can capture the affordances of language to make learning in your classroom a meaningful, dynamic and vibrant process.

OBJECTIVES

At the end of this unit you should be able to:

■ begin to establish participatory and interactive classrooms;
■ begin to set up effective exploratory, dialogic talk;
■ begin to create tasks and activities that generate active reading;
■ support the development of writing in your subject.

Check the requirements of your initial teacher education (ITE) programme to see which relate to this unit.

Creating an interactive classroom

Talk for learning

Talk is the dominant mode of communication between any teacher and their pupils. Teachers typically use talk to explain, give instructions, assess learning and control behaviour. However, talk can also be a powerful tool for learning. It allows us to formulate and express ideas, to reformulate or clarify thinking, to communicate ideas and receive feedback from others, and to reflect on learning (Howe, 1992). Language is thus not only an *intra*personal 'psychological tool' that allows us to crystallise and represent thought to ourselves, but also an *inter*personal 'cultural tool' that provides 'a means for people to think and learn together' (Mercer, 1995, p.4). The implication of this is that an effective classroom is not one in which you, as a teacher, dominate conversation, using talk to channel information from expert to novice, but rather one where you help pupils to use talk to formulate, test and evaluate their own ideas, developing their thinking through conversations with you, the teacher, and each other.

Research over the past 30 years indicates that teachers dominate whole-class talk (Edwards and Westgate, 1994; Galton et al., 1999), and more recent research suggests that the patterns of basic classroom interaction have changed very little (Mercer and Littleton, 2007; Myhill, 2006). The pattern of turn-taking in discussion tends to follow what is often called an IRF or IRE structure: Initiation Response Feedback/Evaluation. Typically, the teacher initiates with a question to which a pupil responds, and the teacher then offers some form of feedback. The consequence of this is that the teachers' voice is consistently dominant, and pupils' involvement in discussion is limited and subordinate. Other factors exacerbate the situation: teachers ask many questions but pupils ask few; questions tend to invite factual recall only; pupil answers tend to be brief; feedback from teachers tends to praise but not explore pupil answers (Alexander, 2001). Furthermore, the fact that teachers often echo or repeat pupil answers reinforces the implicit message that the teacher's voice is the only one to which pupils need to listen. The level of control exerted by teachers is highlighted by Edwards and Westgate (1994, p.46):

> The teacher takes turns at will, allocates turns to others, determines topics, interrupts and reallocates turns judged to be irrelevant to those topics, and provides a running commentary on what is being said and meant which is the main source of cohesion within and between the various sequences of the lesson.

To create more space for learning, consider how far you can provide opportunities 'for the children to develop their individual understanding or ideas' and 'to articulate their thoughts and comments' (Myhill and Warren, 2005, p.67).

You need to plan carefully for whole-class discussion in order to do this. You should consider the balance of closed, factual questions to more open, speculative ones in advance, and check that open questions genuinely invite open responses. It is important to plan sequences of questions that invite pupils to use higher-order thinking skills of analysis, synthesis and evaluation, and to ask 'process' questions that invite them to explain their thinking. You should also actively prompt pupils to ask their own questions about what they are learning. Think about the 'wait time' you allow pupils before they answer – do they have enough time to formulate their ideas? Could they talk through their thoughts with a partner before sharing them with the whole class? Also, consider alternatives to questions. Some research suggests that questions can actually 'inhibit students' intellectual creativity' (Mercer, 1995, p.28), and that teachers can use other kinds of conversational strategies, such as offering your own observations and speculations, in order to prompt pupils to do the same. Most importantly, try to give your full attention to your pupils' responses, explore their thinking and use mistakes as opportunities to collaboratively explore misunderstandings or miscommunication. Task 5.8.1 is designed to help you with this.

Task 5.8.1   Observing and analysing whole-class discussion

Observe a 5-10 minute episode of whole-class discussion.
  Make a note of:

- how many conversational 'turns' the teacher takes;
- how many turns pupils take.

  Reflect and evaluate:

- how far does the pattern of interaction fit the 'IRF' pattern described above?
- what does the teacher do to try to encourage pupil participation in the discussion?
- how successful are they in doing this?

  Discuss your reflections with a peer. Now pair up with a colleague and undertake the same exercise in one of the lessons you are teaching. Were the results what you had planned for? If not, why not?
  Record the outcomes of your reflections and discussions in your professional development portfolio (PDP) or equivalent.

Dialogic talk for learning

Increasingly, dialogic talk is considered as the most powerful kind of talk for teachers to create in the classroom, and recent research has evidenced that in classrooms where teachers are able to use dialogic talk effectively, pupils' outcomes in Maths, English and Science are improved (Education Endowment Foundation (EEF), 2017). Dialogic talk moves away from the routine pattern of IRF exchanges, 'aiming to be more consistently searching and more genuinely reciprocal and cumulative' (Alexander 2004, p.1). While a monologic teacher is characterised by a desire to transmit knowledge, convey information and maintain control of talk, a dialogic teacher is focused on creating authentic conversational exchanges, creating opportunities for pupils to learn through exploration and collaborative talk.

Dialogic talk is founded on five principles: collectivity, reciprocity, support, cumulation and purposefulness (Alexander, 2004, p.27). Teachers and pupils *collectively* address learning tasks together, in groups or as a whole class. They *reciprocate* by sharing ideas, listening to each other and considering alternative views. They are *supportive* in allowing all members of the group to freely express their ideas without fear of embarrassment, and they support each other to reach common understandings. The discussion is *cumulative* in that teachers and pupils respond to each other's ideas, building them into a coherent line of enquiry. The talk is also *purposeful* in that it is planned and steered by the teacher in order to reach a specific educational goal (Alexander, 2004). Skidmore (2000) contrasts this purposeful dialogic pedagogy with the more monologic dialogue, which he calls pedagogic dialogue, in many classrooms (see Table 5.8.1).

Alexander (2017) invites us to consider a repertoire of talk in the classroom, and this acknowledges that some classroom talk will not be dialogic because its purpose is, for example, to explain something or to check recall. He also identifies the nature of the dialogic talk repertoire:

- *interactions*, which encourage pupils to think, and to think in different ways;
- *questions*, which invite more than simple recall;
- *answers*, which are justified, followed up and built upon rather than merely received;
- *feedback*, which, as well as evaluating, leads thinking forward;
- *contributions*, which are extended rather than fragmented or prematurely closed;
- *exchanges*, which chain together into coherent and deepening lines of enquiry;
- *discussion and argumentation*, which probe and challenge rather than unquestioningly accept;

Table 5.8.1 The features of typical pedagogic (monologic) dialogue vs a dialogic pedagogy, drawing on Skidmore (2000)

Pedagogic dialogue	Dialogic pedagogy
Teacher controlled	Teacher managed
Closed interactions	Open interactions
Limited participation	High participation
'Right' answers valued	All answers valued
Teacher owns truth	Shared quest for truth
Teacher talks most	Extended pupil contributions
Closed structure	Open structure

- *scaffolding*, which provides appropriate linguistic and/or conceptual tools to bridge the gap between present and intended understanding;
- *professional mastery of subject matter*, which is of the depth necessary to liberate classroom talk from the safe and conventional;
- *time, space, organisation and relationships*, which are so disposed and orchestrated as to make all this possible.

To enable your pupils to succeed in dialogic talk, you need to explicitly teach a range of skills. They need guidance in how to work together, how to include others, and how to monitor their own contributions (for example, to check that they're not dominating the discussion). They also need to learn about how to express disagreement politely and constructively, how to listen effectively and how to be sensitive to other people's reactions. Such skills are essential for effective group work in all areas of the curriculum, and you should make opportunities to model good (and bad!) practice. Now complete Task 5.8.2.

 Task 5.8.2   Analysing pupil discussions

Read this extract from a whole-class episode in which Year 8 pupils discuss the smoking ban. At the end of each pupil's contribution, they nominate another pupil to continue. Pupil names have been changed.

- What features of dialogic talk are evident?
- What would be a suitable topic of enquiry within your own subject area?
- How would you prepare your pupils to take part in an activity like this?

Record your ideas in your PDP.

Claire: I also think that smoking should be banned because people think it's sexy and cool but really it's just a health hazard. Sarah?

Sarah: But smoking is part of some people's personality, and if you had to say about somebody who smokes, if you had to describe them, you'd probably, one of the first things you'd say is that they smoked, and I feel that if they banned it in public places then it wouldn't be the right of freedom. Jack?

Jack: I also feel that the ban could have been the wrong decision because people may like feel loss of freedom, like they're being told what to do. John?

John: Yeah but it also means less people killed, less people dying because of it, and children are healthier. Ella?

Ella: I agree with John when he says that other people might not want the smoke near them. It's not really the choice of people that do smoke, it's the decision of the government to protect the people that don't smoke against becoming ill. Sophie?

Sophie: I agree with Sarah and Jack. It's not nice if you don't smoke, but like Sarah said it's their personality and their own right of freedom. And you'd kind of feel like you're being bossed around. It's not really free. Jess?

Jess: But I think they should ban it because it's doing everyone a favour, by making people cut down. Even if they do feel bossed around it's better for them. Chris?

Chris: It depends what you think is more important. The right of freedom for smokers, or protecting people who don't smoke, like Ella said.

Record the outcomes in your PDP.

Supporting reading development

Active reading involves readers in engaging with interpreting, questioning, and meaning-making from the texts they read, rather than simply decoding the words on the page (Gough and Tunmer, 1986; Stuart et al., 2008). In order to support reading development, you need to understand a little about the nature of reading and reader behaviour. Constructing meaning from texts involves a complex interaction between the reader, the text being read, and the context in which we are reading. As we read, we bring to the act all our previous reading experiences, our own life experiences and our cultural knowledge and values: there are 'as many different possible readings of text as there are readers' (Stevens and Fleming, 1998, p.64). What we already know influences how we interpret the text: reading a historical account of the reign of Queen Elizabeth I could be influenced by having seen Miranda Richardson's portrayal of her in *Blackadder*; an explanation of volcanic craters could be influenced by a holiday trip to Vesuvius; and it is impossible for post-holocaust readers to read *The Merchant of Venice*, with its cutting anti-Semitism, in the same way as Shakespeare's audience. Cultural influences are significant, too, and we read very much from our own cultural perspective. A description of a loyal dog has many cultural resonances in England, with our view of a dog as 'man's best friend', but many readers from other countries would have very different views of dogs, perhaps as scavenging pests to be deterred. And words and phrases carry many cultural overtones: think about 'afternoon tea', or 'blood sports'. Readers who have English as an additional language or come from different cultural backgrounds may draw different meanings from texts.

Developing comprehension

When we comprehend a text, we "interpret, integrate, critique, infer, analyse, connect and evaluate ideas" (New South Wales (NSW) Education Department, 2010, p.2). This process of constructing meaning is both a reader-led and a text-led issue: problems with comprehension are always the result of a mismatch between the knowledge and skills of the reader and the level of difficulty of a text. All of us can struggle with comprehension at times; common causes of difficulty include layout issues (e.g. font size), grammatical complexity, unfamiliar vocabulary, unfamiliar concepts, or the text not being in our first language (e.g. pupils with English as an additional language (EAL)). Consequently, to ensure that pupils can access and understand the texts you use, you need to first determine what makes them difficult. You may need to break a text down into smaller chunks, or to help pupils to make sense of complex grammatical constructions, or to devise some *pre-reading* activities to explore key concepts, explain key vocabulary or discuss culturally-specific content before reading.

Confident readers make use of a range of strategies to support comprehension, and these strategies can be taught (Snow, 2002). Strong readers know instinctively that we don't read every text in the same way: it would be foolish to read a telephone directory from the beginning, just as it rarely makes sense to begin a novel in the middle of the book. As we read, we anticipate what comes next, drawing both on our life knowledge and our knowledge of similar texts; and we constantly strive towards making sense of the text. This is why, when we are revising our own writing, it is hard to find mistakes in expression: we read what we intended to say, rather than what we have actually written. The strategies that we use to make meaning from texts are both cognitive and metacognitive, that is, they involve both thinking (without a conscious decision to employ a strategy), and thinking *about* thinking (where we consciously and deliberately decide to use a strategy). If you flick back in a text to check a piece of information, or skim over unimportant information, then you are using a cognitive strategy. If you deliberately decide to highlight key words in a text, or choose to summarise information in a table to help you to understand it, then you are using a metacognitive strategy. Teaching comprehension strategies is essentially about enabling pupils to develop better metacognitive control of their reading – it involves making explicit what good readers do instinctively so that all pupils can consciously choose to make use of different strategies to improve their comprehension. Over time, some of these may then become automatic.

The most important strategy is comprehension monitoring (Pressley, 2000; Yuill and Oakhill, 2010). This is always a metacognitive strategy, and involves checking what you do and don't understand in a text, enabling you then to find ways to address what you don't understand (by referring back in a text, or looking for further information, for example). It is an important skill for all readers, including those with Special Educational Needs (Berkeley et al., 2010). As well as comprehension monitoring, other strategies which have been shown to improve reading ability when they are taught explicitly (NSW, 2010) include:

- making connections: comparing ideas within a text, across other texts you've read and with life experiences you have had;
- predicting: anticipating what will happen next;
- visualising: creating mental representations of people, places, activities;
- questioning: asking questions of the text;
- inferring: reading between the lines;
- summarising: putting content into your own words.

Note that these are not teaching strategies, but are rather reading strategies that pupils need to be taught. You can refer to this list when devising a lesson that involves reading, and consider what activities would be relevant to both the text and the development of pupils' reading strategies.

DART – directed activities related to text

Another way to develop comprehension is to use a DART activity (directed activities related to text). These were originally developed by Lunzer and Gardner in 1979 and are particularly relevant to non-fiction texts. They can be used to support the development of reading strategies (e.g. doing a prediction activity, if you highlight to pupils what they are doing, this will develop pupils' understanding of how to use prediction); however, they are, themselves, specific *activities* rather than general *strategies*. You should encourage readers to explain and articulate how they made their decisions so that they become explicitly aware of the reading strategies that they are using as they complete the activities – developing their metacognitive awareness. Choose a DART activity that fits the work you are doing with your class and that naturally accompanies the kind of text you are using or the particular skill or learning that you are hoping to develop. Be clear about what the learning point of any given activity is, otherwise the learning pupils may derive from the activity will be fortuitous rather than planned. Through a successful DART activity, 'the processes of comprehension, of gaining meaning and drawing inferences from text, are brought out into the open, and it is from this that one reader can learn from another how to become a better or more thoughtful creator of meaning' (Harrison, 2004, p.100). The list below groups the DART activities into clusters and explains what reading skills each might develop.

DART activities (see also Unit 5.2) include the following:

Text marking: underlining, annotating, or numbering the text to show sequence. Skills include: skimming or scanning to find specific information; deciding what is relevant; finding the main ideas.

Graphic reorganisation: reading and remodelling the information into another format, such as flow charts, diagrams, grids, lists, maps, charts, or concept maps. Skills include: identifying what is key and relevant; applying what is known in a new context; summary and prioritisation; synthesising information.

Sequencing: reconstructing a text that has been cut into chunks. Skills include: paying close attention to the structure of the text; paying close attention to link words; hunting for the logic or organising principle of the text, e.g. chronological order; using previous experience and earlier reading.

Cloze: gap-filling tasks that involve the reader in actively constructing meaning. Skills include: paying close attention to the meaning of the sentence; choosing a word that fits grammatically; using one's existing knowledge of the topic; working out what is likely from the rest of the text; working out what fits with the style of the text; reading and re-reading.

Prediction: intelligent, informed speculation about what happens next. Skills include: looking for clues in the text to inform prediction; drawing on reader knowledge of other similar texts; justifying decisions with textual evidence.

Text reformulation: re-presenting the information or ideas in a text in a different format. Skills include: selecting key information; sifting the relevant from the irrelevant; awareness of the characteristics of different genres.

Adapted from Department for Education and Skills (DfES), 2002, p.31)

Now complete Task 5.8.3.

Task 5.8.3 Incorporating comprehension strategies into lessons

Take a text for your subject that you might use in a lesson and create a lesson activity that explicitly teaches one of the comprehension strategies outlined above, perhaps using a DART activity.

Write a short paragraph explaining the rationale for the task you have developed.

Include this in your PDP.

Writing like an expert

As a teacher, you are most likely to use talk as a tool for fostering learning; however, it remains the case that the dominant mode of assessment is writing. Your pupils will need to develop an appropriate 'voice' in their writing, following the conventions of your particular subject. In teaching your pupils to write 'like an expert', you should aim to enable them to communicate with authority – both to support their confidence in tackling written exams and assignments, and to raise the quality of their responses. To achieve this, you will need to spend some time unpicking the conventions of writing within your subject, examining the key vocabulary and patterns of language which pupils need to learn, and considering how to interweave the teaching of writing into your subject content.

In terms of mental effort, writing is one of the most sophisticated and complex activities we engage in: Kellogg (2008) argues that writing makes as much demand on our cognitive abilities as playing chess. The reason it is such a challenging task is because all writers are multi-tasking: we have to think about who the writing is for and what we want it to achieve, about structure and organisation, word choices, tone and formality, punctuation and spelling; and we have to physically produce the text, either on paper or digitally. Writers have to learn that writing 'is not simply the language of speech written down' (Perera, 1987, p.17) and have to shape written text to match the writing task set. Secondary school pupils are expected to develop expertise in a range of academic genres, and will rarely develop the repertoire of language that they need to achieve this automatically. Perera noted that 'teachers need to be aware of some of the linguistic difficulties that pupils encounter as they attempt to master a formal written style' (1987, p.22) and Myhill (2009) has shown that writers of differing levels of competence have mastered different linguistic constructions. Many pupils have only vague ideas about how to improve their writing, e.g., 'I need to add more detail'; 'I need to use better words'. It is important, then, to be explicit in your teaching of writing (see Gardner, 2013).

The first thing to make explicit is the key vocabulary needed to communicate ideas with accuracy and precision within your subject. Precise terminology is crucial for conveying expertise and to enable pupils to present their points more concisely. Consider the difference between 'the heart would go faster' and 'the heart rate increases' or between 'people who have moved to work in another place' and 'economic migrants'. It is common practice for classrooms to display key subject vocabulary, though these often tend to be nouns. It is equally important to consider the verbs needed in your subject, as they frequently relate to higher-order thinking skills and to appropriate ways to communicate in your subject. As well as simply displaying vocabulary, you could teach pupils the etymology of key words in order to support their understanding of related words (e.g.

photo-synthesis: light + putting together) or create word-webs of related words to underline relationships: (e.g. geography; geophysical; geothermal). When starting to plan for a new topic, you might like to draw up two vocabulary lists: *entitlement vocabulary*, the words you want all pupils to know, use and spell correctly; and *extension vocabulary*, the words you want your highest attaining pupils to know.

Another way to be explicit is to consider what the written genres for your subject are. Genres in writing are 'how things get done, when language is used to accomplish them' (Martin, 1985, p.250); they are a collectively and implicitly agreed upon set of conventions for writing and 'preferred ways of creating and communicating knowledge within particular communities' (Swales, 1990, p.4). Ask yourself what kinds of writing you ask pupils to complete: it might be evaluations, reports, explanations, argument essays or instructions. Don't get bogged down with naming text types: there are different ways of categorising genres (e.g. Derewianka, 1996; Wing Jan, 1991) but it is more important that you can identify the writing genres for your subject and explain how they work. One way to approach this is to consider the different command words used to frame writing tasks. These might be words like 'describe' 'explain' 'analyse' 'evaluate' or 'explore'. To some extent these words have standard definitions, but there can be variations in what is expected according to subject. For example, the following question and (high level) answer is taken from a GCSE Geography exam.

Question: Using a case study of a quarry you have studied, describe how it has been managed during extraction and restored following the extraction of the resources.

Answer: At Lafarge Cement in Hope in Derbyshire, over 75,000 trees have been planted to make the quarry and cement works less obvious and make it blend in with the environment. Two and a half million tonnes of limestone that could not be used for making cement have been used to help conceal the entrance by altering the landscape. Much is transported by train, so traffic on narrow roads in the countryside is reduced. Road cleaning is arranged to get rid of dust in immediate area. After an area is finished it is restored to farming or a different use, such as fishing lakes, and a 9-hole golf course has been opened.

The command word here is 'describe', but we can also see features typical of 'explanations', particularly in the way in which *reasons* are presented: 'to make the quarry...less obvious'; 'to help conceal'; 'so traffic...is reduced'.

We can look at this example more closely to consider which linguistic features make this answer sound like an expert. Firstly, there is sophisticated vocabulary: 'conceal', 'transported', 'restored'. There is a clear and logical sequence of information signalled by conjunctions related to causation or sequence: 'so', 'After'. There are subordinate clauses which explain the reasons for actions: 'to make...less obvious', 'that could not be used for making cement', 'to get rid of dust'. There are noun phrases in which a single noun is expanded with extra information, to provide precision and detail: '*traffic* on narrow roads in the countryside', 'a 9-hole *golf course*'.

These structures and patterns of language can and should be taught. It is helpful for you as a teacher to model writing for the pupils. Modelling is a scaffolding strategy (Wood et al., 1976) teachers use that gives additional assistance in the early stages of learning and that is later withdrawn. Whittaker et al. (2006) describe the modelling of written genres as a three-step process of deconstruction, joint construction and independent construction:

> From the examination of the purpose, structure and grammatical features of genres (deconstruction), through a critical phase of guided interaction which provided a context in which the 'constructedness' of texts could be explicitly negotiated, and responsibility for the construction of a new text could be shared among peers and with teachers, through to a phase of independent construction and 'control' of the genre.
>
> (Whittaker et al., 2006, p.86)

The benefit of modelling how a genre is constructed is that it makes visible things that writers might not have noticed otherwise and allows them to have more choice and control in designing their writing (Myhill, 2010). But one danger of modelling genres is in teaching writers formulaic approaches to writing, rather like offering them a recipe for writing that they must dutifully follow. Encourage writers to appreciate that there are often a range of ways to fulfil the demands of the genre, and that sometimes being unconventional can be very successful. Now complete Task 5.8.4.

 Task 5.8.4   Deconstructing text

Take an example of a high-level extended writing from your subject and annotate with the genre and linguistic features that you would want pupils to understand and be able to use. Look at the helpful accounts of different genres in Christie and Martin (2005). And then use the following questions as prompts:

- How does this text begin?
- Is it written in the first person or the third person?
- Is it formal or informal?
- Does it use the passive voice?
- Do the sentences tend to be short or long, or have any typical characteristic?
- Are there particular conjunctions or adverbs used to link ideas?
- Is there a vocabulary associated with this kind of text?
- Is there an underlying structure?
- How does this end?
- Is there a particular visual layout of the text?

Then create a teaching episode where you model this text, using the deconstruction, joint construction and independent construction approach.

Put the annotated text and the episode plan in your PDP.

SUMMARY AND KEY POINTS

■ This unit has addressed the primacy of language for learning, and has emphasised the importance of language in creating learning classrooms.

■ Drawing principally on Vygotsky's theory of the relationship between thought and language, the unit outlines how, through developing young people's language, we are simultaneously supporting their development as learners.

■ All three language modes - talking, reading, and writing - play a part in this interrelationship between language and learning, and by addressing language issues in your subject you are also increasing pupil achievement in your subject.

■ The idea of 'language across the curriculum' is not that everyone does the job of the English department, but rather that all teachers understand this integral partnership between language and learning and take seriously how they can strengthen subject-specific language use.

■ This unit, then, is fundamentally about creating language-rich classrooms. To do this, you need to be able to plan explicitly for language activities in the context of your subject.

■ We hope this unit enables you to establish classroom interaction patterns where pupils talk more than teachers, and engage in collaborative and constructive group work.

■ We hope that you will offer pupils activities that help them to become active and critical readers of texts, and that you will identify and model the written genres used in your subject.

■ Finally, we hope that you become a teacher who understands the power of language and knows that language is the very heart of empowered learning.

Check which requirements for your ITE programme you have addressed through this unit.

 ## Further resources

Alexander, R. (2004) *Towards Dialogic Teaching: Rethinking Classroom Talk*, **Cambridge: Dialogos.**
> This short booklet is invaluable in providing a thorough overview of the principles of dialogic teaching, and in offering ways to think about transforming the patterns of classroom talk so that young people are given more dynamic and challenging opportunities to learn.

Coultas, V. (2007) *Constructive Talk in Challenging Classrooms*, **Abingdon: Routledge.**
> This book is full of practical, but principled guidance on how to develop collaborative group work in classrooms where many teachers would avoid it, including where pupils have low levels of literacy or have English as an additional language. Coultas argues that talk is essential for building positive relationships, especially in difficult classrooms.

Creative Grammar Teaching, viewed 3 July 2018, from http://socialsciences.exeter.ac.uk/education/ research/centres/centreforresearchinwriting/grammar-teacher-resources/

Cremin, T. and Myhill, D.A. (2012) *Writing Voices: Creating Communities of Writers*, **Abingdon: Routledge.**
> This book considers writing from a range of perspectives and covers both primary and secondary phases. It offers a sound theoretical review of research on writing in the opening chapter and goes on to consider, for example, the role of talk in writing, agency and ownership, and metacognition in writing. The book is interspersed with vignettes of writing from pre-school writers to professional novelists and journalists.

Dialogic Teaching, http://www.robinalexander.org.uk/

Harrison, C. (2004) *Understanding Reading Development*, **London: Sage.**

Underpinned by a strong grasp of research in reading, this book looks at various elements of reading development in the reading process, comprehension, critical literacy and assessment. It takes a holistic view of reading, addressing issues of reading in both primary and secondary school.

MESHGuides (Mapping Educational Specialist knowHow) (see https://www.meshguides.org)

This website hosts a growing number of research-informed guides for teachers to support teachers becoming evidence-informed practitioners, including specific guides on 'English as an Additional Language (EAL)'; 'Grammar'; 'Reluctant writers'; 'Special Educational Needs and Disabilities (SEND)'; 'Spelling'.

Ross, A. (2006) *Language Knowledge for Secondary Teachers*, **London: David Fulton.**

Many teachers, including English teachers, are not confident with grammar because, for many years, grammar was not taught in our schools. This book is a practical text that can also act as a reference point if you need to brush up on your nouns or clauses!

Appendix 2 lists subject associations and teacher councils and Appendix 3 provides a list of websites.

Capel, S., Leask, M. and Turner, T. (eds.) (2010) *Readings for Learning to Teach in the Secondary School: A Companion to M Level Study*, **Abingdon: Routledge.**

This book brings together essential readings to support you in your critical engagement with key issues raised in this textbook.

Capel, S., Lawrence, J., Leask, M. and Younie, S. (eds.) (2019) *Surviving and Thriving in the Secondary School: The NQT's Essential Companion*, **Abingdon: Routledge.**

This book is designed to support newly qualified teachers in the next phase of development as a teacher. However, you may find it useful as it covers aspects of teaching not included in this book which, nonetheless you experience on your ITE programme.

The subject specific books in the *Learning to Teach (Subject)* series, the *Practical (Subject) Guides, Debates in (Subject)* and *Mentoring (Subject) Teachers* are also very useful.

Any additional resources and an editable version of any relevant tasks/tables in this unit are available on the companion website: www.routledge.com/cw/capel

6 Assessment

Assessment and its reporting are a central issue in teaching and learning throughout education. In England, since the 1988 Education Reform Act, national testing has taken centre stage in monitoring standards in schools.

This chapter addresses the purposes of assessment, their relationships to teaching and learning, and recent changes in assessment practice and reporting. The importance of formative assessment in raising achievement is discussed. Formative assessment is contrasted with summative assessment as is 'low stakes' vs 'high stakes' testing. The concepts of validity and reliability in assessment are addressed, including the tensions between them. Learning objectives that are difficult to assess but educationally important are also considered.

Formative assessment provides information about an individual pupil's progress, helps you devise appropriate teaching and learning strategies and gives parents helpful information about their child's progress. Summative assessments are used to compare pupils, schools and LAs across the country. This chapter also discusses the extent to which any one test can be used to assess pupil progress, the quality of teaching and teachers, and school effectiveness in raising standards.

Unit 6.1, 'In-school summative and minute-by-minute formative assessment in the classroom', gives an overview of the principles of assessment, of formative and summative assessment, diagnostic testing and ideas of validity and reliability. The differences between norm-referenced, criterion-referenced and ipsative assessment are introduced and the nationally set tests discussed in the light of these principles. This unit shows how assessment can be used to identify progress and diagnose problems. The unit compares what could be assessed with what is assessed, linking the issues to public accountability of teachers, school governing bodies, LAs and national educational standards. The chapter also considers the implications of the Department for Education's decision to move away from a 'levels'-based system of assessment for National Curriculum subjects (DfE, 2013d), and suggests some pragmatic ways of assessing pupil progress based on what is known about good practice in assessment.

Unit 6.2, 'External assessment and examinations', considers preparing pupils for public examinations, an important feature of a teacher's work; this unit considers assessment as exemplified by GCSE and GCE Advanced Level. This unit links national monitoring of standards with your classroom work, raising issues of accountability. Public examinations grade pupils on a nationally recognised scale and exercise control over both entry to jobs and higher education. This unit addresses how national standards are maintained and national grades are awarded. Recent national developments in vocational education are discussed and the status of vocational education in relation to academic education is highlighted. Contrasts are drawn between the assessment methods used for vocational courses and academic courses.

6.1 In-school summative and minute-by-minute formative assessment in the classroom

Nikki Booth

Introduction

Assessment is complex, multifaceted and is one of the most debated areas of educational discourse. It covers a wide variety of purposes and uses ranging from nationally recognised external assessments, for example GCSEs and A Levels (see Unit 6.2), to day-by-day, even minute-by-minute, assessments. This unit looks closely at assessments that take place within the classroom with a particular focus on how assessment can be used on a minute-by-minute basis to improve teaching and learning. It is important to state from the outset that every school may see and do assessment differently, and although this unit is research- and practitioner-informed, it is important that it is read in conjunction with your school's assessment policy.

OBJECTIVES

At the end of this unit you should be able to:

- define what assessment is;
- define the four purposes of assessment in schools;
- explain why national curriculum levels were removed;
- explain the differences between summative and formative assessment;
- write clear learning intentions (learning objectives);
- write process success criteria;
- give quality feedback that moves learning forward;
- describe what meaningful self- and peer-assessment is;
- grow self-regulating learners.

Check the requirements of your initial teacher education (ITE) programme to see which relate to this unit.

What is assessment?

Assessment can be defined as the collecting and interpreting of a range of evidences in order to make a judgement of some kind. Although we, as teachers, may use assessment to establish what pupils have *learned* at the end of a unit of work, for example, through the completion of a test (commonly referred to as summative assessment), it is certainly possible, however, to assess pupils prior to this, that is, while they are still *learning*. This type of process-based formative assessment can be in the form of, for example, day-to-day observations of, and learning conversations with, our pupils.

The *Oxford English Dictionary* traces the term 'assessment' from the Latin *ad sedere* which means 'to sit beside'. Sousa (2015) theorises that this could relate to the time of Socrates who would sit beside a pupil and test them through oral questions and conversations, and whether the pupil's response was right or wrong, it would lead to more dialogue, insights and greater depth of understanding of the subject domain; this, in turn, is known as the 'Socratic method'. By using assessment in this way, it acts as a bridge between what is being taught and what is being learned (Wiliam, 2013), and whether teaching is having its intended effect. The term 'assessment', however, can be problematic as it can be viewed as being separate from (Graue, 1993) and more likely to occur *after* (Fautley and Savage, 2008) the teaching and learning cycle. This point is further exemplified at the whole-school level by Ofsted (2015b) who, in their *Common Inspection Framework*, partly judge schools on the quality of their teaching, learning *and* assessment, as if assessment is seen as something separate from day-to-day teaching and learning. Fautley labels this separation as the 'folk view of assessment' (2010, p.3) where the association of classroom-based assessment seems to represent a series of fixed-points throughout the school year in order to determine pupil progression. Although this may happen more frequently in some subjects than others, you may often hear teachers in schools refer to this as 'assessment week' or 'the assessment lesson' as is visually exemplified in Figure 6.1.1.

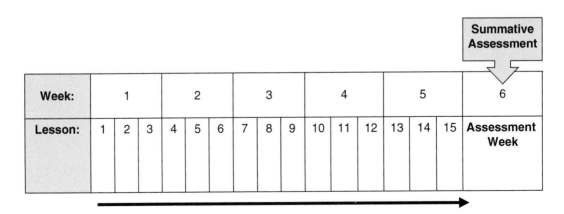

Figure 6.1.1 Teaching *and* assessment

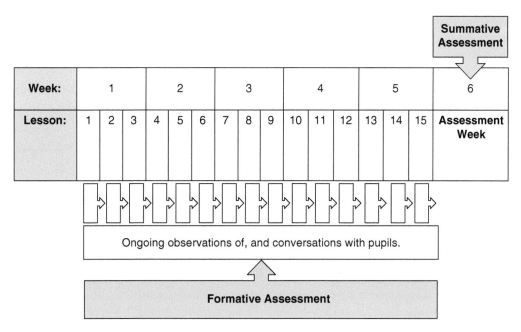

Figure 6.1.2 Teaching *within* assessment

A problem with this 'folk view' of assessment is that it 'downgrade[s] teachers' judgements' (Fautley, 2010, p.4), and yet it is the day-to-day observations and ongoing learning conversations which are essential to pupil progress (Wiliam, 2011). Seen from this perspective, 'to teach *is* to assess' (Swanwick, 1988, p.149) and it, therefore, becomes impossible to separate assessment from teaching. Furthermore, as Figure 6.1.2 shows, when assessment is integrated into teaching, it becomes a key part in day-to-day learning as it can be 'used to help students learn and to improve instruction rather than being used only to rank students or to certify the products of learning' (Shepard, 2000, p.31). What is clear from Shepard's view is that assessment can serve different purposes and although different forms of assessment may commonly judge pupil learning in some way, it is how the information is *used* that can determine its purpose. Regardless of this, though, as Mortimore and Mortimore (1984) assert, it is vital that assessment is the faithful servant and not the dominating master.

What are the purposes of assessment?

The Task Group on Assessment and Testing for England and Wales (TGAT, 1988) reported four generic purposes of assessment and included terminology that are still frequently used in schools today:

- **diagnostic assessment**: to identify pupils' learning needs so remedial help and guidance can be provided;
- **formative assessment**: to support and encourage learning through the discussion of next steps;
- **summative assessment**: to record overall achievement of pupils;
- **evaluative assessment**: to report on the quality of provision in schools and the system as a whole.

Within the classroom, it is the 'formative' and 'summative' purposes of assessment that are most relevant, and even though 'diagnostic assessment' is indeed important for our pupils to progress, it is commonly thought of nowadays as being part of formative assessment. Although distinctions between 'summative' and 'formative' have been familiar since the 1960s (for example, Scriven, 1967), it would appear that these two purposes have not been well understood (James et al., 2006), so they require clarifying and will be dealt with in turn. Before continuing, complete Task 6.1.1.

✏ Task 6.1.1   Identifying summative and formative purposes of assessment

Read each of the scenarios below and try to identify which are for 'summative' purposes and which are for 'formative'. You will be able to check your answers once you have read the in-school summative assessment and minute-by-minute formative assessment sections.

1   The teacher marks a test and gives scores out of 20 back to the pupils.
2   The teacher gives oral comments to a pupil on how they can improve their previous answer.
3   In a group activity, pupils discuss their strengths and weaknesses from the previous lesson.
4   After an end-of-lesson plenary, pupils swap their exit cards and mark how many the other person got right.
5   The teacher collects in and marks pupils' exercise books with a mark of how many answers they got right along with comments on how to improve.

Store the answers in your professional development portfolio (PDP) or equivalent.

In-school summative assessment

Assessment without levels: why were national curriculum levels removed?

National curriculum levels were introduced in 1988 and were originally designed to deliver an assessment process that measured pupils' achievement on a 10- (and later, eight-) level-based national framework. The original intention behind these levels was that teachers would report their pupils' achievement at the end of the Key Stage. This was, in fact, the only legal requirement. Wiliam (2014) posits that the original intention behind levels changed significantly when schools moved from reporting at the end of the Key Stage to reporting levels every year, then every term, and even for individual pieces of work on a lesson-by-lesson basis. Not only this, but the notion of sub-levels (for example '4c') became a common feature within schools for reporting pupil progress. What happened, therefore, was that the level-based framework was being used in such a way that it simply got in the way of quality teaching and learning (Wiliam, 2014).

In 2014, with the revised national curriculum for England, levels were removed and schools were required to establish their own approaches to curriculum assessment. As such, senior leaders were expected to 'use their professional judgement in deciding which approaches work best for their pupils' (DfE 2015c, p.4).

According to the Department for Education's (DfE, 2015c) *Commission of Assessment without Levels*, there are several reasons for this significant change:

1 Despite the intention for use only in statutory national assessments, all too frequently levels also became used for in-school assessment between key stages in order to monitor whether pupils were on track to achieve expected levels at the end of the key stages. This often distorted the purpose of in-school assessment, and in particular day-to-day assessment which was intended to inform teaching and learning.

2 Too often levels became viewed as thresholds and teaching became focused on getting pupils across the next threshold instead of ensuring they were secure in their knowledge and understanding. As a result, depth and breadth of understanding were sometimes sacrificed in favour of pace.

(DfE, 2015c, p.5)

In addition to this, pupils would frequently compare themselves with their peers and also tended to label themselves according to what 'level' they were at. By using levels in this way, pupils would inherit a fixed mindset of their ability, which could be seen as damaging, particularly for those who were told that they were a lower level (Dweck, 2006).

According to Dweck (1986; 2006), a learner with a fixed mindset has the following traits:

■ they have a strong desire to prove themselves over and over again;
■ they evaluate situations in terms of: 'Will I succeed or fail?', 'Will I look smart or dumb?';
■ they become afraid of seeking and taking challenges and risks through potential fear of failure;
■ they are only interested in feedback which relates to their ability;
■ they maintain interest in tasks if they can do them straight away;
■ they focus far more on repairing their self-esteem than the 'failures' of their work.

The notion of removing levels offers pupils the opportunity to develop a growth mindset (Dweck, 1986; 2006) where they:

■ believe that the basic qualities of learning can grow from effort, application and experience;
■ believe that a person's true potential is unknown;
■ believe that they can *become* smart rather than being born smart.

In short, it can be seen that a fixed mindset limits achievement, interferes with thoughts, makes effort disagreeable and leads to inferior learning strategies. A growth mindset, on the other hand, can help pupils understand that learning is a *process* that develops over time (Dweck, 2006) (see Unit 4.3 on cognitive development).

The revised national curriculum provides a basis for a different and a more secure depth of understanding. In the DfE's *Commission* (2015c), it is revealed that the benefits of assessing without levels are that:

1 pupils will be able to take far more responsibility for reflecting on their personal progress through understanding what their current strengths are and be able to clearly identify what they need to do to improve their learning. It is also important to note that this aim also provides parents/carers with a clearer sense on how they can support their child(ren) at home with their learning;

2   teachers will be able to focus far more on providing quality feedback that clearly identifies aspects of the curriculum that are secure and where there are gaps;

3   pupils can change their mindsets regarding their own ability.

What is important to note from this section is the notion that, in a response to assessing without levels, schools have had to come up with their own ways of recording pupil attainment. What you may find, therefore, is that even schools that are very near to each other could have taken very different approaches, and details of this will be written in each school's assessment policy. Despite the wide range of potential approaches, though, in order to record pupil attainment with some sort of 'level', it is likely that pupils would have undergone some form of summative assessment.

What is summative assessment?

Summative assessment (also commonly referred to as Assessment *of* Learning) certifies pupil attainment in some way. As the name suggests, the principal aim of summative assessment is to summarise learning; for example, giving a pupil a mark, level or grade from a test, quiz or end of unit exam. The gathering and interpreting of these 'summaries' may indeed have an impact on the teaching and learning cycle in terms of future planning; however, summative assessment is not carried out with this in mind. Instead, the purpose of this form of assessment is to report attainment at a particular time (Broadfoot, 2008). There are a number of ways in which information from in-school summative assessments can be used throughout the school year including: the internal tracking of pupil progress, informing the pupil, informing parents/carers and informing the pupil's next teacher. The reporting of in-school summative assessments differs from that of external examinations; these results do not lead to accreditation from an external examining body nor selection for employment or higher education. The key notion with summative assessment, whether in-school or external, is that it happens *after* learning has taken place and, therefore, 'looks back on achievement' (Fautley and Savage, 2008, p.27). The publication of marks, levels or grades, or what Broadfoot calls 'dead data' (2008, p.8), to pupils and parents/carers can be problematic with regards to validity and reliability.

Validity can be broken down into several sub-parts:

■   *face validity*: requires that an assessment looks as if it assesses what it claims to assess;

■   *predictive validity*: generalises information from a test to predict future achievement;

■   *construct validity*: requires clarity in the area being assessed so that the assessment tests the construct (for example, mathematical concepts) and not anything else, such as someone's ability to read complex instructions;

■   *consequential validity*: where teachers consider how information from the assessment will be used for teaching, learning and school improvement;

■   *content validity*: which can be regarded as 'the most important kind of validity' (James, 1998, p.151), where assessments are conducive of all relevant subject matter and not just a small sample of it.

In-school, teacher-made summative assessments have been found to lack sufficient validity. This is because they frequently focus on a narrow range of knowledge and information gained (Stobart, 2009), rather than a wide range of learning goals including problem-solving and critical thinking skills. The reason behind this, it has been suggested, is that 'teachers emulate externally-devised tests in creating their own' (Harlen, 2007, p.53). This is an important consideration as not only is there a loss of skill by teachers in writing assessments, which can lead to the poor design of assessment tasks (Harlen, 2002), but there is also a lack of confidence in teachers' ability to make sound judgements of their pupils (Black et al., 2010). Notwithstanding this, *construct validity* is likely to be greater when teachers gather evidence from a range of sources by the coverage of a varied, and far more complete, set of learning goals (Harlen, 2007).

Reliability is not a separate idea, but is interwoven with validity (Andrade and Heritage, 2018) and can refer to the quality of the assessment procedure (Harlen, 2000) where results from assessments can be made more consistent by 'eliminating errors from different sources' (James, 1998, p.157). Such inconsistencies, for example, might come from differences in how a task is presented to different pupils. This is important as it could have a profound impact on the way pupils respond to an assessment. The blend of validity and reliability, then, can be referred to as 'dependability' (James, 1998).

With regards to teacher-made assessments, there can be a trade-off in favour of validity since, through the academic year, no terminal decisions will hang upon this data. As such, as has been mentioned above, our judgements can be based on a range of curricular outcomes. This means that meaningful evidence of learning can come from regular pupil work; it can cover a range of opportunities for pupils to show what they have learned and, furthermore, can reduce anxiety associated with tests (Harlen, 2007). It should be emphasised, however, particularly within large departments of several teachers, that threats to the reliability of the information gathered need to be reduced. In order for our judgements to have more reliability, there is the need for internal, quality-assured school moderation to take place to confirm our decisions, which, unlike testing for external purposes, can enhance teaching and learning (Assessment Reform Group, 2006). It is unfortunate, however, that this is not a consistent practice throughout schools in the United Kingdom (Black et al., 2010).

Due to the pressures set upon schools, current practice seems to be for teachers to show their pupils to be making regular, visible, rapid progress (Harlen, 2008). Depending on your school's assessment policy, it may be the norm for you to show how much your pupils have learned by not only testing them at the end of every topic, but every few lessons, or even at the end of every lesson. Whilst these low-stake tests may inform you as to what pupils can and cannot do as well as inform future lessons, the impact of these frequent summative assessments have been found to have serious consequences on learning. With reference to frequent summative assessments, Harlen and Deakin-Crick (2003) observed that:

- teachers adopt a 'teach to the test' style of teaching;
- the tests reinforce low self-esteem among lower-achievers, particularly with boys;
- pupils become increasingly anxious because of the need to 'perform' well;
- pupils' effort is affected by what they think they are going to achieve;
- pupils adjust their future effort in response to receiving their mark, level or grade;
- pupils become increasingly grade obsessed.

Harlen asks us to appreciate 'that children's learning is not regular and that change in important skills and understanding takes time' (2008, p.149) and:

> to attempt to detect change at more frequent intervals results in focusing on 'surface' learning, such as memorizing facts that are quickly learned and just as quickly forgotten, in frequent tests to demonstrate this learning.

(Harlen, 2008, p.149)

Harlen also asks us to use summative assessment 'only when reports are needed, at the end of the year or half-year, or when major decisions have to be made' (2008, p.150). Similarly, Kohn (1994) suggests that we should never give scores or grades to pupils whilst they are still learning; as soon as they receive them, the learning stops as pupils focus far more on the potential consequences of these marks or grades rather than what they need to do to improve.

Although the negative effects of regular summative assessment are well-documented within assessment literature, their frequency is dependent upon a school's assessment policy. It is important to note that giving marks, levels or grades is very unlikely to improve learning by itself; what is needed, therefore, is formative assessment to move learning forward.

Minute-by-minute formative assessment

Why is formative assessment important?

There is over 40 years' worth of research evidence to suggest that enhancing formative assessment (also commonly referred to as 'Assessment *for* Learning') in the classroom leads to a significant impact on pupil learning (Wiliam, 2016). The early work on formative assessment focused on how teachers would use evidence of their pupils' learning to inform and change their teaching decisions, whilst more recent research (for example, Black and Wiliam, 2012) reports that formative assessment requires a change in roles between teachers and pupils where pupils take a greater responsibility for their own learning. Despite the wealth of research evidence into and exemplification of good formative assessment practice in schools, 'there has been no (or, at best, limited) effect on learning outcomes nationally' (Coe, 2013, p.10). It would appear that the term 'formative assessment' has become a confused term in schools and, thus, requires some clarification.

What is formative assessment?

Within the UK, the term 'formative assessment' tends to be built upon the pioneering work of Black and Wiliam (1998). In their research, they defined formative assessment as 'all those activities undertaken by teachers, and/or their students to modify teaching and learning activities in which they are engaged' (1998, p.8). The key thing to know is that formative assessment is an ongoing *process* and involves working *with* pupils so that they know where they are in their learning, where they need to be and how they are going to get there. In short, formative assessment normally involves a conversation (whether oral or written) that enables teaching and learning to move forward (Booth, 2017).

Within a lesson, on a minute-by-minute basis, if you model what success looks like, observe, and give your pupils constructive comments to improve, you are engaging in formative assessment. As previously mentioned, 'to teach *is* to assess' (Swanwick, 1988, p.149), and although this may not be seen, by some, as assessment, this is exactly what is going on. Formative assessment does not include the giving of marks, levels or grades, nor does it compare pupils with one another. Instead, its focus is on what the next steps in learning are on an individual and personal level. What makes formative assessment truly *formative*, though, is not only the collecting and giving of information, but that the information is actively *used* by you to improve your teaching, and your pupils to improve their learning.

Based on Leahy et al.'s (2005) work, there are a number of formative strategies (each described below) which can be used in the classroom to help support quality, minute-by-minute formative assessment. Before any meaningful learning conversation can take place within a lesson, however, it is important that we know what it is we want our pupils to learn. This is done through the sharing and clarifying of learning intentions.

Beginning with the end: what do clear learning intentions look like?

A common feature within many classrooms today is the sharing of learning intentions (also known as learning objectives) with pupils. Although wording may be different between schools, fundamentally, these fall into three categories, as Table 6.1.1 shows.

Table 6.1.1 Categories of learning intentions

To know...	A learning intention that shows how much a pupil knows about a topic.
To understand... (sometimes used as to know how or know why...)	A learning intention that shows how well (rather than how much) a pupil knows about a topic.
To be able to...	A learning intention that shows how well a pupil can apply knowledge of a topic.

The clarification of the learning intention(s) is essential so that pupils are able to hold a concept similar to that of you, the teacher (Sadler, 1989). Furthermore, as Wiliam and Leahy state:

> Before we can find out what our learners are learning, before we can give feedback, before we can engage learners as resources for one another or as owners of their own learning, we have to be clear about where we are going.
>
> (2015, p.27)

Writing good learning intentions is challenging, even for more experienced teachers, and there are two key aspects that we must take into consideration.

The first relates to the work of Clarke (2005) and the problem of including the *context* within the learning intention itself. For example, in Key Stage 3 English, a learning intention of 'to (be able to) write a letter to your local council to keep your local swimming pool open' would be considered confused. In Clarke's (2005) view, pupils who have been working on this, perhaps for several lessons, are likely to do well – but so what? This is because, as teachers, we may not necessarily be interested in whether pupils can just write about keeping their local pool open *per se*, but whether the knowledge they have acquired throughout a sequence of lessons can be transferred into other contexts, for example, viewpoints regarding fox hunting. Instead, a slightly clearer learning intention could be 'to (be able to) write a letter' where 'to your local council to keep your local swimming pool open' would be the *context*.

Second, we need to have a clear understanding in our planning not only on what the pupils will be *doing* (activities), but what they will be *learning* by doing them. Our clearer learning intention of 'to be able to write a letter' is actually activity focused, not learning focused. What are pupils going to *learn* by writing this letter? Are they, for example, writing to persuade, or argue, is it formal or informal? Depending on where this particular learning intention falls within a unit of work, and what pupils' prior knowledge of writing letters is, possible alternatives could include:

■ to know the key features of a persuasive letter; or
■ to know (understand) how to use persuasive features; or even
■ to be able to write persuasively.

Table 6.1.2 Learning intention with process success criteria

Learning intention:	To be able to write persuasively.
Process Success Criteria:	You need to: ▪ state your point of view ▪ give reasons for your view points, with proof ▪ give alternative view points ▪ use subjective (personal feelings) language ▪ use rhetorical questions ▪ include a summary

Once we have made clear what the destination of our lesson is going to be, the next thing we need to consider is what pupils need to *do* in order to arrive there. This is where sharing and modelling what success looks like becomes an important aspect of quality learning.

What does success look like in the classroom?

If pupils are indeed to come 'to hold a concept of quality similar to that of the teacher' (Sadler, 1989, p.121), then sharing with them what success looks like is a very good idea. As one pupil voices, 'it's like knowing the teacher's secret' (Spendlove, 2009, p.18). Sharing success criteria means that there are regular formative assessment opportunities, for both teachers and pupils, during the lesson, on the journey to fulfilling the lesson's learning intention(s).

Clarke (2005) has been particularly influential, on an international level, with regards to defining two types of success criteria: *process* and *product*. Process success criteria can be seen as a summary of 'the key steps or ingredients the student needs in order to fulfil the learning objective' (Clarke, 2005, p.29). Product success criteria, on the other hand, merely tell pupils what the end product would look like. With our third English learning intention example above, a product success criteria example could be 'the reader will be persuaded by your letter'. To some, this may be fine, but what is it *exactly* pupils need to do in order to be persuasive writers? The table above (Table 6.1.2) shows how the last of our three learning intentions can be supported by process success criteria.

When pupils are clear on what they are learning (learning intentions) and what they need to do in order to get there (success criteria), we are then able to give meaningful feedback through the lesson to support pupils. Task 6.1.2 looks at learning intentions and process success criteria.

 Task 6.1.2   Writing clear learning intentions and process success criteria

Using the information that you have just read, write a clear context-free and learning-focused learning intention with process success criteria for a lesson within a unit of work. Give this to a colleague, who is not a subject specialist, and see if they understand what you propose pupils will be learning and what specifically they will need to do to be successful.

Store this in your PDP to inform your future development in this area.

What is quality feedback?

Feedback is significant for improving learning (Hattie and Yates, 2014) and is, therefore, a key part of formative assessment. Learning gaps can be evidenced through ongoing observations and regular conversations in relation to the learning intention(s) and success criteria. The purpose of giving feedback, whether oral or written, is that it is a two-way dialogue to reduce the gap between a pupil's current performance and the desired outcome. Sadler (1989) makes it clear that simply knowing how work can be improved cannot be considered feedback unless it is actively used.

The notion of giving marks, levels or grades (summative assessment) is important to consider when giving oral or written feedback. In a pioneering, oft-cited experiment, Butler (1988) found that pupils who received comment-only feedback made 30% more progress than pupils who just received a mark and, interestingly, those who received both comments and marks. The reason is simple: when pupils receive a mark, level or grade, with comments, the first reaction is for pupils to look at the standard they have been awarded, the second is to look around and see what other people got. The comments teachers write, therefore, go largely ignored. Reducing feedback to just comments may well seem easy, but it is the *quality* of the comments that makes a difference to moving learning forward.

Hattie and Timperley (2007) have classified four different types of feedback: task (or product), process, self-regulation and self; these are exemplified in Table 6.1.3.

Traditionally, feedback from the teacher has been seen as a one-way-type communication and has been criticised because pupils become too dependent on their teacher (Sadler, 1989). In an

Table 6.1.3 Types of feedback

Feedback Type	Description	How this might look like in the classroom
Task (or product)	This indicates whether a response is right or wrong.	Information is correct (tick) or incorrect (cross).
Process	This shows *how* pupils can correct their mistakes through the use of, for example, prompts to better understand the details of the task in hand.	'You need to re-work your letter using the success criteria so that you are clearly writing to persuade'.
Self-regulation	This is where pupils are able to monitor their own work and make necessary corrections as they go along.	'You already know the key features of a persuasive letter. Check to see if they are in yours'.
Self	This is information that provides personal feedback about the pupil. Hattie and Timperley found this level of feedback 'has too little value to result in learning gains' (2007, p.96); it does not give pupils any useful information about the learning task(s).	'Wow, great effort!'.

ideal world, effective feedback enables pupils to self- and peer-assess their own work (Nicol and Macfarlane-Dick, 2006). You are asked to look at feedback in Task 6.1.3.

 Task 6.1.3   Recognising quality feedback

Following Hattie and Timperley's (2007) types of feedback, ask a colleague to observe part of your lesson and make a tally of the different types of feedback you give to pupils. What does this information tell you about feedback in your lesson?

   Store this information in your PDP to inform your development of feedback.

What is meaningful self- and peer-assessment?

Research suggests (for example, Black and Wiliam, 1998) that when pupils are given a more active role in the assessment process, they are able to develop, use and apply their understanding to improve the quality of their own work through self- and peer-assessment (Butler and Winne, 1995) with increasing autonomy (Swaffield, 2011). This means that when pupils become 'insiders' of the assessment process, they become less dependent on their teacher and, therefore, more effective learners (James and Pedder, 2006). Other research (for example, James et al., 2006) has also shown that pupils make significantly more progress when they evaluate their learning using clearly defined process success criteria (as exemplified above) and not whether something is right or wrong, or whether they enjoyed it or not.

   Self- and peer-assessment is far more than pupils ticking and crossing their own and each other's work. Self- and peer-assessment, can be seen as a 'review process' in which pupils are actively engaged in:

■   reflecting upon past experience;
■   evaluating it and attempting to articulate what has been learned; and
■   identifying, in the light of this reflection, what still needs to be pursued.

(Broadfoot, 2008, p.135)

   Whilst this is a perfectly good description, the issue, from a learning perspective, is that this reflective thinking is done *after* learning, not *during*. Pupils who are able to assess and regulate as learning progresses are engaged in metacognition – thinking about thinking (Hattie, 2009). This is a complex form of learning that takes years of practice (Earl and Katz, 2008). As educators, we, therefore, have the responsibility for growing these skills. What we want, then, is to develop more self-regulating learners in our classrooms.

How can we grow self-regulating learners?

Zimmerman and Schunk (2011) observe that self-regulated learners are those who set their own learning goals during learning, and then monitor and regulate their motivation, behaviour and cognition to reach the desired outcome. There is research evidence (for example, Schunk and Zimmerman, 1998) to suggest that self-regulation can be taught to all pupils in the classroom by means of scaffolding. This scaffolding is powerful and initially comes from the receiving of quality teacher feedback, which is then acted upon by the pupil. As a result, pupils are able to take control of their own learning (Andrade and Heritage, 2018) by answering three questions:

1   **Where am I going?** (What is the learning intention?)
2   **Where am I now?** (Where am I currently within the success criteria?)
3   **Where to next?** (What do I still need to do to meet the learning intention?)

As has been a running theme throughout this unit, for any effective formative assessment to take place and improve learning, it is not only knowing this information that is important, but that it is actively used to make learning better. This, then, is formative assessment in action.

Now complete Task 6.1.4.

Task 6.1.4   Understanding the benefits of assessment tasks

Select one class that you teach and then some tasks that you have given pupils to do in recent lessons.

1   Over a period of several lessons with a class, consider whether your tasks address all the points outlined in this unit.
2   Write a record summarising your analysis and the implications this may have for planning future tasks for your class.
3   Use your analysis and discussion to plan and execute a short unit of work that includes all or most of the benefits you have identified from reflecting on assessment in this unit.

Finally, review the success or otherwise of your planned work, identifying the ideas and/or theories that have influenced your thinking about how you assess pupils' work and progress. Store in your PDP.

SUMMARY AND KEY POINTS

■   Assessment is the collecting and interpreting of a range of evidences in which a judgement of some kind is made about pupil progress and attainment.
■   The four purposes of assessment are:
  ■   **diagnostic**: to identify pupils' learning needs;
  ■   **formative**: to support learning;
  ■   **summative**: to record and report learning;
  ■   **evaluative**: to report on the quality of school provision.
■   National Curriculum levels were removed because:
  ■   in many schools, they were being used to measure pupil progress on a lesson-by-lesson basis, which often distorted good teaching and learning;
  ■   depth and breadth of learning was being overlooked in favour of pace.

- Summative assessment (Assessment *of* Learning) reports on learning; formative assessment (Assessment *for* Learning) is where information is gathered and *used* to improve teaching and learning.
- Learning intentions (learning objectives) can be made clear for pupils if they are context-free and focus on what pupils are going to *learn* rather than what they are going to *do*.
- Process success criteria reveals to pupils what the sequential order of key ingredients are for a quality piece of work.
- Quality feedback can be shown through the clarification as to *how* pupils can improve their work. Feedback is only effective, though, if it is actively used.
- Meaningful self- and peer-assessment relates to the regular reflective practice on learning intentions and success criteria.
- Self-regulating learners can be grown from answering three questions in relation to the learning intentions, success criteria and constructive teacher feedback:
  - Where am I going?
  - Where am I now?
  - Where to next?

Check which requirements for your ITE programme you have addressed through this unit.

 ## Further resources

In addition to the work cited in this unit, the following resources will also be of use:

Assessment Reform Group website: http://www.nuffieldfoundation.org/assessment-reform-group
(Download research papers and buy resources)

Black, P., Harrison, C., Lee, C., Marshall, D. and Wiliam, D. (2003) *Assessment for Learning: Putting It into Practice,* **Maidenhead: Open University Press.**
An insight from a large-scale study of 36 teachers into implementing formative assessment into the classroom.

Dylan Wiliam's website: http://www.dylanwiliam.org/Dylan_Wiliams_website/Welcome.html

Fautley, M. and Savage, J. (2008) *Assessment for Learning and Teaching in Secondary Schools,* **Exeter: Learning Matters.**
Targeted specifically at student teachers, this text links explicitly to the new qualified teacher status (QTS) standards, and the tasks provide opportunities for reflection and for practising the range of skills involved in assessing pupils.

Fautley, M. and Savage, J. (2013) *Lesson Planning for Effective Learning,* **Maidenhead: Open University Press.**
Practical strategies for teachers in order to plan successfully and reflect on practice.

Procter (2013) Assessment for Learning, MESHGuide, viewed 3 July 2018, from http://www.meshguide s.org/assessment-for-learning/

Stobart, G. (2014) *The Expert Learner: Challenging the Myth of Ability,* **Maidenhead: Open University Press.**
This book demolished the idea that ability is fixed and brings together ideas on what being a successful learner is through effective teaching.

Twitter feeds on assessment issues, e.g.

@nbooth2506, @dylanwiliam, @CharteredColl, @BeyondLevels, @Cam_Assessment.

YouTube:

Type, for example, 'Dylan Wiliam', 'formative assessment' and 'assessment for learning' for more information and classroom-based, practical techniques on implementing formative assessment in your classroom.

Appendix 2 lists subject associations and teacher councils and Appendix 3 provides a list of websites.

Capel, S., Leask, M. and Turner, T. (eds.) (2010) *Readings for Learning to Teach in the Secondary School: A Companion to M Level Study*, **Abingdon: Routledge.**

This book brings together essential readings to support you in your critical engagement with key issues raised in this textbook.

Capel, S., Lawrence, J., Leask, M. and Younie, S. (eds.) (2019) *Surviving and Thriving in the Secondary School: The NQT's Essential Companion*, **Abingdon: Routledge.**

This book is designed to support newly qualified teachers in the next phase of development as a teacher. However, you may find it useful as it covers aspects of teaching not included in this book which, nonetheless you experience on your ITE programme.

The subject specific books in the *Learning to Teach (Subject)* series, the *Practical (Subject) Guides*, *Debates in (Subject)* and *Mentoring (Subject) Teachers* are also very useful.

Any additional resources and an editable version of any relevant tasks/tables in this unit are available on the companion website: www.routledge.com/cw/capel

6.2 External assessment and examinations

Cara McLaughlin

Introduction

Principles of assessment were introduced in Unit 6.1. This unit looks at the particular role, function and nature of external assessment and examinations. We suggest you read Unit 6.1 before studying this unit.

This unit aims to provide you with an overview of the framework for external assessment and examinations in secondary schools with a particular focus on England. Issues relevant to Northern Ireland, Scotland and Wales are covered in units in Chapter 7 on the companion website. Although you are familiar with the public examinations that you took in school, there are regular changes and significant developments in assessment methods and in the range of external examinations taken by pupils in secondary schools. In England, each phase of schooling has been the subject of various policy initiatives in recent years. This can mean that the national qualifications can be introduced and withdrawn within a relatively short timescale.

As well as knowing how pupils are assessed throughout their secondary education, it is important to be aware of the many purposes of external assessment and examinations. These purposes can be usefully divided into those associated with candidates and those that have more to do with educational establishments and public accountability. Two important, recurrent themes that arise when discussing external assessment and examinations are validity and reliability. These two concepts, together with the agencies, regulations and processes involved in ensuring consistency in these two areas, are defined in Unit 6.1. Teaching externally examined classes is a challenge for any teacher and demands particular teaching skills and strategies, in addition to the routine elements of good lesson planning and teaching. This aspect of teaching, and the constraints and influence of the accountability agenda on the work of schools, is discussed in the final part of this unit.

OBJECTIVES

At the end of this unit, you should be able to:

■ identify the range of external assessments in secondary schools and access the national qualifications and credit framework;
■ understand the relationship between the national curriculum in a home country and external examinations;
■ explain the main purposes of external assessment;
■ understand the processes involved in the setting of external examinations and the organisations involved;
■ start addressing the issues relating to teaching examination classes;
■ understand the impact of external accountability measures on schools and teaching.

Check the requirements of your initial teacher education (ITE) programme to see which relate to this unit.

Your own experience

A good starting point for this unit is your own experience of external assessment and examinations whilst at school. What did you think was the purpose of sitting examinations, and did preparing for examinations impact on your motivation as a learner? Did the teaching strategies of examination classes differ from non-examination classes? Recalling these impressions may provide a good starting point from which to develop your understanding of the issues pertaining to external assessment and examinations.

Types of assessment

In Unit 6.1, we discussed formative and summative assessment and we remind you of those terms. Formative assessment can be defined as assessment for learning, and summative assessment as assessment of learning (Stobart and Gipps, 1997). External assessment and examinations are generally considered to be forms of summative assessment. There are two important methods used extensively in summative assessment that you need to be familiar with, namely norm-referenced assessment and criterion-referenced assessment.

Norm-referenced assessment has been used extensively throughout the British education system. In norm-referenced assessment, the value of, or grade related to, any mark awarded depends on how it compares with the marks of other candidates sitting the same assessment. The basis for this form of assessment is the assumption that the marks are normally distributed; that is, if you plot the marks awarded against the number of candidates, a bell-shaped curve is produced, providing the sample is big enough. This curve is then used to assign grade boundaries based on predetermined conditions; for example, that 80% of all those sitting the examination pass and 20% fail. In this way, an element of failure is built into the examination. The system of reporting by grades is essentially norm-referenced. For example, if you are awarded the highest grade in a subject in a public examination, this grade does not give any specific information about what you can do in that subject, simply that you were placed within the top group of candidates.

Criterion-referenced assessment, on the other hand, is concerned with what a candidate can do without reference to the performance of others, and so it provides an alternative method to address the limitations of norm-referencing. A simple example of criterion-referenced assessment is that of a swimming test. If someone is entered for a 100-metre swimming award, and swims 100 metres, then they are awarded that certificate irrespective of how many other people also reach this standard. Academic courses, such as General Certificate of Secondary Education (GCSE) Drama, use criterion-referencing when assessing practical skills as part of the teacher assessed element of the course, but the grades are awarded and the results are reported by comparing pupils with other pupils, that is, norm-referenced. Thus, the overall assessment in most examinations is a mixture of criterion-referenced marking together with norm-referenced grading and reporting of the level of achievement.

The framework of external assessment in secondary schools

External assessment in secondary schools is an area that has seen considerable change over a short period of time. We consider, in turn, Key Stage 3 (KS3), GCSE and post-16 education in England. Different arrangements are in place in Northern Ireland, Scotland and Wales. We suggest that you ensure you gather the information relevant to the context in which you are learning to teach. For example, in England, four assessment stages are referred to in this section; that is, Key Stage 2 (KS2), Years 3-6; Key Stage 3 (KS3), Years 7-9; Key Stage 4 (KS4) (that is, GCSE); and post-16 assessment.

Key Stage 3 assessment

On transfer to secondary school, pupils bring with them information obtained from the end of Key Stage 2 assessment. This information has historically been reported as teacher-assessed and externally assessed National Curriculum (NC) levels. The introduction of a new National Curriculum in September 2014 saw the removal of levels and no intention to replace them (DfE, 2014h), see Unit 6.1. Since the introduction of a National Curriculum following the Education Reform Act of 1988, levels have underpinned assessment and reporting progress, particularly across Key Stages 1-3. The stated purposes of the 2014 reform include to 'allow teachers greater flexibility in the way that they plan and assess pupils' learning' and a commitment to 'curriculum freedom' (DfE, 2014h). In practice, this means that summer 2015 was the final year that an end of Key Stage 3 'level' was reported. New National Curriculum tests for Key Stages 1 and 2 were introduced in summer 2016, two years after the start of a new National Curriculum. One purpose of the new Key Stage 2 tests is to test that pupils are 'secondary-ready' by reporting: a scaled score, which will show whether a pupil has met the expected standard and is 'secondary-ready'; ranking in the national cohort (by decile); and the rate of progress from a baseline (DfE, 2014h).

In England, until 2008, assessment at the end of Key Stage 3 took the form of internal teacher assessment for all NC subjects and external written tests, called Standard Assessment Tasks (SATs), for the core NC subjects of English, Mathematics and Science. The SATs were written with reference to the subject Programmes of Study of the NC; the questions in the tests were designed so that the demand on the pupil links closely to the level descriptions. Papers were set for each of the core subjects and tiered assessment was used to allow pupils to be entered for the paper most suited to their achievement. However, the written SATs were limited in what they tested and so had reduced validity in relation to the overall aims of NC subject specifications.

There are no longer external tests set at the end of Key Stage 3 and no public reporting of Key Stage 3 data, the last published tables being in 2007. Since 2014, schools no longer have a statutory requirement to report teacher-assessed levels for each of the core and non-core subjects.

Key Stage 4 assessment (Years 10–11) GCSE

The GCSE examination was introduced in 1986 to be taken at the end of Key Stage 4 to replace the General Certificate of Education (GCE) Ordinary (O) level and Certificate of Secondary Education (CSE), and to provide certification for about 90% of candidates. Similar examinations are in place in Northern Ireland and Wales. The Scottish system has a different structure (see Unit 7.5 on the

companion website).

In the *Importance of Teaching* White Paper (DfE, 2010), the government of the day signalled changes to 'restore confidence in GCSEs'. This statement heralded significant changes to the existing GCSE qualifications. The first change, introduced in September 2012, means that all GCSE courses are assessed by summer terminal examination only; the only exception to this rule is the opportunity to retake examinations in English, English Language and Mathematics GCSEs in November. The practice of pupils taking GCSE examinations by module, sometimes over a period of three years, and retaking individual modules on multiple occasions was withdrawn. Alongside these changes has been a return to the compulsory inclusion of marks for spelling, punctuation and grammar in GCSE examinations.

At the time of writing, the GCSE examinations are reported under two different grading systems and pupils receive a mixture of letter and number grades depending on the subject being assessed. Under the letter grading system, there are eight pass grades, A*–G; the A* grade recognises exceptional performance. In the number grading system there are nine pass grades, 9–1; the 9 grade recognises exceptional performance. The number grading system has been implemented in line with the GCSE reforms and to allow better differentiation between pupils' abilities. By 2019, most grades will be awarded as numbers.

The GCSE examinations are designed to test recall, understanding and skills. The reformed GCSE system still has a tiered assessment pattern for many of the subjects. This enables pupils to be entered for the paper most appropriate for their current achievement. Teachers assess pupils' progress and potential, and advise pupils on which tier of the examination to enter. Tiered papers carry grade limits, thus narrowing the opportunities of pupils. For example, a higher paper may enable pupils to be awarded grades 9–4, while a foundation paper may allow only the award of grades 5–1. Furthermore, if pupils fail to achieve the marks required for the lowest grade in their tier, then they receive an unclassified (U) grade.

Changes to the content and grading of GCSEs were introduced in September 2015. Initially, new specifications in English Language, English Literature and Mathematics were introduced followed by Science, History, Geography, languages and the remaining National Curriculum subjects in September 2016. The grading has been changed from letters to numbers. The use of tiered papers was also reduced. Decisions about the inclusion of tiered papers were considered at a subject level and depended on how effectively a single paper allows all pupils opportunities to demonstrate what they know and can do. In the first three new specifications, Mathematics is the only qualification to have foundation tier (grades 1-5) and higher tier (grades 4-9) papers.

Teacher-assessed coursework was introduced with the GCSE, and, in the early days of GCSE, some courses offered were entirely coursework-based. However, coursework has become progressively restricted by government legislation through the subject specifications and the amount allowed depends on the subject. In the 2015 GCSE reforms, more practically based subjects (for example, Music, Physical Education), a proportion of teacher-based assessment contributes to the final mark. No subject can be assessed only by teacher-assessed coursework, and for most other subjects (for example, Mathematics, Science) there is no coursework. English Language does have a non-examination assessment of spoken English but it does not contribute to the overall GCSE assessment.

Thus, the innovative approaches introduced with the GCSEs have been systematically removed to leave mainly single-tier, linear written examinations taken at the end of two years' study. It is important that you have a clear understanding of how and why GCSEs have changed; Task 6.2.1 asks you to address this issue.

 Task 6.2.1   GCSE examinations

Obtain copies of GCSE specifications from before and after the reforms introduced in 2015. For each specification, read the general introduction and familiarise yourself with the aims, assessment objectives and assessment patterns of the specification. Now turn to the assessment section and compare for each specification:

■ how the subject content differs;
■ how the structure of the qualification differs;
■ what form the assessment takes in each of the specifications;
■ whether there is any assessment outside the final examinations.

Discuss your findings with an experienced teacher in your placement school and find out:

■ their perceptions of how the GCSE assessment has changed in recent years;
■ what impact the changes have had on workload;
■ any impact the changes have had on pupils' motivation, engagement, achievement and attainment.

   A record of your work could be placed in your professional development portfolio (PDP) or equivalent.

Post-16 assessment

Of all of the changes that have followed the Education Reform Act (ERA, 1988), the area that has continued to undergo reorganisation is the provision of post-16 courses and their assessment: General Certificate of Education (GCE) Advanced (A) level courses.

GCE A level courses were first introduced in 1951 and since then have been regarded as the academic 'gold standard' by successive governments. Substantial changes were made to the framework of the 16–19 qualifications following a review, and implemented in September 2000 (Dearing, 1996), with further revisions introduced in 2007 (Ofqual, 2007).

Alongside the GCSE reforms outlined above, new GCE AS and A levels were introduced in schools in England from September 2015. AS assessment usually occurs after one year's study and A levels after two. The courses are no longer divided into modules and there are no exams in January. The AS qualification is now 'stand-alone' and does not contribute to the assessment of the full A level.

The AS- and A-Level specifications include the setting of a broad range of question types to ensure that a wide range of skills is assessed, and a requirement for extended writing to give candidates the opportunity to demonstrate the depth and breadth of their knowledge and understanding. The AS course may be taken as a qualification in itself or it may be used as a foundation to study the A Level. Although, for many years, GCE A levels could be assessed in stages, as in a modular course, or terminally, this practice has now been stopped.

All GCE A-Level courses must include an element of synoptic assessment designed to test a candidate's ability to make connections between different aspects of the course. There is no synoptic assessment at AS level. GCE A-level pass grades range from A*–E, with A* the highest grade. The A* grade was introduced in response to concerns about the standard of GCE A level and the increase in the number of candidates achieving Grade A.

Vocational courses post-16

The main vocational qualifications traditionally encountered in secondary schools in England have been the General National Vocational Qualifications (GNVQs), which were introduced into schools in 1992 and developed from National Vocational Qualifications (NVQs).

The NVQs are work-related, competence-based qualifications, and the courses were designed for people in work or undertaking work-based training. NVQ courses provide job-specific training, the assessment of which takes place in the work environment and is criterion-referenced. Central to the NVQ model is the idea of competence to perform a particular job, where competence is defined as the mastery of identified performance skills.

GNVQs were introduced to provide pupils with an introduction to occupational sectors through school- or college-based courses. Indeed, one of the principal aims of the GNVQ was to provide a middle road between the general academic route and occupational courses, such as the NVQs described above.

One of the main stumbling blocks to the uptake of vocational qualifications by schools was the difference in assessment practice and terminology between academic and vocational courses identified in the report on 16–19 qualifications (Dearing, 1996). The report identified, as well, the need for a coherent qualifications framework encompassing all national qualifications, and one that provides a status for vocational qualifications equivalent to the academic subjects at GCE A level. Following that report, vocational GCSE and vocational GCE A levels were introduced, accompanied by a timetable for the phased withdrawal of GNVQ courses. The vocational GCSE and GCE qualifications were renamed and known as GCSE and GCE in applied subjects with pupils at both levels maintaining their study of core curriculum subjects. The purpose of these developments, together with the other reforms outlined, is to encourage Key Stage 4 pupils and post-16 pupils to broaden their course of study to include vocational courses. The National Qualifications framework in Table 6.2.1 shows how the three qualification strands discussed are intended to overlap.

Table 6.2.1 Framework of national qualifications (entry level to Level 3 only)

Level of qualification	General qualifications
3	GCE A-level grades A–E
2	GCSE grades A*–C
1	GCSE grades D–G
Entry	Certificate of (educational) achievement

The framework for national qualifications has a total of nine separate levels of qualification (entry level to level 8) and shows progression across academic and vocational qualifications.

GCSE qualifications in vocational subjects were first introduced in September 2002 and are offered in eight subjects; for example, Leisure and Tourism, Applied Science.

The vocational sector of qualifications was also subject to significant change in the 2015 reforms. At Key Stage 4, the only qualifications that are recognised in performance tables are technical awards that are 'broad, high quality level 1 and level 2 qualifications in non EBacc subjects that equip pupils with applied knowledge and associated practical skills not usually acquired through general education' (DfE, 2015a, p.3). For post-16 pupils, they follow one of three routes: an academic route, a vocational route or a combined route. Within the vocational route, there are three main types of qualification: applied general qualifications, technical levels and substantial vocational qualifications at level 2. As with the GCSE reforms, there is now a significant level of external assessment.

Further discussion of vocational (applied) courses can be found in Wolf (2011) and Musset and Field (2013).

The purposes of external assessment

There is a long-standing history in the United Kingdom of externally examining pupils at particular stages in their education, which is quite different from the practice in some other countries (QCA, 2008; Wolf, 2011). In recent years in England, this practice has extended to the external assessment of pupils at the end of Key Stage 2. If the time and resources spent on this form of assessment are to be justified, then it is important that the purposes of external assessment are fully understood. The purposes of external, summative assessment can be thought of in terms of certificating candidates and the public accountability of teachers and schools. Another purpose is to categorise candidates in order to select people for higher education, employment, or to recognise achievement. The outcome of national examinations provides pupils with a grade so that they and other people can compare them with other candidates.

One recognised function of external assessment is that of certification. If you hold a certificate, then it is evidence that competence in particular skills or a level of knowledge has been achieved. For example, if you hold a driving licence, this is evidence that in a driving test you successfully performed a hill start, completed a three-point turn, and so on. The significance to pupils, of both the categorising and certification purposes, is evidenced by the fact that an impending examination provides an incentive for pupils to concentrate on their studies and to acquire the relevant knowledge and skills required by the examination for which they are entered. Thus, a consequence of external examinations is to provide motivation for both pupils and teachers. Motivation is discussed in greater detail in Unit 3.2.

Public accountability

Assessment is high on the political agenda because it is inextricably linked with the notion of raising standards, narrowing the attainment gap between different groups of pupils, school improvement and making schools publicly accountable. Schools are statutorily required to publish information on public examination results and school statistics (for example, number on roll, gender balance and uptake of free school meals) each year in what are now known as the performance tables, often referred to simply as the 'league tables'. In 2011, the data reported on KS4 and GCE A level attainment were expanded further to include significantly more data on a school's performance. The tables now include:

- how well disadvantaged pupils perform in each school;
- whether previous high-, middle- and low-achieving pupils continue to make progress;
- how many pupils at each school are entered into the core academic subjects that make up the English Baccalaureate.

The English Baccalaureate is not a qualification in its own right, but was introduced in the 2010 performance tables as a measure of the number of pupils securing a grade C or better in a selected core of academic subjects (DfE, 2017a). The core subjects are closely prescribed, and at the time of writing include English, Mathematics, Science, a language (modern or classical) and either Geography or History. The reasons behind the introduction of this measure are discussed below.

There is a variety of statistical information published each year; currently, schools in England can be placed in rank order based on a number of variables. Once such variable is the percentage of pupils gaining five or more GCSE passes at grades A*-C, including English and mathematics. The high profile given to the performance tables by the different stakeholders in the education process has led schools to implement strategies to increase the percentage of their pupils achieving five or more A*-C grades. For example, schools often target pupils predicted to achieve grade Ds at GCSE for additional tutoring and academic support as part of the school's strategy to increase the number of pupils achieving grade Cs in their GCSE exams.

There has been a dramatic increase in the number of non-academic qualifications taken each year from about 15,000 in 2004 to 575,000 in 2010 (DfE, 2015f). The Wolf Report (2011) explains how this shift was a consequence of two factors: the accountability regime becoming more rigorous and the simultaneous relaxing of National Curriculum requirements at Key Stage 4 (Wolf, 2011). One quotation from the report aptly summarises concerns expressed by the education community for some time:

> For young people, which vocational courses, qualification or institution they choose really can be life-determining. 14-19 education is funded and provided for their sakes, not for the sakes of the institutions who provide it. This may be a truism; but it is one which policy too often seems to ignore.
>
> (Wolf, 2011, p.8)

It is against this backdrop that the English Baccalaureate was introduced and the government announced a series of measures further tightening the qualifications eligible to be included in the league tables. Significant changes to the performance tables took effect from 2016, when schools were required to report four key measures on their website: pupils' progress across eight subjects from Key Stage 2 to Key Stage 4 to be known as Progress 8; an Attainment 8 measure; percentage of pupils achieving a grade C or higher in English and Mathematics; and the percentage of pupils gaining an English Baccalaureate. The Progress 8 and the Attainment 8 measures can include up to three recognised vocational qualifications.

The introduction of external assessment of pupils at the end of Key Stage 2 also had a significant impact on the teaching of pupils in this age range, providing further evidence of the effect that so-called 'high stakes' external assessment has on classroom practice. This impact is reported as a concentration on the curriculum subjects to be assessed through SATs or GCSE at the expense of a broader curriculum (Berliner, 2011; Leckie and Goldstein, 2017).

The term 'high stakes' is used to describe assessment that has significant consequences for either the candidate or the school. Although no longer required to set and publish targets for all pupils aged 11–16 in order to demonstrate year-on-year improvements, in practice, target setting on many different levels has become a feature of school culture. To assist schools in setting targets, from 2017 all schools in England have been able to access the programme Analyse School Performance (ASP). This programme provides interactive analysis of school and pupil performance data across the four Key Stages of the National Curriculum. This package contains benchmark data so that schools can compare whole-school performance with that of schools with similar intakes and profiles; also, it contains contextual value added (CVA) data, which aims to take into account a wide range of variables that may affect a school's performance, for example, number of pupils with SEN or number of pupils entitled to free school meals. The programme allows for primary schools to assess how well their pupils have performed in different aspects of the curriculum. This data then feeds into secondary schools who can then use the same data to identify strengths and weaknesses in their new intake of Year 7 pupils each year.

Validity and reliability

The concepts of validity and reliability are central to understanding an assessment process and are also discussed in Unit 6.1. For all external assessments and examinations, frameworks of regulations have been developed to ensure that the examination process and the results produced are both valid and reliable. To understand this framework, you need to be aware of the organisations and processes involved in this regulation.

Since October 2011, Ofqual is the government agency that approves all course specifications, as well as monitoring examinations through a programme of scrutinies, comparability exercises and probes, and is accountable to the DfE. There are three awarding organisations in England authorised by the government to offer GCSE, GCE A and AS and vocational courses. These are:

▪   Assessment and Qualifications Alliance (AQA): www.aqa.org.uk
▪   Edexcel: www.edexcel.com/
▪   Oxford Cambridge and RSA Examinations (OCR): www.ocr.org.uk/index.html

Following the *Guaranteeing Standards* consultation (Department for Education and Employment (DfEE), 1997), the formation of a single awarding body was considered, but a group of three was thought useful to retain a measure of competition. The key recommendations of the standards' consultation report were:

▪   that for each externally examined course, there is a specification for the core material;
▪   the publication of a detailed code of practice designed to ensure that grading standards are consistent across subjects and across the three awarding bodies, in the same subject, and from year to year;

■ that this code of practice should also set out the roles and responsibilities of those involved in the examining process and the key procedures for setting papers, standardising marking and grading.

Teaching externally assessed courses

All teachers have to think beyond the particular lesson they are teaching to the end of the unit of work, to ensure that pupils can respond successfully to any assessment scheduled to take place. When pupils are assessed externally, the same considerations apply; that is, how to maximise pupils' achievement. However, you do need to be fully aware of the nature of the external assessment for which you are preparing your pupils. It is important not just to teach to the examination, but to hold on to the principles of good classroom practice.

In preparing your pupils for external assessment, you need to be familiar not only with the subject content, but also with the particular demands of the assessment process, such as the types of questions set and the language used in setting questions. Questions are set that often employ words with a specific meaning; for example, they ask candidates to describe, or explain, or use short notes or summarise. Candidates need to know what these command words mean in examination conditions. Task 6.2.2 is designed to help you become familiar with types of questions currently set in examination papers in your own subject and the corresponding reports of examiners.

Once you are familiar with the structure and language used in past papers, you can then integrate this information into your teaching throughout the course. Another important aspect to consider is the development of study skills both in your lessons and throughout the school (see Task 6.2.3). Finally, we ask you to review the influence of public assessment on the way pupils are grouped and taught (see Task 6.2.4).

 Task 6.2.2   Using examination papers in your teaching

Collect a number of examination papers (for example, GCSE or the equivalent in other countries) for your subject together with the mark schemes and specification. Where possible, obtain the relevant examiners' reports. Read through the specification for the examination arrangements. Then address the questions in the paper in the following way:

■ answer the questions on the paper yourself;
■ mark your answers using the mark scheme;
■ evaluate your answers and marking and identify the key knowledge and concepts needed to gain maximum marks. Look back at the examination questions, identify the key words and phrases most often used in the questions;
■ use the examiners' report to review and refine your findings;
■ identify any ideas that might be useful to consider in your day-to-day teaching;
■ repeat the exercise for another year of the same paper, or repeat the exercise using papers from a different level (for example, post-16 course).

The completed task should be placed in your PDP.

Task 6.2.3   Revision study skills

Discuss with your tutor or another experienced teacher in your placement school the whole-school and departmental approaches available to support the development of pupils' revision study skills. These skills include, for example, planning and supporting revision, and time management. Use the information you gain to integrate the teaching of study skills in your own teaching.

File your notes in your PDP.

M

 Task 6.2.4   League tables and pupil grouping

Performance tables ('league tables') have been said to influence not only what is taught in a school, but also how pupils are grouped and the subjects they are offered for study, thus influencing their final qualifications. Investigate whether pupil grouping in the school is affected by the league tables; that is, if teaching and learning is being driven by public accountability. You may find sharing this work with another student teacher helpful.

Check first your understanding of setting, banding, streaming and mixed-ability grouping (see Unit 4.1).

In your placement school (see Unit 4.1 on pupil grouping):

1   for each year cohort 7-11, identify how tutor groups are formed for pastoral purposes and the criteria used to do this;
2   identify in broad terms which subjects reorganise the tutor groups for teaching purposes;
3   for your teaching subject and either English, Mathematics or science in Year 7, find out how pupils new to the school are assessed and placed into teaching groups. Compare the criteria used for each subject;
4   how flexible is the placement? Can pupils move between groups? If so, how is this movement managed in practice?
5   for your teaching subject and either English, Mathematics or Science in Year 10, identify how pupils are grouped for teaching, and which courses the different groups are offered, and the criteria used to do this.

With the information gained from tasks 1-5 above, arrange to interview a number of pupils in Year 10 to elicit their views about subject and course choice and grouping. Choose your subject area and, if time permits, one other subject. How do pupils make their subject/course choices at the end of Year 9? Are pupils:

1   provided with information to help make choices?
2   guided towards particular courses by teachers at the school?
3   aware of the long-term consequences of the courses they select?
4   encouraged to choose courses that help them to achieve five 'good' GCSE passes in English Baccalaureate subjects?

Within the same subject areas, find out what pupils think about the groups they are taught in. Are pupils aware of:

1   the reasons they were allocated to a group in that subject?
2   any advantages to the grouping system?
3   any limitations to their particular group, such as limit on grade at end of their course (for example, GCSE)?

Finally, interview a head of department for one or more subject areas chosen to find out their views about pupil choice of subject in Year 9 and how pupils are grouped for teaching purposes in their subject. You could use the questions you have put to the pupils.

Write a summary of your findings for discussion with your tutors, indicating whether the importance of league tables has had any effect on the way pupils are grouped. Evidence should be kept anonymous. The final document can be filed in your PDP.

SUMMARY AND KEY POINTS

- In this unit, we have linked the framework for external assessment and examinations with the nature and purposes of summative assessment.
- In England, the external examinations utilise aspects of both norm-referenced and criterion-referenced methods, and this is an important feature of assessment of which you need to be aware and understand.
- Norm-referencing and criterion-referencing are factors used in discussions seeking to explain the steady increase in the proportion of candidates achieving A*-C grades.
- The changes recently introduced to all sectors of education regarding external assessments aim to promote the academic attainment of all pupils.
- There are likely to be further innovations in approaches to assessment and, as long as there remains a political focus on raising standards in our schools, external assessment and examinations will maintain their present high profile and powerful influence on educational practice.

Check which requirements for your ITE programme you have addressed through this unit.

 ## Further resources

Black, P. (1998) *Testing: Friend or Foe? Theory and Practice of Assessment and Testing (Master Classes in Education),* **London: RoutledgeFalmer.**
The author was deeply involved in the development of assessment practices for the National Curriculum. This text provides a review of the different issues surrounding assessment. An early text but important in the development of assessment practices.

DfE (Department for Education) (2014h) *National Curriculum and Assessment from September 2014: Information for Schools*, London: DfE, viewed 3 July 2018, from https://assets.publishing.service.gov.uk/government/uploads/system/uploads/attachment_data/file/358070/NC_assessment_quals_factsheet_Sept_update.pdf

DfE (Department for Education) (2017a) *English Baccalereate (EBacc)*, from https://www.gov.uk/government/publications/english-baccalaureate-ebacc/english-baccalaureate-ebacc
A formative website that details attainment measures and the subjects and qualifications that are included within the EBacc.

Isaacs, T., Zara, C., Herbert, G., Coombs, S.J. and Smith, C. (2013) *Key Concepts in Educational Assessment*, London: Sage.

Wolf, A. (2015) *Review of Vocational Education: The Wolf Report: Recommendations final progress report*, DFE-00070-2015, viewed 4 July 2018, from https://www.gov.uk/government/uploads/system/uploads/attachment_data/file/405986/Wolf_Recommendations_Progress_Report_February_2015_v01.pdf
A final, and compressive, review of the recommendations set out by Wolf in 2011.

Appendix 2 lists subject associations and teacher councils and Appendix 3 provides a list of websites.

Capel, S., Leask, M. and Turner, T. (eds.) (2010) *Readings for Learning to Teach in the Secondary School: A Companion to M Level Study*, Abingdon: Routledge.
This book brings together essential readings to support you in your critical engagement with key issues raised in this textbook.

Capel, S., Lawrence, J., Leask, M. and Younie, S. (eds.) (2019) *Surviving and Thriving in the Secondary School: The NQT's Essential Companion*, Abingdon: Routledge.
This book is designed to support newly qualified teachers in the next phase of development as a teacher. However, you may find it useful as it covers aspects of teaching not included in this book which, nonetheless you experience on your ITE programme.

The subject specific books in the *Learning to Teach (Subject)* series, the *Practical (Subject) Guides*, *Debates in (Subject)* and *Mentoring (Subject) Teachers* are also very useful.

Any additional resources and an editable version of any relevant tasks/tables in this unit are available on the companion website: www.routledge.com/cw/capel

6.3 Using feedback and data effectively to move teaching and learning forward

Nikki Booth

Introduction

Feedback and data can be considered as two highly common assessment-related words used in schools today. Although both can be used as a meaningful source of information as to where teaching and learning is currently and should go to next, they can also be problematic. Furthermore, although both feedback and data can be related, they can also serve very different purposes. Both parts of this chapter begin with key information regarding the balancing of workload and what can be done to help reduce it. Each part also considers and critiques some of the key literature surrounding these areas as well as gives practical examples that can be implemented into the classroom. Whilst this chapter offers a wide range of information regarding feedback and data, it is important that it is read in conjunction with your school's assessment and/or marking and feedback policy.

OBJECTIVES

At the end of this unit you should be able to:

- explain the issues surrounding marking workload and how they can be overcome;
- know the difference between marking and feedback;
- understand what research says about feedback;
- explain what quality feedback means;
- confidently implement effective feedback strategies to help move teaching and learning forward;
- explain the issues surrounding data management workload and how they can be tackled;
- explain how data can be used for predicting future achievement and the issues surrounding this;
- know the difference between performance and learning;
- explain how data can be used for summing up pupil learning and the issues surrounding this;
- explain how data can be used formatively for improving teaching and learning.

Check the requirements of your initial teacher education (ITE) programme to see which relate to this unit.

Part 1: feedback

Tackling excessive workload: marking

In the report, *Eliminating unnecessary workload around marking* (DfE, 2016b), for England, the Independent Teacher Workload Review Group (ITWRG) stated that 'marking had become a burden that simply must be addressed, not only for those currently in the profession but for those about to enter it' (2016b, p. 3). As part of their published summary, they listed a range of ineffective marking practices, for example:

- extensive written comments in different coloured pens;
- the use of 'VF' on pupil's work to indicate when verbal feedback had been given;
- marking that fails to help pupils improve their understanding;
- marking that fails to encourage motivation and resilience.

The report also recognises that 'teachers who mark work late at night and at weekends are unlikely to operate effectively in the classroom' (DfE, 2016b, p. 7).

In providing solutions to tackling the marking workload problem, the ITWRG suggest that all marking should be *meaningful*, *manageable* and *motivating*. In the report, marking that is *meaningful*:

> should serve a single purpose – to advance pupil progress and outcomes.... Oral feedback, working with pupils in class, reading their work – all help teachers understand what pupils can do and understand.

> (DfE, 2016b, p.8)

Marking is **not** *manageable*, however, when 'teachers are spending more time on marking than the children are on a piece of work' (DfE, 2016b, pp.8–9). Finally, marking that is *motivating*:

> should help to motivate pupils to progress. This does not mean always writing in-depth comments or being universally positive: sometimes short, challenging comments or oral feedback are more effective. If the teacher is doing more work than their pupils, this can become a disincentive for pupils to accept challenges and take responsibility for improving their work.

> (DfE, 2016b, p.10)

The advice provided by the ITWRG has been brought together with the clear aim of reducing teacher workload. If, during your teaching practice, you find your marking load becoming unmanageable, speak to your subject and/or your professional mentor to see how they can best support you.

Clarifying terminology: is marking different from feedback?

Although often used synonymously within some schools, the terms 'marking' and 'feedback', although connected, do actually differ. Citing the Cambridge Dictionary Online, Didau (2015a) exemplifies the two as:

Marking (noun) (CORRECTING)
    The activity of checking, correcting, and giving a mark to a pupil's work.

Feedback (noun) (OPINION)

> Information or statements of opinion about something, such as a new product, that can tell you if it is successful or liked.

In assessment terms, the definition of 'marking' could be considered more summative in nature, for example, ticks or crosses on a pupil's work or the giving of a percentage at the bottom of the page. 'Feedback', on the other hand, might be considered more formative, as its purpose, in an educational context, is not only to state whether the work has been successful or not, but, more crucially, that the information given, whether oral or written, is then *actively used* to improve what has been produced. This, then, is formative assessment.

The marking and feedback policy within school

Although England's Ofsted (2018b) are clear that they do not expect to see any frequency or volume of marking for inspection, they are specific in that these details are for schools to decide through their assessment and/or marking and feedback policy. Policies can look very different from school to school, and even within different departments within one school. For example, a school's assessment and/or marking and feedback policy may state that pupils' books should be marked with feedback every five lessons. What this could mean, for example, is that if the English department has five lessons a week, its books would be looked at once a week. Within the same school, if a music teacher sees a class only once a week, pupils' work may only be marked and fed back on approximately once a half-term. Within your placement schools it is important that you get a copy of and check the assessment and/or marking and feedback policy to see what this means for your subject. Speak to your subject and/or professional mentor to get a copy.

Is oral feedback better than written feedback?

There are different views to this question. Some, for example Hattie and Clarke, are clear that '[a]nything which happens after the lesson has questionable value compared to what happens in the moment' (2019, p.123). Given that this takes place during the lesson it might be assumed that they are primarily (but not solely) talking about oral feedback. Others' stances, for example Wiliam (2018), often refer to the work of Bjork and Bjork (1992), where feedback can be more effective on long-term learning if it is delayed a little. Here, it might be assumed that we are talking about written feedback. In cognitive science, the idea of providing pupils with feedback a little after the lesson is to do with retrieval strength (how accessible, or retrievable, something is) and storage strength (how well learned something is). The idea is that, at the point of giving pupils the feedback, their retrieval strength is low. What this means is that the re-learning and the re-thinking required to respond to the feedback is said to have positive benefits on storage strength and, therefore, long-term memory. We must be cautious, however, not to favour one mode of feedback over the other; both types are beneficial to learning. Ofsted (2018b) make it clear that both oral and written forms of feedback are important aspects of assessment. What is key, however, is that oral and written forms of feedback to pupils are consistent with the school's assessment and/or marking and feedback policy.

Defining feedback

It has already been discussed within Unit 6.1 that the notion of feedback, whether oral or written, is important for moving teaching and learning forward. It is, therefore, an integral part of the formative assessment process. In defining the term *feedback*, Ramaprasad sees it as 'information about the gap between the actual level of a system which is used to alter the gap in some way' (1983, p.4). This definition was later extended within Sadler's (1989) formative assessment theory where, in order for a pupil to be successful, practice towards meaningful learning requires a 'feedback loop' (1989, p.121). The purpose of this loop is to attempt to close the gap between a pupil's current performance in a task and the desired performance. Both Sadler (1989) and Andrade and Heritage (2018) make it clear, however, that a pupil simply knowing how a task can be improved cannot be classed as feedback unless it is first *understood* and, second, in particular, *actively used* to serve this function. When thought of as a sequence of ongoing loops, the notion of Sadler's (1989) feedback loop is a powerful tool for classroom learning for a number of reasons:

- it tells us, as teachers, about the differing levels of knowledge, understanding and skills already attained and still yet to be attained by a pupil;
- it helps pupils to identify and amend any learning gaps;
- it helps us with the planning of suitable tasks or activities as next steps within the learning process;
- it allows us to modify our teaching and direction of teaching in order to support the closing of pupils' learning gaps.

Whilst it is clear from the information presented above that feedback can indeed be a powerful strategy for moving teaching and learning forward, it is also important to unpick the wealth of research information available on feedback to find out what types of feedback have the most impact on pupil learning.

What does research say about feedback?

In his meta-analysis, Hattie (2018) ranked feedback as 32nd out of 256 influences related to pupil achievement with an effect size of 0.70. An effect size is a quantifiable measure that is calculated by finding the difference between two groups involved in a research project – the experimental group (participants who receive a research intervention that is being investigated) and the control group (participants who do not receive the research intervention being tested). This number is then divided by the standard deviation, that is, the measure of how far the data are from the mean (or average). This calculation then results in an effect size, which can tell us the effectiveness of the intervention being tested. Effect sizes can be useful in that they move us beyond the notion of 'Does it work?' to 'How well does it work?' In Hattie's view, an effect size between 0.15 and 0.4 is believed to be 'what teachers can accomplish in a typical year of schooling' (Hattie, 2009, p.20), and shows effects that 'enhance achievement in such a way that we notice real-world differences' (Hattie, 2009, p.17). By looking at Hattie's research alone it is clear that feedback may significantly enhance pupil achievement. It should be pointed out, however, that Hattie's use of effect sizes within his meta-analyses has come into considerable criticism. Although it is not the place of this chapter to critique the use of effect sizes in meta-analysis, examples of comprehensive and thought-provoking reviews of their use in education can be found in Wiliam (2016) and Slavin (2018).

While it is commonly perceived that feedback enhances learning, Kluger and DiNisi (1996 a,b), however, found that some types of feedback actually lower pupil achievement. In their research, they found that approximately one-third of the studies accepted into the meta-analysis worsened a pupil's performance, particularly when the feedback focused on the person rather than the task. Consider what this means for your practice in the classroom. They also found that in approximately one-third of studies the feedback made no difference on pupil outcomes whether they received it or not. What is perhaps surprising is that only one-third of studies included in the meta-analysis, where feedback given focused on specific aspects of the task, or gave clear and specific guidance on how the work could be improved, led to better pupil outcomes. This, then, leads us to the question of 'what does quality feedback consist of?'

Quality within feedback

In addition to Butler's (1988) study of giving pupils scores, comments or both, cited in Unit 6.1, Elawar and Corno (1985) also looked into the quality of feedback given on pupils' mathematics homework. The feedback included to one group of pupils (experimental group) detailed comments on mistakes and errors, suggestions on how to improve and at least one positive comment. The second group of pupils were split into two sub-groups, half of which received constructive feedback (experimental group), and the other half received just scores (control group). A third group of students received their usual form of feedback on their homework – just the giving of marks (control group). The research found that the pupils who received the constructive feedback learned twice as fast as those in the control groups. What was also found was that in the lessons where pupils had been given constructive feedback, not only did achievement increase, but the gender gap between boys and girls was reduced and there was more of a positive attitude towards learning mathematics (Elawar and Corno, 1985).

In their research about quality feedback, Hattie and Timperley (2007) have provided a useful guide for teachers of four different types of feedback: *task* (or product), *process*, *self-regulation* and *self*. A brief representation of these different types of feedback, and what they might look like in the classroom, has been presented in Unit 6.1, Table 6.1.3. In their research, *task* feedback, also referred to as product or corrective feedback, gives pupils information as to how well they have performed a task. It should be considered that this level of feedback might be thought to be more summative in nature where pupils would, for example, receive a score on the number of correct answers they have at the bottom of the page. *Process* feedback provides information as to how well pupils correct their mistakes and use prompts to better understand the details of the task. Blazer, Doherty and O'Conner (1989), for example, found that process feedback positively effects the quality of deep learning. *Self-regulation* feedback is concerned with ways in which pupils autonomously monitor their own learning. Self-regulatory feedback can be directed at a pupil's effort rather than their ability which has been found to result in higher engagement and better performance (Dohrn and Bryan, 1994). Both *process* and *self-regulatory* feedback are perhaps more akin to the definition of formative assessment discussed in Unit 6.1. Finally, *self* feedback provides information about personality characteristics. Studies suggest that this type of feedback is ineffective, 'has too little value to result in learning gains' (Hattie and Timperley, 2007, p.96) and does not provide the learner with useful information about the task. This is not to say that *self* feedback should never happen in schools; comments such as 'great work!' can be hugely motivational for pupils. What needs to be considered further, though, is what the balance between this type of feedback is compared with, perhaps, more formative types of feedback to improve pupil learning.

Hattie and Timperley's (2007) feedback model also states that, in order for feedback to be effective, three questions need to be answered:

■ Where am I going?
■ How am I doing?
■ Where to next?

(updated version of questions by Hattie, Masters and Birch, 2016, p.10).

The first question relates to the task or goal the pupil needs to accomplish. The second provides them with information on their current level of performance, compared with the goal established. The third relates to the strategy for further learning and improvement in task performance. Hattie and Timperley (2007) argue that these foci for feedback are effective in improving learning where it should relate to the task itself, the processing of the task, self-regulation, or the pupil's confidence. Regardless of the focus, the important factor is increasing the pupil's ability to learn.

Practical examples of impactful feedback

Example 6.3.1: oral group feedback

Concerned with the fact that, during a lesson, the need to give pupils personal and individual oral feedback and spending quality time re-explaining key concepts is a very timely process, a music teacher at Wolgarston High School, Staffordshire, uses more group-based oral feedback. In a lesson, when walking around the room looking at pupils' work, the teacher might spot a small number of pupils who seem to share the same misconception. Instead of stopping and giving each individual pupil feedback, the teacher brings them all together and re-explains in one go. Similarly, when the number of pupils who misunderstand seems to be rather high, this is an excellent opportunity to stop the whole class and address this together. Although there will be pupils who *do* understand, this is a good opportunity to use them as a learning resource to help clarify to others the misconception in question and what needs to be done to correct it.

Example 6.3.2: feedback to the teacher

Although teacher-pupil feedback is indeed an important part of moving learning forward, so is pupil-teacher feedback to move teaching forward. Inspired by the work of Wiliam (2018), a Spanish teacher at Wolgarston High School, Staffordshire, uses 'Learning Logs' as a means of getting pupils to reflect on two of the prompts below, on an 'exit ticket', at the end of the lesson. What makes this strategy particularly impactful is that the teacher then reads the pupils' reflections and, based on the pupils' feedback, plans accordingly for their next lesson. Figure 6.3.1 below shows a PowerPoint slide showing reflective prompts taken from Wiliam, 2018, pp.184-185.

Example 6.3.3: whole class feedback

In geography lessons at Penkridge Middle School, Staffordshire, pupils are frequently given the opportunity to improve their work by acting on feedback given by the teacher. What is particularly important here is that the teacher does not spend time marking each individual book; instead, a list of common errors (for example, spellings) are indicated at the whole-class level, as well as next step

<u>**Para terminar...**</u>

- Today I have learned...
- I was surprised by...
- The most useful thing I will take from this lesson is...
- I was interested in...
- What I liked most about the lesson was...

- One thing I am not sure about is...
- The main thing I want to find out more about is...
- After this lesson, I feel...
- I might have gotten more from this lesson if...

Figure 6.3.1 End of lesson reflective prompts for pupils (used with permission)

tasks for all pupils to act upon. Figure 6.3.2 is an example PowerPoint slide which would be shared with pupils.

Key to abbreviations used in the example:

■   LI = Learning Intention
■   SPAG = Spelling, Punctuation and Grammar

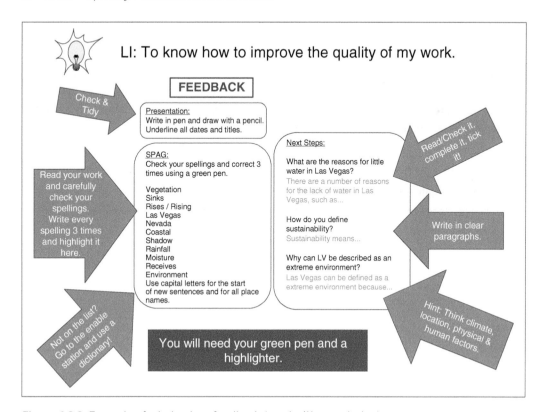

Figure 6.3.2 Example of whole-class feedback (used with permission)

In the teacher's own words:

> The beauty of this approach is that it allows me to teach misconceptions from the front of the room; this allows me to give guidance to pupils as to why they are being asked to respond to these questions. Generally, compared with previous years, this has led to improved pupil responses and more closed gaps in learning. Pupils have responded positively to this approach and feel supported through the learning process. I believe this encourages them to take on challenges and reduces the fear of making mistakes; this type of marking has helped create and prompt a culture of learning from our mistakes.
>
> (Teacher at Penkridge Middle School, Staffordshire, personal communication)

From a teacher workload perspective, what all of these examples of feedback have in common is, as Wiliam says, '[f]eedback should be more work for the recipient than the donor' (Wiliam, 2015). Now do M-Level Task 6.3.1.

Task 6.3.1 Pupil perceptions of feedback

Arrange to meet with a group of five to six pupils, including both genders as well as a range of abilities and backgrounds.

Create a list of about 10 questions and discuss with them what their perceptions of feedback at school are. Some areas for inquiry could include:

1   Do they like receiving feedback from teachers? Why? Why not?
2   Do they understand the feedback they are given?
3   In which subjects do they feel they get more useful feedback than others? Why is this?
4   Are they given time in lessons to read, ask questions about and respond to feedback given?
5   Do they feel that the feedback they are given is beneficial to their learning? Why is this?

Analyse the findings and, in the light of the research mentioned earlier, write a strategy for feedback to guide your work with your pupils. Keep this is in your professional development portfolio (PDP) or equivalent for future reference.

Part 2: data

Tackling excessive workload: data management

In the report, *Eliminating unnecessary workload associated with data management* (DfE, 2016d), for England, the ITWRG identified two key reasons why data management can hinder, rather than help, teaching and learning. The first is *purpose*, that is, how the data being collected is going to improve pupil outcomes, and second, *process*, where data collection is duplicated or requires a lot of time to complete. They go on to say that, '[i]n both cases, a flawed understanding of the validity of different types of data contributes to burdensome practice' (DfE, 2016d, p.6).

What is interesting is that the practices that have been found to be problematic for teacher workload are also considered good practice. They say that anyone who is involved in the production and use of data should start by having clear answers to three questions:

1   Am I clear on the purpose?
     Why is data being collected, and how will it help improve the quality of provision?
2   Is this the most efficient process?
     Have the workload implications been properly considered and is there a less burdensome way to collect, enter, analyse, interpret and present the information?
3   Is the data valid?
     Does the data actually provide a reliable and defensible measure of educational attainment?

(DfE, 2016d, p.8)

By keeping the data management workload down to a manageable level, not only does it mean a more balanced home-to-work life, but it allows us, as teachers, to focus on what we do best – teach great lessons!

Data for the purpose of predicting future achievement

Data that is aimed at predicting pupils' future achievement (for example, providing schools, teachers, parents and pupils with GCSE target grades) is a complex mix of how different groups of pupils within the cohort performed previously (prior attainment) in national tests, for example, in England, Key Stage 2 national tests (taken at age 11), their socio-economic status, as well as other information. The Fischer Family Trust (FFT), is one well-known example within the United Kingdom of an agency which, upon subscription, provides this information to schools. Predictions (for example, GCSE grades) provided by the FFT usually come with probable percentages. This means that each predicted grade for a pupil is accompanied by a percentage indicating the probability of the pupil achieving each grade. The higher the percentage, the more likely it is that they are to achieve that particular grade according to the collection of information.

Although providing schools, teachers, parents and pupils with predicted grades based on a range of factors can be useful, it can also be problematic. For example, since part of the mix of information contains data regarding, for example, Key Stage 2 national test results, this information only factors in a pupil's achievement in English and Mathematics. This becomes an issue for some subjects, such as Music or Art; a pupil's previous achievements in these areas are not at all taken into consideration. Research also suggests that the use of target grades can lead to motivational issues. For example, Booth (2015) found that pupils who were given a low target grade (for example a grade '3') self-reported themselves as disengaged with the subject, as they were already perceived to have 'failed'. The research also showed that some pupils would self-report themselves as less likely to engage in more complex tasks if they had already met their target grade; they saw little value in working harder to potentially achieve higher grades because they were perceived to have 'passed'.

There is also the question of the likelihood of each pupil actually achieving their target grade. In a report by Education DataLab (2015), it was revealed that only 9% of pupils make the expected linear pathways through Key Stage 2 (ages seven to 11), Key Stage 3 (ages 11–14) and Key Stage 4 (ages 14–16). When each Key Stage was analysed separately, it was found that 55% of pupils make the predicted linear progress to reach the Key Stage 2 standard that is anticipated from their Key Stage 1 (ages five to seven) achievement. The remaining 45%, however, either outperform or underperform. Furthermore, the accuracy of predicting a pupil's achievement falls in the secondary context; with 45% of learners making the expected linear progress between Key Stage 2 and Key Stage 3, and only 33% of them making the anticipated linear progress between Key Stage 3 and 4. In other words, when attempting to use a model of linear progression to predict future achievement, most pupils will perform better or worse than their expected Key Stage achievement on one or two occasions, whereas some frequently outperform or underperform throughout their school career. This notion is represented diagrammatically, by Education DataLab (2015), in Figure 6.3.3 below.

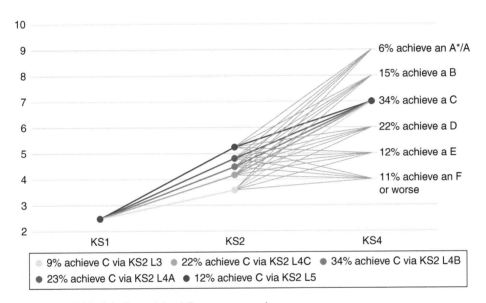

Figure 6.3.3 Model of consistent linear progression

(*Source*: Education Datalab, 2015, p.13, and used with permission)

Separating performance from learning

There is often confusion, in some schools, that when pupils perform well on an end of unit test this means that they have learned the material well. This is not necessarily the case. For example, if a maths teacher has spent the last few weeks teaching their pupils about Pythagoras, providing meaningful activities to practise, giving feedback that has been acted upon and then tests the pupils, they are likely to do well. Within cognitive science (for example, following the work of Bjork and Bjork, 1992), this, however, is *performance* not *learning*. It is *performance* because the material has just been taught and is still likely to have high retrieval strength (how accessible, or retrievable, something is). If the teacher moves on to a different unit of work, for example, statistics, and then re-tests the pupils on Pythagoras questions six weeks later, are they going to get the same result? This is unlikely because now, six weeks later, the Pythagoras material has not been practised, so the retrieval strength is low. Furthermore, the storage strength (how well learned something is) is also low because pupils cannot remember how to answer questions. This has huge implications on the notion of tests and examinations used in schools.

Kirschner, Sweller and Clark (2006) state that learning requires a change in long-term memory. They go on to say that, '[t]he aim of all instruction is to alter long-term memory. If nothing has changed in long-term memory, nothing has been learned' (2006, p.77). This is important for us, as teachers; as we teach our pupils new material, naturally forgetting the previous material is likely to occur. Meta-analysis research (for example, Cepeda et al., 2006) has shown, however, that the use of distributed practice (also called spaced practice or synoptic assessment) can have positive effects on summative tests/examinations and long-term learning. What this means in practice is that instead of solely testing the content covered within a single unit of work, the addition of questions covering previous material allows pupils the opportunity to practise retrieving the information from their long-term memories. By engaging pupils in retrieval practice as a learning strategy, this then helps speed up the retrieval strength so the information is more quickly accessed in future, as well as increasing the likelihood that the information will develop higher storage strength for its potential future use.

The summative use of data to sum-up pupil learning

Entering data into the school's tracking system will differ from school to school. Such data may well include the entry of scores, percentages and/or grades from end of unit tests and/or examinations, and will occur at various points during the school year (again, this differs from school to school). The management information system, SIMS, for example, is a common tool used for entering pupil data (as well as other things), which can then be viewed by the Head of Department and the Senior Leadership Team at both the individual pupil- and cohort-level to see how different classes and particular focus group (for example, in the English context, Pupil Premium) are performing over time. The data entered can then be used for a number of purposes, for example, from whether a pupil needs interventions of learning support – the moving from one set to another – to the decision to enter for a higher or foundation tier examination, and so on. Whilst this data carries with it some key consequences, it is important to remember that, as Koretz makes clear, 'authors of tests sample a small amount of content to represent the larger domain. Most of the domain remains untested' (2017, p.13). The fact that tests and examinations only assess a sample of the content covered in a unit of work is a key point that can often be forgotten when talking about pupil performance, particularly since many high-stakes tests create pressure to raise grades (Harlen, 2007). This notion becomes even more important when it is considered that schools, and in some cases individual teachers, are judged on the basis of the pupils' scores and grades.

Despite the small sample of content being covered in a test or examination, the result the pupil achieves at that moment in time is also subject to a 'margin of error'. We know that pupils have bad days as well as good days, and that pupils who take a test more than once can receive different scores (Koretz, 2017). Although the notion of the margin of error is not often talked about in schools in relation to pupil performance, it has been acknowledged by Her Majesty's current Chief Ofsted Inspector, Amanda Spielman, who acknowledges, 'that the best we can ever expect from GCSEs is to narrow student achievement down to + or − one whole grade!' (cited from Didau, 2015b). Wiliam (2017) also comments about the margin of error in the context of school-based tests:

> A typical school test would have a margin of error of 10 marks or more, and many, perhaps most, teachers would be uncomfortable saying to a parent that the pass mark for a course was 70, and their child scored 65, plus or minus 10. The parent might ask whether their child passed, and all we could say is, 'Probably not. But they may have done.' At this point the parent would probably ask, 'Why don't you know?' to which the only sensible reply would be, 'Because no test is perfectly reliable.' Parents may well ask, 'Can't you make the test more reliable?' and of course the answer is yes. We can make the test more reliable, but this involves making the test longer. Much longer – and we have better things to do with the time, such as teaching.
>
> (Wiliam, 2017, pp.1–2)

Since there are clear issues with reporting a single score, percentage or grade on a test or examination, we are fortunate that we can collect data more regularly to help build up a holistic view of pupil learning as it develops.

The formative use of data to improve teaching and learning

Whilst summative (test/examination) data can indeed be used formatively (so called *the formative use of summative assessment*) to help plan for next teaching and learning steps, data can also be collected prior to the test, that is, *during* the teaching and learning process. This can be done in a number of ways. For example, at the end of a lesson, a teacher may use 'exit tickets' to check whether their pupils have understood the lesson. At the end of the session, pupils respond to a question or small number for questions relating to the learning intention(s). When the exit tickets are collected in, the teacher looks at the pupils' responses and, crucially, uses this information to inform their planning next time. This quick check is not only a strategy that can be useful for us reflecting on whether our teaching has had the desired effect or not, but also helps reduce the amount of marking and individual feedback.

It can also be beneficial to check whether learning is heading in the right direction before the end of the lesson. Effective strategies could include formative conversations with pupils working in groups, for example, where teacher-initiated oral feedback would impact on all members. Depending on the length of the lesson, groups may well receive at least two opportunities for teacher feedback to respond to. Similarly, in some lessons, the use of quick diagnostic 'hinge questions' (see Wiliam, 2018) that require every student to respond would elicit useful information before proceeding with the lesson. When 100% of pupils respond to a teacher question, via a mini-whiteboard, for example, and show their response, they are showing whether they have understood the concept or whether they need further support. Regardless of whether it is one way, the other, or both, it is at this point that formative assessment takes place; not only has data been collected (i.e. I am looking around the room to see how many pupils have got this), but, perhaps more importantly, the data then drives decision making as to what happens next. As such, it is this decision making that drives pupil achievement.

Now do Task 6.3.2.

Task 6.3.2   Using data effectively to promote quality teaching and learning

Collect a range of data for a class that you are going to teach and use this information to inform your planning.

Before the lesson:

■   What do the target grades and any prior attainment data tell you about this class? How can you use this data effectively to plan for differing learning needs?

During the lesson:

■   What sorts of data can you collect during the lesson that will inform you whether learning is on track? What will you do if you identify a group of pupils who have not quite got it yet?

End of the lesson:

■   How will you check that the Learning Intention(s) for the lesson have been met by pupils?

Post-lesson:

■   What does the range of information you gathered both during and at the end of the lesson tell you about where to start with these pupils next time?

Record your analysis in your professional development portfolio (PDP) and repeat the exercise periodically with different classes.

SUMMARY AND KEY POINTS

■   Examples of ineffective marking practices include:
    ■   extensive written comments in different coloured pens;
    ■   use of 'VF' to indicate that verbal feedback has been given;
    ■   marking which does not contribute to improved pupil understanding;
    ■   marking that fails to encourage motivation and resilience.
■   When tackling the marking workload problem, marking should be *meaningful*, *manageable* and *motivating*;
■   The term 'marking' can often have summative connotations, whereas 'feedback' might elicit more of a formative meaning;
■   Marking and feedback should be consistent with the school's assessment and/or marking and feedback policy;
■   Both oral and written forms of feedback are beneficial to learning;
■   Whilst some research suggests that feedback can have a highly positive influence on learning, other research has found some feedback types that actually lower pupil achievement. What matters is the quality of the feedback given;
■   Both feedback to the pupil and feedback to the teacher are important for moving teaching and learning forward;

- Key questions for tackling the data management workload problem include:
  - Am I clear on the purpose?
  - Is this the most efficient process?
  - Is the data valid?
- While target grades are often given and used in schools, these are also problematic due to the information they are based on;
- There is often a confusion, in some schools, between *performance* and *learning*:
  - *performance* relates to how a pupil has done on a test on a particular day;
  - whereas *learning* is seen as a change in long-term memory.
- Although data entry, into a tracking system, of pupils' scores is common in schools the margin of error of the test results is rarely considered;
- Data can be meaningfully used formatively as well as summatively.

Further resources

Department of Education (DfE) (2016b) *Eliminating Unnecessary Workload around Marking*, viewed 10 September 2018, from https://assets.publishing.service.gov.uk/government/uploads/system/upl oads/attachment_data/file/511256/Eliminating-unnecessary-workload-around-marking.pdf
Complete summary of the report from the Independent Teacher Workload Review Group (ITWRG) on marking.

Koretz, D. (2017) *The Testing Charade. Pretending to Make Schools Better*, Chicago, IL: The University of Chicago Press.
An in-depth book on how scores from educational tests can misunderstood and misused.

Wiliam, D. (2018) *Embedding Formative Assessment*, 2nd Edition, Bloomington, IN: Solution Tree Press.
Chapter 5: 'Providing feedback that moves learning forward' is an excellent resource for understanding feedback in a research context as well as its effective use in the classroom.

Appendix 2 lists subject associations and teacher councils and Appendix 3 provides a list of websites.

Capel, S., Leask, M. and Turner, T. (eds.) (2010) *Readings for Learning to Teach in the Secondary School: A Companion to M Level Study*, Abingdon: Routledge.
This book brings together essential readings to support you in your critical engagement with key issues raised in this textbook.

Capel, S., Lawrence, J., Leask, M. and Younie, S. (eds.) (2019) *Surviving and Thriving in the Secondary School: The NQT's Essential Companion*, Abingdon: Routledge.
This book is designed to support newly qualified teachers in the next phase of development as a teacher. However, you may find it useful as it covers aspects of teaching not included in this book which, nonetheless you experience on your ITE programme.

The subject specific books in the *Learning to Teach (Subject)* series, the *Practical (Subject) Guides*, *Debates in (Subject)* and *Mentoring (Subject) Teachers* are also very useful.

Any additional resources and an editable version of any relevant tasks/tables in this unit are available on the companion website: www.routledge.com/cw/capel

7 The school, curriculum and society

This chapter takes you away from the immediacy of teaching to consider the aims of education, how those aims might be identified and, more importantly perhaps, how the curriculum reflects those aims. In the day-to-day urgency of teaching the given curriculum, it is easy to push the 'why' into the background and simply get on with the 'how'. As a prospective teacher you need to be able to explain to pupils and parents what the personal benefit is to them from learning your subject; you also need to understand, for yourself, why your country does things one way and that other countries offer a different approach to educating their young people.

The chapter addresses the ways in which the home countries of the UK organise their education system and the different emphasis placed on various aspects of education by them, for example: the types of schools and the grouping of pupils, on assessment and the role of public examinations in promoting standards, and inspection and accountability. We include on the companion website units that focus on the education systems of the home countries of England, Northern Ireland, Scotland and Wales.

In Unit 7.1, 'Aims of education', a comparative and analytical approach is taken to examine assumptions about education and a consideration of the different purposes of schooling. It discusses the origin of national aims and their translation into school aims and contrasts the aims of society with those of the individual. Unit 7.2, 'The school curriculum', examines the school curriculum in terms of aims and purposes. The unit draws attention to the formal and the informal, or hidden curriculum, and discusses how the formal curriculum of subjects might develop from the broad aims of education and asks, 'Who decides?'

The following four units are available on the companion website and examine the education systems of the home countries, with Unit 7.3 on England, Unit 7.4 on Northern Ireland, Unit 7.5 on Scotland and Unit 7.6 on Wales. Each unit focuses on the 'distinctive' nature of each country's education system, which includes the structure and governance of education in each country, alongside their school curriculum, the requirements of the teaching profession in each country and the future.

If education is 'what is left after most of what you have learned in school is forgotten', then what is education for and who decides? Young people, between the ages of five and 16, spend a substantial part of the formative period of their lives in school and a significant slice of the national budget is channeled into education, so you can expect to be held accountable for what you teach. In meeting the demand for accountability, an understanding of one's own education system and its comparison with those of other countries may help frame your response.

7.1 Aims of education

*Ruth Heilbronn, Janet Orchard
and Graham Haydon*

Introduction

Most student teachers receive an abundance of advice and guidance from all around them when learning to teach concerning the important technical and practical information they need. However, most teachers come into teaching motivated by wider aims and values, and it is important at various points to step back from the business of the day to day to find moments to reflect more broadly on those and at a deeper level. This unit is written in that spirit and focuses on the aims of the educational process in schools. Where do you stand on the explicit aims of the National Curriculum for the educational system in which are planning to teach? Do you know what they are? In England the most recently revised aims are as follows:

> The national curriculum provides pupils with an introduction to the essential knowledge they need to be educated citizens. It introduces pupils to the best that has been thought and said, and helps engender an appreciation of human creativity and achievement
>
> (DfE, 2014i, p.1)

Do you agree with them? Why? Why not?

Thinking through questions like these has a practical as well as philosophical point. For example, we may well ask ourselves what the point of education or schooling is when the going gets tough, and wonder whether teaching really is for us. The question of implicit educational aims matters whenever you ask yourself what, above all, you are trying to achieve as a teacher; when the staff in your school collectively consider whether they are offering anything distinctive that other schools are not; or if a politician complains that schools are not getting good enough exam grades or not doing as well as schools internationally. Teachers in secondary schools often need to be able to justify the aims of schooling and the subjects that they teach in language that is accessible to pupils too; for example, when a pupil asks, 'What's the point of this?' This unit considers the question about aims in some detail and, in conjunction with the next unit, shows that it is not a theoretical question that can be sidelined while you get on with teaching. On the contrary, it plays a fundamental role as it determines the content of and context in which you teach.

OBJECTIVES

At the end of this unit you should be able to:

■ list a variety of actual and possible aims for education;
■ reflect on and formulate your own aims in being a teacher;
■ discuss aims of education with other teachers and with parents.

Check the requirements of your initial teacher education (ITE) programme to see which relate to this unit.

The social and political context of aims

All education systems are governed by underlying aims, whether or not they are stated explicitly. These may be decided at different political or administrative levels. Many countries today have a national education system, at least partly state-funded and state-controlled. In some cases, as once in the Soviet Union, a clearly defined ideology sets aims that the whole education system is meant to promote. However, even in a more decentralised system in which many decisions are taken at a local level, there may be a widely shared sense of what the aims of education should be, for example, across a chain of multi-academy trust schools. These aims will reveal certain values about education. In the early 20th century in the USA, for example, there was a shared understanding that a primary aim of the national education system should be to forge a single nation out of diverse indigenous and migrant communities that had come to settle there. This was expressed most famously by John Dewey, and came to be known as the idea of the 'common school' (Dewey, 1916).

Meanwhile, in Britain today, the aim to promote common values may still be seen in the current requirement that schools create and publish a statement about how they demonstrate and promote values that are 'British' (DfE, 2014j). This requirement has generated a good deal of comment, on the grounds that the values promoted seem not to be exclusively those of one nation but rather general values concerning democracy and 'the rule of law' (e.g. see Lander et al., 2016; Both, 2017; Elton-Chalcraft et al., 2017). The requirement to make a statement of this kind illustrates how, at certain times, some fundamental values might be seen to need reiteration and reinforcement and the belief that schools are places where this should happen (see Unit 4.5 on values in education).

Reflecting on these statements and the way in which they are developed, promoted and exemplified in the school is a useful undertaking. A typical statement might refer to preparing pupils for life in modern Britain, managing the curriculum to provide a vehicle for furthering understanding of the values related to democracy and the rule of law, and giving pupils a range of out of school activities where these values are implicit, such as sporting events and out of school visits. These statements are available on school websites. Some people will believe that a duty of this kind is not the proper purpose of a school, but rather the responsibility of families and communities. Your own response to matters of this kind will be a reflection of your own position on the aims of education, informed by your educational values and principles.

Earlier and through much of the 20th century in Britain, schools enjoyed a good deal of autonomy, from a legal point of view, in setting and pursuing their aims, even if they didn't make them explicit. Local Authorities (LAs) had some control over the curriculum in schools for which they were responsible until gradual changes to the governance of schools in the English education system from the 1980s onwards reduced their involvement to a minimum to allow for greater diversity. Since 2010, there has been a further move to decentralise schooling with less national control, and greater control of school management and organisation by groups of academy schools, on the model of charter schools in the US and Sweden. The national curriculum and its aims remain statutory, but the content has been slimmed down considerably compared with the version that schools were required to follow earlier in the 21st century.

These policy changes illustrate a long-standing debate about the aims underlying the education system, that is, whether governments ought to determine aims for state-funded schools and, if so, what they should be (see Harris, 1999; Pring, 2012; Reiss and White, 2013). On the other hand, schools could be governed less by a national imposition of aims and more focused on devising and making clear their own aims, respectful of the wishes of local parents and relevant to prospective pupils. Do you think that there are 'right' curriculum aims which ought to be imposed for the benefit of all? Do you think the aims of education are a matter of opinion and dependent on context and circumstances? Is your view somewhere in between?

Avoiding here the radical claim that the state has no role to play at all in determining the aims of education and that there are at least some aims that all schools should follow, a position that having a national curriculum with aims implies the question: what should those aims be? There has been a shift since 2010 towards a more traditionally academic curriculum in English schools directed by national policy makers, which some citizens have welcomed, for example, arguing for 'powerful knowledge' that all children and young people should encounter while at school (see Young and Lambert, 2014) and others have criticised. Michael Rosen, for example, has been outspoken about the impact of the more academic nature of the curriculum on the teaching of English. By focusing intensively on academic attainment measured by examination results, it might be said, we lose sight of other educational aims. Examination results may be important for some individuals, and for the wider economy, but a focus on targets and results might overwhelm any wider aims of education, such as preparing young people to take their place as future citizens (Watkins, 2012; Pring, 2012; Ravitch, 2013). Moreover, while schools are judged by Ofsted and required to compete for a place on the national league tables according to particular criteria, and while governments also look to international comparison of results, it is not clear that schools do in fact enjoy much autonomy. Teachers need to be clear where they stand on debates such as these and defend their views with recourse to reasonable arguments.

Politicians do not often explicitly express their views on what the aims of education should be, but when they say that schools should enable Britain to compete economically with other nations, or that schools should inculcate 'British values' or should promote active citizenship, they are in effect recommending certain aims for schools. At this broad level, it is generally assumed that the same aims are shared by schools, creating a potential tension between the possibility of a diversity of aims in different schools, (perhaps because they are serving rather different communities) and the promotion of common aims across the school system as a whole. Therefore, as a student teacher, you are working in a context in which many expectations about aims are already in place, explicitly or implicitly. You do not have a free hand to pursue any aims you like. You might wonder, then, whether there is much point in your doing your own thinking about the aims of education. It is a premise of this unit that good teachers will consider the aims of education and know what they endorse. We suggest two reasons why your own thinking about aims is relevant and you may well think of others.

First, within the constraints of your individual school, curriculum and circumstances, your own thinking about aims influences the way you approach your task as a teacher of a particular subject. (This aspect of aims of education is discussed further in Unit 7.2.) Second, as a citizen, you have the same right as any other citizen to form and express your own view about the aims of education in general, but being a teacher with a duty of care towards young people, you are in a better position than the average citizen to make your views clear and be prepared to argue for them.

Thinking about aims

Tasks 7.1.1 and 7.1.2 are intended to give you some insight into the nature and variety of aims in education, as well as some experience in thinking about aims and their implications and discussing this with others.

   Task 7.1.1   School aims: a comparison

1 What do you consider the aims of education to be? Some other ways into this reflection might be to consider questions such as:

'What is education for?'
'Who is education for?'
'What kind of person do we wish to develop and why?'

2 Think about two schools with which you are familiar, for example: the school in which you received your own secondary education (or the majority of it, if you changed schools) and your current placement school.

   For the first school, your data will be wholly or largely from your own memory. Answer the following questions as far as you can:

■   Did your school have an explicit statement of its aims?
■   Were you as a pupil aware of the school's aims?
■   Roughly what kinds of educational aims did it stand for (e.g. academic learning, promoting community relations, etc.)? In what ways did the particular aims of your school impinge on your experience as a pupil?

   For your placement school, ask:

■   Does your school have an explicit statement of aims – if so, what does it say?
■   Are the pupils you are teaching aware of the school's aims?
■   Does the existence of these aims appear to make any difference to the pupils' experience in the school?

   If you are a parent, you could also identify the aims of your child's school, using the school's documentation and, perhaps, discussion with staff.

   Compare your findings for the two schools. Do you find that aims have a higher profile in one school or the other? Is there any evidence that the existence of an explicit policy on aims enhances the education the school is providing?

3. Go back to your own reflection in (1) and relate the answers you have given for the two schools to these thoughts. You could discuss your findings and your views with other student teachers.

Keep your notes in your professional development portfolio (PDP) or equivalent for use when you are considering what schools to apply to work in and to prepare for an interview for a teaching post (see Unit 8.1).

 Task 7.1.2   The aims statement in your placement school

1   Study the aims statement of your placement school and evaluate how far the aims of the school fit with your own view of the broader aims of education. Refer back to the questions you answered in 7.1.1. *What is education for? Who is education for? What kind of person do we wish to develop?*

2   What do pupils understand the aims of education to be? It is interesting to learn how they experience education and what their views might be. With other student teachers and tutors design some small-scale empirical research that might be undertaken at a later date to find out the views of the pupils. Be mindful of the ethical sensitivities or implications of undertaking any such research on aims/values with pupils and be sure to discuss these as a group.

Store this information in your professional development portfolio (PDP).

Recognising the diversity of aims

We have been talking about the aims of education in this unit. Different people can have different ideas about the aims of education; and these differences may be quite legitimate. These are not matters about which there is a 'right' answer. At the same time, a school, and even a national education system, needs some coherent sense of direction. We might reflect on just how much overall coherence and agreement is needed and how far there is room for internal variation, yet some coherence and agreement seems to be necessary, because of the ways in which conceptions of aims can make a practical difference. They can make a difference, for instance, to:

■   how a whole school system is organised (for example, the movement towards comprehensive education, which began in the 1960s, was driven at least partly by an explicit aim to break down class barriers and distribute opportunities for good education more widely, assuming that the division into grammar and secondary modern schools that preceded comprehensive education was undesirable. The debate about whether or not it is desirable to have selection by ability in education continues);

- how an individual school is run (for example, various aspects of a school's ethos and organisation may be motivated by the aim that pupils should respect and tolerate each other's differences);
- How curriculum content is selected and taught (there is more on this aspect of aims in Unit 7.2).

Given that aims in education can make a practical difference, it is important not just that the diversity of possible aims can be recognised but also that there can be some prospect of reasoned debate over the importance of certain aims rather than others.

Comparing and justifying aims

It can be argued that some aims are inherent in the concept of education, if we take education to mean an initiation into practices relating to being human in the world, as did one highly influential philosopher of education, Richard Peters (1964). We could then differentiate 'education' from 'training', that is, teaching might be considered a form of training when it imparts a certain mode of thinking, or a canon, which cannot be criticised. Training has been defined as *conditioning* or *indoctrination* in contrast with *education*, which is about developing autonomy (Thiessen, 1985; Hocutt, 2005; Snook, 2010).

The distinction between 'education' and 'training' is a live issue, returning to the question about whether education is largely about being trained to pass exams, on one hand, or to be educated into how to live well with others in a community on the other. Perhaps there are certain beliefs or habits or skills that teachers should be trying to inculcate in their pupils in an unquestioning way. If not, why not? Conversely, perhaps teachers should, above all, be aiming to turn pupils into autonomous adults who can think critically about everything they are told and make up their own minds about what to think and what to do in their lives. Again, if so, why should this be the aim?

As there is considerable diversity in views about what teachers and schools should be aiming at, it might be helpful to identify some common ground, as much as possible. One fundamental and common view of education is that it should in some way be improving the quality of life of individuals or of society in general. Otherwise, why bother with it? This general aim still leaves room for more specific discussions over what priority to put on aims that may be best for each individual, or aims to improve society as a whole through education. It hardly needs saying that different people may bring different views to that discussion about what in particular is good for individuals and what the nature is of a good society. (We will come back to the question of whether societal and individual aims necessarily conflict later).

So how can the debate be taken further? What follows is intended to stimulate your own thinking rather than to give any definitive answers. One starting point could be to focus first on a set of aims that are always likely to be very influential in determining what actually happens in education: the aims of government in setting educational policy. Then we can broaden the picture by looking at different people who have aims for education, and at a broader range of possible aims.

Societal and individual aims

Government education policies are inevitably influenced by political priorities. These tend to be driven by concerns to promote economic stability and growth. Parents may think about the aims of education in a similar way as may pupils, seeing the primary point of going to school to be getting qualifications that will lead to further qualifications and/ or a job that will pay relatively well. This may be a view of schooling shared by some people entering the teaching profession, but by no means all. The overall societal aims of education for employment is an important one. However, this does not mean that there is no room for other conceptions of the aims of education as well.

One issue with having 'economic growth' as an educational aim is that it isn't certain that continued economic growth will happen, year on year, especially if we take a global perspective. Consequently, we may argue that governments' responsibilities towards their citizens have to extend beyond material conditions. For one thing, there is evidence that, above some level of minimal provision, increasing affluence does not produce increasing happiness or flourishing (James, 2007). Peoples' aspirations for their own lives may not be purely material, and governments may have a responsibility to protect and promote the well-being of their citizens in a broader than economic sense. Government policy, if it is explicit about aims at all rather than taking certain aims for granted, tends to sketch aims with a broad brush. Teachers (and perhaps parents and pupils themselves) need to be able to think about aims in more detail. While they may see the point of education at least in part in terms of the good of society, their focus is more likely to be aims for individuals: ways in which education can make the lives of individuals better than they would otherwise be. Governments need to take into account the ways, both positive and negative, that people's lives impinge on each other, a consideration that can lead to an explicit concern with values education (see Unit 4.5).

With values education in mind, we might say that education should do more than enable people to gain qualifications and 'transferable skills' for the global economy, because qualifications are only part of the preparation for becoming an adult in any society. It could also be added that technological changes are bringing about such radical social change, so we can no longer predict what kind of employment and challenges young people will be facing as adults. On this view, it follows that education might need to be broadly based, enabling people to adapt what they know, and enjoy what they are able to do, as preparation for life in uncertain times. As well as a core of skills, a deep familiarity with the arts and humanities and a critical and curious approach to problem solving and discussion might be valuable aspects of education in addition to the more instrumental, economic ones (Greene, 1981; Nussbaum, 2010).

On this alternative approach, the question of what aims education ought to have might start differently by asking, 'What should count as an educated young person in this day and age?' To do so is to ask questions about which human qualities we wish to nurture and develop and how education may foster them (Oakeshott, 1972). These might cover the knowledge and understanding required for work, but also for managing one's life and relationships. It is important, too, that people develop a practical capacity and an ability to make sensible and grounded decisions, given changing economic and social conditions. 'Moral seriousness' (Haydon, 2007; Pring, 2012) is a quality that has been highlighted as important for the individual and for society. This might involve having a sense of responsibility for the community, which might include kindness and respect towards others.

This takes us into thinking not only about the knowledge and the skills that schools should aim to inculcate, but also about the kinds of qualities and dispositions we think pupils need to develop. Often, and perhaps increasingly, the language of 'skills' and knowledge tends to dominate (Ball, 2003a,b); Gleeson and Husbands, 2004). This is not to question the value of education that leads pupils towards having certain skills and subject knowledge, and indeed, there are pragmatic reasons for gaining knowledge and skills that may be individual (including earning a living) or societal (including the filling of occupational roles that the society needs). There is also an intrinsic value to some knowledge and skills: that is to say, it may just be interesting to know about certain things, or satisfying to be able to do certain things, regardless of any practical benefit. It is arguable that education should be at least partly about giving people access to such intrinsic sources of satisfaction. To think further and beyond knowledge and skills as the end of education, it is questionable whether all the capacities and qualities that we might want pupils to develop can be captured by the idea of skills and knowledge alone (see Greene, 2011; Pring, 2012).

Up to this point a number of possible aims for education have been mentioned. Some, referred to here as individual aims, are characterised by individual achievements or qualities that contribute towards improving the lives of individuals. Others, referred to as societal aims, are characterised by some possible state of society seen as desirable (such as an affluent society, or a free society, or a society with a strong sense of community). Most people have views about what makes a society 'good' and about what factors contribute to a good life for individuals, which may include: material prosperity, job satisfaction, wide-ranging and satisfying interests outside of work, good relationships with others, being in control of one's own destiny in life – the list is potentially endless.

Thinking about the aims of education is partly an attempt to bring coherence to thinking about such factors; but, crucially, it will be a matter of thinking through how far, and in what ways, the kind of teaching and learning that we associate with school education have a special role to play in realising these positive factors (and in limiting potentially negative ones). What sort of society a person lives in may be largely outside the individual's control, but education may influence how far a person fits into that society or seeks to change it. Life opens up opportunities and risks that may be unforeseen and unavoidable, but education can influence an individual's capacity to take advantage of the opportunities and cope with the risks. Health, for instance, is an important factor in a good life; in relation to health, teachers and schools do not have the same role as doctors and nurses, but there might be things that schools could do to influence a person's chances of having a healthy life, for example, by promoting healthy eating, which policy makers now require all schools to follow as part of a national strategy identified to tackle obesity (see Unit 4.2 on healthy eating in schools).

Two further points before turning to issues about the curriculum and its relationship to aims: first, there is more to be considered about the relationship between aims for individuals and aims for society. This is the topic of Task 7.1.3. Also, there is an assumption to be brought out and considered: that the fundamental aims of education are the same for everyone. This is the topic of the next section.

 Task 7.1.3   Individual and societal aims

This is a task for your individual reflection and group discussion.

There are some combinations of individual and societal aims that seem to fit neatly together: e.g. the societal aim of a society of full employment and the individual aim of giving each individual the knowledge and skills to equip them to do one of the jobs available. There are other combinations where the relationship between societal and individual aims may be problematic: consider, for instance, the societal aim of maintaining a society characterised by traditional ways of doing things, and the individual aim of equipping and encouraging young people to be independent and critical in their thinking.

Can you think of other combinations of societal and individual aims that seem to be 'made for each other'?

And other ways in which there may be conflicts between societal and individual aims?

Do you think societal aims should always have priority over individual ones? Or vice versa?

Do you think that it is easier for societal and individual aims to fit together in some kinds of society as opposed to others? (You could think, for instance, about how authoritarian or democratic a society is.)

Make notes of your discussion and summarise your views about aims. Keep your notes in your professional development portfolio (PDP).

Equal aims for everyone?

Through much of the history of education, it would have been an unquestioned assumption that the aims of education should be different for different people. Plato built his conception of an ideal state (*The Republic*) on the argument that the people in power would need a much more thorough education than anyone else. A similar position was apparent in Victorian Britain, where the expansion of education was driven in part by the aim that the mass of the population should be sufficiently well educated to form a productive workforce but not so well educated that they might rebel against the (differently educated) ruling classes. Until quite recent times, it was usual for the education of boys to have different aims – implicitly and sometimes explicitly – from the education of girls: boys might be educated to acquire the abilities necessary for certain sorts of occupation (which might, in turn, depend on their social position); girls would often be educated on the assumption that professions needing an extensive education were not for them. In the mid-20th century in England, within a system selecting by ability, there were also different aims behind the education offered in different types of schools: secondary modern, technical and grammar. An example that is still pertinent is that the aims of religious schools and the aims of secular schools are unlikely to coincide entirely (see below).

Despite these examples, today the unquestioned assumption is often that the basic aims of education are the same for everyone, even if different methods have to be used with different people in pursuing the same aims; and even if some people go further in the process than others. This assumption underlies many important developments in the promotion of equal opportunities. One of the basic reasons for being concerned with equal opportunities is that, if what you are aiming at is worthwhile, then no one should be excluded from it because of factors such as race or gender, which ought to be irrelevant to achieving these worthwhile aims. But this basic assumption is still not without its problems.

In the area of special educational needs (SEN) in England and Wales, for instance, the Warnock Committee, which was set up in the late 1970s to look into the education of pupils with physical and mental disabilities, argued that the fundamental aims of education are the same for everyone (Department of Education and Science (DES), 1978). This was part of the thinking that led in the 1980s to the integration of an increasing proportion of pupils with SEN into mainstream schools, rather than their segregation in special schools. There has been debate ever since over how far integration can be taken and whether there is still a case for some degree of separation in provision. But the debate is still usually conducted on the assumption that there are underlying aims of education that are the same for all. (See Unit 4.6 for the current position on SEN.)

As regards gender, few people would now suggest that the aim of education for girls should be to produce wives and mothers while the aim of education for boys should be to produce breadwinners. When people today make arguments for single-sex schooling or for dividing teaching groups according to gender, it is usually because they recognise that giving boys and girls an equal opportunity to achieve similar aims may require attention to practical conditions, and this may make a difference to the means of educating them. Even so, some might argue that a degree of differentiation in aims is needed; perhaps, for instance, there should be an attempt to develop assertiveness in girls and sensitivity in boys. (See Unit 4.4 for further discussion of gender issues.)

Turning to different cultural, religious or ethnic groups, it should come as no great surprise that governments expect the same general aims of schooling to be pursued for all; anything else would seem grossly discriminatory. But, at the same time, members of particular groups may have special aims they would like to see pursued for their own children, and this is certainly an issue in relation to schools of a religious character. To some religious believers it may be more important that their children are brought up within the faith of their community than that they are brought up as citizens of a secular society, illustrating the point made in the previous section, that conceptions of the aims of education turn, in the end, on views about what matters in life. To committed religious believers, there is a dimension to what matters in life that is absent for purely secular thinkers and which ought to be respected in schooling, while others question the right of religious groups to promote explicitly religious beliefs in schools that are publicly-funded.

These examples illustrate that, while at one level statements of the aims of education can appear rather platitudinous and bland, there is the potential for controversy when aims are considered in more detail and an attempt is made to see how the pursuit of certain aims can be implemented in practice. Unit 7.2 raises several questions about the relationship between stated aims and curriculum content.

To conclude the present unit, we suggest you address Task 7.1.4, which asks you to reflect on any single published statement of aims.

 M

 Task 7.1.4   Aims and education - a statement of aims

You need a statement of educational aims as a prompt for reflection that you can share with fellow student teachers. It does not have to be one that is currently in use. You might use one taken from another country, or your school, or one of the National Curriculum for England documents, in previous or current forms.

Analyse and evaluate the statement of aims, addressing questions such as the following:

- Does the statement comprise a list of discrete aims in no order of priority, or does it convey that some aims have priority over others?
- Where there are subordinate aims under a broader aim, is there a clear rationale for the particular subordinate aims listed?
- Do the aims listed seem to you to fit together into a coherent idea of what education is about?

If the answer to the last question is 'Yes', can you write one sentence summarising this conception of education?

Finally, consider whether there is anything in this statement of aims that you would not have expected to see there. Is there anything that is likely to prove controversial? Is there anything that you think should be mentioned that is not mentioned?

Discuss your responses with other student teachers, or with your tutor. Keep these notes together with those from Tasks 7.1.1, 7.1.2 and 7.1.3 in your professional development portfolio (PDP).

SUMMARY AND KEY POINTS

- In working as a teacher, you necessarily have some aims, and these are more likely to be coherent and defensible if you have thought them through.
- At the same time, you are operating within the context of aims set by others.
- Aims can exist at different levels, local and national.
- In England, in 2014, there was a revision of the National Curriculum that enabled schools to plan much of their own curricula. The question of aims is therefore open to discussion where planning occurs, and this leaves room for you to form your own view on the most important priorities for education, and to discuss with others how these aims can best be realised.
- It is always possible to raise questions about the justification of educational aims. Ultimately our aims for education rest on our values – our conceptions of what makes for a good life both for individuals and for our society as a whole.
- Because we do not share all of our values with each other, there is always room for debate about the aims of education.

Check which requirements for your ITE programme you have addressed through this unit.

Further resources

Haydon, G. (2007) *Values for Educational Leadership,* **London: Sage.**
This book is also relevant to those who are not in leadership roles. Chapter 2, 'Educational aims and moral purpose', goes in more detail into some of the issues raised in this unit, asking if and how school leaders should be motivated by a sense of moral purpose in pursing the aims of their school and the school curriculum.

Marples, R. (2014) 'What is education for?', in R. Bailey (ed.) *The Philosophy of Education: An Introduction.* **London: Bloomsbury Publishing.**
This chapter discusses three curriculum theories relating to the aims of education, i.e. curricula based on an academic curriculum, a vocational curriculum and one in which pupil well-being is fore-fronted.

National Curriculum documents

England, viewed 5 September 2017, from https://www.gov.uk/government/publications/national-curricul um-in-england-framework-for-key-stages-1-to-4

Northern Ireland, viewed 5 September 2017, from www.nicurriculum.org.uk/

Scotland (Curriculum for Excellence), viewed 5 September 2017, from http://www.gov.scot/Topics/Education/Schools/curriculum

Wales, viewed 5 September 2017, from http://www.wales.gov.uk/topics/educationandskills/schoolshome/curriculuminwales/arevisedcurriculumforwales/?lang=en

Promoting British Values in Schools - Guidance, viewed 13 November 2017, from https://www.gov.uk/government/news/guidance-on-promoting-british-values-in-schools-published

Reiss, M. and White, J. (2013) *An Aims Based Curriculum*, London: IoE Press.
This book, which is relevant to both this unit and Unit 7.2, argues that curriculum design should start from a consideration of aims rather than from the more familiar approach based on subject divisions. It starts by identifying some possible overarching aims of education that might equip learners to lead personally fulfilling lives and help others to do so, too. From these, more specific aims are derived, which cover the personal qualities, skills and understanding needed for a life of personal, civic and vocational well-being. In the second half of the book, the authors focus on the implementation of educational policy based on this view of aims and curriculum.

Standish, P. What Is Education?, viewed 5 September 2017, from www.philosophy-of-education.org/resources/students/video-listing.html
See also other videos on the website of the Philosophy of Education Society of Great Britain, viewed 4 July 2018, from www.philosophy-of-education.org/resources/students/video-listing.html

White, J. (2007) What Schools Are for and Why, Philosophy of Education Society of Great Britain (PESGB) IMPACT pamphlet No. 14, viewed 4 July 2018, from https://onlinelibrary.wiley.com/toc/2048416x/2007/14
This downloadable pamphlet gives a succinct expression of views expressed more fully in the Reiss and White book. Other free pamphlets in this series are also available on the PESGB website at http://www.philosophy-of-education.org/publications/impact.html

Young, M., Lambert, D., Roberts, C., and Roberts, M. (2014) *Knowledge and the Future School: Curriculum and Social Justice*, London: Bloomsbury.
The authors explain recent ideas in the sociology of educational knowledge, particularly drawing on Michael Young's research with Johan Muller. The book explicates three models of the curriculum in terms of their assumptions about knowledge and link the idea of 'powerful knowledge' for all pupils as a curriculum principle for any school. The question of knowledge, it is argued, is closely tied to the issue of social justice. The authors contend that access to 'powerful knowledge' is a necessary component of the education of all pupils.

Appendix 2 lists subject associations and teacher councils and Appendix 3 provides a list of websites.

Capel, S., Leask, M. and Turner, T. (eds.) (2010) *Readings for Learning to Teach in the Secondary School: A Companion to M Level Study*, Abingdon: Routledge.
This book brings together essential readings to support you in your critical engagement with key issues raised in this textbook.

Capel, S., Lawrence, J., Leask, M. and Younie, S. (eds.) (2019) *Surviving and Thriving in the Secondary School: The NQT's Essential Companion*, Abingdon: Routledge.
This book is designed to support newly qualified teachers in the next phase of development as a teacher. However, you may find it useful as it covers aspects of teaching not included in this book which, nonetheless you experience on your ITE programme.

The subject specific books in the *Learning to Teach (Subject)* series, the *Practical (Subject) Guides*, *Debates in (Subject)* and *Mentoring (Subject) Teachers* are also very useful.

Any additional resources and an editable version of any relevant tasks/tables in this unit are available on the companion website: www.routledge.com/cw/capel

7.2 The secondary school curriculum

Shirley Lawes

Introduction

When we talk about the secondary school curriculum today, it is easy to assume that we simply mean the National Curriculum as it currently exists in statute. Teachers have become accustomed to the idea that what will be taught in state schools should be prescribed for them. The centralised curriculum has become the norm, but this has not always been the case. Until the introduction of the National Curriculum in 1988, it was largely teachers who decided for themselves what should be taught, and external examinations, taken by some pupils at the end of their schooling, were a distant goal rather than an ever-present pressure. Over the following three decades, the content of the secondary school curriculum, as well as its aims and purposes, were increasingly prescribed and managed by government purportedly in order to achieve higher standards in educational achievement across the sector.

The introduction of the National Curriculum was a political decision rather than an entirely educational one; its purpose was to standardise the content taught across schools to improve and standardise assessment. This in turn enabled the compilation of league tables detailing the assessment statistics for each school. These league tables, together with the decision to give parents some degree of choice of school for their child (also legislated in the same act) were intended 'to encourage a "free market" by allowing parents to choose schools based on their measured ability to teach the National Curriculum' (Bartlett et al., 2001).

Since 2014, however, the situation is that the National Curriculum is not compulsory for over half of state schools, since the growth of Academy Schools and Free Schools, and does not apply to the independent sector. Moreover, this most recent version of the National Curriculum represents a significant departure from previous versions with respect to the central emphasis placed on subject knowledge. These two changes open up an important opportunity for a new discussion about what should be taught in secondary schools. This unit will consider how teachers might take an active role in shaping the curriculum. In order to do this, it is first worthwhile to take a step back and examine what it meant by the curriculum, and what influences and informs curriculum content.

> ## OBJECTIVES
>
> At the end of this unit, you should be able to:
>
> ▪ appreciate the central importance of the curriculum in education;
> ▪ be familiar with competing views and approaches to the curriculum and its content;
> ▪ have considered how teachers might contribute to the development of the secondary school curriculum.
>
> Check the requirements of your initial teacher education (ITE) programme to see which relate to this unit

What is the curriculum?

How the curriculum is shaped and set out is now very much a product of how political decision-makers and society view the value and purpose of education. This was not always the case. From an historical perspective, there have been numerous curriculum ideologies and models that, to a greater or lesser extent, reflected the historical or social context in which they were developed. These curriculum models were mostly influenced by the academic disciplines taught in universities because that was largely where knowledge was produced and categorised. Historically, and prior to the introduction of the National Curriculum, there was a high degree of consensus that the curriculum was synonymous with subject knowledge drawn from the university disciplines; although, the 1970s saw elements of experimentation in a 'progressive' direction where the value and relevance of an academically-orientated education for all pupils was called into question. Over time, we have come to consider the curriculum to encompass all that is taught and learned in schools. This includes the traditional subject disciplines that still pertain in the secondary school, but also all the activities designed to promote and encourage the intellectual, personal, social and physical development of children. All that falls outside the formal programme of subject study used to be called the 'hidden curriculum'. However, in the past, the 'hidden curriculum' referred to learning that was not planned for directly, but which was passed on informally through the subject disciplines. More recently, those 'hidden' elements have been formalised and their role elevated, partly through the development of Personal, Health and Social Education (known as PHSE, although with a number of variations on the theme). Different schools place different emphases on aspects of the curriculum, and it is interesting to consider what informs the choices that are made, and how they have changed over time. Nevertheless, the point to note here is how the social aspects of education have gained increasing importance in the curriculum in recent times. Now complete Task 7.2.1.

Task 7.2.1   School curricula
Reflect on your own secondary education. List all the traditional subject disciplines that you were taught. Now list what other subjects or activities relating more broadly to your personal and social education were included in your school curriculum. What was their relative importance?   Store this in your professional development portfolio (PDP) or equivalent.

It would not be too strong a claim to make that the curriculum defines the school in that it is through the curriculum that the beliefs and values and views on the purpose of education are expressed. Curriculum theory is a substantial academic body of knowledge that describes, examines and explains the principles that underpin the curriculum and seeks 'justification for the pursuit of an activity' (Barrow and Woods, 1988). There are a number of competing arguments about how the curriculum is established and what it should be in practice. Perhaps a good starting point for exploring some of the arguments would be to ask the following three key questions, and then consider the different ways of answering them:

- What should be taught in schools?
- Why should it be taught? To whom should it be taught?
- What does it mean to be an educated person?

What should be taught in schools?

We might start from the premise that it is in schools that we learn what we don't learn anywhere else; we can then eliminate from the curriculum swathes of information and everyday knowledge born out of experience. As the sociologist of education Michael Young points out, "[I]t is everyday concepts which constitute the experience which pupils bring to school. On the other hand, it is the theoretical concepts associated with different subjects that the curriculum can give them access to" (Lambert et al., 2014). Furthermore, if we see education as being concerned with the intellectual transformation of the individual, then these two principles taken together would inform and direct the content of the school curriculum. This approach would support the notion that there is a body of knowledge that throughout history has been transmitted from one generation to the next, that it is misguided to place 'personal development' on par with the intellectual pursuit of knowledge. In what has become known as a 'knowledge-based' curriculum, the focus is on intellectual growth through subject knowledge. A 'knowledge-based' curriculum embodies a vision of *liberal education* in which all pupils are entitled to be introduced to a range of subject disciplines where the boundaries between the different subjects are relatively clear and stable. Each subject discipline has its own conceptual structure and it is through each subject's core concepts that content is defined on the basis that the purpose of education is to provide all children with the chance to appreciate the intellectual achievements of humanity through the teaching of subjects. The debate around this approach to the curriculum has been developed in depth by Young (2008) and Young and Muller (2016) through his theory of 'powerful knowledge'. Young and a group of academics (notably Johan Muller and Rob Moore) argue from a social realist standpoint that a 'knowledge-based' curriculum does not have to be a curriculum of the past that is often seen as elitist and insists that a progressive case for a subject-based curriculum is possible.

While there is renewed support for this approach to designing the curriculum, the trend over the last 30 years or so has been towards a blurring of subject boundaries, cross-curricular themes and a greater focus on the social development of the child. Drawing on ideas originally from John Dewey, the famous American philosopher and educational reformer of the late 19th century, 'progressive education', as it may be loosely described, emphasises the importance of education as a means of social reconstruction. Dewey, like many other educators since, saw the purpose of education as being essentially about the development of human beings in society. The focus of the curriculum should be based on the interests of the child with due regard to useful knowledge and its application. More recently, curriculum policy-makers with 'progressive' leanings have been more influenced by pedagogy rather than by content and have developed an approach to the curriculum influenced by social learning theories, broadly categorised as *constructivism*. The central idea here is that human learning is constructed, that pupils build new knowledge upon previous learning and, therefore, learning involves constructing one's own knowledge from one's own experiences. Pupils are encouraged to discover principles for themselves and to co-construct knowledge by working to solve realistic problems.

The effect of these ideas on the content of the curriculum is to have a much more fluid view of subjects and the organisation of knowledge, and to elevate experience over substantive knowledge. This broadly child-centred approach to the curriculum has been explored by a number of writers, notably Michael Reiss and John White (2013) and Ken Robinson (2016). Their arguments militate against a subject-based curriculum, which they see as elitist. White (2004), in particular, has been consistent in his critique of the traditional subject curriculum, asserting that 'the curriculum is for all children, not an academic élite, and should be planned accordingly' (2004, p.183). The expansion of the curriculum since the late 1990s, explicitly to include a greater responsibility for the social and mental health of the child, expressed an increasing emphasis on the psychological well-being of pupils, which manifested itself through a whole range of interventions concerned with self-esteem, well-being, resilience, character-building and 'personal capital'. Dubbed by critics as 'the therapeutic turn' (Ecclestone and Hayes, 2009), these additions to the curriculum may be seen to shift the emphasis of the curriculum from developing an understanding of the world, to an understanding of the self: to elevate therapeutic goals over academic aims.

However, whatever the balance between 'subject and social', it is still the case that the range of subject disciplines in the secondary curriculum has remained relatively static since the introduction of comprehensive education in the late 1960s; however, the importance placed on certain subjects has undoubtedly changed as has the content of the curriculum. Perhaps the challenge now is to consider seriously how what 19th century cultural critic and poet Matthew Arnold called 'the best which has been thought and said' (Arnold, 1869) provides us with the intellectual framework for the curriculum of the future, or what other alternatives we might prefer to offer our pupils.

Why should it be taught? To whom should it be taught?

Clearly *what* should be taught needs justification and different curriculum models are based on differing views of the value and purpose of education. The notion that education is a good in itself with no external aims was once dominant, but that is no longer the case. Now, as we have suggested, the emphasis is more on ensuring that young people gain the qualifications and skills needed to take their place in society and to make a contribution to its economic success, with personal well-being also playing a significant role. The instrumental value of education is now a view that dominates decisions about the curriculum and a contingent relationship between education and the needs of the economy is assumed. The words 'relevant' and 'useful' are often applied to curriculum content, certain subjects are privileged over others and instrumentalism is often expressed as 'employability'. The drive to improve standards in education has influenced curriculum choices in terms of what subjects are most likely to lead to the highest GCSE grades. It is entirely legitimate for the school curriculum to cater for a range of abilities and interests and a broad range of subject disciplines. While success in examinations is important for both pupils and schools (partly because of the existence of school league tables), it would be very limiting if the curriculum were designed entirely around GCSE results. It is often said that the curriculum should be 'broad and balanced' and that due attention should be given to the all-around education of all young people.

However, how an 'all-around education' is achieved is another area of discussion. Some teachers and policy-makers would argue that decisions about *who* learns *what* are necessary if all pupils are to achieve what they are capable of and if educational standards are to be maintained. It is here that the notion of 'relevance' is sometimes applied, often with the best intentions, but mostly with the effect of limiting access to some subjects. This may not be much in evidence at Key Stage 3 until choices are made by pupils about which subjects to continue to learn at GCSE level, but the question is raised, often implicitly, whether all pupils really benefit from disciplinary knowledge and are capable of developing conceptual understanding. That is not a question we can easily answer, certainly not here, but it is an important issue to consider and then to ask: what happens if children miss out on academic knowledge? Is it only through the curriculum that schools can provide all children with the chance to appreciate the intellectual achievements of humanity? How far is it the role of the school to prepare young people for work? These questions might lead us to think about the subjects that make up the curriculum in more detail. Task 7.2.2. asks you to compare curricula.

 Task 7.2.2   School curricula: a comparison

Select two schools with which you are familiar, for example:

- the school in which you received your own secondary education;
- the school you are currently teaching in.

From memory, write down briefly what was in the curriculum of the school you attended as a pupil. Then (without referring to documentation at this stage) write down what is in the curriculum of your present school. Compare the two accounts and think about how you might account for any differences.

Keep your notes from this task in your professional development portfolio (PDP).

The subject curriculum

Historically, school subjects evolved out of the subject disciplines of the universities. The way that knowledge has been classified, categorised and structured over time is in itself a wonder to behold and something that we now take utterly for granted. So, for teachers today, the work has been done – or has it? Our knowledge of the world is developing all the time, and the curriculum cannot be set in stone. However, we should recognise the importance of the foundational knowledge – that is conceptual as well as factual knowledge that has endured over time, and which contribute to our understanding of what it means to be educated.

We often talk about 'core' and 'foundation' subjects and other terms at various times that indicate there is at least an agreed upon, basic curriculum that all pupils should experience. Once upon a time, the so-called 'three Rs' (Reading (W)riting and (A)rithmetic) – what would now be called 'basic literacy' and 'numeracy' – was the dominant focus of education for the masses. Over time, changes in social attitudes and economic development fostered more enlightened views and gradually the categories of Sciences, Arts and Humanities emerged as legitimate areas of knowledge for most children to be introduced to. We cannot go into depth here about the development of school subjects (see Standish and Sehgal Cuthbert, 2017 for an exploration of disciplinary knowledge and school subjects), but we should note the emergence of a fairly standard list of subjects that has altered little over the last 50 years or so. What has changed significantly at various points in time is the place particular subjects occupy in the curriculum, and the selection of knowledge that is included in the school subject. So, for example, in the 1970s, partly due to recent membership of the European Economic Community, Modern Foreign Languages were seen by policy-makers as being an important subject to be taught to the majority of pupils. In the intervening years, their importance waned and, by 2005, they became an optional subject in the secondary curriculum and is now a subject area in crisis. Currently, STEM subjects (Science, Technology, Engineering and Mathematics) are arguably the most favoured parts of the secondary school curriculum. Latin, Classical Studies and Philosophy are rarely taught in state schools today and this might be seen as an example of privileging 'useful' knowledge over the supposedly 'useless' knowledge of the past. ICT (Information and Communications Technology), now referred to a computing science, has emerged as a significant addition to the school curriculum in recent years, and much emphasis has been placed on teaching a variety of aspects of the subject area from basic data mining to coding.

The selection of knowledge within subjects, what is seen as important and why, is central to the values, aims and purposes of education and is susceptible to change. It is important for the curriculum to reflect developments in knowledge, but the question of how far the knowledge-content of the curriculum should follow social or political agendas is contentious. We now have a National Curriculum that purports to be broad and balanced, providing an initiation into subject disciplines that draws on knowledge of the past and present, providing insights that inform our vision of the future. But what resources and resourcefulness to reassert a confident focus on knowledge do teachers need? What educational outcomes might we expect for all young people? Although a strong subject-based liberal education is currently favoured by government and a section of the education world, we could also argue that in the fast-changing world in which we live, we cannot predict what knowledge will be needed in the future, and so the school curriculum should focus more on generic learning skills, critical thinking and problem-solving in order to better prepare young people for an uncertain future. Now complete Task 7.2.3.

> ✎ **Task 7.2.3   Reflection on changes to curricula**
>
> Think about the subject(s) that you are learning to teach. From what you know of the Key Stage 3 curriculum, how much similarity is there with what you remember from your own learning experience? What are the differences? How might the differences be explained, do you think? What evidence is there for these differences?
>
> Write down your reflections in your professional development portfolio (PDP) and, if possible, discuss them with another student teacher or teacher in your subject area.

What does it mean to be an educated person?

It was the philosopher of education, Richard Pring, who, in the 2009 Nuffield Review of 14-19 Education and Training (Pring, 2009) posed the question, 'What counts as an educated 19 year old in this day and age?'. This would seem a pertinent question to ask in relation to our discussion of the curriculum. We have already suggested that there has been a growing tendency to see educational success in narrow instrumental terms, that is, measured by examination results, and pointed to the need for the curriculum to go beyond those confines. Curriculum planning is often now built around 'outcomes' and some sort of tangible evidence of learning is expected, often at the end of every lesson. But if we take the 'long view' of education and consider that the accumulation of knowledge in a subject and the development of conceptual understanding cannot be entirely measured, then the school curriculum will reflect longer-term aspirations and the belief in knowledge as personal enrichment. Examination success is undoubtedly important, but the curriculum should provide an enriched experience of subjects that seeks to inspire young people and enliven their curiosity to understand the world through knowledge. Perhaps the one principle that unites almost everyone involved in education is the desire to see all young people succeed to the best of their abilities and to lead fulfilled and successful lives. If we return to the notion of a 'broad and balanced' curriculum, are we in fact supporting the traditional liberal education for the 21st century that Michael Young argues for? What sort of re-thinking is needed to achieve a knowledge-based curriculum? First and foremost, teachers need to be firmly committed to the idea that all pupils are entitled to a knowledge-rich curriculum and are, to a greater or lesser extent, capable of acquiring foundational subject knowledge if they have teachers who are confident to teach it. Every 19-year-old that Pring refers to will not achieve the same things, will not have the same aspirations, opportunities and goals, but they can all be inspired by knowledge. Perhaps the image of young people evoked by John Anderson (1980) as 'the heir to all the ages' is one to reflect upon.

Teachers as curriculum makers

If we were to read about the curriculum as it was understood in the 1970s, as discussed, for example by Hugh Sockett in Designing the Curriculum (1975), we would encounter an entirely different view of how decisions are made about what should be taught. Prior to the introduction of the National Curriculum in 1988, teachers decided for themselves what to teach and the implicit acknowledgement of the broad body of knowledge to be taught was put to question, challenged and alternatives experimented with. That was at a time when teachers were perhaps more professionally confident to take advantage of the freedom to experiment, sometimes successfully, but sometimes with serious failures. The culture of schools has changed considerably over the last 20 years towards a more 'business'-orientated organisation and ethos. The work of the teacher has been closely prescribed as part of an attempt to establish more consistency in the overall quality of education. The drive to 'raise standards' has arguably resulted in a progressive narrowing down of the secondary curriculum, particularly at Key Stage 4, in order to focus on examination preparation. The charge of 'teaching to the test' is a criticism often heard of teachers anxious to ensure pupils are well-prepared for their exams. Student teachers could be forgiven for thinking that, indeed, the curriculum *is* set in stone, as many schools have prioritised examination success over curriculum and pedagogic experimentation. The stakes are high in terms of examination and inspection results for schools but since the 2014 iteration of the National Curriculum is no longer compulsory for more than 50% of schools that are not with the state-maintained sector, that is, all Academies and Free Schools.

A window of opportunity now exists for teachers to be active in the development of the curriculum. The 2014 National Curriculum (DfE, 2014n) gives teachers more freedom to choose what they teach, and for those teaching in an Academy or Free School, there is potentially greater freedom to do things differently – if they dare. Student teachers may feel wary of experimenting and may be discouraged from attempting to break out of the tried and tested schemes of work that schools have been employing for years. This is quite understandable, but this is the very time to be thinking about what different subject content might be introduced in the future, and perhaps make some small steps to experiment and challenge yourself and your pupils. This will mean something different for each curriculum subject, but never underestimate what your pupils are capable of if they are inspired by the knowledge that you have to share.

SUMMARY AND KEY POINTS

- ■ This unit has introduced some of the past and present thinking about the curriculum.
- ■ While some attention has been paid to the National Curriculum, we have attempted to examine some of the broader principles that inform curriculum organisation and practice.
- ■ The 'knowledge-based' curriculum has been presented here in a new light – not as a return to the past, but as a liberating and exciting approach to curriculum planning for the future.
- ■ As student teachers, you are invited to start thinking imaginatively about curriculum content and are urged to begin to take ownership and become curriculum makers rather than curriculum deliverers.

Check which requirements for your ITE programme you have addressed through this unit.

 Further resources

Reiss, M. and White, J. (2013) *An Aims Based Curriculum*, **London: IoE Press.**
This book sets out an alternative to a subject-based curriculum, having as its starting point not subjects but a question about what schools should be for. Reiss and White state this should be to equip each pupil to lead a personally fulfilling life and to help others to do so. From these, they derive more specific aims covering the personal qualities, skills and understanding needed for a life of personal, civic and vocational well-being. This leads to discussion of how curricula could be designed in different ways, in different schools, starting with aims and not subjects.

Standish, A. and Sehgal Cuthbert, A. (eds.) (2017) *What Should Schools Teach? Disciplines, Subjects and the Pursuit of Truth,* **London: UCL Institute of Education Press.**
This book develops a distinctive and robust rationale for, and understanding of, what schools should teach - the curriculum.

Young, M.F.D. and Muller, J. (2016) *Curriculum and the Specialization of Knowledge,* **Abingdon: Routledge.**
This book is an exceptional collection of papers that draw on the sociology of knowledge to examine the curriculum and to think about curriculum priorities in a new way.

Young, M.F.D. and Lambert, D. (eds.) (2014) *Knowledge and the Future School - Curriculum and Social Justice,* **London: Bloomsbury.**
This book explains recent ideas in the sociology of knowledge and explores three models of the curriculum that chart possible future developments in education.

Appendix 2 lists subject associations and teacher councils and Appendix 3 provides a list of websites.

Capel, S., Leask, M. and Turner, T. (eds.) (2010) *Readings for Learning to Teach in the Secondary School: A Companion to M Level Study,* **Abingdon: Routledge.**
This book brings together essential readings to support you in your critical engagement with key issues raised in this textbook.

Capel, S., Lawrence, J., Leask, M. and Younie, S. (eds.) (2019) *Surviving and Thriving in the Secondary School: The NQT's Essential Companion,* **Abingdon: Routledge.**
This book is designed to support newly qualified teachers in the next phase of development as a teacher. However, you may find it useful as it covers aspects of teaching not included in this book which, nonetheless you experience on your ITE programme.

The subject specific books in the *Learning to Teach (Subject)* series, the *Practical (Subject) Guides*, *Debates in (Subject)* and *Mentoring (Subject) Teachers* are also very useful.

Any additional resources and an editable version of any relevant tasks/tables in this unit are available on the companion website: www.routledge.com/cw/capel

8 Your professional development

In this chapter, we consider life beyond your student teaching experience. The chapter is designed to prepare you for applying for your first post and to be aware of the opportunities available to continue your professional development as a teacher after you have completed your initial teacher education course. Society is constantly changing and so the demands society places on teachers change. Consequently, as your career progresses, you will find you need new skills and knowledge about teaching and learning (pedagogy), so you can expect to continue to learn through your career. Professional development is therefore a lifelong process that is aided by regular reflection on practice and continuing education. The chapter also provides an overview of accountability, and contractual and statutory duties. It contains three units.

Getting a job at the end of your initial teacher education is important, time consuming and a high priority for student teachers. Unit 8.1 is designed to help you at every stage of the process of getting your first post. It takes you through the stages of considering, once again, why you want to enter the teaching profession; deciding where, and in what type of school, you want to teach; looking for suitable vacancies; sending for further details of posts that interest you; making an application – asking referees, different methods of application – an application form, letter of application and a curriculum vitae; and preparing for and attending an interview – including teaching a lesson as part of an interview; and accepting a post.

The success of any school depends on its staff. However, although you have successfully met the requirements to qualify as a teacher at the end of your initial teacher education course, you still have a lot to learn about teaching to increase your effectiveness. Unit 8.2 considers your further development as a teacher. It looks at planning your professional development, and the transition from student teacher to newly qualified teacher, focusing on five specific times – before you start the job, starting the job, after the first few weeks, over the course of the first year and continuing professional development beyond the first year. It then focuses on your professional development to help you continue to learn and develop professionally throughout your career.

Unit 8.3 is designed to give you an insight into the system in which many of you will be working as teachers and to your accountability, contractual and statutory duties. We look briefly at where teachers fit within the education system in the structure of the state education system in England and then at teachers' accountability: organisational, legal, professional and moral. This leads into a slightly fuller consideration of the legal duties and responsibilities, highlighting important legislation – including rights and responsibilities, child protection, safeguarding children and young people, the welfare of children and young people, special educational and physical needs, managing pupils' behaviour, and recruitment of teachers and other staff. Finally, the unit considers contractual requirements and statutory duties that govern the work of teachers.

Unit 8.4 focuses on developing as a professional. It starts by considering what it means to become a 'professional'. It then considers your developing teacher identity. The third section focuses on understanding that developing professional judgement is highly complex and requires developmental tools. The unit then looks at working with your school-based mentor to support your development and understanding the importance of learning throughout your teaching career. Developing your professional knowledge, skills and judgement is important to enable you to manage situations that arise with pupils.

8.1 Getting your first post

Julia Lawrence and Susan Capel

Introduction

Gaining employment post-qualification is a challenging activity. Applying for and obtaining your first post is one of the most important decisions you make. It needs to be thought through and considered carefully. The process itself is more than just completing an application form. It involves a number of equally important stages. You need to be clear about why you want to enter the teaching profession, as well as about where and in what type of school you want to teach. You need to look for suitable vacancies, select a post that interests you and request further details. You need to prepare your curriculum vitae (CV), write a letter of application and contact potential referees. Once these have been completed, you need to complete your application, prepare for and attend an interview in order to secure a full-time post.

There is a lot to do, and being organised and prepared are key elements to a successful outcome. There may well be a session or two in your initial teacher education (ITE) programme on applying for jobs. This may include support for writing your CV and letters of application and opportunities for mock interviews. You may be able to access further support from your careers advisors (if university-based), and many schools now contact universities to come to speak to student teachers to share teaching opportunities within their school or across the alliances they may work with. You should make every effort to attend these. The aim of this unit is to offer advice and guidance to support you with the process of getting your first post.

OBJECTIVES

At the end of this unit, you should be able to:

- articulate why you want to enter the teaching profession;
- follow the procedure for, and the process of, applying for your first teaching post;
- make a written application;
- prepare for an interview for a teaching post.

Check the requirements of your ITE programme to see which relate to this unit.

Consider why you want to enter the teaching profession

In many respects, you have already joined the profession in undertaking your ITE programme. However, the type of ITE programme you have undertaken may now start to influence your future career aspirations. Having undertaken substantial periods of school experience, and being aware of the demanding nature of the profession (including workload and stress; see Unit 1.3) you are entering, you should reaffirm the reasons for your decision to pursue a career in teaching, in preparation for questions you may be posed at interview.

Teaching is an attractive choice of career for many reasons, and different people have different reasons for wanting to become a teacher. For many, it is altruistic and intrinsic reasons that motivate them to enter the profession rather than the extrinsic rewards they might get. Your reasons might also influence your choice of post and the type of school in which you wish to teach.

Deciding where, and in what type of school, you want to teach

There are complexities involved in getting your first post; thus, it is best to consider the whole picture before you start applying, rather than finding things out once you have accepted a post. Deciding on the location in which you wish to teach is one of the first major decisions. You may be committed to teaching in a specific area because, for example, family commitments or a desire to stay close to where you have undertaken your ITE programme, where you have set up and established social networks.

If you are committed to a specific area you need to take into consideration a number of factors, for example accommodation, travel time and access to public transport. Of these, one of the key considerations is that of travel time to and from school, as a long journey in your first year of teaching when you are likely to be tired at the end of each day or when you have had a school commitment in the evening can become very wearing.

You also need to recognise that if you are limiting your search to a small and specific location, it may be difficult to find a post, and hence your employment opportunities may be limited. Popular areas may have few schools, low turnover of staff, or have a large number of applicants, especially if they are located close to a number of providers of ITE.

Ask yourself if you can you be flexible as to where you teach. The more flexible you can be increases the number of posts for which you might apply.

A number of student teachers look to teach abroad as a first teaching post. International schools offer many benefits; although, you do need to understand the implication of taking this type of employment in terms of completing any induction period required, contributions to pensions, payment of taxes and so on. Further, many countries require experience prior to appointment. You may be better served completing your first-year post-qualification before heading overseas. You may also want to consider organisations such as Voluntary Service Overseas (VSO).

You should now spend some time thinking about where you want to teach by completing Task 8.1.1.

Task 8.1.1   Where do you want to teach?

Think about where you would like to teach and how flexible you can be in where you can look for a post. List all areas in which you would consider working and find out as much information about these areas as you can; for example, transport networks, travelling time, local facilities, house rent or purchase prices. Talk to anyone you know who lives in these areas. If it is an area you do not know, if possible, visit the area so that you can get a 'general feel of the place'.

Store the information in your professional development portfolio (PDP) or equivalent for later reference.

As well as location, consider the type of school in which you wish to work. During your ITE programme, you should have been placed in different types of school. These might have varied in, for example, the general location (for example, rural or inner-city school), size, ethnic make-up, the general philosophy of the school and independent as well as state sector. Further, over recent years, the range of schools in England has increased, including free schools and academies. (If you are thinking of applying to a school that is part of Multi Academy Trust (MAT), look carefully at the terms and conditions specified, as some may appoint you to the trust rather than a specific school. This might impact on where you end up teaching). You may also have heard about other types of school from others. Gaining an insight into different types of school will help you to identify those in which you would prefer to teach.

Task 8.1.2 asks you to consider what type of school you might wish to work in.

 Task 8.1.2   What type of school do you want to teach in?

Think back to the types of school you have experienced on school experience during your ITE programme. List positive aspects about working in the different types of school, opportunities you are/were able/not able to experience in these different types of school and identify any experiences you felt you would like to focus on in your first teaching post.

From this, identify the types of school you would be happy to teach in (for example, state, independent, specialist school, academy, free school or sixth form college). Identify why you want to teach in that type of school.

Store this information in your professional development portfolio (PDP) for use in planning applications.

Looking for suitable vacancies

The majority of advertisements for teaching posts in the UK are for specific posts in specific schools. Teaching posts are advertised in a number of places: the *Times Educational Supplement* (https://www.tes.com/jobs/), national press, local press/other local publications, school websites and employment websites (for example, www.eteach.com, www.jobsgopublic.com). Sometimes, schools contact ITE providers directly or you may hear details of vacancies via your placement school. Consider signing up for 'alerts', which means that you can receive regular updates on posts becoming available. With the rise in the use of social media, following Twitter feeds from the schools you are interested in can also provide alerts when jobs are being advertised.

Advertisements occur year-round. Traditionally, the majority of posts are for a September start, so the bulk of advertisements are published between March and May because teachers who are leaving at the end of the academic year are required to hand in their notice by the end of May. Try to set aside time each week to check vacancies. Apply for as many jobs as you want but do not apply for a job you do not want because you are panicking that you won't have a job for September. You should not be disheartened if you are unsuccessful for a post for a September start as January start dates are also common. Maternity cover is also worthwhile as you can still undertake your induction. Also, opportunities for work through a teaching supply agency may be available as a short-term solution to gain experience while you wait until opportunities arise within your chosen location. You may find that if you get a long-term supply post, you may be able to use some of this time against your induction period. However, if you are looking at agency work, be clear what the terms and conditions there are in relation to applying for permanent roles in the future, as many agencies charge finder fees to schools.

It is clear that getting a job is not easy. Try and keep open-minded to the range of options available to you and be as flexible as you can.

Check your online professional identity

Throughout your ITE programme, issues around appropriate use of social media and safe-guarding will have been highlighted. It is not uncommon for potential employers to check your online identity (for example, through Twitter, Facebook and LinkedIn). At this point, you should review all information about yourself that is on the Web and consider whether the way you present yourself online is appropriate for the professional you wish to be. Remember, your online identity is visible to potential employers, as well as the press, other teachers, pupils, parents and governors.

Selecting a post that interests you

You cannot start early enough in looking for appropriate posts. If an advertisement interests you, read the application pack if one is provided and contact the school for any further information not included in the pack. You can phone or email the school (the school secretary is a good starting point if the advertisement does not specify a point of contact); for example:

Dear Sir/Madam (or name, if given in the advertisement)

I am interested in the vacancy for a (subject) teacher (quote reference number if one is given) at ABC school, advertised in (publication; for example, *Times Educational Supplement*) of (date) and would be grateful to receive further details of this post.

Yours faithfully (if you use Sir/Madam) or sincerely (if you use a name)

Making an application

If you decide to apply, remember that your application is the first formal contact you have with the school, and first impressions count. An application is an early stage in the selection process, and the decision to call you for interview is based on the quality of this application. Hence, the importance of presenting yourself effectively in your application cannot be overestimated. You need to make sure that you have as much information available to you as possible, both about the school and the particular post, so you can develop a better understanding about the school (for example, its philosophy and organisation). The school website will provide information about the general activities of the school. The latest school inspection report is on the relevant website (see websites for England, Northern Ireland, Scotland and Wales in 'Further resources' and Appendix 3). Accessing the most recent inspection report allows you to develop an impression of how the school is performing. If possible, organise a visit to the school; this allows you to get a better feel for the school and the area and to personalise your application.

Any job advertisement will include a description of the post (job description) and, in most cases, an overview of what they are looking for in the person applying (sometimes referred to as a person specification), which focuses on the main knowledge, skills and experiences the school are looking for. Highlight key words and phrases contained in these. You need to consider whether you have the knowledge, skills, experience and qualities the school is looking for and whether the school meets some or all of your requirements. You need to make sure you highlight your strengths in your application, providing, where possible, examples of where you have demonstrated the skills and experience that they are looking for. For example, if the advertisement identifies strong behaviour management as a requirement, you should include examples of when you have demonstrated this in your teaching: state what you did and why and how you knew it was successful. You should also demonstrate other qualities you have that would contribute to the school's vision (which is why it is important to access as much information about the school as you can) and what makes you distinct from other applicants.

Plan the content of your application before you complete the application form or write a covering letter for a specific post and finalise your CV. If you are making multiple applications, do not be tempted to use the same form, letter or CV. While many applications require the same basic information (for example, previous experience, prior employment), you cannot have a standard application form, letter of application or CV that you use for every application. Each application needs to match your experience and qualifications to the specific requirements of the post, highlighting different points and varying the amount of detail you provide, according to the specific requirements of the post and the school. If you use some of the same information, make sure you have changed all references specific to other applications (this is a common mistake and does result in some applications being rejected). You may want to store relevant information in the form of a Word document, from which you take relevant information for a specific application.

As well as demonstrating why you want the job, a customised application also shows you have taken the effort to find out about a specific post in a specific school, which should help your application to stand out from the others. An application that fails to explain why you are interested in the specific post in the specific school is unlikely to be considered further. Being proactive is a good quality to demonstrate.

Hopefully, you have started to see that the application process is more than just form filling. To do it properly takes time. Two hours is probably the minimum time to complete an application properly without rushing it if you have prepared beforehand and have all the information available. Most applications have a closing date about two weeks after the original advertisement is placed. Getting yourself organised is therefore important, as is starting the application early. Do not leave it to the last minute; otherwise, you might have to rush it. It is usually clear when you have rushed an application. Much of the information you need to include on an application can be prepared in advance. The next section provides examples.

Referees

You are normally asked to supply the names and contact details of at least two people who are willing to act as referees. These are people who have a good knowledge of you as an individual as well as your teaching ability and academic work. Check whether there is one particular person within your ITE provider whom you should name as the first referee and, if not, ask someone who has knowledge of your teaching abilities. Examples might include a tutor from a placement school, a member of staff from your ITE provider or a previous employer. Your second referee should be someone who knows you well and is able to comment on your character, qualities, achievements and commitment to teaching as a career. Family members must not be used.

You should contact your referees before making any application to check they are willing to act for you. You should confirm the contact details of your referees are accurate, including telephone number(s) and email address, and whether there are any dates when they are away and unable to respond should a request arrive. Many schools require references to be taken up prior to interviews, but if not, any offer of employment may be withheld until these have been received.

You will have selected your referees because you feel they will be supportive of your application, so try to give them as much information as possible about you that might be included in the reference; for example, other activities in which you have been involved. It is often helpful for the referee to have a copy of your CV. Also provide them with as much information about the post as you can. While most schools send referees information about the post to which you have applied, this tends to be very close to the interview date. It is therefore useful to send your referees the job description when you submit your application so they have time to complete their reference.

Some schools have a policy of open references; that is, a reference is shown to the applicant in certain circumstances. The referee knows this at the time of writing the reference.

Methods of application

Schools normally require job applicants to submit a completed application form or letter of application and CV. Most frequently, you complete a form plus a letter or a personal statement. In these cases, the form acts as your CV.

Modern technology means that many applications are now made online, rather than either sending hard copy by post or attaching a letter to an email; however, some still require either of these. You need to check what process is expected for the post for which you are applying. If a postal application is required, you need to build time into the process (including getting access to the post office) so that it arrives before, or on, the due date. Avoid leaving things to the last minute though.

An application form

The information required on an application form closely matches that identified for a letter of application and CV (see the companion website, www.routledge.com/cw/capel).

It is likely that one page of the form will be blank for you to explain why you are applying for the post, add additional information and elaborate on the skills and experience that equip you for it. As with a letter of application (see below), unless otherwise stated, this should focus on the specific job you are applying for, on the experience, skills and qualities you have to be able to do the job, and any additional skills you might bring to the post. This section should be written in continuous prose as if it is a section of a letter, following the suggested format and containing the type of information in a letter of application. Adding headings related to the person specification and job description before the relevant text can help those who are shortlisting candidates to see easily that you meet the specification for the post.

When you submit the application, you may need to include a covering letter (this may be included in an email, if appropriate) indicating the post you have applied for and where you accessed information about it. This will generally be very short, but will be written formally, indicating that you have included your application for the post of (subject) teacher as advertised in (publication).

Letter of application

Some schools require you to write a letter of application. This should state clearly your reasons for applying for the post, matching your qualifications, experiences, particular skills and personal qualities to the post as described in the information sent to you from the school. The letter should normally be no more than two sides of A4 in length. A suggested format is given in Figure 8.1.1 on the companion website (www.routledge.com/cw/capel). When completing your letter of application, it is important to check grammar and punctuation. Applications are frequently rejected if either of these are poor.

Your curriculum vitae (CV)

A CV summarises your educational background, qualifications, teaching and other work experience and any other relevant information (for example, interests and activities you enjoy outside of school), as well as any other relevant qualifications (for example, a clean driving licence) or any course you might have attended as part of your development as a teacher (for example, coaching qualifications, first aid). It should always accompany a letter of application and provides detail and further information to support your application. Remember, it is a supportive tool. Figure 8.1.2 (on the companion website, www.routledge.com/cw/capel) provides an editable version of a sample template for a CV.

To consolidate your learning from this section, Task 8.1.3 provides you with an opportunity to compile both a CV and letter of application/form.

 Task 8.1.3   Your CV/application

Draft a specimen letter of application and CV and obtain and complete an application form.

Ask your tutor to check these for you and give formative feedback on any changes they feel are appropriate. Store these in your professional development portfolio (PDP) to use as the basis for all your job applications.

Notes and reminders about applications

With any completed application, indicate clearly (if appropriate) any dates you are unable to attend for interview, for example, because you have an examination. Most advertisements identify the proposed date for interview, so you will have some indication of whether clashes are likely to occur. Examinations must normally take precedence over interviews. If you are concerned, you should contact your ITE tutors immediately to see if there are any alternatives. Holidays do not take precedence over interviews and most schools do not wait until you return from holiday to interview you; therefore, do not book holidays at times when you are likely to be called for interview. Other than for examinations, most ITE providers release student teachers to attend interviews without penalties. If you attend a lot of interviews during one of your school experiences, you may be expected to complete additional days in school to ensure you have completed the required number of days in school for your ITE programme.

Remember, you are not the only person applying for a post; there may be many applicants for some posts. It is therefore important to make sure your application is laid out and presented well, without using jargon. Some electronic forms enable you to complete individual sections and save and return to them prior to submitting the form, rather than having to complete the whole form at one time. Check your application to make sure there are no basic errors such as typing errors, mistakes in spelling, grammar or punctuation, and that the information is accurate and consistent (a common example is using the wrong school name). If the form does not allow you to spellcheck, or does not allow you to use more than a specific number of words, complete the information in another format so that you can spellcheck or count the number of words, and then cut and paste it into the file. This also allows you to spend time focusing on exactly what you want to say, and the words you want to use. Ask someone to read through any application to check for spelling and grammatical errors. Tutors will usually look through your application before you send it off but build this time into the process.

It is also important that you make your application stand out. Consider how you can do this in what and how you write your application. For example, try to use phrases that show your good qualities. For example, 'I successfully led an initiative to introduce a new monitoring system to check pupils' homework' is better than 'I checked pupils' homework'. However, do not exaggerate claims. Make sure you 'sell yourself'. If you do not have a strong letter of application or statement, the school is unlikely to be interested; however, do not sound too arrogant. They do not want you to tell them what they already know about their school. Remember that if you put down additional skills and experiences (for example, that you sing in a local choir), you may be invited to use those skills in school. Also, clearly demonstrate that you have read and understood some of the school policies.

Ensure all relevant information is included. Check that there is no missing information, dates or other details, or questions that you have not answered. Do not leave any sections of the form blank. If there are sections you cannot complete (for example, you have had no previous teaching posts), then just put not applicable (N/A). Remember, you only have one chance to get this right.

Keep a copy of each application with details of the post. If you are called for interview, you will need this information to prepare.

The interview

If you are invited to interview, confirm that you will attend, confirming the post, date and time of interview and the requirements for any lessons you are asked to teach and/or presentations you are asked to give. If your situation changes (for example, if you are unable to attend the interview because of a clash, such as another interview on the same day, or you have had another interview and been offered that post) and you are not going to attend the interview, let the school know as soon as possible (don't just not turn up). This will allow them to invite another candidate if they wish.

For any change, where possible, speak directly to the school contact rather than leave an answerphone message or email, and be honest and explain the situation. Try to avoid ringing on the day of interview unless your problem is illness-related.

Preparing for the interview

Prepare for an interview in advance by refreshing your memory about your application and the school itself and considering the points below.

If you have not already done so, you might wish to visit the school (always organise an appointment) or at least travel to it so that you know where you are going on the actual day.

You might find it helpful to reflect on why you applied for this particular post, so that you can put across the relevant information convincingly at interview. Read through the advertisement, job description, any other information about the post and school and your application again so that you can communicate effectively the information and evidence you consider to be relevant to the post. It also helps to avoid any contradictions between what you say and what you wrote in your application, as each member of the interview panel has a copy of your application so can compare answers. It may be that someone you know has knowledge of the school; if so, talk to them. Access recent reports on the school (see 'Further resources' for relevant websites). Write down any questions you have about the post or the school. While many might be answered during the course of the day, it is always useful to have one or two to ask in the interview.

Make sure that you have all the information you need for teaching a lesson on the day of interview (see teaching a lesson as part of the interview, below). You should be told this in the letter of invitation to interview, but, if not, contact the school and ask. Prepare any resources you might need for your lesson in advance and remember to take them with you! If you are giving a presentation, offer to send it through prior to the interview so that it can be uploaded onto the school system (also, this will mean that you have it in your emails should you forget your memory stick).

As a professional, you are expected to keep as up to date as possible on your subject and education, generally. Read around the subject you are hoping to be employed to teach, as well as about education more generally, so you can discuss the latest educational issues and debates, as well as changes in your subject area. If appropriate, prepare a portfolio of your resources, or attainment against the teaching standards for qualified teacher status or teaching-related activities, such as good lesson plans, examples of pupils' assessed work, worksheets, evaluations, photographs of displays or trips, review of resources and information and communications technology (ICT) skills. This is derived from the professional development portfolio (PDP) you are keeping throughout your ITE programme. Many ITE providers encourage student teachers to complete e-portfolios that allow you to showcase your work and progress over the duration of your ITE programme. On the interview day, you may not have time to show these, but reflecting on them prior to the day may well help relax you and give you good examples of practice to use during the interview itself.

Plan what you are going to wear at the interview. Appearance is important. You should dress professionally, smartly and conservatively, but with appropriate clothing for teaching your lesson.

Attending the interview

The interview starts as soon as you walk into the school and does not finish until you leave the school at the end of the day. Hence, the initial impact you make is very important as interviewers tend to form an overall impression early. You are assessed throughout the day, so your performance, including your verbal and non-verbal communication in each activity, is important and could make the difference between being offered the job or not.

An interview is a two-way affair. The fact that you have been called for interview demonstrates you have the qualifications to do the job. By attending, the school is identifying whether you are what they are looking for, but you are being given the opportunity to identify whether you want to teach at that school. Thus, at the same time as being interviewed, you are, in effect, interviewing the school and deciding whether this is a school in which you could work and, therefore, whether this is a post for you. Take the opportunity to learn as much as you can about the post, the school and the working environment. This requires you to be alert to what is being said and to be prepared to ask as well as answer questions. If at any stage during the day you feel this is not the right post/school for you, you can withdraw, and it is fair to do so.

It is difficult to generalise about interviews because they vary considerably. When you are offered an interview, you should expect to be given information about the format of the day. This might include a tour of the school, a teaching episode (a lesson/part of a lesson), an informal talk or interview with the head of department, a senior teacher or other staff in the department, group interview, individual interview and interview/talk with pupils. It might also include a presentation, group discussion or an activity such as an 'in-tray' exercise or drafting a letter to parents.

For many interviews, all interviewees are required to attend at the same time, while others specify a time for your interview, so you do not meet the other candidates. In some interviews, there is a sifting process, whereby some interviewees are sent home part-way through the day while the others remain for a formal interview. In some interviews, some interviewees teach in the morning and some are interviewed in the morning, then vice versa in the afternoon. You need to understand the processes for the day, and if you are in any doubt, contact the school for clarification. Because of these variations, the format and length of an interview day varies.

Teaching a lesson as part of the interview

It is regular practice for candidates to be asked to teach a lesson or section of a lesson as part of the interviewing process. You should be notified of this when you are called for interview and be given specific information about the age and size of the class, what you are expected to teach and the pupils' ability and prior knowledge, the length of the lesson, what facilities, resources and equipment are available (i.e. all the information you require before teaching any class). If you require further information (for example, the prior learning of the pupils, what level of attainment they are working at, where the lesson fits in to the wider unit of work), then you should contact the school as soon as you receive your initial information. You might also want to do some research on how the school currently delivers lessons (for example, how do they share learning outcomes, how do they assess progress?) so that you can reflect aspects of this in your own delivery or offer activities that develop these principles further.

Plan the lesson carefully, giving attention to learning outcomes, purpose and content of activities, teaching strategies including questioning technique, resources and using as many of the principles you have developed during your ITE programme as possible. It is useful to have copies of the lesson plan available to give to those observing you. This is an opportunity to show the quality of your preparation and planning. Lessons taught as part of the interview process also provide you with the opportunity to demonstrate the level of your subject content knowledge and implementation of appropriate pedagogy so, again, prepare well, particularly if you have been asked to teach a topic with which you are not totally familiar. It is probably best to try to base your interview lesson on something that has been successful on a previous occasion with similar classes. The lesson is also an opportunity for you to show your enthusiasm for teaching, pupils' learning and your subject. This is your opportunity to demonstrate how you develop a rapport with your classes, as well as how you organise and progress lessons. Try to appear confident and relaxed, even though those observing you understand that you probably feel a little nervous!

If possible, practise the lesson before you deliver it. This allows you the opportunity to evaluate and modify your plan based on feedback.

Be prepared to discuss your lesson during your formal interview; for example, how you feel it went, what the pupils learned, how you know they learned this, and what you might change. It might be worth making a few notes about the lesson once you have taught it to help you with this. Be honest and do not be anxious about mentioning it if something has not gone to plan. For example, your timing might have gone astray, or your instructions were not as clear as you had anticipated. Where this is the case, offer examples of developments/improvements you might make. In essence, you are providing a verbal evaluation of the lesson itself. In doing so, you demonstrate your ability to analyse why it happened and how you might change this in the future. This demonstrates your level of reflexivity, but also that you have given serious thought to what you have just done, and hence about your practice.

The interview

As the format of interviews varies across schools, so do the composition and size of interview panels. In some interviews, you are faced by a panel comprising anything between two to three and six to seven people; in others, you have a series of interviews with different people. In either case, these people normally include the following: the head teacher, a (parent) governor, another senior member of the school staff and head of subject department. The length of the panel interview also varies, from about 30 minutes to 90 minutes. Commonly, interviews are scheduled to last for about 45 minutes, with time for you to ask questions yourself.

In the formal interview, the initial impression you make is very important. For example, how will you greet the panel when you arrive? Do not sit down until you are invited to do so. Think about your body language; for example, how you sit (sit comfortably on your chair, looking alert; do not sit on the edge of your chair looking anxious or slouch in your chair looking too relaxed). Look and sound calm, relaxed and confident (even if you are not). Try to be yourself. Try to smile and direct your answers to the person who has asked the specific question, as well as the panel, during discussion. You may want to change your body position slightly to face the person asking the question so that you maintain eye contact when answering questions. Try not to speak too quickly and to keep your answers to the question posed. If you are unsure about how much information to give when answering questions, it is probably better to keep an answer brief and then ask the panel if they would like further information. If you are not sure what the question means, do not hesitate to ask for clarification. If your mind goes blank, ask them to repeat the question. Avoid repetition, but do not worry if you repeat information included in your application, as long as you do not contradict what you wrote.

Interviewers have various degrees of specialist knowledge and understanding. Avoid jargon in explanations but assume interviewers have some knowledge and understanding of your subject area. Aim to provide a balanced picture of yourself, being, on the whole, positive and emphasising your strengths, while acknowledging areas of potential development. Interviewers are trying to form an impression of you as a future teacher and as a person, and so have a number of things they are looking for. These include:

- *Your knowledge and understanding of your subject and your ability to teach it.* Interviewers assess your ability to discuss, analyse, appraise and make critical comment about ideas, issues and developments in your subject and subject curriculum, your personal philosophy about and commitment to the teaching of your subject(s);
- *Your professional development as a teacher.* This is based partly on your school experiences. Interviewers assess your ability to analyse observations of pupils' behaviour and development, your own development and your involvement in the whole life of the school on school experiences, and your ability to discuss, analyse, appraise and make critical comment about educational issues.
- *Your ability to cope with the post.* Interviewers assess your understanding of the different roles you are required to undertake as a teacher and how you would cope (for example, how you have coped or would cope, in a number of different situations, such as disciplining a pupil or class experiencing difficulties, dealing with a concerned parent or with teaching another subject).
- *Your ability to fit into the school and the staffroom and to make contact with and relate to colleagues and pupils.* Interviewers assess your interpersonal skills, verbal and non-verbal communication skills (your written communication skills have been assessed from your application).
- *Your commitment to the specific post.* Interviewers assess the interest and enthusiasm you show for the post to try to find out whether this is a post you really want or whether you see this post as a short-term stop-gap before you can find a post in an area or school where you really want to teach.

After introductions and preliminaries, interviewers normally ask why you have applied for this specific post. They then focus on the information in your application, including your personal experiences, your education, qualifications, teaching skills gained from school experience and other teaching and/or work experience, your interest and activities and other qualifications. Throughout your ITE programme, you should have been encouraged to gain as much wider experience as possible; it is now that you can demonstrate how this has contributed to your own personal development as well as how it will benefit the school as a whole. In addition, you are normally also asked what you feel you can contribute to the school and general questions about professional or personal interests, ideas, issues or attitudes.

Remember that the interview provides you with an opportunity to expand upon information contained in your original application. Consequently, you can predict some of the questions that are likely to be asked based on the job description or person specification. Look back at the initial information you received to identify the parts of the job on which they expect to get information at the formal interview. Try to give practical examples to support your answers. If asked about your approaches to teaching, give examples of how you have used different approaches in your own practice. Talking through an example tends to allow you to demonstrate a deeper level of understanding than writing it down. However, try to remain focused. Make your point as clearly and succinctly as possible and then stop. If the panel want more information, they will probe further.

Therefore, think about areas you want to emphasise or any additional evidence of your suitability for the post that you did not have room to include in your application. Draw on both the university-based part of your ITE programme (for those of you on an ITE programme in partnership with a university) and school experience, other teaching experience and other experience; for example, other work with young people, such as work in a youth club or voluntary work. This demonstrates your commitment to working with young people.

You also need to show that you realise you still have things to learn and that you are committed to continuing your development as a teacher. You should come prepared with examples of potential short-term and longer-term targets for development. For example, you need to consolidate your learning in your first year, perhaps gain further experience of other areas, such as teaching Years 12 and 13 or taking on a tutor group. As you come to the end of your ITE programme, you are expected to develop some form of early professional development/transition planning, so use this to support your answers. You might also wish to consider undertaking an additional academic qualification, for example, studying at master's level (see also Unit 8.2 on continuing professional development). It is helpful to have a career plan, but not to appear so ambitious that you give the school the impression that you will leave at the first opportunity.

Possible interview questions

Questions asked at interview vary considerably; therefore, it is not possible for you to prepare precisely for an interview. However, it is helpful if you identify possible questions in your preparation and prepare some possible outline responses to such questions. It is useful to give a general response to the question to show you are aware of some of the principles and issues and also to refer to examples of your own practice. For example:

> *Interviewer*: How did you set about planning differentiated learning for a class you have taught recently?

> *Candidate*: This is an important way of enabling all pupils to have equal access to the curriculum so that they learn as much as possible and fulfil their individual potential. There are a number of strategies that can be used; for example, differentiation by outcome, by task or by rate of work. During my last school experience, I was teaching a Year 7 class about religious festivals. I did not want to give out several different worksheets as this might have embarrassed some pupils, so I made one worksheet that had some core tasks for all pupils and also some option tasks, which involved different levels of work and different types of activities. I also developed differentiation through my use of questioning...

 Some possible interview questions are included in Figure 8.1.3 on the companion website (www. routledge.com/cw/capel).

Other questions

At the start of the interview you may be asked if you are still a firm candidate for the role. This is an opportunity for the panel to confirm that you are still interested in the job. It is not a trick question.

At the end of the interview, you may be asked whether you have any questions. Asking one or two questions shows a genuine interest in the post and the school. You are likely to forget the questions you wanted to ask if you are nervous; therefore, do not be afraid to prepare a list of questions and take this with you to interview. It is quite acceptable to refer to this at this stage of the interview. You may also wish, at this stage, to seek clarification on any issues that might have arisen during the day, such as whether you would be expected to have a tutor group or deliver across subject areas. You should enquire what arrangements there are for induction of NQTs in the school and what you might expect. You may also want to ask questions about the contract, for example, to check about the type of contract that is being offered (such as fixed term or temporary contract; this should be part of the application information you will have been sent, but be aware that some schools only offer a one year contract for NQT's so it is worth double checking) or, if the school is a MAT, if you are only expected to teach in this school. You can also ask when you would be expected to start (some schools employ staff during the summer term or offer part-time work once you have finished your commitments to your ITE programme).

At some point, you may want to ask about your starting salary (unless this has already been indicated at the application stage). If you are an NQT, there may be little room for negotiation unless you have something the school really needs/wants, for example, if you have been a cover supervisor previously and have specialist behaviour management training above and beyond what you would have covered in an ITE programme. How you describe experience in an application and at interview, therefore, is very important as it may be used to support any claim for increments above the starting salary.

Avoid asking questions just because you think you should; do not ask questions just to impress. If all your questions have been answered during the course of the day and you do not have any questions, just say politely that all the questions you wanted to ask have been answered during the day (or in the interview).

Earlier, we identified the benefits of practising your lesson prior to delivering it at interview. Many ITE providers provide opportunities for you to experience a mock interview. You are encouraged to take up any such opportunity (see also Task 8.1.4).

 Task 8.1.4   A mock interview

Arrange for a mock interview with your tutor. If possible, either have an observer or video the interview so that you and the interviewer can use this to analyse your verbal and nonverbal communication after the interview. Identify ways you could improve and practise these. If possible, organise another mock interview. Store notes in your professional development portfolio (PDP) to refer to later.

Accepting a post

The process of being notified about the outcome of the interview should be explained to you at the end of the interview. If you are not going to be told prior to leaving the school, confirm the best form of contact, for example, your mobile number or landline. You may have to wait several days before being told whether or not you have been successful.

Where all candidates are invited for interview at the same time, you may be offered the post on the same day as the interview. You are normally expected to verbally accept or reject the offer at this time. Schools rarely give you time to think about an offer; therefore, it is important that you consider all the implications of accepting the post before you attend for interview. On rare occasions, it may be that you feel you really need some time to think about the offer. You may want to ask whether you can think about the offer; in which case, be clear about when you will inform the school of your decision (for example, you want to think about it overnight and telephone first thing in the morning). Be prepared for such a request to be rejected. If your request is refused, you have to make the decision there and then or be prepared for the post to be offered to another candidate. Your decision depends on how much you want a particular job and how strong a position you think you are in.

If you are offered a post verbally at or following the interview, the offer of a post must be followed by a written confirmation and a contract. Also, it is normal practice for you to be asked to confirm your verbal acceptance of a post in writing. This might be via the completion of a letter issued by the school or in a formal letter written by yourself.

Do check carefully your contract, your salary and the induction programme. Offers of a post are made on certain conditions and therefore may be conditional until those conditions are met (for example, until you have passed a medical, in which case the school or the local authority sends you details), until references have been received or until you have met legal requirements (for example, undertaken an enhanced check with the Disclosure and Barring Service (DBS); you will have completed one of these as part of your ITE programme).

Once you have signed your contract, you are tied to it, so spending time seeking clarity is important. It is unprofessional to continue to apply for other teaching posts after you have verbally accepted a post, even if you see one advertised that you prefer.

The transition from student teacher to newly qualified teacher is not easy. Being a teacher involves you coming to terms with your new role within a new institutional context with an awareness of the complexities of its organisation, structures and routines, as well as ethos and expectations. This transition may be easier if you have gained employment in one of the schools in which you completed your school experience. If not, make arrangements (with your future mentor, for example) to visit the school again to make preparations to start your post. This is not dissimilar to the preparations you make when you go on school experience. You are able to meet members of the department and find out about facilities in the school. You also need to collect information about your teaching timetable as well as classes and what you will be teaching. You may find it useful to make a few visits to get to know the school culture. For example, you may become involved in some school activities such as sports day or perhaps observe some classes or teach some lessons before you start your post.

If you are not offered a post

It is disappointing when a post is offered to another candidate. However, try not to think of this in terms of failure on your part. There may be many legitimate reasons why the post was offered to the other candidate in preference to you. For example, the other candidate might have relevant teaching experience (which you did not have) in an aspect of the curriculum required for the post. Try to be reflective about the decision and acknowledge where you might need to make improvements next time. For example, can you gain any further experiences to strengthen your application? Can you take up any further opportunities to practise your interview technique? If you are not successful, build this into your learning experience. Most interview panels routinely offer feedback to candidates. If not, you can ask if this is possible, as it helps you identify strengths and areas to develop in preparation for your next interview.

Also, if you are still looking for a job in September, do not be too disappointed and give up. Ask yourself whether you have been too set on obtaining your ideal job and need to reassess your search criteria in terms of area, type of school or age range, for example. You may also want to consider other options, such as part-time work, a job-share, temporary post or supply work. These can give you valuable experience while you continue to search for a permanent full-time post, and can sometimes lead to permanent work in a school. You can find out details about supply work in your chosen area from the LA, schools and teaching supply agencies. If you decide to take such a route, you should check carefully the implications in terms of contracts, pay, your formal induction period and your further professional development. It is also worth maintaining contact with your ITE provider to see whether they are aware of any opportunities. You might even start to consider other teaching-related opportunities. Tasks 8.1.5 and 8.1.6 are designed to help you to reflect on the change from student teacher to newly qualified teacher.

 Task 8.1.5   Moving from student teacher to newly qualified teacher

How do student teachers learn to become teachers? Consider this critically in relation to the literature.

Identify similarities and differences between being a student teacher and being an NQT. Discuss your perceptions with a small number of NQTs. Critically compare their biographical stories with your own considerations for entry into the teaching profession. Store this information in your professional development portfolio (PDP).

  Task 8.1.6   Entering and staying in the profession

Design and conduct a piece of empirical research with selected established teachers in your placement school about the factors that: (a) influenced them to become teachers; and (b) make them stay in the teaching profession. Report critically on your analysis, identifying issues related to the philosophical assumptions underlying the methods of data collection and analysis. Give a critical evaluation of their choice, design and effective use, as well as a critical analysis of the factors identified and comparison with your own personal circumstances. Store this information in your professional development portfolio (PDP).

SUMMARY AND KEY POINTS

This unit is designed to help you realise that, just as with your teaching, you must prepare for obtaining your first teaching post; you cannot leave it to chance or rely on your innate ability to perform well at interview. In this unit, we have tried to lead you through the steps, skills and techniques you need to prepare actively for obtaining your first post, that is:

■ why you want to enter the teaching profession, as well as about where and in what type of school you want to teach;
■ looking for suitable vacancies;
■ selecting a post that interests you and requesting further details;
■ preparing your CV, writing a letter of application or completing an application form and contacting potential referees;
■ completing your application, preparing for and attending an interview in order to secure a full-time post;
■ accepting a post.

   To be successful, you need to:

■ be proactive;
■ be prepared;
■ practise your techniques;
■ be confident.

Check which requirements for your ITE programme you have addressed through this unit.

 Further resources

Ainsworth, P.K. (2012) *Get That Teaching Job*, **London: Continuum.**
   This text covers all aspects of the process of securing employment. Whilst not exclusively for the NQT, it provides guidance on the application process as well as focusing on key questions you might be asked at interview.

The Guardian, **viewed 31 August 2017 at https://www.theguardian.com/teacher-network/teacher-blog/2013/jan/09/teacher-job-tips-write-winning-application**
   An interesting read that gives feedback from teachers about the application process.

Times Education Supplement, **viewed 31 August 2017 at https://www.tes.com/jobs/careers-advice**
   This provides careers advice across your teaching career.

http://jobsearch.about.com/od/jobsearchglossary/g/letterofapplication.htm
   This site provides guidance on writing letters of application. Although quite Americanised, it gives some useful tips.

www.tes.co.uk/article.aspx?storycode=6000318
   This article focuses on how to write a covering letter when applying for a job.

Teaching jobs are advertised on the following websites:

Guardian Education: https://jobs.theguardian.com/jobs/schools/

eTeach: https://www.eteach.com

Education jobs: http://www.education-jobs.co.uk

Jobsgopublic: www.jobsgopublic.com/

Local government: www.lgjobs.com/

Times Educational Supplement: www.tes.co.uk/jobs/

Information about obtaining your first post is available from teaching unions; for example:

Irish National Teachers' Organisation, Northern Ireland: www.into.ie/NI/

National Association of Schoolmasters/Union of Women Teachers, England, Northern Ireland, Scotland and Wales: NASUWT www.nasuwt.org.uk/

National Education Union (NEU): https://neu.org.uk

National Union of Teachers, England and Wales (NUT): www.teachers.org.uk/

Scottish Secondary Teachers' Association, Scotland: www.ssta.org.uk

The Educational Institute of Scotland (EIS), Scotland: www.eis.org.uk/

Ulster Teachers Union, Northern Ireland: www.utu.edu/

Voice, England, Northern Ireland and Wales: www.voicetheunion.org.uk/

School inspection reports and further information about education can be obtained from:

England: Ofsted: www.ofsted.gov.uk; and Department for Education: www.education.gov.uk/

Northern Ireland: The Education and Training Inspectorate Northern Ireland: www.etini.gov.uk/index/inspection-reports.htm; and the Department of Education Northern Ireland: www.deni.gov.uk/

Scotland: Education Scotland: www.educationscotland.gov.uk/scottishschoolsonline/; and the Scottish Government: www.scotland.gov.uk/Topics/Statistics/Browse/School-Education

Wales: Estyn (The Office of Her Majesty's Inspectorate for Education and Training in Wales): www.estyn.gov.uk/; and the Welsh Government: http://wales.gov.uk/topics/educationandskills/?lang=en

Appendix 2 lists subject associations and teacher councils and Appendix 3 provides a list of websites.

Capel, S., Leask, M. and Turner, T. (eds.) (2010) *Readings for Learning to Teach in the Secondary School: A Companion to M Level Study*, Abingdon: Routledge.
This book brings together essential readings to support you in your critical engagement with key issues raised in this textbook.

Capel, S., Lawrence, J., Leask, M. and Younie, S. (eds.) (2019) *Surviving and Thriving in the Secondary School: The NQT's Essential Companion*, Abingdon: Routledge.
This book is designed to support newly qualified teachers in the next phase of development as a teacher. However, you may find it useful as it covers aspects of teaching not included in this book which, nonetheless you experience on your ITE programme.

The subject specific books in the *Learning to Teach (Subject)* series, the *Practical (Subject) Guides*, *Debates in (Subject)* and *Mentoring (Subject) Teachers* are also very useful.

Any additional resources and an editable version of any relevant tasks/tables in this unit are available on the companion website: www.routledge.com/cw/capel

8.2 Developing further as a teacher

Jeanne Keay

Introduction

The main driver of the variation in pupil learning at school is the quality of the teachers.
(Barber and Mourshed, 2007, p.15)

Successfully completing the initial phase of teacher education is a big achievement. It is, however, only the beginning of a continuous process of professional learning that will prepare you for a range of career pathways in education. You have a responsibility as a teacher to ensure that you are developing in ways that not only help you to further your career, but also help you to meet the learning needs of your pupils. Barber and Mourshed (2007), in their review of the best-performing school systems, found that it was teachers who made the difference and that getting the right teachers into the profession and developing them were two of the most important elements of these systems. In a follow-up to this review, they looked at how the world's most improved school systems keep getting better and found that improving system performance essentially comes down to improving pupils' learning experiences (Mourshed et al., 2010). Mizell (2010) is more specific on this point, stating that research has shown that teaching quality and school leadership are the most important factors in raising pupil achievement. As a teacher, you provide learning experiences for your pupils and you are therefore central to their success. You must be aware of your weaknesses, understand what best practice is and must be motivated to improve (Barber and Mourshed, 2007). These elements are reflected in the focus for this unit. However, I would like to promote a positive approach to professional development that not only recognises the need to be aware of weaknesses, but also demands that you know your strengths in order to build on them. This entails taking a reflective approach to your teaching, understanding how you learn, taking responsibility for planning and undertaking professional development, and understanding your professional role as a teacher. These expectations are not meant to scare you, but to encourage you to ask questions that will help you make a successful transition from your initial teacher education (ITE) programme into your induction year. You are not expected to be a perfect teacher at the end of this stage, but you should have a clear view of your strengths and areas for development.

The main purpose of this unit is to help you to prepare for the responsibility you have to support pupils' learning through adopting, from the start of your career, a planned approach to professional development. It considers professional development beyond your ITE programme and focuses particularly on the transition from ITE into your first post and the early years of your teaching career.

OBJECTIVES

At the end of this unit, you should be able to:

■ plan your professional development and keep a record of professional learning;
■ plan a successful transition into your first teaching post;
■ understand and make best use of the range of professional development opportunities available to you during induction;
■ better understand your role as a professional.

Check the requirements of your ITE programme to see which relate to this unit.

Developing further as a teacher

Your professional development as a teacher began when you were at school; as a pupil, you experienced good, and sometimes perhaps not so good, teaching and you entered your ITE programme with professional knowledge gained through this experience, having served what Lortie (1975) called 'an apprenticeship of observation'. You are now progressing through a professional learning process that is enabling you to meet the standards required to embark on a career in teaching. However, this is not the end of your development; it is the beginning of a continuous career-long process. A teaching career is sometimes described as four key stages of professional development: ITE, induction (the first year of teaching), early professional development (the second and third years of teaching) and continuing professional development. However, while this ensures that we think of a teaching career as a long process of development, it presents the stages as discrete elements, which may be problematic. A review of literature in Scotland highlights this point and criticises the compartmentalised nature of teacher education (Menter et al., 2010). The review suggests that teacher education should operate as a continuum, spanning a career. The authors suggest there needs to be much better alignment between schools, local authorities, universities and national organisations to achieve coherent and progressive professional development throughout a teacher's career.

Much is expected of you as a teacher and the quality of your teaching must be high. You will only achieve this through a professional, organised and committed approach to development. You are not expected to achieve this alone and, in the same way as you are supported through your ITE programme, you have specific support from more experienced teachers during your induction year.

Having met the requirements to become a teacher at the end of your ITE programme, during your induction period, you will work towards meeting a further set of expectations. Although arrangements are slightly different depending on the country in which you are teaching, most governments want to be assured that, through induction, you are on the way to becoming a good teacher. An Organisation for Economic Co-operation and Development (OECD, 2014) report found that formal induction programmes are mandatory in half the countries surveyed and that more experienced teaching staff were responsible for supporting new teachers in their first year. Each school has different support systems, but each should provide you with an induction tutor and protected development time. In addition, you should also expect to be observed and to have your performance assessed.

Beyond induction, schools have appraisal and performance management arrangements that continue to provide support. In the United Kingdom, each of the countries have their own standards, expectations and requirements for continuing professional development (Learning Wales, 2016; General Teaching Council for Northern Ireland, 2017; General Teaching Council Scotland, 2012; Department for Education (DfE), 2016i). For example, in England, a separate standard for professional development has been produced, which clearly describes a professional learning context:

> Effective teaching requires considerable knowledge and skill, which should be developed as teachers' careers progress. High-quality professional development requires workplaces to be steeped in rigorous scholarship, with professionals continually developing and supporting each other so that pupils benefit from the best possible teaching
>
> (DfE, 2016i, p.1)

Planning your professional development

You are expected to take control of, and responsibility for, your professional development. This is an expectation in performance management arrangements for all teachers. Planning and keeping a record of professional learning is central to your development as a teacher. During your ITE programme, you are encouraged, and in some places required, to maintain what might be called a professional development profile (PDP). There are different names for this document, and it might simply be a profile in which you record evidence to demonstrate that you are meeting the requirements for becoming a teacher. Profiling your learning also helps you to celebrate achievements and identify areas for development. You may also find it useful to keep a diary of reflective practice, which helps you to consider the impact of your professional development on your pupils' learning and to plan for future learning. Your PDP is a useful record not only in providing evidence during your ITE programme, but also when preparing for job interviews and in professional, subject and career planning; hence, it is worth continuing this after completing your ITE programme.

A practical approach to planning and recording achievement necessitates thinking about the sort of evidence of learning you will collect, as simply undertaking professional development activities is, in itself, not enough. Whatever method you choose to use to record achievement and development, the process should be realistic and achievable. You should record:

- your learning objectives;
- why you decided to focus on a particular area of learning, based on your reflections and other evidence;
- how you will know you have met your objectives;
- what professional development you undertook to meet those objectives.

This process requires you to engage in a cyclical process of reflective practice (see Unit 5.4 for a detailed overview of reflective practice), involving planning, implementation and gathering evidence of success. Task 8.2.1 is designed to help you with this.

   Task 8.2.1   Planning your professional development

Start to gather evidence of professional development as a basis for your planning, using the PDP suggested by your tutor or one you have designed yourself or an equivalent.

Gathering evidence

- If you are at the beginning of your ITE programme, start to plan how you will gather evidence of professional progress.
- If you are at the end of your ITE programme and have not started this process, begin to gather as much evidence of professional progression as possible.

Action planning

- Whatever stage of your ITE programme you are at, develop and start to implement an action plan to extend strengths and address areas identified for development.
- When you are near the end of your ITE programme, review the evidence you have gathered and reflect on what this tells you about your current strengths and areas for development, and start to plan your future development.

Use this action plan to initiate discussions about your professional needs with your tutor and fellow teachers.

In order to engage in this professional learning process, you will need to understand not only how your pupils learn, but also how you learn and take this into consideration in planning professional development activities. In recent years, consideration of complexity thinking has emerged in education literature (e.g. Ovens, Hopper and Butler, 2013; Davis, Sumara and Luce-Kapler, 2008) and applying this perspective to understand teachers' professional development can help to inform and improve this learning process and make it individually relevant. Jess et al. (2016) explore the view that professional learning is non-linear and long-term in nature and that there it should be recognised that teachers' professional learning has different starting points. In a later publication, Carse, Jess and Keay (2017) propose that professional development has to take into account not only the different starting points but also the different contexts in which teachers work. The list in Table 8.2.1 uses principles drawn from complexity thinking to suggest how you might review on your own learning.

Transition into your first teaching post

Moving from your ITE programme into your first teaching post is an exciting, but possibly daunting, prospect. However, you are not expected to demonstrate the attributes of an experienced teacher in one year, and your school should provide you with a support programme. Inevitably, you will be anxious about this phase of your career and you will have expectations based on your current and past experiences in schools. All of this is very normal, and most new teachers embark on induction with concerns that are varied but often include behaviour management issues (Hobson et al., 2009).

Table 8.2.1 Principles from complexity thinking you can use to review your own learning

1   Self-organisation and interaction: You should take individual responsibility for engaging in professional learning, recognising your own individual starting point and organising relevant development activities.
2   Reflection and inquiry: The learning process you engage in should be reflective and based on constant inquiry. You must be inquisitive and concerned about your own and your pupils' learning and how both can be advanced.
3   Identification and negotiation of boundaries: You should identify the challenges to your learning and work to overcome or work around them.
4   Consolidation, challenge and creativity: The learning process you engage in should be one of consolidation, through which you continually practice and develop skills and understanding. You should challenge yourself to go beyond your comfort zone and seek to create solutions to learning needs.
5   Connections: You should exploit and understand the connections between your current and previous learning and look for learning opportunities between different aspects of the curriculum. You should be aware of opportunities to collaborate and connect with other teachers to support your learning. However, connectedness also refers to the nested nature of your position as a teacher and the context in which you work. This context and, inevitably, your role and development will be influenced by your school, regional and national policy demands.

You must be realistic about what you can achieve and recognise that each school is different; any difficulties you have experienced in one school may not be present in another school. Of course, the reverse is also true, and when you start your induction period, circumstances in a different school may present new challenges. Research has been undertaken to explore the resilience of teachers.

Gu and Day (2013, p.39) define this as 'the capacity to manage the unavoidable uncertainties inherent in the realities of teaching'. They identify personal, relational and organisational settings as influences on teachers' capacities to cope with the everyday demands of the job. Beltman et al. (2011), in their review of literature on teacher resilience, suggest that self-efficacy and intrinsic motivation, together with collegial and mentor support, are key protective factors. The ability to sustain an approach to teaching that ensures you successfully meet induction requirements and, at the same time, maintain a proactive and planned approach to development should be your goal. However, you are more likely to achieve this goal if you adopt a reflective approach to teaching, seek support from more experienced teachers and, most importantly, take responsibility for identifying your own development needs.

As you may have experienced during your ITE programme, challenges not only come in the form of pupils. They also occur in your relationships with other staff. As a new member of a subject department, you may be expected to understand the department ethos and work in particular ways before you are accepted as a valued member of the team. Lave and Wenger (1991) called this *legitimate peripheral participation*; that is, as a new member of the community, you are expected to watch from the sidelines and learn the rules before making an effective contribution to the community. This concept can be seen as both problematic and productive. Working collaboratively as a member of a professional learning community, such as a subject group, is a very useful form of professional development. However, if membership of that community simply means adopting community practices instead of contributing to their development, it can be problematic. As Kennedy (2016) maintains, collaborative professional learning can be very positive, but it also has the potential to impose externally driven agendas and to present opportunities for dominant members of the group to exercise undue influence on activities and modes of operation. When you are a qualified teacher, you will need to consider how to balance independence with collaborative working, and how to fit into the department while at the same time making a contribution to the development of practice.

The following sections present some practical considerations that may help you to deal with these challenges.

Before starting the job

A good induction programme will ease you into a career in teaching. However, although induction support is mandatory in most countries, sometimes it is not well organised. While it is a school's responsibility to provide support, it is also your responsibility to ensure that recommended induction processes are in place and used. You need to start preparing for undertaking induction while you are in your ITE programme and you must have a realistic understanding of what can be achieved during this period. A professional development action plan in your PDP will help you to achieve this. Task 8.2.2 is designed to help you with that planning.

 Task 8.2.2   Your induction

Check the expectations of an induction programme for the country in which you are learning to teach. What should be provided? Is this what you expected?

Now that you are aware of induction programme expectations, how can you prepare for induction? Discuss this with your tutor and store it in your PDP.

Starting the job

In the first few days and weeks of any job, you need to focus on familiarising yourself with the school and building on the information you have gained during the job application process and interview and potentially an orientation visit (see Unit 8.1). Initially, you need information that will help you to operate successfully in the school. This may cover a range of issues, such as:

■ teaching and learning expectations and policies;
■ management, administrative arrangements and school policies (for example, staff responsibilities, sickness policy, accessing school buildings);
■ structures and departments (for example, staff responsibilities, line managers);
■ rules, regulations and procedures within the school and your department (for example, behaviour policy, equal opportunities policies, lesson planning and assessment policies, quality assurance activities);
■ health and safety requirements (for example, fire drill, pupil medical information).

During the first term in your new post, you will probably find that you concentrate mainly on becoming confident and competent in your teaching in order to establish yourself in the school. You are busy getting to know your classes, planning units of teaching from the school's schemes of work, preparing lesson plans, teaching, setting and marking homework, undertaking pastoral activities with your tutor group and getting to know the rules, routines and procedures of the school. Research by the Organisation for Economic Co-operation and Development (OECD, 2013a) suggests that new teachers are more likely to feel prepared in subject content than in the pedagogy or classroom practice of their subject field. It is important to acknowledge this as you embark on your teaching career. Task 8.2.3 is designed to help you prepare for your first week in school.

 Task 8.2.3   Gathering information during induction

Make a list of the information you will need to gather at specific points during induction, i.e.:

- before starting your new post;
- during the first week;
- during the first month;
- during the first term.

   Check this list with a teacher who has recently completed induction in your school and use it to inform your professional development planning. Store this in your PDP and use/update as appropriate.

After the first few weeks

Induction must be linked to and develop from your ITE programme. You need to use your induction action plan, which has identified strengths and areas for development, as the starting point for a discussion with your induction tutor (or line manager) about professional development priorities, targets and support. This set of priorities should be revisited regularly throughout your induction year and used to help you to identify and evidence development, as well as to inform future planning of professional development.

   Starting a career in teaching is very demanding, more so than your ITE programme, because you have to sustain your practice over a whole year. Many new teachers experience what has been termed *reality shock* (Veenman, 1984) because, while your ITE programme gives you some experience of teaching, it is not until you are employed as a teacher that you realise the enormity of the role and the scope of responsibility. You will feel tired and it will be a stressful period (see Unit 1.3); however, it is also a time when you can form strong relationships with other members of staff and your pupils, when you can try different teaching approaches and really see the impact of your work with pupils. You will be observed and evaluated, but this will be in relation to your career stage and in the context of managing and supporting your performance. Many schools have well-developed policies for observing teachers in practice that include not only formal observations but also informal visits as part of learning walks by senior managers.

   While you will have the responsibility of being a 'real' teacher, you will be supported on your journey through this period. It is inevitable that you will feel unprepared for some aspects of the role because your ITE programme is only the start of your professional development; it does not cover all eventualities. In your first year of teaching, you undertake a greater range of responsibilities; for example, you have your own groups and classes and can establish your own procedures and practices for classroom management right from the beginning of the school year. In order to help you and to ensure consistency across subjects and year groups, many schools have strict policies for dealing with class management and behaviour (see Unit 3.3). While, as a newly qualified teacher (NQT), you contribute to long-term planning such as developing schemes of work, you are not expected to undertake the full range of a teacher's roles and responsibilities; for example, you may not be expected to deal with some of the more serious pastoral problems or to undertake the full range of administrative demands.

Over the course of the first year

During induction, you face situations and challenges you did not experience as a student teacher. This includes undertaking activities for the first time, such as setting questions for examinations, undertaking supervisory duties or sustaining activities over a long period of time; for example:

■ planning and preparing for a year to incorporate different material, teaching and assessment strategies and approaches to sustain pupil interest and motivation;
■ setting targets to maintain progress in learning over the period of a year;
■ maintaining discipline over a whole year, which is very different to maintaining discipline over a short period of time on school experience.

Providing extracurricular activities may be expected of you, and you can gain a great deal from involvement in such activities. However, you should be careful not to take on too many additional responsibilities as you will be expected to contribute to providing cross-school, additional learning opportunities; you will have assessment and reporting and pastoral responsibilities.

At some points, you may feel that teaching is more difficult than you first thought, and inevitably you may become frustrated and have doubts about whether you can teach and question what you are achieving with the pupils. You may need help from other members of staff to overcome these doubts and continue to develop as a teacher. Although some support may be informal, your induction tutor (or head of department) should provide structured support. You can draw on your tutor's experience to help you answer the numerous questions you have as new situations arise, and to overcome problems with aspects of your teaching. Your tutor can help you to learn as part of your daily routine by identifying and using opportunities available in your everyday work to develop your knowledge, skills and/or understanding. In an ideal world, a tutor is proactive, making a conscious effort to look for opportunities for development. However, your tutor is likely to be busy, and you will spend much of your time in a learning space on your own with pupils; therefore, there may be limited opportunities to work with your tutor.

Most staff are helpful and understanding, especially if you establish good relationships with them, but relationships take time to develop and you need to be sensitive to the environment you are in. Be aware of how you behave; for example, do not try to change something immediately because you think things you have seen in other schools could work better, learn procedures and policies, and operate within the organisational rules. If you do not, for example, enforce school rules, you undermine the system and create tensions between pupils and teachers, and between yourself and other members of staff.

As you settle into the job and work with your classes and learn the procedures, rules and routines, some staff may forget that you are new. This can also be a problem. As the term and year progress, they may treat you as any other member of staff and not offer help and advice. Initially, this might be flattering, but if you need support you must approach staff, talk to them about your concerns and ask for help. You may also find it helpful to form a support group with other NQTs in the school or within the local subject community, through which you can share your concerns and problems, and support and learn from each other. Task 8.2.4 is designed to help you identify experiences of NQTs.

 Task 8.2.4   NQT experience

While you are on school experience during your ITE programme, undertake a small-scale research project (Unit 5.4 looks at undertaking practitioner research) with NQTs in your school. Find out what their experiences of induction have been.

How can you use this information to help you prepare for induction? Store the information in your PDP.

You could also undertake a similar exercise when in your first year of teaching by interviewing a teacher in the second year in order to learn for the next transition.

Continuing professional development (CPD) beyond the first year

Induction should lead seamlessly into your second year of teaching. Your professional development planning should involve consideration, not only of your teaching, but also of how you may want to develop; for example, some new teachers take on posts of responsibility very early in their careers. Is this something you are ready for? Would you like to take responsibility for part of the subject, undertake a pastoral role or be involved in supporting new teachers? You should also consider further qualifications, especially completing a master's programme, if you have not already done so. You may decide to undertake other qualifications; for example, some teachers find they need further support in relation to pupils' special educational needs.

Towards the end of induction, you should find out about the process for appraisal and performance management in your school, as you will now participate in these processes.

Professional development

Professional development can be aimed at achieving career progression (for example, focusing on development to undertake posts of responsibility through undertaking a middle management programme), but it can also be seen as a way to overcome professional challenges encountered in your daily work. Both aspects of professional development are important and should be included in your planning.

There are several challenges to be considered when planning professional development; for example:

■   What counts as professional development?
■   Are planned learning activities relevant to your needs?

■ Does identified development meet your needs or your institution's needs?
■ Do you have access to high-quality learning experiences?
■ How will you measure the impact of your professional learning?
■ What evidence of the impact of your professional learning on pupils' learning will you collect?

Teachers interpret and undertake professional development in different ways, but it is often defined very narrowly. A common definition is 'going on a course' (Bolam and Weindling, 2006) or 'listening to stale talks accompanied by endless slides' (Blank and de las Alas, 2009). When planning professional development, activities should not only match your needs, but should be relevant to your pupils' needs and the school context.

A further problem lies in the questionable quality of some professional development activities (Avalos, 2011) and the lack of evaluation undertaken by providers (Keay and Lloyd, 2009). A good venue and a take-home pack are not always indicative of a good professional development activity. You should be aware of these issues as you plan professional development activities.

One of the most challenging issues you will have to address relates to providing evidence of the impact of your professional development on pupils' learning (Burchell et al., 2002; King, 2013). Development needs must be identified effectively and meeting them must be planned carefully. One way to achieve this is to use a process model that links pupils' learning and professional learning. Such a model, developed by Keay and Lloyd (2011), has been used with teachers in a range of schools. As an integral part of the process, the model demands reflective practice from those using it. As Figure 8.2.1 shows, you are asked to consider the culture and organisation of professional development in your school. This is part of the planning described in the sections above, such as induction support and learning from different members of staff. You are then asked to locate your professional learning in the everyday process of teaching and link your professional development with your pupils' learning by identifying learning outcomes and the evidence of meeting those learning outcomes. It is at this point that you ask yourself whether you have the knowledge, skills and understanding to meet your pupils' needs and, if not, you identify those as professional development needs.

Stages 4, 5 and 6 are similar to the professional development planning process suggested earlier in this unit; with the focus on the clear link you make to your pupils' learning and the identification of evidence of impact identified early in the process, which is therefore consequently easily gathered in Stage 7 of the process (for a more detailed explanation of this process and the contributing research, see Keay and Lloyd, 2011). Task 8.2.5 is designed to help you link your learning with pupils' learning.

 Task 8.2.5   Linking your learning with your pupils' learning

During school experience, try the process suggested in the model, focusing on linking the learning of one pupil with your professional learning. Reflect on the process and whether it might be useful to incorporate in your daily teaching practice. Write notes on what you have learned and store it in your PDP.

Figure 8.2.1 Professional development process model

Source: Keay and Lloyd (2011, p.99)

Teaching: a professional role

Teaching is a professional role, with professional demands and professional values and a specialised knowledge base that is embedded in the standards and demands of the role. However, the way the demands of the role are played out through the adoption of different forms of professionalism in schools affects the way teachers are viewed as professionals.

Menter et al. (2010) identified four models of teacher professionalism emerging from policy and research literature. They found that the *effective* teacher was the dominant model. This emphasises technical accomplishment, which relates to a practical interpretation of professional knowledge. The *reflective* teacher model, which emphasises the need for continuing and collaborative professional development, has been influential for over 20 years and remains popular; it has already been promoted in this and previous units. A third model, which is also highlighted in this book, is the *enquiring* teacher model, which promotes a research orientation within teachers' work. The final model could be linked to the intention behind the process model presented in Figure 8.2.1, as it positions teaching as a transformative activity. However, professionalism has also been considered as *managerial* or *democratic*, and the adoption of each one has an impact on how professional development is enacted in schools, that is, teacher professionalism in action. *Managerial* professionalism values effectiveness, efficiency and compliance, in contrast to a *democratic* form of professionalism, which values a collaborative and inclusive approach within a self-regulating environment. Kennedy (2014)

Table 8.2.2 Professionalism and professional development

Managerial professionalism	Aspects of professional development	Democratic professionalism
External regulation	Control	Self-regulation
Compliance with policy	Authority	Decisions taken by school
Slow to change, reactive, conservative practices	Decision-making	Collaborative, collegial, within an ethical code of practice
External assessment	Performance review	Critically reflective practice
Self-interest of the organisation and individual	Motivation	Pupil-centred
Efficiency, effectiveness	Focus	Inclusive, enquiry-driven, knowledge building

Source: Developed from Keay and Lloyd (2011)

has revised her original thinking (Kennedy, 2007) about models of CPD and proposes that there could be three purposes to professional learning activities with different levels of teacher autonomy. At one end, there is a transmissive purpose, which seeks to redress a deficit, provides little autonomy and is related to a managerial approach. At the other end is a transformative purpose, which focuses on a democratic approach through collaborative models of learning. In the middle, she proposes a 'malleable' group of activities, which could provide autonomy or, alternatively, could be used to transmit required learning, for example that required to be accepted in a group. This is an interesting analysis and one you should be aware of as you engage in learning opportunities. Table 8.2.2 summarises the work of Evetts (2009), Kennedy (2007) and Sachs (2001; 2003), and applies their views of professionalism to professional development.

As a teacher, you are a member of a community, and learning in that community has its advantages and challenges, depending on the culture of professionalism adopted within the school. Task 8.2.6 asks you to think about the culture of the professional learning community in which you are working and how this may support or challenge your developing practice.

 Task 8.2.6   Professionalism and CPD

Use Table 8.2.2 to consider the form of professionalism prevalent in your department while on school experience. Reflect on how this might affect your professional development planning. Record this in your PDP.

SUMMARY AND KEY POINTS

This unit highlights the importance of professional development in providing high-quality learning and teaching in schools. In particular, it emphasises the following points:

■ the process of professional learning is continuous and it is important for you to take responsibility for, and control of, planning your development;

■ using a portfolio to gather evidence to use in subsequent planning will be a practical way of ensuring you develop continuously;

■ in order to make a successful transition into teaching, you need to be knowledgeable about induction expectations and school systems, so preparation for this period during your ITE programme is important;

■ once in your first job, you should expect challenges and prepare to overcome them. This will ensure that you enjoy making a contribution to the learning of the pupils in your classes;

■ your professional development should be relevant not only to your career needs, but also to meeting the needs of your pupils. In order to achieve this, you will need formal support from an induction tutor and to participate in a range of development activities. However, you will also need to use the opportunities to learn in everyday teaching practice;

■ finally, being a teacher means being a member of a community of practice that has both pupils' and teachers' learning at its heart. Understanding the culture of the community and participating and contributing to it is an important element of your teaching role and one that supports your development.

Check which requirements for your ITE programme you have addressed throughout this unit.

 Further resources

Cordingley, P., Higgins, S., Greany, T., Buckler, N., Coles-Jordan, D., Crisp, B., Saunders, L. and Coe, R. (2015) *Developing Great Teaching: Lessons from the International Reviews into Effective Professional Development*, London: Teacher Development Trust.
This publication draws on a range of findings through a detailed review of relevant literature in order to suggest implications for future policy on teacher professional development and learning.

Hobson, A.J., Malderez, A., Tracey, L., Homer, M.S., Tomlinson, P.D., Ashby, P., Mitchell, N., McIntyre, J, Cooper, D., Roper, T., Chambers, G.N. and Tomlinson, P.D. (2009) *Becoming a Teacher: Teachers' Experiences of Initial Teacher Training, Induction and Early Professional Development: Research Report*, DCSF Research Report No. RR115, London: DCSF.
This publication reports on a large-scale longitudinal research project that examined the experiences of teachers during their ITE programme, induction and early career professional development.

The Teacher Education Observatory: http://teachereducationobservatory.org
This website provides a network which can monitor developments across teacher education and provides signposts to resources.

The Teaching and Learning Research Programme (TLRP) webwww.tlrp.org/
This website provides access to a large range of material relating to teaching.

The Stanford Center for Opportunity Policy in Education (SCOPE): https://edpolicy.stanford.edu
This website offers links to a range of education literature and project overviews relating to teaching.

Wenger-Trayner: www.ewenger.com

This website provides an overview of communities of practice and presents a brief introduction to the concept and the characteristics of such communities. This helps you to consider your school as a community of learning and you as a member of that community.

The following organisations, among others, provide support for new teachers in the form of resources, professional development and advice: *Times Education Supplement* (tes.com); NUT (nut.org.uk); NASUWT (nasuwt.org.uk); ATL (atl.org.uk).

Appendix 2 lists subject associations and teacher councils and Appendix 3 provides a list of websites.

Capel, S., Leask, M. and Turner, T. (eds.) (2010) *Readings for Learning to Teach in the Secondary School: A Companion to M Level Study,* **Abingdon: Routledge.**

This book brings together essential readings to support you in your critical engagement with key issues raised in this textbook.

Capel, S., Lawrence, J., Leask, M. and Younie, S. (eds.) (2019) *Surviving and Thriving in the Secondary School: The NQT's Essential Companion,* **Abingdon: Routledge.**

This book is designed to support newly qualified teachers in the next phase of development as a teacher. However, you may find it useful as it covers aspects of teaching not included in this book which, nonetheless you experience on your ITE programme.

The subject specific books in the *Learning to Teach (Subject)* series, the *Practical (Subject) Guides*, *Debates in (Subject)* and *Mentoring (Subject) Teachers* are also very useful.

Any additional resources and an editable version of any relevant tasks/tables in this unit are available on the companion website: www.routledge.com/cw/capel

8.3 Accountability

Leora Cruddas

Introduction

Accountability is the professional obligation of an organisation and individual to account for their actions and activities, accept responsibility for them and disclose the results in a transparent manner. Teaching is a profession. As such, the highest form of accountability is your professional accountability for the quality of your own work and to the children, young people, parents and carers whom the profession serves.

The work of teachers is guided by different accountability frameworks. In England, the government sets national accountability frameworks in the form of legislation and statutory guidance. The role of government is to determine an accountability framework in the interests of the parents and the wider community, incentivising policies and behaviours that contribute to a high-quality education for all.

As part of the overall accountability framework, the government tasks independent bodies to oversee certain aspects of accountability. In England these are:

- **The Office for Standards in Education, Children's Services and Skills (Ofsted)** is responsible for inspecting maintained schools and academies, some independent schools, and other educational institutions in England.
- **The Office of Qualifications and Examinations Regulation** (**Ofqual**) regulates qualifications in England.
- **The National College for Teaching and Leadership** (NCTL) is the regulator of professional standards for teachers in England. It investigates misconduct in the teaching profession and makes decisions about whether individual teachers should be allowed to continue to teach.

You are also accountable to your employer:

- the local authority if you work in a maintained or voluntary-aided school;
- the trust board if you work in an academy or multi-academy trust (MAT);
- the governing board, foundation or trust if you work in a foundation school.

Your contract of employment sets out your contractual responsibilities, but employers also often have their own accountability frameworks that may be in addition to the government's accountability framework.

This unit is designed to help you understand how the education system in state schools in England functions in relation to the accountability of both schools and teachers. It is important that you understand the ways in which the school in which you work will be held to account, as well as your own professional accountabilities. This is because school or organisational accountability can have implications for an individual teacher.

Check the structure of education and the accountability system for each of the four home ocuntries (Units 7.3, 7.4, 7.5 and 7.6 (on the companion website www.routledge.com/cw/capel) look at the education system in England, Northern Ireland, Scotland and Wales, respectively).

OBJECTIVES

At the end of this unit, you should be able to:

■ understand the structure of the state education system in England and the different types of schools;
■ be aware of the full range of accountabilities governing schools and teachers and how they relate to each other;
■ know and understand the specific legal and regulatory, moral and ethical and contractual accountabilities governing teachers and their practice.

Check the requirements of your initial teacher education (ITE) programme to see which relate to this unit.

Overview of different types of schools in the education system in England

The structures of education systems across the world vary quite considerably. Even in the United Kingdom, the structures of the education system in England, Northern Ireland, Scotland and Wales differ in quite significant ways from each other. For example, in Scotland and Wales, local authorities 'maintain' all state schools. This is not the case in England. England has a very diverse system with many different types of schools:

■ schools maintained by local authorities;
■ sponsored and convertor academies;
■ free schools, which are technically academies;
■ university technology colleges and studio schools;
■ faith schools (voluntary aided, voluntary controlled or academy);
■ foundation schools, which grew out of the grant-maintained movement;
■ grammar schools that operate selective policies;

- special schools;
- multi-academy trusts (MATs).

Academies were originally introduced as an improvement initiative for intractable failure by the Labour administration prior to the coalition government in 2010. The coalition government turned this policy on its head, encouraging good and outstanding schools to convert to academy status to take advantage of freedoms and autonomy, for example, curriculum freedoms. An academy is a legal entity, separate from the local authority. It is the direct employer of staff and the holder of land titles. An academy trust is a charitable company limited by guarantee. So, academies are independent state schools, funded by government, but legally separate from local authorities and run by legally constituted trusts. Academies receive their funding directly from government and have their accountabilities set out in a Funding Agreement, which is a contract between the Secretary of State for Education and the Academy Trust.

Free schools are legally academies. They are held accountable through the same mechanism as an academy: a Funding Agreement between the Secretary of State for Education and the Academy Trust, which operates the free school. However, free schools are set up through a specific application process. The requirements to set up a free school are:

- free schools must respond to local demand, which usually means there is a petition from parents in the area naming the school as their first choice;
- free schools are completely *new* state schools, which means that the group that is applying to establish the free school (usually a successful academy or MAT) can decide on the kind of school they want to establish.

A university technical college (UTC) is a type of secondary school that is led by a sponsor university. UTCs combine an academic education with a technical and practical one. Typically, students join a UTC at age 14 or 16.

Studio Schools are also designed for 14–19-year olds. They are small schools usually with around 300 students. They are open all year round, more like a working day than a school day. They offer a range of academic and vocational qualifications and work placements linked directly to local employment opportunities.

UTCs and studio schools are types of 'free schools'.

Faith schools teach a general curriculum but have a particular religious character or formal links with a religious organisation. Voluntary-aided or voluntary-controlled faith schools have to follow the National Curriculum, but they can choose what they teach in religious studies. Voluntary-aided means that a foundation or trust (usually a religious organisation) has substantial influence in the running of the school, employs the staff and has responsibility for pupil admissions. Voluntary-controlled means that a foundation or trust, usually a Christian denomination, has some influence in the running of the school but the employer is the local authority. Faith academies or faith free schools do not have to follow the National Curriculum. Faith schools may have different admissions criteria and staffing policies to state schools; however, any parent can apply for a place for their child.

Foundation schools were set up under the School Standards and Framework Act 1998 (UK Parliament, 1998) to replace grant-maintained schools, which were funded directly by the central government. As with voluntary-aided schools, the governing body employs the staff and has responsibility for pupil admissions.

Grammar schools are state secondary schools to which pupils are admitted on the basis of ability. There are 164 grammar schools in England. In some local authority areas, such as Kent, a grammar-school system is still in operation. This means that a test, the 'eleven plus', is used to identify about a quarter of children to be admitted to grammar schools on the basis of their intellectual ability.

Special schools usually specialise in specific areas of special educational needs, for example, communication difficulties, cognition and learning difficulties, social, emotional and behaviour difficulties, and sensory and physical needs. Typically, only pupils with specific additional needs are admitted to special schools.

A multi-academy trust (MAT) is a single legal entity that is responsible for a group of schools. So, the group of schools is governed through a single set trust board. The MAT makes collaboration across the schools in the group possible, in order to improve educational standards and pupil outcomes.

Each of these have slightly different accountability frameworks. For example, local authority-maintained schools must follow the National Curriculum and teachers' pay is determined by the School Teachers Pay and Conditions Document (STPCD, Department for Education (DfE), 2017f). However, academies do not have to follow the National Curriculum and are not bound by the STPCD.

In Task 8.3.1 you are asked to look at the governance of your school.

 Task 8.3.1   The governance of your school

Consider the school and context in which you are working on school placement. Find out more about the governance of your school.

What type of school is it?

Who is on the governing board? Or if you are part of a MAT, who are the trustees/directors on your Trust board? Does your school have a local governing body? To whom is your school/governing board accountable?

Who is your employer?

Create a diagram showing these relationships. Check that you are aware of any key documents that are relevant to your work by asking your tutor and checking key national websites.

Store this in your professional development portfolio (PDP) or equivalent.

A very short history of accountability in England

Gilbert (2012) and Gibton (2013) argue that origins of accountability as we know it in England can be traced back directly to the 1988 Education Reform Act (ERA,1988). This Act shifted responsibilities for parts of the education system as laid down by the 1944 Education Act (UK Parliament, 1944). It increased the power of the Secretary of State for Education and passed considerable responsibilities to governing bodies and head teachers. It also laid down legislation to establish the National Curriculum and national testing of pupils.

This was followed four years later by the Education (Schools) Act 1992 (UK Parliament, 1992), as part of further reform of the school system accountability. The Education (Schools) Act established what was then called the Office for Standards in Education (Ofsted). It removed school inspection from local authorities.

By the mid-1990s, according to Gilbert (2012), the accountability framework in England was established on the basis of:

- national tests and examination results;
- published performance tables;
- inspection.

These pillars, she says, remain in place to this day. But Gilbert (2012) argues persuasively for a broader definition of accountability. Accountability is more than compliance with a government prescribed framework.

At its simplest, the term 'accountability' describes a relationship whereby one party – sometimes interpreted as an individual, sometimes an institution – has an obligation to account for their actions or performance to another (Brundrett and Rhodes, 2011). Accountability is 'answerability'.

At the beginning of this unit, we said: the highest form of accountability is the teacher's professional accountability for the quality of their own work and to the children, young people, parents and carers whom the profession serves. This is first and foremost, an *ethical* position. It is expressed in part two of the *Teachers' Standards* (DfE, 2011d, p.14): 'Teachers uphold public trust in the profession and maintain high standards of ethics and behaviour'.

Accountabilities governing schools and teachers

The key purpose of school and teacher accountability is to improve the education system. Earley and Weindling (2004) identify four key accountability relationships for schools. Schools have responsibilities for and have to account to:

- pupils (**moral accountability**);
- colleagues (**professional accountability**);
- employers or government (**contractual accountability**);
- the market, where parents and pupils have a choice of school (**market accountability**).

This taxonomy assumes that accountability to the government is contractual, and to a degree, it is. Arguably, however, contractual accountability is primarily through the employment relationship. It is by no means clear that either schools or teachers are accountable to the market. One might argue that market forces increasingly have a *determining effect* on schools, but this is not the same as arguing that school and teachers are accountable to the market.

Collins and Leslie (2016) propose a different taxonomy for accountability:

- **Organisational**: your responsibility to work collaboratively in ensuring compliance with relevant government targets, policies and standards.
- **Legal**: your responsibility to do all that is reasonable to protect the health, safety and welfare of pupils.
- **Professional**: standards defining the minimum level of practice expected of student teachers and teachers from the point of being awarded qualified teacher status, the *Teachers' Standards* (DfE, 2011d).

■   **Moral**: your own values and beliefs and the expectation, as set out in part two of the Teachers' Standards (DfE, 2011d), that you will demonstrate consistently high standards of personal and professional conduct.

This is a more helpful articulation of the different frameworks governing teachers' professional practice. However, it is perhaps not clear enough about the fairly complex infrastructure of the state-determined accountability system.

For this reason, in this unit, accountability is explored under the following headings:

■   **Moral and ethical accountability**: your accountability as a professional to the people you serve and to your colleagues.
■   **Legal and regulatory accountability**: the state-determined infrastructure of accountability.
■   **Employer and contractual accountability**: your accountability to your employer.

We will explore each of these in turn.

Moral and ethical accountability

Teachers come to teaching for a variety of reasons, but many are attracted to the profession in order to make a difference in the lives of children and young people. Teachers are trusted by parents and carers (and, indeed, the wider public) to educate children and to form them into the best they can be. It is therefore reasonable that the public expect teachers to uphold moral and ethical principles. These must be evident in everything you do as a teacher: how you behave in the classroom and with your peers, how you conduct yourselves in the teacher-pupil relationship, the standards of learning and behaviour expected and what you do when difficult decisions need to be made.

In loco parentis

Teachers are *in loco parentis* during the time they are responsible for children and young people. This is the Latin for 'instead of a parent'. There is a statutory basis to this. The Children Act 1989 (UK Parliament, 1989) says that teachers have a duty of care towards the children and young people under their supervision, as well as promoting the safety and welfare of the children and young people in their care. The way this is measured is by that of what a 'reasonable parent' might do.

The Health and Safety at Work Act 1974 (UK Parliament, 1974) places a further obligation on schools and teachers to safeguard the wellbeing and safety of pupils in its care.

Personal and professional conduct; the Teachers' Standards

According to the *Teachers' Standards* (DfE, 2011d, p.14), a teacher is expected to demonstrate consistently high standards of personal and professional conduct by:

■   treating pupils with dignity, building relationships rooted in mutual respect, and at all times observing proper boundaries appropriate to a teacher's professional position;

- having regard for the need to safeguard pupils' well-being, in accordance with statutory provisions;
- showing tolerance of and respect for the rights of others;
- not undermining fundamental British values, including democracy, the rule of law, individual liberty and mutual respect, and tolerance of those with different faiths and beliefs;
- ensuring that personal beliefs are not expressed in ways which exploit pupils' vulnerability or might lead them to break the law.

Teachers must also have proper and professional regard for the ethos, policies and practices of the school in which they teach, and maintain high standards in their own attendance and punctuality. You must have an understanding of, and always act within, the statutory frameworks that set out teachers' professional duties and responsibilities.

The *Teachers' Standards* (DfE, 2011d) are statutory and binding on all teachers in England. They set a bar for minimum expectations of conduct.

The Nolan Principles of Public Life

In 1995, Lord Nolan chaired the first Committee on Standards in Public Life and set out a ministerial code (Nolan, 1995). The code, '7 principles of public life', now apply to anyone who works as a public office-holder. This includes all people appointed to work in education. These principles are summarised in Table 8.3.1 (see also, https://www.gov.uk/government/publications/the-7-principles-of-public-life/the-7-principles-of-public-life--2).

Where the *Teachers' Standards* (DfE, 2011d) outline minimum expectations of conduct, the Nolan Principles offer a very clear statement of ethical behaviour. Arguably, the Nolan Principles are a better guide for teachers when having to make difficult ethical decisions. As teachers, you are accountable not just for your good conduct, but also for the ethics of your decision-making.

Task 8.3.2 asks you to consider an ethical dilemma

Table 8.3.1 The 7 principles of public life

1 **Selflessness**: Holders of public office should act solely in terms of the public interest.
2 **Integrity**: Holders of public office must avoid placing themselves under any obligation to people or organisations that might try inappropriately to influence them in their work. They should not act or take decisions in order to gain financial or other material benefits for themselves, their family, or their friends. They must declare and resolve any interests and relationships.
3 **Objectivity**: Holders of public office must act and take decisions impartially, fairly and on merit, using the best evidence and without discrimination or bias.
4 **Accountability**: Holders of public office are accountable to the public for their decisions and actions and must submit themselves to the scrutiny necessary to ensure this.
5 **Openness**: Holders of public office should act and take decisions in an open and transparent manner. Information should not be withheld from the public unless there are clear and lawful reasons for so doing.
6 **Honesty:** Holders of public office should be truthful.
7 **Leadership**: Holders of public office should exhibit these principles in their own behaviour. They should actively promote and robustly support the principles and be willing to challenge poor behaviour wherever it occurs.

Task 8.3.2   An ethical dilemma

A pupil in your classroom suddenly hits out at another pupil. The second pupil is hurt. The first pupil runs out of the classroom, throwing a chair on his way out, which narrowly misses a third pupil. On his way out, he damages school property. You know this pupil has been in and out of the care system. He is currently accommodated in a children's home. He has been the victim of physical and emotional abuse by his father, who is now in prison.

It is not your decision about whether to exclude this pupil; that is for the head teacher to decide. However, you are asked to write a report on the incident. Further, the pupil has a very good relationship with you, perhaps better than any other teacher in the school, so you have also been asked to advise.

How do you balance the needs of the individual pupils with the rights of rest of the class to a safe and orderly learning environment? Is it possible to serve the interests of both? How do you interpret *in loco parentis* in this case?

Consider the Nolan Principles. How do they help?

Ethics is to do with right and wrong, the moral principles that govern our behaviour and decision-making, but there is no right answer. Ethics requires professional judgement, and you are also accountable for the decisions you make. But your ethical decisions are guided by statutory frameworks. What pieces of legislation and/or statutory guidance do you need to take into account?

Discuss this case with your tutor and check key national websites. Store this in your PDP.

The State and its agencies: legal and regulatory accountability

The State and its agencies

As indicated earlier, the state-determined accountability system, which has its origins in legislative reform in the late 1980s and early 1990s, is a complex infrastructure.

The government determines the national accountability framework. As you have seen, since the mid-1990s, the accountability framework has been based on national tests and published league tables.

Three concepts are now defined and explored:

■ **legislation** is the process of making or enacting laws;
■ **inspection** is the process of inspecting providers to reach judgements about the quality of provision and check they meet legal requirements;
■ **regulation** has to do with taking enforcement action where requirements are not met.

It is important to understand not just to whom you and your school are accountable, but ultimately who can take enforcement action against you or your school when certain standards are not met. Significantly, however, a very high percentage of schools (89% of primary schools and

78% of secondary schools) in England were judged by Ofsted to be good or outstanding in 2016 (Ofsted, 2017a). Therefore, the vast majority of teachers and schools are doing a very good job at providing a good quality education for children and young people. There are only a small minority of schools where standards are not good enough.

So, in accountability terms, the government sets the overall framework for accountability, usually through the prescription of **performance measures** for schools. The government publishes tables of school performance against the measures it sets out.

Task 8.3.3 asks you to research the performance measures in the current accountability framework.

 Task 8.3.3   Performance measures

Use government websites to find out what the headline measures in the accountability framework are. Then, make an assessment of how your school performs against these measures. You may want to talk to the colleague in your school or MAT who leads on data to help you identify websites and performance measures and assess school performance.

Consider Goodhart's law: 'When a measure becomes a target, it ceases to be a good measure'. What are the unintended consequences of the current accountability framework?

Store this in your PDP.

As part of the overall accountability framework, the government tasks certain agencies or individuals to oversee certain aspects of accountability. In England, these agencies are:

- **Ofsted** is responsible for inspecting maintained schools and academies, some independent schools and other educational institutions in England. However, Ofsted cannot take enforcement action if the quality of education is judged not to be good enough.
- **Regional schools' commissioners** are senior civil servants who act on behalf of the Secretary of State to intervene in both maintained schools and academies where standards are not good enough. It is the regional schools' commissioner who can take enforcement action if standards in a school are not good enough, or Ofsted judges the school to be requiring improvement or failing.
- **Ofqual** regulates qualifications in England. Ofqual can take enforcement action both in relation to schools where malpractice has taken place and in relation to exam boards when things go wrong.
- **NCTL** is the regulator of professional standards for teachers in England. It investigates misconduct in the teaching profession and makes decisions about whether an individual teacher should be allowed to continue to teach.

In Task 8.3.4 you are asked to consider the Ofsted inspection for your current placement school.

Task 8.3.4   Inspection

Download the current Ofsted inspection framework (Ofsted, 2018b) and your placement school's most recent Ofsted report.

Make an assessment of how the school performs against the inspection framework and the point that data is a signpost, rather than a destination for inspection (Ofsted, 2017b). You may want to talk to the colleague in your school or MAT who leads on data.

Store this in your PDP.

Government is accountable to the electorate. It sets the broad policy framework.

The Secretary of State for Education is the senior political post holder responsible for education legislation, policy and the work of the Department for Education.

The Secretary of State works with a **ministerial team** who each have portfolios of responsibility for parts of the education system. They are responsible for putting forward legislation and setting the overall accountability framework for schools in England.

Department for Education. The **Permanent Secretary** is the most senior civil servant, charged with running the department on a day-to-day basis. The Department for Education is part of the civil service and supports and advices the ministerial team. The civil service impartially implements a government's policies and laws.

Ofsted: The Office for Standards in Education, Children's Services and Skills. Ofsted inspects and regulates services that care for children and young people and services providing education and skills for learners of all ages. Ofsted is a non-ministerial department meaning that it is independent of government and reports directly to Parliament. It is led by HMCI; Her Majesty's Chief Inspector.	**Ofqual**: The Office of Qualifications and Examinations Regulation regulates qualifications, examinations and assessments in England. It maintains standards and confidence in qualifications in England including GCSEs, A levels, AS levels and vocational and technical qualifications Ofqual is a non-ministerial department meaning that it is independent of government and reports directly to Parliament. It is led by the Chief Regulator.	**The NCTL** is the National College for Teaching and Leadership. It is responsible for regulating the teaching profession in England. It investigate cases of serious teacher misconduct and decides whether to refer a case to a professional conduct panel. The panel then investigates whether a prohibition order should be issued to prevent a teacher from continuing to teach. The NCTL is part of the Department for Education. It is led by a Chief Regulator. It carries out its duties on behalf of the Secretary of State who is directly responsible for regulating the teaching profession in England.

Middle tier bodies that can take enforcement action:

Regional schools commissioners are civil servants and the agents of the Secretary of State in regional areas. Where standards in schools are not good enough, regional schools commissioners have powers to intervene in schools and academies. In specific circumstances, where maintained schools are not performing well, the regional schools commissioner can issue an academy order and require a school to be sponsored by a MAT.

Local authorities also have specific powers of intervention but only in schools they maintain.

Figure 8.3.1 Overview of the government and its agencies in respect of the school accountability system in England

Figure 8.3.1 provides an overview of the government and its agencies in respect of the school accountability system in England.

Safeguarding and child protection

Teachers in schools in England should be familiar with the general principles of the Children Act 1989 (UK Parliament, 1989), which put in place the first significant child protection structures that have considerable relevance to teachers today. Guidance for teachers, governors and schools in England is provided by statutory guidance, *Keeping Children Safe in Education* (DfE, 2016e).

Child protection training is a mandatory requirement for all teachers. In order to be awarded qualified teacher status, you will have to demonstrate a sound understanding of your contractual, administrative and pastoral responsibilities for children and young people.

Newly qualified teachers are expected to be able to identify pupils with special educational needs and demonstrate a sound understanding of the procedures for seeking advice and support from appropriate agencies, such as social workers and healthcare professionals.

You must be fully conversant with the policies and procedures in your school that address issues of children protection, health and safety and bullying (including cyberbullying).

The statutory guidance, *Working Together to Safeguard Children* (HM Goverment, 2015; 2018) reiterates the key tenets of the Children Acts of 1989 and 2004 (UK Parliament, 1989; 2004) in stressing the need for organisations and individuals to work collaboratively to:

■ protect children from maltreatment;
■ prevent impairment of children's health or development;
■ ensure that children grow up in circumstance consistent with the provision of safe and effective care;
■ take action to enable all children to have the best outcomes.

As a teacher, part of your professional responsibility is to help your school create and maintain a safe learning environment for every pupil.

Task 8.3.5 focuses on the document *Keeping Children Safe in Education* (DfE, 2016e)

 Task 8.3.5   Keeping children safe in education

Make sure you have been given a copy of, and have read, part one of *Keeping Children Safe in Education* (DfE, 2016e), your school's child protection policy, staff behaviour policy (or code of conduct) and information about the role of the designated safeguarding lead in your school.

Make notes and store these in your PDP.

Ask your school's designated safeguarding lead if you have any questions. Also, talk to them about their role.

Health and safety

As a member of the school community, you have a responsibility for the arrangements made to meet the health and safety needs of pupils.

The main legislation is the Health and Safety at Work Act 1974 (UK Parliament, 1974) and regulations made under that Act. Your employer is primarily responsible for health and safety; however, teachers have a general duty to look after their own and others' health and safety. Teachers also have a duty under common law to take care of pupils in the same way that a prudent parent would do so (*in loco parentis*).

It is very rare for school staff to be prosecuted under criminal law with regard to accidents involving pupils, as long as they are not negligent.

Task 8.3.6 is designed to support you in understanding risk assessments.

 Task 8.3.6   Health and safety: risk assessments

Ask for a copy of a recent risk assessment undertaken prior to a school visit or trip. Read this carefully. Talk to the teacher who undertook the risk assessment. How did they go about identifying risk? What factors did they consider in how to support pupils to take risks safely?

Annotate the risk assessment and store this in your PDP.

Equalities

The Equality Act 2010 (UK Parliament, 2010) has replaced all equality legislation such as the Race Relations Act, Disability Discrimination Act and Sex Discrimination Act. The DfE (2014l) has published guidance: *The Equality Act 2010 and Schools: Departmental advice for school leaders, school staff, governing bodies and local authorities.*

It is important for you to know and understand responsibilities and accountabilities under this legislation because, in practice, as a teacher you can be held liable for your *own* discriminatory actions.

The Act deals with the way that teachers and schools treat their pupils and prospective pupils. The relationship between one pupil and another is not within the scope of the Act. The DfE (2014l, p.8) guidance says:

> It does not therefore bear directly on such issues as racist or homophobic bullying by pupils. However, if a school treats bullying which relates to a protected ground less seriously than other forms of bullying – for example dismissing complaints of homophobic bullying or failing to protect a transgender pupil against bullying by classmates – then it may be guilty of unlawful discrimination.

In Task 8.3.7 you are asked to focus on the Equalities Act and discrimination.

Task 8.3.7   The Equality Act and discrimination

The departmental advice on equalities (DfE, 2014l) gives the following examples of valid complaints that the curriculum is being delivered in a discriminatory way:

■ a teacher uses the fact that *The Taming of the Shrew* is a set book to make derogatory generalisations about the inferiority of women, in a way which makes the girls in the class feel belittled. Or, in teaching *The Merchant of Venice*, he encourages the class to laugh at a Jewish pupil;

■ in class discussions, black pupils are never called on and the teacher makes it clear that she is not interested in their views;

■ girls are not allowed to do design technology or boys are discouraged from doing food technology. This is not intrinsic to the curriculum itself but to the way in which education is made available to pupils;

■ the girls' cricket team are not allowed equal access to the cricket nets, or the boys' hockey team is given far better resources than the girls' team. This would be less favourable delivery of education rather than to do with the specific sports per se.

Study the definitions of direct discrimination; indirect discrimination; harassment and victimisation on page 9 of the guidance. Consider which of the definitions fits the vignettes above.

Store this exercise in your PDP.

Prevent and British values

The 'Prevent Duty' requires that teachers identify children and young people who may be vulnerable to radicalisation, and know what to do when they are identified. Protecting pupils from the risk of radicalisation is part of a school's wider safeguarding duties, and is similar in nature to protecting pupils from other harms (e.g. drugs, gangs, neglect, sexual exploitation).

Schools are also required to promote 'British values':

■ democracy;
■ the rule of law;
■ individual liberty;
■ mutual respect for and tolerance of those with different faiths and beliefs and for those without faith.

The non-statutory guidance to schools on the Prevent Duty advises that schools can build pupils' resilience to radicalisation by providing a safe environment for debating controversial issues. Schools are now under a duty to promote the spiritual, moral, social and cultural (SMSC) development of pupils and, within this, British values.

In Task 8.3.8 the focus is on British values.

> ✎   **Task 8.3.8   British values**
>
> Find out more about the arrangements your school has in place to promote British values. Talk to your SMSC coordinator (or equivalent post) about this. If your school has a specific policy on this, read a copy of the policy.
>
>   Store this in your PDP.

Employer and contractual accountability

Safer recruitment

As discussed above, all schools have responsibility for safeguarding children and young people. Make sure you a familiar with Safer Recruitment, part three of *Keeping Children Safe in Education* (DfE, 2016e), which sets out the procedures for selection and pre-employment vetting for schools that will provide the framework for all schools' recruitment policies.

Schools have explicit employment policies that take account of national and local safeguarding requirements. Make sure you familiarise yourself with these before writing and submitting an application for a post, to ensure that you comply with all requirements. The school or organisation to which you are applying will require you to apply for Disclosure and Barring Service (DBS) check at the level appropriate to the post (see Unit 8.1 on applying for your first post).

Your contract of employment

Your contract of employment will set out specific responsibilities and accountabilities you have to your employer. Your contract of employment is legally binding, and you should review it carefully, and ask any questions before signing it.

Performance management and performance-related pay

From September 2013, schools have been able to link teachers' pay to performance, allowing them to pay good teachers more. This follows recommendations from the School Teachers' Review Body (STRB).

In response to this, all schools were required to have revised their pay and appraisal policies, setting out how pay progression will be linked to a teacher's performance.

Department advice to schools suggests they can consider the following factors when assessing teachers' performance:

- impact on pupil progress;
- impact on wider outcomes for pupils;
- contribution to improvements in other areas;
- professional and career development;
- wider contribution to the work of the school.

Schools can consider evidence from a range of sources in order to make decisions about performance-related progression. Performance-related pay and pay policies are the focus of Task 8.3.9.

 Task 8.3.9   Performance-related pay and pay policies

Ask your placement school for a copy of the pay policy. Talk to your head of department or other school leader to find out more about factors and evidence that the school uses as part of teachers' appraisal. Consider the evidence you might start collecting as part of your PDP to help you demonstrate your performance (and your development) as a teacher.

Note that you will not be subject to appraisal until after you have completed your induction year.

Accountability to your employer

You have a general responsibility to your employer to perform your duties as a teacher in the context of the wider accountability frameworks outlined above. You must have regard for the ethos, policies and practices of the school or organisation in which you teach and maintain high standards in your own attendance and punctuality.

As a student teacher, and, later, your contract of employment, will require you to work within the school or organisation's policies and procedures. If you do not follow policies or procedures or you fail to meet the standards or responsibilities in the accountability frameworks, it is your employer who will normally take first action.

SUMMARY AND KEY POINTS

The accountability frameworks guiding a teacher's practice are complex in the state-funded education system in England. Because teaching is a profession, like other professions, the job is rightly highly accountable. A teacher is expected to demonstrate consistently high standards of personal and professional conduct, uphold public trust in the profession, have proper and professional regard for the ethos, policies and practices of the school or organisation and act within the statutory frameworks that set out professional duties and responsibilities. All teachers are responsible for the education, health, welfare and safety of the pupils in their care. It is right that teachers are both responsible and accountable.

This unit has considered:

- the structure of the state-funded education system in England;
- your moral and ethical responsibilities and accountabilities; the role of the State and its agencies;
- legal and regulatory accountability frameworks governing your practice;
- your accountability to your employer and your contractual responsibilities.

Check which requirements for your ITE programme you have addressed throughout this unit.

Further resources

Berry, J. (2013) *Teachers' Legal Rights and Responsibilities: A Guide for Trainee Teachers and Those New to the Profession*, 3rd Edition, Hatfield: University of Hertfordshire Press.
This guide provides an overview of the legal issues relevant to teachers to help them understand their rights, responsibilities and professional duties.

The Bristol Guide (2014 edition, updated regularly) *Professional Responsibilities and Statutory Frameworks for Teachers and Others in Schools*, School of Education, University of Bristol, viewed 3 July 2018, from http://www.bristol.ac.uk/education/expertiseandresources/bristolguide/.
Updated regularly, the Bristol Guide is crucial reading for everyone who works with children and young people in school settings. It provides up-to-date guidance on teachers' statutory frameworks and the law that governs professional responsibilities and duties.

You should read and be familiar with the various Acts, legislation and statutory guidance on accountability in England (many of which are identified in this unit) (or in the country in which you are learning to teach), as well as how these are translated into policy and practice in your placement school. In addition, there are numerous advice documents on various aspects of teacher accountability available on the web to which you can refer.

Appendix 2 lists subject associations and teacher councils and Appendix 3 provides a list of websites.

Capel, S., Leask, M. and Turner, T. (eds.) (2010) *Readings for Learning to Teach in the Secondary School: A Companion to M Level Study*, Abingdon: Routledge.
This book brings together essential readings to support you in your critical engagement with key issues raised in this textbook.

Capel, S., Lawrence, J., Leask, M. and Younie, S. (eds.) (2019) *Surviving and Thriving in the Secondary School: The NQT's Essential Companion,* Abingdon: Routledge.
This book is designed to support newly qualified teachers in the next phase of development as a teacher. However, you may find it useful as it covers aspects of teaching not included in this book which, nonetheless you experience on your ITE programme.

The subject specific books in the *Learning to Teach (Subject)* series, the *Practical (Subject) Guides*, *Debates in (Subject)* and *Mentoring (Subject) Teachers* are also very useful.

> **Any additional resources and an editable version of any relevant tasks/tables in this unit are available on the companion website: www.routledge.com/cw/capel**

8.4 Developing as a professional

Caroline Daly and Clare Brooks

Introduction

During the course of your initial teacher education (ITE), you receive a considerable amount of advice, observe many experienced teachers, become familiar with 'requirements' of the role and develop your teaching. However, none of this, and nobody, can tell you exactly how to teach to enhance pupils' learning. That is because teaching is a highly complex *practice*; teachers develop ethical, social and intellectual behaviours that make them increasingly attuned to pupils as young individuals and affect the likelihood of pupils being able to learn. To develop as a teacher means examining your assumptions about how pupils learn and about the teacher's role in this. It means understanding that your development as a teacher depends on deepening your understanding of teaching as a highly complex practice. In other words – it's about *your* learning as a professional.

You may find yourself teaching with considerable energy during your school experiences, but when you look deeply at what your pupils are learning, you may identify some significant gaps between what you set out to teach and what your pupils actually learn. This is completely normal in the early stages of learning to teach. It is important that you resist interpreting this as a problem that pupils have with being able to learn in the ways you want them to. This can be called a 'deficit analysis', where the teacher pays less attention to their own development needs and identifies 'problems' within pupils as the reasons why lessons do not go as anticipated. A frequent problem is when pupils' lack of progression is attributed to a lack of 'ability' (a very common misconception) or their own behaviour issues. This is a major obstacle to student and newly qualified (new) teachers' development. Teachers accept responsibility for the conditions they bring about in the classroom to enable learning. Your development as a teacher depends on how you are able to interrogate deeply what has happened in your lessons and to reject simplified explanations for why pupils do not always learn when you are teaching. Development means that you gradually learn to adapt your teaching based on deepening knowledge of your pupils, within the context of your particular classroom and the subject that you teach. This is based on your developing professional judgement.

This unit explores the ideas of becoming a professional, developing your identity as a teacher and developing your professional judgement. It discusses core ideas about how teachers learn, in relation to your development *as a professional*. Exploring these ideas is not just important at the start of your career; they underpin the ways in which a teacher develops into an expert practitioner and goes on learning throughout their professional life.

OBJECTIVES

At the end of this unit, you should be able to:

■ understand what it means to become a 'professional';
■ reflect on your developing teacher identity;
■ understand that developing professional judgement is highly complex and requires developmental tools (critical reflection, enquiry, the use of evidence, engagement with theory, collaboration, mentor feedback);
■ plan for how to work with your school-based mentor to support your development;
■ understand the importance of learning throughout your teaching career.

Check the requirements of your ITE programme to see which relate to this unit.

Becoming a 'professional'

When we say that no one can tell you how to teach, we are referring to a particular view of what it means to be a teacher, underpinned by an understanding that teaching is a professional practice. The term 'professional' is used in a variety of contexts, often meaning 'paid for' as distinguished from 'amateur'. However, it also has a specific meaning as a distinctive form of occupation.

Our use of the term profession is as a particular category of occupation which plays a specific role in society and which requires specialist expertise not available to a lay-person. Each profession comes with a set of assumptions about the nature of the work and the responsibilities and activities of a professional. Professionals act under an ethical code (see Unit 8.3). In performing a specific role and with specific expertise comes trust, prestige and status in society. (Teaching was once considered a semi-profession (along with nursing, accounting and others), whilst doctors, lawyers and some other specialist occupations were considered professions. However, semi-professions, including teaching, are now generally considered professions.)

So, how do professions look different from other occupations (some of which call themselves professions), what does this mean for new entrants, for your development as a teacher and what is understood by professional practice? Freidson (2001) argues that there are three types of occupations that require different types of training:

■ skilled occupations require work-place training that takes place through an apprenticeship type model, where skill is learnt 'on the job' guided by an experienced crafts-person;
■ technical occupations require specialist training, which takes place both in the work context but also in specialist environments, where the concepts that underpin the technical training are explained to new entrants;

■ professions require additional specialist input, in order to understand how knowledge about the field is created and what counts as valid knowledge: this is why he argues that professions nearly always situate their training, at least in part, in universities.

The entrance requirements for professions also play an important social and gate-keeping role that helps generate professional (and collective) identity. In the current education tradition in England, one could argue that schools play a large role in knowledge generation (particularly through the research-engaged school movement) and that entrance to teaching is now also monitored by other providers, not just universities. The importance of shared research-engagement by schools and universities in the preparation of teachers has featured in a revision of ITE in Wales (Furlong, 2015). This is an example of a policy commitment to teaching as a profession in which participation in generating knowledge and scrutinising knowledge about learning and teaching is regarded as essential to becoming a teacher.

Freidson's (2001) three categories are echoed by a similar categorisation suggested by Orchard and Winch (2015). Placing their analysis in a more contemporary context, they refer to three ways in which teachers and teaching are viewed – not always as a profession. Understanding these categories should help you when your professional status is questioned by people outside the profession.

The first category is where teachers are seen as craft workers, a reductionist and limited view of teaching that focuses on specific skills which can be learnt through an apprenticeship to a more experienced 'master' practitioner. In the second category, teaching is characterised as a highly skilled profession. Orchard and Winch (2015, p.11) argue that this continues to be a fairly impoverished view of teaching, as it positions teachers as executive technicians, who are 'told prescriptively by others what to do, without needing to understand why they are being told to do it'. In both these categories, teachers are viewed as technical workers with a considerable emphasis on the practical aspects of teaching, focussing solely on the observable actions of teachers in the act of teaching.

However, Orchard and Winch promote teachers as professionals:

> The teacher who is able to engage with theory and the findings of educational research shares with the craft worker teacher a capacity for self-direction. By contrast, though, the professional teacher is able to judge right action in various school and classroom contexts from a more reliable basis for judgment than intuition or common sense. A teacher who is able to make good situational judgments does not rely on hearsay or unreflective prejudice. She draws on a well-thought-through and coherent conceptual framework, on knowledge of well-substantiated empirical research, and on considered ethical principles, to arrive at decisions in the classroom context.
>
> (2015, p. 14)

The distinction, then, of teaching as a profession takes into account a more expansive view of teachers' work, acknowledging the complexity of teaching and learning and the number of judgements teachers have to make in the course of their professional practice. This distinction also acknowledges that this specialist expertise comes from a solid knowledge base, grounded in concepts and closely linked with research. The challenge that faces many new teachers is how to develop that knowledge base whilst engaging in the complexity and immediacy of a classroom environment. Additionally, it can be challenging to gain access to high quality knowledge from other sources, and particularly from research that is often described as inaccessible for teachers in both the way it is published and in the way it is written. Subject associations usually publish a professional journal that translates research into practical applications. Once a teacher becomes aware of research a further challenge is to review its quality and the extent to which it is robust evidence, or unreliable 'snake-oil'. Now complete Task 8.4.1.

 Task 8.4.1   Being a learner of your own teaching

According to Hattie (2009), who carried out analysis of over 800 studies of effective teaching:

the biggest effects on student learning occur when teachers become learners of their own teaching.

(p. 22)

Before reading further in this unit, reflect on this statement, then discuss with other student teachers and your tutor:

- What do you think it means for teachers to become 'learners of their own teaching'?
- What activities and processes can help you to become a 'learner' of your own teaching?
- What challenges might you encounter to maintaining a focus on being a learner of your own teaching during your time as a student teacher and beyond?

Record the results of your discussions in your professional development portfolio (PDP).

Being a learner of your own teaching

Part of becoming a professional is maintaining a commitment to your own learning about your own teaching throughout your career. It is therefore important that, as a professional, you remain up-to-date with advances in your field, in subject content and pedagogy and teaching and education more generally. Alongside gaining experience, you are expected to actively seek opportunities to increase your knowledge, skills and often your qualifications. Developing these expectations from the very start of your career will help to orientate you as a member of the teaching profession. See below and other units in this book.

Developing a teacher identity

Becoming a student teacher is a life-changing choice. You will no doubt face many challenges, become extremely tired, possibly emotional at times. Hopefully you will also discover just how resilient you can be (see unit 1.3) and, also, how immensely rewarding the job of teaching is. It is rewarding *because* it is hard, because it is not for everyone, but when it is right for you, you know that your everyday actions make a difference to the young people in your care. When people ask you, 'So, what do you do for a living?' you'll say, 'I am a teacher'. That is saying much more than 'this is my job' or 'this is my skill set'. It is saying something about you as a person, the things you value and the commitments you have made. That is why your development as a teacher is extremely complex and extends far beyond any particular set of standards or criteria that are applied at a particular time.

It is not unusual to hear new teachers use acting metaphors when referring to classroom practice: the classroom becomes a stage, they worry about their performance in a lesson or in their interactions with pupils. In more reflective moments, new teachers might recall occasions when they did (or did not) really 'feel like a teacher'. This is a question of developing a teacher identity.

Your decision to become a teacher has been influenced by your personal history. You start your development as a teacher having already probably spent fourteen years of your life as a pupil, forming a view of what it is that teachers do. Due to your own experiences as a pupil, you already have deeply embedded images of what it means to be a teacher. What are your images of a teacher? These images are formed early in life (Zeichner and Liston, 1987) and are often underpinned by enduring and resistant beliefs about teaching (Pajares, 1992). These images are also closely aligned to the sort of teacher you want to be: both in terms of personal attributes, but also the subject or phase you are specialising in. Research (Brooks, 2016) suggests that these images are grounded in stories which, when analysed, reveal strong values about what being a teacher (for example, a geography teacher) means to you: why you want to teach that subject (or phase), or why teaching attracts you, and how it relates to other values that you have about your personal and professional life. Learning to teach requires you to re-examine these images and beliefs, particularly in the light of experiences in trying to live up to them.

When applicants for ITE are interviewed, they frequently tell stories about how much they want to make a difference, to inspire others to share their love of a subject. Some say they want to do a better job of it than some of the teachers they had at school; others say they want to be as good as the teachers who changed their lives. Whatever you said in your interview, it was informed by your pre-existing perceptions of what it is that teachers do and the values you attach to that. Entrants to teaching convince their interviewers that their values are based on providing opportunity, overcoming barriers to the attainment of young people and giving them a fairer chance in society. Such values will continue to underpin your development during ITE and beyond.

Growth as a *professional* is deeply connected with growth as a *person*. That is why the process can be unsettling as well as exhilarating; you are developing a teacher identity that involves far more than the acquisition of a set of skills. It involves considering the values and beliefs you currently hold about how pupils learn and re-evaluating your own attributes that will help you to become a teacher. This necessarily involves some discomfort and most student teachers find themselves having moments of doubt during the year – about their subject knowledge, skills, capacity to make relationships with learners and about managing the sheer complexity of teaching (see Unit 1.1). It is extremely important to be aware of this process and to maintain a balanced perspective. Now undertake Task 8.4.2.

 Task 8.4.2   Exploring what it means to be a teacher

- Identify two teachers who were excellent teachers for you as a pupil, in any subject or phase. Write two separate lists of all their qualities and characteristics as you remember them (their perceived *attributes*).
- Now compare the lists. It is almost certain they contain some common features, but also contain some different attributes. Some attributes will be more significant for one than the other – some may even not exist for one teacher.

■   If possible, compare your lists with lists developed by another student teacher. Discuss how far you can agree on 'core' attributes that exist across lists. Which attributes do you believe to be 'non-negotiable' – why? How important is it that there are some attributes that are unique to, or more present in, some teachers than others?

Store your findings in your PDP.

Developing professional judgement

The mandatory standards to become a qualified teacher that apply at any particular time are produced within a policy environment that continues to change. They provide a framework for accountability and common benchmarks of what is required to become qualified as a teacher at a particular time, in a particular society.

Your development towards meeting common standards, however, is a highly individual process. It is shaped by your prior experiences as a learner at school and elsewhere, your values, your existing beliefs about how people learn, prior experience of working with young people, etc. Your development, therefore, takes place within a highly complex set of interactions between your personal history, values and the range of experiences to which you are exposed. Your professional judgement – essential to teacher behaviours and actions – is formed from these interactions over time. There is great strength in this; it means your development is based on a unique blend of personal attributes and beliefs, with common benchmarks that you meet to a common standard.

At the same time, there is a problem with this because development is vulnerable to being idiosyncratic. It can be highly dependent on your individual characteristics and the particular contexts in which you practice. It is possible to form very restricted views on how to teach, which lack an evidence-base and lack exposure to alternative viewpoints. This is what is commonly called finding out 'what works' and is a pitfall in the development of new teachers. It is natural to seek what is 'working' in the pressurised context of learning to teach.

Hargreaves (1999) warned against the dangers of attempting to 'transfer' practice from one teacher to another. Instead, teachers learn how to adapt the actions and behaviours they have seen in others or gained from past experiences to the unique context of their own classroom. To develop as a teacher means asking deep questions about what is happening and seeking evidence to help build a picture of the complexity of learning and teaching. Professional judgement is based on *critically informed understanding*.

There are a number of ways in which teachers' professional knowledge has been described and analysed, with differing emphases on knowledge related to teaching the subject, interpreting the classroom environment, working productively with technologies and so on (see, for example, Shulman's (1986; 1987) categories of knowledge on pages 19–22). These identify the 'knowledge base' for teaching. In order to help you 'make sense' of the multiple interactions you encounter and of your own behaviours and responses to what you experience you need to build your own knowledge and understanding of teaching by becoming a learner of teaching. To do this requires a range of professional learning strategies or tools that enable you to develop the judgements that form the basis for professional action. Professional learning tools are complex and underpinned by extensive research and theory (some are explored in other units in this book: see, particularly, Section 5) but are also implicit throughout discussions of all aspects of becoming a teacher. These professional learning tools include:

- critical reflection on your actions and behaviours as a teacher;
- enquiry into your own practice and its effects on your pupils;
- judicious use of a range of evidence that can inform decisions about teaching approaches;
- the use of theory about learning and teaching to inform your developing practice;
- collaboration and interaction with a range of other professionals;
- mentor feedback.

These learning tools underpin your development as a teacher, increasing your capacity to make careful and informed judgements about your behaviours and actions. This requires systematic focus; developing your judgement does not occur naturally in a deep way and cannot be left to chance in the very busy environments of schools, or to operate at a tacit level. These learning tools are vital to overcome 'common sense' approaches to becoming a teacher. It is important to resist simplified 'solutions' to challenges in the classroom; although, these can sometimes offer 'quick wins'. It is essential that you learn to adopt tools for teacher development that do not focus on 'survival' or 'easy solutions' that everyone can copy because they reduce the requirement to think deeply about what is happening to pupils and about your actions and your rationale for them. This is about you becoming a *learner of your own teaching*.

Support for you in being such a learner is available in the ways that your ITE programme has been designed: through reading material and tasks such as those contained in this book, tutor input and feedback, discussion with peers, etc. A critical source of support for your development throughout your school experience is the school-based tutor or 'mentor'. Your relationship with that colleague is discussed in the next section. Professional organisations and associations such as subject associations (http://www.subjectassociations.org.uk) also provide support.

Working with your school-based tutor – your 'mentor'

Throughout this book, the term 'tutor' refers to both school and university staff who support your development. This section looks specifically at the relationship with your school-based tutor, most commonly called a 'mentor'. The term 'mentor' here refers to the nominated individual within your placement school who is responsible for supporting your day-to-day development needs/learning. They are most usually an experienced teacher who shares your subject specialism, although a mentor can occasionally be from another subject area (in which case a different person may advise you on teaching the subject in school) or provided externally. They will be a teacher with more experience than you, which might range from a short period of time to considerable seniority as a teacher. The length of time does not matter because you are not 'copying' practice from someone who has been teaching for years.

It is essential that you know who is responsible for supporting you in this day-to-day capacity. If you are not sure about the roles played by differing school staff members in supporting your development, then ask for this to be clarified as a priority at the start of your school placement (see also Unit 1.2).

All ITE providers should have guidelines for you and your school-based mentor. Ask about these if they are not clear to you. It is much better to have clarity from the start than to discover misunderstandings as your needs for support emerge in response to increased teaching responsibilities. It is also vital to establish the guidelines for your mentoring relationship from the outset; you should work together to support your development.

The importance of dialogue

To support your development as a teacher, school-based mentoring is a relationship that should be open and candid, based on trust and dialogue that explores your developing practice in deep ways. At best, this can be termed 'educative mentoring' (Langdon and Ward, 2015) where the focus is on learning and teaching and the mentoring conversation *explores* what is happening in the student teacher's classroom. It is based on building knowledge together about how the subject is learned and facilitates the development of alternative beliefs and viewpoints. It goes far beyond inducting you into existing school routines and ways of teaching. Student teachers and mentors can discuss, for example:

- the challenges of motivating particular pupils and understanding their individual needs;
- understanding pupils' subject-specific misconceptions;
- how some forms of assessment can help pupils to learn;
- how inclusion of all pupils in lessons can be increased.

Mentoring conversations should be rich discussions. Resist the tendency to view mentor conversations as 'help sessions' to deal with difficulties or as information sessions; it is easy for meetings to be dominated by paperwork and become focused on transferring information. These things are sometimes inevitable, but your development will be supported by deliberately building agenda items that focus on pupils' learning and your developing judgements about how to teach the subject. It is important that you take responsibility for contributing to the agenda.

Avoiding 'fabrication' with your school-based mentor

'Fabrication' has been identified by Hobson and McIntyre (2013) as a major obstacle to student (and newly qualified) teacher development. They define this as a concern amongst student teachers 'to prevent significant others in or associated with their schools from becoming aware of what they felt were inadequacies in their professional practice' (p.345). Two types of fabrication have been identified:

- Fabrication as strategic silence: teachers' reluctance or inability to raise or discuss freely with school-based mentors, line managers or colleagues specific difficulties they were encountering in their practice.
- Fabrication as strategic avoidance: the avoidance by teachers of forms of behaviour and interaction which they feared might draw attention to or lead significant others to identify any chinks in their armour, such as gaps in subject knowledge, e.g. teachers:
  (i) discouraging mentors or line managers from observing them teach classes they found it difficult to manage;
  (ii) ignoring or failing to report problematic pupil behaviour; and
  (iii) focusing in their planning and teaching on aspects of the curriculum about which they felt confident, in order to avoid being asked awkward questions which might reveal gaps in their [subject] knowledge (pp.345–365).

All of these can have a seriously adverse effect on student teacher learning. The key here is to understand the role of your mentor in supporting your development. An experienced mentor will help you to feel relaxed about openly discussing the challenges that are a normal part of learning to teach. It is also part of your own professional responsibility to be open to discussing difficulties and to actively seek to raise issues in mentor conversations. This can be difficult if mentoring happens in a hurry or in only semi-private surroundings. Some student teachers feel acutely aware of how very busy their mentors are within their other school roles and feel reluctant to ask for their time. It is important that you *do* ask for support to discuss concerns and to spend time looking at the sources of difficulties, that is, what mentors expect to do. It is understandable, however, for them to be convinced by 'fabrication' if they are very busy and you are making good progress, but this will not help you to achieve your full potential and can lead to unnecessary worry. So, what should you do?

The most important thing is to *be explicit* about what is on your mind and what is happening as your teaching progresses. Make the time to note down the things you need to talk about in your mentor meetings and make sure that you discuss them. Going through that list can be a routine start to a meeting, to ensure that important issues are part of an agenda. Being explicit is also part of what mentors need to do in giving feedback on your teaching. Be prepared to receive constructive criticism; that is a vital way that student teachers learn. At the same time, student teachers are often extremely sensitive to negative feedback. It has been suggested that, 'If the mentor's feedback isn't 80% positive, the mentee will hear it as 80% negative' (Wright, 2012, p.4). This is why the quality of your dialogue with your mentor is so important. It is important for both you and your mentor to really listen to what each other is saying. Now complete Task 8.4.3.

 Task 8.4.3   Mentoring dialogue

Write down what is happening in this extract from a mentoring dialogue.

Mentor: Do you think the pupils really understood the main concept you were trying to teach in that lesson?

Mentee: Yes, I think so.

Mentor: How do you know?

Mentee: Well, I gave them 'exit cards' at the end and they nearly all ticked a smiley face about the lesson.

Mentor: But in the plenary - they were reluctant to volunteer explanations?

Mentee: There are a lot of shy individuals in that class, they don't like speaking in front of the others. I'm sure they got it from the way they were working in the lesson.

What are the issues here? Try to share your thoughts with another student teacher or, even better, with your mentor.

Store these thoughts in your PDP.

The issues you have identified might include:

- the mentee has decided very quickly that the pupils learned what they wanted them to learn;
- the mentee has shown they have a 'strategy' to obtain immediate feedback from pupils;
- the mentee has shown they have good knowledge of their pupils' personality traits (there are lots of shy individuals), but that replaces thinking deeply about their learning of the concept;
- the mentee has focused on 'what went well' (pupils were 'working'), but this has restricted thinking deeply about whether the concept was really understood.

The student teacher, in this example, has missed an opportunity to think deeply about the mentor's questions. The mentor has asked direct questions to try to prompt thinking about what really happened – whether the pupils really understood the concept. Direct questions are core to mentoring, to enable you to reflect deeply on your teaching. It would be understandable for the student teacher to feel frustrated that the things that stood out for him do not appear to be the main things that the mentor is trying to focus on. The mentor is not satisfied with the initial responses and that is the mentor's job: to push for deeper, critical analysis of teaching. It would be easy for the student teacher to feel defensive and to feel a need to explain why the 'exit cards' and his knowledge about pupils' shyness are important factors. This is where it is easy to become confused. The mentor is not questioning these things, it's just that the student teacher now needs to look more deeply at the impact of their teaching on pupils' learning. This is *not* questioning their competence – they are learning about teaching. But a concern to demonstrate that all went well is an obstacle to the student teacher being able to really listen to the questions.

This is challenging but central to learning to teach. It helps to establish ground rules from the start about mentoring so that anxiety about exploring difficult issues is reduced and mentoring is more likely to be 'educative'. Task 8.4.4 suggests a practical outline for establishing how to get the best out of your school-based mentoring relationship.

 Task 8.4.4   Planning to get the most out of the school-based mentor relationship

At your first mentor meeting, talk with your mentor about how the mentoring relationship will support your development. Hopefully the mentor will already expect to discuss the following ideas. If not, ask to discuss the following issues *that relate to your development* at that meeting or at another very early mentoring session.

- How frequently will meetings be held and where will they take place? Will they follow lessons where your mentor has observed you teaching, or will there be an interval for reflection before you discuss feedback on your teaching?
- How will mentoring sessions be recorded and by whom, to ensure that you fully understand your progress and development goals?
- How will the agenda items be decided, and will they include a specific focus on your development needs at that time?
- How will goals for your progression be monitored?

- How will feedback be discussed to acknowledge strengths and explore how to develop teaching?
- How can you sustain your capacity to learn? What are your plans to maintain work-life balance and your well-being?
- Talk openly about 'fabrication'. Explain your awareness that some student teachers can find it hard to discuss issues where they feel vulnerable. How can you avoid that?
- Gain a shared understanding of how the mentor sessions feed into reporting on your progress.

Store what was agreed in your PDP and refer to it, if needed.

If you are on an ITE programme run in partnership between a university and school(s), it is important to maintain a three-way dialogue between yourself, your school-based mentor and your university tutor (or with any other external source of subject support that is provided within your ITE programme). The more there is a shared and consistent understanding of your development needs and progress, the more you can receive coordinated support for appropriate priorities to help the next stages in your learning.

Aim to keep communication as open as possible in a three-way relationship with these important sources of support.

SUMMARY AND KEY POINTS

Learning to teach is something that continues throughout your career. Your ITE is naturally the focus of your concerns right now, but it is important to look at this in the context of a teacher's complete professional life. Teachers promote curiosity in those they teach; this needs to be equalled by their own curiosity about how learning happens and how they can develop their practice to enable that. You will return to an underlying message throughout this book – that knowledge about how to teach is made by the individual, supported by engaging with pupils and colleagues and by the ways you work with the existing body of professional knowledge about teaching your subject, that is, the knowledge base. This process is facilitated by established professional learning tools that support you to be critical and enquiring in how you work with evidence to support your judgements. In conclusion:

- your experiences as a student teacher should establish you as a *learner of your own teaching*;
- this means taking responsibility for seeking support for your learning and being prepared for challenges to your current beliefs and assumptions about what makes an effective teacher;
- becoming a professional means developing your teacher identity;
- it also means developing the capacity to make informed judgements that affect your behaviours and actions;

- these judgements are individual but not eccentric or idiosyncratic. They involve others in exploration of your teaching and critical reflection on it;
- your development is facilitated by professional learning tools (critical reflection, enquiry, the use of evidence, engagement with theory, collaboration, mentor feedback). These are explored in other units in this book, especially Chapter 5.

Your professional development is therefore a complex mixture of your own history and values as a learner, working within the unique social context of your classroom, supported by sources of expertise in understanding and teaching your subject.

Check which requirements for your ITE programme you have addressed through this unit.

 Further resources

Andrew Pollard – Reflective Teaching

Andrew Pollard has written a substantial amount of print-based and online material on the subject of 'reflective teaching'.

Pollard, A. (2002) *Readings for Reflective Teaching*, London: Continuum.

This book is a collection of extracts from the most important and influential thinkers and researchers into how teachers develop. The readings are short and grouped thematically. They have been chosen for their high relevance to teacher development. Teachers are introduced to relevant theory in a manageable way. The companion text is:

Pollard, A., with Anderson, J., Maddock, M., Swaffield, S., Warin, J. and Warwick, P. (2008) *Reflective Teaching: Effective and Evidence Informed Practice*, 3rd Edition, London: Continuum.

This book provides a comprehensive collection of reflective activities.

These two books should support long-term career development. Extracts from these longer works, including visual summaries, can be found at Andrew Pollard's website: http://reflectiveteaching.co.uk/. Brief activities are provided that support student teachers to develop reflective practice, many of which expand the themes discussed in this unit, for example 'To reflect on your own decision to become a teacher'.

Wright, T. (2012) *Guide to Mentoring. Advice for the Mentor and the Mentee*, Association of Teachers and Lecturers, viewed 8 June 2018, from https://www.atl.org.uk/Images/ATL%20Guide%20to%20mentoring%20(Nov%2012).pdf

This online booklet is a practical resource for both school-based mentors and student teachers (referred to as 'mentees'). A real strength of this resource is that it is intended for both parties. It includes examples of mentoring dialogue for both mentors and mentees to reflect on and suggests ways of sharing teaching between experienced and student teachers so that the mentor relationship is based on striving together to develop effective teaching.

Reflecting on Outstanding Teaching, featuring Dr Russell Grigg. The Teachers TV ITE Lectures, viewed 8 June 2018, from https://www.youtube.com/watch?v=Wg32-PmpROA

In this film (40 minutes), the speaker leads a discussion with student teachers about what it takes to teach effectively and to manage expectations as a qualified teacher about being 'outstanding'. It includes what pupils say about what makes great teaching from their point of view and is a powerful reminder that teachers learn a huge amount by listening to them. The first 10 minutes are especially relevant to those in the early stages of learning to teach, while the whole film is helpful following a period of school experience.

Subject Associations (http://www.subjectassociations.org.uk).

These are a rich source of information about events for teachers, development opportunities and important national developments in the subject. Many provide reviews and summaries of recent research about teaching specific subjects. You may need to be a member to access the whole range of material, but some is freely available. Your school department may be a member of a subject association, meaning that access to resources should be possible while you are learning to teach there.

Appendix 2 lists subject associations and teacher councils and Appendix 3 provides a list of websites.

Capel, S., Leask, M. and Turner, T. (eds.) (2010) *Readings for Learning to Teach in the Secondary School: A Companion to M Level Study*, **Abingdon: Routledge.**
This book brings together essential readings to support you in your critical engagement with key issues raised in this textbook.

Capel, S., Lawrence, J., Leask, M. and Younie, S. (eds.) (2019) *Surviving and Thriving in the Secondary School: The NQT's Essential Companion,* **Abingdon: Routledge.**
This book is designed to support newly qualified teachers in the next phase of development as a teacher. However, you may find it useful as it covers aspects of teaching not included in this book which, nonetheless you experience on your ITE programme.

The subject specific books in the *Learning to Teach (Subject)* series, the *Practical (Subject) Guides, Debates in (Subject)* and *Mentoring (Subject) Teachers* are also very useful.

Any additional resources and an editable version of any relevant tasks/tables in this unit are available on the companion website: www.routledge.com/cw/capel

9 And finally

Marilyn Leask

Introduction

The introduction to this text sets you the challenge of considering what you want to achieve by becoming a teacher and what it means to be a teacher. Each unit has been designed to help you understand the different elements of teaching. This 'whole-part-whole approach' to introducing you to teaching through this text mirrors best practice in teaching – introducing the whole, undertaking work on the parts, then returning to review the learning in the context of the whole.

Here, in the last unit, we return to the issue of how your values and beliefs shape your work as a teacher. Unit 7.1 challenged you to think about the aims of education. Units 1.1 and 4.5 asked you to consider your values to adopt a code of conduct to guide your work as a professional. Over your teaching career, you can expect demands on teachers to be able to demonstrate evidence-informed practice to become the norm. We do not expect doctors to practice without reference to the latest evidence, and learners and their parents and carers, too, can expect evidence-informed practice from you. In Unit 5.4, we made the point that evidence-informed practice = professional judgement + evidence; research is never adopted without reference to the learner and the environment and subject context. The list of websites on pages 558–564 provides information to enable you to keep up to date.

This text has drawn on the evidence base for educational practice in providing information and background, then exploring these through linked tasks. Some tasks provide opportunities to reflect on and examine the practice of other teachers, of yourself and the organisation of schools; others are enquiry-based and generate data or ideas for reflective thinking upon which an understanding of, and an explanation for, the complex world of teaching and learning in schools are built.

The relationship between explanation and practice is a dynamic one; explanations are needed to make sense of experience and inform developing practice. Some explanations will be your own, to be tried and tested against the theories of others, often more experienced teachers. At other times, you may use others' explanations directly. Explanations, in turn, generate working theories, responsive to practice and experience. Theory is important, as it provides a variety of ways of thinking about the complex world of the classroom and directs further personal research into improving the quality of teaching and learning. It also provides a basis for judging both personal and institutional change. The interplay of theory and practice develops your professional judgement and underpins the notion of the reflective and evidence-informed practitioner.

What values will you pass on?

To teach young people is to contribute directly to shaping the society of tomorrow. What values will you pass on to the young people you teach?

At a time when young people who use social media are being targeted by those wishing to manipulate their thinking, your role in helping young people to understand how to protect themselves and to adopt values that support stability in society through respect for others is crucial. As a last task, we ask you to consider the messages in the letter and poem in Tables 9.1 and 9.2.

The letter, 'Dear Teacher' (Table 9.1), was written by a US high school principal, a World War II concentration camp survivor who was separated from her sister and mother whom she never saw

Table 9.1 'Dear teacher'

Dear teacher, I am the survivor of a concentration camp. My eyes saw what no man should witness. Gas chambers built by learned engineers, Children poisoned by educated physicians, Infants killed by trained nurses, Women and babies shot and burned by high school and college graduates. So I am suspicious of education. My request is: Help your students become human. Your efforts must never produce learned monsters, skilled psychopaths, educated Eichmanns. Reading writing and arithmetic are important only if they serve to make our children more human.

Table 9.2 'Children learn what they live'

If a child lives with criticism, he learns to condemn, If a child lives with hostility, he learns to fight, If a child lives with ridicule, he learns to be shy, If a child lives with shame, he learns to feel guilty, If a child lives with tolerance, he learns to be patient, If a child lives with encouragement, he learns confidence, If a child lives with praise, he learns to appreciate, If a child lives with fairness, he learns justice, If a child lives with security, he learns to have faith, If a child lives with approval, he learns to like himself, If a child lives with acceptance and friendship, he learns to find love in the world.

Source: Dorothy Law Nolte

again. She gives the letter to all new staff at her school (Pring, 2004). The poem, 'Children learn what they live' (Table 9.2, Dorothy Law Nolte), is often displayed on staffroom walls. Read the letter and the poem and then complete Task 9.1.

 Task 9.1   What will your pupils learn from you?

Read the poems in Table 9.1 and Table 9.2. Consider the values that you as a teacher will pass on through your teaching and through the relationships you develop with your pupils. Write a note to yourself about what you hope to achieve, and revisit and review your aspirations for yourself as a teacher at the beginning of each term of your teaching. Store this in your professional development portfolio (PDP) or equivalent.

SUMMARY AND KEY POINTS

■ As a teacher, you will have more impact than you will ever know – on the lives of the pupils you teach, their parents and carers, and the communities and societies within which they live.

   ■ We hope that you will help pupils to build the personal self-confidence and skills to cope with adult life and to become autonomous learners and caring members of society.

   ■ We hope, too, that what your pupils learn from you will help them make positive contributions to their world.

■ To achieve these goals, you should expect to carry on learning throughout your professional life.

   ■ As a first step, joining your subject association will ensure you receive publications outlining good practice, and attending your annual subject conference will introduce you to the network of educators taking thinking in your subject forward. You can find your subject association by asking colleagues and tutors or through the Council for Subject Associations (www.subjectassociation.org.uk).

   ■ Teachers are expected to continue to undertake reflective practice and learning beyond their ITE. Teachers in some countries have to have master's level qualifications; in those countries where this is not required, many teachers study part-time to achieve this level of qualification.

■ The issues raised in this unit about the purpose of education and how children learn are areas that you may wish to follow up through engaging with networks of other educators to develop and share the evidence base for professional practice in education.

Check which requirements for your ITE programme you have addressed through this unit.

Further resources

The texts below provide an introduction to some of the debates and thinking that have shaped educational practice in the UK over more than 100 years. The Masterclass texts (www.bloomsbury.com/uk/series/masterclass/) provide materials giving an in-depth examination of issues in particular subject areas.

Aldrich, R. (2006) *Lessons from History of Education: The Selected Works of Richard Aldrich,* **London: Routledge.**
This text provides a useful introduction to recurrent issues in education.

Bruner, J.S. (2006a) *In Search of Pedagogy Volume 1: The Selected Works of Jerome S. Bruner,* **London: Routledge.**

Bruner, J.S. (2006b) *In Search of Pedagogy Volume 2: The Selected Works of Jerome S. Bruner,* **London: Routledge.**
Bruner's work on pedagogy is seminal – changing thinking and practice.

Council for Subject Associations: www.subjectassociation.org.uk/members_links.aspx
This site provides contact details for the major professional associations. Associations run conferences, networks and professional development to help you develop as a teacher. Some are also trade unions.

Dewey, J. (1933) *How We Think,* **Boston, MA: Houghton Mifflin.**
Dewey's ideas endure. This text will challenge you to think to what extent these ideas are now spread across the education system.

Gardner, H. (2006b) *The Development and Education of the Mind: The Selected Works of Howard Gardner,* **London: Routledge.**
This is just one of Gardner's challenging and informative publications.

Marples, R. (2012) *The Aims of Education,* **Abingdon: Routledge.**
This provides a useful introduction and overview of aims of education.

Teaching Councils: Membership is by subscription and confirmation of qualifications. Normally, Councils have a code of conduct members are expected to adhere to.

Appendices 2 and 3 provide further examples of websites you may find useful.

Capel, S., Leask, M. and Turner, T. (eds) (2010) *Readings for Learning to Teach in the Secondary School: A Companion to M Level Study,* **Abingdon: Routledge.**
This book brings together essential readings to support you in your critical engagement with key issues raised in this textbook.

Capel, S., Lawrence, J., Leask, M. and Younie, S. (eds.) (2019) *Surviving and Thriving in the Secondary School: The NQT's Essential Companion,* **Abingdon: Routledge.**
This book is designed to support newly qualified teachers in the next phase of development as a teacher. However, you may find it useful as it covers aspects of teaching not included in this book which, nonetheless you experience on your ITE programme.

The subject specific books in the *Learning to Teach (Subject)* series, the *Practical (Subject) Guides, Debates in (Subject)* and *Mentoring (Subject)* Teachers are also very useful.

Any additional resources and an editable version of any relevant tasks/tables in this unit are available on the companion website: www.routledge.com/cw/capel

Appendix 1

Glossary of terms

Terms shown in bold within a definition have their own entry in the glossary. All URLs were checked July 2018.

A level See **GCE**.

A2 level See **GCE**

Academies A central government political initiative in England to bring sponsors from business, faith or voluntary groups into school management removing local accountability and local authority oversight. See also **State Maintained Schools in England** and **Other State Schools in England.**

ACCAC (Awdurdod Cymwysterau, Cwricwlwm ac Asesu Cymru) formerly the Qualifications, Curriculum and Assessment Authority for Wales. Merged with **DCELLS** in 2006.

AEB See **AQA**.

Annual Review The review of a statement of special educational needs **(SEN)** in England, which an **LA** must make within 12 months of making the statement or from a previous review.

AQA Assessment and Qualifications Alliance. An **Awarding Body** for **GCSE, GCE A** and **AS levels** and **Diplomas**. Online: <http://www.aqa.org.uk>., Formed in 2000 by a merger of City and Guilds GNVQ, Associated Examining Board (AEB), Southern Examining Group (SEG) and Northern Examination and Assessment Board (NEAB).

AS level See **GCE**

Assessment Assessment covers all those activities that are undertaken by teachers and others to measure the effectiveness of their teaching and of pupils learning. See also **Assessment for learning, Assessment of learning, Criterion-referenced assessment, Formative assessment, Ipsative assessment, Norm-referenced assessment** and **Summative assessment.**

Assessment for learning Assessment for which the first priority is to promote pupils' learning. It allows teachers and pupils 'to decide where the learners are in their learning and encourages pupils to take ownership of their learning'. See also **Assessment, Assessment of learning, Formative assessment, Ipsative assessment, Norm-referenced assessment** and **Summative assessment.**

Assessment of learning The periodic, summative assessment of pupils' attainment and progress in a variety of ways and for a variety of purposes. See also **Assessment, Assessment for learning, Criterion-referenced assessment, Formative assessment, Ipsative assessment, Norm-referenced assessment** and **Summative assessment.**

Attainment targets (ATs) of NC for England. The knowledge, skills and understanding that pupils of different abilities and maturities are expected to have by the end of each **Key Stage**. Attainment targets previously consisted of eight **level descriptions** of increasing difficulty, plus a description for exceptional performance above level 8. The latest national curriculum (2014) has removed all level descriptions. See also **Programmes of Study.**

Awarding Body There are three Awarding Bodies that set public examinations in England: the Assessment and Qualifications Alliance (**AQA**); **EdExcel** (Pearson); Oxford and Cambridge Regional (**OCR**).

BA/BSc (QTS)   Bachelor of Arts/Bachelor of Science with **QTS (Qualified Teacher Status)**. A teaching qualification awarded in England – a combined course with route to QTS. Note: your teaching qualification may not be recognised in other countries including in others of the four countries in the UK.

Banding   The structuring of a year group into divisions, each usually containing two or three classes, on grounds of general ability. Pupils are taught within the band for virtually all the curriculum. See also **Mixed ability grouping, Setting** and **Streaming**.

Baseline Testing   Any process that sets out to find out what the learner can do now in relation to the next stage of learning. For example, the assessment of practical skills and familiarity of pupils with equipment and tools prior to a **D and T** course, or the assessment of pupils in Year 1 and reception classes for speaking, listening, reading, writing, mathematics, social skills. See also **Benchmarking**.

BEd   Bachelor of Education, a teacher training qualification in England leading to **QTS**.

Benchmarking   A term used to describe a standard against which comparisons can be made. Can be used by schools, e.g. to measure success of the school in public examinations relative to a national norm.

BESD   Behavioural, Emotional and Social Difficulties. A group of pupils with special educational needs. The term is often applied to pupils whose behaviour is consistently poor and not obviously related to the circumstances and environment in which pupils find themselves. Pupils who are withdrawn also fit into this category. See also **SEN, SEND**.

BTEC   Business and Technician Education Council. Part of **EdExcel Foundation**, which offers courses called BTEC Nationals.

C and G   City and Guilds; see **AQA**.

Career Entry and Development Profile (CEDP)   All **ITT** providers in England are required to provide newly qualified teachers with a **CEDP** to help newly qualified teachers in their first teaching post schools and support **induction**. Details available on line at <.https://www.education.gov. uk/publications/eOrderingDownload/cepd_2011-12_tda0876.pdf >.

Careers Education   Designed to help pupils to choose and prepare for opportunities, responsibilities and experiences in education, training and employment. See National Careers Service: https:// nationalcareersservice.direct.gov.uk/

CPD   Continuing professional development.

CEDP   See **Career entry and development profile**.

CEHR   Commission for Equality and Human Rights; also referred to as Equality and Human Rights Commission.   http://www.equalityhumanrights.com/

Certificate of Achievement (COA)   An examination designed to give a qualification to pupils who may not gain a GCSE grade, offered by the **Awarding Bodies**. Also called **Entry Level Certificate**; see *Directgov* website.

Church and Faith Schools   A faith school is a British school teaching a general curriculum but with a particular religious character, or having formal links with a religious organisation. Regulations differ in detail among constituent countries of Britain. In England, the curriculum, admissions criteria and staffing policies may reflect their religious foundation. See also **State Maintained Schools in England** and **Other State Schools in England.**

Citizenship   A statutory subject of the English **NC** at **Key Stages** 3 and 4. See also **Cross-curricular** elements. See researchbriefings.files.parliament.uk/documents/SN06798/SN06798.pdf

Collaborative group   A way of working in which groups of children are assigned to groups or engage spontaneously in working together to solve problems; sometimes called co-operative group work. See the now archived DCFS Standards website *Grouping pupils for success*. http:// webarchive.nationalarchives.gov.uk/20110809101133/nsonline.org.uk/node/84974

Combined course   A course to which several subjects contribute while retaining their distinct identity (e.g. history, geography and RE within humanities). See also **Integrated Course.**

Comprehensive school   A type of state maintained secondary school which admits pupils of age 11 to 16 or 19 from a given catchment area, regardless of their ability. See also **State Maintained Schools in England** and **Other State Schools in England.**

Community and Foundation special schools For children with specific special educational needs, such as physical or learning difficulties. See also **State Maintained Schools in England** and **Other State Schools in England**.

Community of practice Groups of people who share a concern for something or have knowledge and skills to share. For example, a subject association network or a network of teachers working on solving a particular problem.

Community School A school run by the **LA**, which employs the staff, owns the land and buildings and decides admission criteria. Develops links with community. See also **State Maintained Schools in England** and **Other State Schools in England**.

Continuity A feature of a curriculum and of lesson plans that ensure that learning builds on what has already been taught and experienced and prepares pupils for what is to come. See also **Progression**.

Core skills Skills required by all students following 14-19 courses. See **Functional Skills** and **Personal Learning and Thinking Skills**.

Core subjects Foundation subjects that are taught at both KS3 and KS4 comprising English, Mathematics and Science in the National Curriculum for England. See also **Entitlement subjects.** See also researchbriefings.files.parliament.uk/documents/SN06798/SN06798.pdf

Coursework Work carried out by pupils during a course of study marked by teachers and contributing to the final examination mark. Usually externally moderated.

CPD Continuing professional development.

CRE Commission for Racial Equality; now part of **CEHR**.

Criterion-referenced assessment A process in which performance is measured by relating candidates' responses to pre-determined criteria. See also **Assessment, Assessment for learning, Assessment of learning, Formative assessment, Ipsative assessment, Norm-referenced assessment** and **Summative assessment.**

Cross-curricular elements Additional elements of a curriculum beyond statutory subjects which in England includes careers, **citizenship**, economic education, **key skills**, **personal learning and thinking skills (PLTS)** and personal, social and health education (**PSHE**).

Curriculum A course of study followed by a pupil.

Curriculum guidelines Written guidance for organizing and teaching a particular subject or area of the curriculum. See also **Programmes of Study**.

Church and Faith schools Similar to other **State Maintained Schools** but follow a locally agreed religious education curriculum and have religion-centred admissions criteria and staffing policies. See **Other State Schools in England**.

DCELLS Department for Children, Education, Lifelong Learning and Skills of the Welsh Assembly. **http://www.accreditedqualifications.org.uk/department-for-children-education-lifelong-learning-and-skills-dcells.html**

DES, DfE, DfEE, DfES, DCSF Various names for the ministry of education in England. See **Government education departments and chronology**

Differentiation The matching of work to the differing capabilities and learning needs of individuals or groups of pupils in order to extend their learning.

Disapplication Arrangement for lifting part or all of the **NC** in England requirements for individuals or for any other grouping specified by the Secretary of State.

EAL English as an Additional Language.

EBDD Emotional and behavioural difficulties and disorders. Used with reference to pupils with such difficulties or schools/units that cater for such pupils.

EdExcel Foundation An **awarding body.** Online http://www.edexcel.org.uk

Education welfare officer (EWO) An official of the **LA** concerned with pupils' attendance and with liaison between the school, the parents and the authority.

Entitlement subjects (in English NC) Non-statutory subjects in four curriculum areas, Arts, Design and Technology, Humanities and Modern Foreign Languages (see 'about the School Curriculum: what is statutory?' on DfE website).

Entry Level See **National Qualifications framework;** see **Certificate of achievement. See https ://www.gov.uk/what-different-qualification-levels-mean**

ESL English as a second language.

Exclusion Headteachers of **state maintained schools** and **other state schools** in England are empowered to exclude pupils temporarily or permanently when faced with a serious breach of their disciplinary code. The exclusions are either a fixed term or permanent. Schools may send pupils to a **pupil referral unit (PRU)**.

EYFS Early Years Foundation Stage   (of the **NC** for England).

Formative assessment   Also, assessment for learning, linked to teaching when the evidence from assessment is used to adapt teaching to meet pupil's learning needs. See also **Assessment, Assessment for learning, Assessment of learning, Criterion-referenced assessment, Ipsative assessment, Norm-referenced assessment** and **Summative assessment**.

Forms of entry (FE)   The number of forms (e.g. of 30 pupils) that a school takes into its intake year. From this can be estimated the size of the intake year and the size of the school.

Foundation schools   The governing body of these schools employs the staff and sets the admissions criteria. The school land and buildings are owned by the governing body or a charitable foundation. See **State Maintained Schools** and **Other State Schools in England**.

Functional Skills   Functional skills in the **NC** for England are those core elements of English, Mathematics and **ICT** that provide individuals with the skills and abilities they need to operate confidently, effectively and independently in life, their communities and work. They can be examined individually. See *Directgov* website.

Foundation subjects   Subjects that **state maintained schools** are required by law to teach. In England, four **foundation subjects** are designated **core subjects**. Different subjects are compulsory at different **Key Stages** in England. See **Basic curriculum, Core subjects, Entitlement subjects.**

Free Schools   In England, a political initiative to set up independent, state-funded schools, non-selective and outside **LA** control, established in 2010 under the **Academies Act**. Free schools are set up by parents, teachers, charities or businesses. Grants are available to support the initial setting-up process. They are subject to the Schools Admissions Code of Practice, but priority is given to founders' children. In time, subject to **Ofsted** inspection. See also **State Maintained Schools in England** and **Other State Schools in England**.

GCE   General Certificate of Education – Also called Advanced Level of the GCE. An award after two years of study usually post **GCSE**. Comprises two awards; an AS level taken after one year of study and A2 level after two years of study.

GCSE   General Certificate of Secondary Education.

GNVQ   General National Vocational Qualifications.

Government education department titles   and chronology For England and Wales to 2006, then England.

DES   (Department of Education and Science) Pre-1992

DfE   (Department for Education) 1992–1995; title reappeared 2010–present.

DfEE   (Department for Education and Employment) 1995–2001.

DfES   (Department for Education and Skills) 2001–2007.

DCSF   (Department for Children, Schools and Families) 2007–2010.

Grade-related criteria   The identification of criteria, the achievement of which are related to different levels of performance by the candidate.

Grammar schools   State maintained or independent schools that select all or almost all of their pupils based on academic ability, usually through the 11 plus examination. Parents often pay for extra tuition to give their children a higher chance of being admitted. See also **State Maintained Schools in England** and **Other State Schools in England**.

Group work   A way of organizing pupils where the teacher assigns tasks to groups of pupils, to be undertaken collectively; although, the work is completed on an individual basis.

GTC   General Teaching Council for England. Closed 2010 and duties taken over by **National College of Teaching and Leadership (NCTL)**. Northern Ireland, Scotland and Wales have their own teaching councils.

HEI   Higher Education Institution.

HMCI   Her Majesty's Chief Inspector of Schools in England.

HMI   Her Majesty's Inspectors of Schools in England.

House system   A structure for pastoral care/pupil welfare within a school in which pupils are grouped in vertical units, i.e. sections of the school that include pupils from all year groups. Alternative to the **year system**.

IB International Baccalaureate. A post-16 qualification designed for university entrance.

In-class support Support within a lesson provided by an additional teacher, often with expertise in teaching pupils with special educational, disability or language needs. See also **Learning support, Learning support assistant, Partnership teaching, Withdrawal**.

Inclusion Inclusion involves the processes of increasing the participation of pupils in, and reducing their exclusion from, schools. Inclusion is concerned with the learning participation of all pupils vulnerable to exclusionary pressures, not only those with impairments or categorised as having special educational needs.

Independent school A private school that receives no state assistance but is financed by fees. Often registered as a charity. See also **Public school**.

Induction For teachers, the first stage of **continuing professional development** (**CPD**). A statutory requirement for newly qualified teachers (**NQTs**) in England in the first year of teaching. Successful completion of induction requires NQTs to meet standards set by the regulatory body in the country in which they wish to practice.

Integrated course A course, usually in a secondary school, to which several subjects contribute without retaining their distinct identity (e.g. integrated humanities, which explores themes which include aspects of geography, history and RE). See also **Combined course**.

Integration Educating children with special educational needs together with children without special educational needs in mainstream schools: see **Inclusion**

Ipsative assessment A process in which performance is measured against previous performance by the same person. See also **Assessment, Assessment for learning, Assessment of learning, Criterion-referenced assessment, Formative assessment, Norm-referenced assessment,** and **Summative assessment.**

ITE Initial Teacher Education

ITT Initial Teacher Training.

ITTE Initial Teacher Training and Education.

Key Skills See **Functional skills** and **Personal Learning and Thinking Skills**.

Key Stages (KS) England The periods in each pupil's education to which the elements of the **NC** for England apply. There are four **Key Stages**, normally related to the age of the majority of the pupils in a teaching group. They are: Key Stage 1, beginning of compulsory education to age 7 (Years R (Reception), 1 and 2); Key Stage 2, ages 7-11 (Years 3-6); Key Stage 3, ages 11-14 (years 7- 9); Key Stage 4, 14 to end of compulsory education (Years 10 and 11). Post-16 is a further Key Stage.

LA see **Local Authority**

Language support teacher A teacher provided by the **LA** or school to enhance language work with particular groups of pupils.

Learning objectives What pupils are expected to have learned as a result of an activity, lesson or topic.

Learning outcomes Assessable learning objectives; the action or behaviour of pupils that provides evidence that they have met the learning objectives.

Learning support A means of providing extra help for pupils, usually those with learning difficulties, e.g. through a specialist teacher or specially designed materials. See also **Learning support assistants, In-class support, Partnership teaching, Withdrawal.**

Learning support assistants Teachers who give additional support for a variety of purposes, e.g. general learning support for pupils with **SEND** or **ESL**; most support is given in-class although sometimes pupils are withdrawn from class. See also **Learning support, In-class support, partnership teaching, Withdrawal.**

Lesson plan The detailed planning of work to be undertaken in a lesson. This follows a particular structure, appropriate to the demands of a particular lesson. An individual lesson plan is usually part of a series of lessons in a **Unit of work**.

Level Description (NC for England) A statement describing the types and range of performance that pupils working at a particular level should characteristically demonstrate. Level descriptions have been removed in the latest version of the NC (2014). Level descriptions provide the basis for making judgements about pupils' performance at the end of **Key Stages** 1, 2 and 3. At Key Stage 4, national qualifications are the main means of assessing attainment in National Curriculum subjects.

Levels of attainment in England   Eight levels of attainment, plus exceptional performance, are defined within the National Curriculum **attainment targets** in England. These stop at **Key Stage** 3; see **Level description**.

Local Authority (LA)   An LA has responsibility for local services, including education, libraries and social services. It has a statutory duty to provide education in their area. Many schools have opted out of LA control, see e.g. **Academies** and **Free schools**.

Maintained boarding schools   State funded schools that offer free tuition but charge fees for board and lodging. See also **State Maintained Schools in England** and **Other State Schools in England.**

Middle school   A school that caters for pupils aged from 8–12 or 9–13 years of age. They are classified legally as either primary or secondary schools depending on whether the preponderance of pupils in the school is under or over 11 years of age.

Minority ethnic groups   Pupils, many of whom have been born in the United Kingdom, from other ethnic heritages, e.g. those of Asian heritage from Bangladesh, China, Pakistan, India or East Africa, those of African or Caribbean heritage or from countries in the European Union.

Mixed ability grouping   Teaching group containing pupils representative of the range of ability within the school. See also **Banding**, **Setting**, **Streaming**.

Moderation   An exercise involving teachers representing an awarding body external to the school whose purpose is to check that standards are comparable across schools and teachers. Usually carried out by sampling coursework or examination papers.

Moderator   An examiner who monitors marking and examining to ensure that standards are consistent in a number of schools and colleges.

Module   A definable section of work of fixed length with specific learning objectives and usually with some form of terminal assessment. Several such units may constitute a modular course.

National Assessment Agency (NAA)   Set up as a separate body by QCA in 2004 to deliver and administer **National Curriculum tests**. Closed 2008 and functions subsumed into **QCA**. Later **QCDA** and **STA**.

NC (National Curriculum) for some schools only in England. https://www.gov.uk/national-curriculum. The **core** and other **foundation** subjects and their associated **attainment targets, programmes of study** and assessment arrangements of the curriculum.

National Curriculum Tests   formerly **Standard Assessment Tasks (q.v.).**

National Qualifications Framework (NQF)   A framework that links academic and vocational qualifications and shows their equivalence at several levels of attainment. See **also Awarding Bodies, Vocational Courses, GNVQ, NVQ**. See Directgov website at https://www.gov.uk/what-different-qualification-levels-mean

NEAB   See **AQA.**

NFER   National Foundation for Educational Research. Carries out research and produces educational diagnostic tests.

Non-contact time   Time provided by a school for a teacher to prepare work or carry out assigned responsibilities other than direct teaching.

Norm-referenced assessment   A process in which performance is measured by comparing candidates' responses. Individual success is relative to the performance of all other candidates. See also **Assessment, Assessment for learning, Assessment of learning, Criterion-referenced assessment, Formative assessment, Ipsative assessment, Summative assessment.**

NQT   Newly qualified teacher.

NSG   Non-statutory guidance (**NC** in England). Additional subject guidance but which is not mandatory; to be found attached to National Curriculum Subject Orders such as PSHE, Citizenship.

NVQ   National Vocational Qualifications.

OCR   Oxford and Cambridge Regional **awarding body**. Online <http://www.ocr.org.uk>.

OFQUAL   Set up in 2008. Regulator of examinations and tests in England, taking over that aspect of **QCA**. Independent (of **DfE** ministers) and responsible directly to parliament. https://www.gov.uk/government/organisations/ofqual

OFSTED   Office for Standards in Education. Non-ministerial government department established under the Education (Schools) Act (1992) to take responsibility for the inspection of schools in England. OFSTED inspects pre-school provision, further education, teacher education institutions and **local authorities. Her Majesty's Inspectors (HMI)** form the professional arm of OFSTED. See also OHMCI.

OHMCI Office of Her Majesty's Chief Inspector (Wales). Non-ministerial government department established under the Education (Schools) Act (1992) to take responsibility for the inspection of schools in Wales. **Her Majesty's Inspectors (HMI)** form the professional arm of OHMCI. See also **OFSTED.**

Other State Schools in England These include **academies, community and foundation special** schools, **church and faith** schools (see **Voluntary schools**), **free** schools, **grammar** schools, **maintained boarding** schools, **specialist** schools and **pupil referral units**. See *Directgov* website. See also **State Maintained Schools in England.**

PANDA See **Raiseonline.**

Parent Under section 576 of the Education Act 1996 a parent includes any person who is not a parent of the child but has parental responsibility (see **Parental Responsibility**), or who cares for the child.

Parental responsibility Under section 2 of the Children Act 1989, parental responsibility falls upon:

- all mothers and fathers who were married to each other at the time of the child's birth (including those who have since separated or divorced);
- mothers who were not married to the father at the time of the child's birth;
- and fathers who were not married to the mother at the time of the child's birth, but who have obtained parental responsibility either by agreement with the child's mother or through a court order. Under section 12 of the Children Act 1989, where a court makes a residence order in favour of any person who is not the parent or guardian of the child that person has parental responsibility for the child while the residence order remains in force.

Partnership teaching An increasingly common means of meeting the language needs of bilingual pupils in which support and class teachers plan and implement together a specially devised programme of in-class teaching and learning. See also **Learning support, Learning support assistants, In-class support, Withdrawal.**

Pastoral care Those aspects of a school's work and structures concerned to promote the general welfare of all pupils, particularly their academic, personal and social development, their attendance and behaviour.

PAT Pupil Achievement Tracker. Now part of **Raiseonline.**

Pedagogic content knowledge The skills to transform subject knowledge into suitable learning activities for a particular group of pupils.

PGCE Post Graduate Certificate in Education. The main qualification for secondary school teachers in England and Wales recognised by the **DfE** for **QTS.**

Policy An agreed school statement relating to a particular area of its life and work.

PoS See **Programmes of Study.**

Pre-vocational courses Courses specifically designed and taught to help pupils to prepare for employment.

Profile Samples of work of pupils, used to illustrate progress, with or without added comments by teachers' and/or pupils.

Programme of study (PoS) for NC in England The subject matter, skills and processes that must be taught to pupils during each **Key Stage** in order that they may meet the objectives set out in **attainment targets**. They provide the basis for planning **schemes of work.**

Progression The planned development of pupils' knowledge, skills, understanding and attitudes over time. See also **Continuity.**

Project An investigation with a particular focus undertaken by individuals or small groups of pupils leading to a written, oral or graphic presentation of the outcome.

PSE Personal and social education.

PSHCE Is **PSHE** with a specific, additional **citizenship** component.

PSHE Personal, social, health and education, a non-statutory subject in the English National Curriculum. See also **PSHCE.**

PSHEE   is **PSHE** with a specific additional economic component.

PTA   Parent-teacher association. Voluntary grouping of parents and school staff to support the school in a variety of ways.

PTR Pupil: Teacher Ratio. The ratio of pupils to teachers within a school or group of schools (e.g. 17.4:1).

Public school Independent school   not state funded. So-called because at their inception they were funded by public charity.

Pupil referral units (PRUs)   For children of compulsory school age who may otherwise not receive suitable education, focusing on getting them back into a mainstream school.

Pupil Achievement Tracker (PAT),   see **RAISEonline**.

QCA   The Qualifications and Curriculum Authority. Initiated in 1997 by the merger of **SCAA** and National Council for Vocational Qualifications **(NCVQ)**. Was responsible for overview of the curriculum, assessment and qualifications across the whole of education and training, from pre-school to higher vocational levels. QCA advised the Secretary of State for education on such matters. Aspects of assessment were delegated by QCA to the **NAA**. Dissolved in 2010 the responsibilities shared between **QCDA** and **Ofqual**. The Welsh equivalent of QCA was **ACCAC,** later **DCELLS**.

QCDA   Qualification, Curriculum and Development Agency. Formerly QCA. Set up in 2008. Responsible for the **National Curriculum** and associated assessments, tests examinations. Dissolved in 2012, its functions taken over by the **Standards and Testing Agency (STA).**

QTS   Qualified teacher status. This is usually attained by completion of a Post Graduate Certificate in Education (**PGCE**) or a Bachelor of Education (**BEd**) degree or a Bachelor of Arts/Science degree with Qualified Teacher Status (**BA/BSc (QTS)**). There are other routes into teaching.

RAISEonline   Closed 2017 Reporting and Analysis for Improvement through School Self-Evaluation. In England it provides interactive analysis of school and pupil performance data. It replaces the OFSTED Performance and Assessment (**PANDA**) reports and the Pupil Achievement Tracker **(PAT).** See replacement ideas on DfE website at <https://www.raiseonline.org/login.aspx?ReturnUrl=%2f>.

Record of achievement (ROA)   Cumulative record of a pupil's academic, personal and social progress over a stage of education.

Reliability   A measure of the consistency of the assessment or test item; i.e. the extent to which the test gives repeatable results. See also **Validity**.

RSA   Royal Society of Arts.

SACRE   The Standing Advisory Council on Religious Education in each LA to advise the LA on matters connected with religious education and collective worship, particularly methods of teaching, the choice of teaching materials and the provision of teacher training.

SATs   See **Standard Assessment Tasks**.

Scheme of work   A planned course of study over a period of time (e.g. a **Key Stage** or a Year). In England it contains knowledge, skills and processes derived from the **programmes of study** and **attainment targets** together with **units of work** and **lesson plans**.

School Improvement Plan (SIP)   A coherent plan, required to be made by a school, identifying improvements needed in curriculum, organisation, staffing and resources and setting out action needed to make those improvements.

SEG   See **AQA**.

SEN (Special Educational Needs)   Children have special educational needs if they have a *learning difficulty*. Children have a *learning difficulty* if they:

■ have a significantly greater difficulty in learning than the majority of children of the same age; or

■ have a disability that prevents or hinders them from making use of educational facilities of a kind generally provided for children of the same age in schools within the area of the local authority;

■ are under compulsory school age and fall within the definition at (a) or (b) above or would so do if special educational provision was not made for them. Very able or gifted pupils are not included in SEN. See also **SEND, SENCO**.

SENCO   Special Educational Needs Coordinator in schools. See also **SEN, SEND.**

SEN Code of Practice   Act of Parliament describing and prescribing the regulations for the support of pupils with SEN

SEND   Special Educational Needs and/or Disability. In England a widening of the scope of **SEN** (Ofsted 2010).

Setting   The grouping of pupils according to their ability in a subject for lessons in that subject. See also **banding, mixed ability grouping, streaming.**

Short course   A course in a National Curriculum foundation subject in **Key Stage** 4, which, by itself, does not lead to a full **GCSE** or equivalent qualification. Two short courses in different subjects may be combined to form one full GCSE or equivalent course.

Sixth Form College   A post-16 institution for 16-19-year-olds. It offers **GCSE, GCE A level** and **vocational courses.**

SLD   Specific learning difficulties.

SOA   Statements of attainment (of **NC** subjects).

Special school   See **Community and Foundation special schools.**

Specialist schools   Teach the whole curriculum but with a focus on one subject area such as: arts; business and enterprise; engineering; humanities; language; mathematics and computing; music; science; sports; technology. See **Other State Schools in England.**

STA (Standards and Testing Agency)   An executive agency of the **DfE** set up in 2011. It is responsible for the development and delivery of all statutory assessments from early years to the end of Key Stage 3, which formerly were carried out by **QCDA** (dissolved in March 2012).

Standard Assessment Tasks (SATs)   Externally prescribed **National Curriculum for England** assessments that incorporate a variety of assessment methods depending on the subject and **Key Stage.** The term SAT is not now widely used, having been replaced by '**National Curriculum Tests**', overseen by **STA.**

State Maintained Schools   In England there are four main types of schools, **community** schools, **foundation and trust** schools, **voluntary-aided** and **voluntary controlled** schools. All are funded by **LA** and/or central government. Many of these schools admit pupils from a wide range of ability; see **Comprehensive** schools. Within the four categories are schools with special characteristics; see **Other State Maintained Schools in England.**

Statements of special educational needs   Provided under the 1981 Education Act and subsequent Acts to ensure appropriate provision for pupils formally assessed as having **SEN.** See **SEN Code of Practice** and **SEND.**

Statutory order   A statutory instrument which is regarded as an extension of an Act, enabling provisions of the Act to be augmented or updated.

Streaming   The organisation of pupils according to general ability into classes in which they are taught for all subjects and courses. See also **Banding, Mixed ability grouping, Setting.**

Summative assessment   Assessment linked to the end of a course of study; it sums up achievement in aggregate terms and is used to rank, grade or compare pupils, groups or schools. It uses a narrow range of methods which are efficient and reliable, normally formal, i.e. under examination conditions. See also **Assessment, Assessment for learning, Assessment of learning, Formative assessment, Ipsative assessment,** and **Norm-referenced assessment.**

Supply teacher   Teachers appointed temporarily to fill vacancies.

Support Teacher   See **In-class support** and **Learning support.**

TA   Teaching Agency. Set up in 2012. Responsible for the initial and in-service training of teachers and other school staff in England. Comprises the former bodies **TDA, General Teaching Council for England** and **QCDA.**

TDA   Training and Development Agency for schools for England. Set up in 2005, closed 2010, replacing the **Teacher Training Agency,** now replaced by the **Teaching Regulation Agency.** The TDA had a remit for overseeing standards and qualifications across the school workforce and supporting the quality of teacher training.

Teacher Assessments   **Assessments** made by teachers alongside **National Curriculum Tests** at some **Key Stages** in England.

Teacher's record book   A book in which teachers plan and record teaching and learning for their classes on a regular basis.

Team teaching   The teaching of a number of classes simultaneously by teachers acting as a team. They usually divide the work between them, allowing those with particular expertise to lead different parts of the work, the others supporting the follow-up work with groups or individuals. See also **In-class support, Learning support, Partnership teaching.**

Thinking skills   Additional skills to be promoted in lessons. See also **Cross-curricular elements.**

T Levels (Technical Levels)   These are for vocational courses, which will be on a par with A levels and will provide young people with a choice between technical and academic education post-16. They start in 2020. https://www.gov.uk/government/news/new-t-levels-mark-a-revolution-in-technical-education

Travellers   A term used to cover those communities, some of which have minority ethnic status, and either are or have been traditionally associated with a nomadic lifestyle, and include gypsy travellers, fairground or show people, circus families, New Age travellers, and bargees.

Traveller education   The development of policy and provision that provides traveller children with unhindered access to and full integration in mainstream education.

Trust schools   A **foundation school** supported by a charitable foundation or trust, which appoints school governors. A trust school employs its own staff, manages its own land and assets, and sets its own admissions criteria.

Tutor group   Grouping of secondary pupils for registration and pastoral care purposes.

Unit of work   Medium-term planning of work for pupils over half a term or a number of weeks. The number of lessons in a unit of work may vary according to each school's organisation. A unit of work usually introduces a new aspect of learning. Units of work derive from **schemes of work** and are the basis for **lesson plans**.

Validity   A measure of whether the assessment measures what it is meant to measure – often determined by consensus. Certain kinds of skills and abilities are extremely difficult to assess with validity via simple pencil and paper tests. See also **Reliability.**

Vocational courses   Programmes of study leading to vocational qualifications that are work-related preparing learners for employment. **Awarding Bodies** offer vocational courses. See also **NVQ, GNVQ, BTEC, National Qualifications**.

Voluntary-aided school   Often religious schools. The governing body, often a religious organisation, employs the staff and sets admissions criteria. The school land and buildings are also owned by a charitable foundation. See also **State Maintained Schools in England** and **Other State Schools in England.**

Voluntary-controlled school   Mainly religious or 'faith' schools but run by the LA. The land and buildings are often owned by a charitable foundation, but the LA employs the staff and has primary responsibility for admission arrangements. See also **State Maintained Schools in England** and **Other State Schools in England.**

Voluntary school   School that receives financial assistance from the **LA**, but owned by a voluntary body, usually religious. See **State Maintained Schools in England** and **Other State Schools in England.**

Withdrawal   Removal of pupils with particular needs from class teaching in primary schools and from specified subjects in secondary schools for extra help individually or in small groups. In-class support is increasingly provided in preference to withdrawal. See also **Learning support, Learning support assistants, In-class support, Partnership teaching**.

WJEC   (Welsh Joint Education Committee) provides examinations, assessment, professional development, educational resources, support for adults who wish to learn Welsh and access to youth arts activities. It also provides examinations throughout England.

Work experience   The opportunity for secondary pupils to have experience of a work environment for one or two weeks, usually within school time, during which a pupil carries out a particular job or range of jobs more or less as would regular employees, although with emphasis on the educational aspects of the experience.

Year system   A structure for pastoral care/pupil welfare within a school in which pupils are grouped according to years, i.e. in groups spanning an age range of only one year. An alternative grouping is the **house system**.

Years 1–11   Year of schooling in England. Five-year-olds start at Year 1 (Y1) and progress through to Year 11 (Y11) at 16 years old. See **Key Stages** for details.

Appendix 2

Subject Associations and Teaching Councils

Teachers' Councils

England Chartered College of Teaching (developed in England in 2016) https://chartered.college (replacing the GTCE – General Teaching Council for England, closed by UK government 2011) http://webarchive.nationalarchives.gov.uk/20111213132132/http:/www.gtce.org.uk

Northern Ireland http://www.gtcni.org.uk/

Scotland http://www.gtcs.org.uk/home/home.aspx

Wales http://www.teachertrainingcymru.org/node/26

Subject Associations

The following associations are members of the UK Council for Subject Associations, which acts as a voice for subjects for government and for the press and public.

www.subjectassociations.org.uk

Association membership keeps you up to date through giving you access to specialist education conferences, workshops, professional development sessions and publications. Many associations have international links that aid knowledge flow from country to country.

See the Council for Subject Associations website for live links and further information.

All the URLs here were checked in July 2018.

Art and Design	
National Society for Education in Art and Design (NSEAD)	www.nsead.org
Assessment	
The Association for Achievement and Improvement through Assessment (AAIA)	www.aaia.org.uk
Citizenship	
Association for Citizenship Teaching (ACT)	www.teachingcitizenship.org.uk

Computing and Information Technology	
Technology, Pedagogy and Education Association (previously Information Technology in Teacher Education (ITTE))	www.itte.org.uk
Computing At School (CAS)	www.computingatschool.org.uk
Dance	
One Dance UK	www.onedanceuk.org
Design and Technology	
The Design and Technology Association	www.data.org.uk
Drama	
National Drama (ND)	www.nationaldrama.org.uk
English	
The English Association (EA)	www.le.ac.uk/engassoc
National Association for the Teaching of English (NATE)	www.nate.org.uk
United Kingdom Literacy Association (UKLA)	www.ukla.org
Geography	
The Geographical Association (GA)	www.geography.org.uk
Royal Geographical Society with IBG (RGS)	www.rgs.org
History	
The Historical Association (HA)	www.history.org.uk
Languages	
Association for Language Learning (ALL)	www.all-languages.org.uk
National Association for Language Development in the Curriculum (NALDIC)	www.naldic.org.uk
Mathematics	
Joint Mathematical Council of the United Kingdom	www.jmc.org.uk
Media	
Media Education Association (MEA)	www.themea.org.uk
Music	
Incorporated Society of Musicians	www.ism.org
UK Association for Music Education - Music Mark	www.musicmark.org.uk
Physical Education	
Association for Physical Education (afPE)	www.afpe.org.uk
PSHE	
PSHE Association	www.pshe-association.org.uk
Religious Education	
National Association of Teachers of Religious Education (NATRE)	www.natre.org.uk

Science	
Association for Science Education (ASE)	www.ase.org.uk
Special Educational Needs	
NASEN	www.nasen.org.uk
Professional Association of Teachers of Students with Specific Learning Difficulties (Patoss)	www.patoss-dyslexia.org

Appendix 3
Useful websites

Providers of web resources for teachers do so for a range of purposes. Some sites are professional, such as subject associations sharing knowledge between professionals, others explicitly support government policy, so advice may be changed or withdrawn on ideological grounds, and others are designed to sell you products. The list below includes websites from:

- Professional Associations, Teaching Councils and Unions (see also Appendix 2);
- Charities and University Research Centres and social enterprises;
- Government funded organisations, and;
- Private companies.

For the most part, we have excluded websites apparently linked with just one individual. Exceptions are where the individuals have clearly researched and published widely in the area.

There are formal and informal networks on various social media sites including: Facebook, LinkedIn and Twitter.

You are advised to check the reliability of any advice – on the web or in print. For teaching to be an evidence-informed profession, teachers need to know the strength of evidence for any pedagogical intervention. By strength of evidence we mean:

- Methods and ethics: has the advice been gathered by ethical (see the BERA ethical code www.bera.ac.uk) and reliable research methods (See Unit 5.4 and Patterson's MESHGuides). Usual research instruments are interviews, questionnaires, documentary analysis and observation but there is huge variation of options within each instrument.
- Independence: were the researchers independent? Who funded the research? Were researchers free to publish adverse findings?
- Quality assurance: has the advice been independently peer-reviewed? Peer review, by an independent panel of educators, is the normal form of quality assurance used for professional association and professional journal sites. Materials from other sites may or may not be peer reviewed.
- Sample: what is the size and type of the sample used to provide the evidence? What confidence does this give you in the results?

■ Transferability: how transferable is the advice likely to be? How similar is the research context to your context? This is not at all to say you reject research and evidence from contexts different to your own, but just that you need to bring your professional judgement to bear in applying the findings. Teachers in many countries face similar challenges in maximising the learning of young people and there is a lot to learn from solutions elsewhere.

> All websites listed here were accessed in July 2018.
> Further information is given only where it is not obvious what the website offers.
> The list starts with generic websites followed by a list of sites grouped alphabetically by theme, e.g. Behaviour, Neuroscience, Subject Associations, Unions.

Generic websites (covering a wide range of areas):

■ British Education Research Tool in Education (BERTIE): http://www.bathspa.ac.uk/static/bertie/bertie.html
■ Ed Talks: www.edtalks.org
■ Education Endowment Foundation: see EEF
■ Education Evidence Portal: www.eep.ac.uk (This is a search tool for specific sites but has not been updated since the 2012 decisions of the UK coalition government to close online services for teachers in England. It is useful for historical documents.)
■ Education-line: https://www.leeds.ac.uk/bei/COLN/COLN_default.html
■ Repository of British Education Research Association conferences research papers www.bera.ac.uk
■ EEF (Education Endowment Foundation): https://educationendowmentfoundation.org.uk/
■ ERIC – USA government Education Resources Information Center: http://eric.ed.gov/
■ European SchoolNet: www.eun.org
■ Evidence for Policy and Practice Information Centre: https://eppi.ioe.ac.uk/cms/This has a list of systematic reviews of practice in education.
■ Khan academy – Teaching videos: www.khanacademy.org/
■ MESHGuides (Mapping Education Specialist knowhow): www.meshguides.org
■ National STEM Centre: https://www.stem.org.uk/resources
■ Open University, Open Learn: http://www.open.edu/openlearnworks/course/view.php?id=1490%3F
■ Seneca Learning (www.senecalearning.com) free homework and revision platform
■ Stanford University Teaching Commons – Resources tab: https://teachingcommons.stanford.edu/
■ Teacher Education Observatory: http://teachereducationobservatory.org
■ TED-Ed Lessons Worth Sharing: http://ed.ted.com/
■ Times Educational Supplement: https://www.tes.co.uk/

UK Government:

■ England: Department for Education: www.education.gov.uk/ and inspection: Office for Standards in Education (Ofsted): www.ofsted.gov.uk
■ Northern Ireland: Department of Education Northern Ireland: www.deni.gov.uk and Inspection: The Education and Training Inspectorate Northern Ireland: www.etini.gov.uk/index/inspection-reports.htm

- Scotland: Education Scotland: http://www.educationscotland.gov.uk/index.asp and The Scottish Government: http://www.gov.scot/Topics/Statistics/Browse/School-Education
- Wales: Welsh Government: http://gov.wales/topics/educationandskills/%20?lang=en and Inspection: Estyn – the office of Her Majesty's Inspectorate for Education and Training in Wales: http://www.estyn.gov.uk/.
- YouTube: Teaching Channel and Teachers https://www.youtube.com/user/teachers https://www.youtube.com/user/TeachingChannel

Additional websites by theme:

A

Assessment for learning:

- see specialist MESHGuides www.meshguides.org and for example, Wiliam, D.:http://www.dylan-wiliam.org/Dylan_Wiliams_website/Welcome.html

Autism:

- National Autistic Society: www.nas.org.uk

B

Behaviour:
See DFE advice:

- (September 2014) https://www.gov.uk/government/policies/improving-behaviour-and-attendance-in-schools
- (April 2012) https://www.gov.uk/government/publications/behaviour-and-discipline-in-schools
- (July 2013) Behaviour checklist https://www.gov.uk/government/publications/behaviour-and-discipline-in-schools
- (July 2013) Guidance for governing bodies https://www.gov.uk/government/publications/behaviour-and-discipline-in-schools-guidance-for-governing-bodies
- (July 2013) Use of reasonable force https://www.gov.uk/government/publications/use-of-reasonable-force-in-schools
- (February 2014) Screening, searching and confiscation https://www.gov.uk/government/publications/searching-screening-and-confiscation
- (August 2013) Preventing and tackling bullying https://www.gov.uk/government/publications/preventing-and-tackling-bullying

C

Citizenship:

- British Humanist Association: www.humanism.org.uk/education/education-policy
- Citizenship Foundation: www.citizenshipfoundation.org.uk
- CitizED subject resource bank: www.citized.info
- Jubilee Centre for Character and Virtues: http://www.jubileecentre.ac.uk

Code of practice for teaching – See Teaching Councils
Curriculum – National requirements:

- England https://www.gov.uk/government/publications/national-curriculum-in-england-framework-for-key-stages-1-to-4/the-national-curriculum-in-england-framework-for-key-stages-1-to-4
- Northern Ireland http://www.nicurriculum.org.uk/
- Scotland   http://www.educationscotland.gov.uk/learningandteaching/thecurriculum/whatis curriculumforexcellence/
- Wales http://wales.gov.uk/topics/educationandskills/schoolshome/curriculuminwales/arevise dcurriculumforwales/?lang=en

D

Deaf and Hearing Impaired:

- National Deaf Children's Society: www.ndcs.org.uk;
  BATOD Foundation http://www.batodfoundation.org.uk/

Dialogic teaching:

- Alexander, R. (2015) http://www.robinalexander.org.uk/dialogic-teaching/
  University of Cambridge http://www.educ.cam.ac.uk/research/projects/dialogic/whatis.html

E

English as an additional language:

- Flynn, N., Pim, C. and Coles, S. (2015) *Teaching English as an Additional Language MESHGuide.* University of Winchester, UK: http://www.meshguides.org/guides/node/112
- Equal and Human Rights Commission (EHRC): www.equalityhumanrights.com
- Joseph Rowntree Foundation (focus: poverty and injustice): www.jrf.org.uk

Ethics:

- Professional – See Teaching Councils
- Research – See BERA.

Europe:

- European Schoolnet (EUN): www.eun.org

G

Gifted and Talented:

- National Association for Able Children in Education www.nace.co.uk

H

Handwriting:

- National Handwriting Association: www.nha-handwriting.org.uk

Health:

- British Nutrition Foundation: www.nutrition.org.uk.
- Food Standards Agency: www.eatwell.gov.uk.
- NICE (National Institute for Health and Care Excellence) https://www.nice.org.uk/guidance

I

Intelligence:

- Gardner, H. http://howardgardner.com/multiple-intelligences

L

Lesson Study:

- Dudley, P. http://lessonstudy.co.uk/about-us-pete-dudley/

Learning theories – See the specialist sites in this list:

- Claxton, G (2015) Building Learning Power http://www.buildinglearningpower.co.uk/

N

Names (remembering):

- Buzan: http://www.open.edu/openlearn/body-mind/psychology/buzan-on-how-remember-names-and-faces
- TeacherVision: https://www.teachervision.com/teaching-methods/classroom-management/6708.html

National Qualifications Framework (NQF):

- https://www.gov.uk/what-different-qualification-levels-mean

Neuroscience:

- Blakemore, S. http://www.ted.com/talks/sarah_jayne_blakemore_the_mysterious_workings_of_the_adolescent_brain?language=en
- Centre for Neuroscience in Education led by Professor Usha Goswami http://www.cne.psychol.cam.ac.uk/people/ucg10@cam.ac.uk
- Neuroscience for Kids: http://faculty.washington.edu/chudler/neurok.html
- Royal Society: http://royalsociety.org/policy/projects/brain-waves/education-lifelong-learning

- The Brain from Top to Bottom: http://thebrain.mcgill.ca
- The International Mind, Brain and Education Society: www.imbes.org

M

MESHGuides:

- www.meshguides.org: research summaries to support evidence-informed teaching.

P

Philosophy:

- Philosophy of Education, http://www.philosophy-of-education.org/resources/students/video-listing.html

Projects:

- collaborative projects across Europe - E-twinning: www.etwinning.net/en/pub/index.htm
- WebQuests UK: www.webquestuk.org.uk/

R

Risk:

- CLEAPSS http://www.cleapss.org.uk
- Eaton Vale Schools Activity Centre http://www.eatonvale.co.uk/schools/riskassessments.aspx
- Health and Safety Executive http://www.hse.gov.uk/risk/classroom-checklist.htm

Research methods/research ethics:

- British Educational Research Association (BERA): http://www.bera.ac.uk
- Patterson, E. (2016) *Research Methods 1: How to get started on a Literature Review* MESHGuide, University of Winchester. www.meshguides.org
- Patterson, E. (2016) *Research Methods 2: Developing your Research Design* MESHGuide, University of Winchester. www.meshguides.org
- Patterson, E. (2016) *Research Methods 3: Considering Ethics in your research* MESHGuide, University of Winchester. www.meshguides.org

S

- Safer Internet Day: https://www.saferinternetday.org
- SEND: see also deaf, dyslexia: NASEN (National Association for Special Educational Needs): www.nasen.org.uk/. and www.nasen.org.uk/onlinesendcpd/
- Blamires, M. and others (2014) *Special Educational Needs and Disability: Enabling Pupil Partici-pation MESHGuide*. http://www.meshguides.org/category/special-needs-2/enabling-pupil-partici pation-special-needs-2/

- The Professional Association of Teachers of Students with Specific Learning Difficulties (PATOSS): www.patoss-dyslexia.org
- Royal National Institute for the Blind: www.rnib.org.uk
- Subject Associations: are represented by the Council for Subject Associations www.subject associations.org.uk

T

Teacher Support Network:

- www.teachersupport.info (24-hour confidential counselling)

Teacher Standards:

- England: http://www.legislation.gov.uk/uksi/2003/1662/schedule/2/made
- Northern Ireland: http://www.deni.gov.uk/index/school-staff/teachers-teachinginnorthern ireland_pg.htm
- Scotland: http://www.gtcs.org.uk/standards/
- Wales: http://gov.wales/topics/educationandskills/publications/circulars/becomingateacher/?lang=en

Thinking – See also Dialogic teaching:

- Education Scotland, (2015) Skills in Practice: Thinking Skills http://www.educationscotland.gov.uk/resources/s/skillsinpracticethinkingskills/knowing.asp
- University of Cambridge Thinking Together http://thinkingtogether.educ.cam.ac.uk/ University of Cambridge/Professor Neil Mercer (2015) Thinking together
- http://thinkingtogether.educ.cam.ac.uk/resources/
- Transitions: http://www.dundee.ac.uk/eswce/research/resources/

U

- UK Council for Child Safety (UKCCIS): https://www.gov.uk/government/groups/uk-council-for-child-internet-safety-ukccis

Unions:

- Irish National Teachers' Organisation, Northern Ireland: www.into.ie/NI/
- National Association of Schoolmasters/Union of Women Teachers, England, Wales, Scotland and Northern Ireland: NASUWT www.nasuwt.org.uk/
- National Education Union https://neu.org.uk/best-atl-and-nut
- Scottish Secondary Teachers' Association, Scotland: www.ssta.org.uk
- The Educational Institute of Scotland (EIS), Scotland: www.eis.org.uk/
- Ulster Teachers Union, Northern Ireland: www.utu.edu/
- Voice, previously the Professional Association of Teachers, England, Wales and Northern Ireland: www.voicetheunion.org.uk/

References

Abercrombie, M.L. (1985) *The Anatomy of Judgement*, Harmondsworth: Pelican Books.

Addison, N. and Burgess, L. (eds.) (2007) *Learning to Teach Art and Design in the Secondary School: A Companion to School Experience*, 2nd Edition, Abingdon: Routledge.

Adey, P. (2008) *Let's Think Handbook: Cognitive Acceleration in the Primary School*, London: NFER Nelson.

Adey, P. and Serret, N. (2010) 'Science teaching and cognitive acceleration', in J. Osborne and J. Dillon (eds.) *Good Practice in Science Teaching: What Research Has to Say*, Maidenhead: Open University Press, pp. 82–107.

Adey, P. and Shayer, M. (2013) 'Piagetian approaches', in J. Hattie and E.M. Anderman (eds.) *International Guide to Student Achievement*, New York and Abingdon: Routledge, pp. 28–30.

Adeyemo, D.A. (2005) 'The buffering effect of emotional intelligence on the adjustment of secondary school students in transition', *Electronic Journal of Research in Educational Psychology*, 3(2), 79–90.

Adeyemo, D.A. (2010) 'Educational transition and emotional intelligence', in D. Jindal-Snape (ed.) *Educational Transitions: Moving Stories from Around the World*, New York: Routledge, pp. 33–47.

Akhlaq, M., Amjadz, M. and Mehmoda, K. (2010) 'An evaluation of the effects of stress on the job performance of secondary school teachers', *Journal of Law and Psychology*, September, 43–54.

Akos, P. (2004) 'Advice and student agency in the transition to middle school', *Research in Middle Level Education*, 27, 1–11.

Aldrich, R. (2006) *Lessons from History of Education: The Selected Works of Richard Aldrich*, London: Routledge.

Alexander, R. (2001) *Culture and Pedagogy: International Comparisons in Primary Education*, Oxford: Blackwell.

Alexander, R. (2004) *Towards Dialogic Teaching: Rethinking Classroom Talk*, Cambridge: Dialogos.

Alexander, R. (2008) *Essays on Pedagogy*, Abingdon: Routledge.

Alexander, R. (2015) *Dialogic Teaching*, viewed 10 November 2017, from http://www.robinalexander.org.uk/dialogic-teaching/

Alloway, T.P. and Alloway, R.G. (2015) *Understanding Working Memory*, 2nd Edition, London: Sage Publications.

Ames, C. (1992a) 'Achievement goals and the classroom motivational climate', in D.H. Schunk and J.L. Meece (eds.) *Student Perception in the Classroom*, Hillsdale, NJ: Erlbaum, pp. 327–348.

Ames, C. (1992b) 'Classrooms: goals, structures and student motivation', *Journal of Educational Psychology*, 84, 261–271.

Amos, J.-A. (1998) *Managing Your Time: What to Do and How to Do It in Order to Do More*, Oxford: How to Books.

Anderson, L., Krathwohl, D.A., Airasain, P.W., Cruickshank, K.A., Mayer, R.R., Pintrich, P.R., Raths, J. and Wittrock, M.C. (2001) *Taxonomy for Learning, Teaching and Assessing: A Revision of Bloom's Taxonomy of Educational Objectives*, New York: Longman.

Anderson, J. (1980) *Education and Inquiry*, Oxford: Basil Blackwell.

Anderson, M. (1992) *Intelligence and Development; a Cognitive Theory*, London: Blackwell.

Andrade, H. and Heritage, M. (2018) *Using Formative Assessment to Enhance Learning, Achievement and Academic Self-Regulation*, New York: Routledge.

Archer, L. (2008) 'The impossibility of minority ethnic educational "success"? An examination of the discourses of teachers and pupils in British secondary schools', *European Educational Research Journal*, 7(1), 89-107.

Archer, L. and Francis, B. (2007) *Understanding Minority Ethnic Achievement in Schools*, Abingdon, Oxon: Routledge.

ARG (Assessment Reform Group) (2006) *The Role of Teachers in the Assessment of Learning*, London: Institute of Education, University of London.

Arnold, M. (1869) *Culture and Anarchy: An Essay in Political and Social Criticism*, Oxford: Project Gutenberg.

Arter, J.A. and Jenkins, J.R. (1979) 'Differential diagnosis - prescriptive teaching: a critical appraisal', *Review of Educational Research*, 49, 517-555.

Atkinson, J.W. (1964) *An Introduction to Motivation*, Princeton, NJ: Van Nostrand.

Atkinson, R.C. and Shiffrin, R.M. (1968) 'Human memory: a proposed system and its control processes', in K.W. Spence and J.T. Spence (eds.) *The Psychology of Learning and Motivation: Advances in Research and Theory, Volume 2*, New York: Academic Press, pp. 742-775.

Ausubel, D.P. (1968) *Educational Psychology: A Cognitive View*, New York: Holt, Rinehart and Winston.

Avalos, B. (2011) 'Teacher professional development in teaching and teacher education over ten years', *Teaching and Teacher Education*, 27, 10-20.

Ayers, H. and Prytys, C. (2002) *An A-Z Practical Guide to Emotional and Behavioural Difficulties*, London: David Fulton Publishers.

Baggott la Velle, L.M. Watson, K.E. and Nichol, J.D. (2001) 'OtherScope – The virtual microscope – can the real learning experiences in practical science be simulated?' *International Journal of Healthcare Technology and Management*, 2(5/6), 539-556.

Ball, S.J. (2003a) *Class Strategies and the Education Market: The Middle Classes and Social Advantage*, London: RoutledgeFalmer.

Ball, S.J. (2003b) 'The teacher's soul and the terrors of performativity', *Journal of Education Policy*, 18(2), 215-228.

Bandura, A. (1969) *Social Learning and Personality Development*, London: Holt, Rinehart and Winston.

Bandura, A. (2006) 'Toward a psychology of human agency', *Perspectives on Psychological Science*, 1, 164-180.

Banks, F., Leach, J. and Moon, B. (1999) 'New understandings of teachers' pedagogic knowledge', in J. Leach and B. Moon (eds.) *Learners and Pedagogy*, London: Paul Chapman Publishing, pp. 89-110.

Bar-David, Y., Urkin, J. and Kozminsky, E. (2005) 'The effect of voluntary dehydration on cognitive functions of elementary school children', *Acta Paediatrica*, 94, 1667-1673.

Bar-Or, O., Dotan, R., Inbar, O., Rotshstein, A. and Zonder, H. (1980) 'Voluntary hypohydration in 10 to 12 year old boys', *Journal of Applied Physiology*, 48, 104-108.

Barber, M. and Mourshed, M. (2007) *How the World's Best Performing School Systems Come out on Top*, McKinsey and Company, viewed 8 June 2018, from https://www.mckinsey.com/industries/social-sector/our-insights/how-the-worlds-best-performing-school-systems-come-out-on-top

Barnes, D. (1986) 'Language in the secondary classroom', in D. Barnes, J. Britton and M. Torbe (eds.) *Language the Learner and the School*, Harmondsworth: Penguin, pp. 206-221.

Barnes, I. and Harris, S. (2006) *Special Series on Personalised Learning: An Overview of the Summary Report Findings*, Nottingham: NCSL.

Barnett, R. (1994) *The Limits of Competence*, Maidenhead: Society for Research in Higher Education/Open University Press.

Barnett, R. (1997) *Higher Education, a Critical Business*, Maidenhead: Society for Research in Higher Education/Open University Press.

Barraclough, N. (2015) *First Aid Made Easy*, Bradford: Qualsafe Limited.

Barrow, R. and Woods, R. (1988) *An Introduction to the Philosophy of Education*, London: Routledge.

Bartlett, S.J. and Burton, D.M. (2016) *Introduction to Education Studies*, 4th Edition, London: Sage Publishing.

Bartlett, S. Burton, D. and Peim, N. (2001) *Introduction to Education Studies*, London: Paul Chapman Publishing.

Bartolo, P.A., Janik, I., Janikova, V., Hofsäss, T., Koinzer, P., Vilkiene, V., Calleja, C., Cefai, C., Chetcuti, D., Ale, P., Mol Lous, A., Wetso, G. M. and Humphrey, N. (2007) *Responding to Student Diversity: Teacher's Handbook*, Malta: University of Malta.

Barton, G. (2010) *Grammar Survival: A Teacher's Toolkit*, Abingdon: Routledge.

Battisch, V., Solomon, D. and Watson, M. (1998) 'Sense of community as a mediating factor in promoting children's social and ethical development', Paper presented at the meeting of the American Educational Research Association, San Diego, CA, April 1998, viewed 29 October 2017, from http://tigger.uic.edu/~ln ucci/MoralEd/articles/battistich.html

BBC (British Broadcasting Corporation) *Assessment for Learning*, viewed 11 April 2018 from http://www.bbc.co.uk/northernireland/forteachers/curriculum_in_action/assessment_for_learning.shtml

Becker, W.C., Madsen, C.H., Arnold, C.R. and Thomas, D.R. (1967) 'Contingent use of teacher attention and praise in reducing classroom behavior problems', *Journal of Special Education*, 1(3), 287–307.

Bee, H. and Boyd, D. (2013) *The Developing Child*, 13th Edition, Boston: Pearson Education.

Beghetto, R.A. and Kaufman, J.C. (eds.) (2010) *Nurturing Creativity in the Classroom*, Cambridge: Cambridge University Press.

Bell, J. and Waters, S. (2014) *Doing Your Research Project: A Guide for First Time Researchers*, 6th Edition, Maidenhead: McGraw-Hill.

Beltman, S., Mansfield, C. and Price, A. (2011) 'Thriving not just surviving: A review of research on teacher resilience', *Educational Research Review*, 6(3), 185–207.

Bennett, T. (2017a) *Creating a Culture: How School Leaders Can Optimise Behaviour*, London: DfE.

Bennett, T. (2017b) *Tom Bennett's School Report*, viewed 3 October 2017, from http://behaviourguru.blogspot. co.uk/2017/10/better-behaviour-benefits-everyone-why.html

Bennett, T. (2018) *Behaviour*, viewed 8 July 2018, from http://behaviourguru.blogspot.com/

Benson, P. (2001) *Teaching and Researching Autonomy in Language Learning*, Harlow: Longman.

BERA (British Educational Research Association) (2011) *Ethical Guidelines for Educational Research*, London: BERA, viewed 9 February 2019, from https://www.bera.ac.uk/wp-content/uploads/2014/02/BERA-Ethical-Guidelines-2011-1.pdf?noredirect=1

BERA (British Educational Research Association) (2018) *Ethical Guidelines for Educational Research*, 4th edition, London: BERA, viewed 22 February 2019, from https://www.bera.ac.uk/wp-content/uploads/201 8/06/BERA-Ethical-Guidelines-for-Educational-Research_4thEdn_2018.pdf?noredirect=1

Berger, J. (1972) *Ways of Seeing*, London: Penguin.

Berkeley, S., Scruggs, T.E. and Mastropieri, M.A. (2010) 'Reading comprehension instruction for students with learning disabilities, 1995–2006: A meta-analysis', *Remedial and Special Education*, 31(6), 423–436.

Berliner, D. (2011) 'Rational responses to high stakes testing: the case of curriculum narrowing and the harm that follows', *Cambridge Journal of Education*, 41(3), 287–302.

Bernstein, B. (1977) *Class, Codes and Control, Volume 3: Towards a Theory of Educational Transmissions*, 2nd Edition, London: Routledge and Kegan Paul.

BHF (British Heart Foundation) (2011) *The 21st Century Gingerbread House. How Companies Are Marketing Junk Food to Children Online*, viewed 27 February 2019, from https://www.bhf.org.uk/informationsuppor t/publications/policy-documents/the-21st-century-gingerbread-house

Biggam, J. (2015) *Succeeding with Your Master's Dissertation: A Step by Step Handbook*, 3rd Edition, Maidenhead: Open University Press.

Biggs, J. (1996) 'Enhancing teaching through constructive alignment', *Higher Education*, 32, 347–364.

Biggs, J.B. (2001) 'Enhancing learning: a matter of style or approach?', in R.J. Sternberg and L.F. Zhang (eds.) *Perspectives on Thinking, Learning and Cognitive Styles*, Mahwah, NJ: Lawrence Erlbaum Associates.

Bjork, R.A. and Bjork, E.L. (1992) 'A new theory of disuse and an old theory of stimulus fluctation', in A.F. Healey, S.M. Kosslyn and E.M. Siffrin (eds.) *From Learning Processes to Cognitive Processes: Essays in Honor of Wiliam K. Estes*, Vol. 2, Hillsdale, NJ: Erlbaum, pp. 35–67.

Bjork, R.A., Dunlosky, J. and Kornell, N. (2013) 'Self-regulated learning: beliefs, techniques, and illusions', *Annual Review of Psychology*, 64, 417–444.

Black, P. and Wiliam, D. (1998) *Inside the Black Box: Raising Standards Through Classroom Assessment*, London: King's College School of Education.

Black, P. and Wiliam, D. (2012) 'Developing a theory of formative assessment', in J. Gardner (ed.) *Assessment and Learning: Practice, Theory and Policy*, 2nd Edition, London: Sage.

Black, P., Harrison, C., Hodgen, J., Marshall, B. and Serret, N. (2010) 'Validity in teachers' summative assessments', *Assessment in Education: Principles, Policy and Practice*, 17(2), 215–232.

Black, P., Harrison, C., Lee, C., Marshall, B. and Wiliam, D. (2002) *Working Inside the Black Box: Assessment for Learning in the Classroom*, London: King's College, University of London.

Black, P., Harrison, C., Lee, C., Marshall, B. and Wiliam, D. (2004) 'Working inside the black box: assessment for learning in the classroom', *Phi Delta Kappan*, 86(1), 8–21.

Blamires, M. (ed.) (2014) *Special Educational Needs and Disability: Enabling Pupil Participation*, MESHGuide, viewed 4 December 2017, from http://www.meshguides.org/category/special-needs-2/enabling-pupil-part icipation-special-needs-2/

Blank, R.K. and de las Alas, N. (2009) *Effects of Teacher Professional Development on Gains in Student Achievement: How Meta Analysis Provides Scientific Evidence Useful to Education Leaders*, Washington: Council of Chief State School Officers.

Blatchford, P., Bassett, P., Brown, P., Koutsoubou, M., Martin, P., Russell, A. and Webster, R. with Rubie-Davies, C. (2009) *Deployment and Impact of Support Staff in Schools: The Impact of Support Staff in Schools.*

Results from Strand 2, Wave 2, DCSF Research Report DCSF RR148, viewed 8 June 2018, from http://discovery.ucl.ac.uk/10001336/

Blazer, W., Doherty, M. and O'Conner Jr., R. (1989) 'Effects of cognitive feedback on performance', *Psychological Bulletin*, 106(3), 410–433.

Bloom, A. (2007) 'Me level 4, you level 2 = end of friendship', *Times Educational Supplement*, 9 February, 13.

Bloom, B.S. (ed.) (1956) *Taxonomy of Educational Objectives: Handbook 1: Cognitive Domain*, New York: Longmans Green.

Boaler, J. (1997) *Experiencing School Mathematics: Teaching Style, Sex and Setting*, Maidenhead: Open University Press.

Bochner, S. (1978) 'Ayres, sensory integration and learning disorders: a question of theory and practice', *Australian Journal of Mental Retardation*, 5(2), 41–45.

Bolam, R. and Weindling, D. (2006) *Synthesis of Research and Evaluation Projects Concerned with Capacity Building Through Teachers' Professional Development*, Report for General Teaching Council for England, Birmingham: GTCE.

Booth, N. (2015) *What Are the Main Causes of Stress for Year 11 Students when Being Prepared for Public Examinations?* Masters in Teaching and Learning Thesis, Birmingham: Birmingham City University.

Booth, T. (2017) 'Promoting educational development led by inclusive values in England', in F. Dovigo (ed.) *Special Educational Needs and Inclusive Practices. Studies in Inclusive Education*, Rotterdam: Sense Publishers, pp. 3–20.

Bourdieu, P. (1974) 'The school as a conservative force: scholastic and cultural inequalities', in J. Egglestone (ed.) *Contemporary Research in the Sociology of Education*, London: Methuen and Co. Ltd.

Bourdieu, P. (1986) 'The forms of capital', in J.G. Richardson (ed.) *Handbook of Theory and Research for the Sociology of Education*, New York: Greenwood Press, pp. 241–260.

Bradshaw, J. (2016) *The Well-being of Children in the UK*, 4th Edition, Bristol: Policy Press.

Bradshaw, P. and Younie, S. (2018) 'E-ethics and online identity', in S. Younie and P. Bradshaw (eds.) *Debates in ICT and Computing*, Abingdon: Routledge.

Bransford, J.D., Brown, A. and Cocking, R.C. (eds.) (1999) *'How People Learn: Brain, Mind, Experience and School'*, Washington DC: National Academy Press.

Branzi, A. (2004) Keynote Lecture at the Crossing Boundaries Conference, Reggio Emilia, Italy.

Brindley, S. (ed.) (2015) *Masterclass Series of Texts*, London: Bloomsbury.

British Council/British Broadcasting Corporation (2018) *Learning Styles and Teaching*, viewed 26 September 2018, from www.teachingenglish.org.uk/articles/learning-styles-teaching

Britzman, D.P. (1998) *Lost Subjects, Contested Objects: Toward a Psychoanalytic Inquiry of Learning*, Albany, NY: SUNY Press.

Broadfoot, P. (2008) *An Introduction to Assessment*, London: Continuum International Publishing Group.

Brod, G., Werkle-Bergner, M. and Shing, Y.L. (2013) 'The influence of prior knowledge on memory: a developmental cognitive neuroscience perspective', *Frontiers in Behavioral Neuroscience* 7(13) viewed 31 March 2019, from DOI: 10.3389/fnbeh.2013.00139.

Bronfenbrenner, U. (1979) *The Ecology of Human Development*, Cambridge, MA: Harvard University Press.

Brookfield, S. (1993) *Developing Critical Thinkers*, Oxford: Oxford University Press.

Brookfield, S. (1995) *Becoming a Critically Reflective Teacher*, San Francisco: Jossey-Bass.

Brooks, C. (2016) *Teacher Subject Identity in Professional Practice: Teaching with a Professional Compass*, Abingdon: Routledge.

Brown, A.L. (1994) 'The advancement of learning', *Educational Researcher*, 23, 4–12.

Brown, T. and Summerbell, C. (2009) 'Systematic review of school-based interventions that focus on changing dietary intake and physical activity levels to prevent childhood obesity: an update to the obesity guidance produced by the National Institute for Health and Clinical Excellence', *Obesity Review*, 10, 110–141.

Brundrett, M. and Rhodes, C. (2011) *Leadership for Quality and Accountability in Education*, Abingdon and New York: Routledge.

Bruner, J.S. (1961) 'The act of discovery', *Harvard Educational Review*, 31, 21–32.

Bruner, J. (1966) *Towards a Theory of Instruction*, New York: Norton.

Bruner, J. (1983) *Child's Talk: Learning to Use Language*, Oxford: Oxford University Press.

Bruner, J.S. (2006a) *In Search of Pedagogy Volume 1: The Selected Works of Jerome S. Bruner*, London: Routledge.

Bruner, J.S. (2006b) *In Search of Pedagogy Volume 2: The Selected Works of Jerome S. Bruner*, London: Routledge.

Bryan, H., Carpenter, C. and Hoult, S. (2010) *Learning and Teaching at M Level: A Guide for Student Teachers*, London: Sage.

Bull, S. and Solity, J. (1987) *Classroom Management: Principles to Practice*, London: Croom Helm.

Bullock Report (1975) *A Language for Life*, London: HMSO.

Burchell, H., Dyson, J. and Rees, M. (2002) 'Making a difference: a study of the impact of continuing professional development on professional practice', *Journal of In-Service Education*, 28(2), 219-229.

Burden, K. and Younie, S. (2014) *Using iPads Effectively to Enhance Learning in Schools*, MESHGuide, University of Hull and De Montfort University, viewed 4 December 2017, from http://www.meshguides.org/category/icttechnology/tabletsipad-pedagogy/

Burgess, T. (2004) 'Language in the classroom and curriculum', in S. Capel, R. Heilbronn, M. Leask and T. Turner (eds.) *Starting to Teach in the Secondary School: A Companion for the Newly Qualified Teacher*, 2nd Edition, London: RoutledgeFalmer.

Burke, R.J., Greenglass, E.R. and Schwarzer, R. (1996) 'Predicting teacher burnout over time: effects of work stress, social support and self-doubts on burnout and its consequences', *Anxiety, Stress and Coping*, 9, 261-275.

Burnett, P. (2002) 'Teacher praise and feedback and students' perception of the classroom environment', *Educational Psychology*, 22(1), 5-16.

Burton, N., Brundrett, M. and Jones, M. (2008) *Doing Your Education Research Project*, London: Sage.

Buscemi (date unknown) in P. Reeve (1992) 'The Average Child', Dissertation, Bedford: De Montfort University.

Busch, C.R., Taylor, H.A., Kanarek, R.B. and Holcomb, P.J. (2002) 'The effects of a confectionery snack on attention in young boys', *Physiology & Behavior*, 77(2-3), PII S0031-9384(0002)00882-X.

Butler, D. and Winnie, P. (1995) 'Feedback and self-regulated learning: a theoretical synthesis', *Review of Educational Research*, 65(3), 245-281.

Butler, R. (1988) 'Enhancing and undermining intrinsic motivation: the effects of task-involving and ego-involving evaluation on interest and performance', *British Journal of Educational Psychology*, 58(1), 1-14.

Buzan, T. (2003) *Use Your Memory*, London: BBC Books.

Buzan, T. (2008) *How to Remember Names and Faces*, viewed 11 April 2018, from http://www.open.edu/openlearn/body-mind/psychology/buzan-on-how-remember-names-and-faces

Cain, T., Holmes, M., Larrett, A. and Mattock, J. (2007) 'Literature-informed, one-turn action research: three cases and a commentary', *British Educational Research Journal*, 33(1), 91-106.

Calderhead, J. and Shorrock, S.B. (1997) 'Understanding teacher education: case studies in the professional development of beginning teachers', *British Educational Research Journal*, 24(3), 370-371.

Campbell, E. (2008) 'Review of the literature', *Curriculum Inquiry*, 38(4), 357-385.

Capel, S., Bassett, S., Lawrence, J., Newton, A. and Zwozdiak-Myers, P. (2018) 'How trainee physical education teachers in England write, use and evaluate lesson plans', *European Physical Education Review*, viewed 31 March 2019, from https://doi.org/10.1177/1356336X18785053

Capel, S., Heilbronn, R., Leask. M. and Turner, T. (eds.) (2004) *Starting to Teach in the Secondary School: A Companion for the Newly Qualified Teacher*, 2nd Edition, London: RoutledgeFalmer.

Capel, S., Leask, M. and Turner, T. (eds.) (2010) *Readings for Learning to Teach in the Secondary School: A Companion to M Level Study*, Abingdon: Routledge.

Carli, V., Hoven, C.W., Wasserman, C., Chiesa, F., Guffanti, G., Sarchiapone, M., Apter, A., Balazs, J., Brunner, R., Corcoran, P., Cosman, D., Haring, C., Iosue, M., Kaess, M., Kahn, J.P., Keeley, H., Postuvan, V., Saiz, P., Varnik, A. and Wasserman, D. (2014) 'A newly identified group of adolescents at "invisible" risk for psychopathology and suicidal behaviour: findings from the SEYLE study', *World Psychiatry*, 13, 78-86.

Carr, D. (1993) 'Questions of competence', *British Journal of Educational Studies*, 41(3), 253-271.

Carse, N., Jess, M. and Keay, J. (2017) 'Primary physical education: shifting perspectives to move forwards', *European Physical Education Review*, 24(4), 487-502.

Carter, A. (2015) *Carter Review of Initial Teacher Training*, London: DfE

Cash, R.M. (2016) *Self-regulation in the Classroom: Helping Students Learn How to Learn*, Golden Valley, MN: Free Spirit.

Catterall, J. (1998) 'Risk and resilience in student transitions to high school', *American Journal of Education*, 10(2), 302-333.

CDC (Council for Disabled Children) (2017) *Education, Health and Care Plans: Examples of Good Practice*, viewed 6 January 2018, from https://councilfordisabledchildren.org.uk/help-resources/resources/education-health-and-care-plans-examples-good-practice

Centre for Studies on Inclusive Education (2011) *Index for Inclusion: Developing Learning and Participation in Schools*, viewed 8 June 2018, from www.csie.org.uk/resources/inclusion-index-explained.shtml

Cepeda, N.J., Pashler, H., Vul, E., Wixted, J.T. and Rohrer, D. (2006) 'Distributed practice in verbal recall tasks: a review and quantitative synthesis', *Psychological Bulletin*, 132(2), 354-380.

Chaplain, R.P. (2008) 'Stress and psychological distress among trainee secondary teachers in England', *Educational Psychology*, 28(2), 195-209.

Cheminais, R. (2010) *Developing Inclusive School Practice*, London: Davis Fulton Publishers.

Cherniss, C. (2000) *Emotional Intelligence; What It Is and Why It Matters*, viewed 15 January 2018, from http://www.eiconsortium.org/reports/what_is_emotional_intelligence.html

Child, D. (2007) *Psychology and the Teacher*, 8th Edition, London: Continuum.

Christie, F. and Martin, J.R. (2005) *Genre and Institutions: Social Processes in the Workplace and School*, London: Continuum.

Cian, C., Koulman, N., Barraud, P. A., Raphel, C., Jimnez, C. and Melin, B. (2000) 'Influence of variations in body hydration on cognitive function: effect of hyperhydration, heat stress, and exercise-induced dehydration', *Journal of Psychophysiology*, 14, 29-36.

Clarke, S. (2005a) *Formative Assessment in Action*, London: Hodder Murray.

Clarke, S. (2005b) *Formative Assessment in the Secondary Classroom*, London: Hodder and Stoughton.

Claxton, C. (2001) *Wise Up*, Stafford: Network Educational Press Ltd.

Claxton, G. (2002) *Building Learning Power: Helping Young People Become Better Learners*, Bristol: TLO.

Claxton, G. (2015) *Building Learning Power*, viewed 19 July 2015, from http://www.buildinglearningpower.co.uk/

Claxton, G. (2017) *Building Learning Power*, viewed 10 November 2017, from https://www.buildinglearning power.com

Claxton, G. and Lucas, B. (2015) *Educating Ruby: What Our Children Really Need to Learn*, Camarthan, Wales: Crown House Publishing.

Claxton, G., Chambers, M., Powell, G. and Lucas, B. (2011) *The Learning Powered School: Pioneering 21st Century Education*, Bristol: TLO Ltd.

CLEAPSS (2005) *Managing Risk Assessment in Science Classrooms*, viewed 17 July 2015, from http://www .cleapss.org.uk/attachments/article/0/L196.pdf?Secondary/Science/Guides/

Clough, P. and Nutbrown, C. (2007) *A Student's Guide to Methodology: Justifying Enquiry*, London: Sage.

Clucas, B. and O'Donnell, K. (2002) 'Conjoined twins: the cutting edge', *Web Journal of Current Legal Issues*, 5, viewed 29 November 2017, from http://www.bailii.org/uk/other/journals/WebJCLI/2002/issue5/ index.html

Clunies-Ross, P., Little, E. and Kienhuis, M. (2008) 'Self-reported and actual use of proactive and reactive classroom management strategies and their relationship with teacher stress and student behaviour', *Educational Psychology: An International Journal of Experimental Educational Psychology*, 28(6), 693-710.

Coe, R. (2013) *Improving Education: A Triumph of Hope Over Experience*, Durham: Centre for Education and Monitoring, Durham University.

Coe, R., Aloisi, C., Higgins, S. and Major, E.L. (2014) *What Makes Great Teaching? Review of the Underpinning Research*, Durham: The Centre for Monitoring and Evaluation, Durham University and the Sutton Trust, viewed 24 June 2018, from https://www.suttontrust.com/wp-content/uploads/2014/10/What-Makes-Grea t-Teaching-REPORT.pdf

Coffield, F. (2008) *Just Suppose Teaching and Learning Became the First Priority*, London: Learning and Skills Network, viewed 8 June 2018, from http://weaeducation.typepad.co.uk/wea_education_blog/files/frank_ coffield_on_teach_and_learning.pdf

Coffield, F., Moseley, D., Hall, E. and Ecclestone, K. (2004a) *Learning Styles and Pedagogy in Post-16 Learning: A Systematic and Critical Review*, Report no. 041543, London: Learning and Skills Research Centre, Learning and Skills Development Agency.

Coffield, F., Moseley, D., Hall, E. and Ecclestone, K. (2004b) *Should we be Using Learning Styles? What Research Has to Say to Practice*, London: Learning and Skills Research Centre, Learning and Skills Development Agency.

Cohen, S.A. (1969) 'Studies in visual perception and reading in disadvantaged children', *Journal of Learning Disabilities*, 2, 498-507.

Coleman, S.J. (1988) 'Social capital in the creation of human capital', *American Journal of Sociology*, 94, 95-120.

Collins, S. and Leslie, D. (2016) 'Accountability, contractual and statutory duties', in S. Capel, M. Leask and T. Turner (eds.) *Learning to Teach in the Secondary School: A Companion to School Experience*, 7th Edition, Abingdon: Routledge.

Connolly, P. (2006) 'The effects of social class and ethnicity on gender differences in GCSE attainment: a secondary analysis of the Youth Cohort Study of England and Wales 1997-2001', *British Educational Research Journal*, 32(1), 3-21.

Conway, P.F. and Clarke, C. (2003) 'The journey inward and outward: a re-examination of Fuller's concerns-based model of teacher development', *Teaching and Teacher Education*, 19(5), 466-482.

Coultas, V. (2007) *Constructive Talk in Challenging Classrooms*, Abingdon: Routledge.

Council of Europe (2017) *Council of Europe's Report on Citizenship and Human Rights Education*, viewed 29 November 2017, from https://www.coe.int/en/web/edc/home?desktop=trueConvention

Covington, M.V. (2000) 'Goal theory, motivation and school achievement: an integrative review', *Annual Review of Psychology*, 51, 171-200.

Crothers, L.M., Kanyongo, G.Y., Kolbert, J.B., Lipinski, J., Kachmar, S.P. and Koch, G.D. (2010) 'Job stress and locus of control in teachers: comparisons between samples from the United States and Zimbabwe', *International Review of Education*, 56, 651-669.

CSIE (Centre for Studies on Inclusive Education) (2011) *Index for Inclusion: Developing Learning and Participation in Schools*, viewed 3 July 2018, from www.csie.org.uk/resources/inclusion-index-explained.shtml

Curren, R. (2017) *Why Character Education?* Impact, Oxford: Wiley Blackwell, viewed 29 November 2017, from http://onlinelibrary.wiley.com/doi/10.1111/2048-416X.2017.12004.x/abstract

Dave, R.H. (1975) 'Psychomotor levels', in R.J. Armstrong (ed.) *Developing and Writing Behavioral Objectives*, Tucson: Educational Innovators Press.

Davies, F. and Greene, T. (1984) *Reading for Learning in Science*, Edinburgh: Oliver and Boyd.

Davies, N. (2000) *The School Report: Why Britain's Schools Are Failing*, London: Vintage Books.

Davies, D., Jindal-Snape, D., Collier, C., Digby, R., Hay, P. and Howe, A. (2013) 'Creative learning environments in education—a systematic literature review', *Thinking Skills and Creativity*, 8, 80-91.

Davis, B., Sumara, D. and Luce-Kapler, R. (2008) *Engaging Minds: Cultures of Education and Practices of Teaching*, 3rd Edition, New York and London: Routledge.

Davison, J. and Dowson, J. (eds.) (2003) *Learning to Teach English in the Secondary School: A Companion to School Experience*, 2nd Edition, London: Routledge.

Day, C., Edwards, A., Griffiths, A. and Gu, Q. (2011) *Beyond Survival: Teachers and Resilience*, Nottingham: University of Nottingham.

Day, J.J. and Sweatt, J.D. (2011) 'Epigenetic mechanisms in cognition', *Neuron*, 70(5), 813-829, viewed 25 June 2018, from https://www.cell.com/neuron/fulltext/S0896-6273(11)00433-8

DCSF (Department for Children, Schools and Families) (2008a) *Pedagogy and Practice: Teaching and Learning in Secondary Schools*, London: DCSF.

DCSF (Department for Children, Schools and Families) (2008b) *Guidance on Preventing Underachievement - A Focus on Exceptionally Able Pupils*, London: DCFS.

DCSF (Department for Children, Schools and Families) (2008c) *The National Strategies, Secondary, Key Stage3*, viewed 4 January 2018, from http://webarchive.nationalarchives.gov.uk/20110809091832/http://www.teachingandlearningresources.org.uk

DCSF (Department of Children, Schools and Families) (2009) *Steer Report: Learning Behaviour: Lessons Learned (The Steer Report)*, London: DCSF, viewed 26 October 2014, from http://www.behaviour4learning.ac.uk/ViewArticle2.aspx?ContentId=12597

DDA (2005) *Disability Discrimination Act 2005*, viewed 6 January 2018, from https://www.legislation.gov.uk/ukpga/2005/13/contents

de Bono, E. (1972) *Children Solve Problems*, London: Penguin Education.

Dearing, R. (1996) *Review of Qualifications for 16-19 Year Olds (Full Report)*, London: School Curriculum and Assessment Authority.

Deci, E.L. and Ryan, R.M. (1985) *Intrinsic Motivation and Self-Determination in Human Behavior*, New York: Plenum.

Deci, E.L., Nezlek, J. and Sheinman, L. (1981) 'Characteristics of the rewarder and intrinsic motivation of the rewardee', *Journal of Personality and Social Psychology*, 40, 1-10.

Degener, T (2016) 'Disability in a human rights context', *Laws*, 5(3), 35, viewed 25 February 2019, from https://doi.org/10.3390/laws5030035

Delamont, S. (1991) 'The hit list and other horror stories', *Sociological Review*, 39(2), 238-259.

Derewianka, B. (1996) *Exploring the Writing of Genres*, Royston: United Kingdom Reading Association.

DES (Department of Education and Science) (1978) *Special Educational Needs*, London: HMSO.

DES (Department of Education and Science) (1989) *Memo to National Curriculum Working groups*, para 4.1, London: DES.

Dewey, J. (1909) *The Moral Principles in Education, The Middle Works of John Dewey, 1899-1924*. Volume 4: 1907-1909, Essays, Carbondale and Edwardsville, IL: Southern Illinois University Press.

Dewey, J. (1916) 'Democracy and education', in J.-A. Boydson (ed.) *The Middle Works of John Dewey, 1899-1924 Volume 9. The Collected Works of John Dewey, 1882-1953*, Carbondale, IL: Southern Illinois University Press.

Dewey, J. (1916) *Democracy and Education*, New York: Free Press.

Dewey, J. (1933) *How We Think*, Boston: Houghton Mifflin.

DfE (Department for Education) (2011) *Families in the Foundation Years*, viewed 17 July 2017, from https://www.gov.uk/schools-colleges-childrens-services/early-years.

DfE (Department for Education) (1994a) *The Code of Practice on the Identification and Assessment of Special Educational Needs*, London: DfE.

DfE (Department for Education) (1994b) *The Education of Children with Emotional and Behavioural Difficulties (Circular 9/94)*, London: DfE.

DfE (Department for Education) (2010) *The Importance of Teaching, The Schools White Paper 2010*, London: DfE, viewed 4 July 2018, from https://assets.publishing.service.gov.uk/government/uploads/system/uploads/attachment_data/file/175429/CM-7980.pdf

DfE (Department for Education) (2011a) *About the School Curriculum*, London: Department for Education, viewed 30 May 2012, from http://www.education.gov.uk/schools/teachingandlearning/curriculum/b00200366/about-the-school-curriculum

DfE (Department for Education) (2011b) *Achievement for All: National Evaluation*, London: Department for Education.

DfE (Department for Education) (2011c) *Getting the Simple things Right - Charlie Taylor's Behaviour Checklists*, viewed 4 December 2017, from https://www.gov.uk/government/uploads/system/uploads/attachment_data/file/283997/charlie_taylorchecklist.pdf

DfE (Department for Education) (2011d) *Teachers' Standards in England from September 2012*, London: HMSO, viewed 3 July 2018, from https://www.education.gov.uk/publications/eOrderingDownload/teachers%20standards.pdf

DfE (Department for Education) (2011e) *The Overall Aims of the National Curriculum*, London: DfE, viewed 1 June 2012, from http://www.education.gov.uk/publications/eOrderingDownload/QCA-99-457.pdf

DfE (Department for Education) (2012a) *Aims, Values and Purposes of the National Curriculum for England (2012)*, viewed 1 April 2012, from http://www.education.gov.uk/schools/teachingandlearning/curriculum/b00199676/aims-values-and-purposes

DfE (Department for Education) (2012b) *Behaviour and Discipline in Schools: Guidance for Governing Bodies*, viewed 3 July 2018, from http: //www.gov.uk/government/publications/behaviour-and-discipline-in-schools-guidance-for-governing-bodies

DfE (Department for Education) (2012c) *National Curriculum for England (2012)*, Viewed 1 April 2012, from http://www.education.gov.uk/schools /teachingandlearning/curriculum

DfE (Department for Education) (2013a) *National Curriculum in England: Citizenship Programmes of Study, Statutory Guidance*, viewed 4 July 2018, from https://www.gov.uk/government/publications/national-curriculum-in-england-citizenship-programmes-of-study

DfE (Department for Education) (2013b) *National Curriculum in England: Complete Framework for Key Stages 1 to 4 - for Teaching from September 2016*, viewed 3 July 2018, from https://www.gov.uk/government/publications/national-curriculum-in-england-framework-for-key-stages-1-to-4

DfE (Department for Education) (2013c) *National Curriculum in England: Computing Programmes of Study, Statutory Guidance*, viewed 2 July 2018, from https://www.gov.uk/government/ publications/national-curriculum-in-england-computing-programmes-of-study/national-curriculum-in-england-computing-programmes-of-study

DfE (Department for Education) (2013d) *Statutory Guidance National Curriculum in England: Framework for Key Stages 1 to 4*, viewed 5 January 2014, from http://www.gov.uk/government/publications/national-curriculum-in-england-framework-for-key-stages-1-to-4

DfE (Department for Education) (2013e) *Teachers' Standards*, viewed 18 February 2018, from https://www.gov.uk/government/uploads/system/uploads/attachment_data/file/665520/Teachers_Standards.pdf

DfE (Department for Education) (2013f) *The National Curriculum*, London: DfE, viewed 3 March 2015, from http://www.gov.uk/national-curriculum

DfE (Department for Education) (2013g) *Use of Reasonable Force in Schools: Advice for Headteachers, Staff and Governing Bodies*, London: DfE, viewed 3 July 2018, from http://www.gov.uk/government/publications/use-of-reasonable-force-in-schools

DfE (Department for Education) (2014a) *Behaviour and Discipline in Schools: Advice to Headteachers and School Staff (Status: Departmental advice, February 2014)*, viewed 1 November 2014, from http://www.gov.uk/government/publications/behaviour-and-discipline-in-schools

DfE (Department for Education) (2014b) *Behaviour and Discipline in schools: Advice to Headteachers and School Staff, Status: Departmental advice (Updated 2016)*, viewed 7 July 2018, from http: //www.gov.uk/government/publications/behaviour-and-discipline-in-schools

DfE (Department for Education) (2014c) *Child Poverty Strategy 2014-17*, London: HMSO.

DfE (Department for Education) (2014d) *First Statistical Release. Special Educational Needs in England*, January, 2014, London: DfE.

DfE (Department for Education) (2014e) *Guidance for Schools to Prevent and Respond to Bullying as Part of their Overall Behaviour Policy (Updated 4 July 2017)*, viewed 7 July 2018, from http://www.education. gov.uk/schools/pupilsupport/behaviour/bullying/f007689 9/preventing-and-tackling-bullying

DfE (Department for Education) (2014f) *Health and Safety: Advice on Legal Duties and Powers*, viewed 18 February 2018, from https://www.gov.uk/government/uploads/system/uploads/attachment_data/file/ 335111/DfE_Health_andSafety_Advice_06_0214.pdf

DfE (Department for Education) (2014g) *Improving Behaviour and Attendance in Schools*, viewed 23 April 2015, from http://www.gov.uk/government/policies/improving-behaviour-and-attendance-in-schools

DfE (Department for Education) (2014h) *National Curriculum and Assessment from September 2014: Information for Schools*, London: DfE, viewed 3 July 2018, from https://assets.publishing.service.gov.uk/ government/uploads/system/uploads/attachmentdata/file/358070/NCassessment_quals_factsheet_ Sept_update.pdf

DfE (Department for Education (2014i) *National Curriculum in England: Framework for Key Stages 1 to 4*, updated 2 December 2014, London: DfE, viewed 3 July 2018, from https://www.gov.uk/government/publications/national-curriculum-in-england-framework-for-key-stages-1-to-4 /the- national-curriculum-in-england-framework-for-key-stages-1-to-4#inclusion

DfE (Department for Education) (2014j) *Promoting Fundamental British Values as part of SMSC in Schools*, London: DfE, viewed 4 July 2018, from https://www.gov.uk/government/publications/ promoting-fundamental-british-values-through-smsc

DfE (Department for Education) (2014k) *SEND Code of Practice: 0-25 Years*, London: DfE. (Updated May 2015), viewed 7 July 2018, from http://www.gov.uk/government/publications/send-code-of-practice-0-to-25

DfE (Department for Education) (2014l) *The Equality Act 2010 and Schools: Departmental Advice for School Leaders, School Staff, Governing Bodies and Local Authorities*, viewed 18 February 2018, from https://www. gov.uk/government/uploads/system/uploads/attachment_data/file/315587/Equality_Act_Advice_Final.pdf

DfE (Department for Education) (2014m) *The GCSE and Equivalent Attainment by Pupil Characteristics in England, 2012/13*, viewed 3 July 2018, from https://www.gov.uk/government/statistics/gcse-and-equivalent-attainment-by-pupil-characteristics-2012-to-2013

DfE (Department for Education) (2014n) *The National Curriculum in England Framework Document*, viewed 3 July 2018, from https://www.gov.uk/government/uploads/system/uploads/attachment_data/file/ 210969/NC_framework_document_-_FINAL .pdf

DfE (Department for Education) (2015a) *2017 Key Stage 4 Performance Tables: Qualifications in the Technical Award Category*, viewed 7 January 2018, from https://www.gov.uk/government/upload/system/uploads/ attachment_data/file/448760/TechnicalAwards_2017_list_July_2015.pdf

DfE (Department of Education) (2015b) *Carter Review of Initial Teacher Training (ITT)*, viewed 10 June 2018, from www.gov.uk/government/publications/carter-review-of-initial-teacher-training

DfE (Department for Education) (2015c) *Final Report of the Commission on Assessing Without Levels*, September 2015, London: DfE, viewed 4 July 2018, from https://assets.publishing.service.gov.uk/ government/uploads/system/uploads/attachmentdata/file/483058/Commission_on_Assessment_ Without_Levels_-_report.pdf

DfE (Department for Education) (2015d) *Government Response to the Carter Review of Initial Teacher Training*, London: Crown.

DfE (Department for Education) (2015e) *Government Response to the Workload Challenge*, London: Crown.

DfE (Department for Education) (2015f) *School and College Performance Tables*, viewed 7 January 2018, from https://www.gov.uk/education/school-performance-tables-and-ofsted-reports

DfE (Department for Education) (2015g) *SEND Code of Practice: 0 to 25 Years*. London: DfE, viewed 24 September 2017, from https://www.gov.uk/government/uploads/system/uploads/attachment_data/file/3 98815/SEND_Code_of_Practice_January_2015.pdf

DfE (Department for Education) (2015h) *Teacher Guidance: Preparing to Teach about Mental Health and Emotional Wellbeing*, London: Department for Education.

DfE (Department for Education) (2015i) *The Prevent Duty: Departmental Advice for Schools and Childcare Providers*, viewed 18 February 2018, from https://assets.publishing.service.gov.uk/government/uploads/ system/uploads/attachment_data/file/439598/prevent-duty-departmental-advice-v6.pdf

DfE (Department for Education) (2015j) *Workload Challenge: Analysis of Teacher Consultation Responses*, London: DfE, viewed 3 March 2015, from http://www.gov.uk/government/publications/workload-chal lenge-analysis-of-teacher-responses

DfE (Department for Education (2016a) *Behaviour and Discipline in Schools: Advice to Headteachers and School Staff*, viewed 3 July 2018, from www.gov.uk /government/publications/behaviourand-discipline-in-schools

DfE (Department for Education) (2016b) *Eliminating Unnecessary Workload around Marking: Report of the Independent Teacher Workload Review Group*, viewed 8 July 2017, from https://www.gov.uk/government/uploads/system/uploads/attachment_data/file/511256/Eliminating-unnecessary-workload-around-marking.pdf

DfE (Department for Education) (2016c) *Eliminating Unnecessary Workload around Planning and Teaching Resources. Report of the Independent Teacher Workload Review Group*, viewed 10 June 2018, from www.gov.uk/government/publications/reducing-teacher-workload-planning-and-r esources-group-report

DfE (Department for Education) (2016d) *Eliminating Unnecessary Workload Associated with Data Management*, viewed 10 September 2018, from https://assets.publishing.service.gov.uk/government/uploads/system/uploads/attachment_data/file/511258/Eliminating-unnecessary-workload-associated-with-data-management.pdf

DfE (Department for Education) (2016e) *Keeping Children Safe in Education*, viewed 18 February 2018, from https://www.gov.uk/government/uploads/system/uploads/attachment_data/file/550511/Keeping_children_safe_ineducation.pdf

DfE (Department for Education) (2016f) *Mental Health and Behaviour in Schools. Departmental Advice for School Staff*, London: DfE, viewed 2 July 2018, from https://assets.publishing.service.gov.uk/government/uploads/system/uploads/attachment_data/file/508847/Mental_Health_and_Behaviour_-_advice_for_Schools_160316.pdf

DfE (Department for Education) (2016g) *Provisional GCSE and Equivalent Results in England*, 2015 to 2016, viewed 3 January 2018, from https://www.gov.uk/government/uploads/system/uploads/attachment_data/file/5 59919/SFR48_2016.pdf

DfE (Department for Education) (2016h) *Revised GCSE and Equivalent Results in England, 2014 to 2015*, viewed 3 January 2018, from https://www.gov.uk/government/uploads/system/uploads/attachment_data/file/494073/SFR01_2016.pdf

DfE (Department for Education) (2016i) *Standard for Teachers' Professional Development*, London: DfE, viewed 4 July 2018, from https://assets.publishing.service.gov.uk/government/uploads/system/uploads/attachment_data/file/537030/160712_-_PD_standard.pdf

DfE (Department for Education) (2017a) *English Baccalereate (EBacc)*, viewed 7 January 2018, from https://www.gov.uk/government/publications/english-baccalaureate-ebacc/english-baccalaureate-ebacc

DfE (Department for Education) (2017b) *Literacy and Numeracy Catch-Up Strategies*, London: Crown Copyright, viewed 24 June 2018, from https://assets.publishing.service.gov.uk/government/uploads/system/uploads/attachmentdata/file/659067/Literacy_andnumeracy_catchup_strategies_amended_13.11.17.pdf

DfE (Department for Education) (2017c) *National Curriculum in England: Design and Technology Programmes of Study*, viewed 3 July 2018, from https://www.gov.uk/government/publications/national-curriculum-in-england-design-and-technology-programmes-of-study/national-curriculum-in-england-design-and-technology-programmes-of-study

DfE (Department for Education) (2017d) *Preventing and Tackling Bullying: Advice for Headteachers, Staff and Governing Bodies*, viewed 2 July 2018, from https://assets.publishing.service.gov.uk /government/uploads/system/uploads/attachmentdata/file/623895/Preventing_and_tackling_bullyingadvice.pdf

DfE (Department for Education) (2017e) *School Teachers' Pay and Conditions Document 2017 and Guidance on School Teachers' Pay and Conditions (Valid from 1 September 2017)*, viewed 4 July 2018, from https://www.gov.uk/government/uploads/system/uploads/attachment_data/file/636389 /School_teachers__pay_andconditions_document2017.pdf

DfE (Department for Education) (2017f) *SEN Support: Research Evidence on Effective Approaches and Examples of Current Practice in Good and Outstanding Schools and Colleges*, viewed 3 July 2018, from www.sendgateway.org.uk

DfE (Department for Education) (2017g) *Teacher Workload Survey 2016*, viewed 1 May 2018, from https://www.gov.uk/government/uploads/system/uploads/attachment_data/file/592499/TWS_2016_FINALResearch_report_Feb2017.pdf

DfE (Department for Education (2018a) *Screening, Searching and Confiscation: Advice for Headteachers, School Staff and Governing Bodies*, viewed 3 July 2018, from www.gov.uk/government/publications/searching-screening-and-confiscation

DfE (Department for Education) (2018b) *Qualified Teacher Status (QTS) Skills Test*, viewed 17 July 2017, from http://sta.education.gov.uk

DfE/DoH (Department for Education/Department of Health) (2014) *Special Educational Needs Code of Practice*, London: DfE.

DfE/ONS (Department for Education/The Office of National Statistics) (2017) *Special Educational Needs in England 2017 SFR/2017*, viewed 21 September 2017, from https://www.gov.uk/government/uploads/system/uploads/attachment_data/file/633031/SFR37_2017_Main_Text.pdf

DfEE (Department for Education and Employment) (1997) *Guaranteeing Standards: A Consultation Paper on the Structure of Awarding Bodies*, London: DfEE.

DfEE (Department for Education and Employment) (1999) *Social Inclusion: Pupil Support* (Circular 10/99), London: DfEE.

DfES (Department for Education and Skills) (2001a) *Education and Skills: Delivering Results – A Strategy to 2006*, Sudbury, Suffolk: DfES.

DfES (Department for Education and Skills) (2001b) *Inclusive Schooling*, London: DfES.

DfES (Department for Education and Skills) (2001c) *The Special Educational Needs Code of Practice*, London:DfES.

DfES (Department for Education and Skills) (2002) *Guided Reading in English at Key Stage 3*, Ref. DfES 0044/2002, London: DfES.

DfES (Department for Education and Skills) (2003a) *Every Child Matters*, London: DfES.

DfES (Department for Education and Skills) (2003b) *Key Stage 3 Strategy: Key Messages about Assessment and Learning*, London: DfES.

DFES (Department for Education and Skills) (2004a) *Pedagogy and Practice: Teaching and Learning in the Secondary School, Unit 6 Modelling*, London: DfES.

DFES (Department for Education and Skills) (2004b) *Pedagogy and Practice: Teaching and Learning in the Secondary School, Unit 7 Questioning*, London: DfES.

DFES (Department for Education and Skills) (2004c) *Pedagogy and Practice: Teaching and Learning in the Secondary School, Unit 8 Explaining*, London: DfES, viewed 2 July 2018, from http://webarchive.nationalarchives.gov.uk/20110813104232/http://nsonline.org.uk/node/174694?uc=forceuj

DFES (Department for Education and Skills) (2004d) *Pedagogy and Practice: Teaching and Learning in Secondary Schools, Unit 10 Group Work*, London: DFES, viewed 2 July 2018, from http://webarchive.nationalarchives.gov.uk/20110809211306/http://nsonline.org.uk/node/174698

DFES (Department for Education and Skills) (2004e) *Pedagogy and Practice: Teaching and Learning in the Secondary School, Unit 18 Improving the Climate for Learning*, London: DfES.

DFES (Department for Education and Skills) (2004f) *Pedagogy and Practice: Teaching and Learning in Secondary Schools, Unit 19 Learning Styles*, London: DfES.

DfES (Department for Education and Skills) (2005) *Key Stage 3 National Strategy: Leading in Learning: Developing Thinking Skills at Key Stage 3*, DfES 0036 – 2005 G, viewed 29 December 2018, from https://webarchive.nationalarchives.gov.uk/20110809211717/http://nsonline.org.uk/node/175300

DfES (Department for Education and Skills) (2006) *Highlights: Personalised Learning*, London: DfES.

DfES (Department for Education and Skills) (2006a) *National Strategies: Grouping Pupils for Success*, viewed 2 July 2018, from http://webarchive.nationalarchives.gov.uk/20110812191333/http://nsonline.org.uk/node/84974

DfES/QCA (Department for Education and Skills/Qualifications and Curriculum Authority) (2004) *The National Curriculum Handbook for Secondary Teachers in England*, London: QCA, viewed 2 July 2018, from http://webarchive.nationalarchives.gov.uk/20130401151715/http://www.education.gov.uk/publications/eOrderingDownload/QCA-04-1374.pdf

Dillon, J. and Maguire, M. (eds.) (2001) *Becoming a Teacher: Issues in Secondary Teaching*, 3rd Edition, Maidenhead: Open University Press.

Dix, P. (2010) *The Essential Guide to Taking Care of Behaviour: Practical Skills for Teachers*, London: Longman.

Dohrn, E. and Bryan, T. (1994) 'Attributional instruction', *Teaching Exceptional Children*, 26, 61–63.

Donaldson, M. (1978) *Children's Minds*, London: Fontana.

Donaldson, M. (2013) *A Study of Children's Thinking*, Abingdon: Routledge.

Driver, R. (1983) *The Pupil as Scientist*, Milton Keynes: Open University Press.

Duckworth, A. (2016) *Grit: The Power of Passion and Perseverance*, London: Edbury Publishing.

Duckworth, A., Peterson, C., Matthews, M. and Kelly, D.R. (2007) 'Grit: Perseverance and passion for long-term goals', *Journal of Personality and Social Psychology*, 92(6), 1087–1101.

Dudek, M. (2000) *Architecture of Schools: The New Learning Environments*, Boston: Architectural Press.

Dudley, P. (2011) *Lesson Study: A Handbook*, viewed 6 February 2019, from http://lessonstudy.co.uk/lesson-study-a-handbook/

Dudley, P. (2014) *Lesson Study: Professional Learning for Our Time*, Abingdon: Routledge, viewed 21 July 2015, from http://lessonstudy.co.uk/about-us-pete-dudley/

Dufrene, B.A., Lestremau, L. and Zoder-Martell, K. (2014) 'Direct behavioral consultation: effects on teachers' praise and student disruptive behavior', *Psychology in the Schools*, 51(6), 567–580.

Dunne, J. (2003) 'Arguing for teaching as a practice: a reply to Alasdair MacIntyre', *Journal of Philosophy of Education*, 37(2), 353–369.

Dweck, C.S. (1986) 'Motivational processes affecting learning', *American Psychologist*, 41(10),1040–1048.

Dweck, C.S. (1999) *Self Theories: Their Role in Motivation, Personality and Development*, Philadelphia, PA: Psychology Press.

Dweck, C.S. (2006) *Mindset: The New Psychology of Success*, New York: Ballantyne Books.

Dweck, C.S. (2012) *Mindset: How You Can Fulfill your Potential*, London: Robinson.

Dweck, C.S. and Leggett, E. (1988) 'A social-cognitive approach to motivation and personality', *Psychological Review*, 95, 256–273.

DWP (Department for Work and Pensions) (2016) *Family Resources Survey*, viewed 20 December 2017, from https://www.gov.uk/government/collections/family-resources-survey--2

Dyson, A. (2001) 'Special needs in the twenty-first century: where we've been and where we're going', *British Journal of Special Education*, 28(1), 24–29.

Earl, L. and Katz, S. (2008) 'Getting to the core of learning: Using assessment for self-monitoring and self-regulation', in S. Swaffield (ed.) *Unlocking Assessment: Understanding for Reflection and Application*, Abingdon: Routledge.

Eaton Vale Schools Activity Centre (2015) *Risk Assessments*, viewed 17 July 2015, from http://www.eatonvale.co.uk/schools/riskassessments.aspx

Eccles, J.S. and Midgley, C. (1989) 'Stage-environment fit: developmentally appropriate classrooms for young adolescents', in C. Ames and R. Ames (eds.) *Research on Motivation in Education: Goals and Cognitions*, Volume 3, New York: Academic Press, pp. 139–186.

Ecclestone, K. and Hayes, D. (2009) *The Dangerous Rise of Therapeutic Education*, Abingdon: Routledge.

Education DataLab (2014) *Seven Things You Might not Know about Schools*, viewed 14 September 2018, from http://universityofhullscitts.org.uk/scitts/ass_supp_primary/downloads/assessment/EduDataLab.pdf

EEF (Education Endowment Foundation) (2018) *Setting or Streaming*, viewed 8 January 2018, from https://educationendowmentfoundation.org.uk/pdf/generate/?u=https://educationendowmentfoundation.org.uk/pdf/toolkit/?id=127&t=Teaching%20and%20Learning%20Toolkit&e=127&s=

Education Scotland (2015) *Skills in Practice: Thinking Skills*, viewed 18 July 2015, from http://www.educationscotland.gov.uk/resources/s/skillsinpracticethinkingskills/knowing.asp

Edwards, A.D. and Westgate, D.P.G. (1994) *Investigating Classroom Talk*, 2nd Edition, London: Falmer.

EHRC (Equality and Human Rights Commission) (2010) *How Fair is Britain? Equality, Human Rights and Good Relations in 2010*, viewed 1 February 2015, from http://www.equalityhumanrights.com/key-projects/how-fair-is-britain/full-report-and-evidence-downloads

EHRC (Equality and Human Rights Commission) (2013) *Gender Pay Gaps 2012*, London: Government Equalities Office.

Elawar, M. and Corno, L. (1985) 'A factorial experiment in teachers' written feedback on student homework: Changing teacher behaviour a little rather than a lot', *Journal of Educational Psychology*, 77(2), 162–173.

Elliot, A.J. and McGregor, H.A. (2001) 'A 2 × 2 achievement goal framework', *Journal of Personality and Social Psychology*, 80, 501–519.

Elliott, J. (1998) *The Curriculum Experiment: Meeting the Challenge of Social Change*, Maidenhead: Open University Press.

Ellis, S. and Tod, J. (2009) *Behaviour for Learning. Proactive Approaches to Behaviour Management*, Abingdon: Routledge

Elton-Chalcraft, S., Lander, V., Revell, L., Warner, D. and Whitworth, L. (2017) 'To promote, or not to promote fundamental British values? Teachers' standards, diversity and teacher education', *British Educational Research Journal*, 43, 29–48.

Entwistle, N.J. (1990) *Handbook of Educational Ideas and Practices*, London: Routledge.

Entwistle, N.J. (2009) *Teaching for Understanding at University: Deep Approaches and Distinctive Ways of Thinking*, Basingstoke: Palgrave Macmillan.

ERA (Education Reform Act) (1988) *Education Reform Act, 29 July 1988; Section 1,2 Aims of the School Curriculum*, viewed 4 January 2018, from http://www.legislation.gov.uk/ukpga/1988/40/pdfs/ukpga_19880040_en.pdf

Ericsson, A. and Pool, R. (2016) *Peak: Secrets from the New Science of Expertise*, Boston: Houghton Mifflin Harcourt.

Erikson, E.H. (1980) *Identity and the Life Cycle*, New York: Norton.

Evans, C. (2004) 'Exploring the relationship between cognitive style and teaching style', *Educational Psychology*, 24(4), 509-530.

Evetts, J. (2009) 'The management of professionalism: a contemporary paradox', in S. Gewirtz, P. Mahony, I. Hextall and A. Cribb (eds.) *Changing Teacher Professionalism: International Trends, Challenges and Ways Forward*, Abingdon: Routledge, pp.19-30.

Fairclough, S., Hackett, A., Davies, I., Gobbi, R., Mackintosh, K., Warburton, G., Stratton, G., Sluijs, E. and Boddy, L. (2013) 'Promoting healthy weight in primary school children through physical activity and nutrition education: a pragmatic evaluation of the change! Biomedical central', *Public Health*, 13, 626.

Fantilli, R.D. and McDougall, D.E. (2009) 'A study of novice teachers: challenges and supports in the first years', *Teaching and Teacher Education*, 25, 814-825.

Farah, M. with Andrews, T.J. (2013) *Twin Ambitions: My Autobiography*, London: Hodder and Stoughton Ltd.

Farooqi, I.S., Bullmore, E., Keogh, J., Gillard, J., O'Rahilly, S. and Fletcher, P.C. (2007) 'Leptin regulates striatal regions and human eating behavior', *Science*, 317(5843), 1355-1355.

Faultey, M. (2010) *Assessment in Music Education*, Oxford: Oxford University Press.

Fautley, M. and Savage, J. (2008) *Assessment for Learning and Teaching in Secondary Schools*, Exeter: Learning Matters Ltd.

Fautley, M. and Savage, J. (2013) *Lesson Planning for Effective Learning*, Maidenhead: Open University Press.

Fernet, C., Guay, F., Senécal, C. and Austin, S. (2012) 'Predicting intraindividual changes in teacher burnout: the role of perceived school environment and motivational factors', *Teaching and Teacher Education*, 28, 514-525.

Fisher, R. (2013) *Creative Dialogue: Talk for Thinking in the Classroom*, 2nd Edition, Abingdon: Routledge.

Fitzgerald, R., Finch, S. and Nove, A. (2000) *Black Caribbean Young Men's Experiences of Education and Employment, Report No. RR186*, London: DfEE.

Flavell, J.H. (1982) 'Structures, stages and sequences in cognitive development', in W.A. Collins (ed.) *The Concept of Development: The Minnesota Symposia on Child Psychology*, 15, 1-28.

Fletcher-Campbell, F. (2004) 'Pupils with moderate learning difficulties', in A. Lewis and B. Norwich B (eds.) *How Specialist Is Teaching Children with Difficulties and Disabilities?* Maidenhead: Open University Press.

Flynn, N., Pim, C. and Coles, S. (2015) *English as an Additional Language*, MESHGuide, from www.MESHGuides.org

Freakly, M., Burgh, G., MacSporran, L. (2008) *Values Education in Schools: A Resource Book for Student Inquiry*, Victoria, Australia: Acer Press.

Freeman, N.H. and Parsons, M.J. (2001) 'Children's intuitive understanding of pictures', in B. Torff and R.J. Sternberg (eds.) *Understanding and Teaching the Intuitive Mind: Student and Teacher Learning*, London: Lawrence Erlbaum Associates.

Freidson, E. (2001) *Professionalism, the Third Logic: On the Practice of Knowledge*, Chicago, IL: University of Chicago Press.

Freud, S. (1901) 'The psychopathology of everyday life', republished in 1953 in J. Strachey (ed.) *The Standard Edition of the Complete Psychological Works of Sigmund Freud*, Volume 6, London: Hogarth.

Frost, J. (2010) *Learning to Teach Science in the Secondary School : A companion to School Experience*, 3rd edition, Abingdon: Routledge.

Frost, J. and Turner, T. (2005) *Learning to Teach Science in the Secondary School: A Companion to School Experience*, 2nd Edition, London: RoutledgeFalmer.

Fuller, F.F. and Brown, O.H. (1975) 'Becoming a teacher', in K. Ryan (ed.) *Teacher Education (Seventy-Fourth Yearbook of the National Society of Education)*, Chicago: University of Chicago Press, pp. 25-52.

Furlong, J. (2015) *Teaching Tomorrow's Teachers: Options for the Future of Initial Teacher Education in Wales*, Oxford: University of Oxford.

Gagne, R.M. (1977) *The Conditions of Learning*, New York: Holt International.

Gallard, D. and Cartmell, K.M. (2015) *Psychology and Education*, London and New York: Routledge.

Galton, M. (2010) 'Moving to secondary school: what do pupils in England say about the experience?', in D. Jindal-Snape (ed.) *Educational Transitions: Moving Stories from Around the World*, New York: Routledge, pp. 107-124.

Galton, M., Hargreaves, L., Comber, C., Wall, D. and Pell, T. (1999) 'Changes in patterns of classroom interaction in primary classrooms: 1976-1996', *British Educational Research Journal*, 25(1), 23-37.

Gardner, H. (1983) *Frames of Mind: The Theory of Multiple Intelligences*, New York: Basic Books.

Gardner, H. (1991) *The Unschooled Mind*, London: Harper Collins.

Gardner, H. (1993) *Frames of Mind: The Theory of Multiple Intelligences*, 2nd Edition, London: Fontana.

Gardner, H. (2006) *The Development and Education of the Mind: The Selected Works of Howard Gardner*, London: Routledge.

Gardner, H., Kornhaber, M. and Wake, W. (1996) *Intelligence: Multiple Perspectives*, Fort Worth, TX: Harcourt Brace.

Garner, P. (2011) *Promoting the Conditions for Positive Behaviour to Help Every Child Succeed*, Nottingham: NCSL, viewed 8 July 2018, from http://dera.ioe.ac.uk/12538/1/download%3Fid%3D158591%26filen ame%3Dpromoting-the-conditions-for-positive-behaviour-to-help-every-child-succeed.pdf

Garner, P., Kauffman, J. and Elliott, J. (2014) *The Handbook of Emotional and Behavioural Difficulties*, London: Sage.

Gathercole, S. (2008) 'Working memory in the classroom: the President's Award lecture to the Annual Conference of the British Psychological Society', *The Psychologist*, 21(5), 382–385.

Gervis, M. and Williams, T. (2017) *The Coaches Guide to Mindmapping. The Fundamental Tools to Become an Expert Coach and Maximize your Players' Performance*, London: Meyer and Meyer Sport (UK) Ltd.

Gessell, A. (1925) *The Mental Growth of the Preschool Child*, New York: Macmillan.

Giallo, R. and Little, E. (2003) 'Classroom behaviour problems: the relationship between preparedness, classroom experiences and self-efficacy in graduate and student teachers', *Australian Journal of Educational and Developmental Psychology*, 3(2), 21-34.

Gibton, D. (2013) *Law, Education, Politics, Fairness: England's Extreme Legislation for Education Reform*, London: Institute of Education.

Gibton, D. (2016) *Researching Education Policy, Public Policy and Policymakers – Qualitative Methods and Ethical Issues*, Abingdon: Routledge.

Gilbert, C. (2012) *Towards a Self-improving System: The Role of School Accountability*, Nottingham: National College for School Leadership.

Gilham, B. (ed.) (1986) *The Language of School Subjects*, London: Heinemann.

Gillborn, D. and Gipps, C. (1996) *Recent Research on the Achievements of Ethnic Minority Pupils: OFSTED Reviews of Research*, London: HMSO.

Gillborn, D. and Mirza, H.S. (2000) *Educational Inequality: Mapping Race, Class and Gender; A Synthesis of Research Evidence*, London: Ofsted.

Giroux, H. (2011) *On Critical Pedagogy*, London: Continuum

Gleeson, D. and Husbands, C. (2004) *The Performing School*, London: Routledge.

Goleman, D. (1995) *Emotional Intelligence: Why It Can Matter More than IQ for Character, Health and Lifelong Achievement*, New York: Bantam Press.

Goleman, D. (2006) *Emotional Intelligence: Why It Can Matter more than IQ*, 10th Anniversary Edition, New York: Bantam Books.

Good, T. and Brophy, J. (2007) *Looking in Classrooms*, 10th Edition, New York: Addison-Wesley Longman.

Goswami, U. (2008) *Cognitive Development: The Learning Brain*, Hove and New York: Psychology Press.

Goswami, U. (2017) *Centre for Neuroscience in Education*, viewed 10 November 2017, from http://www.cne. psychol.cam.ac.uk/people/ucg10@cam.ac.uk

Gough, P.B. and Tunmer, W.E. (1986) 'Decoding, reading and reading disability', *Remedial and Special Education*, 7, 6-10.

Gould, S.J. (1981) *The Mismeasure of Man*, New York: Norton and Co.

Goulding, M. (2005) 'Pupils learning mathematics', in S. Johnston-Wilder, P. Johnston-Wilder, D. Pimm and J. Westwell (eds.) *Learning to Teach Mathematics in the Secondary School: A Companion to School Experience*, 2nd Edition, London: Routledge.

Gov.uk (2013) *Public Health England: Sedentary Lifestyles and too much Screen Time Affect Children's Wellbeing*, viewed 6 February 2019, from https://www.gov.uk/government/news/sedentary-lifestyles-and-too-much-screen-time-affect-childrens-wellbeing

Gov.uk (2014) *Department for Education: New School Food Standards*, viewed 6 February 2014, from https://www.gov.uk/government/news/new-school-food-standards

Gov.uk (2015) *Public Health England: Change4Life and Disney's 10 Minute Shake Up Campaign Launches with Release of New Study on the Benefits of Physical Activity for Children*, viewed 6 February 2019, from https://www.gov.uk/government/news/study-finds-physically-active-children-are-happier-and-more-confident

Gov.uk (2016a) *Childhood Obesity: A Plan for Action*, viewed 1 March 2019, from https://www.gov.uk/govern ment/publications/childhood-obesity-a-plan-for-action

Gov.uk. (2016a) *Ofsted: Not Enough Physical in Physical Education: Beyond 2012 Outstanding Physical Education for All*, viewed 6 February 2019, from https://www.gov.uk/government/news/not-enough-physical-in-physical-education

Gov.uk. (2016b) *Public Health England: Diabetes*, viewed 6 February 2019, from https://www.gov.uk/government/news/38-million-people-in-england-now-have-diabetes

Graue, M. (1993) 'Integrating theory and practice through instructional assessment', *Educational Assessment*, 1(4), 283-309.

Green, J. (2011) *Education, Professionalism and the Quest for Accountability: Hitting the Target but Missing the Point*, Abingdon: Routledge.

Greene, M. (1981) 'Aesthetic literacy in general education', in *80th Yearbook of the National Society for the Study of Education*, Chicago: University of Chicago Press, pp. 115-141, viewed 27 October 2017, from http://www.scribd.com/doc/26620361/Greene-Maxine-Aesthetic-Literacy-in-General-Education#scribd

Greenhalgh, P. (1994) *Emotional Growth and Learning*, London: Routledge.

Griebel, W. and Niesel, R. (2001) 'Transition to school child: what children tell us about school and what they teach us', Paper presented at the 11th European Conference on Quality of Early Childhood Education, Alkmaar, the Netherlands, 29 August-1 September.

Grossman, P.L., Wilson, S.M. and Shulman, L.S. (1989) 'Teachers of substance: subject matter knowledge for teaching', in M.C. Reynolds (ed.) *Knowledge Base for the Beginning Teacher*, Oxford: Pergamon Press, pp. 23-36.

GTCNI (General Teaching Council for Northern Ireland) (2011) *Teaching: The Reflective Profession*, viewed 21 June 2017, from http://www.gtcni.org.uk/index.cfm/area/information/page/profstandard

GTCS (General Teaching Council for Scotland) (2012a) *Code of Professionalism and Conduct*, viewed 21 July 2015, from http://www.gtcs.org.uk/web/FILES/teacher-regulation/copac-0412.pdf

GTCS (General Teaching Council for Scotland) (2012b) *Standards for Career Long Professional Learning: Supporting the Development of Teacher Professional Learning*, viewed 21 June 2017, from http://www.gtcs.org.uk/web/FIL ES/the-standards/standard-for-career-long-professional-learning-1212.pdf

GTCS (General Teaching Council for Scotland) (2015) *Code of Professionalism and Conduct*, viewed 8 June 2018, from http://www.gtcs.org.uk/standards/copac.aspx

Gu, Q. and Day, C. (2013) 'Challenges to teacher resilience: conditions count', *British Educational Journal*, 39(1), 22-44.

Habermas, J. (1971) *Knowledge and Human Interests*, London: Heineman.

Hallam, S. (2002) *Ability Grouping Schools: A Literature Review*, London: Institute of Education, University of London.

Halpern, D. (1998) 'Teaching critical thinking for transfer across domains', *American Psychologist*, 53, 449-455.

Halstead, M. and Taylor, M. (2000) 'Learning and teaching about values: a review of recent research', *Cambridge Journal of Education*, 30(2), 169-202.

Hammill, D., Goodman, L. and Wiederholt, J.L. (1974) 'Visual-motor processes: can we train them?' *The Reading Teacher*, 27(5), 469-478.

Hand, M. (2003) 'The meaning of spiritual education', *Oxford Review of Education*, 29(3), 391-401.

Hand, M. and Levinson, R. (2011) 'Discussing controversial issues in the classroom', *Educational Philosophy and Theory*, 44, 6.

Handscomb, G. (2013) 'Empowering teachers!...through practitioner research', *Education Today*, 63(3), 3-11.

Hansen, D. (1995) 'Teaching and the moral life of classrooms', *Journal for a Just and Caring Education*, 2, 59-74.

Hargreaves, A. and Fullan, M. (2012) *Professional Capital: Transforming Teaching in Every School*, New York: Teachers College Press.

Hargreaves, D.H. (1999) 'The knowledge-creating school', *British Journal of Educational Studies*, 47(2), 122-144.

Hargreaves, D.H. (2005) *About Learning: Report of the Learning Working Group*, London: Demos.

Harlen, H. and Deakin-Crick, R. (2003) 'Testing and motivation to learn', *Assessment in Education*, 10, 170-207.

Harlen, W. (1997) 'Making sense of the research on ability grouping', *Newsletter No 60* (Spring), Scottish Council for Research in Education (SCRE).

Harlen, W. (2000) *Teaching Science in the Primary Schools*, London: David Fulton.

Harlen, W. (2007) *Assessment of Learning*, London: Sage.

Harlen, W. (ed.) (2008) *Student Assessment and Testing*, London: Sage.

Harris, K. (1999) 'Aims, whose aims?' in R. Marples (ed.) *The Aims of Education*, London: Routledge, pp. 1-14.

Harrison, C. (2004) *Understanding Reading Development*, London: Sage

Harrison, C. and Killion, J. (2007) 'Ten roles for teacher leaders', *Educational Leadership - Teachers as Leaders*, 65(1), 74-77.

Hartley, B. and Sutton, R. (2010) 'Children's development of stereotypical gender-related expectations about academic engagement and consequences for performance', Poster presented at the British Educational Research Association (BERA) Annual Conference, University of Warwick, September 1-4.

Hartley, B. and Sutton, R. (2013) 'A stereotype threat account of boys' academic underachievement', *Child Development*, 84, 1716-1733.

Hatcher, R. (1998) 'Class differentiation in education: rational choices?' *British Journal of Sociology of Education*, 19(1), 5-24.

Hattie, J. (2009) *Visible Learning: A Synthesis of over 800 Meta-analyses Relating to Achievement*, Abingdon: Routledge.

Hattie, J. (2012b) 'Know thy impact', *Feedback*, 70(1), 18-23.

Hattie, J. (2018a) *Hattie Ranking: 252 Influences and Effect Sizes Related to Student Achievement*, viewed 14 September 2018, from https://visible-learning.org/hattie-ranking-influences-effect-sizes-learning-achievement/

Hattie, J. and Clarke, S. (2019) *Visible Learning Feedback*, Abingdon: Routledge.

Hattie, J. and Timperley, H. (2007) 'The power of feedback', *Review of Educational Research*, 77(1), 81-112.

Hattie, J. and Yates, G. (2014) *Visible Learning and the Science of How We Learn*, Abingdon: Routledge.

Hattie, J., Masters, D. and Birch, K. (2016) *Visible Learning into Action: International Case Studies of Impact*, Abingdon: Routledge.

Haydn, T. (2012) *Managing Pupil Behaviour: Improving the Classroom Atmosphere*, 2nd Edition, Abingdon: Routledge.

Haydon, G. (2006a) *Values in Education*, London: Continuum.

Haydon, G. (2006b) *Education, Philosophy and the Ethical Environment*, London: Faber and Faber.

Haydon, G. (2007) *Values in Education*, London: Bloomsbury Publishing.

Haydon, G. and Hayward, J. (2004) 'Values and citizenship education', in S. Capel, M. Leask and T. Turner (eds.) *Starting to Teach in the Secondary School: A Companion for the Newly Qualified Teacher*, 2nd Edition, London: RoutledgeFalmer.

Heatherley, S.V., Hancock, K.M.F. and Rogers, P.J. (2006). 'Psychostimulant and other effects of caffeine in 9- to 11-year-old children', *Journal of Child Psychology and Psychiatry*, 47(2), 135-142.

Heilbronn, R. (2008) *Teacher Education and the Development of Practical Judgement*, London: Continuum.

Heilbronn, R., Jones, C., Bubb, S. and Totterdell, M. (2002) 'School based induction tutors: a challenging role', *School Leadership and Management*, 22(4), 371-387.

Higgin, S. (2015) *Fact Check: Is the Pupil Premium Narrowing the Attainment Gap?* Viewed 3 April 2015, from http://theconversation.com/fact-check-is-the-pupil-premium-narrowing-the-attainment-gap-39601

Higgins, S., Katsipataki, M., Kokotsaki, D., Coleman, R., Major, L.E. and Coe, R. (2013) *The Sutton Trust-Education Endowment Foundation Teaching and Learning Toolkit*, London: Education Endowment Foundation, viewed 18 December 2014, from http://www.educationendowmentfoundation.org.uk/toolkit/

Hinds, E., Jones, L.B., Gau, J.M., Forrester, K.K. and Biglan, A. (2015) 'Teacher distress and the role of experiential avoidance', *Psychology in the Schools*, 52(3), 284-297.

HM Government (2015) *Working Together to Safeguard Children A Guide to Inter-agency Working to Safeguard and Promote the Welfare of Children 2015*, viewed 18 February 2018, from https://assets.publishing.service.gov.uk/government/uploads/system/uploads/attachment_data/file/592101/Working_Together_to_Safeguard_Children_20170213.pdf

Hobson, A. and McIntyre, J. (2013) 'Teacher fabrication as an impediment to professional learning and development: the external mentor antidote', *Oxford Review of Education*, 39(3), 345-365.

Hobson, A.J., Malderez, A., Tracey, L., Homer, M.S., Tomlinson, P.D., Ashby, P., Mitchell, N., McIntyre, J., Cooper, D., Roper, T., Chambers, G.N. and Tomlinson, P.D. (2009) *Becoming a Teacher: Teachers' Experiences of Initial Teacher Training, Induction and Early Professional Development: Research Report*, DCSF Research Report No. RR115, London: DCSF.

Hocutt, M. (2005) 'Indoctrination v. education', *Academic Questions*, Springer.

Holliday, A. (2007) *Doing and Writing Qualitative Research*, London: Sage.

Hook, P. and Vass, A. (2000) *Confident Classroom Leadership*, London: David Fulton Publishers.

Hopkins, D. (2008) *A Teacher's Guide to Classroom Research*, 4th Edition, Milton Keynes: Open University Press.

Howard-Jones, P.A. (2014). 'Neuroscience and education: myths and messages', *Nature Reviews Neuroscience*, 15(12), 817-824.

Howard-Jones, P.A., Jay, T., Mason, A. and Jones, H. (2016) 'Gamification of learning deactivates the default mode network', *Frontiers in Psychology*, 6(16).

Howard, R.W., Berkowitz, M.W., Shaeffer, E.F. (2004) 'Politics of character education', *Educational Policy*, 18(1), 188-215, viewed 29 March 2019, from https://doi.org/10.1177/0895904803260031

Howe, A. (1992) *Making Talk Work*, London: Hodder and Stoughton.

Hoyle, E. and John, P. (1995) *Professional Knowledge and Professional Practice*, London: Cassell.

Hoyle, E. (1974) 'Professionality, professionalism and control in teaching', *London Educational Review*, 3, 13-19.

Hromek, R. and Roffey, S. (2009) 'Promoting social and emotional learning with games: "it's fun and we learn things"', *Simulation and Gaming*, 40(5), 626-644.

HSE (Health and Safety Executive) (2015) *Health and Safety Checklist for Classrooms*, viewed 17 July 2015, from http://www.hse.gov.uk/risk/classroom-checklist.htm

HSE (Health and Safety Executive) (2016) *Work Related Stress, Anxiety and Depression Statistics in Great Britain 2016*, Liverpool: Health and Safety Executive.

Hughes, H. and Vass, A. (2001) *Strategies for Closing the Learning Gap*, Stafford: Network Educational Press.

Huitt, W. and Hummel, J. (2003) Piaget's Theory of Cognitive Development, Educational Psychology Interactive. Valdosta, GA: Valdosta State University, viewed 31 December 2011, from http://www.edpsycinteractive.org/topics/cognition/piaget.html

IPSEA (Independent Parental Special Education Advice) (2017) *Education Health and Care Plans: Examples of Good Practice*, viewed 18 November 2017, from https://councilfordisabledchildren.org.uk/help-resources/resources/education-health-and-care-plans-examples-good-practice

Ireson, J.M. and Hallam, S. (2001) *Ability Grouping in Education*, London: Paul Chapman.

Ireson, J.M., Hallam, S. and Hurley, C. (2005) 'What are the effects of ability grouping on GCSE attainment?', *British Educational Research Journal*, 31, 443-458.

Ireson, J.M., Hallam, S., Hack, S., Clark, H. and Plewis, I. (2002) 'Ability grouping in English secondary schools: effects on attainment in English, mathematics and science', *Educational Research and Evaluation*, 8(3), 299-318.

ISMA (International Stress Management Association) (nd) *The 60-Second Tranquiliser*, viewed 8 June 2018, from https://isma.org.uk/nsad-free-downloads

Izuma, K., Saito, D.N. and Sadato, N. (2008) 'Processing of social and monetary rewards in the human striatum', *Neuron*, 58(2), 284-294.

Jackson, C. and Warin, J. (2000) 'The importance of gender as an aspect of identity, from key transition points in compulsory education', *British Educational Research Journal*, 26(3), 375-391.

James, O. (2007) *Affluenza: How to Be Successful and Stay Sane*, London: Ebury Publishing

Jackson, C.A., Henderson, M., Frank, J.W. and Haw, S.J. (2012) 'An overview of prevention of multiple risk behaviour in adolescence and young adulthood', *Journal of Public Health*, 34: 131-141.

Jackson, P. (1968) *Life in Classrooms*, New York: Holt, Rinehart and Winston.

James, M. (1998) *Using Assessment for School Improvement*, Oxford: Heinemann Educational Publishers.

James, M. and Pedder, D. (2006) 'Beyond method: assessment and learning practices and values', *The Curriculum Journal*, 17, 109-138.

James, M., Black, P., Carmichael, P., Conner, C., Dudley, P., Fox, A., Frost, A., Honour, L., MacBeath, J., McCormick, R., Marshall, B., Pedder, D., Procter, R., Swaffield, S. and Wiliam, D. (2006) *Learning How to Learn: Tools for Schools*, London: Routledge.

Jenkins, K., Smith, H. and Maxwell, T. (2009) 'Challenging experiences faced by beginning casual teachers: here one day and gone the next!', *Asia-Pacific Journal of Teacher Education*, 37(1), 63-78.

Jess, M., Carse, N. and Keay, J. (2016) 'The primary physical education curriculum process: more complex than you might think!!', *Education 3-13*, 44(5), 502-512.

Jindal-Snape, D. (ed.) (2010a) *Educational Transitions: Moving Stories from Around the World*, New York: Routledge.

Jindal-Snape, D. (2010b) 'Moving on: integrating the lessons learnt and the way ahead', in D. Jindal-Snape (ed.) *Educational Transitions: Moving Stories from Around the World*, New York: Routledge, pp. 223-244.

Jindal-Snape, D. (2010c) *Moving to Secondary School, Board Game for Facilitating Primary-Secondary School Transition*, viewed 5 February 2012, from http://www.dundee.ac.uk/eswce/people/djindalsnape/transitions/

Jindal-Snape, D. (2010d) 'Setting the scene: educational transitions and moving', in D. Jindal-Snape (ed.) *Educational Transitions: Moving Stories from Around the World*, New York: Routledge, pp. 1-8.

Jindal-Snape, D. (2012) 'Portraying children's voices through creative approaches to enhance their transition experience and improve the transition practice', *LEARNing Landscapes*, 6(1), 223-240.

Jindal-Snape, D. (2018) 'Transitions from early years to primary and primary to secondary schools in Scotland', in T. Bryce, W. Humes, D. Gillies and A. Kennedy (eds.) *Scottish Education*, 5th Edition, Edinburgh: Edinburgh University Press Ltd.

Jindal-Snape, D., Baird, L. and Miller, K. (2011) *A Longitudinal Study to Investigate the Effectiveness of the Guitar Hero Project in Supporting Transition from P7-S1*, Dundee: Report for Learning and Teaching Scotland.

Jindal-Snape, D. and Foggie, J. (2006) *Moving Stories: A Research Study Exploring Children/Young People, Parents and Practitioners' Perceptions of Primary-Secondary Transitions*, Report for Transitions Partnership Project, Dundee: University of Dundee.

Jindal-Snape, D. and Foggie, J. (2008) 'A holistic approach to primary-secondary transitions', *Improving Schools*, 11, 5–18.

Jindal-Snape, D. and Hannah, E.F.S. (2014) 'Promoting resilience for primary-secondary transitions: supporting children, parents and professionals', in A.B. Liegmann, I. Mammes and K. Racherbäumer (eds.) *Facetten von übergängen im bildungssystem: nationale und internationale ergebnisse empirischer forschung*, Munster: Waxmann, pp. 265–277.

Jindal-Snape, D. and Ingram, R. (2013) 'Understanding and supporting triple transitions of international doctoral students: ELT and SuReCom Models', *Journal of Perspectives in Applied Academic Practice*, 1(1), 17–24.

Jindal-Snape, D. and Miller, D.J. (2008) 'A challenge of living? Understanding the psycho-social processes of the child during primary-secondary transition through resilience and self-esteem theories', *Educational Psychology Review*, 20, 217–236.

John, P.D. (2006) 'Lesson planning and the student teacher: re-thinking the predominant model', *Curriculum Studies*, 38(4), 483–489.

Johnson, B., Down, B., Le Cornu, R., Peters, J., Sullivan, A., Pearce, J., Hunter, J., Day, C. and Lieberman, A. (2016) *Promoting Early Career Teacher Resilience: A Socio-cultural and Critical Guide to Action*, Abingdon: Routledge.

Johnston-Wilder, S. and Lee, C. (2008) 'Does articulation matter when learning mathematics?' Proceedings of the British Society for Research into Learning Mathematics, 2008, *British Society for Research into Learning Mathematics*, 28(3), 54–59.

Johnston-Wilder, S. and Lee, C. (2010) 'Developing mathematical resilience', BERA Annual Conference 2010, 1–4 Sep 2010, University of Warwick, viewed 18 July 2015, from http://oro.open.ac.uk/24261/2/3C23606C.pdf

Joint Council for Qualifications (2016) *GCE Entry Trends 2016*, viewed 16 May 2017, from http://www.jcq.org.uk/examination-results/a-levels/2016

Jones, M.V., Meijen, C., McCarthy, J. and Sheffield, D. (2009) 'A theory of challenge and threat states in athletes', *International Review of Sport and Exercise Psychology*, 2(2), 161–180.

Joseph Rowntree Foundation (2016) *UK Poverty: Causes, Costs and Solutions*, viewed 3 January 2018, from https://www.jrf.org.uk/report/uk-poverty-causes-costs-and-solutions

Joseph Rowntree Foundation (2016) *Special Educational Needs and Their Links to Poverty*, viewed 6 February 2019, from https://www.jrf.org.uk/report/special-educational-needs-and-their-links-poverty

Kane, M.J. and Engle, R.W. (2002) 'The role of prefrontal cortex in working-memory capacity, executive attention, and general fluid intelligence: an individual-differences perspective', *Psychonomic Bulletin and Review*, 9(4), 637–671.

Kavale, K.A. and Forness, S.R. (1987). 'Substance over style: assessing the efficacy of modality testing and teaching', *Exceptional Children*, 54, 228–239.

Kayser, C., Petkov, C.I., Augath, M. and Logothetis, N.K. (2007). 'Functional imaging reveals visual modulation of specific fields in auditory cortex', *Journal of Neuroscience*, 27(8), 1824–1835.

Keay, J. and Lloyd, C. (2009) 'High quality professional development in physical education: the role of a subject association', *Professional Development in Education* (previously *Journal of In-Service Education*), 35(4), 655–676.

Keay, J. and Lloyd, C. (2011) *Linking Children's Learning with Professional Learning: Impact, Evidence and Inclusive Practice*, Rotterdam: Sense.

Keenan, T., Evans, S. and Crowley, K. (2016) *An Introduction to Child Development*, London and New York: Sage.

Kellogg, R.T. (2008) 'Training writing skills: A cognitive developmental perspective', *Journal of Writing Research*, 1(1), 1–26.

Kelly, G.A. (1955) *The Psychology of Personal Constructs*, New York: Norton.

Kemmis, S. and McTaggart, R. (1988) *The Action Research Planner*, 3rd Edition, Geelong: Deakin University Press.

Kennedy, A. (2007) 'Continuing professional development (CPD) policy and the discourse of teacher professionalism in Scotland', *Research Papers in Education*, 22(1), 95–111.

Kennedy, A. (2014) 'Understanding continuing professional development: the need for theory to impact on policy and practice', *Professional Development in Education*, 40(5), 688–697.

Kennedy, A. (2016) 'Professional learning in and for communities: Seeking alternatives discourses', *Professional Development in Education*, 42(5), 667–670.

Kerry, T. (2004) *Explaining and Questioning*, Cheltenham: Nelson Thornes.

Keuchel, T. and Beaudry, J. and Ritz-Swain, S. (2015) *Visual Literacy, MESHGuide*, University of Southern Maine, viewed 6 February 2019, from http://www.meshguides.org/meshguides-full-list/

King, F. (2013) 'Evaluating the impact of teacher professional development: an evidence-based framework', *Professional Development in Education*, 40(1), 89-111.

King, P. and Kitchener, K. (1994) *Developing Reflective Judgement*, San Francisco: Jossey-Bass.

Kirschner, P.A., Sweller, J. and Clark, R.E. (2006) 'Why minimal guidance during instruction does not work: An analysis of the failure of constructivist, discovery, problem-based, experiential, and inquiry-based teaching', *Educational Psychologist*, 46(2), 75-86.

Kitching, K., Morgan, M. and O'Leary, M. (2009) 'It's the little things: Exploring the importance of commonplace events for early-career teachers' motivation', *Teachers and Teaching: Theory and Practice*, 15(1), 43-58.

Klaasen, R.M. (2010) 'Teacher stress: the mediating role of collective efficacy beliefs', *The Journal of Educational Research*, 103, 342-350.

Klaasen, R.M. and Chui, M.M. (2010) 'Effects on teachers' self efficacy and job satisfaction: teacher gender, years of experience and job stress', *Journal of Educational Psychology*, 102(3), 741-756.

Kluger, A. and DeNisi, A. (1996a) 'The historical effects of feedback interventions on performance: a historical review', *Psychological Bulletin*, 119(2), 254-284.

Kluger, A. and DeNisi, A. (1996b) 'The effects of feedback interventions on performance: a historical view, a meta-analysis, and a preliminary feedback intervention theory', *Psychological Bulletin*, 119(2), 254-284.

Knapp, M., Hall, J. and Horgan, T. (2014) *Non-Verbal Communication in Human Interaction*, 8th Edition, Boston, MA: Wadsworth/Cengage Learning.

Knowles, C. (2015) *Achievement for All 3As*, MESHGuide, London: Achievement for All 3As (www.meshguides.org).

Knutson, B., Adams, C.M., Fong, G.W. and Hommer, D. (2001) 'Anticipation of monetary reward selectively recruits nucleus accumbens', *Journal of Neuroscience*, 21(RC159), 1-5.

Kohlberg, L. (1976) 'Moral stages and moralization: the cognitive-developmental approach', in T. Lickona (ed.) *Moral Development and Behaviour: Theory, Research and Social Issues*, New York: Holt, Rinehart and Winston.

Kohlberg, L. (1985) 'The just community: approach to moral education in theory and practice', in M. Berkowitz and F. Oser (eds.) *Moral Education: Theory and Application*, Hillsdale, NJ: Lawrence Erlbaum Associates Inc.

Kohn, A. (1994) 'Grading: The issue is not how but why', *Educational Leadership*, 52(2), 38-41.

Kolb, D.A. (1976) *The Learning Style Inventory: Technical Manual*, Boston: McBer and Co.

Kolb, D.A. (1984) *Experiential Learning*, New York: Prentice Hall.

Kolb, D.A. (2015) *Experiential Learning: Experience as the Source of Learning and Development*, 2nd Edition, New Jersey: Pearson Education.

Koretz, D. (2017) *The Testing Charade. Pretending to Make Schools Better*, Chicago, IL: University of Chicago Press.

Krathwohl, D.R., Bloom, B.S. and Masia, B.B. (1973) *Taxonomy of Educational Objectives, the Classification of Educational Goals. Handbook II: Affective Domain*, New York: David McKay Co., Inc.

Kratzig, G.P. and Arbuthnott, K.D. (2006). 'Perceptual learning style and learning proficiency: a test of the hypothesis', *Journal of Educational Psychology*, 98(1), 238-246.

Kutnick, P., Hodgkinson, S., Sebba, J., Humphreys, S., Galton, M., Steward, S., Blatchford, P. and Baines, E. (2006) *Pupil Grouping Strategies at Key Stage 2 and 3: Case Studies of 24 Schools in England*, DFES Research Report RR796, London: DfES.

Kutnick, P., Sebba, J., Blatchford, P., Galton., M. and Thorp, J. (2005) *The Effect of Pupil Grouping: A Literature Review*, DfES Research Report RR 688, London: DfES (copyright the University of Brighton).

Lam, S.F., Yim, P.S., Law, J.S.E and Cheung, R.W.Y. (2004) 'The effects of competition on achievement motivation in Chinese classrooms', *British Journal of Educational Psychology*, 74, 281-296.

Lambert, D., Young, M., Roberts, C. and Roberts, M. (2014). *Knowledge and the Future School: Curriculum and Social Justice*, London: Bloomsbury Academic Press.

Lander, V. Elton-Chalcraft, S. and Revell, L. (eds) (2016) *Special Issue Journal of Education for Teaching: Introduction to Fundamental British Values 42*, 3.

Lander, V., Elton-Chalcraft, S., Revell, L. Warner, D and Whitworth, L. (2016) 'To promote or not to promote fundamental British values? Teachers' standards, diversity and teacher education', *British Educational Research Journal*, 43(1), 29-48.

Langdon, F. and Ward, L. (2015), 'Educative mentoring: a way forward', *International Journal of Mentoring and Coaching in Education*, 4(4), 240-254.

Latta, S. (2003) *Hitting the Wall*, viewed 27 February 2019, from https://www.marathonandbeyond.com/choices/latta.htm

Lave, J. and Wenger, E. (1991) *Situated Learning: Legitimate Peripheral Participation*, Cambridge: Cambridge University Press.

Leahy, S., Lyon, C., Thompson, M. and Wiliam, D. (2005) 'Classroom assessment: Minute-by-minute and day-by-day', *Educational Leadership*, 63(3), 18-24.

Learning Wales (2016) *Induction for Newly Qualified Teachers in Wales*, viewed 21 June 2017, from http://learning.gov.wales/resources/collections/professional-standards?lang=en#collection-3

Leask, M. and Moorehouse, C. (2005) 'The student teacher's role and responsibilities', in S. Capel, M. Leask and T. Turner (eds.) *Learning to Teach in the Secondary School: A Companion to School Experience*, 4th Edition, Abingdon: Routledge, pp.18-31.

Leask, M. and Younie, S. (2014) 'National models for CPD: the challenges of twenty-first century knowledge management', *Journal for Professional Development in Education (PDiEJ)*, 39(2), 273-287.

Leckie, G. and Goldstein, H. (2017) 'The evolution of school league tables in England 1992-2016: "contextual value-added", "expected progress" and "progress 8"', *British Educational Research Journal*, 43(2), 193-212.

Lee, C. and Johnston-Wilder, S. (2015) 'Mathematical resilience: what is it and why is it important?', in S. Chinn (ed.) *The International Handbook of Dyscalculia and Mathematical Learning Difficulties*, Abingdon: Routledge, pp. 337-345.

Legislation.gov.uk (2013) *The Education School Teachers' Qualifications, England, Regulations 2003*, viewed 29 December 2018, from http://www.legislation.gov.uk/uksi/2003/1662/schedule/2/made

Leung, S.S.K., Chiang, V.C.L., Chui, Y.-Y., Lee, A.C.K. and Mak, Y.-W. (2011) 'Feasibility and potentials of online support for stress management among secondary school teachers', *Stress and Health*, 27, e282-e286.

Levinson, R. (2005) 'Planning for progression in science', in J. Frost and T. Turner (eds.) *Learning to Teach Science in the Secondary School: A Companion to School Experience*, 2nd Edition, London: RoutledgeFalmer.

Levinson, R. (2005) 'Science for citizenship', in J. Frost and T. Turner (2005) *Learning to Teach Science in the Secondary School: A Companion to School Experience*, 2nd Edition, London: RoutledgeFalmer.

Lewis, A. and Norwich, B. (2004) *Special Teaching for Special Children? Pedagogies for Inclusion*, Maidenhead: Open University Press.

Lickona, T. (1983) *Raising Good Children*, New York: Bantam Books.

Lindsay G., Cullen, M.A., Cullen, S., Dockrell, J., Strand, S., Arweck, E., Hegarty, S. and Goodlad, S. (2011) *Evaluation of Impact of DfE Investment in Initiatives Designed to Improve Teacher Workforce Skills in Relation to SEN and Disabilities*, DfE RR115, London: DfE.

Liu, S. and Meng, L. (2009) 'Perceptions of teachers, students and parents of the characteristics of good teachers: a cross-cultural comparison of China and the United States', *Educational Assessment, Evaluation and Accountability*, 21(4), 313-328.

Lortie, D. (1975) *Schoolteacher*, Chicago, IL: University of Chicago Press.

Lu, M.-L. (1998) *English-Only Movement: Its Consequences for the Education of Language Minority Children*, Bloomington: University of Indiana, An ERIC Clearinghouse digest No 139 (EDO-CS-98-12 Nov 1998), viewed 15 November 2015, from http://www.ericdigests.org/1999-4/english.htm

Lucey, H. and Reay, R. (2000) 'Identities in transition: anxiety and excitement in the move to secondary school', *Oxford Review of Education*, 26, 191-205.

Lunzer, E.A. and Gardner, K. (1979) *The Effective Use of Reading*, London: Heinemann.

Luthar, S.S. (2006) 'Resilience in development: a synthesis of research across five decades', in D. Cicchetti and D.J. Cohen (eds.) *Developmental Psychopathology. Volume 3: Risk, Disorder and Adaptation*, New York: John Wiley and Sons, pp. 739-795.

Luthar, S.S. and Barkin, S.H. (2012) 'Are affluent youth truly "at risk"? Vulnerability and resilience across three diverse samples', *Development and Psychopathology*, 24, 429-449.

Lymperopoulou, K. and Parameshwaran, M. (2014) *How Are Ethnic Inequalities in Education Changing? Dynamics of Diversity: Evidence from the 2011 Census*, Manchester: Centre on Dynamics of Ethnicity.

Machino, T. and Yoshizawa, T. (2006). 'Brain shrinkage due to acute hypernatremia', *Neurology*, 67, 880-880.

Mager, R. (2005) *Preparing Instructional Objectives*, 3rd Edition, Atlanta, GA: Center for Effective Performance.

Maker, C.J. and Nielson, A.B. (1995) *Teaching/Learning Models in Education of the Gifted*, 2nd Edition, Austin, TX: Pro-Ed.

Manouchehri, A. (2004) 'Implementing mathematics reform in urban schools: a study of the effect of teachers' motivational style', *Urban Education*, 39(5), 472-508.

Martin, J. (1985) *Factual Writing*, Geelong, Victoria: Deakin University Press.

Martin, J.R. (1976) 'What should we do with a hidden curriculum when we find one?' *Curriculum Inquiry*, 6, 131-151.

Maslow, A.H. (1970) *Motivation and Personality*, 2nd Edition, New York: Harper and Row.

Masten, A.S. (2014) 'Global perspectives on resilience in children and youth', *Child Development*, 85(1), 6-20.

McCarthy, C., Lambert, R. and Ullrich, A. (eds.) (2012) *International Perspectives on Teacher Stress*, Greenwich, CO: Information Age Publishing.

McClelland, D.C. (1961) *The Achieving Society*, Princeton, NJ: Van Norstrand.

McCormack, A. and Gore, J. (2008, Nov-Dec) '"If only I could just teach": early career teachers, their colleagues and the operation of power', Paper presented at the Annual Conference of the Australian Association for Research in Education, Brisbane.

McGregor, D. (1960) *The Human Side of Enterprise*, New York: McGraw-Hill.

McLaughlin, T. (2004) 'Philosophy, values and schooling: principles and predicaments of teacher example', in W. Aiken and J. Haldanne (eds.) *Philosophy and Its Public Role. Essays in Ethics, Politics, Society and Culture*, Exeter, UK and Charlottesville, USA: Imprint Academic.

McNiff, J. and Whitehead, J. (2002) *Action Research: Principles and Practice*, London: Routledge.

Mead, G.H. (1934) *Mind, Self, and Society*, Chicago: University of Chicago Press.

Mehrabian, A. (1972) *Non-Verbal Communication*, New York: Aldine Atherton.

Menter, I., Hulme, M., Elliot, D. and Lewin, J. (2010) *Literature Review on Teacher Education in the 21st Century*, Edinburgh: Scottish Government, Schools Research, Education Analytical Services.

Mercer, N. (1995) *The Guided Construction of Knowledge*, Clevedon: Multilingual Matters.

Mercer, N. (2015) *Thinking Together Project Materials*, University of Cambridge Faculty of Education, viewed 8 June 2018, from https://thinkingtogether.educ.cam.ac.uk/

Mezirow, J. (1997) 'Transformative learning: theory to practice', *New Directions for Adult and Continuing Education*, 74, 5-12.

Miles, M. and Huberman, M. (1994) *Qualitative Data Analysis: A Sourcebook of New Methods*, Thousand Oaks, CA: Sage.

Miller, N. and Boud, D. (1996) 'Animating learning from experience', in D. Boud and N. Miller (eds.) *Working with Experience*, London: Routledge.

Mills, S. (1995) *Stress Management for the Individual Teacher*, Lancaster: Framework Press.

Mizell, H. (2010) *Why Professional Development Matters*, viewed 21 June 2017, from https://learningforward.org/docs/pdf/why_pd_matters_web.pdf

Monk, J. and Silman, C. (2011) *Active Learning in Primary Classrooms - A Case Study Approach*, Harlow: Longman.

Moon, J. (2005) *Reflection in Learning and Professional Development*, London: RoutledgeFalmer.

Moon, J. (2008) *Critical Thinking: An Exploration of Theory and Practice*, Abingdon: Routledge.

Morgan, B. (2011) 'Consulting pupils about classroom teaching and learning: policy, practice and response in one school', *Research Papers in Education*, 26(4), 445-467.

Morgan, N. and Ellis, G. (2011) *A Kit Bag for Promoting Positive Behaviour in the Classroom*, London: Jessica Kingsley Publishers.

Morgan, N. and Saxton, J. (1991) *Teaching Questioning and Learning*, London: Routledge.

Morris, C. (2004) 'Towards an evidence-based approach to quality enhancement - a modest proposal', A Discussion Paper for the Higher Education Academy.

Mortimore, J. and Mortimore, P. (1984) *Secondary School Examinations: Helpful Servant or Dominating Masters?* Bedford Way Papers: 18, London: Institute of Education.

Mosston, M. and Ashworth, S. (2002) *Teaching Physical Education*, 5th Edition, New York: Macmillan College Publishing OR Maxwell Macmillan International.

Mourshed, M., Chijioke, C. and Barber, M. (2010) *How the World's Most Improved School Systems Keep Getting Better*, London: McKinsey and Company.

Mruk, C. (1999) *Self-Esteem: Research, Theory and Practice*, London: Free Association Books.

Muijs, D. and Reynolds, D. (2005) *Effective Teaching: Evidence and Practice*, 2nd Edition, London: Paul Chapman.

Muijs, D. and Reynolds, D. (2011) *Effective Teaching: Evidence and Practice*, 3rd Edition, London: Sage.

Murdock, T.B. (1999) 'The social context of risk: social and motivational predictors of alienation in middle school', *Journal of Educational Psychology*, 91, 1-14.

Musset, P. and Field, S. (2013) *A Skills Beyond School Review of England*, Paris: OECD.

Myhill, D.A. (2002) 'Bad boys and good girls? Patterns of interaction and response in whole class teaching', *British Educational Research Journal*, 28(3), 339-352.

Myhill, D.A. (2006) 'Talk, talk, talk: teaching and learning in whole class discourse', *Research Papers in Education*, 21(1), 19-41.

Myhill, D.A. (2009) 'Becoming a designer: trajectories of linguistic development', in R. Beard, D. Myhill, J. Riley and M. Nystrand (eds.) *The Sage Handbook of Writing Development*, London: Sage, pp. 402–414.

Myhill, D.A. (2010) 'Ways of knowing: grammar as a tool for developing writing', in T. Locke (ed.) *Beyond the Grammar Wars: A Resource for Teachers and Students on Developing Language Knowledge in the English/Literacy Classroom*, Abingdon: Routledge, pp. 129–148.

Myhill, D.A. and Jones, S. (2006) '"She doesn't shout at no girls": pupils' perceptions of gender equity in the classroom', *Cambridge Journal of Education*, 36(1), 99–113.

Myhill, D.A. and Warren, P. (2005) 'Scaffolds or straitjackets? Critical moments in classroom discourse', *Educational Review*, 57(1), 55–69.

NASUWT (2016) *The Big Question 2016: An Opinion Survey of Teachers and School Leaders*, viewed 6 February 2019, from https://www.nasuwt.org.uk/uploads/assets/uploaded/c316d25b-d8d7-4595-bbb0f9 181d0427d1.pdf

National STEM Centre (2015) *Concept Cartoons*, viewed 19 July 2015, from http://www.nationalstemcentre.org.uk/elibrary/resource/1482/concept-cartoons

NCSL (National College of School Leadership) *Personalising Learning*, viewed 18 July 2015, from www.nationalcollege.org.uk/index/leadershiplibrary/leadingschools/personalisedlearning/about-personalised-learning/what-is-personalised-learning.htm

Newman, T. and Blackburn, S. (2002) *Transitions in the Lives of Children and Young People: Resilience Factors*, Edinburgh: Scottish Executive Education Department.

Newsom, J. (1963) *Half Our Future*, Report to the Ministry of Education, viewed 8 June 2018, from http://www.educationengland.org.uk/documents/newsom/newsom1963.html#05

Newton, A. and Bowler, M. (2015) 'Assessment for and of learning', in Capel, S and Whitehead, M. (Eds) *Learning to Teach PE in the Secondary School: A Companion to School Experience*, 4th Edition, Abingdon: Routledge.

NHS (National Health Service) (2010), *Exercise, Genetics and Obesity*, viewed 6 January 2019, from https://www.nhs.uk/news/obesity/exercise-genetics-and-obesity

NHS (National Health Service) (2014) *Brits Eating too much Salt, Sugar and Fat*, viewed 6 February 2019, from https://www.nhs.uk/news/food-and-diet/brits-eating-too-much-salt-sugar-and-fat/

NICE (National Institute for Health and Care Excellence) (2013) *Attention Deficit Hyperactivity Disorders: Quality Standards*, viewed 30 December 2017, from https://www.nice.org.uk/guidance/qs39/chapter/list-of-quality-statements

Nicholls, J.G. (1984) 'Achievement motivation: conceptions of ability, subjective experience, task choice and performance', *Psychological Review*, 91, 328–346.

Nicholls, J.G. (1989) *The Competitive Ethos and Democratic Education*, Cambridge, MA: Harvard University Press.

Nicholson, N. (1987) 'The transition cycle: a conceptual framework for the analysis of change and human resources management', *Research in Personnel and Human Resources Management*, 5, 167–222.

Nicol, D. and Macfarlane-Dick, D. (2006) 'Formative assessment and self-regulated learning: a model and seven principles of good feedback', *Studies in Higher Education*, 31(2), 199–218.

Nixon, J. (1996) *Encouraging Learning: Towards a Theory of the Learning School*. Milton Keynes: Open University Press.

Nolan, M. (1995) *Standards in Public Life: First Report of the Committee on Standards in Public Life*, London: HMSO, viewed 18 February 2018, from https://assets.publishing.service.gov.uk/government/uploads/system/uploads/attachment_data/file/336919/1stInquiryReport.pdf

Norman, K. (ed.) (1992) *Thinking Voices: The Work of the National Oracy Project*, London: Hodder and Stoughton.

Norwich, B. (1993) 'Ideological dilemmas in special needs education: practitioners' views', *Oxford Review of Education*, 19(4), 527–545.

Noyes, A. (2003) 'Moving schools and social relocation', *International Studies in Sociology of Education*, 13(3), 261–280.

Nucci, L. (1987) 'Synthesis of research on moral development', *Educational Leadership*, 44(5), 86–92.

Nucci, L. (2007) *Moral Development and Moral Education: An Overview/Kohlberg's Theory*, viewed 29 November 2011, from http://tigger.uic.edu/~lnucci/MoralEd/overview.html#kohlberg

Nussbaum, M. (2010) *Not for Profit: Why Democracy Needs the Humanities*, Princeton, NJ: Princeton University Press.

O'Keeffe, G.S. and Clarke-Pearson, K. (2011) 'The impact of social media on children, adolescents and families', *Pediatrics*, 127, 800–804.

Oakeshott, M. (1972) 'Education: the engagement and its frustration', in T. Fuller (ed.) (1989) *The Voice of Liberal Learning*, New Haven and London: Yale University Press.

OECD (Organisation for Economic Cooperation and Development) (2005) *Teachers Matter: Attracting, Developing and Retaining Effective Teachers*, Education and Training Policy, Paris: OECD Publishing.

OECD (Organisation for Economic Co-operation and Development) (2011) *Divided We Stand: Why Inequality Keeps Rising*, Paris: OECD Publishing, viewed 1 February 2015, from http://dx.doi.org/10.1787/97892641 19536-en

OECD (Organisation for Economic Cooperation and Development) (2013a) 'Do new teachers feel prepared for teaching?', *Teaching in Focus*, viewed 23 June 2017, from http://www.keepeek.com/Digital-Asset-Management/oecd/education/do-new-teachers-feel-prepared-for-teaching980b f07den#.WUy3XsaZPos#page1

OECD (Organisation for Economic Co-operation and Development) (2013b) *TALIS 2013 Results: An International Perspective on Teaching and Learning*, Paris: OECD, viewed 1 May 2018, from https://read.oecd-ilibrary.org/education/talis-2013-results_9789264196261-en#page1

OECD (Organisation for Economic Cooperation and Development) (2014) *Education at a Glance 2014*, OECD Indicators, Paris: OECD Publishing.

OECD (Organisation for Economic Cooperation and Development) (2015) *The Teaching and Learning International Survey*, Paris: OECD, viewed 8 June 2018, from http://www.oecd.org/edu/school/talis.htm

Ofsted (The Office for Standards in Education, Children's Services and Skills) (1993) *The New Teacher in School: A Survey by Her Majesty's Inspectorate in England and Wales*, 1992, London: HMSO.

Ofsted (The Office for Standards in Education, Children's Services and Skills) (1996) *The Annual Report of Her Majesty's Chief Inspector of Schools*, London: HMSO.

Ofsted (The Office for Standards in Education, Children's Services and Skills) (2002) *Good Teaching; Effective Departments*, London: Ofsted.

Ofsted (The Office for Standards in Education, Children's Services and Skills) (2004) *Promoting and Evaluating Pupils' Spiritual, Moral, Social and Cultural Development*, viewed 3 July 2018, from http://webarchive.nationalarchives.gov.uk/20141107081413/http://www.ofsted.gov.uk/resources/promoting-and-evaluating-pupils-spiritual-moral-social-and-cultural-development

Ofsted (The Office for Standards in Education, Children's Services and Skills) (2007) *The Annual Report of Her Majesty's Chief Inspector of Education, Children's Services and Skills 2006/07*, London: The Stationery Office, viewed 30 May 2012, from http://www.Ofsted.gov.uk/

Ofsted (The Office for Standards in Education, Children's Services and Skills) (2008) *Assessment for Learning: The Impact of National Strategy Support*, viewed 21 July 2015, from http://dera.ioe.ac.uk/9309/1/Assessment%20for%20learning%20-%20the%20impact%20of%20National%20Strategy%20support.pdf

Ofsted (The Office for Standards in Education, Children's Services and Skills) (2010) *The Special Educational Needs and Disability Review: A Statement Is Not Enough*, Manchester: Ofsted, viewed 3 July 2018, from http://dera.ioe.ac.uk/1145/1/Special%20e ducation%20needs%20and%20disability %20review.pdf

Ofsted (The Office for Standards in Education, Children's Services and Skills) (2011a) *ICT in Schools 2008-2011: An Evaluation of Information and Communication Technology Education in Schools in England 2008-11*, Manchester: Ofsted.

Ofsted (The Office for Standards in Education, Children's Services and Skills) (2011b) *The Annual Report of Her Majesty's Chief Inspector of Education, Children's Services and Skills 2010/11*, viewed 18 March 2015, from http://www.gov.uk/government/uploads/system/uploads/attachment_data/file/379294/Ofsted_20Annual20Report_ 2010- 11_20-_20full.pdf

Ofsted (The Office for Standards in Education, Children's Services and Skills) (2012a) *Beyond 2012: Outstanding Physical Education for All*, viewed 9 February 2019, from https://assets.publishing.service.gov.uk/government/uploads/system/uploads/attachment_data/file/413187/Beyond_2012_-_outstanding_physical_education_for_all.pdf

Ofsted (The Office for Standards in Education, Children's Services and Skills) (2012b) *Questioning to Promote Learning*, viewed 20 March 2015, from www.fromgoodtooutstanding.com/2012/05/ofsted-2012-questioning-to-promote-learning

Ofsted (The Office for Standards in Education, Children's Services and Skills) (2012c) *The Shape of School Inspection from 2012*, viewed 6 February 2019, from https://webarchive.nationalarchives.gov.uk/20141106183252/https://www.ofsted.gov.uk/news/shape-of-school-inspection-2012?news=17353

Ofsted (The Office for Standards in Education, Children's Services and Skills) (2013) *Unseen Children: Access and Achievement 20 Years On*, London: Ofsted.

Ofsted (The Office for Standards in Education, Children's Services and Skills) (2014a) *Common Inspection Framework: Education, Skills and Early Years from September 2015*, viewed 2 July 2017, from http://www.ofsted.gov.uk/resources/framework-for-school-inspection

Ofsted (The Office for Standards in Education, Children's Services and Skills) (2014b) *Note for Inspectors: Use of Assessment Information during Inspections in 2014/15*, viewed 8 June 2018, from https://

www.gov.uk/government/publications/note-for-inspectors-use-of-assessment-information-during-inspections-in-201415

Ofsted (The Office for Standards in Education, Children's Services and Skills) (2015a) *School Inspection Handbook: Guidance for Inspecting Schools under the Common Inspection Framework*, Manchester: Ofsted.

Ofsted (The Office for Standards in Education, Children's Services and Skills) (2015b) *The Common Inspection Framework: Education, Skills and Early Years*, Manchester: Ofsted, viewed 3 July 2018, from https://assets.publishing.service.gov.uk/government/uploads/system/uploads/attachmentdata/file/717953/The_common_inspection_framework_education_skills_and early_years-v2.pdf

Ofsted (The Office for Standards in Education, Children's Services and Skills) (2016) *School Inspection* (Updated January 2017), viewed 12 February 2019, from https://www.gov.uk/government/publications/schools-inspection-newsletter-2015-to-2016.

Ofsted (The Office for Standards in Education, Children's Services and Skills) (2017a) *Official Statistics: Maintained Schools and Academies Inspection Outcomes as at 31 August 2016* (Updated 25 October 2017), viewed 8 June 2018, from https://www.gov.uk/government/publications/maintained-schools-and-academies-inspections-and-outcomes-as-at-31-august-2016/maintained-schools-and- academies-inspection-outcomes-as-at-31-august-2016.

Ofsted (The Office for Standards in Education, Children's Services and Skills) (2017b) *School Inspection Handbook*, viewed 18 February 2018, from https://www.gov.uk/government/uploa ds/system/uploads/attachment_data/file/678967/School_inspection_handbook_se ction5.pdf

Ofsted (The Office for Standards in Education, Children's Services and Skills) (2017c) *School Inspection Update: Special Edition September 2017*, viewed 18 February 2018, from https://assets.publishing.service.gov.uk /government/uploads/system/uploads/attachmentdata/file/643178/SIU_special_edition_5_September_final.pdf

Ofsted (The Office for Standards in Education, Children's Services and Skills) (2018a) *Ofsted Inspections: Myths*, viewed 14 September 2018, from https://www.gov.uk/government/publications/school-inspection-handbook-from-september-2015/ofsted-inspections-mythbusting

Ofsted (The Office for Standards in Education, Children's Services and Skills) (2018b) *School Inspection Handbook for Inspecting Schools in England Under Section 5 of the Education Act 2005*, Manchester: Ofsted, viewed 18 December 2018, from https://assets.publishing.service.gov.uk/government/uploads/system/uploads/attachmentdata/file/730127/School_inspectionhandbook_section_5_ 270718.pdf

Ofsted (The Office for Standards in Education, Children's Services and Skills) (2018d) *The Annual Report of Her Majesty's Chief Inspector of Education, Children's Services and Skills 2016/17*, viewed 18 February 2018, from https://www.gov.uk/government/uploads/system/uploads/attachment_data/file/666871/Ofsted_Annual_Report_2016-17_Accessible.pdf

Ofqual (Office for Qualifications and Examination Regulation) (2007) *Changes to A Levels*, viewed 7 January 2018, from http://webarchive.nationalarchives.gov.uk/20110206091107/http://www.ofqual.gov.uk/qualification-and-assessment-framework/89-articles/13-a-and-as-levels

Oliver, M. (1990) *The Politics of Disablement: A Sociological Approach,* St Martin's Press (summary of his views of the definitions), viewed 6 January 2017, from http://disability-studies.leeds.ac.uk/files/library/Oliver-i n-soc-dis.pdf

Olweus, D. (1993) *Bullying at School*, Oxford: Blackwell.

ONS (Office for National Statistics) (2012a) *Ethnicity and National Identity in England and Wales: 2011*, viewed 16 May 2017, from https://www.ons.gov.uk/peoplepopulationandcommunity/culturalidentity/ethnicity/articles/ethnicityandnationalidentityinenglandandwales/2012-12-11

ONS (Office for National Statistics) (2012b) *Integrated Household Survey April 2011 to March 2012*, viewed 1 February 2015, from http://www.ons.gov.uk/ons/rel/integrated-household-survey/integrated-household-survey/april-2011-to-march-2012/stb-integrated-household-survey-april-2011-to-march-2012.html

ONS (Office for National Statistics) (2016) *Social Survey Division, Annual Population Survey, July 2015-June 2016* (computer file), Colchester, Essex: UK Data Archive, viewed 25 May 2017, from http://dx.doi.org/10.5255/UKDA-SN-8054-1

ONS (Office for National Statistics) (2017) *Explore the Gender Pay Gap and Test Your Knowledge*, viewed 20 December 2017, from https://visual.ons.gov.uk/explore-the-gender-pay-gap-and-test-your-knowledge/#interactive

Open University, Open Learn (nd) *Self Regulated Learning*, viewed 6 February 2019, from http://www.open.edu/openlearncreate/local/ocwsearch/customgsearch.php?q=self+regulated+learning&headersearchbutton=

The Open University's Open Learn website, viewed 29 December 2018, from http://www.open.edu/openlearn/education/educational-technology-and-practice/educational-practice

Orchard, J. and Winch, C. (2015) 'What training do teachers need?: Why theory is necessary to good teaching', *Impact*, 22, 1-43.

Orchard, J., Heilbronn, R. and Winstanley, C. (2016) 'Philosophy for teachers (P4T): developing new teachers applied ethical decision making', *Ethics and Education*, 11(1), 42–54.

Organisation for Economic Co-operation and Development (OECD) (2013)

Ovens, A. Hopper, T. and Butler, J. (2013) *Complexity Thinking in Physical Education: Reframing Curriculum, Pedagogy and Research*, Abingdon: Routledge.

Oversby, J. (2012) 'Science education research: a critical appraisal of its contribution to education', in J. Oversby (ed.) *ASE Guide to Research in Science Education*, Herts: ASE.

Owen-Jackson, G. (ed.) (2008) *Learning to Teach Design and Technology in the Secondary School: A Companion to School Experience*, 2nd Edition, Abingdon: Routledge.

Oxfam (2012) *The Perfect Storm: Economic Stagnation, the Rising Cost of Living, Public Spending Cuts and the Impact on UK Poverty*, Oxford: Oxfam GB.

Paechter, C. (2000) *Changing School Subjects: Power, Gender and Curriculum*, Maidenhead: Open University Press.

Pajares, M.F. (1992) 'Teachers' beliefs and educational research: cleaning up a messy construct', *Review of Educational Research*, 62(3), 307–332.

Panadero, E. (2017) 'A review of self-regulated learning: six models and four directions for research', *Frontiers in Psychology*, 8, 422.

Parkinson, B. and Simons, G. (2012) 'Worry spreads: interpersonal transfer of problem-related anxiety', *Cognition and Emotion*, 26(3), 462–479.

Patterson, E. (2016) *Research Methods 1: How to Get Started on a Literature Review*, MESHGuide, University of Winchester.

Patterson, E. (2016) *Research Methods 2: Developing Your Research Design*, MESHGuide, University of Winchester.

Patterson, E. (2016) *Research Methods 3: Considering Ethics in Your Research*, MESHGuide, University of Winchester.

Pearce, S. (2005) *You Wouldn't Understand: White Teachers in the Multiethnic Classroom*, Stoke on Trent: Trentham Books.

Pease, A. and Pease, B. (2011) *Body Language in the Workplace*, London: Orion, viewed 4 December 2017, from http://www.peaseinternational.com/index.php?route=news/headlines

Perera, K. (1987) *Understanding Language*, Sheffield: NAAE.

Personal, Social, Health Education Association (2016), viewed 6 January 2019, from https://www.pshe-association.org.uk/

Peters, R.S. (1964) *Education as Initiation*, London: Evans for the University of London Institute of Education.

Peters, S. (2010) *Literature Review: Transition from Early Childhood Education to School*, Report commissioned by the Ministry of Education, Wellington: Ministry of Education.

Piaget, J. (1932) *The Moral Judgment of the Child*, New York: Simon and Schuster.

Piaget, J. (1954) *The Construction of Reality in the Child*, New York: Basic Books.

Pickering, J., Daly, C. and Pachler, N. (2007) *New Designs for Teachers' Professional Learning*, London: Institute of Education.

Pietarinen, J., Pyhältö, K. and Soini, T. (2010a) 'A horizontal approach to school transitions: a lesson learned from Finnish 15-year-olds', *Cambridge Journal of Education*, 40(3), 229–245.

Pietarinen, J., Soini, T. and Pyhältö, K. (2010b) 'Learning and well-being in transitions – how to promote pupils' active learning agency?' in D. Jindal-Snape (ed.) *Educational Transitions: Moving Stories from around the World*, New York: Routledge, pp. 143–158.

Pittman, C.M. and Karl, E.M. (2015) *Rewire Your Anxious Brain*, Oakland, CA: New Harbinger Publications.

Plummer, D.M. (2014) *Helping Adolescents and Adults Build Self-Esteem*, 2nd Edition, London: Jessica Kingsley Publishers.

Pollard, A. (2002) *Readings for Reflective Teaching*, London: Continuum.

Pollard, A. with Anderson, J., Maddock, M., Swaffield, S., Warin, J. and Warwick, P. (2008) *Reflective Teaching: Effective and Evidence Informed Practice*, 3rd Edition, London: Continuum.

Postlethwaite, K. (1993) *Differentiated Science Teaching: Responding to Individual Differences and Special Educational Needs*, Milton Keynes: Open University Press.

Poulson, L. and Wallace, M. (eds.) (2004) *Learning to Read Critically in Learning and Teaching*, London: Sage.

Powell, E. (2005) 'Conceptualising and facilitating active learning: teachers' video-stimulated reflective dialogues', *Reflective Practice*, 6(3), 407–418.

Power, S., Edwards, T., Whitty, G. and Wigfall, V. (2003) *Education and Middle Class*, Maidenhead: Open University Press.

Pressley, M. (2000) 'What should comprehension instruction be the instruction of?' in M.L. Kamil, P.B. Mosenthal, P.D. Pearson and R. Barr (eds.) *Handbook of Reading Research*, Volume 3, Mahwah, NJ: Erlbaum, pp. 545-561.

Pring, R. (2009) *Nuffield Review of 14-19 Education and Training*, viewed 15 January 2018, from http://www.nuffieldfoundation.org/14-19review

Pring, R. (2012) *The Life and Death of Secondary Education for All*, Abingdon: Routledge.

Procter, R. (2013) *Assessment for Learning*, MESHGuide, University of Bedfordshire, viewed 24 July 2015, from www.MESHGuides.org

Prosser, M. and Trigwell, K. (1999) *Understanding Teaching and Learning: The Experience in Higher Education*, The Society for Research into Higher Education, Maidenhead: Open University Press.

PSHE (Personal, Social and Health Education) Association (2016) *PSHE Education Programme of Study Key Stages 1-5*, viewed 28 February 2019, from https://www.pshe-association.org.uk/system/files/PSHE%2 0Education%20Programme%20of%20Study%20%28Key%20stage%201-5%29%20Jan%202017_2.pdf

Public Health England (2015) *Promoting Children and Young People's Emotional Health and Well-Being*, London: Public Health England.

Public Health England (2016) *National Diet and Nutrition Survey: Results from Years 5 and 6 (Combined) of the Rolling Programme (2012/2013 - 2013/2014)*, London: Crown Copyright.

Putnam, R.D. (2000) *Bowling Alone: The Collapse and Revival of American Community*, New York: Simon and Schuster.

QCA (Qualifications and Curriculum Authority) (2001) *Supporting School Improvement: Emotional and Behavioural Development*, London: QCA.

QCA (Qualifications and Curriculum Authority) (2007) *Geography Programme of Study and Attainment Target*, London: QCA, viewed 4 January 2018, from http://media.education.gov.uk/assets/files/pdf/g/g eography%202007%20programme%20of%20study%20for%20key%20stage%203.pdf

QCA (Qualifications and Curriculum Authority) (2008) *National Curriculum Key Stages 3 and 4*, viewed 7 January 2018, from www.education.gov.uk/schools/teachingandlearning/curriculum/secondary

Ramaprasad, A. (1983) 'On the definition of feedback', *Behavioral Science*, 28(1), 4-13.

Ravitch, D. (2013) *Reign of Error: The Hoax of the Privatization Movement and the Danger to America's Public Schools*, New York: Alfred A. Knopf.

Reardon, S. (2011) 'The widening academic achievement gap between the rich and the poor: new evidence and possible explanations', in G. Duncan and R. Murnane (eds.) *Whither Opportunity? Rising Inequality, Schools and Children's Life Chances*, New York: Russell Sage Foundation.

Reinke, W.M., Lewis-Palmer, T. and Merrell, K. (2008) 'The classroom check-up: a classwide teacher consultation model for increasing praise and decreasing disruptive behavior', *School Psychology Review*, 37(3), 315-332.

Reiss, M. and White, J. (2013) *An Aims-Based Curriculum*, London: IoE Press.

Riding, R.J. and Burton, D. (1998) 'Cognitive style, gender and behaviour in secondary school pupils', *Research in Education*, 59, 38-49.

Riding, R.J. and Cheema, I. (1991) 'Cognitive styles: an overview and integration', *Educational Psychology*, 11, 193-215.

Robertson, J. (1996) *Effective Classroom Control: Understanding Teacher-Student Relationships*, 3rd Edition, London: Hodder and Stoughton.

Robinson, K. and Aronica L. (2016) *Creative Schools: Revolutionizing Education from the Ground Up*, London: Penguin.

Rogers, B. (2002) *Classroom Behaviour*, London: Paul Chapman Publishing.

Rogers, B. (2015) *Classroom Behaviour: A Practical Guide to Effective Teaching, Behaviour Management and Colleague Support*, 4th Edition, London: Sage.

Rogers, C.R. (2007) 'The necessary and sufficient conditions of therapeutic personality change', *Psychotherapy: Theory, Research, Practice, Training*, 44(3), 240-248. Reprinted article originally appeared in *Journal of Consulting Psychology*, 1957(Apr), 21(2), 95-103.

Rogoff, B. (1990) *Apprenticeship in Thinking: Cognitive Development in Social Context*, Oxford: Oxford University Press.

Roosevelt, F.D. (1933) "Inaugural Address, March 4, 1933", *World Affairs*, 96(1), 26-28.

Rose, J. (2009) *Identifying and Teaching Children and Young People with Dyslexia and Literacy Difficulties*, London: DCSF.

Rose, R. (2004) 'Towards a better understanding of the needs of pupils who have difficulties accessing learning', in S. Capel, R. Heilbronn, M. Leask and T. Turner (eds.) *Starting to Teach in the Secondary School: A Companion for the Newly Qualified Teacher*, 2nd Edition, London: RoutledgeFalmer, pp.139-148.

Rosenthal, R. and Jacobson, L. (1968) *Pygmalion in the Classroom*, New York: Holt, Rinehart and Winston.

Roosevelt, F.D. (1933) "Inaugural Address, March 4, 1933", *World Affairs*, 96(1), 26-28.

Rowland, T. (2004) 'The childhood obesity epidemic: putting the dynamics into thermodynamics', *Pediatric Exercise Science*, 16, 86-93.

Royal College of Psychiatrists (2013) *Whole-Person Care: From Rhetoric to Reality - Achieving Parity between Mental and Physical Health* (Occasional paper OP88), London: Royal College of Psychiatrists, viewed 6 February 2019, from http://publichealthwell.ie/node/436048?&content=resource&member=6841&catalogue=Research%20and%20Evaluation,Report&collection=Mental%20Health%20&tokens_complete=true

Rudduck, J. (2004) *Developing a Gender Policy for Secondary Schools*, Maidenhead: Open University Press.

Rudduck, J., Brown, N. and Hendy, L. (2006) *Personalised Learning and Pupil Voice*, The East Sussex Project, London: DFES.

Rudman, D. (2018) *Learning and Memory*, London and New York: Sage.

Ryan, R.M. and Deci, E.L. (2000a) 'Intrinsic and extrinsic motivations: classic definitions and new directions', *Contemporary Educational Psychology*, 25, 54-67.

Ryan, R.M. and Deci, E.L. (2000b) 'Self-determination theory and the facilitation of intrinsic motivation, social development and well-being', *American Psychologist*, 55, 68-78.

Ryan, R.M. and Stiller, J. (1991) 'The social contexts of internalization: parent and teacher influences on autonomy, motivation and learning', in P.R. Pintrich and M.L. Maehr (eds.) *Advances in Motivation and Achievement*, **Volume 7**. Greenwich, CT: JAI Press, pp. 115-149.

Sachs, J. (2001) 'Teacher professional identity: competing discourses, competing outcomes', *Journal of Education Policy*, 16(2), 149-161.

Sachs, J. (2003) *The Activist Teaching Profession*, Maidenhead: Open University Press.

Sadler, R. (1989) 'Formative assessment and the design of instructional systems', *Instructional Science*, 18, 119-144.

Sage, R. (2000) *Class Talk*, Stafford: Network Educational Press.

Säljö, R. (1979) *Learning in the Learner's Perspective. 1: Some Common-Sense Conceptions* (Report No.76), Göteborg: Institute of Education, University of Göteborg.

Salmon, P. (1988) *Psychology for Teachers: An Alternative Approach*, London: Hutchinson.

Salovey, P. and Mayer, J.D. (1990) 'Emotional intelligence', *Imagination, Cognition and Personality*, 9, 185-211.

Savage, M., Devine, F., Cunningham, N., Taylor, M., Li, Y., Hjellbrekke, J., Le Roux, B., Friedman, S., Miles, A. (2013) 'A new model of social class? Findings from the BBC's great British class survey experiment', *Sociology*, 47(2), 1-32.

Sawyer, S.M., Afi fi, R.A., Bearinger,L.H., Blakemore,SJ., Dick, B. Ezeh,A.C and Patton, G.C. (2012) 'Adolescence: a foundation for future health', *The Lancet*, 379(9826), 1630-1640.

Scherger, S. and Savage, M. (2010) 'Cultural transmission, educational attainment and social mobility', *The Sociological Review*, 58(3), 406-428.

Schunk, D. and Zimmerman, B. (eds.) (1998) *Self-Regulated Learning: From Teaching to Self-Reflective Practice*, New York: Guilford Press.

Schmeck, R. (ed.) (2015) *Learning Strategies and Learning Styles*, New York: Springer Science and Business Media.

Scholes, S. (2016) *Health Survey for England (2015) Physical Activity in Children*, NHS Digital, viewed 6 February 2019, from https://files.digital.nhs.uk/publicationimport/pub22xxx/pub22610/hse2015-child-phy-act.pdf

Schon, D.A. (1983) *The Reflective Practitioner: How Professionals Think in Action*, New York: Basic Books.

School Sport in England (2017), viewed 6 January 2019, from https://www.fit-to-study.org

Schwab, J.J. (1964) 'Structure of the disciplines: meaning and significance, in G.W. Ford and L. Pugno (eds.) *The Structure of Knowledge and Curriculum*, Chicago, IL: Rand McNally, pp. 6-30.

Scott, D. (2000) *Reading Educational Research and Policy*, London: RoutledgeFalmer.

Scottish Government (2010) *Assessment for Curriculum for Excellence: Strategic Vision, Key Principles*, Edinburgh: Scottish Government.

Scottish Government (2017) *Parent Zone*, viewed 10 June 2018, from https://education.gov.scot/parentzone/additional-support/What%20are%20additional%20support%20needs?

Scriven, M. (1967) 'The methodology of evaluation', in R.W. Tyler, R.M. Gangé and M. Scriven (eds.) *Perspectives of Curriculum Evaluation*: Volume 1, Chicago: Rand McNally.

SEED (Scottish Executive Education Department) (1999) *Review of Assessment in Pre-School and 5-14*, Edinburgh: HMSO.

Seddon, C. (2003) *Adolescent Health*, London: British Medical Association.

Seligman, M. (2003) *Authentic Happiness: Using the New Positive Psychology to Realise Your Potential for Lasting Fulfilment*, London: Nicholas Brealey Publishing.

Seligman, M. (2011) *Flourish: A New Understanding of Happiness and Well-being - and How to Achieve Them*, London: Nicholas Brealey Publishing.

Selman, R.L. (1980) *The Growth of Interpersonal Understanding*, New York: Academic Press.

SFT (School Food Trust) (2012), viewed 6 January 2019, from http://www.gov.uk/government/publications

SFT (School Food Trust) (2012) *Annual Report and Financial Statements*, London: The Stationary Office, viewed 28 February 2019, from https://assets.publishing.service.gov.uk/government/uploads/system/upl oads/attachment_data/file/246932/0491.pdf

Shakespeare, T. and Watson, N. (2002) 'The social model of disability: an outdated ideology?' *Research in Social Science and Disability*, 2, 9–28.

Shayer, M. (2008) 'Intelligence for education: as described by Piaget and measured by metrics', *British Journal of Educational Psychology*, 78(1), 1–29.

Shayer, M. and Adey, P. (eds.) (2002) *Learning Intelligence: Cognitive Acceleration across the Curriculum from 5 to 15 Years*, Maidenhead and Philadelphia: Open University Press.

Shepard, J. (2000) *The Role of Classroom Assessment in Teaching and Learning*, Los Angeles: Centre for the Study of Evaluation, National Centre for Research on Evaluation, Standards and Student Testing, Graduate School of Education and Information Studies, University of California.

Shing, Y.L. and Brod, G. (2016) 'Effects of prior knowledge on memory: implications for education', *Mind, Brain and Education*, 10(3), 153–161.

Short, G. (1986) 'Teacher expectation and West Indian underachievement', *Educational Research*, 27(2), 95–101.

Shulman, L. (1986) 'Those who understand: knowledge growth in teaching', *Educational Researcher*, 15, 4–14.

Shulman, L. (1987) 'Knowledge and teaching: foundation of a new reform', *Harvard Review*, 57, 1–22.

Siegel, D. (2010) *Mindsight: Transform Your Brain with the New Science of Kindness*, London: Oneworld Publications.

Sifft, J.M. and Khalsa, G.C.K. (1991). 'Effect of educational kinesiology upon simple response-times and choice response-times', *Perceptual and Motor Skills*, 73(3), 1011–1015.

Skidmore, D. (2000) 'From pedagogical dialogue to dialogic pedagogy', *Language and Education*, 14(4), 283–296.

Skinner, B.F. (1953) *Science and Human Behavior*, New York: Macmillan.

Slavin, R. E. (2018) *Effect Sizes: How Big Is Big?* viewed 14 September 2018, from https://robertslavinsblog .wordpress.com/2018/04/12/effect-sizes-how-big-is-big/

Smith, E. (2005) *Analysing Underachievement in Schools*, London: Continuum Books.

Smith, R. and Standish, P. (eds.) (1997) *Teaching Right and Wrong: Moral Education in the Balance*, Stoke on Trent: Trentham.

Smyth, J. (1989) *Rationale for Teachers' Critical Pedagogy: A Handbook*, Geelong: Deekin University Press.

Snook, L.A. (ed.) (2010) *Concepts of Indoctrination*, Abingdon: Routledge.

Sousa, D. (2015) *Brain-Friendly Assessments: What They Are and How to Use Them*, West Palm Beach: Learning Sciences International.

Spendlove, D. (2009) *Putting Assessment for Learning into Practice*, London: Continuum.

Standish, A. and Sehgal Cuthbert, A. (eds.) (2017) *What Should Schools Teach? Disciplines, Subjects and the Pursuit of Truth*, London: UCL Institute of Education Press.

Stanford University (2015) *Teaching Commons: Blooms Taxonomy of Educational Objectives*, viewed 10 June 2018, from http://teachingcommons.stanford.edu/resources/course-preparation-resources/course-des ign-aids/bloom%E2%80%99s-taxonomy-educational-objectives

Stenhouse, L. (1975) *An Introduction to Curriculum Research and Development*, London: Heinemann.

Stenhouse, L. (1983) *Authority, Education and Emancipation*, London: Heinemann

Stern, D.N. (1985) *The Interpersonal World of the Infant*, New York: Basic Books.

Stobart, G. (2009) 'Determining validity in national curriculum assessments', *Educational Research*, 51(2), 161–179.

Stobart, G. (2014) *The Expert Learner: Challenging the Myth of Ability*, Maidenhead: Open University Press.

Stobart, G. and Gipps, C.V. (1997) *Assessment: A Teachers' Guide to the Issues*, London: Hodder and Stoughton.

Strand, S. (2008) *Minority Ethnic Pupils in the Longitudinal Study of Young People in England*, Report DCSF-RR029, London: Department for Children, Schools and Families.

Strand, S. (2011) 'The limits of social class in explaining ethnic gaps in educational attainment', *British Educational Research Journal*, 37, 197–229.

Strand, S. (2014) 'Ethnicity, gender, social class and achievement gaps at age 16: intersectionality and 'getting it' for the white working class', *Research Papers in Education*, 29(2), 131-171.

Struppert, A. (2010). '"It's a whole new fun different way to learn". Students' perceptions of learning with an electronic simulation', *International Journal of Learning*, 17(9), 363-375.

Stuart, M., Stainthorp, R. and Snowling, M. (2008) 'Literacy as a complex activity: deconstructing the simple view of reading', *Literacy*, 42, 59-66.

Sullivan, J. (1972) 'The effects of Kephart's perceptual motor-training on a reading clinic sample', *Journal of Learning Disabilities*, 5(10), 32-38.

Sutherland, K.S., Wehby, J.H. and Copeland, S.R. (2000) 'Effect of varying rates of behavior-specific praise on the on-task behavior of students with EBD', *Journal of Emotional and Behavioral Disorders*, 8(1), 2-8, 26.

Sutton, C. (1981) *Communicating in the Classroom*, London: Hodder and Stoughton.

Swaffield, S. (2011) 'Getting to the heart of authentic assessment for learning', *Assessment in Education: Principles, Policy and Practice*, 18(4), 433-449.

Swales, J. (1990) *Genre Analysis*, Cambridge: Cambridge University Press.

Swanwick, K. (1988) *Music, Mind and Education*, London: Routledge.

Sylva, K., Melhuish, E., Sammons, P., Siraj-Blatchford, I. and Taggart, B. (2004) *The Effective Provision of Pre-School Education (EPPE) Project – The Final Report: Effective Pre-School Education*, Technical Paper 12, London: DfES/Institute of Education.

Tackey, N., Barnes, H. and Khambhaita, P. (2011) *Poverty, Ethnicity and Education*, York: Joseph Rowntree Foundation.

Tafarodi, R.W. and Vu, C. (1997) 'Two-dimensional self-esteem and reactions to success and failure', *Personality and Social Psychology Bulletin*, 23, 626-635.

Tait, M. (2008) 'Resilience as a contributor to novice teacher success, commitment and retention', *Teacher Education Quarterly*, 35(4), 57-75.

TDA (Training and Development Agency for Schools (nd) *ITT Trainees: The Pillars of Inclusion*, viewed 7 July 2019, from http://dera.ioe.ac.uk/13816/2/e5_itt_pillars.pdf

TeacherVision (2015) *Learning Students' Names Quickly*, viewed 17 July 2015, from https://www.teachervision .com/teaching-methods/classroom-management/6708.html

TED talk, Blakemore, S-J. (2012) *The Mysterious Workings of the Adolescent Brain*, viewed 6 February 2019, from http://www.ted.com/talks/sarah_jayne_blakemore_the_mysterious_workings_of_the_adolescent_ brain?language=en

TED talk, Dweck, C. (2014) *The Power of Believing That You Can Improve*, viewed 2 January 2018, from https:// www.ted.com/talks/carol_dweck_t e_power_ofbelievingthat_you_can_improve

TED talk, Kanwisher, N. (2014) *A Neutral Portrait of the Human Mind*, viewed 2 January 2018, from https:// www.ted.com/talks/nancy_kanwisher_thebrain_is_a_swiss_army_knife

TED talk, Robinson, K. (2006) *Do Schools Kill Creativity?*, viewed 9 January 2018, from https://www.ted.com/ talks/ken_robinson_says_schools_kill_creativity

TED talk, Robinson, K. (2010) *Bring on the Learning Revolution*, viewed 6 February 2019, from http://www.ted. com/talks/sir_ken_robinson_bring_onthe_revolution?language=en

Terzi, L. (2008) 'Beyond the dilemma of difference: the capability approach in disabilities and special educational needs', in L. Florian and M. McLaughlin (eds.) (2008) *Disability Classification in Education: Issues and Perspectives*, CA: Corwin Press, pp. 244-260.

TGAT (Task Group on Assessment and Testing) (1988) *The Task Group on Assessment and Testing: A Report*, London: DfES.

Tham, E.K.H., Lindsay, S. and Gaskell, M.G. (2015) 'Markers of automaticity in sleep-associated consolidation of novel words', *Neuropsychologia*, 71, 146-157.

The Children's Society (2012) *The Good Childhood Report: A Review of Our Children's Well-Being*, viewed 3 February 2012, from http://www.childrenssociety.org.uk/what-we-do/research/well-being/good-chil dhood-report-2012

The Teaching College New Jersey (2015) *Anti-Violence Measures*, viewed 21 July 2015, from http://oavi.tcn j.edu/tools-for-everyone/assertiveness/assertive-nonassertive-and-aggressive-behaviors/

Thiessen, E.J. (1985) 'Initiation, indoctrination and education', *Canadian Journal of Education/Revue Canadienne de l'Éducation*, 10(3), 229-249.

Tinson, A., Ayrton, C., Barker, K., Born, T.B., Aldridge, H. and Kenway, P. (2016) *Monitoring Poverty and Social Exclusion 2016*, viewed 16 May 2017, from www.jrf.org.uk/mpse-2016

Titchmarsh, A. (2012) Personal communication.

TLRP (Teaching and Learning Research Programme) (2006) *Learning How to Learn – In Classrooms, Schools and Networks*, viewed 19 July 2015, from http://www.tlrp.org/pub/documents/no17_james.pdf

Tobin, K. (1987) 'The role of wait time in higher cognitive functioning', *Review of Higher Education Research*, 57(1), 69–75.

Tod, J. and Powell, S. (2004) *A Systematic Review of How Theories Explain Learning Behaviour in School Contexts*, London: EPPI.

Tomlinson, C. (2014) *The Differentiated Classroom: Responding to the Needs of All Learners*, 2nd Edition, Alexandria, Virginia: Association for Supervision and Curriculum.

Turner, S. (1995) 'Simulations', in J. Frost (ed.) (1995) *Teaching Science*, London: The Woburn Press.

UK Parliament (1944) *Education Act*, London: HMSO.

UK Parliament (1974) *Health and Safety at Work Act*, London: HMSO.

UK Parliament (1988) *ERA (Education Reform Act)*, 29 July 1988, London: HMSO.

UK Parliament (1989) *The Children Act*, London: HMSO.

UK Parliament (1992) *Education (Schools) Act*, London: HMSO.

UK Parliament (2004) *The Children Act*, London: HMSO.

UK Parliament (2010) *The Equality Act*, London: HMSO.

Underwood, A., Turner, R., Whyte, S. and Rosenberg, J. (2015) *Acoustic Accessibility*, MESHGuide, viewed 4 December 2017, from http://www.meshguides.org/category/general-pedagogy/acoustics-listening-and-learning/

Van Manen, M. (1991) *The Tact of Teaching: The Meaning of Pedagogical Thoughtfulness*, Albany: State University of New York Press.

Veenman, S. (1984) 'Perceived problems of beginning teachers', *Review of Educational Research*, 54, 143–178.

Vernon-Feagans, L., Odom, E., Panscofar, N. and Kainz, K. (2008) 'Comments on Farkas and Hibel: a transactional/ecological model of readiness and inequality', in A. Booth and A.C. Crouter (eds.) *Disparities in School Readiness*, New York: Lawrence Earlbaum Associates, pp. 61–78.

Voice Care Network (nd) *More Care for Your Voice*, viewed 23 April 2015, from http://www.voicecare.org.uk

Volante, L. (2004) 'Teaching to the test: what every educator and policy-maker should know', *Canadian Journal of Educational Administration and Policy*, 35, viewed 8 June 2018, from http://eric.ed.gov/?id=EJ848235

Vygotsky, L. (1962) *Thought and Language*, Cambridge, MA: MIT Press.

Vygotsky, L.S. (1978) *Mind in Society: The Development of Higher Psychological Processes*, London: Harvard University Press.

Vygotsky, L.S. (1979) *Mind in Society*, Cambridge, MA: MIT Press.

Vygotsky, L.S. (1986) *Thought and Language*, trans. and ed. A. Kozulin, Cambridge, MA: MIT Press.

Vygotsky, L.S. and Kozulin, A. (2012) *Thought and Language*, London and Cambridge, MA: MIT Press.

Walker v Northumberland County Council (1994) EWHC QB 2 (England and Wales High Court (Queen's Bench Division) Decisions) (16 November 1994), viewed 1 May 2018, from http://www.bailii.org/ew/cases/EWHC/QB/1994/2.html

Walker, S. (2004) 'Interprofessional work in child and adolescent mental health services', *Emotional and Behavioural Difficulties*, 9(1), 189–204.

Wallace, B. (2000) *Teaching the Very Able Child*, London: NACE/David Fulton.

Wallace, B., Leyden, S., Montgomery, D., Winstanley, C., Pomerantz, M. and Fitton, S. (2009) *Raising the Achievement of all Pupils within an Inclusive Setting: Practical Strategies for Developing Best Practice*, Abingdon: Routledge.

Walsh, J. (nd) *How Can Quality Questioning Transform Classrooms?*, viewed 20 March 2015, from www.sagepub.com/upm-data/6605_walsh_ch_1.pdf

Wang, M.-T. and Holcombe, R. (2010) 'Adolescents' perceptions of school environment, engagement and academic achievement in middle school', *American Educational Research Journal*, 47, 63.

Wasserman, D. (2001) 'Killing Mary to save Jodie: conjoined twins and individual rights', *Philosophy and Public Policy Quarterly*, 21, 9–14.

Waters, E., De Silva-Sanigorski, A., Hall, B.J., Brown, T., Campbell, K.J., Gao, Y., Armstrong, R., Prosser, L. and Summerbell, C. (2011) *Interventions for Preventing Obesity in Children*, Cochrane Database Systematic Review, 12, viewed 6 February 2019, from https://www.cochrane.org/CD001871/PUBHLTH_interventions-for-preventing-obesity-in-children.

Watkins, C., Carnell, E. and Lodge, C. (2007) *Effective Learning in Classrooms*, London: Paul Chapman.

Watkins, W. (2012) *The Assault on Public Education*, Columbia, NY: Teachers College Press.

Weare, K. (2004) *Developing the Emotionally Literate School*, London: Paul Chapman Publishing.

Webster, R. (2018) *Are SEN Teaching Assistants Effective?*, viewed 6 July 2018, from http://www.ucl.ac.uk/ioe/research/featured-research/teaching-assistants

Wegerif, R., Li, L. and Kaufman, J.C. (eds.) (2015) *The Routledge International Handbook of Research on Teaching Thinking*, London and New York: Routledge.

Welsh Government/Llywodraeth Cymru (2018) 02/22-last update, *Digital Competence Framework*, viewed 2 July 2018, from http://learning.gov.wales/resources/browse-all/digital-competence-framework/?lang=en

Weichselbaum, E. and Buttriss, J. (2011) 'Nutrition, health and schoolchildren', British Nutrition Foundation, *Nutrition Bulletin*, 36, 295-355.

Weiten, W. (2010) *Psychology: Themes and Variations*, 8th Edition, Boston Mass: Cemgage Learning.

Wellings, C. and Wood, A. (2012) *Closing the Achievement Gap in England's Secondary Schools*, London: Save the Children.

Weiner, B.J. (1972) *Theories of Motivation*, Chicago, IL: Markham.

Wentzel, K. (1997) 'Student motivation in middle school: the role of perceived pedagogical caring', *Journal of Educational Psychology*, 89, 411-417.

White, J. (1998) *Do Howard Gardner's Multiple Intelligences Add Up?*, in the series Perspectives on Education Policy, London: The Institute of Education, University of London.

White, J. (2005) *Howard Gardner: The Myth of Multiple Intelligences*, London: The Institute of Education, University of London, Viewpoint Number 16 (October).

White, J. (ed.) (2004) *Rethinking the School Curriculum: Values, Aims and Purposes*, London: RoutledgeFalmer.

Whittaker, R., O'Donnell, M. and McCabe, A. (eds.) (2006) *Language and Literacy: Functional Approaches*, London: Continuum.

Wiedmaier, D., Moore, C., Onwuegbuzie, A., Witcher, A., Collins, J. and Filer, C. (2007) 'Students' perceptions of characteristics of effective college teachers', *American Educational Research Journal*, 44: 113L, viewed 28 December 2011, from http://aer.sagepub.com/content/44/1/113

Wigfield, A., Eccles, J.S., MacIver, D., Redman, D.A. and Midgley, C. (1991) 'Transitions during early adolescence: changes in children's domain-specific self-perceptions and general self-esteem across the transition to junior high school', *Developmental Psychology*, 27, 552-565.

Wigfield, A. and Eccles, J. (2000) 'Expectancy-value theory of achievement motivation', *Contemporary Educational Psychology*, 25, 68-81.

Wiliam, D. (2001) *Level Best? Levels of Attainment in National Curriculum Assessment*, London: ATL.

Wiliam, D. (2011) *Embedded Formative Assessment*, Bloomington, IN: Solution Tree Press.

Wiliam, D. (2013) 'Assessment: the bridge between teaching and learning', *Voices from the Middle*, 21(2), 15-20.

Wiliam, D. (2014) *Planning Assessment without Levels*, viewed 31 July 2017, from https://thehub.walthamforest.gov.uk/news/planning-assessment-without-levels-article-dylan-wiliam

Wiliam, D. (2015) *Feedback for Learning: Make Time to Save Time*, viewed 14 September 2018, from https://www.dylanwiliamcenter.com/feedback-for-learning-make-time-to-save-time/

Wiliam, D. (2016) *Leadership for Teacher Learning*, West Palm Beach, FL: Learning Sciences International.

Wiliam, D. (2017) 'Editorial', *Impact - Journal for the Chartered College of Teaching*, 1(1), 1-2.

Wiliam, D. (2018) *Embedded Formative Assessment*, 2nd Edition, Bloomington, IN: Solution Tree Press.

Wiliam, D. and Leahy, S. (2015) *Embedding Formative Assessment*, West Palm Beach: Learning Sciences International.

Willis, P. (1977) *Learning to Labour: How Working Class Kids Get Working Class Jobs*, Aldershot: Gower.

Wilson, E. (2009) *School-Based Research: A Guide for Education Students*, London: Sage.

Wilson, H., Pianta, R. and Stuhlman, M. (2007) 'Typical classroom experiences in first grade: The role of classroom climate and functional risk in the development of social competencies', *The Elementary School Journal*, 108(2), 81-96.

Wing Jan, L. (1991) *Write Ways: Modelling Writing Forms*, Melbourne: Oxford University Press.

Winch, C. (1998) *The Philosophy of Human Learning*, London, Routledge.

Winstanley, C. (2010) *The Ingredients of Challenge*, Stoke-on-Trent, Staffs: Trentham Books.

Winter, B., Breitenstein, C., Mooren, F.C., Voelker, K., Fobker, M., Lechtermann, A. and Knecht, S. (2007) 'High impact running improves learning', *Neurobiology of Learning and Memory*, 87, 597-609.

Winter, E. (2006) 'Preparing new teachers for inclusive schools and classrooms', *Support for Learning*, 21(2), 85-91.

Wirebring, L.K., Wiklund-Hornqvist, C., Eriksson, J., Andersson, M., Jonsson, B. and Nyberg, L. (2015) 'Lesser neural pattern similarity across repeated tests is associated with better long-term memory retention', *Journal of Neuroscience*, 35(26), 9595-9602.

Wittgenstein, L. (1961) *Tractatus Logico-Philosophicus*, trans. D.F. Pears and B.F. McGuinness, London: Routledge and Kegan Paul.

Wolf, A. (2011) *Review of Vocational Education: The Wolf Report*, DFE-00031-2011, viewed 6 February 2019, from www.education.gov.uk/publications/standard/publicationDetail/Page1/DFE-00031-2011

Wood, D. (1988) *How Children Think and Learn*, Oxford: Blackwell.

Wood, D., Bruner, J. and Ross, G. (1976) 'The role of tutoring in problem-solving', *Journal of Child Psychology*, 17, 89–100.

Woodward, W. (2003) 'Poverty hits exam scores', *The Guardian*, 21 April, viewed 8 June 2018, from http://www.guardian.co.uk/uk/2003/apr/21/politics.schools

WHO (World Health Organization) (2016), viewed 6 January 2019, from https://www.who-int/end-childhood-obesity-report

Wragg, E.C. (ed.) (1984) *Classroom Teaching Skills*, London: Croom Helm.

Wragg, E.C. (ed.) (2004) *The RoutledgeFalmer Reader in Teaching and Learning*, London: RoutledgeFalmer.

Wragg, E.C. and Brown, G. (2001) *Questioning in the Secondary School*, London: RoutledgeFalmer.

Wright, T. (2008) *How to Be a Brilliant Trainee Teacher*, Abingdon: Routledge.

Wright, T. (2012) *Guide to Mentoring. Advice for the Mentor and the Mentee*, Association of Teachers and Lecturers, viewed 12 January 2018, from https://www.atl.org.uk/Images/ATL%20Guide%20to%20mentoring%20(Nov%2012)pdf

Young, C.B., Wu, S.S. and Menon, V. (2012) 'The neurodevelopmental basis of math anxiety', *Psychological Science*, 23(5), 492–501.

Young, M.F.D. (2008) *Bringing Knowledge Back In*, Abingdon: Routledge.

Young, M. and Lambert, D. (eds.) (2014) *Knowledge and the Future School - Curriculum and Social Justice*, London: Bloomsbury.

Young, M.F.D. and Muller, J. (2016) *Curriculum and the Specialization of Knowledge*, Abingdon: Routledge.

Younger, M., Warrington, M. and Williams, J. (1999) 'The gender gap and classroom interactions: reality and rhetoric?' *British Journal of Sociology of Education*, 20(3), 325–341.

Younie, S. and Leask, M. (2013) *Teaching with Technologies: The Essential Guide*, Maidenhead: Open University Press.

Yuill, N. and Oakhill, J. (2010) *Children's Problems in Text Comprehension: An Experimental Investigation*, Cambridge: Cambridge University Press.

Zaretskii, V.K. (2009) 'The Zone of Proximal Development: what Vygotsky did not have time to write', *Journal of Russian and East European Psychology*, 47(6), 70–93.

Zeichner, K.M., and Liston, D.P. (1987) 'Teaching students teachers to reflect', *Harvard Educational Review*, 57(1), 23–49.

Zimmerman, B. (2002) 'Becoming a self-regulated learner: an overview', *Theory Into Practice*, 41(2), 64–70.

Zimmerman, B. and Schunk, D. (eds.) (2011) *Handbook of Self-Regulation of Learning and Performance*, New York: Routledge.

Zimmerman, B. and Schunk, D. (1989/2001) *Self-Regulated Learning and Academic Achievement: Theoretical Perspectives*, New York: Routledge.

Zwozdiak-Myers, P. (2009) *An Enquiry into How Reflective Practice Influenced the Professional Development of Teachers as They Engaged in Action Research to Study Their Own Teaching*, PhD Thesis, London: Brunel University.

Author index

Subject index